ELEMENTS OF AERODYNAMICS OF SUPERSONIC FLOWS

THE MACMILLAN COMPANY
NEW YORK · BOSTON · CHICAGO
DALLAS · ATLANTA · SAN FRANCISCO

MACMILLAN AND CO., LIMITED
LONDON · BOMBAY · CALCUTTA
MADRAS · MELBOURNE

THE MACMILLAN COMPANY
OF CANADA, LIMITED
TORONTO

ELEMENTS OF AERODYNAMICS OF SUPERSONIC FLOWS

ANTONIO FERRI

OHIO STATE UNIVERSITY

THE MACMILLAN COMPANY: NEW YORK

1949

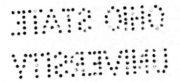

PREFACE

Classical aerodynamics is based upon two fundamental hypotheses: (a) Air is a perfect fluid, (b) Air is an incompressible fluid. These two hypotheses permit the universal assumption of the existence of potential flow, thus permitting extensive mathematical treatment of the phenomena.

When the variations of pressure generated by aerodynamic phenomena are large (which occurs when the velocity of flow increases), the hypothesis of incompressible flow is no longer correct because the corresponding changes in density are important, producing large changes in the flow velocity. It is possible to include the effect of variation of density in the general phenomena, and to extend with some modifications the theories of incompressible flow to those of compressible flow. However, these extensions are generally approximations to the real flow if the speed of sound is not exceeded in any part of the flow. This mathematical treatment usually changes when the local speed of sound is reached or exceeded. In this case new and complicated phenomena occur which completely change the physical characteristics of the flow and require a different mathematical treatment.

The case of the flow which, initially subsonic, becomes supersonic only in some parts, is especially difficult, while the case of the flow which originally has a velocity greater than the speed of sound is, in some cases, mathematically simpler.

This part of aerodynamics that can be called *aerodynamics of supersonic flow* is considered in elementary form, from the aeronautical point of view, in this book.

ANTONIO FERRI

Langley Field, Virginia

v

CONTENTS

ELEMENTS OF AERODYNAMICS OF SUPERSONIC FLOWS

1

GENERAL CONSIDERATIONS

General Equation of Fluid Motion. Irrotational and Rotational Flow.

Euler's Equations. Consider a perfect compressible flow in steady motion, absolute or relative, with respect to the orthogonal axis of reference xyz (Figure 1). Because the motion is steady, all characteristics of the flow, such as velocity, pressure, density, etc., are functions only of the independent variables x, y, z. In order to determine the fluid motion, it is necessary to determine the laws that connect these characteristics of the flow as functions of the position (x, y, z) for known conditions of the boundaries of the flow. Assume

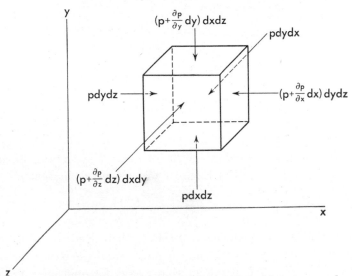

Fig. 1. *Equilibrium of the elementary volume.*

that the characteristics of the flow change gradually (discontinuities do not occur), so it is possible to assume finite the derivative of the entity considered, and consider an infinitesimal parallelepiped $dx\ dy\ dz$. By the momentum theorem applied to the surfaces $dydz$, $dxdz$, and $dxdy$ there are obtained

$$\frac{\partial p}{\partial x} = - \rho \frac{du}{dt}$$

$$\frac{\partial p}{\partial y} = - \rho \frac{dv}{dt} \tag{1}$$

$$\frac{\partial p}{\partial z} = - \rho \frac{dw}{dt}$$

or in vectorial form,

$$\frac{1}{\rho} \operatorname{grad} p = - \frac{dV}{dt} \tag{1a}$$

where u, v, and w are the components of the velocity V along the axis xyz, t is the time, p the pressure, and ρ the density, and the forces are positive if they have the same direction as the axis. (Mass forces are not considered.) By the hypothesis of a steady flow,*

$$\frac{du}{dt} = \frac{\partial u}{\partial x} \frac{\partial x}{\partial t} + \frac{\partial u}{\partial y} \frac{\partial y}{\partial t} + \frac{\partial u}{\partial z} \frac{\partial z}{\partial t} \tag{1b}$$

because

$$\frac{\partial u}{\partial t} = 0.$$

Therefore (Euler's equation)

$$\frac{1}{\rho} \frac{\partial p}{\partial x} = - \frac{\partial u}{\partial x} u - \frac{\partial u}{\partial y} v - \frac{\partial u}{\partial z} w$$

$$\frac{1}{\rho} \frac{\partial p}{\partial y} = - \frac{\partial v}{\partial x} u - \frac{\partial v}{\partial y} v - \frac{\partial v}{\partial z} w$$

$$\frac{1}{\rho} \frac{\partial p}{\partial z} = - \frac{\partial w}{\partial x} u - \frac{\partial w}{\partial y} v - \frac{\partial w}{\partial z} w \tag{1c}$$

Continuity Equation and Energy Equation. The equation of continuity applied to the parallelepiped of Figure 1 for continuous motion is

$$\frac{\partial (\rho u)}{\partial x} + \frac{\partial (\rho v)}{\partial y} + \frac{\partial (\rho w)}{\partial z} = 0. \tag{2}$$

The equation of energy for the mass of the parallelepiped states that the work produced by the pressure in the time dl must equal the variations of kinetic and internal energy. If U is the internal energy for unit mass, the resulting equation is

$$- dx \, dy \, dz \, dt \left[\frac{\partial}{\partial x} (pu) + \frac{\partial}{\partial y} (pv) + \frac{\partial}{\partial z} (pw) \right] =$$
$$\rho dx \, dy \, dz \, (dU + VdV) \tag{3}$$

* The symbol d/d indicates total derivative and ∂/∂ indicates partial derivative.

but from equation (2) we obtain

$$\frac{\partial}{\partial x}(pu) + \frac{\partial}{\partial y}(pv) + \frac{\partial}{\partial z}(pw) = u\frac{\partial p}{\partial x} + v\frac{\partial p}{\partial y} + w\frac{\partial p}{\partial z}$$

$$-\frac{p}{\rho}\left(u\frac{\partial \rho}{\partial x} + v\frac{\partial \rho}{\partial y} + w\frac{\partial \rho}{\partial z}\right)$$

and

$$u\frac{\partial p}{\partial x} - u\frac{p}{\rho}\frac{\partial \rho}{\partial x} = u\rho\frac{\partial}{\partial x}\left(\frac{p}{\rho}\right).$$

Therefore from an equation similar to (1b) (in which p/ρ is derived instead of u), can be obtained

$$\frac{\partial}{\partial x}(pu) + \frac{\partial}{\partial y}(pv) + \frac{\partial}{\partial z}(pw) = \rho\frac{d}{dt}\left(\frac{p}{\rho}\right) \tag{4}$$

and equation (3) becomes

$$\frac{d}{dt}\left(\frac{p}{\rho} + U\right) + \frac{1}{2}\frac{d(V^2)}{dt} = 0 \tag{5}$$

or

$$\frac{p}{\rho} + U + \frac{1}{2}V^2 = \text{constant.} \tag{5a}$$

If the motion is steady, the trajectories of the particles of flow coincide with the stream lines, but by equation (5) the total energy of a given particle of flow is constant for the entire motion; therefore the total energy of the unit mass is constant along every stream line.

Thermodynamic Concepts. For perfect gases, the equation of state gives

$$p = R g \rho T \tag{6}$$

where g is the acceleration of gravity, T is the absolute temperature, and R is the gas constant, the dimensions of which are length per degree of temperature.

Using mechanical units for c_p and c_v, the constant R can be expressed in the form

$$R = c_p - c_v \tag{7}$$

where c_p and c_v are the specific heats at constant pressure and at constant volume respectively (work per degree per unit weight).

The first law of thermodynamics yields the energy balance

$$dQ = g c_v dT + p d\left(\frac{1}{\rho}\right) \tag{8}$$

or

$$dQ = dU + p d\left(\frac{1}{\rho}\right) \tag{8a}$$

where dQ is the quantity of heat added in work per unit mass of gas. If the total heat I (enthalpy) is introduced (work per unit mass), that is defined by

$$\frac{I}{g} = c_p T = \frac{U}{g} + \frac{p}{g\rho}. \tag{9}$$

From equation (6) the following expression can be obtained:

$$I = \frac{c_p}{R}\frac{p}{\rho} = \frac{\gamma}{\gamma - 1}\frac{p}{\rho} \tag{9a}$$

where c_p and c_v are assumed constant and

$$\gamma = \frac{c_p}{c_v}. \tag{10}$$

For air, γ in all numerical applications will be considered equal to 1.40.

Using equations (9), equation (5) can be written in the form

$$I + \frac{1}{2} V^2 = \text{constant} \tag{11}$$

or

$$\frac{\gamma}{\gamma - 1}\frac{p}{\rho} + \frac{1}{2} V^2 = \text{constant}. \tag{11a}$$

Equation (11) can be applied whenever an adiabatic transformation is considered in the flow. From the equation, it is shown that for flow at rest $(V = 0)$ the temperature T_0 of the flow is constant, independent of the transformations that the flow has undergone.

Equations for Rotational Flow. From the first of equations (1c), by adding and subtracting $v\dfrac{dv}{dx}$ and $w\dfrac{\partial w}{\partial x}$ is obtained

$$-\frac{1}{\rho}\frac{\partial p}{\partial x} = \frac{1}{2}\frac{\partial V^2}{\partial x} - 2v\,\omega_z + 2w\,\omega_y \tag{12}$$

and in a similar way

$$-\frac{1}{\rho}\frac{\partial p}{\partial y} = \frac{1}{2}\frac{\partial V^2}{\partial y} - 2w\,\omega_x + 2u\,\omega_z$$

$$-\frac{1}{\rho}\frac{\partial p}{\partial z} = \frac{1}{2}\frac{\partial V^2}{\partial z} - 2u\,\omega_y + 2v\,\omega_x$$

where

$$\omega_x = \frac{1}{2}\left(\frac{\partial w}{\partial y} - \frac{\partial v}{\partial z}\right) = \frac{1}{2}\,(w_y - v_z) \tag{13}$$

$$\omega_y = \frac{1}{2}\left(\frac{\partial u}{\partial z} - \frac{\partial w}{\partial x}\right) = \frac{1}{2}\,(u_z - w_x)$$

$$\omega_z = \frac{1}{2}\left(\frac{\partial v}{\partial x} - \frac{\partial u}{\partial y}\right) = \frac{1}{2}\,(v_x - u_y)$$

ω_x, ω_y, ω_z are the components of a vector ω that represents the rotation of the flow V and can be written in the form $\frac{1}{2}$ curl V.

Equations (12) can be written in vectorial form and become*

$$\text{grad}\left(P + \frac{1}{2}V^2\right) = V \times \text{curl } V \tag{14}$$

where

$$P = \int \frac{dp}{\rho} \cdot$$

For the first theorem of thermodynamics, if S is the entropy (work per degree of temperature per unit mass) and T is the absolute temperature (equations 8 and 9),

$$TdS = dI - \frac{dp}{\rho} \cdot \tag{15}$$

Considering a variation along a line l, from equations (14) and (15) is obtained

$$- T\frac{dS}{dl} + \frac{d}{dl}\left(I + \frac{1}{2}V^2\right) = V \times \text{curl } V. \tag{16}$$

$\left(I + \frac{1}{2}V^2\right)$ is the energy for a unit mass and is constant along a stream line;

therefore $\frac{d}{dl}\left(I + \frac{1}{2}V^2\right) = 0$, and along the streamline

$$- TdS = (V \times \text{curl } V) \cdot dl \tag{17}$$

but the vector $V \times$ curl V is normal to the stream line; therefore the term $(V \times \text{curl } V) \cdot dl$ is zero, and the entropy is constant along every stream line.

If no discontinuities occur in the flow in a perfect compressible fluid, the entropy is constant along every stream line.

Consider now equation (14) as applied along a line n normal to a stream line.

$$- T\frac{dS}{dn} + \frac{d}{dn} \cdot \left(I + \frac{1}{2}V^2\right) = V \times \text{curl } V. \tag{18}$$

If the flow around the body is steady and the body does not move, the flow has constant energy, because the body cannot produce or absorb work, being fixed; therefore the flow has constant energy along every stream line.

---

* The symbol $\times$ indicates a vectorial product. If A and B are two vectors of components $A(x_1 y_1 z_1)$ and $B(x_2 y_2 z_2)$ the vectorial product $A \times B$ represents another vector C of components $C(x_3 y_3 z_3)$ defined by the following equations:

$$x_3 = (y_1 z_2 - y_2 z_1)$$
$$y_3 = (z_1 x_2 - z_2 x_1)$$
$$z_3 = (x_1 y_2 - x_2 y_1)$$

and directed in normal direction to the plane of the vectors A and B.

If the flow is uniform to infinity, the energy is constant everywhere, and therefore for every stream line the energy is the same, and

$$\frac{d}{dn}\left(I + \frac{1}{2}V^2\right) = 0.$$

Therefore

$$- T\frac{dS}{dn} = V \times \text{curl } V. \tag{19}$$

If in the flow the entropy is not constant for all stream lines and therefore a normal gradient of entropy exists, the flow is rotational.

It will be demonstrated later that in supersonic flow some discontinuities of flow characteristics exist that are called *shock waves*. When shock waves exist in the flow, a variation of entropy across the shock is produced that depends on the intensity of the shock. If the shock does not produce the same variation of entropy in the entire flow, the stream lines no longer have equal entropy, and an entropy gradient normal to the stream lines exists; therefore the flow behind the shock is rotational.

Lagrange-Thompson Theorem.   Consider a closed line l in the flow and made up of the same particles of flow. The line l, locus of the particles considered, changes with the time. If dl is an element of the line l and V the velocity of a point, the value

$$\Gamma = \int_l V \cdot dl \tag{20}$$

is the circulation of the line l. Consider now the variation of circulation with time:

$$\frac{d\Gamma}{dt} = \frac{d}{dt}\int_l V \cdot dl = \int_l \frac{dV}{dt} \cdot dl + \int_l V \cdot \frac{d}{dt}(dl) \tag{21}$$

but

$$\int_l V \cdot \frac{d}{dt} dl = \int_l \frac{1}{2} dV^2 = 0$$

because the integral is extended along the closed line l, and V is a single value function; therefore

$$\frac{d\Gamma}{dt} = \int_l \frac{dV}{dt} \cdot dl \tag{21a}$$

and for equation (1a)

$$\frac{d\Gamma}{dt} = -\int \frac{dp}{\rho} . \tag{21b}$$

If the density is a function of the pressure only, the term in the integral of the second part of equation (21b) is a total differential, the integral along l is zero, and the variation of circulation is zero. But at infinity $\Gamma = 0$; therefore Γ remains zero in the whole field, and the movement is irrotational. If density is a function also of other variables, the value of the integral is no longer zero, the value $\dfrac{d\Gamma}{dt}$ is other than zero, and the flow can become rotational even if it is initially irrotational to infinity.

The Speed of Sound and Mach Number. When the flow velocity in the aerodynamic phenomena analyzed is large, and it is necessary to consider air a compressible fluid, two quantities become important:

    (a) The speed of sound,
    (b) The Mach number.

In general, the speed of sound in a fluid is the speed with which a small disturbance (infinitesimal) of the physical conditions of the fluid, generated at a point of the fluid, is transmitted to the whole flow surrounding the point. The Mach number of the flow at any point is the ratio of the velocity of the fluid, absolute or relative, at this point to the velocity of sound at the same point. The reason the speed of sound is important when compressibility effects are being considered can be clarified by the following considerations: In aerodynamic phenomena, the effects of compressibility can be important if the variations of volume caused by the variations of pressure which occur in the flow are of the same order of magnitude as the variations of velocity which correspond to the variations of pressure.

Now consider a stream tube of length dl (Figure 2). The mass contained in the space dl moves in the time dt from position 1-2 to position 3-4. The mass flow does not change. Therefore, if D is the volume of the flow, and ρ the density,

$$\rho D = \text{Mass flow} = \text{Constant}$$

or

$$\rho dD + D d\rho = 0. \qquad (22)$$

The work done by the pressures on the surfaces 1-2 in going from position 1-2 to 3-4 must be equivalent to the change of energy of the flow, ignoring mass forces; therefore if p is the pressure and V the velocity, from equations (5) and (8) (dQ is zero) is obtained

$$- dp = \rho V dV. \qquad (23)$$

From equation (22) can be obtained

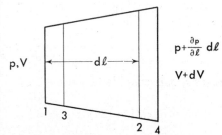

Fig. 2. *Elementary stream tube.*

$$dp = - \rho \, \frac{dp}{d\rho} \frac{dD}{D}.$$ (22a)

If it is assumed that

$$\frac{dp}{d\rho} = c^2$$ (24)

from equations (23) and (22a) it can be shown that

$$\frac{dD}{D} \bigg/ \frac{dV}{V} = \frac{V^2}{c^2}.$$ (25)

Therefore when the velocity V is of the same order of magnitude as c, the variation of volume dD/D is of the same order of magnitude as the variation of the velocity dV/V. The quantity c must be a velocity because the left-hand side of equation (25) is nondimensional. It is possible to show that c is equal to the velocity of sound of the flow.

Consider a cylindrical tube of unit section with a piston traveling at a very low speed u (Figure 3). If the fluid is compressible, the motion does not start instantaneously in the entire fluid mass, but it

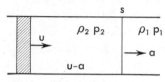

is possible at every instant to determine a section s which divides the region in which motion is propagated from the region in which motion is not propagated. The position of this section changes with time. Call a the velocity of displacement of the section s. The velocity a is the velocity of sound because it is the velocity with which small variations produced by the piston are transmitted to the flow. If a system of coordinate axes which moves with s is taken, the relative velocity ahead of the section s is $V_1 = -a$, and the velocity of flow contained between the piston and s is $(V_2 = u - a)$. If ρ_1 and ρ_2 are the densities of the two flows separated by the section s, then by the equation of continuity,

Fig. 3. *Piston moving in cylindrical tube.*

$$- \rho_1 a = \rho_2 (u - a) = m.$$ (26)

Indeed, the mass flow which crosses every section of the tube must remain constant.

Call p_2 and p_1 the pressures corresponding to the flow before and after the section s, and consider the equation of the variation of momentum across the section s. Since the change of momentum of the flow which crosses the section s must be equal to the variation of pressure in the two zones before and after s, it is possible to write

$$p_2 - p_1 = - mu$$ (27)

but from equation (26)

$$- a = \frac{m}{\rho_1}$$ (28)

$$\rho_2 u + \frac{\rho_2}{\rho_1} m = m \tag{28a}$$

$$u = \frac{m}{\rho_2} - \frac{m}{\rho_1}. \tag{28b}$$

Therefore

$$p_2 - p_1 = m^2 \left(\frac{1}{\rho_1} - \frac{1}{\rho_2} \right) \tag{29}$$

and

$$p_2 + \frac{m^2}{\rho_2} = p_1 + \frac{m^2}{\rho_1} = p_2 + \frac{a^2 \rho_1^2}{\rho_2} = p_1 + a^2 \rho_1 \tag{29a}$$

By hypothesis, u is small; therefore the variations of pressure and density are small. Thus, if we let

$$\rho_2 = \rho_1 + d\rho = \rho_1 (1 + \epsilon)$$

the quantity ϵ is small and ϵ^2 is negligible.

$$p_2 = p_1 + \frac{dp}{d\rho} d\rho = p_1 + \frac{dp}{d\rho} \epsilon \rho_1$$

but by definition c^2 is equal to $\frac{dp}{d\rho}$; therefore

$$p_2 + \frac{a^2 \rho_1^2}{\rho_2} = p_1 + \epsilon \rho_1 c^2 + \frac{a^2 \rho_1}{1 + \epsilon}. \tag{30}$$

But

$$\frac{1}{1 + \epsilon} = 1 - \epsilon + \epsilon^2 - \epsilon^3 \dots \dots \dots = 1 - \epsilon$$

since in the series expansion the other terms are negligible. Therefore from equation (30),

$$p_2 + \frac{a^2 \rho_1^2}{\rho_2} = p_1 + \epsilon \rho_1 c^2 + a^2 \rho_1 - a^2 \rho_1 \epsilon$$

and for equation (29a), $p_2 + \dfrac{a^2 \rho_1^2}{\rho_2} = p_1 + a^2 \rho_1$; therefore $\epsilon c^2 \rho_1$ must be equal to $a^2 \rho_1 \epsilon$, and

$$c^2 = a^2 \tag{31}$$

The velocity $c = \sqrt{dp/d\rho}$ is therefore the velocity of sound of the flow.
Conclusion: The compressibility effect in the flow depends on the ratio of the flow velocity to the velocity of sound. The ratio is called the *Mach number* and is usually indicated by the symbol M.

Compressibility Effects in Isentropic Transformations. If an isentropic transformation occurs in the flow,

$$\frac{p}{\rho^\gamma} = \text{constant.} \tag{32}$$

Therefore the velocity of sound, because

$$\frac{dp}{d\rho} = \gamma \frac{p}{\rho}$$

becomes

$$a = \sqrt{\frac{dp}{d\rho}} = \sqrt{\frac{\gamma p}{\rho}} = \sqrt{gR\gamma T}. \tag{33}$$

Equation (33) shows that the velocity of sound changes with change of temperature, and decreases if temperature decreases. Therefore the compressibility effects become more important for high-altitude flight, because the temperature and the speed of sound decrease, and for the same speed of flight, the Mach number increases. If p_0 and ρ_0 are the pressure and density corresponding to zero velocity, from the energy equation (11a) it may be shown that:

$$\frac{\gamma}{\gamma - 1} \frac{p_0}{\rho_0} = \frac{\gamma}{\gamma - 1} \frac{p}{\rho} + \frac{V^2}{2} \tag{34}$$

or

$$\frac{p_0}{\rho_0} = \frac{p}{\rho}\left(1 + \frac{\gamma - 1}{2} M^2\right). \tag{34a}$$

But from equation (32)

$$\frac{p_0}{\rho_0{}^\gamma} = \frac{p}{\rho^\gamma}.$$

Therefore

$$\frac{\gamma}{\gamma - 1} \frac{p}{\rho}\left[\left(\frac{\rho_0}{\rho}\right)^{(\gamma - 1)} - 1\right] = \frac{1}{2} V^2 \tag{35}$$

and because $a = \sqrt{\gamma \dfrac{p}{\rho}}$

$$\left(\frac{\rho_0}{\rho}\right)^{\gamma - 1} = 1 + \frac{\gamma - 1}{2}\left(\frac{V}{a}\right)^2. \tag{36}$$

If the velocity is the same as the velocity of sound, $V = a$, and

$$\left(\frac{\rho_0}{\rho_*}\right)^{\gamma - 1} = \frac{1 + \gamma}{2}. \tag{37}$$

The density corresponding to the speed equal to the speed of sound is

$$\rho_* = \left(\frac{2}{1 + \gamma}\right)^{\frac{1}{\gamma - 1}} \rho_0 \tag{38}$$

and the corresponding pressure becomes

$$p_* = \left(\frac{2}{\gamma + 1}\right)^{\frac{\gamma}{\gamma - 1}} p_0$$

if $\gamma = 1.40$, $p_* = 0.528 p_0$, and $\rho_* = 0.634 \rho_0$. $\qquad$ (39)

From equation (35) the following expression can be obtained (Reference 1)*:

* See list of numbered Specific References in the Appendix.

$$V = a\sqrt{\frac{2}{\gamma + 1}\left[\left(\frac{p_0}{p}\right)^{\frac{\gamma-1}{\gamma}} - 1\right]} \qquad (40)$$

or

$$M = \sqrt{\frac{2}{\gamma - 1}\left[\left(\frac{p_0}{p}\right)^{\frac{\gamma-1}{\gamma}} - 1\right]} \qquad (41)$$

In Table 1 of the appendix some values of p/p_0, T/T_0, and ρ/ρ_0 as functions of M are given.

One-Dimensional Phenomena. If a stream tube with uniform velocity distribution across all the sections is considered (one-dimensional theory) for the continuity equation,

$$\rho s V = \text{constant} \qquad (42)$$

where s is the cross section of the stream tube, or

$$\frac{d\rho}{\rho} + \frac{ds}{s} + \frac{dV}{V} = 0 \qquad (43)$$

but

$$\frac{d\rho}{\rho} = \frac{d\rho}{dp}\frac{dp}{\rho} = \frac{1}{a^2}\frac{dp}{\rho} \qquad (44)$$

and from the energy equation

$$\frac{dp}{\rho} = -VdV. \qquad (45)$$

Therefore

$$\frac{d\rho}{\rho} = \frac{1}{a^2}\frac{dp}{\rho} = -\frac{V}{a^2}dV = -M^2\frac{dV}{V} \qquad (46)$$

and from equation (43)

$$\frac{ds}{s} = (M^2 - 1)\frac{dV}{V} \qquad (47)$$

but

$$\frac{dM}{M} = \frac{dV}{V} - \frac{da}{a}$$

and for isentropic transformations,

$$\frac{da}{a} = \frac{1}{2}\left(\frac{dp}{p} - \frac{d\rho}{\rho}\right) = \frac{1}{2}\frac{d\rho}{\rho}(\gamma - 1) = \frac{1}{2}\frac{dp}{p}\left(1 - \frac{1}{\gamma}\right). \qquad (48)$$

Therefore

$$\frac{dM}{M} = \frac{dV}{V} - \frac{\gamma - 1}{2}\frac{d\rho}{\rho} \qquad (49)$$

or

$$\frac{dM}{M} = \frac{dV}{V}\left(1 + \frac{\gamma - 1}{2}M^2\right). \qquad (49a)$$

Substituting equation (49a) in equation (47) (Reference 2),

$$\frac{ds}{s} = \frac{M^2 - 1}{1 + \dfrac{\gamma - 1}{2} M^2} \frac{dM}{M} \tag{50}$$

or in finite form

$$\frac{s_1}{s_2} = \frac{M_2}{M_1} \left(\frac{M_1^2 + \dfrac{2}{\gamma - 1}}{M_2^2 + \dfrac{2}{\gamma - 1}} \right)^{\frac{\gamma + 1}{2(\gamma - 1)}} . \tag{51}$$

Equations (46), (47), and (50) permit some interesting considerations:

If the velocity in the stream tube is subsonic, the term $(M^2 - 1)$ in equations (47) or (50) is negative; therefore ds, dV, and dM are of opposite sign ($\gamma > 1$), while if the velocity is supersonic $(M^2 - 1) > 0$, ds, dV, and dM are of the same sign. This means that in subsonic flow, in order to increase the velocity in a stream tube, it is necessary to decrease the section, or to have converging stream lines, but in supersonic flow, in order to increase the velocity, it is necessary to have diverging stream lines (Figure 4). It is also

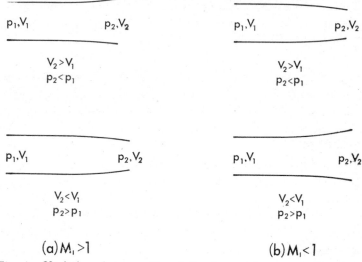

Fig. 4. *Variation of cross section of the stream tube corresponding to variation of velocity of given sign in* (a) *supersonic, and* (b) *subsonic flow.*

shown (equation 46) that for $(M > 1)$ the speed increases less rapidly than the corresponding decrease in density. Therefore, in order to obtain expansion in a flow in supersonic velocity, it is necessary to produce a divergence of the stream lines, and vice versa, if an expansion is produced, the stream lines tend to diverge (increase the section of the stream tube). For isentropic compression the phenomenon is inverse.

The minimum cross section of the stream tube corresponds to $(M = 1)$ (equation 50).

If s_* is the section of stream tube in which Mach number one is reached,

$$\frac{s}{s_*} = \frac{1}{M} \left[\frac{\dfrac{\gamma - 1}{2} M^2 + 1}{\dfrac{\gamma + 1}{2}} \right]^{\frac{\gamma+1}{2(\gamma - 1)}} \tag{51a}$$

In Table I of the appendix some values of s_*/s as a function of Mach number are shown.

The hypothesis of isentropic flow is, in general, valid for flow velocities below the velocity of sound except for regions within the boundary layer where the viscosity, neglected in this analysis, is of paramount importance. For supersonic flow, the isentropic hypothesis is not equally valid even if the viscosity is neglected. In this case, the hypothesis of isentropic flow is valid, neglecting viscous effects when expansion occurs, but, in general, it is not valid if the velocity of flow decreases and the pressure increases, because new physical phenomena, characteristic of supersonic flow, can occur, that are governed by laws other than the isentropic. In this case equation (51) cannot be applied.

Diversity of the Phenomena in Subsonic and Supersonic Flow. In the preceding considerations it is shown that small disturbances in a flow are transmitted with the velocity of sound. As a consequence of this law, the aerodynamic phenomena in the case in which a body moves in a flow with velocity less than the speed of sound are different from those in the case in which the speed is greater than the speed of sound.

Consider a uniform perfect flow and assume that a continuous small (infinitesimal) change in pressure is produced at a point P that moves in the flow with the velocity V (Figure 5). The disturbance is transmitted to the flow with the velocity of sound; therefore, if the positions 1, 2, 3, and 4 of the point P are considered after 1, 2, 3, and 4 seconds from the time at which P was in the position 0, it is possible to construct for the time at which the point P is at 4, the limit of the zone influenced by the variation of pressure produced by the point P in the four positions considered.

If the velocity of the point P is less than the velocity of sound, the phenomenon is as shown in Figure 5a. The point is at 4. The variations in pressure produced by P are extended in spherical waves of radius $r = a \times$ time (a, speed of sound). The variation of pressure is very small, and it is possible to assume that the speed of sound does not change in the flow. Because the speed of the point P is less than the speed of sound, every wave overtakes the point P and also influences a zone in front of the point P. Therefore, in moving, the point P finds a flow that *knows* of the presence of the point P, and

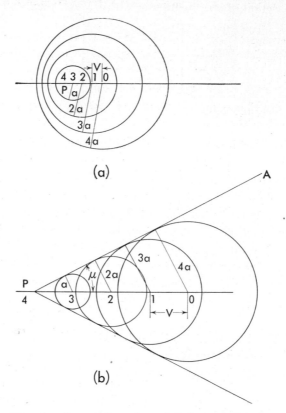

(a)

(b)

Fig. 5. *Propagation of an infinitesimal disturbance in* (a) *subsonic, and* (b) *supersonic stream.*

because of its presence has undergone some variations. The waves are separated from each other and therefore the change is gradual. In the case where the velocity of the point P is greater than the velocity of sound, the phenomenon is different (Figure 5b). The disturbances generated by P in the preceding positions 3, 2, 1, and 0 cannot overtake the point P, which is in position 4, therefore P finds in moving, a flow that does not *know* of the presence of the point P, and which therefore has the characteristics of an undisturbed flow. All the disturbances are extended only to the flow contained in a cone with vertex at P and having an angle μ that is defined by

$$\sin \mu = \frac{a}{V} = \frac{1}{M} \,. \tag{52}$$

The angle μ is called the *Mach angle* and the cone is called the *Mach cone*.

All the disturbance waves are tangent to the line PA (*Mach line*), and across the line PA a variation of flow characteristics occurs. In regions outside the cone of which PA is the generator, the fluid is unaffected by the motion of the point P.

The Mach angle and the Mach cone are relative to the small disturbances that are transmitted with sound waves, but it is clear that similar phenomena must occur for finite variations of flow characteristics. In this case, the phenomena are more complicated, and mathematical treatments are possible only in some cases that will be discussed later, but qualitatively the phenomena can be considered now.

Consider, for example, a plane AB wetted by a flow with relative or absolute supersonic velocity (Figure 6a), and assume that at a point P a finite variation of pressure is produced (at C the pressure is different than along AB). Assume that the finite variation of pressure is produced gradually, and consider first the case in which the variation of pressure is negative. At P an expansion occurs. When a variation of pressure dp is produced at P this variation of pressure pertains to a zone of the flow that, for considerations analogous to those used for Figure 5b, is limited by a line PL_1 that starts from P and is inclined at a Mach angle. In the field CPL_1, the flow has a lower pressure than in the zone APL_1. The transformation that occurs across the line PL_1 for the small variation of p can be considered isentropic; therefore (equations 48 and 46) across PL_1 the speed of sound decreases $(\gamma > 1)$, and the velocity and the Mach number increase.

As shown previously for supersonic flow, expansion occurs with increase of section of stream tube; therefore the direction of velocity across the line PL_1 tends to turn from the direction AB with direction of rotation $PD \rightarrow PC$.

When a second expansion dp is produced, this expansion, because it takes place in the region CPL_1, occurs at a Mach number higher than the undisturbed Mach number; therefore the zone pertaining to the second expansion must be limited by a line PL_2 more inclined than PL_1, because μ_2 is smaller than μ_1 ($\sin \mu = 1/M$) and the velocity V_2 behind PL_1 is rotated with respect to V_1. For all successive expansions the same phenomenon occurs; therefore the expansion occurs in the zone PL_1L_n gradually. The line PL_1 corresponds to the Mach line for the Mach number in ABL_1, and PL_n is the corresponding Mach line in CPL_n, but considered with respect to the velocity V_n in CPL_n which is in a different direction, and with respect to the local Mach number which is higher.

Consider now a positive variation of pressure. The phenomenon in this case is different. The first variation of pressure dp (Figure 6b) is transmitted to a zone of flow limited by a line PL_1 inclined at the Mach angle with respect to the direction AB. But in the zone CPL_1 the Mach number decreases and the velocity tends to turn in the direction from PD to PL_1. Therefore the successive compression dp must be limited by a line PL_2 less inclined than the preceding. But in this case, the Mach number decreases and the velocity turns also in the zone L_2PL_1; therefore the line PL_1 changes position and

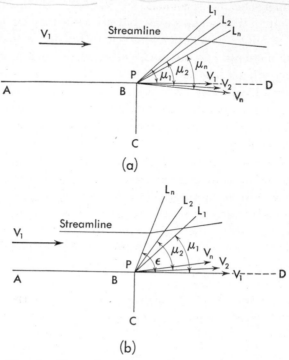

(a)

(b)

Fig. 6. *Expansion* (a), *and compression* (b), *of a supersonic two-dimensional stream.*

reaches the line PL_2. If the pressure at P continues to increase, all the limiting lines PL of the compressions Δp tend to attain the same position PL_n which is less inclined $(\epsilon > \mu)$ than the Mach line with respect to V. Across the line PL_n, a finite variation of pressure occurs, and the law of compression is not isentropic. The finite compression occurs, in this case, not gradually, but with a discontinuity. The surface of the discontinuity is called a *shock wave*. Across the shock wave a decrease of velocity and Mach number and increase of pressure, density, temperature, and entropy occur; it is possible to demonstrate that the process is not reversible.

All variations of the physical quantities of the flow are governed by a law that will be developed later. The intensity of the shock is defined if the Mach number and the inclination of the shock with respect to the velocity are known.

The formation of shock is explained in the case of finite variation of pressure in a point, but, in general, shock can occur also if a gradual compression is produced. Consider for example a flow at supersonic speed along a curved wall (Figure 7). At A a small variation of stream tube cross section occurs; therefore a small variation of pressure is generated which is transmitted in the flow behind a Mach line AA_1. Behind the line AA_1 the Mach number is smaller than in front; therefore if another small variation in section occurs, the relative Mach line is less inclined than AA_1 and meets the line AA_1 at A_1. Across the line A_1B_1 a variation in pressure and direction occurs corresponding to that from A to B. At C and D the same is true; therefore the conclusion is that an envelope is formed across which the variation is finite and a shock wave is generated. It is possible in some particular cases to avoid

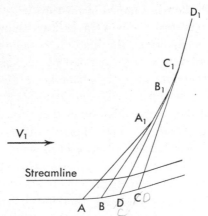

Fig. 7. *Compression of a supersonic two-dimensional stream along a curved surface.*

this envelope, and in this case the recompression can be considered gradual, but formation of shock waves in transformations of compression in supersonic flow is the more general case.

In the preceding considerations, steady phenomena were analyzed, but transmission of a finite variation of pressure in the flow also occurs with expansion waves and shock waves in an analogous manner for unsteady phenomena. Consider a cylinder in which a piston moves with velocity V, the velocity V increasing from zero to a final value V_1 (Figure 8). At the time zero, the piston moves with velocity dV and a compression wave is generated that moves with the speed of sound a_c. In front of the compression wave, the flow

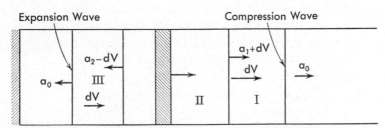

Fig. 8. *Transmission of compression or expansion waves, produced in a cylinder by the movement of a piston initially at rest.*

is undisturbed; and behind the first compression wave in zone I, the flow moves with velocity dV and undergoes an infinitesimal increase of pressure. If the speed of the piston increases, other compression waves are generated, but the speed of sound a_1 in zone I is greater than the speed of sound a_0, in the undisturbed flow (because in I, the temperature or the value p/ρ is larger), and the flow in I moves in the tube with the velocity dV; therefore the succeeding compression waves travel faster than the first (speed $a_1 + dV$), and after some time overtake the first. The same phenomenon occurs for succeeding compression waves generated by successive increases of the speed of the piston. Therefore when the piston has attained the velocity V_1, all variation of pressure occurs in the flow across a shock wave that is generated by superimposition of the compression waves that unite, and that travel at a speed greater than the speed of sound. For the other side of the piston the phenomenon is different, and the variation of pressure (expansion) occurs gradually, because the first expansion wave decreases the speed of sound in zone III. The subsequent expansion waves travel more slowly than the preceding because the speed of sound a_2 in III is less than in the undisturbed flow a_0, and the flow in III has a velocity dV of opposite sign than the velocity with which the disturbance travels in the tube. No meeting of two expansion waves therefore occurs in the tube.

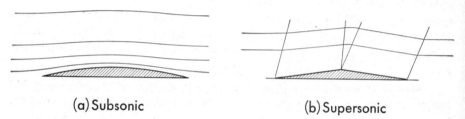

(a) Subsonic   (b) Supersonic

Fig. 9.   *Differences of aerodynamic phenomena in* (a) *subsonic, and* (b) *supersonic flow.*

From all these considerations, it appears that large differences exist between supersonic and subsonic flow. If the body moves in a flow at subsonic speed, some variations in the flow are produced by the presence of the body; but these variations are important for the zone near the body and decrease with the decrease of distance of the point considered from the body (Figure 9a). The variations are gradual, all transformations for perfect flow are isentropic, and all losses (drag) are generated by viscous friction. In supersonic flow, the phenomena are different; in the flow in front of the body no variations occur (Figure 9b). The variations are extended to infinity (for perfect flow) if other variations of opposite sign are not generated in the flow. Losses (drag) occur also for perfect flow, because the transformations are not always isentropic. Consequently, a new form of drag must be considered, called *shock drag.*

CHAPTER

2

THEORY OF TWO-DIMENSIONAL FLOW

POTENTIAL FLOW — CHARACTERISTIC

SYSTEM — SMALL DISTURBANCES

Differential Equations for Potential Flow. Consider a phenomenon in which all physical quantities pertaining to the flow are equal for all particles of the flow that are situated at the same time along every straight line perpendicular to a plane. In this case, it is sufficient to consider the variations of the physical quantities which occur in this plane to determine the value of the physical quantity in the entire space; therefore the phenomenon can be defined as two-dimensional, because it depends only on two spacial coordinates x and y.

Assume that the flow is a steady perfect isentropic flow, therefore a flow the characteristics of which are independent of time, and which is irrotational. With these hypotheses the continuity equation, and Euler's equation, can be written in the following form:

$$\frac{\partial(\rho u)}{\partial x} + \frac{\partial(\rho v)}{\partial y} = 0 \tag{53}$$

$$u\frac{\partial u}{\partial x} + v\frac{\partial u}{\partial y} = -\frac{1}{\rho}\frac{\partial p}{\partial x}$$

$$u\frac{\partial v}{\partial x} + v\frac{\partial v}{\partial y} = -\frac{1}{\rho}\frac{\partial p}{\partial y} \tag{54}$$

but

$$\frac{\partial p}{\partial \rho} = a^2$$

and

$$\frac{\partial \rho}{\partial x} = \frac{\partial \rho}{\partial p}\frac{\partial p}{\partial x} = \frac{1}{a^2}\frac{\partial p}{\partial x}.$$

Therefore, from equations (53) and (54),

$$\frac{\partial u}{\partial x}\left(1 - \frac{u^2}{a^2}\right) + \frac{\partial v}{\partial y}\left(1 - \frac{v^2}{a^2}\right) - \frac{uv}{a^2}\left(\frac{\partial u}{\partial y} + \frac{\partial v}{\partial x}\right) = 0 \qquad (55)$$

and because the flow is irrotational,

$$\text{curl } V = 0$$

or (equation 13)

$$\frac{\partial u}{\partial y} - \frac{\partial v}{\partial x} = 0. \qquad (56)$$

Therefore there exists a function Φ (potential of velocity) defined by the following condition:

$$u = \frac{\partial \Phi}{\partial x} \text{ and } v = \frac{\partial \Phi}{\partial y}. \qquad (57)$$

Equation (55), using equations (56) and (57), becomes

$$\left(1 - \frac{u^2}{a^2}\right)\frac{\partial^2 \Phi}{\partial x^2} + \left(1 - \frac{v^2}{a^2}\right)\frac{\partial^2 \Phi}{\partial y^2} - \frac{2uv}{a^2}\frac{\partial^2 \Phi}{\partial xy} = 0. \qquad (58)$$

All physical quantities of the flow are determined if a function $\phi(xy)$, which respects the boundary conditions, is determined in the entire field. Indeed, from the value of the velocity, it is possible to determine the value of pressure with the energy equation (11a), and the temperature and density from the equation of isentropic transformation and the general equation of a perfect gas. The boundary conditions usually give the value of all flow quantities in a zone of the fluid (for example, at infinity), and give the condition that the flow must be tangent to a body of given form, and therefore give the value of $\partial \Phi / \partial x$, $\partial \Phi / \partial y$ in a zone of the field; if the stream is parallel to the x axis at infinity, this boundary condition is expressed in the form

$$\left(\frac{\partial \Phi}{\partial x}\right)_\infty = V_1, \quad \left(\frac{\partial \Phi}{\partial y}\right)_\infty = 0$$

and gives the condition that the normal gradient of ϕ, $\partial \phi / \partial n$, must be zero along a line that defines the section of the body in the plane considered. Because the phenomenon considered is two-dimensional, the body considered must be two-dimensional; therefore it must be a cylinder.

Equation (58) permits some interesting considerations: if the value of the velocity is small in comparison with the velocity of sound, it is possible to assume the terms u^2/a^2, v^2/a^2, uv/a^2, equal to zero. In this case, the equation becomes

$$\frac{\partial^2 \Phi}{\partial x^2} + \frac{\partial^2 \Phi}{\partial y^2} = 0$$

which is the equation of motion for incompressible flow. Equation (58) is a partial differential equation of the second order, linear in terms of the second derivative, and is of the type of the Monge-Ampere equation (Reference 3).

Three types of Monge Ampere equations exist: the elliptical, parabolic, and hyperbolic types. The difference between these three types depends on the value of equation (59):

$$\left(1 - \frac{u^2}{a^2}\right)\left(1 - \frac{v^2}{a^2}\right) - \frac{u^2 v^2}{a^4} = 1 - \frac{u^2 + v^2}{a^2} = 1 - \frac{V^2}{a^2}. \tag{59}$$

If equation (59) is greater than, equal to, or less than zero, the equation is, respectively, of elliptical, parabolic, or hyperbolic type. Now, if the phenomenon is all subsonic ($V < a$), equation (59) is greater than zero, and equation (58) is of elliptical type; if the phenomenon is all supersonic ($V > a$) and equation (59) is less than zero, equation (58) is of hyperbolic type. If in the phenomenon the flow is in part supersonic and in part subsonic, the equation is partly of the elliptical type, partly of the parabolic type, and partly of the hyperbolic type. The difference in the type of the equation is connected with differences in the general integral of equation (58), and therefore with substantial differences in the resultant configuration of the flow, that corresponds to the fact that substantial physical differences exist for the phenomena in the two fields of velocity.

The use of equation (58) is possible when in the entire flow, the equation is of one type alone, but becomes more difficult when, in the field, the type of the equation changes, as happens in the case of transonic phenomena.

Case of Flow Supersonic throughout the Entire Field — Characteristic Lines. It was shown in Chapter 1 that in supersonic flow the small disturbances produced in a point of the field influence a zone contained in a cone that has a vertex at the point and an angle equal to the Mach angle. Consider now a two-dimensional flow that wets a plane, and assume that at the point A (Figure 10) a small deviation occurs that produces expansion. The deviation is in accord with the hypothesis that the phenomenon is isentropic, because the expansion occurs gradually, and therefore if the flow is

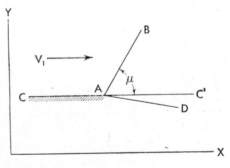

Fig. 10. *Deviation of expansion in a two-dimensional flow.*

isentropic in the part in front of AB, it remains isentropic after the deviation in A. Because the disturbance starts from a line perpendicular to the plane in A, the disturbance must be transmitted to a zone contained in the dihedral BAC', where BAC' is the Mach angle. If the velocity of the undisturbed flow is V_1, the value of the velocity in the zone AB must change, because in the zone BAD, as a consequence of the small deviation, the flow is expanded and changes direction. Now consider this phenomenon in terms of the differential equation (58) of potential flow. In the zone CAB the potential is

$$\Phi_1 = V_1 x.$$

In the zone BAD the potential must be different:

$$\Phi = \Phi_2.$$

Along the line AB, because the movement is continuous, the functions Φ_1 and Φ_2 must have the same value, and the first derivatives of the functions (the velocity components), must also have the same value. As a consequence of this consideration, two possible solutions must exist for equation (58), solutions that are coincident for all points of the line AB, and which also have the first derivative, that corresponds to the velocity, coincident. The Cauchy theorem (Reference 3) shows that the integral of a partial differential equation of the second order, such as equation (58), is, in general, universally defined if its value and the value of its first derivatives are known for all points on a line. This does not occur only if the line is a *characteristic variety* of the equation. In this case, because there are two solutions for equation (58), Φ_1 and Φ_2, having the same value and the same derivative along AB, it can be concluded that the Mach lines in the flow are the characteristic lines of the differential equation that define the potential function. Therefore it is possible to determine the position of the characteristic lines of the equation on the basis of the physical meaning of these lines.

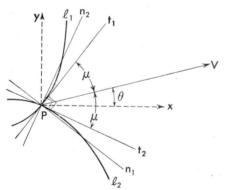

Fig. 11. *The characteristic lines of the two different families.*

Equations of the Characteristic Lines. * From the preceding considerations it is shown that the characteristic lines of equation (58) are coincident with the Mach lines; therefore, if the flow is not at a constant Mach number in the entire field, the characteristic lines are curved at all the points on the line. Now if a point P in the flow is considered (Figure 11) and V is the velocity of the point, the tangent t to the characteristic line must be inclined at the angle μ (Mach angle at the point P) with respect to the direction of the

* For the method of characteristics for two-dimensional flow see Reference 4. For the analytical treatment used see Reference 5.

velocity. Because two lines l_1 and l_2 exist at P the tangents of which are inclined at the angle μ with respect to V, it can be concluded that for every point P of the flow, two characteristic lines exist that are defined by the condition that the tangents are inclined at an angle μ to the direction of velocity, where μ is defined by

$$\sin \mu = \frac{1}{M_p}.$$

If dl is an elementary arc of components dx and dy of the line l, and θ is the inclination of the velocity with respect to the x axis,

$$\left(\frac{dy}{dx}\right)_{l_1} = \tan (\theta + \mu); \left(\frac{dy}{dx}\right)_{l_2} = \tan (\theta - \mu). \tag{60}$$

Equations (60) can be expressed in Cartesian coordinates, if $t_{1,2}$ are the tangents to the characteristic lines and $n_{1,2}$ are the normal to the lines $l_{1,2}$ at P (Figure 11),

$$\cos (xV) = \frac{u}{V} ; \cos (yV) = \frac{v}{V}$$

$$\cos (t_1 x) = + \frac{dx}{dl} ; \cos (t_1 y) = \frac{dy}{dl} \tag{61}$$

$$\cos (n_{1,2}V) = \sin \mu = \frac{a}{V} = \frac{1}{M} \tag{62}$$

but

$$\cos (n_{1,2}V) = \frac{u}{V}\frac{dy}{dl} - \frac{v}{V}\frac{dx}{dl}.$$

Therefore

$$\frac{a}{V} = \frac{u}{V}\frac{dy}{dl} - \frac{v}{V}\frac{dx}{dl} \tag{63}$$

or

$$1 = \frac{u}{a}\frac{dy}{dl} - \frac{v}{a}\frac{dx}{dl}$$

but

$$(dx)^2 + (dy)^2 = (dl)^2 \tag{64}$$

and

$$\left(\frac{dx}{dl}\right)^2 + \left(\frac{dy}{dl}\right)^2 = 1.$$

Therefore substituting the square of equation (63) in equation (64) instead of one, the result is

$$\left(\frac{dx}{dl}\right)^2 + \left(\frac{dy}{dl}\right)^2 = \frac{u^2}{a^2}\left(\frac{dy}{dl}\right)^2 - \frac{2uv}{a^2}\frac{dx}{dl}\frac{dy}{dl} + \frac{v^2}{a^2}\left(\frac{dx}{dl}\right)^2 \tag{65}$$

or
$$\left(1 - \frac{u^2}{a^2}\right)\left(\frac{dy}{dx}\right)^2 + \frac{2uv}{a^2}\frac{dy}{dx} + \left(1 - \frac{v^2}{a^2}\right) = 0. \tag{66}$$

Assuming
$$H = 1 - \frac{u^2}{a^2} \;\; ; \;\; L = 1 - \frac{v^2}{a^2} \;\; ; \;\; K = -\frac{uv}{a^2} \tag{67}$$

$$\left(\frac{dy}{dx}\right)_1 = \lambda_1 \qquad \left(\frac{dy}{dx}\right)_2 = \lambda_2 \tag{68}$$

where λ_1 and λ_2 are the solutions of quadratic equation (66) and are

$$\lambda_1 = \frac{K}{H} - \frac{1}{H}\sqrt{K^2 - HL}$$

$$\lambda_2 = \frac{K}{H} + \frac{1}{H}\sqrt{K^2 - HL}. \tag{69}$$

From equation (69) it is evident that if in the flow $(K^2 - HL)$ is less than zero, as it is for the case of equations of the elliptical type, the angular coefficients of the characteristics have imaginary values, and therefore characteristic lines do not exist.

Equations (60), (68), and (69) give the equations of the characteristic lines.

Law of Variation of the Mach Number, of the Pressure, and of the Velocity along a Characteristic Line.

Equation (58) can be written using equations (67) in the form

$$H\frac{\partial u}{\partial x} + 2K\frac{\partial v}{\partial x} + L\frac{\partial v}{\partial y} = 0. \tag{70}$$

If du and dv are the variations of the velocity components along a characteristic line,

$$\left.\begin{aligned}
du &= \frac{\partial u}{\partial x}dx + \frac{\partial u}{\partial y}dy = \left(\frac{\partial u}{\partial x} + \lambda\frac{\partial u}{\partial y}\right)dx \\
dv &= \frac{\partial v}{\partial x}dx + \frac{\partial v}{\partial y}dy = \left(\frac{\partial v}{\partial x} + \lambda\frac{\partial v}{\partial y}\right)dx
\end{aligned}\right\} \tag{71}$$

Where λ is defined by the equations (68) and (69), but

$$\frac{\partial u}{\partial y} = \frac{\partial v}{\partial x} \text{ (irrotational flow).}$$

Therefore from equation (71) is obtained

$$\frac{\partial u}{\partial x} = \frac{du}{dx} - \lambda\frac{\partial u}{\partial y} \;\; ; \;\; \frac{\partial v}{\partial x} = \frac{\partial u}{\partial y} = \frac{dv}{dx} - \lambda\frac{\partial v}{\partial y} \tag{72}$$

and substituting the second part of equation (72) in the first produces

$$\frac{\partial u}{\partial x} = \frac{du}{dx} - \lambda \frac{dv}{dx} + \lambda^2 \frac{\partial v}{\partial y} . \tag{73}$$

Substituting equation (73) in (70),

$$H \frac{du}{dx} + (2K - H\lambda) \frac{dv}{dx} + \frac{\partial v}{\partial y} (H\lambda^2 - 2K\lambda + L) = 0 \tag{74}$$

but λ is defined by equation (69) and is the solution of the equation

$$H\lambda^2 - 2K\lambda + L = 0$$

which gives

$$2K - H\lambda_1 = \lambda_2 H$$
$$2K - H\lambda_2 = \lambda_1 H.$$

Therefore equation (74) for the first characteristic defined by

$$\frac{dy}{dx} = \lambda_1$$

becomes

$$du + \lambda_2 dv = 0 \tag{75a}$$

and for the second characteristic defined by

$$\frac{dy}{dx} = \lambda_2$$

becomes

$$du + \lambda_1 dv = 0. \tag{75b}$$

Equations (75) are integrable because λ_1 and λ_2 are functions of u and v.

Considering polar coordinates, the values of λ_1 and λ_2 are given by equation (60)

$$\lambda_1 = \tan (\theta + \mu)$$
$$\lambda_2 = \tan (\theta - \mu)$$

and du and dv correspond to the following expressions:

$$du = dV \cos \theta - V \sin \theta d\theta$$
$$dv = dV \sin \theta + V \cos \theta d\theta \tag{76}$$

where V is the velocity having the components u and v. Substituting the values of du and dv given by equation (76), the value of λ given by equation (60) and the value $1/M$ for the value $\sin \mu$, from equation (75a) the following expression is obtained:

$$\frac{dV}{d\theta} \sqrt{1 - \frac{1}{M^2}} = + \frac{V}{M} \tag{77a}$$

and from (75b)

$$\frac{dV}{d\theta} \sqrt{1 - \frac{1}{M^2}} = - \frac{V}{M} \tag{77b}$$

but from the hypothesis of isentropic flow, the velocity of sound a is

$$a^2 = \gamma \frac{p}{\rho} = \frac{dp}{d\rho}$$

and

$$- V dV = \frac{dp}{\rho} \text{ (energy equation).}$$

Therefore

$$\frac{dM}{M} = \frac{dV}{V}\left(1 + \frac{\gamma - 1}{2} M^2\right) \tag{78}$$

and

$$d\theta = \pm \frac{dM}{M\left[1 + \frac{\gamma - 1}{2} M^2\right]} \sqrt{M^2 - 1}. \tag{79}$$

Equation (79) can be integrated

$$\pm d\theta = dM \frac{M^2 - 1}{M\sqrt{M^2 - 1}\left(1 + \frac{\gamma - 1}{2} M^2\right)}$$

and substituting for M^2 the equivalent $\left(\frac{\gamma + 1}{2} - \frac{\gamma - 1}{2}\right) M^2$,

$$\pm d\theta = dM\left[\frac{\gamma + 1}{2} \frac{M}{\sqrt{M^2 - 1}\left(1 + \frac{\gamma - 1}{2} M^2\right)}\right] - \frac{dM}{M\sqrt{M^2 - 1}}.$$

Performing the integration, the following expression is obtained:

$$\pm\theta = \cos^{-1} \frac{1}{M} + \frac{1}{2}\sqrt{\frac{\gamma + 1}{\gamma - 1}} \cos^{-1}\left(1 - \frac{\gamma + 1}{1 + \frac{\gamma - 1}{2} M^2}\right) + \text{constant} \tag{80}$$

or changing the value of the constant of the quantity $\frac{\pi}{2}\sqrt{\frac{\gamma + 1}{\gamma - 1}}$,

$$\pm\theta = \cos^{-1} \frac{1}{M} - \sqrt{\frac{\gamma + 1}{\gamma - 1}} \tan^{-1}\left(\sqrt{M^2 - 1}\sqrt{\frac{\gamma - 1}{\gamma + 1}}\right) + \text{constant.} \tag{81}$$

Equations (80) or (81) give the value of the Mach number as a function of
the direction of the velocity along a characteristic line. From the value of the
Mach number, it is possible, with the energy equation, to determine the value
of the pressure, and subsequently to determine all other flow quantities.
Equations (80) and (81) have important application in calculations for
isentropic two-dimensional supersonic flow.

The following considerations explain the use of equations (80) or (81).
Consider a uniform supersonic flow that runs parallel to the wall AB (Figure
12), having a Mach number M_1 and pressure p_1. Assume that in the zone BC

a uniform pressure p_2 smaller than p_1 exists.* The flow is expanded at the corner B. The expansion begins along the line BD inclined at an angle μ_1 with respect to the line AB. The line BD is a straight line because the flow in front has constant direction and Mach number.

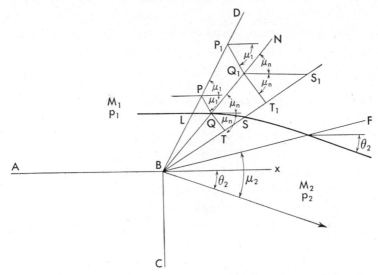

Fig. 12. *Analysis of the flow around a corner with the characteristic system.*

Across every Mach line the flow undergoes an infinitesimal variation of pressure. When the flow crosses the Mach line BD the pressure of the flow does not become equal to p_2, but attains a value $(p_1 + dp)$ where dp is the infinitesimal variation of pressure that is propagated in the flow along BD. Therefore the flow must continue to expand, and the next expansion dp will occur across another Mach line BN that must pass through B because the variation of pressure is transmitted in the flow from the point B; the line NB must be less inclined than BD, and must be a straight line because the Mach number in front is constant. In a similar way, all variations of pressure $(p_2 - p_1)$ will be transmitted in the flow across a series of Mach lines from BD to BF, each of which transmits in the flow a variation of pressure dp. The Mach lines BD and BF correspond to the characteristic lines of the first family, and because no variation of pressure occurs along each characteristic line, the variation of velocity is also zero along each of these lines. The lines are all straight lines. At every point P of the first Mach line BD there passes also a characteristic line of the second family PQ inclined at an angle μ_1 with the direction of the velocity. Because along BD the velocity has constant

* Supersonic flow around a corner was treated originally in Reference 6.

intensity and direction, the characteristic lines of the second family for every point on BD are parallel to each other. The same consideration can be applied to all points of every characteristic line BN of the first family. Therefore in order to consider the variation of velocity along all characteristic lines of the second family, it is sufficient to consider the variation along only one characteristic line PQT of the second family. The variation along PQT in this case corresponds also to the variation along the stream lines because the velocity at P is the same as at L, the velocity at T is the same as at S, and the variation of velocity along the stream line LQS is the same as along the characteristic line PQT. The variation of velocity along a characteristic line of the second family can be analyzed with equations (80) or (81). The values of the constants of equation (80) or (81) can be calculated from the Mach number M_1 and from the value θ, in the zone ABD (assuming the value of θ to be measured from the x-axis, θ is equal to zero in the zone ABD), and then for every value of θ the corresponding value of M can be obtained. Because the second characteristic family is considered, the plus sign must be assumed in equations (80) and (81) (θ is negative). When a value of M is determined for a fixed value of θ, the corresponding line BN can be determined, because from the value of M the value of μ can be determined, and the line BN corresponding to the given value of θ must be inclined at $(\mu + \theta)$ with the x-axis (θ is negative). From the energy equation it is possible to determine the value of the Mach number M_2 of the flow when the pressure p_2 is attained:

$$\frac{V_1^2}{2} + \frac{\gamma}{\gamma - 1}\frac{p_1}{\rho_1} = \frac{V_2^2}{2} + \frac{\gamma}{\gamma - 1}\frac{p_2}{\rho_2}$$

and because $\qquad \rho V^2 = \gamma p M^2 \qquad$ and $\qquad \dfrac{p_2}{\rho_2^{\gamma}} = \dfrac{p_1}{\rho_1^{\gamma}}$

$$\left(\frac{p_2}{p_1}\right)^{\frac{\gamma - 1}{\gamma}} = \frac{M_1^2 + \dfrac{2}{\gamma - 1}}{M_2^2 + \dfrac{2}{\gamma - 1}}. \tag{82}$$

From the value of M_2 with equation (80) or (81) the corresponding value of θ_2 can be calculated, and the line BF, along which the expansion is accomplished, can be determined. The line BF is inclined at an angle $(\theta_2 + \mu_2)$ with respect to the x-axis.

The problem can be inverted if the variation of direction is known; from the value of the final angle θ_2, the value of M_2 can be determined, and from this, the value of the pressure. Also, the streamlines can be designed. From the case of expansion around a sharp edge, it is easy to extend to the case of continued expansion along a curved surface (Figure 13). Indeed, for every point N on the surface, the value of θ_N is known, and from the value of M_1, for which θ_1 is zero, it is possible to determine the value of the constant in equation (81); therefore, from θ_N it is possible to determine M_N and μ_N. Along

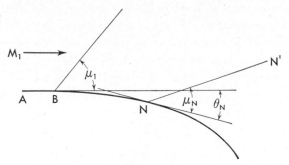

Fig. 13. *Analysis of the flow along a curved surface with the characteristic system (case of expansion).*

NN', the direction of velocity is constant; therefore M_N is constant and the characteristic line is straight. At N the value of pressure is determined by the value of M_N from equation (82).

Equation (81) can be used also in some cases of compression, but we must remember that this equation is obtained from the hypothesis of isentropic flow without discontinuity, and therefore it is not valid in the zone in which shock waves occur. In a curved wall in which compression occurs (Figure 14),

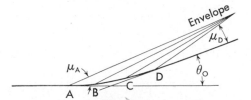

Fig. 14. *Analysis of the flow along a curved surface (case of compression).*

the characteristic lines tend to increase the angle with respect to the horizontal, because μ increases (M decreases) and θ increases; therefore the characteristic lines make an envelope, and the variations across the envelope are no longer infinitesimal, but finite. The phenomenon is no longer continuous, and equation (81) is no longer valid.

The values of θ as a function of M can be determined and tabulated in order to avoid making long calculations. Assume that the initial Mach number is equal to one, and for this value the deviation is zero. The values of the deviation θ corresponding to all other Mach numbers, and the corresponding variations of pressure can be calculated. Because the expansion begins from a fixed Mach number ($M = 1$), the deviation will be designated by another symbol (ν). Some values of Mach number, corresponding to the variations of directions ν, from M equal to one, are given in Table 2 of the appendix. The corresponding values of Mach angle and pressure ratio with respect to the pressure p_* corresponding to ($M = 1$) are also given. This table can be used very easily. Indeed, if a case is considered in which the undisturbed Mach number is M_1, and the flow undergoes a deviation of expansion θ, in order to determine the corresponding Mach number it is sufficient to determine the value of ν_1 corresponding to M_1 in the table, and the corresponding value of p_1/p_*. Then, from the value of ($\nu_2 = \nu_1 + \theta$) it is possible to determine the value of M_2, corresponding to the deviation of θ, and the value of p_2/p_*. The variation of pressure is given by

$$\frac{p_1}{p_2} = \frac{p_1}{p_*} \frac{p_*}{p_2} .$$

The Critical Velocity and the Limiting Velocity. Consider a tank with air at a pressure p_0 and density ρ_0, and assume that the gas is expanded isentropically in a nozzle. In the subsonic part, the nozzle is converging, and in the minimum section, the speed of sound is obtained. Using equations (34), (38), and (39) it is possible to determine the velocity in the minimum section. This velocity is called the *critical velocity* to indicate that it is the velocity of sound in the flow for ($M = 1$), and its value is indicated as the symbol V_c. The value of V_c is given by

$$V_c^2 = \frac{2\gamma}{\gamma + 1} \frac{p_0}{\rho_0} . \tag{83}$$

The velocity in every point is given by the expression (equation 34)

$$V^2 = \frac{2\gamma}{\gamma - 1} \frac{p_0}{\rho_0} \left[1 - \left(\frac{p}{p_0} \right)^{\frac{\gamma - 1}{\gamma}} \right] . \tag{84}$$

The maximum velocity that it is possible to obtain for the air in the tank is that which corresponds to discharge of the air from the tank in a place at static pressure equal to zero. If in equation (84) the term p becomes zero, the speed becomes

$$V_l^2 = \frac{2\gamma}{\gamma - 1} \frac{p_0}{\rho_0} = \frac{\gamma + 1}{\gamma - 1} V_c^2. \tag{85}$$

Because in adiabatic transformations p_0/ρ_0 is constant, the value of V_c is constant also. Equation (84), in terms of equation (85) becomes

$$\frac{V^2}{V_l^2} \equiv 1 - \left(\frac{p}{p_0} \right)^{\frac{\gamma - 1}{\gamma}} . \tag{85a}$$

Because from equation (41)

$$\left(\frac{p_0}{p}\right)^{\frac{\gamma-1}{\gamma}} - 1 = \frac{\gamma-1}{2} M^2$$

then

$$\frac{V_l^2}{V^2} = 1 + \frac{2}{\gamma-1}\frac{1}{M^2} \cdot \qquad (85b)$$

The value of V_l is the maximum possible value of velocity that the air can attain, and is called *limiting velocity*. It is interesting to determine from equation (80), the maximum theoretical value of the deviation that it is necessary to obtain from a given Mach number the limiting velocity. Suppose that the deviation begins from ($M = 1$). For $M = 1$, ν and θ are zero, and the value of the constant of equation (80) for $\gamma = 1.40$ is

$$C = -220.455°.$$

If, in equation (80), for the value of M the expression given by equation (41) is substituted

$$M = \sqrt{\frac{2}{\gamma-1}\left[\left(\frac{p_0}{p}\right)^{\frac{\gamma-1}{\gamma}} - 1\right]} \qquad (41)$$

then

$$\pm\theta = \cos^{-1}\frac{1}{\sqrt{\frac{2}{\gamma-1}\left[\left(\frac{p_0}{p}\right)^{\frac{\gamma-1}{\gamma}} - 1\right]}}$$
$$+ \frac{1}{2}\sqrt{\frac{\gamma+1}{\gamma-1}}\ \cos^{-1}\left[1 - (\gamma+1)\left(\frac{p}{p_0}\right)^{\frac{\gamma-1}{\gamma}}\right] - 220.455° \qquad (86)$$

If, in equation (86), p becomes zero, the first term becomes $\cos^{-1} 0$, which corresponds to $\pi/2$.

The second term becomes $\cos^{-1} 1 = 0$; therefore,

$$\nu_{\text{limit}} = 130.455°. \qquad (87)$$

A perfect supersonic flow cannot turn through $360°$; therefore a part of the space theoretically cannot be filled by the flow. For the velocity V_l, M is

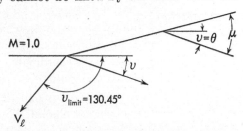

Fig. 15. *The maximum value of the deviation of expansion.*

infinity; therefore μ is zero, and the Mach line is in the same direction as the direction of velocity; the velocity is radial (Figure 15). If the initial Mach number is other than zero, in order to obtain the θ_{limit}, it is sufficient to determine the ν corresponding to the value of the initial Mach number, because

$$\theta_{\text{limit}} = \nu_{\text{limit}} - \nu_{M_1}.$$

It is evident that existence of a maximum value of ν depends on the hypothesis of perfect flow, but air at very low pressures cannot be considered similar to a perfect homogeneous flow; therefore these considerations are theoretical.

Geometrical Interpretation of the Characteristic Equation. Equation (80) can be transformed into an expression which is a function of arc sines in place of a function of arc cosines. Indeed, for every angle α

$$\sin^{-1} \alpha = \frac{\pi}{2} - \cos^{-1} \alpha$$

and

$$\cos 2\alpha = 2 \cos^2 \alpha - 1.$$

Therefore, in place of $\cos^{-1} \dfrac{1}{M}$, it is possible to write $\dfrac{1}{2} \cos^{-1}\left(\dfrac{2}{M^2} - 1\right)$; then, changing the value of the constant, equation (80) becomes

$$\mp 2\theta = \sqrt{\frac{\gamma + 1}{\gamma - 1}}\, \sin^{-1} \frac{\dfrac{\gamma - 1}{2} M_1^2 - \gamma}{\dfrac{\gamma - 1}{2} M_1^2 + 1} + \sin^{-1}\left(\frac{2}{M^2} - 1\right) + c \qquad (88)$$

and, using equations (83) and (85b), equation (88) becomes

$$\mp 2\theta = \sqrt{\frac{\gamma + 1}{\gamma - 1}}\, \sin^{-1}\left[(\gamma - 1)\frac{V^2}{V_c^2} - \gamma\right]$$
$$+ \sin^{-1}\left[(\gamma + 1)\frac{V_c^2}{V^2} - \gamma\right] + c. \qquad (89)$$

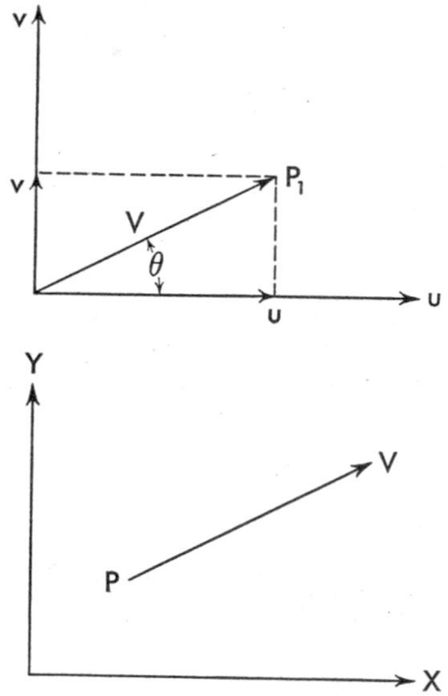

Equation (89) permits a graphical representation of the expansion phenomena (Reference 7). Consider a system including an axis parallel to the coordinate system (Figure 16) and take along the axis, parallel to x, a segment corresponding to the component u of the velocity at a point P, and in a perpendicular direction, a segment corresponding to the component v of the velocity at P. For every point P of the physical plane, a corresponding vector V exists in the new plane considered, the coordinates of which are the

Fig. 16. *Physical and hodograph plane.*

components u and v of the velocity in the direction of the axis x and y in the plane of movement. The vector V determines a point P_1 in the plane determined by u and v, and called the *hodograph plane*.

Now, if in the hodograph plane equation (89) is plotted, a curve is obtained that gives the variation of the velocity as a function of the angle θ along a characteristic line. Because the value of the sines must be between -1 and $+1$, it must be true that

$$- 1 \leq (\gamma - 1)\frac{V^2}{V_c^2} - \gamma \leq 1$$

$$- 1 \leq \frac{V_c^2}{V^2}(\gamma + 1) - \gamma \leq 1$$

and therefore V cannot be less than V_c nor greater than V_l (equation 85). Therefore the curve which represents equation (89) must be contained in the space between two circles of radius V_c and V_l (Figure 17). From equation (89), it appears that to every value of c there corresponds a given curve, and the value of c determines the position of the point of the curve in the circle

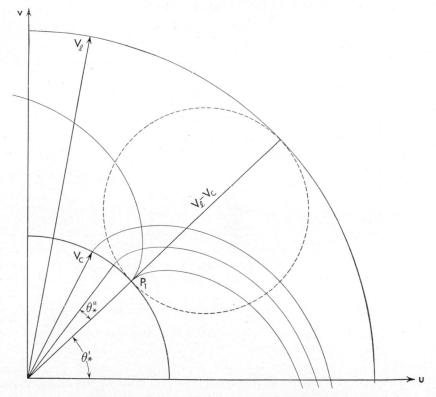

Fig. 17. *Construction of the epicycloid diagram.*

$(V = V_c)$. Every curve that can be obtained by changing the value of c can be also obtained from the preceding curve with the expression

$$\theta_v = \theta_v{}' + \theta_*$$

in which θ_* is a constant and where θ_v and $\theta'{}_v$ are values correspondent to the same value of V_1. Therefore every curve for a fixed sign, of equation (89), is identical to all other curves corresponding to other values of the constants and is obtained by rotation of one of the curves around the point 0, corresponding to $(V = 0)$.

Equation (89) corresponds to the equation of an epicycloid in polar coordinates, and therefore the curve which gives V as a function of θ can be obtained in the following manner: Plot in the hodograph plane the circles $(V = V_l)$ and $(V = V_c)$ (Figure 17) and fix the value of the constant c, that is, the value of θ_* for $(V = V_c)$. Plot the circle of diameter $(V_l - V_c)$ tangent at $(\theta = \theta_*)$ to the circles $(V = V_l)$ and $(V = V_c)$. Roll the circle $(V_l - V_c)$ around the circle $(V = V_c)$. From the point P two curves are obtained corresponding to the two possible directions of rolling of the circle, that correspond to the two signs of equation (89), and therefore to the two families of characteristic lines. Changing gradually the value of the θ_* (which corresponds to the change of the value of c) two families of curves, corresponding to the two families of characteristic lines, are obtained.

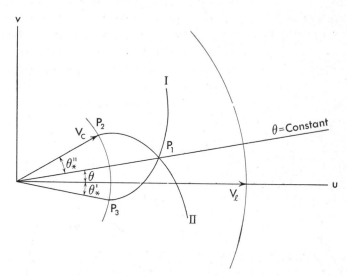

Fig. 18. *The two families of epicycloid curves that pass through a point of the hodograph plane.*

For every point P of the hodograph plane contained in the space of real values of V, two epicycloids pass, one for every family. These epicycloids are symmetrical with respect to the line ($\theta =$ constant) that passes through P_1 (Figure 18). Indeed, for the characteristic line I, calculating the value of the constant in terms of the value θ_* of the point P_3 on the circle ($V = V_c$), equation (89) becomes

$$+ 2\theta = \sqrt{\frac{\gamma + 1}{\gamma - 1}} \sin^{-1}\left[(\gamma - 1)\frac{V^2}{V_c^2} - \gamma\right] + \sin^{-1}\left[(\gamma + 1)\frac{V_c^2}{V^2} - \gamma\right]$$
$$+ 2\theta_*' - \sqrt{\frac{\gamma + 1}{\gamma - 1}}\frac{3\pi}{2} - \frac{\pi}{2}. \tag{90}$$

For characteristic line II, if θ_*'' is the value of θ for the point P_2 of the line II in the circle ($V = V_c$)

$$+ 2\theta = \sqrt{\frac{\gamma + 1}{\gamma - 1}} \sin^{-1}\left[(\gamma - 1)\frac{V^2}{V_c^2} - \gamma\right] + \sin^{-1}\left[(\gamma + 1)\frac{V_c^2}{V^2} - \gamma\right]$$
$$- 2\theta_*'' - \sqrt{\frac{\gamma + 1}{\gamma - 1}}\frac{3\pi}{2} - \frac{\pi}{2}. \tag{90a}$$

Therefore, at the point P_1, $2(\theta - \theta_*') = -2(\theta - \theta_*'')$, and the curves I and II are symmetrical with respect to the line ($\theta =$ constant).

From the preceding considerations it is shown that through every point P of the plane of movement, pass two characteristic lines, I and II, inclined at angle μ with respect to the direction of the velocity. For every point P of the plane of flow, there is a corresponding point P_1 in the hodograph plane that gives the dimension of the velocity. Through every point P_1 of the hodograph two epicycloids pass that give the law of variation of the velocity along the corresponding characteristic lines at P. In order to determine the epicycloid corresponding to a given family of characteristics, equations (75) that are the differential equations of (81) must be considered.

From equations (75) for the first characteristic line,

$$\left(\frac{du}{dv}\right)_{\mathrm{I}} = -\lambda_2 = -\left(\frac{dy}{dx}\right)_{\mathrm{II}}.$$

Therefore

$$\left(\frac{dv}{du}\right)_{\mathrm{I}}\left(\frac{dy}{dx}\right)_{\mathrm{II}} = -1 \tag{91}$$

and in a similar way for the second characteristic line,

$$\left(\frac{dv}{du}\right)_{\mathrm{II}}\left(\frac{dy}{dx}\right)_{\mathrm{I}} = -1. \tag{91a}$$

Equations (91) impose the condition that the tangent to the characteristic line I (dy/dx) must be perpendicular to the epicycloid II (dv/du), and that the tangent to the characteristic line II must be perpendicular to the epicycloid I;

therefore it is possible from this condition to determine in the diagrams the correspondence between the characteristic and epicycloid. The tangent t_2 to the characteristic II in the xy plane (Figure 19) must be parallel to the normal n_1 to the epicycloid of the first family in the hodograph plane and the tangent t_1 in the plane xy must be parallel to n_2 in the plane u, v.

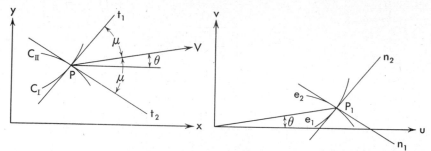

Fig. 19. *Correspondence between characteristic lines in the physical plane and epicycloid curves in the hodograph plane.*

For practical use, it is better to consider θ always positive, and, because the maximum possible deviation is 130.45° it is practical to take the value of θ for the undisturbed flow equal to 200.

Every characteristic can be distinguished by the value of the constant c of equation (88). In this case, for the first characteristic, the equation is

$$- \theta = + f(v) - c_1 \qquad (92)$$

where $2c_1$ is the absolute value of the constant that in equation (88) is negative, and for the second,

$$+ \theta = + f(v) - c_2. \qquad (92a)$$

From equations (92) and (92a),

$$\theta = \frac{c_1 - c_2}{2} \qquad (93)$$

$$f(v) = \frac{c_1 + c_2}{2}. \qquad (94)$$

Therefore, if every epicycloid is indicated with a number C in such a manner that the direction of the velocity for every point is given by the difference of the two numbers of the two epicycloids that in the hodograph plane pass through the point, then the intensity of the velocity is a function of the sum of the two numbers. Every pair of epicycloids, C_1 and C_2, for which the difference of the numbers is equal to a constant must cross each other along the radius (θ = constant), and because $f(V)$ is constant, the epicycloids of every pair having the same value of $(C_2 + C_1)$ cross each other along a circle (V = constant). Figure 20 gives a practical diagram that uses the system of numbers explained before. In Table 2 of the appendix, the number in the first column corresponds to the value $(C_1 + C_2)$, and therefore to the value of the velocity in the hodograph plane.   From Figure 20 it is possible, in terms of

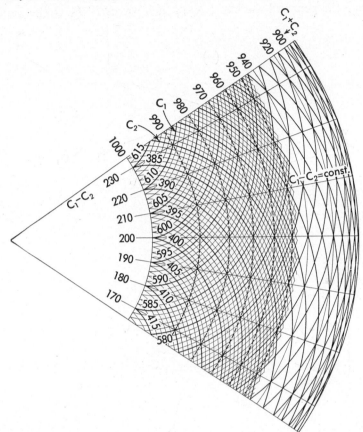

Fig. 20.   *The epicycloid diagram and the corresponding characteristic numbers.*

the value $(C_1 + C_2)$, to determine the value of the corresponding V/V_l.   The diagram is plotted to a large scale in Chart 1 of the appendix.

The epicycloid diagram can be used to determine graphically the characteristic lines for two-dimensional phenomena, and the values of the physical quantities of the flow if the phenomenon is continuous.

A practical example of calculations is given in Figure 21 where the flow along a curved wall is analyzed.   The flow properties are known at the point P_0. In terms of the value of the Mach number and of the velocity direction at P_0, the corresponding point P_0' in the epicycloid diagram can be determined, because the value of M gives the value of $(C_2 + C_1)$ (Table 2), and the direction gives the value of $(C_1 - C_2)$.   Therefore the numbers C_1 and C_2 of the epicycloids that pass through P_0' can be calculated.   The value of V/V_l, and therefore the value of the radius OP_0' can also be evaluated from the value of M at P_0, using equation (85b). If an expansion occurs along the surface $P_0 Q_0$ (Figure 21a), from the points of the line $P_0 Q_0$, Mach waves $P_0 P_1$, $Q_0 Q_1$ are produced

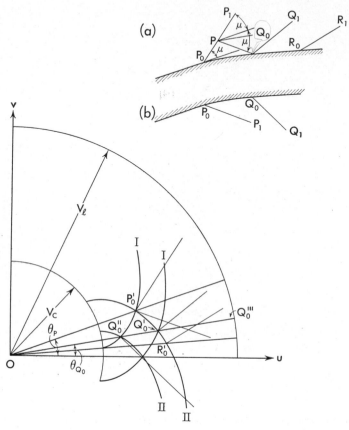

Fig. 21. *The practical use of the epicycloid diagram in order to analyze the flow around a curved surface.*

that are characteristic lines of the first family. Along the characteristic lines $P_0 P_1$ and $Q_0 Q_1$ the velocity is constant. Therefore along every characteristic line of the second family the same variation of velocity occurs. Also along the stream line $P_0 Q_0$ the same variation of velocity occurs as along every characteristic line PQ_0. Therefore, because at Q_0 the direction of the velocity θ_{Q_0} is known in the hodograph plane, the radius OQ_0''' of coordinate θ_{Q_0} can be drawn. The normal at P_0' to the epicycloid of the second family must be parallel to the characteristic line $P_0 P_1$; therefore, the epicycloid of the second family and the point Q_0' along OQ_0''' can be determined. The expansion along $P_0 Q_0$ is represented by the epicycloid $P_0' Q_0'$, and the normals at $P_0' Q_0'$ to the epicycloid give the Mach lines P_0P_1 and Q_0Q_1. If the case of Figure 21b is analyzed, the Mach line P_0P_1 corresponds to a characteristic line of the second family and is parallel to the normal at P_0' to the epicycloid $P_0' Q_0''$. Therefore the variation of velocity is given in the hodograph plane by the epicycloid $P_0' Q_0''$, and along P_0Q_0 the velocity decreases (a compression occurs).

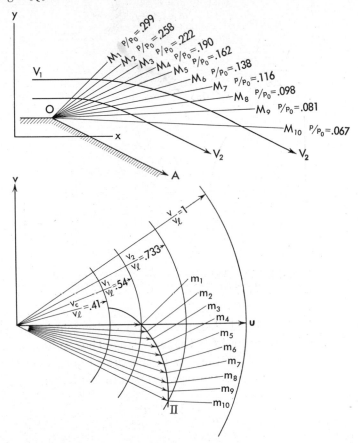

Fig. 22. *Numerical example of analysis of the flow around a corner by use of the epicycloid diagram.*

An example of expansion around a corner is represented in Figure 22. The lines m_1 and m_n in the plane of the hodograph correspond to the lines M_1 and M_n in the physical plane. The values of p/p_0 are determined in terms of the value of the velocity at m_1 and of the value of p/p_0 at m_1. The flow along the characteristic lines is uniform. In Figure 23 is shown an expansion along a curved surface. The entire phenomenon can be determined in the same way, analytically by equation (81), or by using the values calculated in Table 2 of the appendix.

Small Disturbances Theory. In many aerodynamic problems the deviation of the stream lines from the free stream direction is very small, and therefore small variations of pressure and velocity occur in the flow. In these cases in which the disturbances produced in the flow are small, a simplified

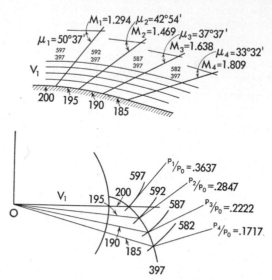

Fig. 23. *The flow along a curved wall analyzed by use of the epicycloid diagram.*

hypothesis can be introduced that permits an easier solution of the flow motion without reducing appreciably the precision of the results (Reference 8).

If the undisturbed velocity of the flow V_1 is assumed in the direction of the x-axis, the velocity components can be expressed in the form:

$$\frac{\partial x}{\partial t} = V_1 + u$$

$$\frac{\partial y}{\partial t} = v \tag{95}$$

The components u and v can be called *disturbance components*. If the components u and v are small quantities in comparison with the undisturbed velocity V_1 and if the variation of the velocity components occurs gradually in such a manner that the derivatives of the velocity components are also small quantities, the hypothesis can be accepted that the second and higher powers of the quantities u and v and, accordingly, of the velocity component derivatives, may be neglected. The variations of the velocity components are gradual when the derivatives $\partial u/\partial x$, $\partial v/\partial y$, and $\partial u/\partial y$ of the velocity components are of the same order of magnitude as the ratios u/l and v/l, where l is a length

of reference connected with the phenomenon; for example, the thickness of
the body, or

$$\frac{\partial u}{\partial y} \approx \frac{\partial u}{\partial x} \approx \frac{u}{l} \; ; \qquad \frac{\partial v}{\partial y} \approx \frac{v}{l} \cdot$$

Therefore, if the variations of the velocity component are gradual, the terms
$u \dfrac{\partial u}{\partial x}$ and $u \dfrac{\partial u}{\partial y}$, etc., are of the same order as u^2/l and v^2/l, etc. Now if the terms
of the order of magnitude of u^2/V_1^2 and v^2/V_1^2 can be neglected, the equation
of motion (equation 58)

$$\left(\frac{a^2}{V_1^2} - \frac{V_1^2 + u^2 + 2uV_1}{V_1^2}\right)\frac{\partial u}{\partial x} + \left(\frac{a^2}{V_1^2} - \frac{v^2}{V_1^2}\right)\frac{\partial v}{\partial y} - \frac{2(V_1 v + uv)}{V_1^2}\frac{\partial u}{\partial y} = 0$$

becomes

$$\left(\frac{V_1^2}{a^2} - 1\right)\frac{\partial^2 \phi}{\partial x^2} = \frac{\partial^2 \phi}{\partial y^2} \cdot \tag{96}$$

The velocity of sound can be expressed using the energy equation (11a) in
the form:

$$a^2 = a_1^2 - \frac{\gamma - 1}{2}\left[(V_1 + u)^2 + v^2 - V_1^2\right] \tag{97}$$

or in the approximation accepted

$$\frac{a^2}{V_1^2} = \frac{a_1^2}{V_1^2} - (\gamma - 1)\frac{u}{V_1} \tag{97a}$$

Substituting equation (97a) in equation (96) and neglecting the terms of
superior order, equation (97) becomes

$$\left(M_1^2 - 1\right)\frac{\partial^2 \phi}{\partial x^2} = \frac{\partial^2 \phi}{\partial y^2} \cdot \tag{98}$$

In this approximation, equation (69) becomes

$$\lambda_1 = \frac{1}{\sqrt{M_1^2 - 1}} = \tan \mu_1 \tag{99}$$

$$\lambda_2 = \frac{1}{\sqrt{M_1^2 - 1}} = \tan \mu_1$$

because

$$\tan \theta = \frac{v}{V_1 + u} \cdot$$

In this approximation

$$\theta = \frac{v}{V_1} \cdot \tag{100}$$

Therefore, from equations (75) and (76),

$$\frac{dV}{V_1} = \mp \, d\theta \, \tan \mu_1.$$

(101)

The pressure coefficient is given by

$$c_p = \frac{\Delta p}{\frac{1}{2}\rho_1 V_1{}^2} = -\frac{\rho V dV}{\frac{1}{2}\rho_1 V_1{}^2} = \pm \frac{2 \tan \mu_1 \Delta\theta}{\rho_1 V_1} \rho V$$

but

$$\frac{\rho_1}{\rho} = 1 + \frac{d\rho}{\rho} = 1 - M^2 \frac{dV}{V_1}$$

(102)

and

$$\frac{V}{V_1} = 1 + \frac{dV}{V_1}.$$

Therefore in the approximation accepted,

$$c_p = \pm \, 2\Delta\theta \, \tan \mu_1 = \pm \frac{2\Delta\theta}{\sqrt{M_1{}^2 - 1}}.$$

(103)

CHAPTER

3

THEORY OF SHOCK WAVES

It was shown from the preceding considerations (Chapters 1 and 2) that when a recompression occurs in a flow with supersonic velocity, the Mach lines tend to converge and to form an envelope. If the envelope occurs, the corresponding disturbance passes from infinitesimal to finite, producing a discontinuity in the flow which is called *shock wave*. The flow across the shock wave undergoes a change of all its physical quantities, and the variations are no longer governed by isentropic law. In order to determine the variation of the quantities across a shock wave, an adiabatic stationary phenomenon will be considered (independent of time and without exchange of heat between the flow and the external). The flow will be assumed to be a perfect flow.

Shock Wave Equations in Stationary Phenomena.* Consider a supersonic flow at Mach number M_1, pressure p_1, density ρ_1, temperature T_1, and entropy S_1; assume that at a point A of the flow a shock wave exists (Figure 24). All flow quantities behind the shock will change. Indicating these quantities with subscript 2, consider the intersection of the shock with the plane that contains the velocity V_1 in front of the shock, and the velocity V_2 behind the shock at A. In this plane at the point A, consider the tangent t to the curve inter-

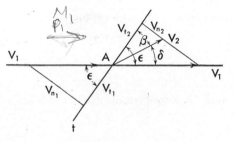

Fig. 24. *Velocity components before and behind a shock wave.*

section of the front of the shock (Figure 24). If ϵ is the angle between V_1 and t, and β is the angle between V_2 and t, in the general case β will be different from ϵ, and therefore a deviation ($\delta = \epsilon - \beta$) of flow direction will

* The first correct treatment of shocks was given by Hugoniot (Reference 9). Hugoniot considered only normal shocks. The general treatment of shock waves was given by Meyer, Th. (Reference 10). For the following analytical treatment see Reference 11.

exist. Projecting the velocities V_1 and V_2 in the direction n normal to the shock and t tangent to the shock, and indicating with the subscripts n and t the corresponding components,

$$\left. \begin{aligned} V_1{}^2 &= V_{n1}{}^2 + V_{t1}{}^2 = M_1{}^2\,\gamma\,\frac{p_1}{\rho_1} \\[2mm] V_2{}^2 &= V_{n2}{}^2 + V_{t2}{}^2 = M_2{}^2\,\gamma\,\frac{p_2}{\rho_2} \end{aligned} \right\} \tag{104}$$

$$\left. \begin{aligned} V_{n1} &= V_1 \sin \epsilon \\ V_{n2} &= V_2 \sin \beta \\ V_{t1} &= V_1 \cos \epsilon \\ V_{t2} &= V_2 \cos \beta \end{aligned} \right\} \tag{105}$$

For the continuity law, the mass of flow across the surface of the shock can be written in the following form:

$$\rho_1 V_{n1} = \rho_2 V_{n2}. \tag{106}$$

The momentum theorem applied to the direction normal to the surface and to the direction tangent to the surface, gives

$$p_1 + \rho_1 V_{n1}{}^2 = p_2 + \rho_2 V_{n2}{}^2 \tag{107}$$

$$\rho_1 V_{n1} V_{t1} = \rho_2 V_{n2} V_{t2}. \tag{108}$$

The law of conservation of energy states that the total energy of the flow in front of the shock and behind the shock must be the same; therefore

$$\frac{\gamma}{\gamma - 1}\frac{p_1}{\rho_1} + \frac{1}{2}V_1{}^2 = \frac{\gamma}{\gamma - 1}\frac{p_2}{\rho_2} + \frac{1}{2}V_2{}^2 \tag{109}$$

but from equations (106) and (108) are obtained

$$V_{t1} = V_{t2} \tag{110}$$

$$\frac{V_2}{V_1} = \frac{\cos \epsilon}{\cos \beta} \tag{111}$$

and therefore equation (109) becomes

$$\frac{2\gamma}{\gamma - 1}\frac{p_1}{\rho_1} + V_{n1}{}^2 = \frac{2\gamma}{\gamma - 1}\frac{p_2}{\rho_2} + V_{n2}{}^2 \tag{112}$$

but

$$\rho_1{}^2 V_{n1}{}^2 = \rho_1{}^2 V_1{}^2 \sin^2 \epsilon = \rho_1 M_1{}^2 \gamma p_1 \sin^2 \epsilon. \tag{113}$$

Therefore equation (106) becomes

$$\rho_1 p_1 M_1{}^2 \sin^2 \epsilon = \rho_2 p_2 M_2{}^2 \sin^2 \beta, \tag{114}$$

equation (107) becomes

$$p_1 \left(1 + \gamma M_1{}^2 \sin^2 \epsilon\right) = p_2 \left(1 + \gamma M_2{}^2 \sin^2 \beta\right), \tag{115}$$

and equation (112) becomes

$$\frac{p_1}{\rho_1}\left(\frac{2}{\gamma-1}+M_1^2\sin^2\epsilon\right)=\frac{p_2}{\rho_2}\left(\frac{2}{\gamma-1}+M_2^2\sin^2\beta\right). \tag{116}$$

It is possible to eliminate the values of p_1/p_2 and ρ_1/ρ_2 in the three equations (114), (115), (116), and to obtain one equation in $M_1\sin\epsilon$ and $M_2\sin\beta$ which, if $M_1\sin\epsilon$ is different from $M_2\sin\beta$ (case of flow with shock), is

$$\left(M_1^2\sin^2\epsilon-\frac{\gamma-1}{2\gamma}\right)\left(M_2^2\sin^2\beta-\frac{\gamma-1}{2\gamma}\right)=\left(\frac{\gamma+1}{2\gamma}\right)^2 \tag{117}$$

or

$$\left(\frac{1}{M_1^2\sin^2\epsilon}+\frac{\gamma-1}{2}\right)\left(\frac{1}{M_2^2\sin^2\beta}+\frac{\gamma-1}{2}\right)=\left(\frac{\gamma+1}{2}\right)^2. \tag{118}$$

Equation (117) combined with equation (115), (transformed in terms of p_2^2 and p_1^2), gives the following:

$$p_1^2\left(M_1^2\sin^2\epsilon-\frac{\gamma-1}{2\gamma}\right)=p_2^2\left(M_2^2\sin^2\beta-\frac{\gamma-1}{2\gamma}\right) \tag{119}$$

and in a similar way

$$\frac{1}{\rho_1^2}\left(\frac{1}{M_1^2\sin^2\epsilon}+\frac{\gamma-1}{2}\right)=\frac{1}{\rho_2^2}\left(\frac{1}{M_2^2\sin^2\beta}+\frac{\gamma-1}{2}\right). \tag{120}$$

Combining equations (119) and (120) with equations (117) and (118) the following expressions are obtained:

$$\frac{p_2}{p_1}=\frac{2\gamma}{\gamma+1}\left(M_1^2\sin^2\epsilon-\frac{\gamma-1}{2\gamma}\right) \tag{121}$$

$$\frac{\rho_1}{\rho_2}=\frac{2}{\gamma+1}\left(\frac{1}{M_1^2\sin^2\epsilon}+\frac{\gamma-1}{2}\right). \tag{122}$$

From equations (108) and (110) is obtained

$$\frac{\rho_1}{\rho_2}=\frac{V_{n2}}{V_{n1}}=\frac{V_{n2}}{V_{t2}}\frac{V_{t1}}{V_{n1}}-\frac{\tan\beta}{\tan\epsilon} \tag{123}$$

and therefore

$$\frac{\tan\beta}{\tan\epsilon}=\frac{2}{\gamma+1}\left(\frac{1}{M_1^2\sin^2\epsilon}+\frac{\gamma-1}{2}\right) \tag{124}$$

and

$$\frac{\tan\epsilon}{\tan\beta}=\frac{2}{\gamma+1}\left(\frac{1}{M_2^2\sin^2\beta}+\frac{\gamma-1}{2}\right). \tag{125}$$

Equation (125) can be transformed, because $\beta=\epsilon-\delta$, into the form:

$$\frac{1}{\tan\delta}=\left[\frac{\gamma+1}{2}\frac{M_1^2}{M_1^2\sin^2\epsilon-1}-1\right]\tan\epsilon. \tag{126}$$

Equations (121), (122), (125), and (126) permit calculation of all physical characteristics of the flow behind the shock as functions of similar characteristics in front of the shock if one condition of shock is known. Usually, either the value of δ (deviation of the flow) or the value of p_2 is known, from which it is possible to determine the inclination of the shock and all other variations that occur across the shock.

Equations (121) to (126) permit some considerations. If M_1 is substituted with $1/\sin \mu$ in equation (121), it is found that ϵ is larger than μ, because p_2

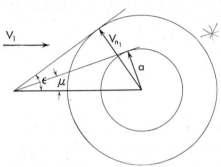

Fig. 25. *The velocity of propagation of a shock wave in comparison with the velocity of the sound.*

is larger than p_1 (necessary condition for shock); therefore the shock wave is always in front of the Mach line. In terms of the scheme of Chapter 1 it can be concluded that (Figure 25) the speed of transmission of a finite disturbance is greater than the speed of sound and depends on the amplitude of the perturbation. If ϵ is equal to μ (Mach angle), $M_1^2 \sin^2 \epsilon$ is equal to one, and from equations (124) or (126), $\delta = 0$, $\beta = \epsilon$, and the shock is a simple Mach wave. If ϵ increases and M_1 is constant, M_2 decreases (equation 125). For a given value of $(\epsilon = \epsilon_s)$, M_2 corresponds to one.

If the value of ϵ continues to increase, M_2 decreases and becomes less than one, and the speed after the shock becomes subsonic. For ϵ equal to $\pi/2$ (equation 126) δ becomes zero, the flow does not change direction, and the shock is normal to the direction of the velocity. This particular case of shock is called *normal shock* and is the shock that gives the maximum pressure ratios across the shock for a given Mach number in front of the shock. In this case, equations (121), (122), and (117) become

$$\frac{p_{2n}}{p_1} = \frac{2\gamma}{\gamma + 1} M_1^2 - \frac{\gamma - 1}{\gamma + 1} \tag{127}$$

$$\frac{\rho_1}{\rho_{2n}} = \frac{2}{\gamma + 1} \frac{1}{M_1^2} + \frac{\gamma - 1}{\gamma + 1} \tag{128}$$

$$M_{2n}^2 = \left(\frac{\gamma + 1}{2\gamma}\right)^2 \frac{1}{M_1^2 - \dfrac{\gamma - 1}{2\gamma}} + \frac{\gamma - 1}{2\gamma} \tag{129}$$

Some data for normal shock are given in Table 3 of the appendix as functions of the stream Mach number. The value of δ passes from a value zero for $(M_2 = M_1)$ (no shock) to a positive value for $(M_2 \neq M_1)$, and becomes zero again for a normal shock; therefore there must be a maximum value for every given value of M_1. The values of δ that correspond to $(M_2 = 1.0)$, and to the maximum value of δ, can be determined as a function of M_1. For M_2 equal to one, by eliminating β from equation (125) and from equation (124) is obtained:

$$2 \sin^2 \epsilon_s \cos^2 \epsilon_s - \left(\sin^2 \epsilon_s - \frac{1}{M_1^2} \right) \left[1 - \frac{2}{\gamma + 1} \left(\sin^2 \epsilon_s - \frac{1}{M_1^2} \right) \right]$$
$$= \frac{1}{M_1^2} \cos^2 \epsilon_s \quad (130)$$

where ϵ_s is the value of ϵ for which M_2 is equal to one. From equation (130) the following expression is obtained:

$$\sin^2 \epsilon_s = \frac{1}{\gamma M_1^2} \left[\frac{\gamma + 1}{4} M^2 - \frac{3 - \gamma}{4} \right.$$
$$\left. + \sqrt{(\gamma + 1) \left(\frac{9 + \gamma}{16} - \frac{3 - \gamma}{8} M_1^2 + \frac{\gamma + 1}{16} M_1^4 \right)} \right] \quad (131)$$

For M_1 equal one, ϵ is $\pi/2$, and M_2 is equal to one. For M_1 equal to infinity, $\sin^2 \epsilon_s$ is equal to $(\gamma + 1)/2\gamma$. The value ϵ_m of ϵ corresponding to the maximum value of δ can be obtained by differentiating equation (124). The differentiation gives

$$\frac{1}{\cos^2 \beta} \frac{d\beta}{d\epsilon} = \frac{\tan \beta}{\tan \epsilon} (\tan \epsilon^2 - 1) + 2 \left(\frac{\gamma - 1}{\gamma + 1} \right)$$

and because

$$\frac{d\delta}{d\epsilon} = 1 - \frac{\partial \beta}{\partial c}$$

then

$$\frac{d\delta}{d\epsilon} = \cos^2 \beta \left[\frac{4}{\gamma + 1} - (1 + \tan \epsilon \tan \beta) \left(1 - \frac{\tan \beta}{\tan \epsilon} \right) \right]. \quad (132)$$

The maximum value of δ corresponds to a value of ϵ, ϵ_m, given by the equation

$$\frac{d\delta}{d\epsilon} = 0$$

or (equation 132)

$$4 - (\gamma + 1)(1 + \tan \epsilon_m \tan \beta_m) \left(1 - \frac{\tan \beta_m}{\tan \epsilon_m} \right) = 0. \quad (133)$$

Eliminating β from equation (133) with equation (124), and resolving, the following is obtained:

$$\sin^2 \epsilon_m = \frac{1}{\gamma M_1^2} \left[\frac{\gamma + 1}{4} M_1^2 - 1 \right.$$
$$\left. + \sqrt{(\gamma + 1) \left(1 + \frac{\gamma - 1}{2} M_1^2 + \frac{\gamma + 1}{16} M_1^4 \right)} \right]. \quad (134)$$

For $(M = 1)$, ϵ_m is equal to $\pi/2$, and for M_1 equal to infinity, $\sin^2 \epsilon_m$ is equal to $(\gamma + 1)/2\gamma$ and coincides with ϵ_s; for M equal to infinity $1/\tan \delta_m$ is equal to

$\sqrt{(\gamma - 1)(\gamma + 1)}$, and $\delta_m = 45°22'$, which is the maximum deviation possible. For intermediate values ϵ_s is smaller than ϵ_m. Calculating the value of δ corresponding to ϵ_m and then the value of M_{2m}, the resulting value of M_{2m} corresponding to the maximum deviation is less than one for every value of M; therefore the maximum deviation corresponds to a subsonic flow behind the shock. The differences between ϵ_m and ϵ_s and between M_{1m} and M_{1s} for the

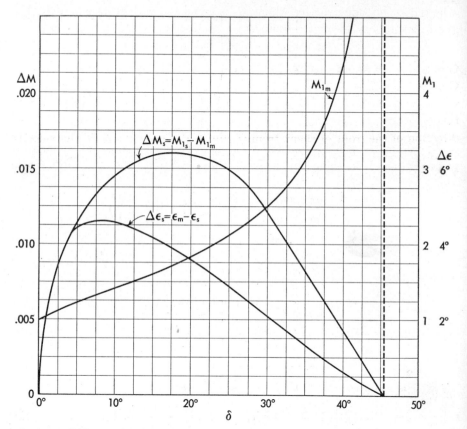

Fig. 26. *Difference between M_{1m} and M_{1s}, ϵ_m and ϵ_s corresponding to the same deviation across the shock as a function of the deviation δ across the shock (from Reference 11).*

same δ are very small and are plotted in Figure 26. Some values of δ_m, δ_s, ϵ_m, ϵ_s, M_{2m} are given as functions of the stream Mach number M_1 in Table 4 of the appendix. Because the value of δ for every value of M_1 goes from the value zero for $(\epsilon = \mu)$ to a maximum for $(\epsilon = \epsilon_m)$ and to zero again for $(\epsilon = \pi/2)$, for every value of δ, two possible values of ϵ exist, one obtained in the zone between μ and ϵ_m, and the second in the zone between ϵ_m and $\pi/2$. The first value of ϵ is smaller and therefore gives a pressure ratio p_2/p_1 smaller (equation 121) than the second value of ϵ.

For the second value of ϵ there is a corresponding value of M_2 below one, and a high pressure ratio, therefore a correspondingly "strong" shock, while the first value of the ϵ corresponds, in general, to a supersonic flow behind the shock. Only in a small zone near ($\epsilon = \epsilon_m$) is there also a corresponding subsonic flow behind the shock for the first value of ϵ (lower pressure ratio).

Table 5 of the appendix gives some values of δ, p_2/p_1, and M_2 as functions of ϵ and M_1.

Graphical Solution of Equations of Shock Waves — Shock Polar Curves. From equation (110) it is apparent that the variation across the shock occurs only for the component normal to the shock in the plane V_1, V_2; therefore, if in Figure 27 a segment OA equal to V_1 is taken, while OB is the direction of the front of shock from O, and BA is normal to OB, the velocity V_2 must be given by a vector OC that ends along the line BA, because $V_{t_2} = V_{t_1}$. Now if u_2 and v_2 are the components in the direction of the x and y axes,

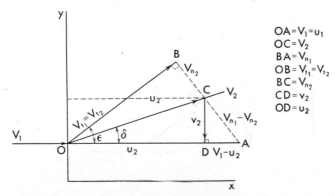

Fig. 27. *The variation of the velocity components across the shock.*

respectively, of the velocity V_2 behind the shock, it is possible to obtain from this consideration an equation that connects the component u_2, v_2 with the velocity V_1. Indeed, from equations (107) and (106),

$$p_2 - p_1 = \rho_1 \, V_{n1} \, (V_{n1} - V_{n2}) \qquad (135)$$

or from the similar triangles OBA and CDA of Figure 27,

$$p_2 = p_1 + \rho_1 \, V_1 \, (V_1 - u_2). \qquad (136)$$

The conservation of energy law requires that

$$\frac{\gamma}{\gamma - 1} \frac{p_1}{\rho_1} + \frac{1}{2} V_1^2 = \frac{\gamma}{\gamma - 1} \frac{p_0}{\rho_0} = \text{constant}.$$

If we substitute for the value of p_0/ρ_0, the corresponding value of V_c given by equation (83),

$$\left.\begin{array}{l} p_1 = \rho_1 \left(V_c^2\,\dfrac{\gamma+1}{2\gamma} - V_1^2\,\dfrac{\gamma-1}{2\gamma} \right) \\[3mm] p_2 = \rho_2 \left[V_c^2\,\dfrac{\gamma+1}{2\gamma} - (v_2^2 + u_2^2)\,\dfrac{\gamma-1}{2\gamma} \right] \end{array}\right\} \tag{137}$$

From the similar triangles CDA and OBA and from equation (106) (Figure 27) the following expression is obtained:

$$\frac{\rho_2}{\rho_1} = \frac{V_1\,(V_1 - u_2)}{u_2\,(V_1 - u_2) - v_2^2}. \tag{138}$$

Substituting equations (137) and (138) in (136), and resolving the equation in terms v_2, results in the expression

$$v_2^2 = (V_1 - u_2)^2\,\frac{u_2 - \dfrac{V_c^2}{V_1}}{\dfrac{V_c^2}{V_1} + \dfrac{2}{\gamma+1}V_1 - u_2} \tag{139}$$

Equation (139) gives a relation which connects the components u_2 and v_2 of velocity behind the shock with the value of the velocity in front of the shock.

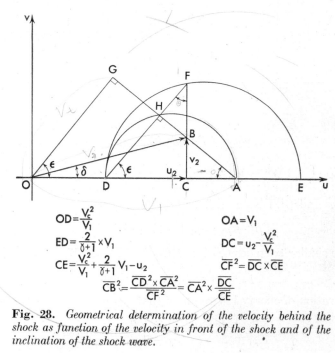

$$OD = \frac{V_c^2}{V_1} \qquad\qquad OA = V_1$$

$$ED = \frac{2}{\delta+1} \times V_1 \qquad\qquad DC = u_2 - \frac{V_c^2}{V_1}$$

$$CE = \frac{V_c^2}{V_1} + \frac{2}{\delta+1} V_1 - u_2 \qquad\qquad \overline{CF}^2 = \overline{DC} \times \overline{CE}$$

$$\overline{CB}^2 = \frac{\overline{CD}^2 \times \overline{CA}^2}{\overline{CF}^2} = \overline{CA}^2 \times \frac{\overline{DC}}{\overline{CE}}$$

Fig. 28. *Geometrical determination of the velocity behind the shock as function of the velocity in front of the shock and of the inclination of the shock wave.*

For every value of V_1 and V_c it is possible to determine many values of v_2 and u_2 that satisfy equation (139). In the hodograph plane (plane u and v) equation (139) can be represented by a curve that is the locus for given values of V_1 and V_c of all the points that define the values of V_2 which conform to the laws of shock (Reference 12). The curve which is the locus of the end of the vector V_2 for given values of V_1 and V_c is easily constructed, and is called a *strophoid* or *cartesian leaf*. The construction can be obtained in the following way:

For a given condition of the flow in front of the shock, the values $\dfrac{V_c^2}{V_1}$, $\dfrac{V_c^2}{V_1} + \dfrac{2}{\gamma+1} V_1$ and V_1 are known, and (Figure 28) therefore along the u axis the segments OD, OA, ED can be taken, respectively, equal to $\dfrac{V_c^2}{V_1}$, V_1 and $\dfrac{2}{\gamma+1} V_1$. The circles that have for diameters DA and DE must be constructed. For every point F of the larger circle, a segment DF can be drawn which intersects the smaller circle at H. The segment AH is normal to DF because DHA is a semicircle. If from F the normal to the axis FC is drawn, a point B can be determined from the intersection of the segments HA and FC. Because CFE is a semicircle, the angle DFE is a right angle, and therefore the segment CF is given by:

$$CF^2 = DC \times CE$$

But the triangles DFC and CBA are right triangles and are similar; therefore,

$$CB^2 = \frac{CD^2 \times CA^2}{CF^2} = CA^2 \times \frac{DC}{CE}$$

and from the definition of OA, OD, and ED,

$$CB = (V_1 - OC)^2 \frac{OC - V_c^2/V_1}{\dfrac{V_c^2}{V_1} + \dfrac{2}{\gamma+1} V_1 - OC}.$$

Therefore OC and CB are the components of the vector V_2 which conform to the law given by equation (139). Because V_2 is given by the segment OB, and V_1 by the segment OA, OG perpendicular to BA gives the value of the tangential velocity V_{t_2} equal to V_{t_1}. Therefore DF, which is parallel to OG, gives the direction of the front of the shock, and the angle FDA is equal to ϵ. By changing the position of the point F along the circle DFE, the values at V_2 and ϵ change, and the position of B moves along a curve which is a strophoid. The form of the curve appears in Figure 29. The curve is symmetrical with respect to the u-axis, which corresponds to the two signs of δ and ϵ, and therefore to the two possibilities of the inclination of the shock for the same intensity of velocity behind the shock. The curve intersects the u-axis at two points, the point D and the point A. The point A corresponds to $(V_2 = V_1)$ (Figures 28 and 29), and therefore to absence of shock. The point D corresponds to

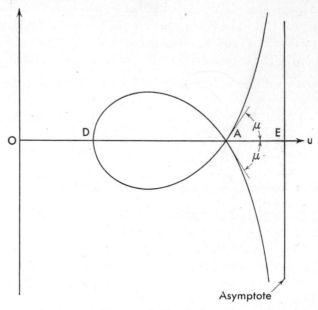

Fig. 29. *The strophoid (shock polar curve).*

zero deviation and therefore to normal shock, for which the value of V_2 is a minimum, and is given by

$$V_{2n} = u_{2n} = \frac{V_c^2}{V_1}. \tag{140}$$

At A the curve has a double point, and the tangent to the curve at A is inclined at the complement of the Mach angle μ_1 corresponding to V_1. This is in accord with the fact that for the point A, V_2 is equal to V_1, and the shock coincides with a Mach wave (ϵ coincides with μ). At A the strophoid has the same tangent as the epicycloid designed for the same velocity OA (inclined at μ with respect to the u axis), and therefore in the neighborhood of the point A the variation in intensity of the velocity, for the same variation of direction, is equal for gradual compression or for compression with shock. For larger variations of direction, the epicycloid which corresponds to isentropic transformation gives different values than the strophoid.

From A the curve continues with two branches that are asymptotically tangent to the line

$$u = \frac{V_c^2}{V_1} + \frac{2}{\gamma + 1} V_1.$$

These parts of the curve that give values of V_2 larger than V_1 are not useful, because they do not correspond to the physical phenomena.

It is possible to design the shock polar curves for some value of V_1 and to obtain a graph which can be very useful for practical calculation of the variation of physical quantities across the shock, because it eliminates use of equations (121) to (126). Because, in supersonic phenomena, the Mach number is usually more interesting than the velocity, it is useful to plot equation (139) in the following form by dividing all terms by a_1^2:

$$v_2^2 \frac{V_2^2}{a_1^2} = \left(M_1 - \frac{u_2}{a_1}\right)^2 \frac{\dfrac{u_2}{a_1} - \dfrac{\dfrac{V_c^2}{a_1^2}}{M_1}}{\dfrac{V_c^2}{a_1^2}{M_1} + \dfrac{2}{\gamma + 1} M_1 - \dfrac{u_2^2}{a_1}}. \tag{141}$$

In this case the segment OA represents M_1, and the segment OB (Figure 28) represents, on the same scale, $M_2 \dfrac{a_2}{a_1}$, where a_2 and a_1 represent the speed of sound behind and in front of the shock, respectively. The segments GA and GB represent, respectively, M_{1n} and $M_{2n} \dfrac{a_2}{a_1}$, from which the value of $\dfrac{a_2}{a_1}$ can be obtained. Indeed, from equation (112),

$$\frac{2}{\gamma - 1} + M_{1n}^2 = \frac{2}{\gamma - 1} \frac{a_2^2}{a_1^2} + M_{2n}^2 \frac{a_2^2}{a_1^2} \tag{142}$$

and therefore

$$\frac{a_2^2}{a_1^2} = \frac{\gamma - 1}{2} \left[\left(\frac{GA}{OA}\right)^2 - \left(\frac{GB}{OA}\right)^2 \right] M_1^2 + 1. \tag{143}$$

The ratio of the density before and behind the shock is given by equation (106)

$$\frac{\rho_1}{\rho_2} = \frac{V_{n2}}{V_{n1}} = \frac{GB}{GA}. \tag{144}$$

The ratio of pressure before and behind the shock is given by equations (144) and (143)

$$\frac{p_2}{p_1} = \frac{\rho_2 a_2^2}{\rho_1 a_1^2} = \left\{ \frac{\gamma - 1}{2} \left[\left(\frac{GA}{OA}\right)^2 - \left(\frac{GB}{OA}\right)^2 \right] M_1^2 + 1 \right\} \frac{GA}{GB} \tag{145}$$

A diagram of the shock polars is given in the appendix, Chart 2. In the diagram the segment OE is maintained constant for all Mach numbers. Now the segment $\left[V_1 \div OE = \dfrac{V_c^2}{V_1} + \dfrac{2}{\gamma + 1} V_1 \right]$ corresponds (equation 85b) to the condition V_1 equal to V_l, and therefore to M_1 equal to infinity. If the value of

V_l, and therefore the value of the segment OE, is assumed constant, for every Mach number the length OA which gives the corresponding value of V_1 can be determined using equation (85b). In this case p_0/ρ_0 is constant for every value of M_1, and for ($M_1 = 1$), V_1 is equal to V_c. The diagram of Chart 2 of the appendix is drawn with this criterion, and the value of M_1 obtained from equation (85b) is written in place of the value of V_1.

Physical Considerations for Interpretation of the Shock Polar Curves.
With the help of shock polars, it is possible to determine all physical conditions of the shock if the conditions in front of the shock and one condition that defines the shock are known. When the known quantity behind the shock is the pressure p_2, it is possible, from equation (121), to determine the value of the inclination of the front of the shock, and from the shock polar with equations (142), (143), and (144) to determine the other quantities. The value of p_2 can vary from the value of p_1 to a maximum equal to p_{2n}. If $p_2 = p_1$, and $M_2 = M_1$, ϵ is equal to μ, the point C is at A, and no deviation occurs (Figure 30). The value of p_2 for a fixed Mach number in front of the shock is maximum if ϵ is equal to $\pi/2$ (equation 121); in this case the shock is a normal shock, and the point C coincides in Figure 30 with D. No deviation occurs across the shock.

If the value of p_2 is greater than $p_{2\max}$, a stationary equilibrium in the flow cannot exist. The shock changes position with time and moves toward the flow, stopping only if it can find in the flow a Mach number that permits a stationary equilibrium with the condition behind the shock.

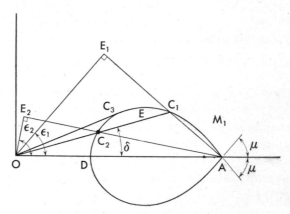

Fig. 30. *The two possible equilibrium conditions corresponding to a given deviation across the shock.*

In aerodynamic phenomena, the boundary conditions (the shape of a body, or what is equivalent, the form of a streamline) are given more often than the value of the pressure p_2. In this case, the value of deviation δ can be determined, which must define the shock. From the shock polar it appears that, for every Mach number in front of the shock and for every value of deviation, two kinds of shock are possible (Figure 30), OE_1 and OE_2, for which there are two corresponding velocities behind the shock, OC_1 and OC_2, and two pressures. The problem apparently is indeterminate. But the indetermination can be solved by the following considerations:

Consider a flow at Mach number M_1 moving along a wall OA parallel to the flow (Figure 31). In this case, the deviation of the stream is zero, but also in this case two conditions of equilibrium are given in Figure 30: the condition OA that corresponds to undisturbed flow, and the condition OD that corresponds to flow behind a normal shock. Normal shock can be produced only by an increase of the back pressure, because it corresponds to zero deviation. Now, if the direction of the flow is changed by rotation of the wall

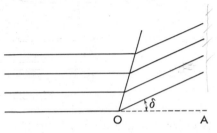

Fig. 31.   *Attached shock.*

OA (Figure 31) through an angle δ, the new stable condition of equilibrium is the condition that corresponds to the minimum variation of the initial condition. In this case, it is the condition that corresponds to the minimum of the square of variation of the velocity which corresponds to the minimum variation of the pressure on the wall. Therefore, if the condition of the flow in Figure 30 before rotation was OA, the new condition is OC_1; if it was OD, it is OC_2. If, in the flow, a deviation δ is produced (Figure 31) and no other conditions are imposed, it is the condition OC_1 that is stable, a condition that gives a value of M_2 greater than the speed of sound. In this case, if all streamlines have the same speed and the same variation in front of the shock, the entire flow undergoes the same deviation δ, and the streamlines behind the shock are also parallel and have the same speed. The shock is straight. If the deviation of the stream increases, the point C_1 moves in the direction of C_3 (Figure 30) which corresponds to the maximum deviation possible for the shock polar considered, and therefore for the Mach number considered for undisturbed flow. At the point C_3 the problem is determined because only one condition of equilibrium exists. For the condition C_3 the flow behind the shock is subsonic. The condition ($M_2 = 1$) is very near the condition of maximum deviation, and the difference from the two corresponding deviations is very small. If the deviation imposed on the flow is higher than the maximum possible, the shock wave moves in front of the point A (Figure 32) in which the deviation is imposed, because at A a condition of equilibrium is not possible (detached shock). In this case, the shock in D is a shock produced by back pressure, because at D no deviation occurs; therefore at D the shock becomes a normal shock. Behind the shock the flow is subsonic; therefore the streamlines can turn without limitation and it is possible to obtain a flow that wets the surface DAC. Because the flow is subsonic, the streamlines are no longer

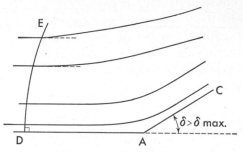

Fig. 32. *Detached shock.*

parallel but have different curvature. The pressure is also no longer constant and since the back pressure is not constant (the perturbation in subsonic flow is propagated with an intensity which decreases with distance), the shock is curved (ϵ is not constant). At some distance from D along the shock (point E of Figure 32) the speed behind the shock becomes again supersonic. Along the shock from D to E all the conditions from the normal shock (point D) to supersonic flow behind the shock exist, and therefore also the condition C_3 of Figure 30 considered before. In order to determine the condition across the shock, it is necessary to determine the conditions of the flow in the field DEA, but this flow is subsonic flow and depends on the initial conditions that correspond to the variation across the shock. The problem therefore is complicated because it is necessary to determine the subsonic flow that is physically possible with the body BAC and with a shock from Mach number M_1, the shape of which is not known.

The Nature of the Transformation That the Flow Undergoes across the Shock. In order to determine the type of transformation that occurs in the flow across a shock wave, it is possible to determine from equations (121) and (122) a relation between the pressure ratio and the density ratio. Eliminating $M_1 \sin \epsilon$ from the two equations, the following expression which is called the *Hugoniot equation* is obtained:

$$\frac{p_2}{p_1} = \frac{1 - \dfrac{\gamma + 1}{\gamma - 1}\dfrac{\rho_2}{\rho_1}}{\dfrac{\rho_2}{\rho_1} - \dfrac{\gamma + 1}{\gamma - 1}} .$$

(146)

It is evident that the transformation that occurs across the shock is not an isentropic, because the form is different from the equation

$$\frac{p_2}{p_1} = \left(\frac{\rho_2}{\rho_1}\right)^{\gamma} \tag{147}$$

and therefore an increase of entropy must occur across the shock. For small variations of density, the two laws, as was shown on page 52, give equivalent results, and therefore the increase of entropy is not important. Indeed, if

$$\rho_2 = \rho_1 + \Delta\rho$$

developing equation (146) in series,

$$\frac{p_2}{p_1} = \frac{1 + \dfrac{\gamma + 1}{2}\dfrac{\Delta\rho}{\rho_1}}{1 - \dfrac{\gamma - 1}{2}\dfrac{\Delta\rho}{\rho_1}} = \left(1 + \frac{\gamma + 1}{2}\frac{\Delta\rho}{\rho_1}\right)\left[1 + \frac{\gamma - 1}{2}\frac{\Delta\rho}{\rho_1}\right.$$

$$\left. + \left(\frac{\gamma - 1}{2}\right)^2\frac{\Delta\rho^2}{\rho_1{}^2} + \cdots\right]$$

or

$$\frac{p_2}{p_1} = 1 + \gamma\frac{\Delta\rho}{\rho_1} + \frac{\gamma(\gamma - 1)}{2}\frac{\Delta\rho^2}{\rho_1{}^2}\cdots \tag{148}$$

while developing in series equation (147),

$$\frac{p_2}{p_1} = \left(\frac{\rho_2}{\rho_1}\right)^{\gamma} = 1 + \gamma\frac{\Delta\rho}{\rho_1} + \frac{\gamma(\gamma - 1)}{2}\frac{\Delta\rho^2}{\rho_1{}^2}\cdots \tag{149}$$

Therefore for a shock of very small intensity, the law of isentropic transformations can be used, but the use is no longer correct if the variation of density or pressure is large. In this case, it is necessary to consider the law given by equation (146) that is exact for the shock, in connection with stationary phenomena in perfect flow.

The variation of entropy across the shock is given in mechanical units by equation (8)

$$d\Delta S = g\,c_p\frac{dT}{T} - gR\frac{dp}{p}$$

or

$$\Delta S = \frac{Rg}{\gamma - 1}\left(\log_e\frac{p_2}{p_1} + \gamma\log_e\frac{\rho_1}{\rho_2}\right) = \frac{gR}{\gamma - 1}\log_e\frac{p_2}{p_1}\left(\frac{\rho_1}{\rho_2}\right)^{\gamma} \tag{150}$$

in which p_2/p_1 and ρ_1/ρ_2 are given by equations (121) and (122), and are constant if $M_1\sin\epsilon$ is constant. Therefore if the value of $M_1\sin\epsilon$ is constant, the variation of entropy ΔS across the shock is constant. Because

$$\log_e\frac{p_2}{p_1} + \gamma\log_e\frac{\rho_1}{\rho_2}$$

is other than zero, the transformation occurs with variation of entropy. It is evident that finite negative variation of pressure (expansion shocks) cannot occur because in this case the entropy must decrease and that is thermodynamically impossible. Shock occurs with increase of entropy, and therefore is an irreversible process.

If in place of p_2/p_1 and ρ_1/ρ_2 equations (121) and (122) are used, the value of ΔS increases if the value of ϵ increases, and is zero for $\epsilon = \mu$ (Mach wave), while it becomes maximum if ϵ is equal to $\pi/2$. Therefore the variation of entropy increases if the intensity of the shock or the variation of pressure across the shock increases. From equation (150) and equations (121) and (122), it also appears that if the flow is isentropic in front of the shock and M_1 sin ϵ is constant, the variation ΔS across the shock is constant, and the flow behind the shock is also isentropic. If M_1 is constant in front of the shock, the condition of M_1 sin ϵ corresponds to the condition of straight shock. If the shock is not straight but curved and ϵ changes from point to point, or more generally if M_1 sin ϵ is not constant, the value of ΔS is different from point to point of the shock, and therefore the flow behind the shock is no longer isentropic, and from the consideration of Chapter 1 the flow is rotational. The rotation is dependent on the variation of ΔS from point to point, a variation that depends on the intensity and on the curvature of the shock. If, therefore, the shock is strong and is curved, it is no longer correct to consider the flow behind the shock a potential flow. When the shock is detached and the flow behind the shock is subsonic, the shock is curved and therefore the subsonic flow behind the shock is always rotational.

Consequence of the Variation of Entropy across the Shock. Shock Drag. Independent of the kind of transformation that the flow undergoes, if energy is not carried away or injected into the flow from the outside, the first term

$$\frac{\gamma}{\gamma - 1} \frac{p_0}{\rho_0} = \frac{V_i^2}{2}$$

of the energy equation remains constant. Therefore if behind the shock the flow undergoes an isentropic transformation from the velocity that it has behind the shock to zero velocity, two new values of pressure and density p_0' and ρ_0' are obtained that must conform to the relation

$$\frac{\gamma}{\gamma - 1} \frac{p_0}{\rho_0} = \frac{\gamma}{\gamma - 1} \frac{p_0'}{\rho_0'}$$

or

$$V_i^2 = \text{constant, and } T_0 = \text{constant.} \tag{151}$$

Now assume that the flow behind the shock undergoes isentropic expansion from the pressure p_2 behind the shock to the pressure p_1 of the flow in front of the shock. The velocity V_1' of the flow behind the shock at the pressure p_1 is given by the energy equation (equation 85a)

$$\frac{V_1'^2}{V_i^2} = 1 - \left(\frac{p_1}{p_0'}\right)^{\frac{\gamma-1}{\gamma}} \tag{152a}$$

where the velocity V_1 in front of the shock is given by

$$\frac{V_1^2}{V_i^2} = 1 - \left(\frac{p_1}{p_0}\right)^{\frac{\gamma-1}{\gamma}}. \tag{152}$$

For equation (85b),

$$\frac{V_i^2}{V_1^2} = 1 + \frac{2}{\gamma-1}\frac{1}{M_1^2} = 1 + \frac{2}{\gamma-1}\sin^2\mu \tag{153}$$

Therefore, from equations (152) the following expression can be obtained:

$$\frac{V_1^2 - V_1'^2}{V_1^2} = \frac{2}{\gamma-1}\sin^2\mu\left[\left(\frac{p_0}{p_0'}\right)^{\frac{\gamma-1}{\gamma}} - 1\right] \tag{154}$$

but

$$\frac{p_1}{\rho_1^\gamma} = \frac{p_0}{\rho_0^\gamma}, \text{ and } \frac{p_2}{\rho_2^\gamma} = \frac{p_0'}{\rho_0'^\gamma}$$

by definition of p_0, ρ_0, p_0', ρ_0'. Equation (150) can therefore be written with equation (151) in the following form:

$$\Delta S = \frac{gR}{\gamma-1}\log_e\left[\frac{p_0'}{p_0}\left(\frac{\rho_0}{\rho_0'}\right)^\gamma\right] = \frac{gR}{\gamma-1}\log_e\left(\frac{p_0}{p_0'}\right)^{\gamma-1}. \tag{155}$$

Therefore

$$\left(\frac{p_0}{p_0'}\right)^{\gamma-1} = e^{\frac{(\gamma-1)\Delta S}{Rg}}. \tag{156}$$

Using equation (156), equation (154) becomes

$$\frac{1}{2}\frac{V_1^2 - V_1'^2}{V_1^2} = \frac{1}{\gamma-1}\sin^2\mu\left[e^{\frac{\Delta S(\gamma-1)}{\gamma Rg}} - 1\right]$$

$$= \frac{1}{\gamma-1}\sin^2\mu\left[e^{\frac{\Delta S}{g\gamma c_v}} - 1\right]. \tag{157}$$

Developing in series the term $e^{\frac{\Delta S(\gamma-1)}{\gamma Rg}}$,

$$\frac{1}{2}\frac{V_1^2 - V_1'^2}{V_1^2} = \frac{1}{\gamma-1}\sin^2\mu\left[\frac{\Delta S}{\gamma c_v g} + \frac{1}{2}\left(\frac{\Delta S}{\gamma c_v g}\right)^2 \cdots\right]. \tag{158}$$

Equation (158) shows that when the flow again attains behind the shock the pressure p_1 that it has in front of the shock, the corresponding velocity V_1' is less than the velocity that the flow has in front of the shock, and the difference between the two velocities increases if the variation of entropy across the shock increases. Therefore, for the same value of the pressure, the kinetic energy of the mass unit of the flow is less behind the shock than in front of the shock (Reference 13).

Now consider a flow that moves with a velocity V_1 and a pressure p_1 and wets a body at supersonic velocity. When shock waves are produced by the presence of the body, a variation of entropy occurs in the flow. When the flow at some distance from the body again attains the pressure p_1 it has a velocity V_1' which is less than the initial velocity V_1. If a closed surface that contains the entire zone disturbed by the flow is considered, the pressure at this surface is equal to p_1, and the resultant of the pressure is therefore zero. A variation of momentum exists, however, because the velocity V_1' behind the shock is different from the velocity V_1 in front, and therefore a resultant force exists that is in the direction opposite to the velocity V_1. By the principle of action and reaction, the body that produces the shock must undergo an equal force in the opposite direction; this force, because it is in the velocity direction, corresponds to a drag. Therefore in supersonic perfect flow, a form of drag independent of the friction drag can occur, a drag which is generated by the formation of shock waves, and which is called *shock drag*. The shock drag depends on the mass of flow influenced by the variation of entropy and on the

variation of velocity $(V_1 - V_1')$. The variation of velocity increases as ΔS increases (equation 158), and therefore increases if the angle ϵ of the shock increases. Therefore, for equal extension of the shock, the maximum drag occurs for a normal shock, for which the maximum variation of entropy occurs. Because the intensity of the shock increases if the angle of deviation of the flow increases, it is evident that for supersonic flow, a body of good aerodynamic shape must have a sharp nose, and not a blunt nose. A sharp nose produces light shock, and a blunt nose produces a strong shock, because the deviation is larger than the maximum possible and the shock must be detached (Figure 33). In order to reduce the intensity of the shock, the thickness of the body must be reduced. The shock drag that is characteristic of supersonic flow is an important part of the total drag, and therefore it is natural that in supersonic flow even with appropriate form of the body, drag coefficients higher than in subsonic flow must be expected.

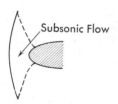

Fig. 33. *Sharp leading edge and blunt leading edge in supersonic flow.*

If, in equation (158), only the first term of the series is considered, it is possible to substitute for $\sin^2 \mu$ the expression $\gamma R g T / V^2$, and the following expression can be obtained:

$$\frac{1}{2}\left(V_1^2 - V_1'^2\right) = \frac{1}{\gamma - 1}\frac{\gamma R T_1}{\gamma c_v} \Delta S = T_1 \Delta S \tag{159}$$

because

$$R = c_p - c_v, \text{ and } \gamma = \frac{c_p}{c_v} \text{ (mechanical units)}.$$

Therefore the loss of kinetic energy per unit mass across the shock is proportional to the absolute temperature in front of the shock and to the variation of entropy. Substituting for the entropy its expression as a function of the heat,

$$\frac{1}{2}\left(V_1^2 - V_1'^2\right) = \int_1^1 T dS = \int_1^1 dQ = \frac{c_p}{g}(T_1' - T_1) \tag{160}$$

where c_p has the dimension of work per unit weight per degree. The variation of kinetic energy is equal to the heat necessary to heat the unit mass of flow at a constant pressure p_1 from the temperature (absolute) T_1 in front of the shock to the temperature T_1' behind the shock. The losses are therefore transformed into heat, and at the same pressure the flow behind the shock has a higher temperature and therefore a lower density.

The Effect of the Viscosity and of the Conductivity in the Shock Wave Formation. In the preceding considerations in which the hypothesis of perfect flow was accepted, a discontinuity in the flow was found, which has been called a *shock wave*, across which an increase of pressure and temperature occurs. The variations occur when the flow crosses the surface that constitutes the front of the shock, which (with the hypothesis accepted) has zero thickness. The existence of two zones of flow near each other with a finite difference of temperature seems to be a mathematical fiction very far from the reality of the phenomena. It is necessary, therefore, to investigate the effect of viscosity and conductivity in the extension of the zone in which the compression occurs and to determine the true thickness of the shock wave.

The calculations of motion with viscosity and conductivity are complex because they require a relation between conductivity coefficient and viscosity coefficient, and therefore the kinetic theory of gases must be used. The results, even if not absolutely exact, show that the thickness of the shock is of the order of a few mean free paths of the molecules of the gas and therefore because the variations occur in a very small thickness, the shock can be considered a physical discontinuity (References 14 and 15).

Consider for simplicity of treatment a normal shock. In this case, if the motion occurs along the x-axis for the continuity equation,

$$u\frac{d\rho}{dx} + \rho\frac{du}{dx} = 0. \tag{161}$$

The momentum equation in the presence of viscosity can be written with good approximation in the form:

$$\rho u \frac{du}{dx} + \frac{dp}{dx} - \frac{4}{3} m \frac{d^2u}{dx^2} = 0 \tag{162}$$

where m is the viscosity coefficient, while the energy equation in presence of viscosity and conduction becomes

$$u g \rho c_v \frac{dT}{dx} = - \left(p - \frac{4}{3} m \frac{du}{dx} \right) \frac{du}{dx} + \Lambda \frac{d^2T}{dx^2} \tag{163}$$

where Λ is the conductivity coefficient in mechanical units. If the following relation for Λ and m is accepted

$$\Lambda = \frac{4}{3} m c_p \tag{164}$$

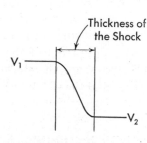

Fig. 34. *Thickness of the shock.*

it is possible to obtain a solution of the three equations and to calculate the thickness of the shock waves. For atmospheric conditions and for the following pressure ratios, π, across the shock, the following thicknesses of the shock are found (see Figure 34):

$\pi =$	2	5	10	100	1000
$d =$	447	117	66	16.5	5.2×10^{-7} cm

The calculations are not exact because equations (162), (163), and (164) are approximate. More exact calculations give greater thicknesses but of the same order, and of the order of the length of the mean free path of the gas molecule (about 4 mean free paths for pressure ratio 5, and 3 for pressure ratio 10). For weaker shocks the thickness increases, but is of the same order. Therefore shock can be considered, with very good approximation, as a physical discontinuity and the laws of shock obtained with the hypothesis of perfect flow are practically correct.

The phenomena of shock can be different for very low density, where the hypothesis of homogeneous flow is no longer correct. In this case the study of the phenomena must be made with the kinetic theory of gases.

CHAPTER

4

THEORY OF TWO-DIMENSIONAL FLOW —

INTERACTION AND REFLECTION OF SHOCK

WAVES AND EXPANSION WAVES

Possibility of Interaction or Reflection of Shock Waves and Expansion Waves. Isolated expansion waves and shock waves in a perfect flow are extended to infinity with the same intensity, and if dissipation is not considered, the streamlines corresponding to every isolated expansion or shock wave are all parallel. However, in aerodynamic phenomena, if expansions and compressions occur in the same flow, it is possible that expansion waves and shock waves may cross; therefore it is necessary to consider what happens when interaction of shock waves and expansion waves occurs. In some cases it is also possible that expansion waves or shock waves are extended to a rigid wall, or to a zone of flow with different velocity or without velocity,

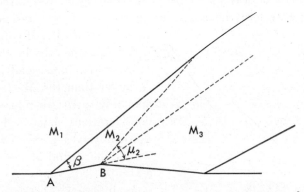

Fig. 35. *Example of interference between shock wave and expansion waves.*

which produces phenomena of reflection of the waves. This case must also be considered. The interaction of shock waves and expansion waves occurs, for example, whenever the streamlines undergo a deviation of direction and later return to the same direction as before the deviation. In this case expansion and compression occur and the waves must interfere. Indeed, if a deviation of compression occurs and a shock is generated at a point A (Figure 35), the Mach number behind the shock, M_2, is smaller than the Mach number in front, M_1, and if the flow behind the shock is supersonic, the corresponding Mach angle μ_2 is larger than the angle of the shock with respect to the velocity behind the shock, β; indeed, if in equation (125) $\sin \mu_2$ is substituted for M_2, $\sin \beta$ is smaller than $\sin \mu_2$, because if shock occurs, ϵ must be larger than β; therefore, if a successive expansion is produced at B expansion waves cross

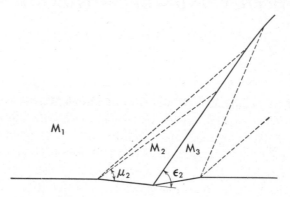

Fig. 36. *Example of interference between expansion waves and a shock wave.*

the shock wave. If expansion waves precede a shock wave, the inclination μ_2 of the last expansion wave is smaller than the inclination ϵ_2 of the shock wave (Figure 36); therefore the shock wave crosses the expansion waves and interferes with it. If two shock waves occur subsequently in the same flow (Figure 37), the second has an angle ϵ_2, larger than the Mach angle corresponding to M_2; therefore for the same considerations developed for the expansion waves generated after shock waves, the second wave meets the first and interferes.

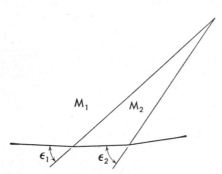

Fig. 37. *Example of interference between shock waves.*

An interaction between a rigid wall and expansion or compression waves can occur, for example, when a supersonic flow into a channel is considered (Figure 38). At A, the shock produced at A_0 meets a rigid wall, and at B, expansion waves generated at B_0 meet a rigid wall. The velocity behind the waves AA_0 and BB_0 is not parallel to the wall; therefore the wall must interfere with the flow, changing its characteristics and producing reflected waves.

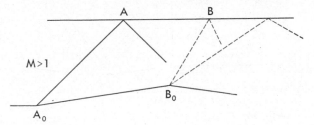

Fig. 38. *Example of interference between shock waves or expansion waves and a rigid wall.*

If a flow with supersonic velocity is not extended to infinity but is contained in a finite region where the shock or the expansion waves attain the boundary of the flow, the equilibrium in the boundary must be considered. For example, in a supersonic jet that overflows into the air, if the internal pressure is different from the external pressure of the flow around the jet, shock waves ($p_1 < p_a$) (Figure 39) or expansion waves ($p_1 > p_a$) (Figure 40) are generated at the end of the wall of the jet. These waves cross in the center of the jet (point A)

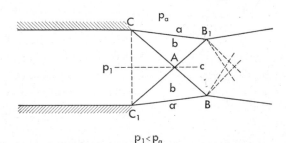

Fig. 39. *Example of interference of shock waves with a boundary constituted by flow having different speed (zero speed).*

similar waves that start from the opposite part of the jet; therefore an interaction between the two waves must be considered. The waves then continue to the boundary of the jet (boundary that is made up of a flow of different physical property), and because the flow with supersonic velocity has, corresponding to compression or expansion waves, zones with different pressure (zones b and c), while the flow at the boundary (zone a) must have a constant pressure, equilibrium is not possible, and the boundary interferes with the flow, producing reflected waves in the flow.

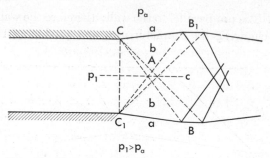

Fig. 40. *Example of interference between expansion waves with boundary constituted by flow having different speed (zero speed).*

A particular case of this interaction which is very important for aerodynamic phenomena is when compression waves or shock waves meet a body in which a boundary layer is generated. If, for example, in a channel with supersonic flow a shock wave is generated at O (Figure 41), the shock at A and B meets

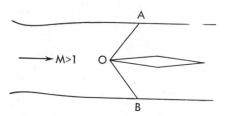

Fig. 41. *Example of interference between shock waves with boundary layer.*

a wall, but along the wall a boundary layer exists in which the velocity is different and partly subsonic; therefore the equilibrium of the point A or B must be determined by considering the shock boundary-layer interaction (which has a different velocity) and not by considering only the interaction between shock waves and wall. This occurs because the laws of transformation of the flow in the boundary layer are different from the flow outside the boundary layer.

Interactions or reflections for two-dimensional phenomena can be considered with the theory of characteristics for potential flow and with the theory of shock waves, but it is necessary to remember that when interaction between shock and expansion is considered, the shock becomes curved, and the flow behind the shock usually becomes rotational; therefore if the curvature of the shock is large, for the flow behind the shock the theory for rotational flow must be used (Chapter 5). In order to analyze the interaction between adjacent flows at different velocity, if one part of the flow is subsonic, as happens when supersonic flow in presence of boundary layer is considered, it is necessary to consider both supersonic and subsonic theories, and if for subsonic flow the viscosity is important, as when the subsonic flow is the flow in the boundary layer, the problem becomes very difficult and a quantitative analysis is not yet possible.

Interaction of Expansion Waves. Interaction of expansion waves can occur only between waves of opposite families (inclined at an angle of opposite sign with respect to the direction of velocity) (Figure 40). The interaction of expansion waves occurs, for example, in supersonic effusers where the expansion waves are generated from the two walls. Determination of the physical properties of the flow can be made by using the characteristic system. The expansion in the flow is continuous, but for simplicity of calculation it is possible to substitute for an infinite number of expansion waves of infinitesimal strength a finite number of waves of finite strength and to assume that the expansion occurs only along these waves. Every wave usually represents a constant value of deviation, and the flow between two expansion waves has in this approximation a constant intensity and direction. For example, in order to determine the flow in zones II, III, and IV (Figure 42), if the flow in I is known, and the value of the deviation represented by the waves a_1, b_1, a_2, b_2 is known, because the wave a_2 represents a deviation of expansion of value $\Delta\theta$ from the Mach number at I, the Mach number at I can be determined with equation (80) or the equivalent Table 2 of the appendix. The characteristic a_2 between the zones I and II must be inclined with respect to the direction of the velocity at I at the angle $(-\mu + \Delta\theta/2)$, where μ is the Mach angle $(\mu_1 + \mu_2)/2$ corresponding to $(M_I + M_{II})/2$. The direction of the velocity at II is rotated with respect to the velocity at I at an angle $\Delta\theta$, and the sign of $\Delta\theta$

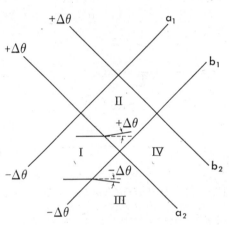

Fig. 42. *Analysis of interference between expansion waves of opposite families.*

is defined by the fact that an expansion occurs; therefore θ at II must be larger than at I. For determination of the flow in III the same consideration can be applied. The wave b_1 transmits a deviation of opposite sign from a_2; therefore the direction is rotated by $-\Delta\theta$ with respect to the direction in I. The Mach number is the same as in II; therefore the wave b_1 is inclined in the zone between I and III at $(\mu - \Delta\theta/2)$, where μ is the Mach angle corresponding to $(M_I + M_{III})/2$. The flow in IV can be determined either from III or from II. From III the deviation is given by the wave a_2 and is equal to $+\Delta\theta$; going from II to IV the wave b_1 is crossed and the variation is $-\Delta\theta$. When the line b_1 crossing a_2 changes direction, the direction is determined as explained previously. A rapid system for determining the Mach numbers and the direction of the waves is that which uses the values of column 1 in Table 2 of the appendix, which correspond to the sum of the values of the constants in the epicycloid diagram. This can also be determined by either the analytical or graphical methods explained in Chapter 2. For every Mach number there is a corresponding number in column 1. For example, if a direction of reference which corresponds to the number 200 of the characteristic system is fixed, and it is assumed that every characteristic line represents a degree of deviation, the direction and the velocity are rapidly determinable. Assuming the Mach number at I is 1.775, the number corresponding in the table is 980 (Figure 43). The number must be divided in two

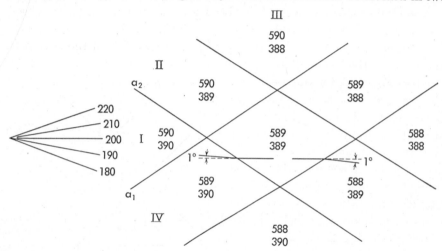

Fig. 43. *Analysis of interference between expansion waves of opposite families by use of the characteristic numbers.*

parts and the difference of the two parts must be equal to the number that gives the value of the direction. If at I the velocity is parallel to the axis of reference, the difference must be 200; therefore the two numbers are 590 and 390. At II an expansion of 1° occurs because a characteristic line is crossed; therefore the sum of the two numbers in II must be 979, but θ_{II} is larger than θ_I because the wave a_2 is an expansion; therefore the difference must be 201 and the numbers become 590 and 389; at III they become for the same reason, 590 and 388. In order to go from zone I to zone IV a characteristic of the other family is crossed; but the wave a_1 is an expansion of opposite sign to a_2; therefore the upper number decreases because the variation of direction indicates that the difference of the two numbers must decrease to 199. With this system, it is easy to assign the values of the two numbers in the relative spaces. The sum of the two values gives the Mach number using Table 2 of the appendix (columns 1 and 3) and the difference gives the direction in degrees with respect to the undisturbed velocity which has a direction of 200°. The inclination of the characteristic is also easy to determine, because it is given by the value of the Mach angle in Table 2, column 5, corresponding to the number in column 1 equal to the average of the sum of the numbers of the two zones, divided by the characteristic line considered; for example, in the line between I and II the Mach angle corresponding to the number 979.5 must be taken. The direction θ is given by the average of the difference of the two numbers of the two zones divided by the characteristic considered. The inclination of the characteristic line with respect to the axis of reference is $(\theta - \mu)$ for the second family, and $(\theta + \mu)$ for the first. For example, the line between I and II must be inclined with respect to the reference axis at $+ \frac{1}{2}° - 33°54'$, and the line between I and IV at $- \frac{1}{2}° + 33°54'$.

The construction of the characteristic lines can also be obtained rapidly using the epicycloid diagram. If the direction and the intensity of velocity in I are known, the corresponding point I' in the epicycloid diagram can be determined.

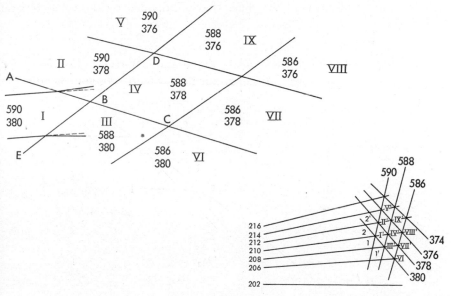

Fig. 44. *Analysis of interference between expansion waves of opposite families by use of the epicycloid diagram.*

Through the point I' (Figure 44) two epicycloids pass which give the law of variation of the velocity and the direction of the lines *AB* and *EB*. In II a positive deviation of $\Delta\theta$ occurs; therefore, placing the value of $\Delta\theta$ in the hodograph plane, the line 0II' is determined, and the point II' is determined along the epicycloid 590. Indeed, the velocity at II must be greater and along the epicycloid 380, for the $\Delta\theta$ considered, the velocity decreases. AB must be normal to the line I′ II′ at the point of polar coordinate $\Delta\theta/2$. In III the deviation is of opposite sign; therefore the point III″ and the line EB can be determined in a similar way by plotting $\Delta\theta$ in the opposite direction. From III to IV the variation corresponds to the epicycloid III′ IV′, and BC is normal to III′ IV′. BD corresponds to the normal to II′ IV′. If the numbers system is used in I, two numbers must be written which correspond to the numbers of epicycloids 1 and 2, and therefore the two numbers immediately define the point I′. In III the number of epicycloid 1 decreases by $\Delta\theta$; therefore epicycloid 1′ is determined by the new number. In II, the number of epicycloid 2 decreases by $\Delta\theta$; therefore epicycloid 2′ is determined. The construction in this way becomes mechanical. Along every line ABC the number of epicycloid 2 remains constant, and along every line EBD the number of epicycloid I remains constant. Every two numbers determine a point on the epicycloid diagram, and the characteristic line is given by the normal to the part of the epicycloid that connects the two points in the epicycloid diagram corresponding to the numbers of the zones that are divided by the characteristic line considered.

Interaction between Shock and Expansion Waves. Consider, for example, a body which moves in supersonic flow (Figure 45), and examine the

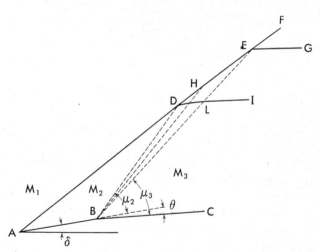

Fig. 45. *Analysis of interference between a shock wave and expansion waves of the same family.*

flow at a point in which the shock that occurs in front is intersected by expansion waves. The shock is produced at A, behind the shock at B an expansion occurs, and the Mach line that starts from B crosses the shock wave at D. In the zone ABD the flow is uniform and the velocity is parallel to AB. At B the flow turns, and an expansion θ occurs. The Mach number M_3 is determined by the theory of characteristics in terms of values of M_2 and θ. The expansion is completed along a line EB, inclined at μ_3, (sin $\mu_3 = 1/M_3$) with respect to the direction of final velocity BC. For every value of M' between M_2 and M_3 it is possible to determine the corresponding characteristic line BH. If M' is fixed, the corresponding μ is known, and the expansion θ' necessary to go from M_2 to M' is also known, either from equation (80), from Table 2 of the appendix, or from the epicycloid diagram; therefore the corresponding direction of velocity θ' with respect to AB is known, and the line HB inclined with respect to AB at the angle $(\mu' - \theta')$ can be drawn.

In order to determine what happens when a generical expansion wave BH meets the shock wave, the equilibrium condition of the flow at H must be determined. This can be obtained from the following considerations: At H (Figure 46) the equations of the shock give, for a given M_1, a value of pressure

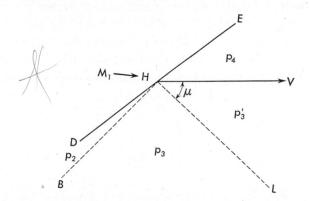

Fig. 46. *Determination of the reflected waves.*

p_2 behind the shock as a function of the value of the deviation of the velocity across the shock (equations 121 through 126). In order to have equilibrium of the flow at H, it is necessary that along HV, if HV is the streamline that starts from H, in the zone EHV and in the zone BHV, the direction of the velocity be the same and the pressure be the same. Because the line BH is an expansion wave the deviation across the shock at HE must be less than at DH; therefore the shock HE must be weaker than the shock DH.

If δ is the deviation across the shock DH, $\Delta_1\theta$ is the expansion across the expansion waves BH, and no reflection of the wave BH occurs at H, the deviation of V at H must be $(\delta - \Delta_1\theta)$; therefore the deviation across the shock HE must also be $(\delta - \Delta_1\theta)$. However, to have equilibrium it is necessary to consider the pressure along HV. If the pressure in DHB is p_2, in HBL is p_3, and in EHV is p_4,

$$p_3 = p_2 - \Delta p_1; \qquad p_4 = p_2 - \Delta p_2$$

where Δp_1 is the variation of pressure connected with a variation of direction $\Delta_1\theta$, considered in terms of the isentropic law along HB, while Δp_2 is the variation of pressure connected with the same variation of direction $\Delta_1\theta$, but calculated by the law of shock along HE. Δp_1 is, in general, different from Δp_2, and therefore a reflected wave of small intensity HL must exist. The difference between Δp_1 and Δp_2 is very small and in general can be neglected; in this case, the value of deviation across HE is known because it is equal to $(\delta - \Delta_1\theta)$; therefore the direction of HE can be determined from equation (126). Because HE is a shock weaker than BH, in EHV the speed is greater than in BHV, and the entropy is less; therefore a vortex line starts from H, and the flow in the zone of interaction of shock waves and expansion waves is rotational.

If the reflected wave HL is considered, and $\Delta_2\theta$ is the variation of direction across HL, the pressure in VHL and the direction in VHL can be determined in this way: For every value of $\Delta_2\theta$, the direction of velocity and the pressure in the zone VHL can be determined from the conditions in BHL with equation (81) or from the corresponding Table 2. From the pressure along HV the direction of the velocity in EHV $(\delta - \Delta_1\theta - \Delta_2'\theta)$ can be determined by eliminating ϵ from equations (121) and (126).

$$\frac{1}{\tan(\delta - \Delta_1\theta - \Delta_2'\theta)} = \left[\frac{\gamma M_1^2}{\dfrac{p_3'}{p_1} - 1} - 1 \right] \sqrt{\frac{(\gamma + 1)\dfrac{p_3'}{p_1} + \gamma - 1}{2\gamma M_1^2 - (\gamma + 1)\dfrac{p_3'}{p_1} - \gamma + 1}} \quad (165)$$

where p_3' is the pressure in LHV corresponding to a given value of $\Delta_2\theta$. When $\Delta_2'\theta$ is equal to $\Delta_2\theta$ which corresponds to the value of p_3' in equation (165), the direction in VHE is equal to the direction in VHL, and the corresponding $\Delta_2'\theta$ in the $\Delta_2\theta$ for which equilibrium exists; then the deviation across the shock HE is known and the inclination of HE can be determined from equation (126).

The practical calculation of the zone BDE and of the shock EF can be made by designing the lines BD and BE (Figure 45) and some line BH in which a finite expansion is supposed to concentrate. Therefore the flow is assumed to be at a constant velocity and direction in the zone contained between the two lines BD and BH, and a finite expansion is assumed to be concentrated on the line BH. For the actual gradual expansion, an expansion of finite increments is substituted. In practical calculations the reflected waves HL are usually neglected, or considered only in few points of the zone DE.

Interaction of Shock Waves. Two kinds of interaction between shock waves can occur: interaction of two shocks produced by deviations of different sign, and interaction of two shocks produced by deviations of the same sign. The first kind of interaction occurs, for example, when the shocks are produced by the opposite walls of a channel (Figure 47). The shock AB is

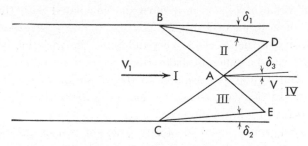

Fig. 47. *Analysis of the interference between shock waves of opposite families.*

produced by a deviation δ_1 of opposite sign to the deviation δ_2 that produces the shock AC. The interaction of the other kind occurs when two shocks of the same sign subsequently are produced, for example, by a surface of the type shown in Figure 48. The shock at C has different inclination from the shock at B and, as shown on page 64, meets the first. The flow conditions at II and III for the first kind of interaction can be determined from the values of δ_1 and δ_2 as functions of the flow conditions in I, while the flow conditions in zone IV can be determined by considering the condition of equilibrium at the point A (Figure 47). The direction in II is different from the direction of III by the angle $(\delta_1 + \delta_2)$. The deviation of the stream lines across the shock AD from II to IV must be related to the deviation across the shock AE from III to IV in such a manner that the direction of the velocity AV in IV must coincide after the two deviations. Also the pressure along AV in the zone DAV and the zone EAV must be the same; therefore from the two conditions the transformation along AD and AE can be determined.

If δ_3 is the deviation in IV with respect to the direction in I, while $-\delta_1$ is in II, and $+\delta_2$ is in III, a deviation $(\delta_3 + \delta_1)$ must occur across the shock AD and a deviation $(\delta_2 - \delta_3)$ must occur across AE. From equations (121) through (126) or from equivalent equation (165) for every deviation of compression, the corresponding value of pressure in IV can be determined from II and III. Therefore if p_{3II} is the pressure corresponding to a value of δ_3 calculated from the conditions in II, and p_{3III} the value of p_3 calculated for the same value of δ_3 from the condition in III, equilibrium exists when p_{3II} is equal to p_{3III}. For every value of δ_3 it is possible to plot a diagram of p_{3II} and p_{3III} as a function of δ_3, and when p_{3III} is equal to p_{3II}, the equilibrium conditions at A are determined. From the corresponding values of $(\delta_2 - \delta_3)$ and $(\delta_3 + \delta_1)$, the inclination of AE and AD can be determined from equation 121 or equation 126.

In some cases, the line BE or CD may be an expansion line; in this case the deviation $(\delta_2 - \delta_3)$ or $(\delta_3 + \delta_1)$ is negative and therefore represents an expansion, and the value of $p_{3_{II}}$ or $p_{3_{III}}$ must be calculated with the expansion equation (81) or in terms of Table 2.

If the intensity of the shocks is very different, the variation of entropy in the zone EAV can be different from the variation in VAD, and different velocity and density may correspond to the condition of equal pressure in the two zones. In this case, along the line AV a discontinuity occurs which produces a vortex of infinite intensity.

In order to determine the effect of interaction of two shocks corresponding to deviations of the same sign, the equilibrium of the flow along the streamline which starts from A must be considered (Figure 48). Across the streamline

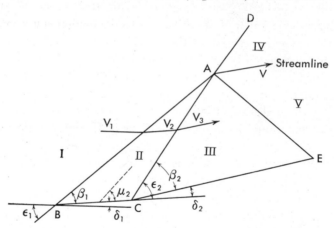

Fig. 48. *Analysis of interference between shock waves of the same family.*

AV no discontinuity of pressure must occur. Now, if behind the shock AD the direction of the stream is assumed the same as the direction in III when the deviation across AD is equal to $(\delta_1 + \delta_2)$, it is found that the pressure in IV is different from that in III, because in III the compression is obtained across two shocks and in IV only across one shock, with larger losses, because the compression across AD is further from isentropic compression than is the compression across BA and CA. If the compression occurs with infinite number of shocks of infinitesimal entity, the compression is isentropic. In order to obtain along AV the same pressure and the same direction, it is necessary to change slightly the direction and the pressure of the flow in III; therefore a reflected wave AE must start from the point A. Determination of the reflected wave can be made by using the same system used in paragraph 3. The reflected wave AE is usually very small and in many cases can be neglected, and the shock AD can be determined in terms of the direction of the flow in IV, assumed equal to the direction of the flow in III, therefore assuming across AD a deviation $(\delta_1 + \delta_2)$. Along the stream line AV a discontinuity of velocity occurs which produces vorticity at A.

A case that can be included in this paragraph is that of the formation of a shock wave from an envelope of some compression waves of infinitesimal intensity. Across the compression waves the transformation is isentropic, but when the envelope occurs, a finite variation of pressure and direction occurs; therefore the law of shock must be considered. For every compression wave that meets the shock wave the system of calculation is the same as for the case of interference of expansion waves and shock waves.

For the case of shock generated by an envelope of compression waves the following consideration is interesting. Assume that a curved surface AC produces a gradual compression (Figure 49); the compression waves form an

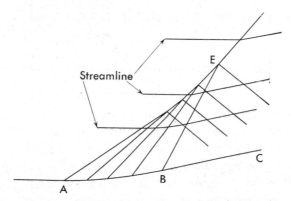

Fig. 49. *Shock wave produced by an envelope of compression waves.*

envelope, and therefore form a shock wave, and the deviation that occurs gradually along AB occurs at E across a shock wave. At E the variation of pressure is obtained with the law of shock, while along AB the variation occurs isentropically; therefore the direction at E and B cannot be the same, but some reflected waves must start from the points at which the compression waves attain the shock wave. The type of reflected waves can be different and change with the Mach number. Although the velocity behind the shock is always less than behind an isentropic compression corresponding to the same deviation of the stream, the isentropic compression can give for the same deviation of the stream, for some Mach numbers, a variation of pressure less than the variation that can be obtained with shock waves. The differences of the two pressures can be determined in this way: The variation of pressure connected with the variation of direction of velocity can be obtained, in the case of isentropic variation and in the case of shock, by a power series, as will be indicated in Chapter 7; for the isentropic variation the equation has the form

$$\frac{\Delta p_1}{\rho_1 V_1^2} = \pm c_1\theta + c_2\theta^2 \pm c_3\theta^3 + \dots \tag{166}$$

where the sign $(+)$ indicates a compression and the sign $(-)$ indicates an expansion. If the variation of direction θ occurs across a shock, an equation for Δp can be obtained that has the form

$$\frac{\Delta p_2}{\rho_1 V_1^2} = + c_1\theta + c_2\theta^2 + (c_3 - D)\,\theta^3 + \dots \tag{167}$$

Therefore the difference of the two pressures corresponding to the same deviation θ is given by

$$\frac{\Delta p_1 - \Delta p_2}{\rho_1 V_1^2} = D\theta^3 + \dots \tag{168}$$

The coefficient D is a function of the Mach number and is given by the expression

$$D = \frac{\dfrac{\gamma + 1}{24} M^4}{(M^2 - 1)^{3.5}}\left[\frac{5 - 3\gamma}{4}\left(M_1^2 - \frac{6 - 2\gamma}{5 - 3\gamma}\right)^2 - \frac{\gamma^2 - 1}{5 - 3\gamma}\right]. \tag{169}$$

Now for Mach numbers between 1.24 and 2.54 (for air) D is negative; therefore in this field Δp_2 is larger than Δp_1, and the pressure behind the shock is greater than behind the isentropic compression of the same deviation. In this field of Mach numbers, along BC, the pressure is less than at E; therefore the reflected waves are compression waves, while for Mach numbers outside of this field the reflected waves are expansion waves.

Reflection of Expansion Waves and Shock Waves on a Rigid Wall. Consider a body that moves with supersonic velocity near a wall in a direction parallel to the wall (Figure 50). From the body, shock waves and expansion waves start that can reach the wall; it is interesting to study the interaction between the waves and the wall. Suppose that BA and $B'A'$ represent two expansion waves. If V_1 is the velocity in front of the expansion waves, the velocity behind the expansion waves is V_2, inclined with respect to V_1. Along the wall the flow cannot have different direction from AA'; therefore at the wall the flow must undergo a transformation which changes the velocity from the direction that it has, V_2, to the direction AA'. The transformation must be produced in the zone AA' and therefore must be transmitted by waves inclined at the Mach angle with respect to the wall in direction opposite to the direction of the waves BA and B_1A' (waves of different family from the incoming waves). Since the deviation across the reflected waves must be of opposite sign from the deviation across the incoming waves, the reflected

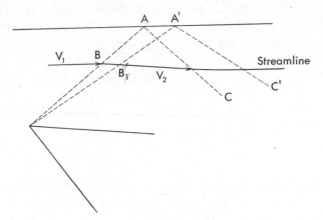

Fig. 50. *Analysis of the reflection of expansion waves from a rigid wall.*

waves must also be expansion waves; therefore expansion waves are reflected by a rigid plane wall as expansion waves of the same intensity of deviation and of opposite family. In order to avoid reflection of the waves from the wall in a channel, it is necessary to turn the wall in the same direction as the streamline which passes through the point A, when crossing the incoming expansion waves. In this case, the flow wets the wall and no reflection occurs.

The reflection of expansion waves can be considered with the same system as the interaction of expansion waves. The direction of the wall can also be

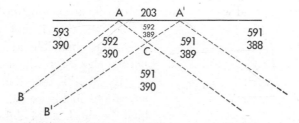

Fig. 51. *Analysis of the reflection of expansion waves from a flat rigid wall by use of the characteristic numbers.*

expressed by the same system. For example, if the wall is inclined at 3° to the reference direction, at the wall the difference of the two characteristic numbers must be 203 (Figure 51); therefore the number in ACA' is easily determined from the number in $BB'AC$. In order to avoid reflection of the expansion waves, if the expansion wave BA' (Figure 52) represents 1° of

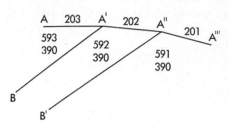

deviation with respect to the direction of AA', it is enough to turn the wall in the zone $A'A''$ at −1°. In this case the direction of $A'A''$ corresponds to the number 202, which is the direction of the velocity in the zone $BB'A'A''$. In order to avoid reflection of the expansion waves $B'A''$, it is necessary to turn the wall at $A''A'''$ at −2° with respect to the direction of AA' to obtain the direction 201.

Fig. 52. *Analysis of the reflection of expansion waves from a curved wall by use of the characteristic numbers.*

An analogous phenomenon occurs when a shock wave meets a plane rigid wall (Figure 53). At A a shock wave is generated, and in the zone ABC the flow has the direction AC. However, at B the flow cannot change direction; therefore at B another shock wave is generated having the same deviation δ, but in opposite direction. Since the value of δ is known, the value of M_2 is determinable, from which the value of M_3 and the direction of BC are determinable in terms of the deviation δ. If the deviation δ is large the value of δ

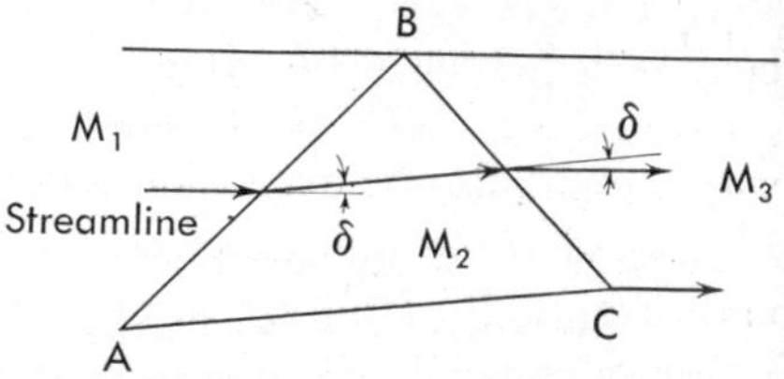

Fig. 53. *Analysis of the reflection of a shock wave from a rigid wall.*

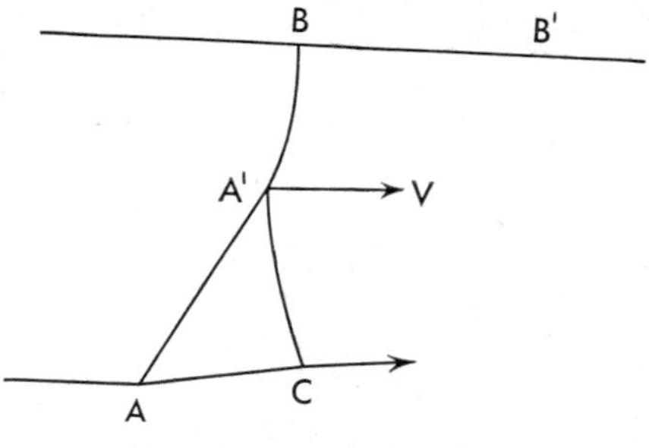

may be larger than the maximum deviation possible for M_2. In this case the reflection BC is no longer possible and the phenomenon must change. At the wall no deviation must occur; therefore if the reflection is not possible, the only shock possible at the wall is a normal shock for which the deviation is zero. In this case the phenomenon appears as in Figure 54. The flow behind the shock $A'B$ is subsonic; therefore it is possible to have equilibrium along $A'C$ and BB', because the stream lines in the zone $A'BB'$ are not parallel. At A' the flow is not parallel to the wall BB'_3; therefore the deviation across $A'C$ is less than across $A'A$.

Fig. 54. *Interference between a rigid wall and a shock wave, when reflection at the wall is not possible.*

Reflection of Expansion Waves and Shock Waves in a Fluid Zone with Different Velocity. Consider a flow which has a pressure p_1 and a supersonic velocity V_1, and which overflows from a tube into a chamber at constant pressure p_2 (Figure 55); the external air has no velocity. If the pressure p_2 is less than p_1, the flow tends to expand, because along the streamlines AC

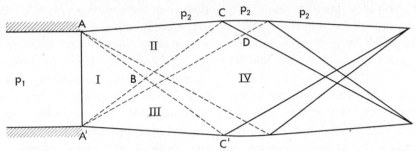

Fig. 55.   *Reflection of expansion waves from a boundary constituted by air at rest.*

and $A'C'$ the pressure must be equal to p_2. From A and $A'_{\downarrow}$ expansion waves are generated which cross in the middle of the jet. In the jet four zones can be considered: zone I in which the pressure p_1 exists, zones II and III in which after expansions from p_1 the pressure p_2 exists, and zone IV between II and III. When the flow goes in the zone IV in terms of the considerations of page 69 it undergoes another expansion; therefore in IV the pressure is less than in III. However in the boundary of the jet, the pressure cannot be different from p_2; therefore the expansion waves must be reflected by the boundary layer as compression waves, because at every point C the pressure must be equal to p_2, while the pressure at D is less than p_2. Therefore the expansion waves are reflected as compression waves, and the compression waves must produce the same variation of pressure as the expansion waves and can thus be determined with these criteria.

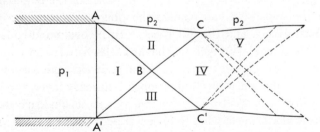

Fig. 56.   *Reflection of a shock wave from a boundary constituted by air at rest.*

If p_2 is larger than p_1 (Figure 56), a shock wave starts from A which increases the pressure from p_1 to p_2; in II and III the pressure is equal to p_2; in IV the pressure increases because the two shock waves cross in the middle of the jet. Since at C, and in zone V, the pressure must be equal to p_2, expansion waves must be generated which decrease the pressure to the value p_2. Therefore shock waves are reflected as expansion waves of the same variation of pressure at the boundary.

The problem becomes more complicated when the pressure p_2 is a function of the pressure p_1 and the conditions in the boundary are not known. This case, which is very important for aerodynamic phenomena, occurs when expansion or shock waves interfere with the boundary layer, because the pressure in the boundary layer is a function of the pressure outside the boundary layer as well as of the velocity and viscosity in the boundary layer. The phenomenon in this case is very complicated and has not yet been solved analytically, but it can be examined qualitatively. The boundary layer is a zone of flow of variable and lower velocity, and near the surface the flow is subsonic; therefore in part of the boundary layer, subsonic flow must be considered in which the variation of pressure must permit an equilibrium with the external flow. If an expansion wave meets the boundary layer, and since a diminution of pressure occurs across the expansion wave, at the boundary layer an expansion must also occur. The equilibrium in the boundary layer is connected with the equilibrium outside, but the phenomenon in presence of boundary layer cannot be very different from the phenomenon of reflection at a solid wall, because the boundary layer can change the direction of the stream very slightly at the point at which the expansion wave meets the boundary layer. Since an expansion occurs, there cannot be separation, and the variation of thickness of the boundary layer cannot be so large as to have the possibility of changing the shape of the streamlines. Because at the point of meeting of the expansion waves and the boundary layer the direction of the streamlines must be about equal to the direction of the wall and cannot undergo a large variation, the effect of the presence of the boundary layer on the zone of the expansion can change the phenomenon only a very small amount quantitatively, and the differences can be evaluated considering the thickness of the boundary layer at the wall. It is, on the contrary, very important in the case of shock waves. When a shock wave occurs in the flow and the flow wets a surface with a developed boundary layer, the presence of the boundary layer changes the aerodynamic phenomenon. In order to understand the physical scheme of what happens, suppose at first that the boundary layer can be represented by a flow having constant subsonic velocity in equilibrium with the flow with constant supersonic velocity in front of the shock. If EA (Figure 57) is the surface of the wall and BC is the streamline that divides the supersonic flow from the subsonic flow, for equilibrium in the zone $BCEA$, it is necessary that along BC the pressure in the supersonic and in the subsonic part be the same. If at CF a shock wave occurs, in the supersonic flow, across the shock wave, a discontinuity of the pressure occurs, and at F_1 behind the shock a greater pressure than at F exists. If the shock is extended near the boundary layer at C, in order to have equilibrium also in the boundary layer there must be the same change in pressure. However, in subsonic flow, discontinuity of pressure is not possible, and the higher pressure of C_1 is transmitted upstream in the subsonic flow in the zone $CBEA$. For equilibrium in the zone CB, also in the supersonic part, the pressure must increase, and in order to have equilibrium it is necessary that the variation of pressure in the supersonic zone near the boundary layer be gradual, which is possible only in the subsonic part. Therefore from the boundary layer

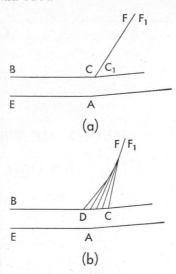

Fig. 57. *Interaction between shock and boundary layer.*

many compression waves start (Figure 57*b*) that form an envelope in the shock. When the variation of pressure across the shock waves is large, a large pressure gradient occurs in the boundary layer; if the boundary layer is extended, separation can occur in the zone of the shock and therefore the phenomenon changes notably from the case without boundary layer. The presence of the boundary layer changes the pressure in the zone AE (Figure 57*b*), and if the boundary layer exists, a gradual compression along AE occurs, and at the wall the pressure cannot have discontinuity. In the actual phenomena the variation of the velocity in the thickness of the boundary layer is gradual and does not occur abruptly as it was assumed, but the necessity for gradual compression near the wall and the possibility of separation remain, and the actual shock is similar to the scheme considered.

The possibility of large variations of the thickness of the boundary layer and the possibility of separation make the phenomenon of shock waves in the presence of boundary layer difficult to analyze, because many different parameters must be considered as to the type of motion in the boundary layer (laminar or turbulent), the thickness and corresponding Reynolds number, and the kind of successive transformations that the boundary layer must undergo. The phenomenon of reflection of shock waves on boundary layer can be, in some cases, similar to reflection from a rigid wall where the shock wave is reflected as a shock wave, while in some other cases the reflection can be similar to reflection from constant-pressure boundary where the shock wave is reflected as an expansion wave. All the intermediate cases are possible in particular boundary conditions.

5

THEORY OF TWO-DIMENSIONAL FLOW—
CHARACTERISTIC THEORY
FOR ROTATIONAL FLOW

When the flow behind a curved shock wave is considered, the flow is no longer a potential flow because the variation of entropy which exists from one streamline to the other produces vorticity in the flow. Usually the presence of vorticity does not change the phenomena very much quantitatively, and therefore usually the potential flow theory can still be used as a good approximation. However, when the variation of entropy is important it can be taken into account in the analysis because it is possible to determine a differential equation that gives the law of the transformation of the flow in this case. The equation of motion for rotational flow in the supersonic part permits determination of characteristic lines similar to those obtained for potential flow, and by application of the characteristic theory it is possible to proceed to determination of the flow at particular points or in the entire field, with a step-by-step calculation. The calculation is more complicated than in the case of potential flow, and therefore is often used only locally in the zone in which the variation of entropy is very large.

The Special Stream Function for Rotational Flow and the Differential Equation for Rotational Flow. (Reference 16.) From the equations of rotational flow (Chapter 1) it was shown that along every streamline, if no shock occurs, the transformation is isentropic (equation 17), and the entropy is constant.

$$(V \times \operatorname{curl} V) \cdot V = 0. \tag{17}$$

Equation (18) can be written using equation (33) in the form

$$+ \operatorname{grad} S = \frac{\operatorname{curl} V \times V}{a^2} \gamma R g \tag{18}$$

because $(I + \dfrac{1}{2} V^2)$ is constant in the entire flow. Projecting equation (18) along the x-axis and along the y-axis*,

$$+ \frac{dS}{dx} = - \frac{v(v_x - u_y)}{a^2} gR\gamma$$

$$\frac{dS}{dy} = + \frac{u(v_x - u_y)}{a^2} gR\gamma$$

and because

$$\frac{d^2S}{dxdy} = \frac{d^2S}{dydx}$$

then

$$\frac{\partial}{\partial x}\left[\frac{u(v_x - v_y)}{a^2}\right] + \frac{\partial}{\partial y}\left[\frac{v(v_x - v_y)}{a^2}\right] = 0. \tag{170}$$

The equation of continuity (2) for the two-dimensional stationary case is

$$\frac{\partial(\rho u)}{\partial x} + \frac{\partial(\rho v)}{\partial y} = 0.$$

The continuity equation can be transformed to the form

$$\frac{\partial u}{\partial x} + \frac{\partial v}{\partial y} + \left(\frac{u}{\rho}\frac{\partial \rho}{\partial x} + \frac{v}{\rho}\frac{\partial \rho}{\partial y}\right) = 0. \tag{171}$$

Multiplying equation (171) by $a^{\frac{2}{\gamma - 1}}$ and using equation (48) along the stream line equation (171) becomes

$$\frac{\partial}{\partial x}\left(ua^{\frac{2}{\gamma - 1}}\right) + \frac{\partial}{\partial y}\left(va^{\frac{2}{\gamma - 1}}\right) = 0. \tag{172}$$

In order to use nondimensional coefficients, it is possible to divide equations (170) and (172) by the square of the limiting velocity defined by equation (85). If, as unit velocity, the limiting velocity V_l is assumed, and W is the velocity in the new units ($W = V/V_l$), by (equation 85b),

$$\frac{V_l^2}{V^2} = 1 + \frac{2}{\gamma - 1}\frac{a^2}{V^2}$$

or

$$V_l^2 - V^2 = \frac{2}{\gamma - 1} a^2 = (1 - W^2)(V_l^2). \tag{173}$$

If u' and v' are the components of the velocity W along x and y, substituting equation (173) in (170) and in (172), because V_l is constant, gives

---

* The symbols with the subscripts x, y, xx, xy, and yy define the first and the second derivatives with respect to the x and y axis, of the quantities represented by the symbols without subscripts.

$$\frac{\partial}{\partial x}\left[u'\,\frac{v'_x - u'_y}{1 - W^2}\right] + \frac{\partial}{\partial y}\left[v'\,\frac{v'_x - u'_y}{1 - W^2}\right] = 0 \tag{174}$$

$$\frac{\partial}{\partial x}\left[u'\,(1 - W^2)^{\frac{1}{\gamma-1}}\right] + \frac{\partial}{\partial y}\left[v'\,(1 - W^2)^{\frac{1}{\gamma-1}}\right] = 0 \tag{174a}$$

and from (174) and (174a)

$$u'\,\frac{\partial}{\partial x}\left[\frac{v'_x - u'_y}{(1 - W^2)^{\frac{\gamma}{\gamma-1}}}\right] + v'\,\frac{\partial}{\partial y}\left[\frac{v'_x - u'_y}{(1 - W^2)^{\frac{\gamma}{\gamma-1}}}\right] = 0. \tag{175}$$

Equation (175) shows that the term in brackets is constant along the stream-lines. Since $(v'_x - u'_y)$ represents the rotation in the flow, the rotation along every streamline must be proportional to $(1 - W^2)^{\frac{\gamma}{\gamma-1}}$. Because along the streamline an isentropic transformation occurs, the pressure is proportional to this factor [equation (85a)]. The rotation along the streamlines in two-dimensional flow is therefore proportional to the value of the pressure.

Assuming a new function ψ defined by the expressions

$$\psi_y = u'\,(1 - W^2)^{\frac{1}{\gamma-1}}; \qquad \psi_x = -\,v'\,(1 - W^2)^{\frac{1}{\gamma-1}} \tag{176}$$

equation (174a) is automatically satisfied. From (176),

$$W^2\,(1 - W^2)^{\frac{2}{\gamma-1}} = \psi^2_x + \psi^2_y = (\text{grad } \psi)^2 \tag{177}$$

$$\frac{u'}{v'} = -\,\frac{\psi x}{\psi y}. \tag{178}$$

The values of u' and v' obtained from (176) and (178) can be substituted in equation (175), and an equation of the third order in ψ is obtained. But from (176) it is possible to obtain immediately the first integral of the equation, because by definition it is

$$u'\psi_x + v'\psi_y = 0. \tag{179}$$

Therefore equation (175) is satisfied only when

$$\frac{v'_x - u'_y}{(1 - W^2)^{\frac{\gamma}{\gamma-1}}} = f(\psi). \tag{180}$$

From equation (19) using mechanical units for the entropy, if n is the normal direction to the streamline and

$$a'^2 = \frac{g\gamma RT}{V_l^2}$$

then

$$\frac{W\,(v'_x - u'_y)}{a'^2} = \frac{1}{g\gamma R}\,\frac{dS}{dn}. \tag{181}$$

From equation (179) it is found that grad ψ is at a right angle to the stream-lines; therefore equation (177) gives

$$W (1 - W^2)^{\frac{1}{\gamma - 1}} = \frac{d\psi}{dn} \tag{182}$$

or remembering equation (173)

$$\frac{v'_x - u'_y}{(1 - W^2)^{\frac{\gamma}{\gamma - 1}}} = f(\psi) = \frac{\gamma - 1}{2\gamma g} \frac{1}{R} \frac{dS}{d\psi}. \tag{183}$$

Differentiating the expressions of ψ_x and ψ_y from (176) produces

$$(1 - W^2)^{\frac{1}{\gamma - 1}} \left[u'_y - \frac{2u'W}{(\gamma - 1)(1 - W^2)} W_y \right] = \psi_{yy} \tag{184}$$

or

$$(1 - W^2)^{\frac{1}{\gamma - 1}} u'_y = \frac{u'W (1 - W^2)^{\frac{1}{\gamma - 1}}}{a'^2} W_y + \psi_{yy} \tag{185}$$

and from the second part of (176)

$$(1 - W^2)^{\frac{1}{\gamma - 1}} v'_x = \frac{v'W (1 - W^2)^{\frac{1}{\gamma - 1}}}{a'^2} W_x - \psi_{xx}. \tag{186}$$

From (185) and (186)

$$- (1 - W^2)^{\frac{1}{\gamma - 1}} (v'_x - u'_y) = \psi_{xx} + \psi_{yy} + \frac{W (1 - W^2)^{\frac{1}{\gamma - 1}}}{a'^2} (u'W_y - v'W_x). \tag{187}$$

From equation (177) is obtained also

$$W(1 - W^2)^{\frac{2}{\gamma - 1}} \left(1 - \frac{2}{\gamma - 1} \frac{W^2}{1 - W^2} \right) \text{grad } W = \psi_x \text{ grad } \psi_x + \psi_y \text{ grad } \psi_y \tag{188}$$

or

$$W(1 - W^2)^{\frac{1}{\gamma - 1}} \left(1 - \frac{W^2}{a'^2} \right) \text{grad } W = - v' \text{grad } \psi_x + u' \text{grad } \psi_y. \tag{189}$$

Therefore the last term of equation (187) becomes

$$W(1 - W^2)^{\frac{1}{\gamma - 1}} \left(1 - \frac{W^2}{a'^2} \right) (u'W_y - v'W_x) = v'^2 \psi_{xx} - 2u'v' \psi_{xy} + u'^2 \psi_{yy} \tag{190}$$

and then (187) becomes

$$(1 - W^2)^{\frac{1}{\gamma - 1}} (v'_x - u'_y)$$
$$= \frac{1}{1 - \frac{W^2}{a'^2}} \left[\left(1 - \frac{u'^2}{a'^2} \right) \psi_{xx} - \frac{2u'v'}{a'^2} \psi_{xy} + \left(1 - \frac{v'^2}{a'^2} \right) \psi_{yy} \right]. \tag{191}$$

Substituting in equation (183) gives

$$\left(1 - \frac{u'^2}{a'^2}\right)\psi_{xx} - \frac{2u'v'}{a'^2}\psi_{xy} + \left(1 - \frac{v'^2}{a'^2}\right)\psi_{yy}$$

$$= (1 - W^2)^{\frac{\gamma+1}{\gamma-1}}\left(\frac{w^2}{a'^2} - 1\right)f(\psi). \tag{192}$$

In the coefficients of (192) the expressions u'^2/a'^2, v'^2/a'^2, W'^2/a'^2 are non-dimensional; therefore equation (192) can be written in the form

$$\left(1 - \frac{u^2}{a^2}\right)\psi_{xx} - \frac{2uv}{a^2}\psi_{xy} + \left(1 - \frac{v^2}{a^2}\right)\psi_{yy}$$

$$= \left[1 - \left(\frac{V}{V_l}\right)^2\right]^{\frac{\gamma+1}{\gamma-1}}\left(\frac{v^2}{a^2} - 1\right)f(\psi). \tag{193}$$

Equation (193) is similar to equation (58) and differs only in the last term.

The Characteristic System for Rotational Flow. For equation (193) the considerations made in Chapter 2 can be repeated. Equation (193) is a Monge-Ampere equation and in supersonic flow it is a hyperbolic equation (see Reference 3); and some lines which are characteristic varieties of the equation exist (Reference 17).

Using the symbols H, L, K, as for the case of potential flow and defined by equation (67), and the symbol G defined by

$$G = -\left(1 - \frac{V^2}{V_l^2}\right)^{\frac{\gamma+1}{\gamma-1}}\left(\frac{V^2}{a^2} - 1\right)f(\psi) \tag{194}$$

H, L, K, G are functions only of ψ, ψ_x, and ψ_y. Proceeding in a similar form as for potential flow, the following equations for the two characteristic families can be obtained

$$\frac{dy}{dx} = \lambda_1; \qquad H\psi_{xx} + H\lambda_2\psi_{xy} + G = 0 \tag{195}$$

$$\frac{dy}{dx} = \lambda_2; \qquad H\psi_{xx} + H\lambda_1\psi_{xy} + G = 0 \tag{196}$$

where the quantities λ_1 and λ_2 are defined by equation (69). Using the same transformations that are used for potential flow, equations (195) and (196) become

$$\frac{dy}{dx} = \tan(\mu + \theta) \tag{197}$$

$$\psi_{xx} + \tan(\theta - \mu)\psi_{xy} + \frac{G}{H} = 0 \tag{197a}$$

$$\frac{dy}{dx} = \tan(\theta - \mu) \tag{198}$$

$$\psi_{xx} + \tan(\theta + \mu)\,\psi_{xy} + \frac{G}{H} = 0. \tag{198a}$$

The first terms of equations (197) and (198) are the same as for potential flow, and the characteristic line can be obtained in the same form. However, the law that gives the variation of velocity along the characteristic line is different because it contains another term G/H which does not appear in the equation for potential flow and which contains the variation of entropy. Equations (197a) and (198a) can be transformed into more practical form. Substituting equations (185) and (186) in (197a) and (198a) (and a similar one obtained from (176) by differentiating ψ_x with respect to y),

$$- v'_x + \lambda u'_x + \frac{W}{a'^2}(v' - \lambda u')\,W_x + \frac{G}{H(1 - W^2)^{\frac{1}{\gamma - 1}}} = 0. \tag{200}$$

If θ is the angle between the velocity and the x-axis, the term W_x is given by the expression

$$W_x = \frac{u'}{W}u'_x + \frac{v'}{W}v'_x = u'_x\cos\theta + v'_x\sin\theta. \tag{201}$$

The term $\dfrac{W}{a'^2}(v' - \lambda u')$ can be written in the form

$$\frac{W}{a'^2}(v' - \lambda u') = \frac{V^2}{a^2}(\sin\theta - \lambda\cos\theta) = \frac{\sin\theta - \lambda\cos\theta}{\sin^2\mu}. \tag{202}$$

Substituting (201) and (202) in (200), and expressing u'_x and v'_x in the form

$$\left.\begin{aligned} u'_x &= \frac{dW}{dx}\cos\theta - W\sin\theta\,\frac{d\theta}{dx}\\[2mm] v'_x &= \frac{dW}{dx}\sin\theta + W\cos\theta\,\frac{d\theta}{dx} \end{aligned}\right\} \tag{203}$$

the following expression results:

$$\frac{dW}{dx}(\sin\theta - \lambda\cos\theta)\frac{1}{\tan^2\mu} - W\frac{d\theta}{dx}(\lambda\sin\theta + \cos\theta)$$
$$+ \frac{G}{H(1 - W^2)^{\frac{1}{\gamma - 1}}} = 0. \tag{204}$$

Dividing by W and substituting the corresponding values for λ_1 and λ_2, equation (204) becomes

$$\frac{dW}{W} \mp d\theta\tan\mu + \frac{G}{HW}\,dx\,\frac{\tan^2\mu}{(\sin\theta - \lambda\cos\theta)(1 - W^2)^{\frac{1}{\gamma - 1}}} = 0. \tag{205}$$

The third term of equation (205) can be expressed as a function of dS/dn in terms of equations (194), (181), (182), and (183), and the following equations can be obtained for the two characteristics:

$$\frac{dy}{dx} = \tan(\theta + \mu) \tag{206}$$

$$\frac{dW}{W} - d\theta \tan \mu + \frac{\sin^3 \mu}{\cos(\theta + \mu)} \frac{dS}{dn} \frac{dx}{\gamma Rg} = 0 \tag{206a}$$

$$\frac{dy}{dx} = \tan(\mu - \theta) \tag{207}$$

$$\frac{dW}{W} + d\theta \tan \mu - \frac{\sin^3 \mu}{\cos(\theta - \mu)} \frac{dS}{dn} \frac{dx}{\gamma Rg} = 0. \tag{207a}$$

Equations (206) and (207) are very similar to equations (75) but an analytical solution has not been found; therefore in order to determine the quantities in the flow, a step-by-step calculation is necessary. This step-by-step calculation, similar to the calculations for axial symmetrical flow (Chapter 13), is long, but permits taking into account the effect of variation of entropy. The step-by-step calculation can be developed in this way: Assume that the conditions at two points P_1 and P_2 near each other are known (Figure 58). From P_1 it is possible to design the tangent to the first characteristic line inclined at $(\mu + \theta)$ with respect to the x-axis, and from P_2 the tangent to the second characteristic line. If the points P_2 and P_1 are near each other it is

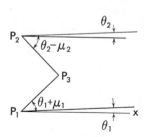

possible to substitute for the characteristic line its tangents, and then a point P_3 can be determined along the two characteristic lines. The values of θ and W (which can be obtained from the corresponding value of M) for the point P_3 can be determined from equations (206) and (207). For practical use, equations (206) and (207) can be transformed into an expression containing only the value of the variation of θ and W with respect to the value that exists in P_1 as functions of the quantities in P_1 and P_2. If the subscript 1 indicates the quantities at the point

Fig. 58. *Construction of the characteristic net.*

P_1, and the subscript 2 indicates the quantities at the point P_2, equations (206) and (207) can be written in the following form:

$$\frac{dy_1}{dx_1} = \tan(\theta_1 + \mu_1) \tag{208}$$

$$\frac{\Delta W_1}{W_1} - \Delta\theta_1 \tan \mu_1 + \frac{\sin^3 \mu_1}{\cos(\theta_1 + \mu_1)} \left(\frac{\Delta S}{\Delta n}\right)_1 \frac{\Delta x_1}{\gamma Rg} = 0 \tag{208a}$$

$$\frac{dy_2}{dx_2} = \tan(\theta_2 - \mu_2) \tag{209}$$

$$\frac{\Delta W_2}{W_2} + \Delta\theta_2 \tan \mu_2 - \frac{\sin^3 \mu_2}{\cos (\theta_2 - \mu_2)} \left(\frac{\Delta S}{\Delta n}\right)_2 \frac{\Delta x_2}{\gamma Rg} = 0 \qquad (209a)$$

where infinitesimals of second and higher order are neglected. But if the variation of entropy between P_1 and P_2 is small and occurs gradually, the gradient of entropy can be considered constant between the two points. In this case

$$\frac{dS}{dn} = \frac{S_3 - S_1}{x_3 - x_1} \frac{\cos (\theta_1 + \mu_1)}{\sin \mu_1}$$

$$= \frac{S_2 - S_1}{(x_3 - x_1) \dfrac{\sin \mu_1}{\cos (\mu_1 + \theta_1)} + \dfrac{(x_3 - x_2) \sin \mu_2}{\cos (\theta_2 - \mu_2)}} \cdot \qquad (210)$$

Assuming

$$x_1 - x_2 = \zeta_1; \qquad \frac{\sin \mu_1}{\cos (\mu_1 + \theta_1)} = e$$

$$x_3 - x_1 = \zeta_0; \qquad \frac{\sin \mu_2}{\cos (\theta_2 - \mu_2)} = f$$

$$1 + \frac{\zeta_1}{\zeta_0} = d$$

equations (206) and (207) can be transformed into the following:

$$\left(\tan \mu_2 + \frac{W_1}{W_2} \tan \mu_1\right) d\theta_1 = 1 - \frac{W_1}{W_2} - (\theta_1 - \theta_2) \tan \mu_2$$

$$+ \frac{S_2 - S_1}{g\gamma R} \frac{fd \sin^2 \mu_2 + \dfrac{W_1}{W_2} e \sin^2 \mu_1}{e + fd} \qquad (211)$$

$$\frac{dW_1}{W_1} = \tan \mu_1 d\theta_1 - \frac{S_2 - S_1}{\gamma Rg} \frac{e \sin^2 \mu_1}{e + fd} \qquad (212)$$

$$S_3 = S_1 + e\gamma Rg \frac{S_2 - S_1}{\gamma Rg} \frac{1}{e + fd} \qquad (213)$$

$$\theta_3 = \theta_1 + d\theta \text{ (radians).} \qquad (214)$$

With equations (211) to (214) it is possible to determine the flow properties for every point P_3 obtained from the intersection of two characteristic lines of different families from two points, P_1 and P_2, in which the flow properties are known.

If a large variation of flow quantities occurs between P_1 and P_2, another approximation can be obtained by designing the lines P_1P_3 and P_2P_3 as average inclinations of the characteristic lines at P_1 and P_3, P_2 and P_3, and using an average value for the coefficients, assuming at P_3 the values obtained by the first approximation. A better approximation can also be obtained for

dS/dn by determining the streamline that passes through P_3 and therefore the corresponding value of entropy. Usually this approximation is not necessary.

Equations (211) to (214) permit determination of the flow properties and the form of the shock waves when rotation is important. For example, if $ABCDQ$ (Figure 59) is the body considered and at A a shock wave AO occurs, the flow behind OA is rotational because OA is not straight. In order to determine the

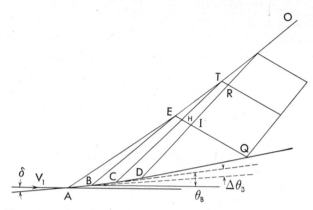

Fig. 59. *Practical application of the characteristic system for rotational flow.*

flow behind the shock AO and the shape of the shock, taking into account the variation of entropy, calculations can be conducted in the following manner. At A a shock wave is produced with inclination AE determined by the inclination δ with respect to the undisturbed velocity of the tangent to the body at A (equation 126). The Mach number M_A at A behind the shock can be determined by using equation (125) and the variation of entropy ΔS across the shock by using equation (150). The entropy along every streamline is constant; therefore along the body (points $ABCDQ$) the entropy is constant and equal to the entropy at A. If B is a point near A and at B the tangent to the body is inclined at $\Delta\theta_B$ with respect to the tangent at A ($\theta_B = \delta + \Delta\theta_B$ with respect to the undisturbed velocity), because an isentropic compression occurs along AB, the Mach number and the Mach angle at B can be determined using either equation (81) or the values of Table 2, remembering that $\Delta\theta_B$ is a deviation of compression and therefore M_B is smaller than M_A. At B the characteristic line BE, inclined at the Mach angle with respect to the tangent to the body at B, is drawn, and the point E on the tangent to the shock at A can be determined. At E the equations of the shock must be satisfied, and along BE equation (208) must be satisfied; therefore the value of W and θ at E can be calculated. For practical calculations it is useful to determine for the given Mach number M_1 in front of the shock, the value of M_2 and the corresponding

W (equation 85b), the value of δ, and the value of ΔS for different values of ϵ, using equations (121), (125), (126), and (150), or the corresponding Table 5. In this case the values of ϵ and δ must increase from the values they have at A. The values of W, ΔS, and ϵ can be plotted as functions of the corresponding deviation across the shock δ. The diagrams that give W and ΔS as functions of δ can be differentiated and two other diagrams that give $dW/d\delta$ and $d\Delta S/d\delta$ as functions of δ can be obtained. Now, if at B the direction of the stream is $(\theta_B = \delta_A + \Delta\theta_B)$, and at E the direction is $(\theta_E = \theta_B + \Delta\theta_E)$, equation (208) can be transformed as follows: If $\Delta\theta_E$ is zero, the deviation across the shock at E is known and is equal to θ_B; therefore the corresponding values of W, ΔS, $dW/d\delta$, and $d\Delta S/d\delta$, which can be called $W_{\theta B}$, $\Delta S_{\theta B}$, $\left(\dfrac{dW}{d\delta}\right)_{\theta B}$, and $\left(\dfrac{d\Delta S}{d\delta}\right)_{\theta B}$, respectively, can be obtained from the diagrams. If $\Delta_{\theta E}$ is not zero, the value of the velocity and the entropy at E can be expressed in this form:

$$W_E = W_{\theta B} + \left(\frac{dW}{d\delta}\right)_{\theta B} \Delta\theta_E$$

$$\Delta S_E = \Delta S_{\theta B} + \left(\frac{d\Delta S}{d\delta}\right)_{\theta B} \Delta\theta_E$$

where only the value of $\Delta\theta_E$ is unknown; therefore equation (208) can be transformed to the form

$$\frac{W_{\theta B} - W_B}{W_B} + \left(\frac{dW}{d\delta}\right)_{\theta B}\frac{\Delta\theta_E}{W_B} - \tan\mu_B\Delta\theta_E$$
$$+ \frac{\sin^2\mu_B}{g\gamma R}\left[\Delta S_{\theta B} - \Delta S_B + \left(\frac{d\Delta S}{d\delta}\right)_B \Delta\theta_E\right] = 0. \quad (215)$$

In equation (215), all quantities are known except the value of $\Delta_{\theta E}$, which can be determined. When the value of $\Delta_{\theta E}$ has been determined, the deviation across the shock at (E, θ_E) can be determined, and all other quantities can be obtained from the diagrams. If it is necessary, the value of θ_E in a second approximation can be calculated by assuming for the inclination of the lines AE and BE the average value between the direction of the shock at A and E and the direction of the characteristic lines at E and B, and using in place of the quantities at B the averages between the corresponding quantities at E and B in equation (215). From E the tangent can be drawn to the second characteristic line EH, and from C (determined in the same way as B was determined), the tangent to the first characteristic line CH. Then with equations (211), (212), (213), and (214) the point H can be determined. From H the points I and Q can be determined. For the point I the calculations are the same as the calculation for H, and for Q equations (209) and (209a) must be used. Indeed, at Q the direction of the flow is given by the shape of the body, and therefore θ_Q is known and the value of ΔS is known ($\Delta S_Q = \Delta S_A$). Therefore in equation (209a), ($\Delta \theta = \theta_Q - \theta_1$), and ($d\Delta S = \Delta S_1 - \Delta S_A$) are known, dn can be calculated, and with equation (209a) ΔW can be determined. Proceeding in the same way, the entire flow and the shock can be determined.

6

MEASUREMENT OF THE PHYSICAL

QUANTITIES OF A SUPERSONIC FLOW

Measurement of the Physical Quantities of the Flow in Aerodynamic Phenomena. When movements of a gas are analyzed, the physical properties of the gas which are most important for the knowledge of aerodynamic phenomena produced by the movements, are static pressure, density, temperature, and vectorial velocity of the flow. From these properties it is possible to learn all other characteristics of the flow such as the mass flow, energy of the flow, the law of transformation along the streamlines and the like, without making other measurements in the particular flow analyzed, but using the general knowledge available for the gas considered in the flow. Therefore, in aerodynamic phenomena it is important to study the possibility of determining these properties at given points of the flow or in the entire flow. While measurement of the value of static pressure and of vectorial velocity is possible in steady phenomena by use of suitable instruments, direct determination of the density is more complicated and is possible only in some particular cases, but no practical instrument or system is yet known for direct measurement of temperature in points of a flow at high speed.

If the values of pressure and density are known at every point, the temperature can be obtained by using the equation of the state of the gas; while if the law of transformation that occurs along the streamlines is known, it is possible to obtain density and temperature along all the streamlines by determining only the pressure along the streamlines and measuring temperature or density only at a single point, as for example, a point at which the velocity is zero, and calculating from the value of pressure the corresponding values of temperature and density in terms of the law of transformation. In many aerodynamic problems the law of transformation along the streamlines is known; therefore measurement of pressure is the only measurement necessary if the initial conditions are known. If the law of transformation is not known, the density must also be determined. The measurement of density can be obtained in some cases with optical systems.

Determination of the Value of the Static Pressure and of the Mach Number with Pressure Measurements. Determination of the value of the static pressure at a point P of the flow at supersonic speed, if the direction of the velocity is known, can be effected in different ways. A sharp wedge with an orifice in one side very near the edge can be used (Figure 60). The orifice must be perpendicular to the surface of the wedge, which must be placed parallel to streamlines of the flow. If the wedge is sharp enough, an attached shock occurs at the opposite side of the orifice, but the flow is not disturbed by the presence of the instrument along the surface that has the orifice; therefore by connecting the orifice to a manometer the value of the static pressure at P can be determined. For this determination it is necessary to know the direction of the velocity because if the surface of the instrument in which the orifice is located is not parallel to the streamlines, expansion or compression occurs in the flow and the value of the pressure at P changes. It is also necessary that the instrument have a thin and sharp leading edge to avoid a detached shock occurring in front (Figure

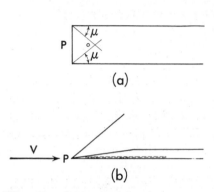

(a)

(b)

Fig. 60. *Instrument for the measurement of static pressure.*

60b) which would change the value of the pressure at P. The wedge can have very small transversal dimensions (Figure 60a), and the pressure orifice can be very near the leading edge of the wedge. The orifice must be in front of the two Mach waves from the ends of the leading edge.

The instrument does not disturb a large extent of flow in front of the point of measurement; therefore it is useful when the measurement occurs in proximity to shock waves (as will be discussed later), but is very sensitive to variations of angle of attack. For this reason the direction of the stream velocity at the point of the measurement must be known with precision. In order to avoid errors due to small angles of attack, often two symmetrical instruments separated by a relatively small distance are used in place of one, and pressures in two parallel surfaces are measured. If the two pressure tubes give different values of pressure, the instrument has an angle of attack that can be evaluated as shown in the next paragraph and the value of the static pressure can be found.

In place of the wedge determination of the static pressure can be made by using a cylindrical tube with a conical tip of small included angle (Figure 61). The pressure orifices of the instrument must be placed in the cylindrical part of the instrument in correspondence to two perpendicular diameters of the cross section. If the total angle of the cone is small (of the order of 8–10°) and the position of the orifices is far (6–10 diameters) from the end of the

Fig. 61. *Instrument for the measurement of static pressure.*

cone, the value of the pressure on the cylinder practically corresponds to the value of the static pressure of the undisturbed stream. This instrument has very low sensitivity to small angles of attack, and therefore it is not necessary to know very exactly the direction of the stream, but the distance between the apex of the cone and the position of the orifices is large, and in this zone the flow velocity must be uniform; therefore tubes of very small diameter must be used.

Determination of the Mach number at a point of the flow, when the direction of the flow is known, can be made from measurement of two pressures. The pressures most suitable for the determination are the static pressure and the pressure in a total-head tube. The ratio of the two pressures permits calculation of the Mach number. Indeed, in front of a total-head tube a normal shock is produced (Figure 62a); therefore the static pressure p_{2n} and the Mach number M_{2n} behind the shock can be determined with the equations for normal shock (equations 127 and 129) or Table 3, columns 2 and 3; the flow behind the shock is subsonic and the compression from the Mach number M_{2n} to zero velocity occurs isentropically. The ratio of the total pressure P_T read by the total-head tube, to the pressure P_{2n}, can be calculated as a function of M_{2n} with equation (41). Combining equation (41) with equa-

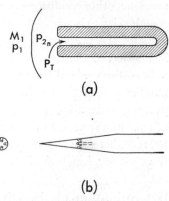

(a)

(b)

Fig. 62. *Total head tube.*

tions (127) and (129), the following expression can be obtained, which gives the value of the pressure in a total-head tube as a function of the Mach number and of the static pressure in the stream.

$$\frac{p_T}{p_1} = \frac{1}{2}\left[\frac{(\gamma+1)^{\frac{\gamma+1}{\gamma-1}} M_1^{\frac{2\gamma}{\gamma-1}}}{(4\gamma M_1^2 - 2\gamma + 2)^{\frac{1}{\gamma-1}}}\right]. \tag{216}$$

The value of p_T/p_1 can be obtained from the ratio of the values of column 4 of Table 3 and column 2 of Table 1 of the appendix.

$$\frac{p_T}{p_1} = \frac{p_T}{p_0}\bigg/\frac{p_0}{p_1}.$$

The value of the pressure in a total-head tube does not change sensibly for small angularity of the total-head tube with respect to the direction of the velocity, and therefore it can also be used if the direction of the stream is not known exactly. In this case for the determination of another pressure, the cylindrical static pressure tube previously described can be used. If a shorter instrument is necessary, in place of the cylindrical pressure tube, another instrument that has also low sensitivity to angle of attack can be used. The instrument is a cone of small included angle which has four orifices for pressure measurements in a normal section of the cone near its apex (Figure 62*b*). The orifices are placed at the ends of two diameters of the cross section perpendicular to each other and are connected to a manometer in such a manner that the average pressure of the four orifices can be read. If the cone has its axis parallel to the stream, the pressure is the same for all four orifices, and this value depends on the value of the angle of cone and on the static pressure and the Mach number of the stream. If the axis of the cone is at a small angle with respect to the direction of the velocity, the pressures at the four orifices are different, but the differences are small and the average value is practically the same, other conditions being the same, as the value of the pressure when the cone has its axis parallel to the stream (Chapter 12). Therefore the average value of the pressure is independent, for small values of inclination, of the inclination of the axis of the cone with respect to the stream, and depends only on the angle of the cone, which is known, and on the values of the Mach number and of the static pressure of the stream. The ratio of the average pressure to the static pressure can be determined analytically for a given angle of cone as a function of Mach number by equations given in Chapters 11 and 12, and therefore the values of the ratio of the p_T to the average pressure of the cone as a function of the Mach number can be obtained.

Determination of the Direction of Velocity with Pressure Measurements. For determination of the direction of the flow, a wedge with two pressure orifices at opposite sides of the wedge can be used. If the plane of the stream is known, at the point in which the direction must be determined, only one wedge is necessary, while if the direction of the streamline must be determined with respect to two planes perpendicular to each other, two mutually perpendicular wedges must be used. In the first case, the wedge AOB (Figure 63) must be placed with the edge OO' perpendicular to the plane of the stream; if the direction of the velocity is VO, the velocity is inclined at δ_B with respect to the surface OB and at δ_A with respect to the surface OA where the value $\delta(\delta = \delta_A + \delta_B)$ is known. If the instrument can be rotated around the axis O, the direction of the flow is given by the axis OC of the wedge when p_A is equal to p_B; if the instrument cannot rotate, the direction of the velocity can be determined in terms of the ratio of the pressures p_A and p_B if the Mach number in front is known. For the deviations δ_A and δ_B the equations of the shock, or of the expansion if δ_A or δ_B are negative, can be used (equations 126 and 121), and therefore for every Mach number in front of the wedge and for

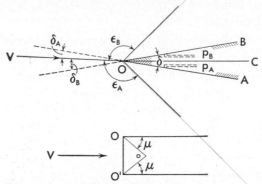

Fig. 63. *Instrument for the measurement of the flow direction.*

a given value of δ, the values of the angles δ_A and δ_B can be determined; however, the use of equations (126) and (121) is complicated because the angles ϵ_A and ϵ_B of the shock must be determined; therefore an equation that relates the pressure ratio p_A/p_1 or p_B/p_1 directly to the deviation δ_A or δ_B is more useful. This relation can be obtained in form of series as will be shown in Chapter 7, and in the case that the deviation δ_A produces a shock, it has the form (δ_A is in radians)

$$\frac{p_A - p_1}{p_1 M_1^2 \gamma} = c_1 \delta_A + c_2 \delta_A{}^2 + (c_3 - D)\, \delta_A{}^3 \dots \tag{217}$$

while in the case that the deviation δ_A produces expansion it has the form

$$\frac{p_A - p_1}{p_1 \gamma M_1^2} = - c_1 \delta_A + c_2 \delta_A{}^2 - c_3 \delta_A{}^3 \dots \tag{217a}$$

The terms c_1, c_2, c_3, and D are functions of the Mach number in front of the wedge, and therefore are known and are given by equations (244), (249), and (169). Usually the values of the angles δ_A or δ_B are small, because the angle of the wedge is small, and the direction of the stream is known in first approximation; therefore only the first term or the first two terms of the expansion in series are necessary. In this case, assuming δ_A or δ_B negative corresponding to an expansion, the following equation can be obtained:

$$\frac{p_A}{p_B} = \frac{1 + c_1 \gamma M_1^2 \delta_A + c_2 \gamma M_1^2 \delta_A{}^2}{1 + c_1 \gamma M_1^2 (\delta - \delta_A) + c_2 \gamma M_1^2 (\delta - \delta_A)^2} \tag{218}$$

where the terms $M_1^2 c_1$ and $M_1^2 c_2$ are known.

Because the expansion in series is not valid for detached shock, the angle

δ of the wedge must be small and the direction of axis OO' must be about the same as that of the stream.

The span of the wedge can be very small; the only necessary precaution is that the orifices must be located outside the zone disturbed by the end of the wedge, a zone that is defined by the lines inclined at Mach angle from the end of the wedge (Figure 63).

When the plane of the stream at the point considered is not known, another wedge in a plane perpendicular to the first wedge must be used. In this case the value of M_1 of equation (218) changes with the inclination of the stream Δ with respect to the plane normal to the wedge (Figure 64), and therefore

determination of the direction requires successive approximations. When the inclination of the velocity in the two planes using the value of the stream Mach number is determined in first approximation from equation (218), a second approximation can be obtained by determining the actual value of the Mach number in

Fig. 64. *Determination of the flow direction in the general case.*

a direction normal to the wedge M_Δ in terms of the inclination Δ measured with the other wedge (Figure 64). With the new value a second approximation for the value of Δ can be obtained.

In order to determine the direction of the stream it is possible also to use a body of revolution and to determine the pressure in different positions of a cross section of the body. The body can be, for example, a cone with four pressure orifices in a cross section. The cone and a total-head tube permit determination of the Mach number and direction of the stream, but the sensitivity of the instrument for determination of direction is much less than the sensitivity of the two wedges, because the variation of pressure with the variation of direction for a body of revolution is less than for a two-dimensional body.

These instruments described are useful in zones of streams in which gradual variation of physical characteristics occurs because in this case, the finite dimensions of the instruments are not practically important, but they are not useful for determining the physical properties near the zone of discontinuity corresponding to shock waves. When shock waves are present in the flow, the instrument can interfere notably with them, and therefore the determinations can be erroneous. The errors are usually very large if the instruments of measurement cross, in some part, shock waves, because along the surface of the instrument no deviation can occur, and the instrument records a value of pressure different from the value of the local pressure in the flow in absence of the instrument. If, for example, the static pressure must be determined in front of or behind a shock wave, determination is very difficult with pres-

sure tubes even if the velocity direction is known.   Indeed, if s is the front of
the shock (Figure 65a), a variation of pressure and direction occurs in the
flow across s.   If the static tube that must determine the pressure in front of

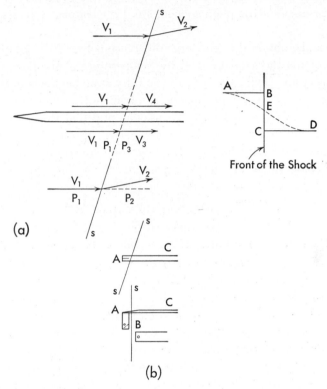

Fig. 65.   *Pressure measurement in the proximity of shock waves.*

the shock crosses the shock, it gives a wrong indication because in the boundary layer the discontinuity does not exist, and at the surface of the tube the
pressure changes in a different way than across the shock; therefore for an
extended zone in front of and behind the shock the pressure on the tube is
different from the pressure in the flow in absence of the tube; along the tube,
instead of having a pressure diagram $ABCD$, a diagram AED exists (Figure
65a).   In order to avoid interference, it is necessary to use a static tube that
is on only one side of the shock, as in Figure 65b (the support AC must produce
an attached shock that must not interfere with the pressure measurement).

Measurement of Temperature.   Direct measurement of temperature in
the flow at high speed is impossible with the usual thermometric systems
because of the presence of the boundary layer.   If a thermometer is placed

in the flow, on the surface of the thermometer a boundary layer is formed which changes notably the temperature on the surface of the thermometer with respect to the temperature of the stream, and therefore the thermometer registers a value much larger than the temperature of the flow. (For a more complete discussion of the phenomenon, see, for example, References 18 and 19).

An idea can be obtained of the large difference between the temperature at the surface of the thermometer and the temperature of the flow, depending on the viscosity and conductivity of the flow, by applying the equation of conservation of energy to the phenomenon. For simplicity, assume that the phenomenon is adiabatic and two-dimensional, and that the stream is in the direction of the axis (x-axis) of the thermometer. If m is the viscosity coefficient, Λ the conductivity coefficient, and T the temperature of the flow, the equation of conservation of energy in presence of viscosity and conductivity has the form

$$\rho \frac{d}{dt}\left(\frac{u^2}{2} + I\right) = \frac{\partial}{\partial y}\left(\Lambda \frac{\partial T}{\partial y} + \frac{m}{2}\frac{\partial u^2}{\partial y}\right) \tag{219}$$

where y is the direction normal to the direction of the stream. But

$$I = C_p T$$

and for an ideal gas it can be assumed that

$$\frac{mC_p}{\Lambda} = \sigma = \text{constant.}$$

Therefore equation (219) becomes

$$\rho \frac{d}{dt}\left(\frac{u^2}{2} + I\right) = \frac{\partial}{\partial y}\left[\frac{\Lambda}{C_p}\frac{\partial}{\partial y}\left(I + \sigma \frac{u^2}{2}\right)\right]. \tag{219a}$$

If the coefficient σ is equal to one, equation (219) admits a particular value of integral, that is given by

$$I + \frac{u^2}{2} = \text{constant.} \tag{220}$$

Outside of the boundary layer, equation (220) is valid, because it is the equation of energy in the absence of viscosity, and on the wall it is also valid because

$$- \Lambda \operatorname{grad} T = - \frac{\Lambda}{C_p} \operatorname{grad} I = \frac{\Lambda}{2C_p}\frac{\partial u^2}{\partial y} = u T_{xy}$$

where T_{xy} is the tangential force dependent on the viscosity, and u on the wall is zero; therefore if σ is equal to one, the solution (220) is also valid in the boundary layer, but

$$I + \frac{u^2}{2} = I_0 = C_p T_0. \tag{221}$$

On the surface u is zero; therefore the surface of the thermometer or of any body placed in the flow, if no heat exchange exists, has, for $\sigma = 1$, the temperature T_0 of the gas in the tank.

If the value of σ is different from one, the consideration is no longer exact. If σ is less than one, the temperature on the surface of the plate is less than T_0, and the temperature is greater for σ greater than one. The value of σ for air is 0.74 in a laminar boundary layer, and therefore the temperature on the body is less than the temperature in the tank. But the difference is not very large. If the boundary layer is turbulent, the quantity σ assumes the value of one, and therefore at the surface a perfect compensation occurs for the thermal content I, and the temperature is equal to T_0.

Practically, measurements of temperature are very doubtful, because the temperature on the thermometer is much different from the temperature in the flow, therefore transmission of heat and radiation on the thermometer can exist that change the value of the reading. Theoretically, for determination of the temperature in the flow, the temperature of a flat plate can be used if the boundary layer is turbulent. In this case the pressure at the point considered gives the value of p_1, the value of M_1 gives the ratio p_1/p_0, and from p_1/p_0 it is possible to determine T_1 because the thermometer gives the value of T_0. For the determination of T_0 it is more practical to use a thermometer which determines the value of the temperature inside the total-head tube. In a total-head tube the temperature is T_0 because the velocity is zero; therefore a thermometer placed inside a total-head tube must give the value of T_0 (Figure 66). The measurement of the temperature T_0 with a total-head tube is also difficult, because the temperature of the air in the tube is in part a function of the temperature of the tube which can transmit heat and therefore can change the value of T_0. Radiation from zones at different temperatures can also interfere with the precision of the measurements. The errors can be reduced if a flow at low velocity goes across the tube, because in this case the tube tends to assume the stagnation temperature of the air (Figure 66). In order to determine exactly the temperature at a point, a thermometer must be

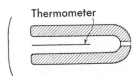

Fig. 66. *Instrument for the measurement of the stagnation temperature.*

used with zero relative velocity with respect to the point, but this system is usually very difficult because the thermometer must move with the flow at the same speed.

Measurement of Density. Determination of the value of density in the flow field can be made by using special optical instruments. By means of optical instruments it is possible in the general case to obtain a qualitative indication of the variation of the density in the flow, while for two-dimensional phenomena or for axial symmetrical phenomena a quantitative evaluation of the density is also possible. In the optical instruments the property used is that the index of refraction of a gas depends almost entirely on the density of the gas. The absolute index of refraction of a gas is the ratio between the speed of light in vacuum and the speed of light in the gas considered, and with good approximation it can be expressed in the form of the law of Arago Biot Lorenz:

$$\frac{\pi - 1}{\rho} = \text{constant.} \tag{222}$$

Because the velocity of light changes when the density of the gas changes (π change), if the light crosses two zones of gas of different density, ρ and ρ_0, after a given time the light has crossed zones of gases of different depth. The difference in depth can be calculated by using equation (222). If l_0 and l are the depth of the two zones and π_0 and π the corresponding indices of refraction

$$\frac{\pi - 1}{\rho} = \frac{\pi_0 - 1}{\rho_0}$$

or

$$\pi - \pi_0 = \frac{\rho - \rho_0}{\rho_0} (\pi_0 - 1) \tag{223}$$

and

$$l_0 - l = l \frac{\pi - \pi_0}{\pi_0} = l \frac{\rho - \rho_0}{\rho_0} \frac{\pi_0 - 1}{\pi_0}. \tag{224}$$

The difference $l_0 - l$ is very small in absolute value and therefore cannot be measured directly in order to determine the value of the density; but it is of the order of the wavelength of light and therefore can be determined with special instruments that can compare the differences of trajectories with the wavelength of light.

In order to have an idea of the differences $(l_0 - l)$ that can be expected for variations of the density of the order of those that occur in aerodynamic phenomena, it is sufficient to remember that for air at atmospheric pressure and temperature the value of $(\pi_0 - 1)$ is

$$\pi_0 - 1 = 290 \times 10^{-6} \text{ for red light of 8000 Angstroms}$$

$$\pi_0 - 1 = 297 \times 10^{-6} \text{ for violet light of 4000 Angstroms}$$

Therefore the difference of trajectory of the light $(l_0 - l)$ is (equation 224)

$$l_0 - l = l \frac{\rho - \rho_0}{\rho_0} \times 297 \times 10^{-6} \text{ for violet light}$$

$$l_0 - l = l \frac{\rho - \rho_0}{\rho_0} \times 290 \times 10^{-6} \text{ for red light}$$

and therefore it is very small. But the difference is of the order of the wave-length; indeed, in wavelengths it is

$$l_0 - l = 297 \times 10^{-6} \frac{10^4}{4} \frac{\rho - \rho_0}{\rho_0} l \text{ wavelengths (for violet light 4000 A)}$$

$$l_0 - l = 290 \times 10^{-6} \frac{10^4}{8} \frac{\rho - \rho_0}{\rho_0} l \text{ wavelengths (for red light 8000 A)}$$

where l is expressed in millimeters; therefore for a thickness of flow l equal to 100 millimeters (about 4 inches) a variation of the density in the air of one per cent corresponds to the variation of trajectory of 0.74 wavelengths for violet light and a variation of 0.33 wavelengths for red light.

The instruments that measure the differences of travel of light in order to determine the density of gas in aerodynamic phenomena are called *interferometers;* these instruments are used in large extent in optics for different purposes.

Interferometers. (References 20, 21, 22, 23.) The interferometer usually used for aerodynamic purposes is one with a wedge of air, which is based upon the following principle: Consider a flat semitransparent glass of constant thickness and a flat mirror and place the two surfaces inclined one with respect to the other as in Figure 67. Consider at a point P a point source of light and a ray PA from P. The ray is divided in two parts by the semitransparent

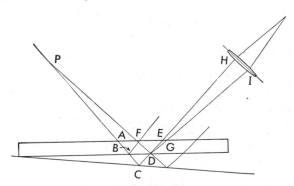

Fig. 67. *Interferometric phenomena in a wedge of air.*

surface; one part is reflected at B and one (PBC) is reflected at C. The reflected ray CDE crosses the glass again and enters a collector at H. Consider now another ray PD emitted by the same point P. The ray PD also is divided in two parts. Consider the part reflected at D, that enters the collector at I. The length of the trajectories of the ray PFD is different from the length of the trajectory PCD; therefore if the rays EH and GI are superimposed again by a collector the rays interfere with each other. If the difference of the two paths is equivalent to a whole number of wavelengths, the two rays are in phase; but if the difference is equivalent to an odd number of half wavelengths, the waves are in opposition, and when the two rays are superimposed the light of the two rays disappears. The same phenomenon occurs for all similar pairs of rays; therefore where the rays are superimposed, a corresponding black zone occurs. If σ is the angle of the wedge, the distance between the zone in which the difference of paths produces the same kind of interference is (Figure 68)

$$\xi = \frac{\Lambda}{2\sigma} \tag{225}$$

where Λ is the wavelength of the light. Indeed, if l_1 (ABC) is the difference of optical travel for the rays 1 and 2 produced by the same path P, 3 and 4 are

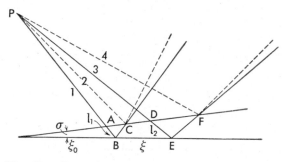

Fig. 68. *Determination of the distance between interference lines.*

two others rays that produce the same interference, and l_2 is the difference of the optical travel between the rays 3 and 4 (DEF), in order to have the same kind of interference, the condition $(l_2 - l_1 = \Lambda)$ must be satisfied. Therefore, because σ is small, the result is

$$\frac{DE - AB}{AB} = \frac{\xi}{\xi_0}$$

or

$$\frac{l_2 - l_1}{l_1} = \frac{\xi}{\xi_0}$$

but

$$l_1 = 2\sigma\xi_0.$$

Therefore

$$\xi = \frac{\Lambda\xi_0}{l_1} = \frac{\Lambda}{2\sigma}.$$

The distance of the interference zone is a function of the angle of the wedge. If a system of parallel rays is considered, for every ray for which the difference of travel l is equal to an odd number of half wavelengths, the interference phenomenon occurs; therefore if the two glasses are flat and the density of the air in the wedge is constant, the interferences occur along straight lines parallel to the edge of the wedge at a constant distance of ξ (equation 225); and if the light is collected in a screen, a system of bright and dark parallel straight lines appears. The principle of interferometers therefore consists in dividing the rays of a parallel light along two optical paths of different length, using a semitransparent glass and superimposing the two parts again on a screen. When the paths differ by an odd number of half wavelengths, the two parts of the ray cancel each other, and therefore a dark zone appears on the screen. For aerodynamic use it is necessary, in order to measure the density, to be able to place the zone of flow with different density in the path of one of the rays; therefore the wedge must be made by a different scheme. A scheme used by Mach (Reference 20) and useful for aerodynamic problems is shown in Figure 69. At the four corners of a rectangle are placed two flat mirrors S_1 and S_2 and two flat semitransparent glasses of constant thickness P_1 and P_2. Mirrors and glass are perfectly parallel and inclined at about 45° with respect to the sides of the rectangles. At the point S, a point source of light is placed in the focus of a lens. Every one of the rays R emitted by S reaches the glass P_1 and is divided into two parts: a part which crosses the glass and has the trajectory $ABCD1$, and the other part which is reflected at A and has the trajectory $AEFD1$. Part of the light is also reflected at B and has the trajectory $ABGM$-$LK2$, or because a second reflection occurs at G, has a trajectory along $ABGHIK2$. At D another reflection can occur and a part of the light has the trajectory $AEFDLK2$. All rays are in phase

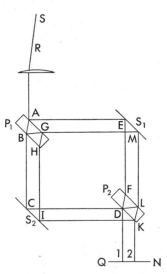

Fig. 69.   *Scheme of the Mach interferometer.*

at 1 or 2 because the surfaces are all parallel and all rays at 2 have crossed the glass twice, while the rays at 1 have crossed the glass once.

Now if a glass or a mirror changes position slightly and turns with respect to the original position around an axis perpendicular to the design, a wedge is generated, and the lengths of the trajectories of the rays that meet at 1 or 2 change, and an interference occurs. When the rays indicated by 1 have a difference of path equal to 1 or 3 or 5 half lengths of the wavelength of the light, the rays eliminate each other, and if all the rays are received on a screen, a black zone occurs corresponding to the place in which the difference of paths is an odd number of half wavelengths, and a white zone in the place in which the difference is equal to an even number of half wavelengths. Also the rays at 2 interfere with each other, but the light of 2 is much less than the light of 1 and the interference of the rays at 2 is of the second order and can be eliminated by using a thick glass which increases the distance between 1 and 2 on the optical screen. The optical interference of the rays at 1 produces at the screen QN a zone with light and a zone without light; the zones are at a constant distance ξ which depends on the angle of wedge. These zones are parallel if the glasses are of constant thickness and all surfaces are plane; therefore there appears on the screen a series of straight black lines separated by zones

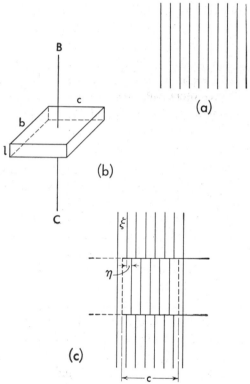

Fig. 70. *Schematic reproduction of the interference phenomena when a constant variation of density is produced in a zone of flow of constant thickness.*

of light. The lines are at equal distances and parallel to the axis of rotation of the glass or mirror (Figure 70a). Now, if along the line BC a flow space bcl of thickness l is placed with different density ρ (Figure 70b), the difference of path of the rays BC and EF changes, and therefore the position of the interference line changes, corresponding to the zone in which the ray BC crosses the flow at different density. If ρ_0 is the density outside the space $b_x c_x l$ and ρ is the density in $b_x c_x l$, the variation of the position of the line of interference is given by

$$\eta = \frac{l}{\sigma} \frac{\rho - \rho_0}{\rho_0} (\pi_0 - 1) \quad \text{or} \quad \eta = \frac{l(\pi_0 - 1)}{\Lambda} \xi \frac{\rho - \rho_0}{\rho_0}. \tag{226}$$

Therefore, because Λ, ξ, π_0, ρ_0, and l are known, from the displacement of the interference line it is possible to determine the density in the space $b_x c_x l$.

$$\frac{\rho - \rho_0}{\rho_0} = \frac{\eta}{\xi} \frac{\Lambda}{l(\pi_0 - 1)}. \tag{227}$$

If the density at $b_x c_x l$ is constant, the lines are displaced by a constant value η and the interference pictures appear as shown in Figure 70c. With this system it is possible to determine the density in a flow at a constant density, such as a uniform jet or a stream in a supersonic tunnel. It is evident that if the jet is a closed jet, the wall must be made of glass of constant index of refraction and perfectly isotropic, therefore not strained. In this case, two other glasses of the same type must be placed along the ray EF of Figure 69 to compensate the absorption of the two glasses along BC.

Determination of Density for Two-Dimensional and Axial Symmetric Phenomena.

With an interferometric system it is possible to determine the value of the density in every point of the flow of a two-dimensional phenomenon by the same principle used to determine the density in a uniform flow. Consider a channel in which a uniform flow of density ρ_1 moves, and assume that the value of the density ρ_1 is known. The value of ρ_1 can be determined by the system indicated before for a uniform stream. When disturbances are produced in supersonic flow, the flow in front of the shock waves or expansion waves produced by the disturbances does not undergo any variation of characteristics; therefore if an axis x parallel to the undisturbed stream is considered, the value of ρ is always known in a zone of the axis in front of the disturbance, because in this zone ρ is equal to ρ_1. In this zone in which the flow is uniform, the interference lines are at constant distance; but when a variation of density is produced in the flow, the interference lines in the zone of different density become curved (Figure 71a). The distance of the interference lines along every x-axis permits determination of the density distribution along the axis.

Consider a Cartesian coordinate system (Figure 71b) where densities are plotted as ordinates and distances as abscissas. At the distance corresponding to the value ρ_1 of the density of the undisturbed stream, consider two axes x_1 and x_2. Along the axis x_1 plot the distances between the interference lines

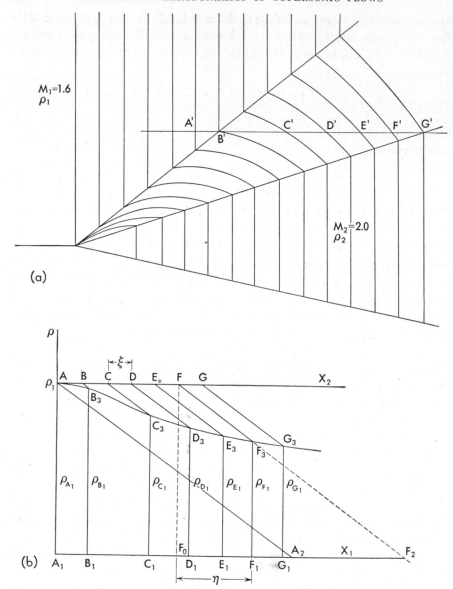

Fig. 71.   (a) *Schematic reproduction of interference phenomena produced by an expansion around a corner, and* (b) *graphical determination of the value of the density.*

along the axis x obtained from Figure 71a.   Call A_1 the position of the inter-section of an interference line in the undisturbed zone, and B_1 C_1 . . . the subsequent intersections of the lines in the zone in which the density must be determined.   Along axis x_2 plot the distances between the same lines for the case of undisturbed flow.   Because if disturbances are not produced in the flow the density is constant, the distance between the interference lines along x_2 is constant, and is equal to ξ.   At A the density does not change because of the presence of disturbances in the flow; therefore the point A is on the normal to x_1 at A_1.   The point F_1 is displaced by η with respect to F.   If l is the thickness of the flow or the length of the two-dimensional phenomenon in direction normal to the design, Λ is the length of the light wave (monochromatic), and π_1 is the index of refraction at the density ρ_1, then from equation (226),

$$\eta = \frac{\rho_1 - \rho}{\rho_1} \; l \; \frac{\pi_1 - 1}{\Lambda} \xi. \qquad (228)$$

The expression $l \dfrac{\pi_1 - 1}{\Lambda} \xi$ is a distance, and is constant; therefore the following construction can be drawn: along the axis x_1 a distance A_1A_2 corresponding to $l \dfrac{\pi_1 - 1}{\Lambda} \xi$ can be plotted, and the point A_2 can be connected with A; the lines BB_2, CC_2, DD_2 parallel to AA_2 must be drawn from the points $BCDE \ldots$ of the x_2 axis; straight lines normal to x_1 axis at the points B_1, C_1, D_1, E_1 also must be drawn, and then the points B_3, C_3, D_3, E_3 are determined by the intersection of corresponding lines parallel to the line AA_2 and normal to the x_1 axis.   The points $D_3, E_3 \ldots$ give the values of the density at D_1, E_1, F_1, etc.; indeed, if the distance between the x_1 and x_2 axes is equal to ρ_1, it is possible to write

$$\eta = \frac{\rho_1 - F_1F_3}{\rho_1} \; F_0F_2$$

but

$$F_0F_2 = A_1A_2 = l \frac{\pi - 1}{\Lambda} \xi.$$

Therefore the diagram B_3G_3 gives the density distribution along the x-axis. By changing the position of the x-axis, the density at every point of the flow can be determined.

From the density distribution it is possible to determine the pressure or temperature distribution if the law of transformation is known; therefore in many experiments it is possible to obtain the pressure distribution by means of optical systems.   With interferometric measurements the entire phenomenon considered can be determined from one test without the necessity of placing instruments in the flow; therefore the system is very useful in many practical problems, because it permits a very rapid measurement of the quantities in the entire flow without interference of instruments.

For axial symmetric phenomena the interferometric system still can be used, because the density is constant along every circle that has its center along the axis and is in a plane normal to the axis. In this case the analysis of the results can be made, for example, in the following way: Consider an interferometric picture, obtained with rays normal to the axis of the body, and in the picture a plane QQ (Figure 72a) perpendicular to the axis of the body. Consider now some circular zones corresponding to the position of the interference lines along the line QQ (Figure 72b). Assume that the density

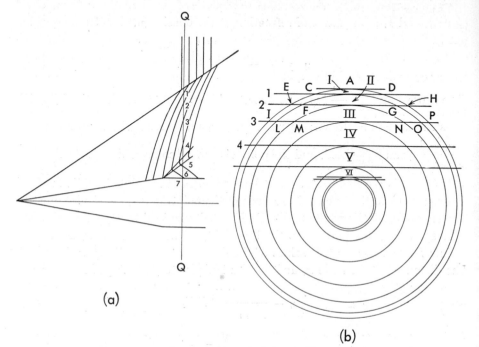

(a)

(b)

Fig. 72.   *System of determination of the flow density for a body of revolution.*

in the zones I, II, III, etc., is constant and equal to ρ_2, ρ_3, ρ_4, etc. The density is known outside of zones of disturbances produced by the body (ρ_1); therefore the density in I can be determined from the deviation in Figure 72a of the interference line corresponding to 1 and determined as for the two-dimensional case. Indeed, the value of l of equation (228) is given by CD, and therefore can be determined by the design in Figure 72b. Therefore the value of ρ' can be calculated from the value of the corresponding deviation η. The interference line 2 undergoes a deviation η_2 which in the zones EF, and HG depends on ρ', and in the zone FG depends on ρ''. But ρ' is known from the preceding determination; the lengths EF and HG can be determined from the design; therefore the deviation in EF and HG can be determined. By the difference from η_2 the deviation corresponding to the path FG can be calculated, and with equation (228) the value of ρ'' can be determined.   Proceeding with the same system, all values of the density along QQ can be determined. The value of the density is more accurate if the number of circles increases, and therefore if the number of interference lines increases. From the value of density calculated by average values in the zone between the two circles it is possible to deduce a corresponding diagram of density with continuous variation, and to determine more exact values with a second approximation.

Assuming the law of the transformation known in the flow, it is possible to determine the pressure distribution in the entire field. The system has been used to determine the pressure distribution along projectiles (Reference 21). By shooting the projectiles in front of an interferometer, the interferometric picture was determined. From the shape of the shock, the variation of pressure across the shock was determined. Behind the shock, the transformation is isentropic; therefore from the density the pressure was determined without use of pressure tubes, which in this case was impossible.

The direction of the interference lines with respect to the direction of the stream can be changed, changing the regulation of the interferometer, and must be chosen case by case in order to increase the precision of the results in the zone of the flow analyzed. Other schemes for interferometric determinations can be also considered and used, but the application is of the same type.

Determination of Density Variation with Methods Using Deviation of the Rays.

The interferometric system uses the variation of phases of light to determine the value of the density in the flow, but it is also possible to examine the density distribution in the flow by using the deviation of light, produced by the variation of the index of refraction (References 20, 21, 23, 24). If the indices of refraction in two zones of flow are π_1 and π_2, respectively, and ϕ is the angle that the ray forms with the normal n to the surface that separates the two zones at different densities (Figure 73), the ray is refracted at an angle ψ given by the law

$$\sin \phi : \sin \psi = \pi_2 : \pi_1. \quad (229)$$

When the density ρ_2 is not constant but changes, the value of π_2 changes, and it is possible to write the value of π_2 in the form

$$\pi_1 = \pi_2 - \left(\frac{\partial \pi}{\partial l}\right)_2 dl \quad (230)$$

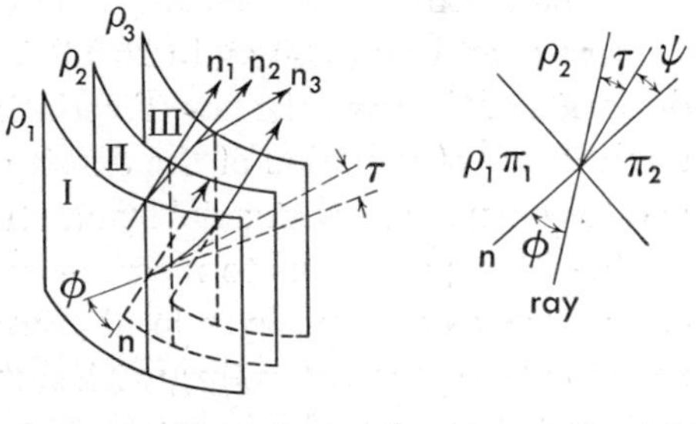

in which dl is the trajectory of the ray. If the difference between ϕ and ψ is small and equal to τ, it is possible to write

Fig. 73. *Deviation of the rays produced by a pressure gradient.*

$$\sin \psi = \sin \phi - \tau \cos \phi \quad (231)$$

and equation (229) becomes

$$\tau \cos \phi = \sin \phi \, \frac{\partial \pi}{\partial l} \frac{\partial l}{\pi}. \tag{232}$$

But if the gradient of the index of refraction G, along the normal n, is used

$$G = \frac{\partial \pi}{\partial n} = \frac{\partial \pi}{\partial l} \frac{\partial l}{\partial n} = \frac{\partial \pi}{\partial l} \frac{1}{\cos \phi} \tag{233}$$

then

$$\tau = \frac{G}{\pi} \sin \phi \partial l. \tag{234}$$

The rotation of the ray is proportional to the length of the trajectory and to the gradient of the index of refraction.

The curvature of the ray at every point of the trajectory is given by

$$\frac{1}{r} = \frac{\tau}{\partial l} = \frac{G \sin \phi}{\pi} \tag{235}$$

or using the value of the density (from equation 223)

$$\frac{\partial \rho}{\partial n} = \frac{\rho_0}{\pi_0 - 1} \frac{\partial \pi}{\partial n} = \frac{\rho_0}{\pi_0 - 1} G$$

then

$$\frac{1}{r} = \frac{\partial \rho}{\partial n} \frac{\sin \phi}{\pi} \frac{\pi_0 - 1}{\rho_0}$$

or

$$\frac{1}{r} = \frac{\partial \rho}{\partial n} \frac{\sin \phi \, (\pi_0 - 1)}{\rho_0 + \rho \, (\pi_0 - 1)}. \tag{236}$$

The rotation of the rays is proportional to the gradient of the density and to the length of the trajectory.

From equations (235) and (236) it appears that the deviation of the ray is very small also for large variations of density.

From equations (235) and (236) it is possible to determine, from the law of deviation of the rays, the law of variation of the index of refraction, and therefore the law of variation of the density of air for two-dimensional phenomena and for phenomena with axial symmetry. But at present there is no practical method that permits us to measure experimentally the variation of direction of the rays as affected by a local gradient of density. Different systems are used to attempt to determine, with sufficient precision, the value of deviation, such as the system of using a screen with lines at uniform distance, or using the astigmatism of a lens; but practically the deviation of the rays is used at present in representative methods rather than for determination of the value of the density. The representative systems most often used are the shadow system and the schlieren system.

Shadow System. The shadow system utilizes a point source of light which illuminates a body and then is collected on a transparent screen. The screen is of uniform illumination if the rays do not undergo any deviation, but if the rays pass through a zone with different optical density, they undergo a deviation which changes the intensity of the light on the screen from point to point. For example (Figure 74), if a system of rays crosses a zone l of density ρ, different from the outside density, the rays are deflected, and at AB the light increases, and at DC it decreases. It is evident that if the variation of density is extended throughout the entire field a direction normal to the rays, all rays are deviated by the same amount, and the screen has uniform illumination. Because the deviations of the rays are proportional to the first derivative of the variation of the density, and the variation of illumination is proportional to the derivative of the deviation, the result is that in the shadow system the variation of the light is proportional to the second derivative of the density in the same direction. Therefore when an abrupt variation of density occurs in the flow, as happens in the presence of shock waves, the shadow system permits determination of the position of the zone in which the variation occurs, with high sensitivity.

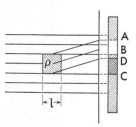

Fig. 74. *Shadow effect produced by a density gradient.*

Schlieren System. The schlieren system has the following scheme: A point source of light P is placed at the focus of a lens or of a mirror (Figure 75), which produces parallel light. The light crosses the zone in which the variation of density will be produced, and is collected on a second lens or mirror

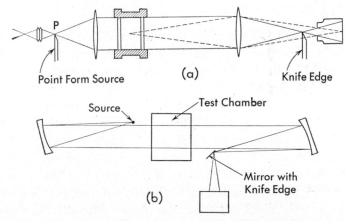

Fig. 75. *Scheme of schlieren apparatus* (a) *using lenses,* (b) *using mirrors.*

which converges all rays to a focus. When a variation of density is produced in the flow, a deviation of rays occurs, and therefore some rays are no longer concentrated at the focal point. Now if a knife edge is interposed in the beam of light in such a way as to intercept some of the deviated rays that do not pass

Fig. 76.   *Shadow photograph for a body of revolution at M = 2.45.*

through the focal point, a change in the pattern of illumination occurs in the sensitive collecting apparatus. Dark areas appear where deviated rays have been intercepted by the knife edge, and bright areas appear where such rays have not been intercepted.

If the source is not a point, but has finite dimensions, an image of the source is produced at the focal point; this image also can be partially obscured by the knife edge. In this way the total intensity of light in the sensitive apparatus and the intensity of the uniform illumination on the screen can be reduced gradually without reducing the intensity of those rays that have been deviated as a result of the variation in density but which have not been intercepted by the knife edge. The result is an increase in the contrast on the screen, and therefore an increase in the sensitivity of the system.

Because the rays that are eliminated from the screen pattern are those that are deviated in the area occupied by the knife edge, the increase or decrease in illumination on the corresponding area of the screen depends upon the variation in direction of the rays in the area in question, in a direction perpendicular to the knife edge. In the schlieren system the variation of intensity of illumination of the screen is proportional to the first derivative of the retardation of the light in a direction perpendicular to the knife edge.

Fig. 77. *Schlieren photograph for a body of revolution at M = 2.45, horizontal knife edge below the focus point.*

Because the deviations are of opposite sign, if the variation of density is of opposite sign, expansions and compressions generate opposite variations of light. The schlieren system is usually used in supersonic tests for determination of the shape of shocks and to examine the physical scheme of the phenomena. The system can use mirrors or lenses and can have very different practical forms.

In Figure 76 a shadow, and in Figures 77, 78, and 79 schlieren determinations of the same phenomenon are shown. As it appears from the pictures, optical methods show the scheme of the phenomenon very well, and therefore are particularly useful for aerodynamic investigations.

Fig. 78. *Schlieren photograph for a body of revolution at* $M = 2.45$, *vertical knife edge from the right side.*

Fig. 79. *Schlieren photograph for a body of revolution at* $M = 2.45$, *vertical knife edge from the left side.*

SUPERSONIC PROFILES

Determination of the Properties of Supersonic Profiles Using the Characteristic Theory and the Theory of Shock Waves.

General Shape of Supersonic Profiles. It was shown in Chapter 3 that at supersonic velocity when shock waves are generated a drag occurs, shock drag, which depends on the losses across the shock, and that exists also for perfect flow. The shock drag, if the extent of the shock and of the other conditions does not change, increases if the variation of entropy across the shock increases, as occurs when the inclination ϵ of the shock increases, and is a maximum when the shock is normal shock. This consideration indicates that in order to reduce the shock drag of supersonic profiles, strong shocks must be avoided, and therefore the profiles must have sharp noses.

Indeed, if a profile has a round nose (Figure 80), the deviation of the streamline at the point A is of the order of 90°. Therefore, no matter how high the Mach number, the deviation is greater than the maximum possible across a shock; thus no equilibrium is possible with shock in A. The disturbances move upstream and a strong shock occurs at B. In the zone AB the flow is subsonic, and therefore can wet the body. But in this case, the shock is very strong (at B it is a normal shock) and the variation of entropy is large. For this reason, this type of profile is not suitable for supersonic flow, and therefore it is logical to suppose that a supersonic profile must be one with a sharp leading edge and an attached shock. In this case, behind the shock which occurs on the leading edge the flow is still supersonic and it is possible to use the theories considered in Chapter 2.

Fig. 80. *Detached shock in front of a wing leading edge.*

It is evident that a sharp leading edge is more convenient only if the shock is an attached shock, and the differences between sharp and round leading edges decrease when the radius of the round leading edge decreases. If the shock is a detached shock, because the deviation required at the leading edge is larger than the maximum allowable deviation, the flow behind the shock in the zone of the leading edge is subsonic; therefore if the stagnation point is not at the leading edge (for example, due to a small angle of attack), a vortex is produced at the leading edge which generates a local separation (Figure 80b) and a subsequent shock (shock a of Figure 80b). The drag in this case is large and can be reduced by using a finite radius of curvature at the leading edge.

In the following paragraphs the phenomena will be considered first by assuming the flow a perfect flow; therefore the pressure drag, the lift, and moment of profiles of different shape will be determined by assuming that no friction drag or separation exists. Later, the effect of viscosity will be considered and a qualitative discussion of the effect of viscosity on the drag, lift, and moment coefficient of the profiles will be made. When the pressure distribution along the profile is known from the perfect flow theory, the friction drag can be evaluated by using the boundary layer theory. However, it is very difficult to evaluate the effect of the separation. The friction drag and the separation at the trailing edge are functions of the Reynolds number and of the pressure distribution along the profile, and their effect can change somewhat the conclusions obtained by analyzing only the pressure forces in a perfect flow, especially the conclusions connected with the determination of the shape of minimum drag; therefore the conclusions based on the pressure drag only, in some cases must be considered as indicative. By analyzing the pressure distribution, it is possible to make an estimate of the relative intensities of the variations due to boundary layer and separation between profiles of different shapes; therefore determination of the pressure drag in perfect flow is an important element for the choice of the most convenient profile shape.

For supersonic flow, because the flow is divided at the leading edge into two parts which do not interfere with each other, the study of the profile can be separated into two zones, the upper zone corresponding to the upper surface and the lower zone corresponding to the lower surface. Because the direction of the stream along the profile is known, the pressure distribution can be obtained for any type of profile, using the shock theory and the characteristic theory.

Flat Plate at Supersonic Speed. The simplest profile to consider is a flat plate of zero thickness and of infinite depth, placed with the leading edge perpendicular to the flow. If the angle of incidence α of the plate with respect to the undisturbed velocity is small, a supersonic flow occurs on both faces of the plate (α less than or equal to the deviation for which $M_2 = 1$). If AB is the cross section of the flat plate (Figure 81), at the point A an expansion occurs for the upper surface, and a compression occurs for the lower surface. The expansion and compression are due to the deviation of α, and therefore

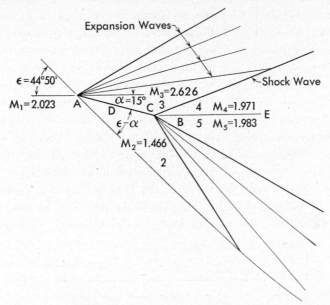

Fig. 81. *The flow around a flat plate.*

can be calculated. In zone 3 the speed is higher and the pressure is lower than in the undisturbed stream, and the values of M_3 and p_3 can be determined either from equations (81) and (41) or from the corresponding Table 2 of the appendix, as functions of α. If ν is the value in the table corresponding to M_1, M_3 corresponds to $\nu + \alpha$. The variation of pressure can be obtained in the same way. On the upper surface at B, the flow undergoes a compression. The condition in zone 4 depends on the conditions in zones 3 and 5. With good approximation it is possible to assume that at B, the flow again attains the direction of the undisturbed stream, and therefore the compression corresponds to a deviation α. The pressure along ACB is constant for all values of M_1 and α.

At A, on the surface ADB, a compression occurs; M_2 is less than M_1, and p_2 is greater than p_1. From the shock polar it is possible to determine the value of ϵ, the inclination of the shock, and the values of M_2 and p_2; the values of M_2 and p_2 can also be obtained analytically from equations (121) to (126) or from Table 5 of the appendix. On the surface ADB the pressure is constant.

At *B* an expansion occurs, and the condition at 5 can be determined with good approximation by assuming that the direction of the velocity at 5 is the

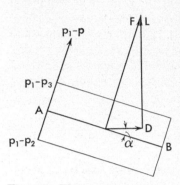

Fig. 82. *The pressure distribution along a flat plate.*

same as that of the undisturbed stream. On the profile two shocks occur; therefore a drag must be found. The drag can be easily determined from the pressure distribution. Indeed, the pressure distribution is as appears in Figure 82. An expansion occurs on the upper surface and a compression occurs on the lower surface. The diagram of $(p_1 - p)$ is rectangular; therefore the lift, if F is the resultant of the pressure, is $(L = F \cos \alpha)$, and the drag is $(D = F \sin \alpha)$. The center of pressure is at 50 per cent of the chord, and its position is constant and independent of M_1 and α, if α is less than the deviation for which $M_2 = 1$, because

changing α changes only the value of the pressure but not its distribution. In Figure 83, the value of C_L is plotted as a function of C_D for different values of M_1 (2, 3, 5) for a flat plate. Because the value C_L/C_D is a function

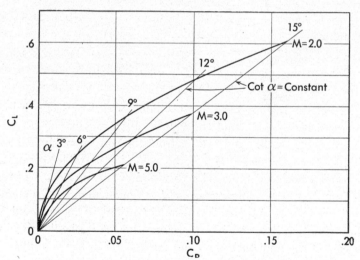

Fig. 83. *Lift coefficient versus drag coefficient for a flat plate at different stream Mach number.*

only of the angle of attack and $(C_L/C_D = \cot \alpha)$, for the same incidence α all points for all Mach numbers must be in the same straight line which starts from the origin of the axis C_L, C_D.

From the diagram it is evident that the value of C_L is very small in comparison with values of C_L possible at subsonic velocities for the same angle of attack.

It is interesting to examine more accurately the general phenomenon. Across the shock wave an increase of entropy occurs. If the shock is extended to infinity with the same intensity, the mass flow that would undergo the variation of entropy would be infinite; therefore the drag would also be infinite. However, the drag has a finite value. This means that a shock of finite intensity must be limited to a finite length. This is shown in Figure 81. At a finite distance the shock interferes with the expansion waves which start from the other edge of the profile, and decreases in intensity. When all expansion waves are eliminated, the flow has the same direction as the undisturbed flow, and therefore no shock exists.

In order to determine the equilibrium at 4 and 5 more exactly, the following considerations can be made. The flow at 4 has undergone an expansion of α degrees from M_1, and then a compression with shock from the Mach number M_3 (larger than M_1). At 5 the flow has undergone a compression with shock from M_1 to M_2, and then an expansion from M_2 to M_5. Because the shock from M_3 occurs for a different Mach number than on the lower surface, the losses across the shocks are different, and therefore the speeds at 4 and 5 are different. At the point B, a discontinuity of velocity occurs in a direction normal to the velocity; therefore the streamline that starts from B represents a line of infinite vorticity. Practically, the viscosity in the flow renders an infinite vorticity at B impossible and produces a vorticose wake which starts from B. Because the transformations on the upper surface and on the lower surface are different for the same deviations across the expansion and shock at A and B, the pressures at 4 and 5 are different; therefore the streamline BE must have, in general, a different direction than the undisturbed velocity. If σ is the difference in direction, the value of σ can be determined because the pressures and the Mach numbers at 4 and 5 can be calculated from the values of 3 and 2 for σ equal to zero; from the difference of pressure between 4 and 5 it is possible by the law of isentropic transformation to determine the value of σ. Indeed, if Δp is the difference in pressure between 4 and 5 for ($\sigma = 0$), $(\partial p/\partial\theta)_4$ is the elemental variation of pressure for the Mach number at 4, and $(\partial p/\partial\theta)_5$ is the elemental variation in pressure for the Mach number at 5, by the isentropic law

$$\sigma \left(\frac{\partial p}{\partial \theta}\right)_4 + \sigma \left(\frac{\partial p}{\partial \theta}\right)_5 = \Delta p$$

where the sign of Δp fixes the sign of σ. The value of σ is very small, and therefore the isentropic law can be considered for expansion and compression.

For example, if a flat plate at 10 degrees of incidence (Figure 84) is considered, and at $M = 2.0683$, the values of M_3 and M_2 are 2.4625 and 1.704, respectively, p_3 is $0.5434p_1$, and p_2 is $1.7252p_1$. For a variation of direction at B of 10 degrees, M_5 is 2.056 and M_4 is 2.053, p_5 is $1.002p_1$, and p_4 is $1.0058p_1$.

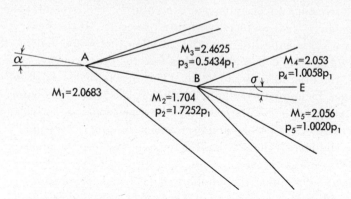

Fig. 84. *Determination of the downwash behind a flat plate.*

To determine the sign of σ which corresponds to a variation of $\Delta p = (1.0058 - 1.0020)p_1$, it is enough to consider that the velocity at 4 must increase and the pressure decrease; therefore σ is positive and BE rotates from 4 to 5. The value of σ can be determined by considering that, in the field $M = 2.05$, the pressure for 1 degree of isentropic transformation changes with respect to the original pressure by the ratio 1.057 (from Table 2); therefore

$$\frac{\partial p}{p\partial \theta} = 0.057/\text{deg}$$

or

$$\left(\frac{\Delta p}{\Delta \theta}\right)_4 = 0.057 \times 1.0058p_1$$

and

$$\left(\frac{\Delta p}{\Delta \theta}\right)_5 = 0.057 \times 1.0020p_1.$$

Therefore

$$\Delta p = 0.058\sigma + 0.057\sigma = 0.115\sigma = -0.0038p_1$$

$$\sigma = -\frac{0.0038}{0.115}.$$

σ corresponds to a deviation of 1.98' positive (downwash).

Supersonic Profile of Any Shape. In a similar way it is possible to determine the pressure distribution along a profile of any shape if the hypothesis that the flow is always supersonic is satisfied (attached shock in front). Consider, for example, the profile shown in Figure 85. If the Mach number in front, M_1, is known at A in terms of the value of δ_1 and θ_1, the form of the shock and of the expansion, and the values of M and p at 2 and 4 can be determined. In the zone AB AD no deviation occurs; therefore the pressure is

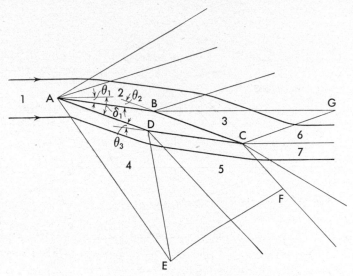

Fig. 85. *The flow around a diamond-shaped profile.*

constant. At B and D an expansion occurs. The values of the deviations of expansion θ_2, θ_3 are known from the geometry of the profile, the values of M_2 and M_4 are also known; therefore from the equation of the expansion, the Mach numbers and the pressures at 3 and 5 can be determined. In the zones BC and DC the pressures are constant. The conditions at 6 and in 7 can be determined by the same system used for the flat plate. Also, in this case, the direction at 6 or 7 is almost exactly the same as the direction of the undisturbed velocity. The pressure at ABC is independent of the form of the body along ADC because at A the flow can be divided into two separate parts; therefore the phenomenon can be examined independently. The expansion that starts from B and D crosses the shock waves at G and E, and therefore the flow in the zone that is inside the Mach wedge from E and G is no longer potential flow, because at G and H the shocks change direction. In this case, the wedge is far from the profile; therefore along the profile the flow is entirely potential flow and the calculations are exact.

If the profile has a curved surface, it is possible to determine the pressure distribution in the same way, but the determination is more complicated. Consider a profile as in Figure 86 formed by a plane and a circular arc surface; at A on the lower part a shock occurs which is the same as that for the flat plate, and the phenomenon along ADC is also the same. On the upper surface at A a shock occurs that corresponds to the deviation at the point A, and is determined by the law of shock. ·Proceeding from A to a point B, near A, the flow changes direction and a gradual expansion occurs. Therefore, for

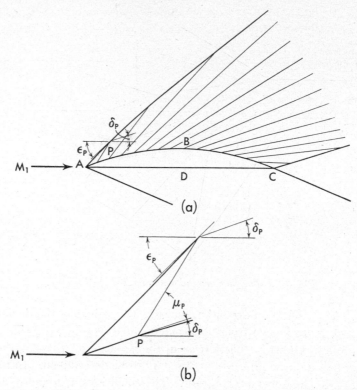

Fig. 86. *Determination of the flow around a circular arc plane profile.*

every point from A to B an expansion wave starts and the velocity of the flow increases. The expansion waves meet the shock and change its direction; thus the shock bends, and the curvature begins at point A. The flow behind the shock is rotational. An exact determination of the shock shape and of the pressure distribution must be made in terms of the considerations of Chapter 5. Usually the deviation that produces the shock is small and the variation of ΔS across the shock is small; in this case it is evident that the variation of the value of the entropy along the shock wave is of small importance for the phenomenon, and therefore it is not necessary to use the chararteristic system for rotational flow because it is possible to assume, with good approximation, that the flow is potential flow. In equation (211), $(S_2 - S_1)$ is very small. With the approximation of potential flow, determination of the pressure distribution is easy. Indeed, from the shape of the profile for every point P of the profile, the value of the angle θ_P that the tangent at P to the profile makes with the tangent at A to the profile is known. If the profile is a circular arc, θ_P is given by the angle corresponding to the arc AP. Since the Mach number behind the shock at A is known, it is possible to determine the value of ν_A from Table 2 of the appendix, corresponding to the Mach number at A, and from this value to determine the pressure ratio p/p^* and the Mach number at every point P corresponding to the value ν_P equal to $(\nu_A + \theta_P)$. Because the value of p_A/p^* is given by the table for the value ν_A, the ratio p_P/p_A can be determined for every point of the profile, and therefore the value p_P/p_1 can also be determined. In order to design the shock wave shape using the same approximation of potential flow, it is possible to design the characteristic line for every point P. Where the characteristic line meets the shock wave, Figure 86b, the shock wave must have an inclination ϵ_P which corresponds to a deviation across the shock for which the flow behind the shock has the same direction as at P. Therefore δ_P is known, and the value of ϵ is determinable by using the shock polar curve. Determination of the characteristic lines and of the Mach number along the profile ABC can also be accomplished graphically by using the epicycloid diagram shown in Chart 1 of the appendix. The pressure distribution for a profile of this type is as in Figure 87.

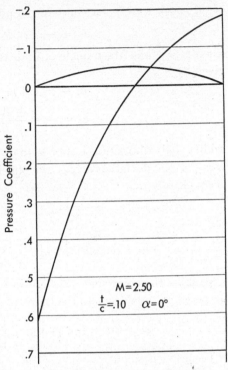

Fig. 87. *The pressure distribution along the chord of a circular arc profile.*

Analytical Determination of the Lift and Drag Coefficients of the Profiles. If the deviation of the stream produced by the profile is small, it is possible with good approximation to assume that all the terms are negligible that have the same order of magnitude as the cube of the angle of the deviation of the stream produced by the profile. In this case it is possible to obtain in analytical form the pressure distribution along the profile and therefore to obtain analytical expressions for the aerodynamic coefficients (References 25 and 26).

In Chapters 2 and 3 it was found that for small deviations the equation of the shock wave and the equation of isentropic compression are coincident, and therefore for small disturbances the epicycloid that regulates the compression must be tangent to the corresponding polar curve. For $(\delta = 0)$ the two curves have the same value and the same tangent. Expanding equation (139) of the shock wave polar curve into a power series of $(u_2 - V_1)$ (Reference 25),

$$v_2 = a_1 (u_2 - V_1) + a_2 (u_2 - V_1)^2 + \ldots \tag{237}$$

where if μ_1 is the Mach angle of undisturbed stream, the coefficients a_1, a_2 are given by

$$a_1 = - \cot \mu_1 \tag{238}$$

$$a_2 = - \frac{\gamma + 1}{4 V_1} \frac{1}{\cos \mu_1 \sin^3 \mu_1}. \tag{239}$$

Adding and subtracting $V_1 \tan \eta$, to equation (237), because η is the absolute value of the deviation across the shock which is assumed small, and $\tan \eta$ is equal to v_2/u_2,

$$(u_2 - V_1) (a_1 - \tan \eta) + a_2 (u_2 - V_1)^2 - V_1 \tan \eta = 0 \tag{240}$$

or

$$\frac{u_2 - V_1}{V_1} = - \tan \mu_1 \tan \eta - \tan^2 \mu_1 \left[\frac{\gamma+1}{4} \frac{1}{\cos^2 \mu_1 \sin^2 \mu_1} - 1 \right] \tan^2 \eta + \ldots \tag{241}$$

Expanding the epicycloid equation into a power series, the first two terms of the series are analogous to the terms of equation (241).

$$\frac{u_2 - V_1}{V_1} = \pm \tan \mu_1 \tan \eta - \tan^2 \mu_1 \left[\frac{\gamma+1}{4} \frac{1}{\cos^2 \mu_1 \sin^2 \mu_1} - 1 \right] \tan^2 \eta \tag{242}$$

or because η is small

$$\frac{u_2 - V_1}{V_1} = \pm c_1 \eta - c_2 \eta^2 \ldots \tag{243}$$

where

$$c_1 = \frac{1}{\sqrt{M_1^2 - 1}} \tag{244a}$$

$$c_2 = \frac{1}{M_1^2 - 1} \left[\frac{(\gamma + 1) M_1^4}{4(M_1^2 - 1)} - 1 \right]. \tag{244b}$$

Equation (243) is valid for expansion and for compression, because the isentropic law agrees with the shock law for the first two terms of the series. The plus or minus sign depends on the type of deviation; the first term is positive for expansion and negative for compression. The value of the pressure coefficient can be obtained from equation (136),

$$\frac{p_2 - p_1}{\rho_1 V_1^2} = \frac{V_1 - u_2}{V_1}. \tag{245}$$

Therefore from equation (243)

$$\frac{p_2 - p_1}{\rho_1 V_1^2} = \mp c_1\eta + c_2\eta^2 + \ldots \tag{246}$$

where the minus sign corresponds to an expansion and the plus sign to a compression. With the approximation accepted, equation (246) is valid for isentropic variation and for compression with shock, because the two laws differ only in the third term of the series. If the term that contains η^3 is considered, for isentropic transformation we obtain the expression

$$\frac{\Delta p}{\rho_1 V_1^2} = \pm c_1\eta + c_2\eta^2 \pm c_3\eta^3 - \ldots \tag{247}$$

and for compression across the shock

$$\frac{\Delta p}{\rho_1 V_1^2} = + c_1\eta + c_2\eta^2 + (c_3 - D)\eta^3. \tag{248}$$

The term D is the first term of the series that considers the increase of entropy across the shock, which is not considered in the approximation accepted.

The coefficient c_3 has the value

$$c_3 = \frac{1}{12(M^2-1)^{3.5}} \left[(\gamma+1)M^8 + (2\gamma^2 + 7\gamma - 5)M^6 + 10(\gamma+1)M^4 - 12M^2 + 8\right]. \tag{249}$$

D is the expression given in Chapter 4, equation (169). The coefficients c_1, c_2, and c_3 are all positive, while D is negative for Mach numbers between 1.24 and 2.54, in which field the increase of pressure across the shock is greater for the same deviation than the increase in pressure obtained with isentropic compression.

If in equation (246) the first term is the only one considered (small disturbances theory), the value of $(p_2 - p_1)/\rho_1 V_1^2$ becomes equal and of opposite sign for expansion and compression, while the second term $c_2\eta^2$ which is always positive, changes the absolute value of $(p_2 - p_1)/\rho_1 V_1^2$ corresponding to the two transformations for the same value of η.

In order to determine the aerodynamic force, if the undisturbed velocity is in the direction of the x-axis, for every element of the profile ds of the upper surface of components dx and dy can be written (Figure 88).

$$\frac{dL}{\frac{1}{2}\rho_1 V_1^2} = -\frac{(p_2 - p_1)}{\frac{1}{2}\rho_1 V_1^2} dx \tag{250}$$

$$\frac{dD}{\frac{1}{2}\rho_1 V_1^2} = -\frac{(p_2 - p_1)}{\frac{1}{2}\rho_1 V_1^2} dy \tag{251}$$

where L is the lift and D is the drag. Considering the profile with respect to the chord, if α is the incidence of the profile,

$$\eta = \alpha + \eta' \tag{252}$$

where η' is the inclination of the tangent to the element of the profile ds with

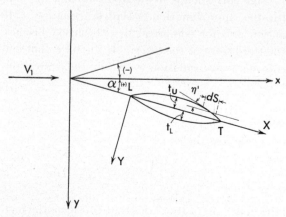

Fig. 88. *Definition of the coordinates XY and of the deviation η'.*

respect to the chord. If Y and X are the coordinates of the profile with respect to the chord, the value of η' is

$$\eta' = \frac{dY}{dX} \tag{253}$$

where the Y axis must be directed as in Figure 88, if the convention is accepted that the angles are positive in the direction of α. With this convention, in equation (247), the minus sign must be chosen for points on the upper surface and the plus sign for points on the lower surface. In this case for the upper surface, the elemental lift and drag are

$$\frac{dL_U}{\rho_1 V_1^2} = (c_1\eta' + c_1\alpha - c_2\eta'^2 - c_2\alpha^2 - 2c_2\alpha\eta')\, dx \tag{254a}$$

$$\frac{dD_U}{\rho_1 V_1^2} = (c_1\eta' + c_1\alpha - c_2\eta'^2 - c_2\alpha^2 - 2c_2\alpha\eta')\,(\alpha + \eta')\, dx \tag{254b}$$

because

$$\frac{dy}{dx} = \eta = \eta' + \alpha$$

and

$$L_U = \int_L^T dL_U; \quad D_U = \int_L^T dD_U.$$

But the term dX differs from the term dx by terms of the order of magnitude of η^2, $\left[dX \cos \alpha = dx = dX(1 - \dfrac{\alpha^2}{2} + \ldots) \right]$ and in equations (254) the term dx is multiplied by the term of the order of η; therefore it is possible with the approximation accepted to replace dx by dX. Then

$$\int \eta' dx = \int \eta' dX = \int \frac{dY}{dX} \, dX.$$

The integral $\int \eta' dX$ is extended along the upper or the lower surface of the profile from the leading edge L to the trailing edge T; therefore

$$\int_L^T \frac{dY}{dX} \, dX = 0$$

and using for the upper surface the symbols

$$D_2 = \frac{1}{c} \int_L^T \left(\frac{dY}{dX}\right)^2 dX; \quad D_3 = \frac{1}{c} \int_L^T \left(\frac{dY}{dX}\right)^3 dX \tag{255}$$

where c is the chord of the profile, the lift and drag for the upper surface are given by the following expressions, in which the subscripts U indicate the values for the upper surface:

$$\frac{L_U}{c\rho_1 V_1{}^2} = (c_1\alpha - c_2\alpha^2 - c_2 D_2) \tag{256}$$

$$\frac{D_U}{c\rho_1 V_1{}^2} = (c_1\alpha^2 - c_2\alpha^3 - 3c_2\alpha D_2 + c_1 D_2 - c_2 D_3). \tag{257}$$

In an analogous way it is possible to obtain the following expressions for the lower surface, where the subscripts L indicate the values corresponding to the lower surface:

$$\frac{L_L}{c\rho_1 V_1{}^2} = (c_1\alpha + c_2\alpha^2 + c_2 F_2) \tag{258}$$

$$\frac{D_L}{c\rho_1 V_1{}^2} = (c_1\alpha^2 + c_2\alpha^3 + 3c_2\alpha F_2 + c_1 F_2 + c_2 F_3) \tag{259}$$

where

$$F_2 = \frac{1}{c} \int_L^T \left(\frac{dY}{dX}\right)^2 dX \quad F_3 = \frac{1}{c} \int_L^T \left(\frac{dY}{dX}\right)^3 dX \tag{260}$$

for the lower surface.

The terms containing η^3 in equations (257) and (259) are exact also if in the approximation accepted only the terms which contain η^2 are considered for the pressure coefficient. The drag and lift coefficients of the profile are

$$C_L = 4c_1\alpha + 2c_2 (F_2 - D_2) \tag{261}$$

$$C_D = 4c_1\alpha^2 + 6c_2\alpha (F_2 - D_2) + 2c_1 (F_2 + D_2) + 2c_2 (F_3 - D_3). \tag{262}$$

The coefficients c_1 and c_2 are independent of angle of attack and shape of the profile (equations 244) and are functions only of the Mach number of the undisturbed stream. The functions F_2 and D_2 are geometrical functions, which depend only on the shape of the profile.

From equation (261), it is shown that in supersonic flow the lift coefficient is a linear function of the angle of incidence, as happens in subsonic flow. However, in subsonic incompressible flow the lift-curve slope is of the order of 2π, while in supersonic flow it is given by

$$\frac{dC_L}{d\alpha} = 4c_1 = \frac{4}{\sqrt{M^2 - 1}} \qquad (263)$$

which is much lower and is decreasing as the Mach number increases. For example, for $M = 1.5$, $dC_L/d\alpha$ is equal to 3.58; for $M = 2$, it is 2.3; and for $M = 4$, it is 1.03. It is important to remember that equations (261) and (262) are valid if the flow is supersonic at every point, and therefore are not valid in the field $(M \to 1)$, where for small deviations the flow becomes subsonic at some point, if shock occurs.

From equation (261), it is possible to determine the angle of zero lift α_0.

$$\alpha_0 = -\frac{c_2}{2c_1}(F_2 - D_2) \qquad (264)$$

The term c_2 is positive and decreases if M increases (equation 244); c_1 is also positive; therefore the sign of α_0 depends on the sign of $(F_2 - D_2)$. The values of F_2 and D_2 depend on the curvature of the upper and lower surfaces equations (260) and (255). If the lower surface is more curved than the upper surface, D_2 is smaller than F_2 and α_0 is negative. The value of α_0 becomes positive if the upper surface is more curved than the lower surface.

This consideration indicates that for $(\alpha = 0)$ the profile with positive camber (in which the upper surface is more curved than the lower surface), has negative lift, which is exactly the opposite of what occurs in subsonic flow. The angle of zero lift, in supersonic flow, has opposite sign to that in subsonic flow. For a given profile shape, the angle of zero lift changes with the change of the Mach number and the change is given by c_2/c_1,

$$\frac{c_2}{c_1} = \frac{1}{\sqrt{M_1^2 - 1}}\left[\frac{(\gamma + 1)M_1^4}{4(M_1^2 - 1)} - 1\right], \qquad (265)$$

which increases as the Mach number increases (c_1 approaches zero if M goes to infinity, and c_2 becomes equal to $(\gamma + 1)/4$ if M goes to infinity). Therefore, in supersonic flow, the angle of zero lift for a given profile increases as the flight Mach number increases. The angle of zero lift for supersonic flow has a much smaller absolute value than for subsonic flow, and is of the order of the average curvature multiplied by the relative thickness, while in subsonic flow it is of the order of the average curvature.

Equations (261) and (262), neglecting the terms of higher order, can be written in the following forms:

$$C_D = \frac{C_L^2}{4c_1} + \frac{c_2}{2c_1} (F_2 - D_2) C_L + C_{D0} \tag{266}$$

$$C_{D0} = 2c_1 (F_2 + D_2) + 2c_2 (F_3 - D_3). \tag{267}$$

The drag coefficient for zero lift decreases as the Mach number increases.

Applications of the Equations for Determination of Lift and Drag Coefficients to Profiles of Particular Shape.

Flat Plate. For the flat plate, the terms F and D are zero; therefore with the approximation of paragraph 2, equations (261), (262), (266), and (267) give

$$\left.\begin{aligned}
C_L &= 4c_1\alpha = \frac{4\alpha}{\sqrt{M^2 - 1}} \\
C_D &= \frac{C_L^2}{4c_1} = C_L\alpha = \frac{4^2\alpha}{\sqrt{M^2 - 1}} = \frac{\sqrt{M^2 - 1}}{4} C_L^2 \\
C_{D_{L=0}} &= 0.
\end{aligned}\right\} \tag{268}$$

The value of C_D for given values of C_L and M_1 is the minimum possible for a profile.

Circular-Arc Profile. Consider a profile which has a circular-arc cylinder for upper and lower surfaces. In this case, the profile is symmetrical with respect to an axis perpendicular to the chord through the center and the values of dY/dX for points at equal distances from this axis are equal and of opposite sign. Therefore the terms D_3 and F_3 are zero. This is true for all the profiles that have an axis of symmetry perpendicular to the chord line. If t_U is the thickness of the upper surface of the profile, and t_L the thickness of the lower surface for a circular-arc profile, the expressions D_2 and F_2, in the approximation used, become

$$\left.\begin{aligned}
D_2 &= \frac{1}{c} \int_L^T \left(\frac{dY}{dX}\right)_U^2 dX = \frac{1}{3}\left(\frac{4t_U}{c}\right)^2 \\
F_2 &= \frac{1}{c} \int_L^T \left(\frac{dY}{dX}\right)_L^2 dX = \frac{1}{3}\left(\frac{4t_L}{c}\right)^2
\end{aligned}\right\} \tag{269}$$

Substituting equations (269) in equations (261), (262), (264), (266), and (267),

$$C_{D_0} = \frac{32}{3}\left[\frac{t_U^2}{c^2} + \frac{t_L^2}{c^2}\right]\frac{1}{\sqrt{M_1^2 - 1}}$$

$$\alpha_0 = -\frac{8}{3\sqrt{M_1^2 - 1}}\left[\frac{(\gamma + 1)M_1^4}{4(M_1^2 - 1)} - 1\right]\left[\frac{t_L^2}{c^2} - \frac{t_U^2}{c^2}\right]$$

$$C_L = \frac{4}{\sqrt{M_1^2 - 1}}(\alpha - \alpha_0) \qquad\qquad (270)$$

$$C_D = \frac{\sqrt{M^2 - 1}}{4}C_L^2 - \alpha_0 C_L + C_{D_0}$$

The thicknesses of the profiles are given by the expression (Figure 88)

$$\frac{t}{c} = -\frac{t_U}{c} + \frac{t_L}{c}$$

Therefore the value of C_{D_0} for a given value of t/c becomes a minimum when

$$\frac{t_U}{c} = -\frac{t_L}{c}$$

or when the profile is symmetrical. For symmetrical circular-arc profiles, the values of F_2 and D_2 are identical, and equation (270) becomes

$$C_{D_0} = \frac{16}{3}\frac{\left(\frac{t}{c}\right)^2}{\sqrt{M_1^2 - 1}}$$

$$\alpha_0 = 0$$

$$C_L = \frac{4}{\sqrt{M_1^2 - 1}}\alpha \qquad\qquad (271)$$

$$C_D = \frac{C_L^2\sqrt{M_1^2 - 1}}{4} + C_{D_0}$$

If the profile has a flat lower surface and a circular arc on the upper surface, t_L is zero, t_U is equal to t, and equation (270) becomes

$$C_{D_0} = \frac{32}{3}\frac{t^2}{c^2\sqrt{M_1^2 - 1}}$$

$$\alpha_0 = \frac{8}{3\sqrt{M_1^2 - 1}}\left[\frac{(\gamma + 1)M_1^4}{4(M_1^2 - 1)} - 1\right]\frac{t^2}{c^2}$$

$$C_L = \frac{4}{\sqrt{M_1^2 - 1}}(\alpha - \alpha_0) \qquad\qquad (272)$$

$$C_D = \frac{C_L^2\sqrt{M_1^2 - 1}}{4} - \alpha_0 C_L + C_{D_0}$$

From equations (270), (271), and (272) it appears that the drag for zero lift is proportional to the square of the relative thickness; therefore it is necessary that, in supersonic flow, the maximum thickness of the wing be very small. For $(M = 2)$ and a relative thickness equal to 0.10, the minimum drag coefficient for a circular arc is equal to 0.0308; it becomes 0.0534 for $(M = 1.41)$. These values of drag coefficients include only pressure drag and do not consider the losses due to friction.

Profile of Minimum Pressure Drag for a Given Thickness. Diamond-Shaped Profile and Profile Made by Circular Arcs of Different Radii. In order to determine the profile of minimum pressure drag, it is necessary to find the profile corresponding to the minimum value of equation (267). In equation (267), C_{D_0} is given by the sum of two terms. Since the first term, $2c_1 (F_2 + D_2)$, is much larger than the second, for determining the minimum drag initially only the first term is considered. If the thickness is fixed, C_{D_0} is given by two terms which are functions of t_U/c and t_L/c. Fixing t_U/c and t_L/c, the maximum values of Y for the curves that give the profiles of the upper and lower surfaces are known from the values of the maximum thickness. But if $Y = f(X)$ is the expression of the curve that gives the surface, while L is the leading edge, M is the point of maximum thickness, and T is the trailing edge, the expression F_2 can be written in the following form (Figure 89):

$$F_2 = \frac{1}{c} \int_L^T \left(\frac{dY}{dX}\right)^2 dX = \frac{1}{c} \int_L^M \left(\frac{dY}{dX}\right)^2 dX + \frac{1}{c} \int_M^T \left(\frac{dY}{dX}\right)^2 dX$$

The expression that gives F_2 can be transformed assuming as axis of reference the axis LM for the first integral, and the axis MT for the second integral. If η_1 and η_2 are the angles between the line LM and the X-axis, and between the line MT and the X-axis respectively, and X_1, Y_1, X_2, and Y_2 are the new coordinates of the curve, the expression becomes

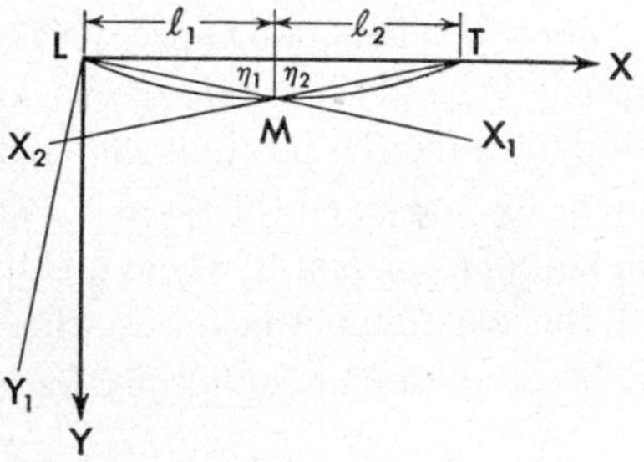

Fig. 89. *Definition of the reference axes* X_1 *and* X_2.

$$F_2 = \frac{1}{c} \int_L^M \left(\frac{dY}{dX}\right)^2 dX + \frac{1}{c} \int_M^T \left(\frac{dY}{dX}\right)^2 dX$$

$$= \frac{1}{c} \int_L^M \left(\frac{dY_1}{dX_1}\right)^2 dX_1 + \frac{1}{c} \int_L^M \eta_1^2 dX_1 + \frac{1}{c} \int_M^T \left(\frac{dY_2}{dX_2}\right)^2 dX_2 + \frac{1}{c} \int_M^T \eta_2^2 dX_2 \quad (273)$$

because

$$\int_L^M \frac{dY_1}{dX_1}\, dX_1 = 0$$

and

$$\frac{dY}{dX}\, dX = \left(\frac{dY_1}{dX_1} + \eta_1\right) dX_1$$

with the approximation accepted before.

Because the values of η_1 and η_2 are determined by the position of the point M and therefore are fixed when M is fixed, equation (273) shows that, for every position of the point M, or for every position of the maximum thickness of the profile, the value F_2 and therefore of C_{D_0} are minimum when

$$\int_L^M \left(\frac{dY_1}{dX_1}\right)^2 dX_1 + \int_M^T \left(\frac{dY_2}{dX_2}\right)^2 dX_2 = 0$$

or when the profile is formed by two straight lines LM and MT. Thus, for a given relative thickness and for a given position of the maximum thickness, with the approximation accepted, the profile of minimum drag is a profile obtained from four straight lines which connect the trailing edge and the leading edge with the point of the extremity of the maximum thickness. This profile is usually called a *diamond-shaped profile*.

The result does not change if the second term is considered in the expression (267), because in an analogous way it is possible to demonstrate that the second term is also minimum if the profile is diamond-shaped.

For the diamond-shaped profile, the position of the maximum thickness (point M) and the values of t_U/c and t_L/c can change; therefore it is necessary to determine the position that reduces the value of C_{D_0} to the absolute minimum for the given thickness. The position of the thickness divides the chord in two parts, l_1 and l_2, where l_1 is the part from the leading edge to the position of the maximum thickness; therefore for a diamond profile from equation (273) and similar equations for F_3 the following expressions are obtained:

$$F_2 = \frac{l_1}{c}\, \eta_1{}^2 + \frac{l_2}{2}\, \eta_2{}^2 \tag{274}$$

$$F_3 = \frac{l_1}{c}\, \eta_1{}^3 - \frac{l_2}{c}\, \eta_2{}^3 \tag{275}$$

but in the approximation accepted

$$\eta_1 = \frac{t_L}{l_1} = \eta_2 = \frac{t_L}{c - l_1}.$$

Therefore (equation 267)

$$C_{D_{0F}} = \frac{2t_L}{c} c_1 [\eta_1 + \eta_2] + \frac{2t_L}{c} c_2 [\eta_1^2 - \eta_2^2]$$

$$C_{D_{0F}} = c_1 \frac{2l^2_L}{c} \left[\frac{1}{l_1} + \frac{1}{c - l_1} \right]$$

$$+ 2c_2 \frac{l^3_L}{c} \left[\frac{1}{l_1} + \frac{1}{c - l_1} \right] \left[\frac{1}{l_1} - \frac{1}{c - l_1} \right]. \quad (276)$$

An expression similar to equation (276) can be obtained for the upper part of the wing; therefore the total drag is given by

$$C_{D_0} = C_{D_{0F}} + C_{D_{0U}}. \quad (277)$$

If the value of l_1 is equal for the upper and lower surface

$$+ \frac{t}{c} = - \frac{t_U}{c} + \frac{t_L}{c}.$$

Therefore the value of C_{D_0} for a given value of l_1 is minimum when

$$- \frac{t_U}{c} = + \frac{t_L}{c} = \frac{t}{2c}$$

or when the profile is symmetrical, as can be shown by differentiating equation (277). In order to obtain an absolute minimum the value of l_1 corresponding to a minimum must be found. Substituting for l_1 and l_2 the values

$$l_1 = \frac{c}{2} (1 + e)$$

$$l_2 = \frac{c}{2} (1 - e)$$

the value of C_{D_0} becomes

$$C_{D_0} = \frac{4c_1 l^2}{c^2} \left[\frac{1}{1 - e^2} - \frac{2c_2 l}{c_1 c} \frac{e}{(1 - e^2)^2} \right]. \quad (277)$$

Assuming e small and not considering the terms in e higher than the second order terms, expression (277) can be transformed into

$$C_{D_0} = \frac{4c_1 l^2}{c^2} \left[1 + e^2 - \frac{2c_2 l}{c_1 c} e \right]. \quad (277)$$

The minimum value of C_{D_0} is obtained when dC_{D_0}/de is zero or

$$e = \frac{c_2 l}{c_1 c}.$$

The position of maximum thickness for the value of minimum drag is

$$l_1 = \frac{c}{2} \left(1 + \frac{c_2 l}{c_1 c} \right) \quad (278)$$

and the value of the drag coefficient for zero angle of attack is

$$C_{D_{0\min}} = \frac{4c_1 l^2}{c^2}\left[1 - \frac{c_2{}^2}{c_1{}^2}\frac{l^2}{c^2}\right]. \tag{279}$$

For 10 per cent thick profile and $M = 2$, C_{D_0} is 0.0226, in comparison with the value of 0.0308 obtained for a circular arc. From equation (278) it appears that the value l_1/c is larger than $\frac{1}{2}$; therefore the maximum thickness is always nearer to the trailing edge than to the leading edge. For $M = 2$ and 10 per cent relative thickness, l_1/c is 0.56.

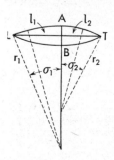

Fig. 90. *Circular arc profile with the maximum thickness behind the point at the 50 per cent of the chord.*

In an analogous way, it is possible to demonstrate that for a circular-arc profile of a given maximum thickness, the minimum drag coefficient decreases if the profile is a symmetrical profile with its maximum thickness beyond the 50 per cent chord.

Consider a profile formed by arcs of circles of different radii, (Figure 90), but with the centers along a line perpendicular to the chord. For the upper surface LAT, it is possible to calculate the values of D_2 and D_3, which are not zero because the axis AB is not an axis of symmetry. Indeed, if r_1 is the radius, σ_1 the angle of the arc LA, r_2 and σ_2 the corresponding values of the arc AT, and l_1 and l_2 the corresponding portions of the chord, then with the approximation accepted before

$$D_2 = \frac{1}{c}\int_L^T \left(\frac{dY}{dX}\right)^2 dX = \frac{r_1\sigma_1{}^3}{3c} + \frac{r_2\sigma_2{}^3}{3c} = \frac{4}{3}\frac{t_U{}^2}{c}\left(\frac{1}{l_1} + \frac{1}{l_2}\right)$$

$$D_3 = \frac{1}{c}\int_L^T \left(\frac{dY}{dX}\right)^3 dX = -\frac{r_1\sigma_1{}^4}{4c} + \frac{r_2\sigma_2{}^4}{4c} = -\frac{2t_U{}^3}{c}\left(\frac{1}{l_1{}^2} - \frac{1}{l_2{}^2}\right).$$

For equation (267), the drag of the upper part of the profiles is minimum when the value of $(c_1 D_2 - c_2 D_3)$ is minimum or when

$$\frac{4c_1}{3}\frac{t_U{}^2}{c}\left(\frac{1}{l_1} + \frac{1}{l_2}\right) + \frac{2t_U{}^3}{c}\left(\frac{1}{l_1{}^2} - \frac{1}{l_2{}^2}\right)c_2 \tag{280}$$

is minimum. The minimum of expression (280) corresponds to a value of l_1/c given by

$$\frac{l_1}{c} = \frac{1}{2}\left(1 + \frac{3c_2}{c_1}\frac{t_U}{c}\right) \tag{281}$$

but for a given thickness, the optimum occurs when $-t_U = t_L$; therefore the maximum thickness of the profile must be at a distance from the leading edge given by

$$\frac{l_1}{c} = \frac{1}{2}\left(1 + \frac{3}{2}\frac{c_2}{c_1}\frac{t}{c}\right). \tag{282}$$

The corresponding drag coefficient is

$$C_{D0} = \frac{16}{3}c_1\left[\frac{t^2}{c^2}1 - \frac{9}{4}\frac{t^2c_2^2}{c_1^2c^2}\right]. \tag{283}$$

Equation (282) is similar to equation (278) for a diamond-shaped profile, and indicates that the position of maximum thickness must move to the rear as the value of the percentage thickness increases and as the Mach number increases (the value of c_2/c_1 increases). For $M_1 = 2$ and $t/c = 0.1$, l_1/c is equal to 0.59, and C_{D0} is equal to 0.0297.

Profile Formed by Two Trapezoids. Consider a profile formed by two trapezoids of heights t_U and t_L and longer base c (Figure 91). The aerodynamic coefficients of this kind of profile can be obtained from equations (261) and (262) where the expressions F_2, D_2, F_3, and D_3 can be directly determined. If l_{1U} is the front part of the chord AB, l_{2U} is the central part BC, and l_{3U} is the back part CD, of the upper surface, and if l_{1L}, l_{2L}, and l_{3L} are the corresponding parts of the lower surface, the expressions F_2, D_2, F_3, and D_3 can be calculated as for the diamond profile.

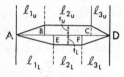

Fig. 91. *Trapezoidal profile.*

$$
\left.
\begin{aligned}
F_2 &= \frac{t_L^2}{c}\left(\frac{1}{l_{1L}} + \frac{1}{l_{3L}}\right) \\
D_2 &= \frac{t_U^2}{c}\left(\frac{1}{l_{1U}} + \frac{1}{l_{3U}}\right) \\
F_3 &= \frac{t_L^3}{c}\left(\frac{1}{l_{1L}} - \frac{1}{l_{3L}}\right)\left(\frac{1}{l_{1L}} + \frac{1}{l_{3L}}\right) \\
D_3 &= \frac{t_U^3}{c}\left(\frac{1}{l_{1U}} - \frac{1}{l_{3U}}\right)\left(\frac{1}{l_{1U}} + \frac{1}{l_{3U}}\right).
\end{aligned}
\right\} \tag{284}
$$

If the profile is symmetrical, $-t_U$ is equal to t_L, equal to $t/2$, then $l_{1U} = l_{1L}$, $l_{2U} = l_{2L}$, $l_{3U} = l_{3L}$, and the drag coefficient becomes

$$C_{D0} = \frac{c_1t^2}{c}\left(\frac{1}{l_1} + \frac{1}{l_3}\right)\left[1 + \frac{tc_2}{2c_1}\left(\frac{1}{l_1} - \frac{1}{l_3}\right)\right] \tag{285}$$

For given values of c, l_2, and t, the drag coefficient becomes a minimum when (equation 278)

$$\frac{l_1}{l_1 + l_3} = \frac{1}{2}\left(1 + \frac{c_2}{c_1}\frac{t}{l_1 + l_3}\right) \tag{286}$$

and becomes

$$C_{D0} = \frac{4c_1t^2}{c(l_1 + l_3)}\left[1 - \frac{t^2c_2^2}{(l_1 + l_3)^2c_1^2}\right].$$ (287)

All the considerations developed before show that the drag coefficient increases practically with the square of the relative thickness; therefore in order to have low drag, the supersonic wing must have very small values of relative thickness. In the design of a wing, the thickness of the profile is chosen in terms of structural considerations. When the relative thickness decreases, the structural problem becomes difficult and it is very probable that because small thickness must be used, the wing in supersonic flight will be of homogeneous material or very near to this type. In this case, the parameter that becomes more important as a term of comparison is the moment of inertia of the profile with respect to the chord, while the parameter of maximum thickness is no longer directly connected with structural necessity; therefore it is interesting to compare drag coefficients of profiles for equal moments of inertia. For a symmetrical trapezoid profile, the moment of inertia with respect to the chord is given by the expression

$$I = \frac{t^3}{48}\left[4c - 3(l_1 + l_3)\right].$$ (288)

Therefore equation (287) defining C_{D_0} in terms of moment of inertia becomes

$$C_{D_0} = \frac{16c_1}{c(l_1 + l_3)}\left[\frac{6I}{4c - 3(l_1 + l_3)}\right]^{\frac{2}{3}}$$
$$\left\{1 - \frac{4c_2^2}{c_1^2(l_1 + l_3)^2}\left[\frac{6I}{4c - 3(l_1 + l_3)}\right]^{\frac{2}{3}}\right\}.$$ (289)

Equation (289) permits determination of the value of $(l_1 + l_3)$ which gives the minimum value of C_{D_0} for a given moment of inertia of profile and for a given chord.

In equation (289), the second term of the subtraction in the expression on the right side is much smaller than the first term for thin profiles; therefore for the consideration of minimum drag it is a good approximation to consider the first term only. In this case, C_{D_0} is minimum when the expression

$$c(l_1 + l_3)\left[4c - 3(l_1 + l_3)\right]^{\frac{2}{3}}$$

is maximum, which occurs when

$$l_1 + l_3 = \frac{4}{5}c, \text{ and } l_2 = \frac{1}{5}c.$$

In this case, equation (287) becomes

$$C_{D_0} = \frac{5t^2c_1}{c^2}\left(1 - \frac{25}{16}\frac{t^2c_2^2}{c^2c_1^2}\right)$$ (290)

and the corresponding moment of inertia is

$$I = \frac{1}{30} \frac{t^3}{c^3} c^4 \tag{291}$$

For a 10 per cent thick diamond-shaped profile, the trapezoidal profile of the same moment of inertia and minimum drag is 8.5 per cent thick, and for $M = 2$, the drag of a diamond-shaped profile is 0.0228, while for the trapezoidal profile it is 0.0205. For a circular-arc profile, the moment of inertia, if the percentage thickness is small, can be determined by the expression

$$I = \frac{4}{105} \frac{(t/c)^3}{1 + (t/c)^2} c^4 \tag{292}$$

For a circular-arc profile of 10 per cent thickness, the corresponding trapezoidal profile of the same moment of inertia must have a percentage thickness of 10.352, and for $M = 2$ the drag coefficients are 0.0308 for circular-arc profile and 0.0301 for trapezoidal profile.

From all the preceding considerations, it is possible to conclude that, in supersonic flow, for thin profiles, the minimum drag coefficient is dependent on the percentage thickness by a law which is nearly quadratic; the profile giving maximum percentage thickness of minimum drag is a symmetrical profile, which has the maximum thickness beyond 50 per cent of the chord. The shape of the profile is dependent on the criteria of comparison. If the comparison is made for constant thickness, the optimum shape is the diamond shape; but if the comparison is made for constant moment of inertia, which is nearer to the practical problem, the optimum shape is no longer the diamond profile but a profile which has a very small variation of thickness in the central zone of the chord. Viscosity changes the physical phenomena, and therefore more accurate theoretical investigations are not very useful, because the small differences of pressure drag can be easily eliminated or changed in sign when the boundary layer and the separation at the trailing edge are considered. The friction drag of a profile changes if the pressure distribution along the surface changes, and therefore is a function of the shape of the profile.

Profile of Maximum L/D. From equations (266) and (267) it is possible to obtain for the value of L/D the following expression

$$\frac{1}{L/D} = \frac{C_L}{4c_1} + \frac{c_2}{2c_1} (F_2 - D_2) + \frac{C_{D_0}}{C_L}. \tag{293}$$

Equation (269) has a minimum value for a value of C_L given by

$$C_L = 2\sqrt{c_1 C_{D_0}} \tag{294}$$

and the corresponding minimum value of D/L is

$$\left(\frac{D}{L}\right)_{min} = \frac{c_2}{2c_1}(F_2 - D_2) + \sqrt{\frac{C_{D_0}}{c_1}}. \tag{295}$$

If the value of maximum thickness is fixed, it is possible to repeat the considerations made for the profile of minimum drag and to demonstrate that the profile of maximum L/D, for a given maximum relative thickness, is a diamond profile. Because the profile must have a lift coefficient other than zero the profile is not symmetrical, and the thickness of the upper part is greater than the thickness of the lower part. For the optimum condition, the maximum thickness is at the same percentage chord as for the profile of minimum drag (equation 278), and the thickness is divided between the upper and lower parts by the following law:

$$\frac{t_U}{c} = -\frac{t_L}{c}\left(1 + \frac{2c_2}{c_1}\frac{t}{c}\right) \tag{296}$$

or

$$\frac{t_L}{c} = \frac{t}{2c}\left(1 - \frac{c_2}{c_1}\frac{t}{c}\right) \geq 0.$$

The profiles therefore are nonsymmetrical, with the upper parts thicker than the lower parts. From equation (296) it appears that the asymmetry of the profile increases with increase of the Mach number (because c_2/c_1 increases) and with increase of thickness, but for small thickness the asymmetry is very small. For $M = 2$ and maximum thickness of 10 per cent, t_U/c is 5.6 and t_L/c is 4.4 per cent; c_2 for M increasing to infinity becomes equal to $\gamma + 1/4$, and c_1 becomes zero; therefore for very high Mach numbers the profile tends to become triangular, and t_L approaches zero, but it is necessary to remember that the considerations are not quantitatively correct because for very high Mach numbers the hypothesis that the terms containing η^3 are negligible on the pressure distribution is no longer correct.

The maximum L/D for a diamond profile which conforms to the relation shown in equation (296) is given by the expression

$$\left(\frac{D}{L}\right)_{min} = 2\frac{t}{c} - 2\left(\frac{c_2}{c_1}\right)^2\left(\frac{t}{c}\right)^3. \tag{297}$$

From equation (297) it is evident that for a thin profile, L/D decreases nearly proportionally to the increase of the maximum relative thickness and L/D increases as the Mach number increases, but the increase is very small.

For $M = 2$ and for a 10-per cent-thick profile, the maximum L/D without friction is 5.1, and occurs for C_L of 0.1. The value of C_L for maximum efficiency is very small and decreases slowly as the Mach number increases (equation 294).

Analytical Determination of the Pitching-Moment Coefficient and of the Focus of the Profile. If ds is an element of the upper part of the profile, the moment produced by the pressure distribution along ds with reference to the leading edge of the profile is

$$\frac{dM_U}{\rho_1 V_1^2} = \frac{p - p_1}{\rho_1 V_1^2} XdX = -(c_1\eta - c_2\eta^2) XdX \qquad (298)$$

From the considerations in paragraph 3 (Figure 88) the angle η can be resolved into two parts (equation 252) and the following expression can be obtained:

$$-\frac{dM_U}{\rho_1 V_1^2} = (c_1\alpha + c_1\eta' - c_2\alpha^2 - 2c_2\alpha\eta' - c_2\eta'^2) XdX \qquad (299)$$

Where X and Y are the coordinates of the profile referred to a system of axes in which the X-axis is the chord (Figure 88). From (299) is obtained

$$-\frac{M_U}{\rho_1 V_1^2} = c_1\alpha \frac{c^2}{2} + c_1 \int_L^T \left(\frac{dY}{dX}\right) XdX - c_2\alpha^2 \frac{c^2}{2}$$

$$- 2c_2\alpha \int_L^T \left(\frac{dY}{dX}\right) XdX - c_2 \int_L^T \left(\frac{dY}{dX}\right)^2 XdX. \qquad (300)$$

The expression can be changed because

$$\int_L^T \left(\frac{dY}{dX}\right) XdX = \left[YX\right]_L^T - \int_L^T YdX = -c^2 s_U \qquad (300a)$$

where $c^2 s_U$ is the area of the upper part of the profile and s_U is the nondimensional value proportional to the area; s_U by the convention accepted for the sign of η is positive if the upper surface is below the chord line and negative in the other case. Calling the expression

$$\frac{1}{c^2} \int_L^T \left(\frac{dY}{dX}\right)^2 XdX = U \text{ for the upper surface} \qquad (301)$$

and

$$\frac{1}{c^2} \int_L^T \left(\frac{dY}{dX}\right)^2 XdX = L \text{ for the lower surface}$$

the following equations are obtained:

$$\frac{-M_U}{\rho_1 V_1^2} = c_1\alpha \frac{c^2}{2} - (c_1 - 2c_2\alpha)c^2 s_U - c_2\alpha^2 \frac{c^2}{2} - c_2 U c^2 \qquad (302)$$

and

$$\frac{-M_L}{\rho_1 V_1^2} = c_1\alpha \frac{c^2}{2} - (c_1 + 2c_2\alpha)c^2 s_L + c_2\alpha^2 \frac{c^2}{2} + c_2 L c^2 \qquad (303)$$

where $c^2 s_L$ is the area of the lower surface of the profile, positive if the lower surface is below the chord line and negative if above the chord line; therefore the moment coefficient is

$$- C_M = - \frac{M}{\frac{1}{2}\rho_1 V_1^2 c^2} = 2c_1\alpha - 2c_1(s_L + s_U)$$
$$- 4c_2\alpha \, (s_L - s_U) + 2c_2 \, (L - U). \quad (304)$$

The area of the section of the profile is $(s_L - s_U)$. It is useful to give the value of C_M as a function of C_L using equation (261)

$$C_M = \frac{1}{2}\left[\frac{2c_2}{c_1} \, (s_L - s_U) - 1\right] C_L - c_2 \, (D_2 - F_2)$$
$$+ 2c_1 \, (s_L + s_U) + 2c_2 \, (U - L) \quad (305)$$

or

$$C_M = BC_L + C_{M_f} \quad (306)$$

where

$$B = \frac{1}{2}\left[\frac{2c_2}{c_1} \, (s_L - s_U) - 1\right] \quad (307)$$

and

$$C_{M_f} = 2c_1 \, (s_L + s_U) + 2c_2 \, (U - L) - c_2 \, (D_2 - F_2) \quad (308)$$

Considering a point F which is at a position x/c from the leading edge equal to $-B$, the moment with respect to the point F is

$$C_{MF} = C_M - BC_L = C_{M_f} = \text{constant.}$$

Therefore the point F is the point for which the moment is constant, and therefore F is the focus of the profile and C_{M_f} is the moment with respect to the focus.

It is interesting to compare the distance $-B$ of the focus of the profile with the equivalent distance for a subsonic profile. For subsonic velocity, the value of B is about equal to $\frac{1}{4}$ of the chord; for supersonic velocity, B is about $\frac{1}{2}$ of the chord because in expression (307) the term $2c_2/c_1 (s_L - s_U)$ is of the order of magnitude of $\frac{2c_2}{c_1}\frac{t}{c}$ and is small in comparison to one. The center of pressure moves in the direction of the leading edge if the area of the profile increases, or if the Mach number increases. For a symmetrical circular-arc profile of 10 per cent maximum thickness, the area of the profile is

$$c^2 \, (s_L - s_U) = \frac{2}{3} \left(\frac{t}{c}\right) c^2 = 0.066c^2$$

and for $M = 2$, $-B = 0.416$; for $M = 4$, $-B = 0.342$. From equation (308) it appears that the value of C_{M_f} depends very much on the thickness of the profile, and for the same shape and curvature of the mean line, when the maximum percentage thickness increases, C_{M_f} increases and becomes zero for zero thickness, independent of the curvature of the mean line. For a symmetrical profile, C_{M_f} is zero.

Experimental Results of Supersonic Profiles. In the considerations of the preceding section, the hypothesis was assumed that the flow is perfect; therefore the effect of the presence of the boundary layer was not considered. The presence of the boundary layer changes the phenomena somewhat and therefore changes the value of the results quantitatively.

The effect of the boundary layer is particularly important for the zone near the trailing edge, because in this zone, the presence of shock waves and of boundary layer can cause separation to occur. Indeed, for every profile of finite thickness compression occurs at the trailing edge, on one or both surfaces (see Figure 92). The boundary layer formed along the surface ACB does not

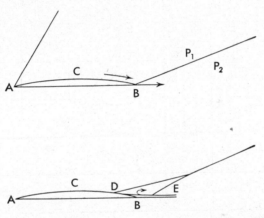

Fig. 92. *Scheme of the separation phenomenon at the trailing edge.*

have sufficient kinetic energy to undergo the variation of pressure which occurs across the shock wave and cannot undergo a recompression with shock wave, because the flow in the boundary layer is at lower velocity than outside the boundary layer and is partly subsonic; therefore, a separation can occur. The pressure p_2 is transmitted in the boundary layer ahead of the point B, and at the boundary layer the compression is gradual. In D a gradual compression begins and in the zone DE, also outside of the boundary layer, a deviation of compression occurs. For equilibrium the pressure must be equal at the two sides of the streamline $DE;$ therefore the deviation produced by DE must be connected with the increase in pressure in the boundary layer. A thick wake is formed in the zone DEB, which changes the pressure distribution in the zone *DBE*. The thickness of the wake is greatly dependent on the condition of the boundary layer (laminar or turbulent boundary layer) and therefore on the Reynolds number and on the variation of pressure across the shock. The separation in the zone *DE* avoids expansion in this zone, which is considered in the theoretical investigation, and the pressure at *DE* is larger than the pressure foreseen by the theory. As a consequence, the lift is less than the lift calculated theoretically, and the pressure drag is smaller. Experimental tests confirm the preceding considerations.

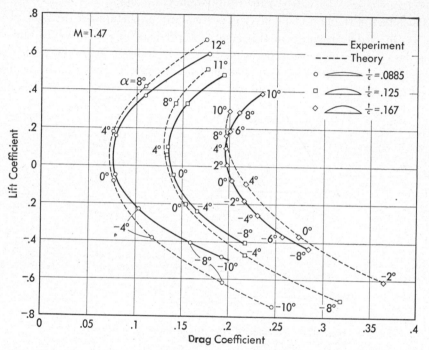

Fig. 93. *Lift coefficient versus drag coefficient for three plane circular-arc profiles of different thicknesses (from Reference 27).*

In order to give an idea of the importance of the boundary layer in aerodynamic phenomena for two-dimensional profiles, some experimental results obtained in wind tunnels at Göttingen (Germany) and at Guidonia (Italy) are shown in the figures beginning with Figure 93 (References 27 and 28). The results are obtained from small scale models. For comparison, the theoretical results obtained from the pressure calculations are also shown. The results shown in Figures 93 to 97 were obtained at Göttingen in an intermittent tunnel having a 2.36- by 2.87-inch test section operating at a Mach number of 1.47 (Reference 27).

In Figure 93 the drag and lift coefficients for plane circular-arc profiles of different thickness are shown. As it appears from the curve, the lift-coefficient-curve slope is less than the theoretical, and the angle of zero lift is negative but is less than the theoretical. The drag coefficient is of the same order as the theoretical value, and the differences increase with increase of the angle of attack. Because the theoretical values do not consider the friction

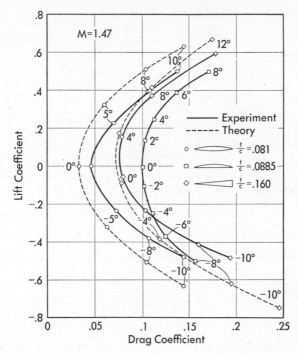

Fig. 94. *Lift coefficient versus drag coefficient for a plane circular-arc profile, a symmetrical circular-arc profile, and a wedge (from Reference 27).*

drag which exists in the experimental data, the experimental pressure drag must be less than the theoretical pressure drag.

If a symmetrical circular-arc profile is compared with a plane circular-arc profile of about the same thickness, comparison shows that the symmetrical arc profile has a much lower minimum drag coefficient (Figure 94). In Figure 95 some experimental results for profiles used at subsonic speeds are shown. (The profiles are the Göttingen profiles M 622, 623, 624.) As is natural, the blunt noses of the profiles produce a large rise of drag at supersonic speeds. If the same profile is tested with the trailing edge in place of the leading edge, the drag decreases notably (Figure 96), because an attached shock is produced

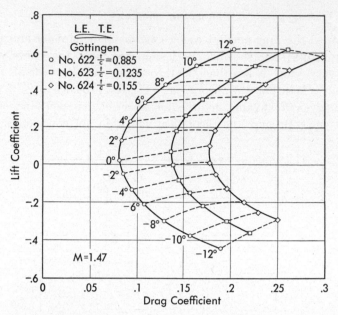

Fig. 95. *Lift coefficient versus drag coefficient for three subsonic profiles at M = 1.47 (from Reference 27).*

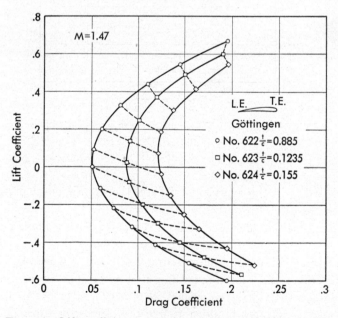

Fig. 96. *Lift coefficient versus drag coefficient for three profiles obtained from the profiles of Figure 95 reversing the flight direction (from Reference 27).*

at the leading edge, and for the same thickness, the drag is less than for plane circular-arc profiles.   In Figure 97 the results of the tests for a circular cylinder

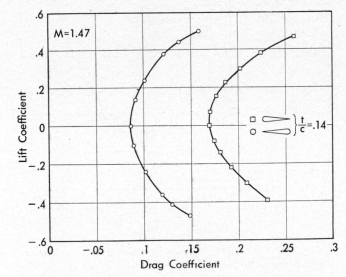

Fig. 97. *Lift coefficient versus drag coefficient for a cylinder with a fairing before and behind the cylinder (from Reference 27).*

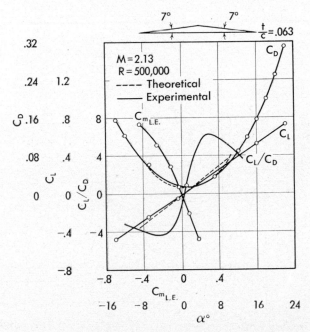

Fig. 98. *Lift, drag, and pitching-moment coefficient for a plane circular-arc profile at M = 2.13 (from Reference 28).*

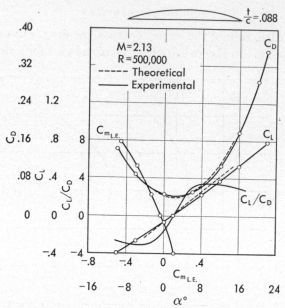

Fig. 99. *Lift, drag, and pitching-moment coefficient for a triangular profile at* $M = 2.13$ *(from Reference 28).*

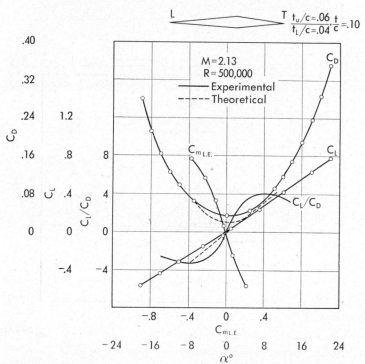

Fig. 100. *Lift, drag, and pitching-moment coefficient for a diamond-shaped profile at* $M = 2.13$ *(from Reference 28).*

with a fairing in front and behind the cylinder are given. While the fairing behind the cylinder is very efficient for subsonic speed, it is no longer efficient in supersonic speed, where it is necessary to have a fairing in front of the cylinder.

Figure 98 and following show some of the results obtained at Guidonia (Reference 28). The tests were made in a continuous tunnel 16 by 20 inches at a Reynolds number of about 5×10^5 and at a Mach number of 2.13. In the figures, the theoretical values are also shown. As appears from Figures 98, 99,

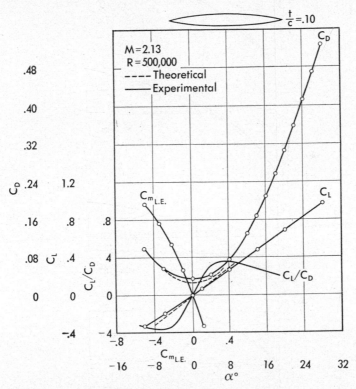

Fig. 101. *Lift, drag, and pitching-moment coefficient for a symmetrical circular-arc profile at M = 2.13 (from Reference 28).*

100, and 101 the lift-coefficient-curve slope is lower than the theoretical, and the drag coefficient is of the same order of magnitude as the theoretical.

The pressure distributions and the schlieren photographs for the symmetrical arc and plane circular-arc shapes provide an explanation of the differences between theory and experiments. Some pressure distributions are shown in Figures 102 and 103. For comparison, the theoretical values are also plotted. The theoretical values are determined by the potential-flow theory.

As appears from Figures 102 and 103, the measured pressure distributions agree very well in the front part of the profiles with the theoretical values, but a large discrepancy is found near the trailing edge. The pressure near the

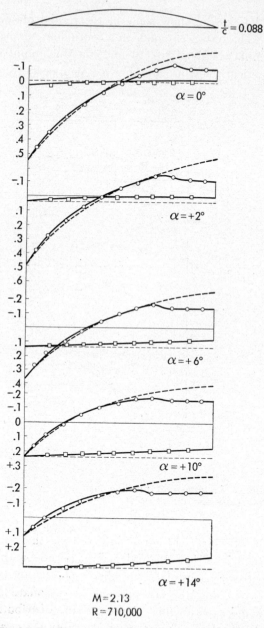

Fig. 102. *Pressure distribution along a circular-arc profile at M = 2.13 (from Reference 28).*

trailing edge is less than the static pressure of the undisturbed flow, and
theoretically a shock wave must occur at the trailing edge; the experimental
data show that the value of the pressure near the trailing edge is larger than

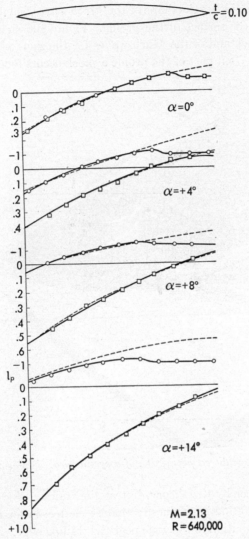

Fig. 103. *Pressure distribution along a symmetrical circular-arc profile at* $M = 2.13$ *(from Reference 28).*

the theoretical value, and that the recompression begins gradually in a zone
in front of the trailing edge, after which the pressure remains about constant.
The differences between theoretical and experimental values due to the separa-

tion at the trailing edge increase when the theoretical value of the pressure at the trailing edge decreases, or when the theoretical intensity of the shock at the trailing edge increases. Schlieren and shadow photographs for a circular-arc profile appear in Figures 104 and 105.

In order to individuate the shape of the Mach waves, small disturbances are produced along the surface of the profile. Figure 106 shows the theoretical shape of the shock and of the Mach waves for the same profile. The figures show that in the front part of the profile a shock occurs followed by an expan-

Fig. 104. *Schlieren photograph of a symmetrical circular-arc profile.*

sion, as was foreseen by the theory, but at the trailing edge corresponding to the shock, a separation is produced; that is the reason for the divergence of the pressure distribution in the zone near the trailing edge. The separation is generated by the presence of the boundary layer. The wake that is produced by the profile has a direction nearly parallel to the stream velocity, as was foreseen by the theory. The separation at the trailing edge decreases the expansion in this zone, and therefore decreases the value of the normal component and the value of the tangent component of the aerodynamic force. Therefore the lift and the pressure drag are less, for the experimental results,

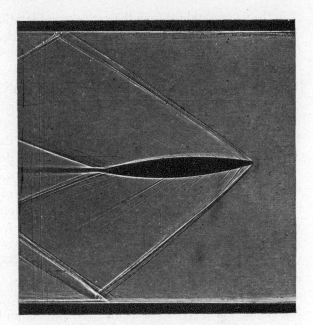

Fig. 105. *Shadow photograph of a symmetrical circular-arc profile at 4° angle of attack.*

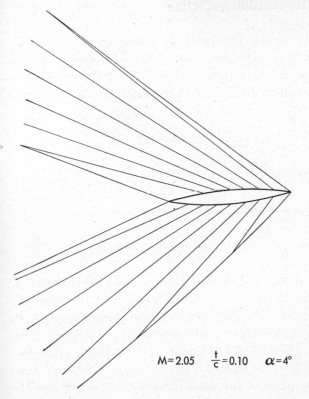

M=2.05 $\frac{t}{c}$=0.10 α=4°

Fig. 106. *Theoretical shape of shock waves and expansion waves for the phenomenon considered in Figure 105.*

153

than the value obtained from theoretical considerations. Because the pressure distribution changes, the experimental moment coefficients are also different from the theoretical moment coefficients.

The Supersonic Biplane. The theoretical analysis and the experimental results for supersonic profiles have shown that, different from that for subsonic profiles, the drag of supersonic profiles increases materially with increase of the maximum thickness of the profiles (about with the square of the thickness). The best profile from the viewpoint of minimum drag or of optimum L/D is the flat plate. For practical aerodynamic problems, it is impossible for structural exigency to reduce the maximum thickness of the wings below a minimum. Therefore a special scheme of a biplane using wings of finite thickness, which is theoretically equivalent to a flat plate from the viewpoint of the pressure drag, is of great interest. The special biplane, which has theoretically the same pressure drag as a flat plate at the same incidence, is a biplane which uses, opportunely, the interaction between the two wings and is based upon an observation of Busemann. Thus this configuration is usually called the Busemann biplane (Reference 25). The Busemann biplane is one example of the use of the interference between different bodies in order to reduce the shock drag.

The basic idea of the Busemann biplane is the following. Consider two profiles which have flat surfaces and sharp noses. The two profiles are placed near each other, with the flat surfaces external and parallel (see Figure 107). The flow that wets the biplane can be divided into two parts: the flow that wets

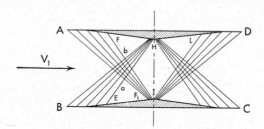

Fig. 107. *Aerodynamic design of a supersonic biplane.*

the external surfaces BC and AD, and the flow that goes into the channel BA, HI, CD. Because the noses of the profiles A and B are sharp, the phenomenon along AD is the same as for the upper surface of a flat plate of same length and of the same incidence with respect to the undistrubed velocity. Along BC the flow is the same as along the lower surface of a flat plate. Therefore for the external part of the flow, the biplane is equivalent, as to pressure drag, lift, and moment, to a flat plate of the same incidence. Consider now the internal flow. Along the profiles BE and AF a compression is generated. The compression can be gradual if the shapes BE and AF vary gradually. Therefore from the parts BE and AF of the two profiles, compression waves are generated that tend to form an envelope. Each family of compression waves crosses the other family generated by the opposite profile and meets the opposite profile. If the distance between the profiles is small, it is possible that the compression waves may reach the opposite profile before forming an envelope. It is possible, also, to avoid reflection of the compression wave on the wall by giving the profile an appropriate shape. If the wall, at the point at which the compression wave touches the profile B, has the same direction as the flow, the compression wave will disappear (see Figure 107). Therefore the flow is compressed isentropically across two families of compression waves, which disappear when meeting the opposite profiles. But it is also possible to expand the flow isentropically with two families of expansion waves and to attain again the conditions that the flow had before compression; in this case, in the tube $ABCD$, an isentropic transformation occurs, and the flow leaves the tube with the same velocity and direction that it had when it went into the tube. Thus the aerodynamic action of the internal flow is zero, and therefore the biplane is equivalent to a flat plate. A practical scheme for the design on a Busemann biplane appears in Figure 107. Along the points BE and AF the velocity undergoes a continuous deviation of compression which generates two families of compression waves a and b. The compression waves cross each other and change direction. When the first compression wave meets the opposite profile at F_1, the direction of the profile at F_1 must turn, and beyond the point F_1 must have the direction of the stream after the compression wave from A_A. Because the compression wave AF_1 is generated by a deviation of opposite sign to the deviation generated by BE, the wall at F_1 turns in an opposite direction from before, and at the point F_1, the shape of the profile has a change in the sign of curvature. When the last compression wave meets the opposite profile at I, the flow has a larger pressure, and therefore in order to obtain the conditions that it had before crossing the compression wave a and b, the flow must undergo an expansion. If $-\eta_1$ is the maximum deviation of compression generated by the profile AHD, and η is the maximum deviation generated by the profile BIC, at I and H the profiles and the stream have an inclination $(\eta - \eta_1)$. In order to obtain conditions of undisturbed flow, it is necessary to expand the flow with an expansion of $(\eta + \eta_1)$ (equal to the compression) and turn the flow at an angle $(-\eta + \eta_1)$. If, from the upper profile, a gradual expansion of η_1 degrees is generated, and, on the lower profile, an expansion of $-\eta$ degrees is generated, the two expansions are of opposite sign; therefore the direction of the velocity changes by $(-\eta + \eta_1)$, and the flow after the two expansions attains the conditions of undisturbed velocity.

From H to D along the upper profile the flow undergoes a deviation of expansion equal to η_1. At L, the first expansion wave generated by the lower profile meets the upper profile, and in order to avoid reflection, the profile must change curvature and must have a point of inflection at L. When all expansion waves are eliminated, the shape of the profile has the same direction as at A, and therefore it is possible to obtain a closed profile. Assuming for simplicity that all expansions and compressions are transmitted across only one characteristic line, it is easy to design the scheme of a biplane for different angles of attack or Mach numbers. Some schemes are shown in Figure 108.

It is interesting to observe that if the compression occurs with a shock, as happens if the leading edge of the profile has a finite value for the edge, it is possible to design a Busemann biplane in which the transformation in the internal flow is no longer isentropic, but the differences from isentropic transformation are very small, and therefore have a pressure drag very nearly that of a flat plate. This type of biplane presents a more practical possibility because it does not need edges of zero angle. A design of such a biplane appears in Figure 109 (Reference 29).

The Busemann biplane is very interesting from the theoretical viewpoint; however its application is difficult for the following reasons: The theoretical design can be made for one angle of attack and for one Mach number only;

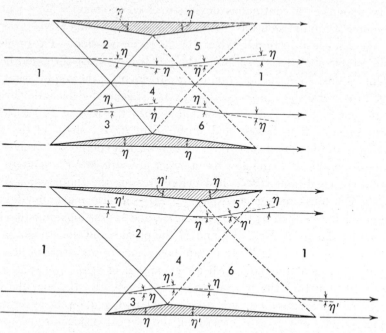

Fig. 108 (a). *Schemes of supersonic biplanes at zero angle of attack (from Reference 29).*

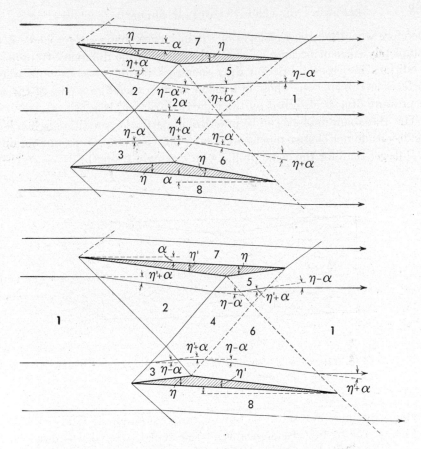

Fig. 108 (b). *Schemes of supersonic biplanes at an angle of attack (from Reference 29).*

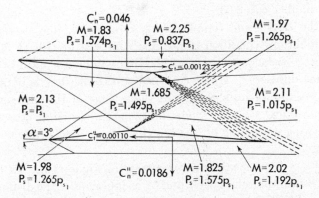

Fig. 109. *A practical design of supersonic biplane (from Reference 29).*

therefore when the speed changes or the incidence changes the scheme is not completely efficient because efficiency decreases as the difference from design conditions increases. Friction drag increases notably because the wetted surfaces are about twice those of a usual profile; therefore a part of the gain in pressure drag is absorbed by the increased friction drag.

The Busemann biplane can be practical in particular conditions when flight conditions do not change much, because in this case it is possible to obtain an L/D larger than for the usual profile with the same strength.

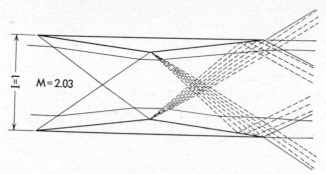

Fig. 110. *The design and aerodynamic analysis of the biplane used in the tests (from Reference 30).*

Some experimental results of a biplane tested at Guidonia (Italy) are shown in Figures 111 to 113 (Reference 30). The biplane tested was designed for zero angle of attack (symmetrical biplane with two similar wings) (Figure 110). The biplane was tested for different angles of attack and for different gap distances I between the two wings, in order to have some data of practical efficiency for conditions of flight other than for the design conditions. The test Mach number was 2.03.

During the tests some complications were found, due to the fact that another equilibrium condition is possible with a strong shock in front and subsonic flow in the channel (a condition that will be discussed in the chapter on supersonic diffusors). However, when supersonic flow is obtained in the channel the results of tests show that the scheme of the phenomena agrees with the theoretical scheme. Some divergence was found near the trailing edge of the wing depending on the boundary layer that produces separation as on wings.

The results of force measurements appear in Figure 111. In Figures 112 and 113 are shown the values of C_D and C_L as functions of the distance between the wings for different angles of attack. The surfaces of reference are the surfaces of the two wings. The theoretical values of the coefficients are also shown for comparison. For a distance between the two wings equal to 1.85, the two wings do not interfere, and the drag coefficient of a wing becomes

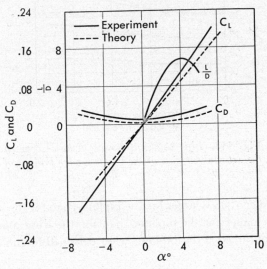

Fig. 111. *Lift and drag coefficient of the biplane of Figure 110 at Mach number 2.03 (from Reference 30).*

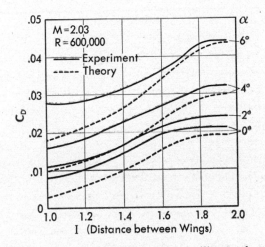

Fig. 112. *Drag coefficient versus distance between the external surfaces of the wings for the biplane of Figure 110 (from Reference 30).*

0.0216. The minimum drag of the biplane for the design condition ($I = 1$) is 0.0164, for the same surface of reference. Therefore, the diminution in drag

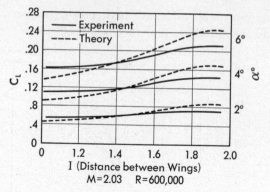

Fig. 113. *Lift coefficient versus distance between the external surfaces of the wings for the biplane of Figure 110 (from Reference 30).*

is important, and $dC_L/d\alpha$ is larger for the biplane than for the wing alone. The value of L/D is higher for the biplane than for the wing alone, and a larger gain would be obtained if the biplane were designed for an angle of attack.

CHAPTER

8

TWO-DIMENSIONAL EFFUSORS

Effusors and Diffusors. In the practical application of supersonic aerodynamics two different kinds of phenomena connected with the flow into tubes must be considered: the phenomena that occur when the flow is decelerated from high speed to low speed, and the phenomena connected with the opposite transformation when the flow is accelerated from low speed to supersonic speed. The apparatus used to decelerate the flow from high speed to low speed is usually called a *diffusor*, while the apparatus used to accelerate the flow from low speed to high speed is usually called an *effusor*. A supersonic effusor can be divided into two parts: the first part is the subsonic part in which the flow increases in speed from low values to the speed of sound, and the second part in which the flow is accelerated from the speed of sound to supersonic speed. The first part is made up of a converging tube, because in subsonic speed the increase in velocity is greater than the corresponding decrease of density; the second part is made up of a diverging tube because, for supersonic speed, the increase in velocity is less than the corresponding decrease of density (Chapter 1, equation 51a). At the minimum section (throat) the speed attains values of the order of the speed of sound. If the velocity is uniform across the entire section, the velocity at the throat is exactly equal to the speed of sound.

The study of effusors and diffusors is particularly important for design of supersonic tunnels, and for design of supersonic jets for jet-propelled airplanes. For analysis, effusors and diffusors can be divided into two types, the two-dimensional effusor or diffusor and the three-dimensional effusor or diffusor. A two-dimensional effusor or diffusor is a tube formed by two parallel walls and two walls made by a cylindrical surface of curved shape with all the generatrices perpendicular to the parallel walls. In this case, if the boundary layer is not considered at the parallel walls, all flow quantities are constant along every line perpendicular to the parallel walls; and therefore it is enough to study the transformation of the flow in a plane, so that the two-dimensional theory can be used.

The physical schemes of the phenomena for three-dimensional effusors and diffusors are similar to those analyzed in the two-dimensional case, but quantitative analysis is much more complicated and is possible only in particular cases. Some of those will be considered when flow with axial symmetry is analyzed.

In analysis of supersonic effusors two problems are usually encountered:

(a) The problem of the design of such a supersonic effusor that for given flow quantities at the beginning of the effusor, and a given pressure on the end of the tube. there is a given velocity distribution at the end of the tube. Usually a uniform velocity is requested at the end of the tube.

(b) The problem of determining the flow quantities at the end of the effusor for a given shape of the effusor and for a given value of the pressure at the beginning and at the end of the effusor.

The first problem for the two-dimensional case is important for design of supersonic tunnels. In tunnels, generally, the direction and intensity of the velocity of the subsonic part of the effusor is known, and it is necessary to design the supersonic part in such a way as to obtain uniform pressure and velocity distribution at the end of the effusor which corresponds to the test section. Because the flow is supersonic, small variations of velocity and pressure in the test section occur with formation of expansion or shock waves which extend across the whole section and complicate analysis of the phenomena and the optical investigation. Such an effusor can be designed without formation of shock waves, and in this case, for a given pressure ratio at the ends of the effusor, the momentum of the flow at the end is maximum; an effusor with isentropic transformation and uniform velocity at the end is called a *perfect effusor*.

Theoretical Design of the Supersonic Part of a Two-Dimensional Effusor. For design of a perfect effusor, the velocity and pressure distribution along a cross section at the beginning of the effusor in a zone in which the flow is supersonic at all points, and the final pressure or the final Mach number must be known.

Sometimes determination of the velocity distribution in the section at the beginning of the tube is not known; and the hypothesis is assumed that, at the minimum section of the tube, the velocity is uniform and equal to sonic velocity. This hypothesis is approximate enough if the subsonic part has a very gradual variation of cross section near the minimum but if, in the subsonic part, a rapid variation of cross section occurs near the minimum, the actual distribution of velocity is very different from the distribution assumed in the design of the effusor, and therefore the results obtained experimentally can be very different from those determined analytically. In general, determination of the velocity distribution in one cross section is very useful to obtain satisfactory results.

For the design of the effusor, the characteristic theory is used. The condition of a uniform velocity distribution at the end of the effusor is equivalent to the condition that the end section of the effusor must not be crossed by compression or expansion waves; therefore, because in the effusor an expansion occurs, it is necessary that the effusor have such a shape that all the expansion waves produced be eliminated before the end section. It was shown in the preceding chapters that, if an expansion wave meets a wall and the wall at the point of meeting undergoes the same variation of direction that the velocity undergoes across the wave, the expansion wave is not reflected, but disappears. Therefore in order to obtain a perfect effusor this concept can be used, and the following scheme can be adopted: Some expansion waves are generated on the wall, the expansion waves cross the flow, and meet the opposite wall; there they are eliminated; when all the expansion waves are eliminated, the flow is uniform and parallel. For practical design for an infinite number of expansion waves of infinitesimal intensity, some line that represents a finite expansion must be substituted with an average inclination corresponding to the average Mach number that the line represents. The substitution is equivalent to assuming that the expansion occurs in small finite steps instead of being a continuous expansion. Using the numbering system of Chapter 2, it is possible to proceed in the following way: Assume that at the beginning of the diffusor the velocity is uniform and equal to sonic velocity, and consider a symmetrical effusor (Figure 114). At A and B the Mach

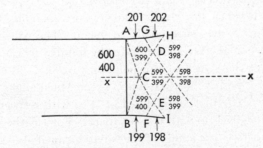

Fig. 114. *Construction of the characteristic net in order to design a supersonic effusor.*

number is one, and the direction is the undisturbed direction. With the system of numbering used in Chapter 2, at A and B there are two corresponding numbers, the sum of which is 1000, and if the direction is the undisturbed direction, the difference of the two numbers must be 200. Therefore, the two numbers are 600 and 400. Along the xx-axis, because the effusor is symmetrical, the velocity must be in the direction of xx; therefore along the xx-axis the number must have a constant value of difference equal to 200. If the angle between xx and xA, is considered positive and the angle between xx and xB is considered negative, when the direction of the velocity is inclined at a positive angle with respect to xx, the difference of the numbers must be larger than 200, and must be smaller in the other case. If a deviation of expansion is produced in A and B, expansion waves are generated from A and B, and, substituting for the continuous expansion a line that corresponds, for example, to a deviation of 1°, it is possible to design the line AC. After the expansion of 1°, the Mach number corresponds to the numbers 600 and 399. Therefore the line AC corresponds to the number 999.5. From Table 2 of the appendix it is possible to determine the Mach number and the Mach angle corresponding to 999.5. The direction of the wave AC is $(-\mu + 0.5°)$. Behind the line AC the Mach number corresponds to the number 999, and the direction of the velocity corresponds to 201; therefore behind AC the flow is defined by the number 600/399. The line BC can be designed with the same interim but, because across AC an expansion occurs in the negative direction, the number behind BC is 599/400. At C the two expansion waves meet each other at the axis. The wave BC represents an expansion of 1° in the negative direction; therefore the flow across CD must expand and turn at 1° in the negative direction, and both the difference and the sum of the two numbers must decrease by 1; therefore the numbers become 599 and 399. Across CE the deviation is 1° positive; therefore the sum must decrease by 1 (expansion of 1°), and the difference must increase by 1; the numbers are 599 and 399. In order to design CD it is necessary to consider that CD represents the average expansion wave between the Mach numbers corresponding to 999 and 998; therefore the Mach wave corresponds to 998.5. The Mach wave must be inclined at a Mach angle corresponding to the number 599.5/399 with respect to the direction of the velocity corresponding to 200.5. If θ is the direction of the velocity ($\frac{1}{2}°$ positive for CD) and μ is the Mach angle, all the waves of the same family as CD that are inclined at $+\mu$ with respect to the velocity must be inclined at $(\theta + \mu)$ with respect to xx. For CE the value of μ is the same, but it is negative (the family of the waves inclined at $-\mu$), and the direction in front is $+\theta$; therefore for the waves of the same family as CE the inclination with respect to xx is $(\theta - \mu)$ (θ for CE is $\frac{1}{2}°$ negative). If at G and F another expansion of 1° occurs, the wall must rotate 1° and the corresponding number must be 202 for GH and 198 for FI. GD is the expansion wave corresponding to the number 600/398.5; its inclination with respect to the xx-axis is $(\theta - \mu)$ because it is of the family for which μ is negative (θ in this case is positive, $\theta = 1.5°$). If at D an expansion wave of opposite direction is crossed, at DH the sum and the difference of the numbers decrease by 1; therefore it is the upper number which decreases by 1 unit.

The procedure therefore is very easy: when moving in the direction of the stream, if an expansion line is crossed which is generated by the lower wall, the upper number decreases by 1 unit, and when an expansion line is crossed that is generated by the upper wall, the lower number decreases by 1 unit (the unit corresponds to the value of deviation in degrees which the expansion line represents; in our example, the unit is 1).

For design of the expansion line that divides the two zones, the Mach angle and the direction of the stream must be determined. The Mach angle is given by the average of the sums of the two numbers corresponding to each zone, while the direction is given by the average of the differences of the two numbers of each zone minus the value of the direction corresponding to the undisturbed flow (200 in the numbering system accepted). The inclination with respect to xx-axis corresponds to an angle equal to $(\theta + \mu)$ for the expansion line generated by the lower surface and to $(\theta - \mu)$ for the lines generated by the upper surface. For design of the effusor the final Mach number or the final pressure is given, therefore, in terms of the final value; the value of the angle of expansion must be fixed. The value of the maximum angle of expansion can be determined, using the following criteria. The final Mach number is known, because, if the value of the static pressure at the ends of the effusor is given, the Mach number can be determined from the pressure ratio for isentropic transformation. For the final Mach number, a value of the angle ν of expansion from M equal to one is given (Table 2 of the appendix). Therefore, the expansion necessary to obtain the given Mach number corresponds to ν. Because the deviation of expansion occurs on the two walls, the expansion at one wall plus the expansion at the other wall must correspond to ν. Therefore, if the effusor is symmetrical, each wall must rotate at $\nu/2°$.

When the expansion line has crossed all the opposite expansion lines in the tube, it meets the opposite wall. Behind the expansion line the direction of the flow is known; in order to avoid reflection of the expansion line at the wall, it is necessary to give to the wall the same direction as the velocity behind the expansion line; therefore it is necessary to curve the wall at the point of meeting at an angle equal to the angle which the expansion wave represents. The expansion wave is generated by a deviation of expansion produced at the opposite wall, and therefore of opposite sign from the expansion which is produced at the wall considered; therefore in order to eliminate the reflection of an expansion line when the waves meet the opposite wall, the wall must decrease curvature with respect to the xx-axis. When all the opposite expansion waves are eliminated, if the effusor is symmetrical the wall is parallel to the xx-axis. In order to check the design, it is desirable to compare the end sections ratio of the effusor with the value given by equation (51) or the corresponding Table 1 in the appendix.

From the preceding considerations it is evident that the first part of the supersonic diffusor can be designed with different lengths and that the second part, in which the expansion waves meet the opposite wall, is calculated from the geometry of the first part. It is possible to concentrate all the expansion $\nu/2$ at the two points A and B (Figure 115); in this case, the effusor presents at

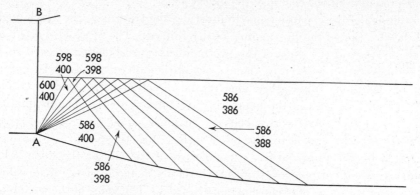

Fig. 115.   *Effusor of minimum length.*

a corner A and B, and the length of the effusor is the minimum possible. This kind of effusor is not very practical because of the precision necessary and because of the presence of the boundary layer, which probably has a more important effect in it than in the longer effusors in which the flow undergoes a gradual expansion.

If the length of the effusor is fixed, the effusor can be designed by predetermining the velocity distribution along the axis and deriving from this the shape of the walls. The system of calculation is the same (Figure 116). From

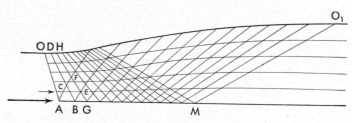

Fig. 116.   *Effusor of given length.*

the part of the wall corresponding to the minimum section O the characteristic corresponding to the first step of expansion must be designed, and from the point on the wall corresponding to the end section O_1 the characteristic of the opposite family corresponding to the last step of expansion must be designed. Two points on the axis are determined, A and M, from the intersection of the two characteristic lines. Fixing the law of variation of velocity between these two points, it is possible to determine the shape of wall. Indeed, when the velocity at $A\ B\ G\ M$ is known, from A and B the point C can be determined, and from C, the point D; from C, B, G, the points E, F, and H can be obtained, and proceeding with the same system the shape of the wall can be designed. In predetermining the velocity distribution along the axis ABM, it is necessary to remember that the expansion along the axis must be gradual and must be more gradual than, or at the maximum equal to, that for the effusor considered in Figure 115, which represents a limit.

In an analogous way a perfect effusor can be designed without symmetry with respect to the direction of the flow at the beginning of the tube. The principle is the same, and the value of the total expansion of the flow must be determined in the same manner. In Figure 117, for example, a perfect effusor

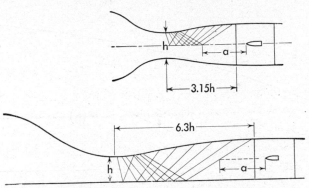

Fig. 117. *Effusor having a straight wall.*

is designed with a straight wall and a curved wall. The effusor is equivalent to one-half of a symmetrical diffuser, and therefore is twice as long for the same section as a symmetrical effusor.

If the velocity at the beginning is not uniform and the distribution of the velocity is known (direction of velocity and intensity of velocity are known at all points), the system of design does not change. Indeed, for every point of the beginning section the two numbers which define the velocity are known, and for every point it is possible to design the two characteristics which pass through the point. After choosing for simplicity the points of the section at which the Mach number corresponds to an exact number N, it is possible to design by the same criteria all the characteristic lines and the shape of the wall (Figure 118). In supersonic tunnels in which effusors for different Mach numbers must be designed, it is practical to maintain the shape of the subsonic

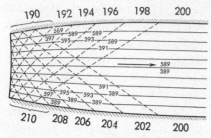

Fig. 118. *Example of design of an effusor when a nonuniform velocity distribution is given in a section (from Reference 7).*

part identical (or similar) for every diffusor and to obtain experimentally the distribution of the velocity (intensity and direction) in a cross section in the zone of the throat. The section chosen for the determination of the velocity distribution, if the determination is obtained from pressure measurements, must be in the supersonic part of the effusor in a zone in which the speed is large enough so that the instruments used will not change the value of the velocity upstream producing detached shocks; if optical systems are used, the velocity distribution can be obtained in the zone of Mach number equal to one. With the velocity distribution deter-

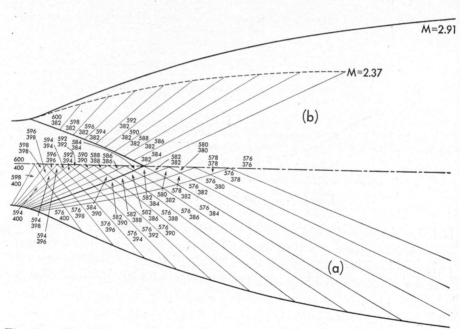

Fig. 119. *The characteristic net that permits direct design of a perfect effusor for every Mach number.*

mined experimentally it is possible to design a net of characteristic lines as in Figure 119 from which can be obtained very rapidly the shape of the effusor for every Mach number. Indeed, for every Mach number considered the last two expansion waves that must be produced by the walls are determined. The sum of the numbers corresponding to the flow after the waves have crossed the axis must be equal to the number corresponding in Table 2 of the appendix to the Mach number considered. Therefore the shape of the effusor can be determined by extending to the opposite wall every wave with the same direction that it has when it crosses the two waves determined before, and curving the wall in the point of intersection with the waves as the direction of the flow. Figure 119*b* gives an example of the construction.

Analysis of Supersonic Two-Dimensional Jets. In the study of supersonic flow it is interesting to examine the phenomena for a jet which overflows into the free air.

Consider a tank with air at high pressure and a nozzle which allows the compressed air to overflow into the free air, and assume at first that the nozzle is a subsonic nozzle with converging walls and decreasing sections from the beginning to the end. If p_0 is the pressure in the tank (Figure 120*a*) and p_a is atmospheric pressure, when p_0 is larger than p_a the air flows from the tank

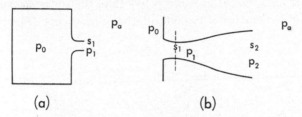

Fig. 120. *Two-dimensional jets from converging and diverging nozzles.*

into the air. If p_0/p_a is less than the critical ratio, p_0/p_* (equation 39), the pressure p_1 corresponds to the pressure p_a; and when the pressure p_0 increases, the speed at the section s_1 increases. When the pressure p_0 becomes equal to 1.886 p_a, the speed at s_1 corresponds to the speed of sound, and the pressure at p_1 corresponds to p_a. A one-dimensional transformation without losses is assumed in the effusor. If the pressure p_0 overtakes the value which at s corresponds to the speed of sound and the external pressure is equal to p_a, the flow at s_1 does not increase speed because in order to obtain supersonic velocity it is necessary to increase the section of the nozzle with respect to the section in which the speed of sound is obtained; therefore at s_1 the speed of sound still exists. If no losses occur, in order to obtain the speed of sound, the value of p_0/p_1 must be equal to 1.886. Since p_0 is larger than 1.886 p_a, the pressure p_1 must be greater than the pressure p_a; therefore the flow coming from the nozzle undergoes an expansion from the pressure p_1 to the pressure p_a, an expansion which occurs outside of the nozzle. If to the converging effusor a diverging part is added (Figure 120b), the expansion can be obtained in the nozzle, and if the pressure p_0 is high enough with respect to p_a, supersonic flow exists in the diverging part.

If at the end of the effusor (section s_2) the flow is supersonic, the flow phenomena in the tube are independent of the value of p_a, and the pressure p_2 at s_2 is a function only of the geometry of the effusor and of the pressure in the tank p_0. If the velocity is assumed constant at the sections s_1 and s_2, the pressure ratio p_0/p_1 is equal to 1.886, and the Mach number at s_2 is given by equation (51a), while the pressure p_2 is given by equation (41). Therefore there exists only one value of p_0 for which the static pressure at the end of the effusor is equal to atmospheric pressure. For values of p_0 different from this, the pressure p_2 is different from p_a; and therefore expansion or compression must occur in the flow outside of the effusor, or the flow at s_2 can no longer be supersonic.

Jet in Which the End Static Pressure Is Higher than the External Pressure. If the external pressure is less than the static pressure at the end of the effusor an expansion outside of the tube occurs (Figure 121). The

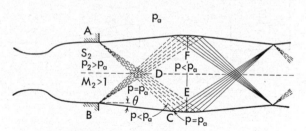

Fig. 121. *Jet from a nozzle having at the discharge static pressure higher than the external pressure.*

expansion begins at the points A and B and is transmitted in the flow by a family of expansion waves which start at A and B. If the speed in the section S_2 is uniform (the effusor is a perfect effusor), the Mach waves are plane and meet each other in the center. If the velocity is not constant and some other waves cross the section S_2, an interaction by the expansion waves generated at A and B and the waves existing at the section S_2 occurs, which can be determined. From the values of M_2 and p_2 it is possible to determine the Mach number corresponding to p_a. From the value of the expansion it is also possible to determine the value of the deviation θ of the streamline that passes through A and B (the expansion is isentropic).

All the expansion waves cross the jet; but when the two families have crossed the jet the expansion in the jet (zone DEF) is larger than at B because the flow has undergone the two families of expansion waves that are generated at B and at A, each of which corresponds to the expansion from p_2 to p_a. Therefore, the flow in the zone FDE is overexpanded with respect to the external air. When the first expansion wave meets the external flow (point C of Figure 121) it is reflected as a compression wave, because at C the pressure must be equal to p_a, and behind the expansion wave the pressure is less than p_a. When a deviation of compression occurs at C, the streamline changes shape. The same phenomenon occurs for all other expansion waves, and two families of compression waves are generated. For the same reason the compression waves are reflected as expansion waves and these expansion waves are reflected again as compression waves; therefore the waves extend theoretically to infinity. Naturally, in the practical case, at the boundary of the jet a strong turbulence is generated because along the boundary of the jet, theoretically, an infinite gradient of velocity exists, and therefore a zone of mixing flow is produced by the viscosity. The zone increases with increase of the extent of the surface of contact; therefore after a finite distance, in practical cases, the expansion waves or compression waves disappear. The

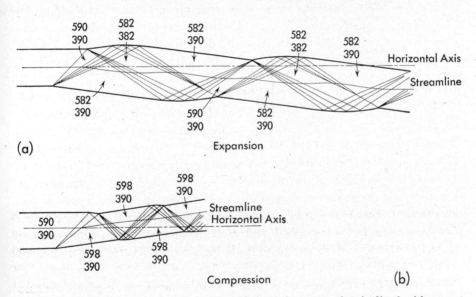

Fig. 122. *Discharge from an effusor having the end cross section inclined with respect to the direction of the stream.*

waves can be determined analytically with the characteristic theory, and the determination is also easy if the effusor is not a perfect effusor or if the effusor does not have the end section perpendicular to the end of the jet. In this case (Figure 122*a*) the expansion occurs in a different way for the two parts of the jet, and a deviation of the direction of the jet, and consequently of the thrust of the jet, occurs, a deviation that changes when the difference between p_2 and p_a changes.

Jet in Which the Static Pressure at the End of the Nozzle Is Less than the External Pressure.

When the external pressure p is greater than the static pressure corresponding to expansion in the entire effusor for a given value of the pressure in the tank (supersonic flow at the end of the diffusor), the phenomenon is more complicated because the boundary layer on the wall of the effusor has an important part in the phenomenon, and therefore a theoretical quantitative analysis is more difficult. Consider at first a perfect flow (no boundary layer) and, for simplicity, a perfect effusor. Also assume that the pressure at the end of the effusor is equal to the external pressure. In this case at the points A and B of Figure 123 no variation of pressure occurs; therefore no deviation occurs and the flow does not change physical characteristics. If the pressure p_0, and

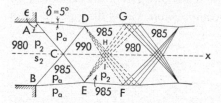

Fig. 123. *Supersonic jet from a nozzle having at the discharge static pressure lower than the external pressure.*

therefore the pressure p_2, decrease, a compression must occur in the flow, at A and B a compression which is transmitted in the flow with a shock wave (Figure 123). The intensity of the shock is determined by the Mach number in front of the shock M_2 and by the variation of pressure from p_2 to p_a; therefore with equations (121) and (125) the inclination of the shock and the deviation across the shock can be determined. The streamline AD is inclined at an angle δ with respect to the velocity at AB, and the shock wave AC at an angle ϵ. The shock waves generated at A and B cross each other at C, and at D and E meet the boundary of the jet. The waves CD and CE can be determined by considering the equilibrium in C (Chapter 4). In the zones BCE and ACD the flow has the same pressure as p_a, but in the zone CDE the pressure is higher because the flow undergoes another compression across CD and CE.

Because at DCE the pressure is greater than atmospheric, expansion occurs at D and E. The expansion is transmitted by a family of expansion waves, and from DE the phenomenon is equal to the phenomenon from BA of Figure 121 for the case in which the external pressure is less than p_2. If, in the first approximation, all transformations are supposed isentropic, the numbering system can be used and the entire determination becomes easier.

If the difference between p_a and p_2 increases, the intensity of the shocks

AC and *BC* increases and the Mach number in the zones *ACD* and *BCE* decreases. But the shocks *CD* and *CE* are shocks which correspond to the same deviation that occurs across *BC* and *AC*. The phenomenon considered is symmetrical with respect to the *x*-axis, and at *DCE* the direction of the velocity is constant and parallel to the axis of the jet; therefore when the Mach number at *ACD* decreases, a value can be obtained for which the maximum deviation is correspondingly less than the deviation which must occur across *CD*, *CE*. When this Mach number is attained, the shock *CD* is impossible and the scheme of the phenomenon must change. When the reflection of the shock at the point *C* cannot occur in the central part of the jet, a compression with one shock alone must occur there, and because at the axis (point *C*) no deviation can occur as the jet is symmetrical, there a normal shock must exist (Figure 124). At the point *A* the flow must undergo a shock fixed by the pressure p_a; therefore the shock at *A* is an inclined shock. At *ADF* the flow is supersonic because the pressure p_0 is decreased by a small quantity with respect to the case in which reflection was possible at *C*; and therefore the shocks *AD* and *BE* must be weak shocks. For equilibrium, a point *D* must be found in which a reflected shock, *DF* or *EG*, is possible for the Mach number which exists at *ADF*. The reflection is possible only if the direction of the streamlines *DI* or *EH* is not parallel to the axis but inclined at an angle with respect to the *xx*-axis, because if the streamlines are parallel to the *xx*-axis at *D* and *E*, the same conditions as those at *C* would occur, and therefore reflection would not be possible. If the streamlines *DI* and *EH* are inclined with respect to the *xx*-axis, the deviation across the reflected waves *EG* and *DF*, at *D* and *E*, is less than the deviation across *BE* and *AD*. Therefore the shocks are physically possible for the Mach number existing in *BEG* and *ADF*. Because at *D* and *E* a deviation of the streamline must occur, the strong shock of the central part must produce at *D* and *E* a deviation, and therefore there must be an inclined shock at *D* and *E*, and the shock *DCE* must be curved. The flow in *IDEH* is subsonic flow at a lower speed than in the zone *FDI* and *HEG*. The position of the point *D* or *E* depends on the equilibrium along the streamline *DI* or *EH*, and therefore on the Mach number in *BEG* and *ADF* and the deviations across the shocks *AD* and *BE*, quantities that depend on the value of the pressure p_a with respect to p_2. If the value of p_2 decreases with respect to p_a the distance between *D* and *E* increases, because the deviation across *AD* and *BE* increases while the Mach number at *ADF* or in *BEG*

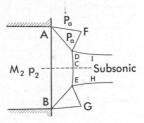

Fig. 124. *Scheme of the shock waves pattern at the discharge of a supersonic jet for the case in which reflection of the shock waves at the axis cannot exist.*

decreases; and therefore the inclination of the streamlines DI and EH with respect to the x-axis must be larger.

If the pressure p_0 continues to decrease, a value is attained for which the points D and E are coincident with A and B, and the reflected waves disappear. For this value of p_0 a strong shock occurs across the entire end section, that, when the pressure p_0 decreases, tends to become a normal shock.

If the value of the pressure p_0 in the tank decreases with respect to the value for which a normal shock occurs at AB, an equilibrium with expansion in the whole effusor (also with the hypothesis of no separation from the wall) is no longer possible, and the strong shock must move inside the effusor. In this case, if no separation occurs, the position of the shock is defined by the ratio p_a/p_0 and by the geometry of the nose. Indeed, for a given p_0, for every position of the shock the values of M_3 and p_3 (Figure 125) are known at every point in front of the shock because they are functions of the geometry of the

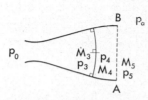

Fig. 125. *Scheme of the flow into the nozzle, assuming no boundary layer at the walls, and shock inside the nozzle*

effusor. Therefore, it is possible to determine the values of M_4 and p_4 behind the shock; no deviation is possible across the shock at the wall because perfect flow is assumed, and therefore the shock must be normal to the wall. From p_4 and M_4 and from the position of the shock, the values of p_5 and M_5 can be determined as functions of the geometry of the effusor. Because the flow is subsonic after the shock, M_5 is smaller than M_4. The position of the shock for which p_5, at B and A, is equal to p_a gives the position of equilibrium.

When p_0 decreases the shock moves upstream in the flow and decreases in intensity because the Mach number in front decreases, and the diffusion becomes more important. When the shock attains the throat of the effusor the intensity of the shock is zero, the supersonic part has disappeared, and the whole nozzle is subsonic.

The preceding considerations are developed with the hypothesis that no boundary layer exists on the walls of the effusor and that separation of the flow cannot occur on the walls. Practically, the boundary layer exists, and when the pressure p_a is greater than the pressure p_2, the boundary layer plays an important part in the flow equilibrium in the effusor. Indeed, when p_2 is greater than p_a, the boundary layer is formed in an expanding flow and no separation can be generated; so the boundary layer has only the effect of slightly changing the geometry of the effusor with no change in the physical scheme of the phenomenon. But when p_2 is less than p_a, the boundary layer, if it exists, modifies the formation of shock waves that are generated at A and B because the boundary layer produces a separation (see Chapter 4) of the stream from the wall, a separation which becomes more important when the difference between p_a and p_2 increases. The separation changes the practical geometry of the effusor, and consequently changes the scheme of the phenomenon very much, and the phenomena in the boundary layer fix the position of the shock in the effusor. Because the boundary layer depends on the variation of the pressure along the walls of the effusor, the position of the shock depends on the shape of the effusor; and the position changes if the length or the law of variation of cross section of the effusor changes. In order to understand the importance of the boundary layer it is interesting to consider the limiting case opposed to the case considered above. In the preceding considerations, an effusor was considered in which separation of the stream from the wall cannot

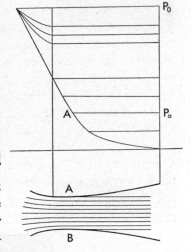

Fig. 126. *The flow pattern into a nozzle assuming that the boundary layer cannot undergo any compression.*

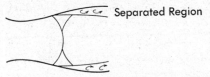

Fig. 127. *Actual scheme of the shock pattern into the nozzle in presence of boundary layer.*

occur; now an effusor will be considered in which separation is supposed to occur every time the conditions necessary to have separation exist, and therefore every time a positive pressure gradient exists in the flow. If the possibility of separation is so large that no recompression can occur in the flow without separation, the equilibrium conditions of the flow are easily determined; indeed, (Figure 126) for every value of p_0, points A and B can be found in the effusor in which the pressure is equal to the value of the external pressure p_a. At these points the flow separates from the walls, and a free jet occurs with constant pressure p_a at the boundary. If the pressure p_0 increases, the points A and B move in the direction of the stream, but no shock occurs at the jet. When the points A and B reach the end of the jet the effusor corresponds to the effusor without separation, in which p_2 is equal to p_a. Actual practical effusors are somewhere between the two limiting cases because the boundary layer can, in part, undergo a gradual compression without separation, but tends to separate if the pressure increase is of a large value. Because the phenomena are stabilized only in the boundary layer, the equilibrium condition depends on the geometry of the effusor. Generally, for small differences of pressure between p_a and p_2 the phenomena are near the case in which

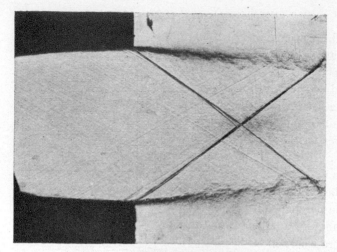

Fig. 128. *Schlieren photograph of the discharge of the flow from nozzle designed for an end Mach number of 1.92; ratio of the tank pressure to the external pressure, 5.08.*

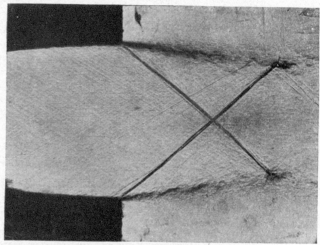

Fig. 129. *Schlieren photograph of the discharge of the flow from a nozzle designed for an end Mach number of 1.92; ratio of the tank pressure to the external pressure, 4.18.*

Fig. 130. *Schlieren photograph of the discharge of the flow from a nozzle designed for an end Mach number of 1.92; ratio of the tank pressure to the external pressure, 3.84.*

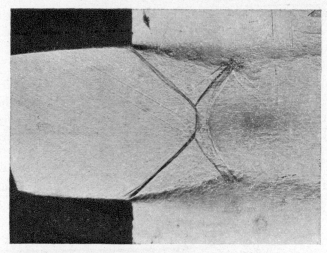

Fig. 131. *Schlieren photograph of the discharge of the flow from a nozzle designed for an end Mach number of 1.92; ratio of the tank pressure to the external pressure, 3.67.*

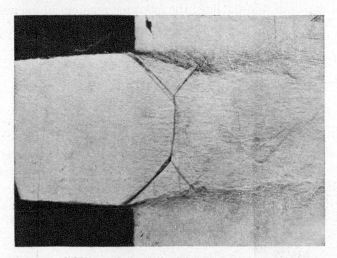

Fig. 132. *Schlieren photograph of the discharge of the flow from a nozzle designed for an end Mach number of 1.92; ratio of the tank pressure to the external pressure, 3.54.*

separation does not occur; inclined shock waves occur at the end of the jet. But if the difference in pressure increases, the separation from the wall becomes larger, and a shock with the conformation shown schematically in Figure 127 occurs, which moves into the effusor in the direction opposite to the stream when the value of p_0 decreases.

Figures 128 to 132 show some schlieren photographs of the flow in a two-dimensional open jet with different pressure ratios p_0/p_a. The jet is designed for $M = 1.92$, and the static pressure at the end of the nozzle is equal to the external pressure when $p_0/p_a = 6.91$.

Impulse of Jets at Supersonic Velocity. Consider a supersonic jet with a uniform velocity at the end of the effusor. If p_2, S_2, and ρ_2 are the pressure, the section of the jet, and the density at the end of the effusor, respectively, and V_2 is the corresponding velocity, the flow that overflows from the jet is

$$m = \rho_2 V_2 S_2.$$

If the pressure p_2 is equal to the external pressure p_a, no variation occurs at the end of the jet, and therefore the impulse of the jet is given by

$$i = \rho_2 V_2^2 S_2 = p_2 M_2^2 S_2 \gamma. \tag{309}$$

If the pressure p_2 is different from the external pressure p_a, the flow undergoes a transformation at the end of the jet. If S_a, V_a, and ρ_a are the cross section of the jet, the axial velocity, and the density of the flow, respectively, when the pressure p_a is attained in the flow, the following relation can be written:

$$\rho_2 V_2 S_2 = \rho_a V_a S_a \quad \text{(Continuity equation)} \tag{310}$$

$$(p_2 - p_a) S_2 + \rho_2 V_2^2 S_2 = \rho_a V_a^2 S_a \quad \text{(Momentum theorem)} \tag{311}$$

Substituting equation (310) in equation (311)

$$p_2 - p_a = \rho_2 V_2 (V_a - V_2). \tag{312}$$

Knowing the values of p_2, p_a, and V_2 from equation (312), the value of V_a can be determined. Equation (312) shows that the velocity V_a is less than the velocity corresponding to p_a for isentropic transformation, and as a consequence, the impulse is less when transformation occurs outside the jet than when the end pressure of the jet is equal to atmospheric pressure. The differences increase with increase of the difference $(p_2 - p_a)$.

SUPERSONIC DIFFUSORS

Perfect Diffusors. The design of supersonic turbojets and ramjets and of supersonic tunnels is directly connected with the possibility of decelerating the flow from supersonic to subsonic speed. Indeed, an air stream at low velocity is required in front of the compressor of a turbojet or of the burner of a ramjet, while in a supersonic tunnel the air must be decelerated from the high speed it has in the test chamber to the low speed required in the return or at the exit.

Deceleration of flow from high speed to low speed occurs usually with losses (part of the kinetic energy is transformed into heat instead of into potential energy) which depend on formation of shock waves and on friction. While it is possible theoretically to avoid shock losses, shock losses must exist in practical diffusors for stability reasons. These losses tend to increase with increase of Mach number, therefore it is very difficult to design high efficiency diffusors at high Mach numbers.

In the phenomena of diffusors the shape of the diffusor is very important, but a general analysis of the possibility of approaching the perfect diffusor (diffusor without shock losses) can be made independently of the shape of the diffusor. Therefore the following considerations can be applied to any kind of diffusor even though the analysis is developed by considering a two-dimensional diffusor.

A perfect diffusor can be defined as a diffusor in which no shock losses occur; therefore a diffusor in which isentropic transformation occurs outside the boundary layer. It is easy to show that a perfect diffusor is theoretically possible. For example, if a supersonic perfect effusor with gradual expansion is considered (Figure 133) and if it is assumed that the direction of the stream is reversed, an ideal diffusor will be obtained. Indeed, the flow that has the speed M_2 undergoes a compression of small entity at A and B, which is transmitted in the flow by two compression waves. The two waves end at C and D, and have the same inclination as the expansion waves that are generated at C and D and end at A and B in the corresponding effusor. At E and F

two other compression waves are produced which interfere with the preceding compression waves generated at A and B. Since for the same Mach number and direction of velocity the compression waves and expansion waves are coincident (coincident to the Mach waves because the compression or expan-

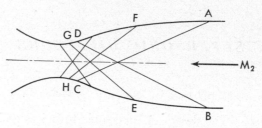

Fig. 133. *Scheme of a perfect diffusor.*

sion is infinitesimal or gradual), the scheme of the diffusor is equivalent to the scheme of the effusor; therefore at the throat a constant velocity is obtained for the flow, and the corresponding Mach number is 1. If a subsonic diffusor is connected with a supersonic diffusor, a very efficient compression must be obtained, and the efficiency must be of the same order as that for subsonic diffusors, because the only difference is the friction in the supersonic part. A difference between a perfect diffusor and a perfect effusor exists in the boundary layer because in the effusor the boundary layer undergoes an expansion, while in the diffusor the boundary layer undergoes a compression, and therefore tends to separate; but independently of the phenomena in the boundary layer a perfect diffusor cannot be realized practically for the following reasons: The aerodynamic scheme of the theoretical diffusor is found to be physically possible if supersonic flow is assumed to be established in the diffusor. When the possibility of the establishment of this supersonic flow is considered, it is found that, when the undisturbed stream in front of the diffusor attains the Mach number M_1^* (corresponding to the theoretical scheme), from lower values, the establishment is not possible. Another condition of equilibrium, with shock in the flow, is the only one possible (the diffusor does not "start"). Supersonic flow into the diffusor can be established only if the value M_1^* is attained by decreasing the speed from a much higher value of Mach number in front of the diffusor, or if the geometry of the diffusor is changed. Moreover, if supersonic flow can be established in the diffusor, this condition of equilibrium is not stable and tends to be transformed by disturbances in the flow to the other condition of equilibrium, with subsonic flow into the diffusor and with shock losses. Because disturbances usually exist in the flow, produced by the diverging part of the diffusor or by the boundary layer, a perfect diffusor cannot be realized practically.

The Two Different Equilibrium Conditions for a Diffusor (References 31 and 32). Consider a diffusor formed, for simplicity of discussion, by a reverse of a perfect effusor for final Mach number M_1^* (Figure 134). S_2 is the final section and S^* is the minimum section of the effusor and therefore the inlet section and the minimum section of the diffusor; if the velocity is constant in the sections S_2 and S^*, the ratio S_2/S^* is a function of M_1^*, and is given by equation (51a) of Chapter 1. The phenomena in the diffusor will be examined in terms of the assumption that the speed of the undisturbed stream corresponding to Mach number M_1 is attained by increasing the speed from the value zero to the value corresponding to M_1, which is the general case for airplanes and for tunnels. Later the phenomena will be examined in terms of the condition that the speed corresponding to M_1 is attained by decreasing the speed from a value higher than M_1 to the velocity corresponding to M_1. The two different conditions of attaining the Mach number M_1 correspond to two possible different equilibrium conditions for the diffusor.

For simplicity of treatment, the velocity will be considered uniform in all cross sections of the diffusor. If the velocity of the undisturbed stream increases from the value zero to a subsonic value in the diffusor, the velocity of the flow increases, and the maximum speed is attained at S^*. The mass flow which goes into the diffusor is given by the expression

$$m = S_2 \rho_2 V_2 = S_2 M_2 \sqrt{\gamma p_2 \rho_2} \tag{313}$$

where S_2 is the inlet section and V_2 the corresponding velocity; and for the continuity equation is obtained

$$S_2 M_2 \sqrt{\gamma p_2 \rho_2} = S^* M^* \sqrt{\gamma p^* \rho^*}. \tag{314}$$

If the undisturbed velocity increases or the pressure at the end of the subsonic part of the diffusor (section S_1) decreases, the speed at the minimum section increases and the mass flow that goes into the diffusor increases, as the other physical properties of the undisturbed flow do not change. If friction is not considered, the transformation that occurs in the diffusor is isentropic, and ρ^*/ρ_2, p^*/p_2, and M^*/M_2 are functions of S^*/S_2. At low velocity M^* is less than one, and in this case M_2 corresponding to the section S_2 can be less than, equal to, or greater than the Mach number of the undisturbed stream M_1, depending on the pressure at the end of the diffusor. If the value of M_2 increases, the value of M^* must also increase, because S_2/S^* does not change. The maximum value possible for M^* is one, because the diffusor is a converging subsonic diffusor (see considerations in Chapter 1); therefore M_2 has a maximum value which is fixed by the value of S^*/S_2 in terms of M^* equal to one. When M_2 has attained this value, the reduction of the pressure at the end of the diffusor (S_4) cannot change the mass flow that goes into the diffusor, and the value of M_2 remains constant. If the value of M_1 increases and M_1 is higher than the maximum value possible for M_2, a recompression must occur in front of the diffusor. The undisturbed flow is still subsonic, and the transformation is still an isentropic transformation.

If the speed of the undisturbed flow increases, the recompression in front of the diffusor increases (Figure 134), and when M_1 is equal to one, if the friction losses are not considered, the section S_1 of the stream tube is equal to S^*.

If the speed becomes supersonic and M_1 is less than M_1^*, the compression in the flow cannot be isentropic, but must occur also outside of the diffusor and with shock. Indeed, if it is assumed that no shock occurs outside of the diffusor, the stream lines must continue parallel until the beginning of the diffusor, and therefore the mass flow that goes into the diffusor must equal $M_1 S_2 \sqrt{\rho_1 p_1 \gamma}$. But the diffusor is designed for the Mach number M_1^*, which is greater than M_1, and for M_1^* at the throat, M^* is equal to one. For M_1 less than M_1^* the contraction ratio is too large for isentropic transformation. Indeed the maximum contraction ratio possible increases with the increase of the stream Mach number, and is given by equation (51a); therefore S^* is too small and no isentropic transformation is possible. If between S_2 and S^* the transformation is other than isentropic, the mass flow that passes across S^*, as will be shown later, is still less than the corresponding mass for isentropic transformation. Therefore, the mass cannot go into the diffusor, and some compression must occur outside in order to reduce the value of M at S_2.

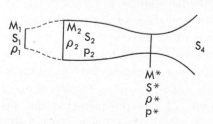

Fig. 134. *Scheme of converging diverging diffusor in subsonic flow.*

The compression that must occur in front of the diffusor can be obtained in some particular design by producing in front of the diffusor a deviation of the stream, and therefore obtaining the compression for deviation; but in the general case, the compression in front of the diffusor is produced only by an increase of back pressure, which moves upstream from the intake of the diffusor, and therefore is a compression which produces a strong shock. In the middle of the diffusor, because only an increase of pressure must occur and the direction of the stream cannot change, the compression must occur with a normal shock (Figure 135). The flow behind the strong shock is subsonic; therefore behind the shock the preceding considerations for M_2 less than one can be applied. The cross section S_1 of the stream tube at the undisturbed velocity that goes into the diffusor is less than S_2 (Figure 135); therefore the shock is extended also at the flow outside the stream tube and therefore is a curved shock, the shape of which depends on the Mach number M_1, which fixes the form of the stream line AB. The external flow also undergoes a variation of entropy; therefore an external shock drag exists. The internal flow undergoes a strong shock which is very near the normal shock for which the variation of entropy is large, and therefore the efficiency of the diffusor is low, because a large part of the kinetic energy is transformed into heat.

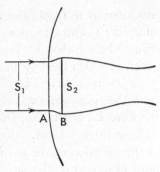

Fig. 135. *Converging diverging diffusor in supersonic flow, below the starting conditions.*

When the Mach number increases, the shock at the point A approaches the intake of the diffusor because the velocity behind the shock decreases (equation 129) and the length of the stream line AB decreases. The velocity in the front part of the diffusor is subsonic, but it is independent of the pressure at the end of the diffusor, as long as M^* is equal to one.

When the Mach number M_1^* is attained in the undisturbed stream, the scheme that gives isentropic compression is theoretically possible for the shape of the diffusor considered; therefore at first sight it seems possible that the phenomena must change and supersonic flow must occur in the diffusor, (if the pressure at the end of the diffusor is not too high). But an exact analysis shows that the theoretical scheme is not yet possible because the diffusor cannot start, and the flow into the diffusor does not have the practical possibility of changing from a subsonic to a supersonic flow. Indeed, consider the diffusor at a Mach number M_1 less than, but very near M_1^*. A strong

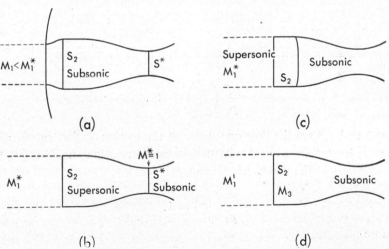

Fig. 136. *Four different conditions of the flow in the diffusor existing during the starting process.*

shock occurs in front, and the flow in the diffusor is subsonic (Figure 136a). In order to obtain a supersonic flow in all the converging parts of the diffusor (Figure 136b), when M_1 becomes equal to M_1^*, a condition of transition must occur, in which the flow in the converging part must be in part subsonic and in part supersonic. Therefore there must be a surface of separation, which from the considerations of Chapter 3 must be a shock wave that travels in the direction of the flow from the original position towards the throat of the diffusor (Figure 136c). Because the velocity in front of the shock decreases in the direction of the motion, the intensity of the shock also decreases and must disappear at the throat. Consider the condition for which the shock is at the inlet of the diffusor (Figure 136d). If this condition exists, the mass flow that must go into the diffusor is $M_1^* S_2 \sqrt{p_1 \rho_1 \gamma}$, because in front of the inlet the flow is undisturbed flow. The throat S^* is proportioned in such a way as to permit the mass $M_1^* S_2 \sqrt{\gamma p_1 \rho_1}$ to pass at M^* equal to one, and for isentropic compression. Now if shock occurs in the flow, in order that the mass $M_1^* S_2 \sqrt{\gamma p_1 \rho_1}$ may pass across the throat, the minimum section must be larger than S^*; therefore the mass $M_1^* S_2 \sqrt{\gamma p_1 \rho_1}$ cannot pass at S^*. The flow into the diffusor cannot become supersonic for the Mach number M_1^*, but only for a Mach number higher than M_1^*. The fact that the maximum value of the mass flow which crosses the throat S^* for given initial flow conditions M_2, ρ_2, p_2 occurs when the flow undergoes an isentropic transformation between M_2 and M^* can be shown in this way.

The maximum mass flow which can cross S^* occurs when the velocity is uniform and is equal to the speed of sound in the entire section S^*. If the velocity is less than or greater than the speed of sound, the section of the stream tube is larger, as well as the unit mass (equation 51a). If the transformation is not isentropic an increase of entropy must occur between S_2 and S^*. Therefore for transformation other than isentropic it is necessary that (equation 150)

$$\frac{p_s^*}{p_2} \left(\frac{\rho_2}{\rho_s^*} \right)^\gamma > 1$$

where ρ_s^* and p_s^* are the flow quantities at the section S^* for transformation other than isentropic, while for isentropic transformation the density ρ^* and the pressure p^* at the throat are given by

$$\frac{p^*}{p_2} \left(\frac{\rho_2}{\rho^*} \right)^\gamma = 1.$$

Therefore ·

$$\frac{p_s^*}{(\rho_s^*)^\gamma} > \frac{p^*}{(\rho^*)^\gamma}. \tag{315}$$

The law of conservation of energy between S_2 and S^* gives (equation 11)

$$\frac{\gamma}{\gamma - 1}\frac{p_2}{\rho_2} + \frac{1}{2}\gamma M_2^2\frac{p_2}{\rho_2} = \frac{\gamma}{\gamma - 1}\frac{p^*}{\rho^*} + \frac{1}{2}\gamma M^{*2}\frac{p^*}{\rho^*}$$

$$= \frac{\gamma}{\gamma - 1}\frac{p_s^*}{\rho_s^*} + \frac{1}{2}\gamma M_s^{*2}\frac{p_s^*}{\rho_s^*} \qquad (316)$$

and because $M^* = M_s^* = 1$

$$\frac{p^*}{\rho^*} = \frac{p_s^*}{\rho_s^*} \quad \text{or} \quad T_s^* = T^*. \qquad (317)$$

Therefore from equation (315)

$$\rho_s^* < \rho^*. \qquad (318)$$

The mass across the section S^* for isentropic transformation is given by

$$m = \rho^* S^* \sqrt{\gamma g R T^*} \qquad (319a)$$

and for the different transformation by

$$m_s = \rho_s^* S^* \sqrt{\gamma g R T_s^*}. \qquad (319b)$$

Therefore, from equations (318) and 319b), $m_s < m$. The difference between m_s and m and therefore the ratio between the minimum section $S^*{}_s$, that permits the mass m of equation 319a to pass at the density ρ_s^*, and S^*, can be expressed as a function of the losses across the shock. Indeed, from equations (319)

$$\rho^* S^* \sqrt{g\gamma R T^*} = \rho_s^* S_s^* \sqrt{g\gamma R T_s^*}$$

or from equation (317)

$$\frac{S_s^*}{S^*} = \frac{\rho^*}{\rho_s^*}.$$

But from equation (316)

$$\frac{p_0}{\rho_0} = \frac{p_{0s}}{\rho_{0s}}$$

where p_{0s} and ρ_{0s} are stagnation pressure and density corresponding to the condition behind the shock. Because

$$M^* = M_s^* = 1$$

$$\frac{\rho_s^*}{\rho^*} = \frac{\rho_{0s}}{\rho_0} = \frac{p_{0s}}{p_0}.$$

Therefore

$$\frac{S_s^*}{S^*} = \frac{p_0}{p_{0s}}. \qquad (320)$$

From equation (320) it appears that the contraction ratio S_s^*/S, necessary in a stream tube in order to pass from a Mach number M, in a section S, to every Mach number M^*, when the transformation is not isentropic, is given by

$$\frac{S_s^*}{S} = \frac{S^*}{S}\frac{p_0}{p_{0s}} \qquad (320a)$$

where S^*/S is the contraction ratio necessary for the same variation of Mach number and isentropic transformation, and p_0/p_{0s} is the ratio of the stagnation pressures at the section S and S_s^*. The ratio p_0/p_{0s} is other than one because variation of entropy occurs in the transformation between the two sections.

In order to determine the Mach number M_1, at which supersonic flow can begin to exist in the converging part of the diffusor, the following considerations can be made. When the shock travels along the diffusor, the Mach number in front of the shock decreases; therefore the losses across the shock decrease, the transformation becomes more nearly isentropic, and the value of S_s^* at the throat, required to permit the mass flow $M_1 S_2 \sqrt{\gamma p_1 \rho_1}$ to pass, decreases. Therefore if the shock can become attached at the entrance of the diffusor, continue to travel into the diffusor, and pass in the diverging part of the diffusor. The value of the Mach number of the undisturbed stream M_1' for which the diffusor can start is given by the condition of equilibrium for which the normal shock can be attached at the entrance of the diffusor. In the entire consideration a gradual change of velocity is assumed, and therefore the equations for steady phenomena are used. If this condition is possible, the diffusor becomes supersonic at the converging part. The normal shock can be attached at the diffusor (Figure 136d) when a Mach number M_3 is obtained behind the normal shock, corresponding to the mass flow $M_3 S_2 \sqrt{\gamma p_3 \rho_3}$ which can pass across S^* at $M^* = 1$. But S_2/S^* is known, and the transformation from M_3 to M^* is known, because it is practically isentropic; therefore from the value of S_2/S^* the value of M_3 can be determined (M^* is equal to one and M_3 is less than one), using equation (51a) or Table 1, column 5. From the value of M_3, using equation (129) for normal shock, or Table 3, column 2, the value of M_1' can be obtained. The differences between M_1^* and M_1' are very large and increase with the increase of M_1'. In Figure 137 are plotted the theoretical contraction ratio S^*/S_2 as a function of the Mach number M_1^* and the contraction ratio which for the same value of the undisturbed Mach number allows the diffusor to start. For comparison, some experimental data obtained for two- and three-dimensional (circular-section) diffusors of small dimension are plotted, data which agree very well with the theoretical consideration (Reference 31). The relation between the two curves is given by equation (320a), where p_0/p_{0s} corresponds to the variation of p_0 across a normal shock at the stream Mach number M_1 and is given by Table 3, column 4, or by equation (216).

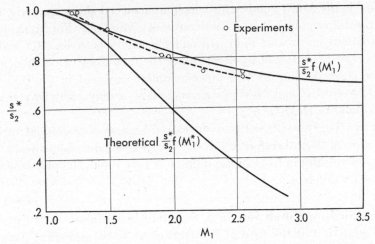

Fig. 137. *Isentropic contraction ratio and contraction ratio required by the starting conditions of a converging diverging diffusor as a function of the Mach number (from Reference 31).*

When supersonic flow is obtained in the diffusor, it is possible to reduce the value of the Mach number of the undisturbed velocity and to maintain supersonic flow in the front part, if the back pressure is not too high, because the diffusor has started. Decreasing the value of M_1 decreases the value of M^*, which for M_1' is greater than one. The minimum Mach number M_1 which it is theoretically possible to obtain with supersonic flow in the diffusor is equal to M_1^*; for M_1^* the speed of sound is attained in the throat. If the value of M_1 decreases below the value of M_1^* the value of the contraction is too high, and therefore the flow becomes subsonic in the diffusor, and a normal shock appears in front. It is evident that for M_1^* the supersonic flow in the diffusor is not stable, because every small (infinitesimal) variation of the flow condition at the end of the diffusor or in front of the inlet produces a normal shock in front of the diffusor, which is stable, and which remains also when the infinitesimal variation disappears.

The preceding considerations permit the conclusion that for a supersonic diffusor two flow conditions are possible, the condition in which a strong shock occurs in front of the diffusor and the converging part of the diffusor is subsonic, and the condition in which the flow in the converging part is supersonic. The first condition occurs always for Mach numbers less than the Mach number M_1^*, defined as the Mach number, which, in order to obtain sonic velocity at the throat with isentropic compression, requires a contraction of the stream tube as existing in the converging part of the diffusor. If the stream Mach number is attained by increasing the speed of the flow, this condition occurs also for a Mach number larger than M_1^* and less than M_1', where M_1' is the Mach number for which an attached shock can exist at the inlet of the diffusor on the basis of the continuity equation. For Mach number of the free stream greater than M_1' and for values between M_1^* and M_1', when the speed is attained by decelerating the flow from values higher than the value corresponding to M_1', supersonic flow can exist in the converging part. Between M_1^* and M_1' the supersonic flow is only partially stable and has zero stability at M_1^*.

The preceding considerations are developed by assuming gradual variation of the value of M_1; therefore using the laws for steady phenomena; if the variation of velocity in front of the diffusor is very rapid, the phenomena can be somewhat different.

The Equilibrium Condition in a Supersonic Diffusor as a Function of the Condition at the End of the Diffusor.

In the preceding paragraph the equilibrium conditions of a diffusor were considered as functions only of the geometry of the diffusor. They depend also on the conditions existing at the end of the diffusor; therefore in this paragraph the converging and the diverging parts of the diffusor will be considered together, and the different equilibrium conditions will be considered in terms of existing conditions at the end of the diffusor. Consider a diffusor (Figure 138) in which the initial

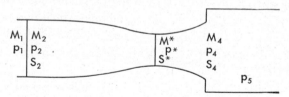

Fig. 138. *Equilibrium condition in a supersonic diffusor as a function of the end conditions.*

conditions are M_1 and p_1 and the final pressure at the end section S_4 is p_4, and assume that the value of the external pressure p_5 can be changed. Assume that the flow in the front part is supersonic. The section S^* is large, as is necessary to "start" the diffusor at a Mach number less than or equal to M_1. If p_5 is very small and is less than or equal to the pressure for which the flow can be supersonic at S_4, between S^* and S_4 the flow continues to expand, and at S_4 attains maximum velocity, which depends only on the geometry of the diffusor.

If the final pressure p_5 increases, phenomena identical to that considered for the effusors occur in the diffusor because in the zone S^*S_4 the subsonic diffusor corresponds to a supersonic effusor. Shocks occur at the ends of the section S_4, which become stronger when the back pressure increases. For higher pressure the shock becomes a normal shock at the center, with the configuration of Figure 127, and travels against the flow direction; p_4 becomes equal to p_5. Because the Mach number at which the shock occurs decreases when the shock moves upstream, when the pressure p_5 increases, the new equilibrium conditions correspond to a change of the position of the shock in the direction of the throat. When the shock occurs at the throat the Mach number at which this occurs is the minimum which it is possible to obtain in the diffusor; therefore the value of p_5 is the maximum possible. If the pressure p_5 still increases, an equilibrium is no longer possible. The shock moves in the diverging part, and the Mach number at which the shock occurs increases; therefore the final pressure decreases, because the losses are larger. The total pressure p_0' behind the shock decreases (equation 156), while the velocity at S_4 increases, as can be shown with considerations similar to those of page 185. In this case the flow cannot overflow at the pressure p_5, and the shock travels in front of the diffusor.

The position of the shock in front of the diffusor depends on the law that relates the pressure p_5 at the end of the diffusor to the mass flow. In supersonic tunnels the supersonic stream is produced by an effusor that is connected with the diffusor; therefore the shock travels into the effusor and a new equilibrium condition can be attained without change of mass flow, because the losses across the shock decrease when the shock moves upstream into the effusor (the Mach number in front of the shock decreases).

In ramjets and turbojets the pressure p_5 is a function of the mass flow at the section S_4; therefore when the shock goes outside the diffusor, the pressure p_5 decreases because the mass flow into the diffusor decreases, and it is the relation between mass flow and pressure that fixes the position of the shock.

It is important to observe that the considerations of the preceding paragraph show that the diffusor starts only if an equilibrium condition can exist with normal shock at the section S_2. Now for this condition the pressure p_5' must be less than $p_{5\text{max}}$ corresponding to the condition of normal shock at the throat; therefore the values of back pressure between p_5' and $p_{5\text{max}}$ can be obtained only by increasing the value of p_5' after the diffusor has started. As a consequence, when the shock goes outside the diffusor from the throat, the pressure recovery and the mass flow that goes inside the diffusor decrease suddenly.

For a given value of the Mach number M_1 of the undisturbed stream, the contraction ratio S^*/S_2 can be decreased if the diffusor can be started at values of M_1 greater than the value considered. Decreasing S^* the Mach number in front of the shock into the diffusor decreases, and therefore the losses decrease. A diffusor started at higher Mach number and with higher contraction ratio must be, all other conditions being equal, more efficient than a diffusor starting at the Mach number considered; therefore p_{5max} must be higher. However, the diffusor is not stable with the shock very near the throat, because if a small disturbance pushes the shock outside, the diffusor does not start again.

Efficiency of a Supersonic Diffusor. The efficiency of a supersonic diffusor depends on the losses in the shocks that occur in the supersonic part and on the losses in the boundary layer. The losses in the supersonic part depend on the form of the compression that occurs, when the speed of the flow changes from the value M_1 to a subsonic velocity. These losses are very large when the compression occurs with a strong shock, while they become zero if the compression occurs with compression waves, for which the transformation is isentropic. In order to increase the efficiency of the supersonic part, it is necessary to adopt a scheme of compression that reduces to the minimum the intensity of the shocks. If a diffusor must start at a given Mach number M_1, the maximum contraction ratio possible is lower than the theoretical, for which M^* is one; therefore a strong shock must always occur in the divergent part, which produces large losses. The losses are minimum when the shock is at the throat and increase if the value of the Mach number at the throat increases with respect to the value one; therefore the losses increase and the pressure recovery decreases with the increase of the Mach number M_1, since the corresponding value of M^* becomes larger, because of the starting conditions. The compression from M_1 to M^* can be very efficient because it occurs practically with small oblique shocks or with compression waves that give a transformation very nearly isentropic. However, in some cases the flow is carried at the intake of the diffusor in a channel; therefore a thick boundary layer can exist at the walls. In this case the compression from M_1 to M_1^* cannot be very efficient, because the boundary layer tends to separate during compression and the separation changes the shape of the stream tube and notably increases the losses.

If no boundary layer is present at the beginning of the diffusor, the shock losses, especially at low Mach number, are given chiefly by the strong shock at the throat. The efficiency of the subsonic part depends practically on the boundary layer. The boundary layer increases in thickness along the wall and, corresponding to the shock in the divergent part near the throat, tends to separate, as is considered in Chapter 4. The separation tends to produce a large wake at the walls; therefore in order to reduce the losses it is necessary to reduce the angle of divergence of the subsonic part of the diffusor, especially near the throat, to a very small value.

The efficiency η of a diffusor can be defined by the ratio of the kinetic energy recovered after the diffusion to the kinetic energy of the flow at the entrance of the diffusor. If the flow at the entrance of the diffusor has the conditions M_1, and p_1 and at the end of the diffusor the conditions are p_4, and M_4, it is possible to determine the efficiency of the diffusor in the following way: The kinetic energy of the flow at the entrance of the diffusor can be expressed as a function of the tank pressure p_0, which for an isentropic expansion to the pressure p_1 gives the Mach number M_1, and as a function of the tank pressure p_0', which for an isentropic expansion to the pressure p_4 gives the Mach number M_4. p_0' corresponds to the total head because M_4 is subsonic. The variation of kinetic energy for unit mass is

$$\frac{1}{2}\left(V_1^2 - V_1'^2\right) = \frac{1}{2}V_1^2\left(1 - \eta\right)$$

where V_1' is the velocity obtained by isentropic transformation from the pressure p_0' to p_1, but

$$\frac{V_1^2}{V_i^2} = 1 - \left(\frac{p_1}{p_0}\right)^{\frac{\gamma-1}{\gamma}} \; ; \; \frac{V_1'^2}{V_i^2} = 1 - \left(\frac{p_1}{p_0'}\right)^{\frac{\gamma-1}{\gamma}}$$

or (equation 154)

$$\frac{1}{2}\frac{V_1^2 - V_1'^2}{V_1^2} = \frac{2}{\gamma-1}\frac{1}{M_1^2}\left[\left(\frac{p_0}{p_0'}\right)^{\frac{\gamma-1}{\gamma}} - 1\right] = 1 - \eta \qquad (321)$$

and

$$\eta = 1 - \frac{2}{\gamma-1}\frac{1}{M_1^2}\left[\left(\frac{p_0}{p_0'}\right)^{\frac{\gamma-1}{\gamma}} - 1\right] \qquad (322)$$

but from equation (156)

$$\left(\frac{p_0}{p_0'}\right)^{\frac{\gamma-1}{\gamma}} = e^{\frac{\Delta S}{\gamma C_v}} . \qquad (323)$$

Therefore it is evident that the efficiency of the supersonic diffusor decreases with increase of the variation of entropy. For a diffusor with fixed geometry, which must start at the Mach number M_1, it is possible to assume that the losses in the supersonic part occur only at the throat, corresponding to strong shock, and that the other part of the compression is practically isentropic. Thus it is possible to calculate the efficiency of the supersonic part in terms of the law of normal shock (Reference 32). The values obtained in this way do not consider friction losses. In Figure 139 the value of p_0'/p_0 as calculated by using the preceding hypothesis is given for different values of Mach number in front of the diffusor for different values of the starting Mach number M_1'. It is evident that the maximum p_0'/p_0 for every Mach number in front of the diffusor corresponds to the diffusor that has $M_1 = M_1'$; therefore an optimum value of p_0'/p_0 exists for every value of M, which corresponds to the starting conditions. In Figure 140 the value of the theoretical optimum efficiency is plotted as a function of M. For comparison, the efficiency that can be obtained, assuming that the compression occurs with a normal shock at the

Mach number in front of the diffusor (divergent diffusor without the convergent part) is also plotted.

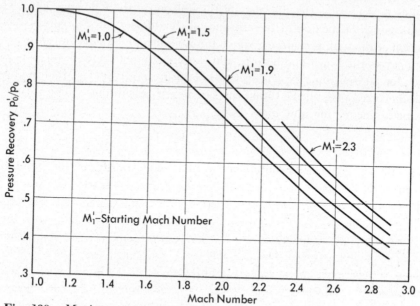

Fig. 139. *Maximum pressure recovery as a function of the Mach number for diverging converging diffusors with different contraction ratio (the friction losses are assumed zero and the compression in front of the normal shock isentropic) (from Reference 32).*

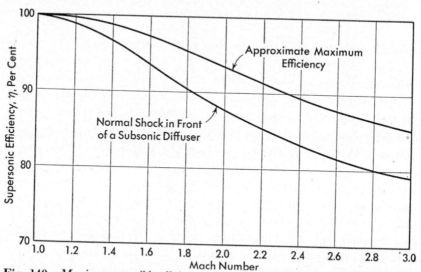

Fig. 140. *Maximum possible efficiency versus Mach number for subsonic diffusors and converging diverging diffusors with zero friction losses and isentropic compression in front of the normal shock (from Reference 32).*

Diffusors with Variable Geometry and Diffusors with External Compression. The considerations of paragraphs 2 and 4 show that one of the conditions that does not permit a supersonic diffusor to have high efficiency is the "starting" requirement. This condition limits the maximum contraction ratio of the stream tube which enters the diffusor, and therefore imposes the condition that in the diffusor the compression must occur in large part with a strong shock and with losses. While, for stability reasons, it is not possible to eliminate completely the losses produced by the strong shock in the diffusor, it is evident they can be reduced practically if the "starting" limitations are in some way eliminated or reduced.

A system which can be used to eliminate the starting limitations is that of using diffusors with variable geometry. The working scheme of a variable geometry diffusor is the following: When the diffusor is started and the converging part of the diffusor is supersonic, the geometry in the diffusor is changed and the area of the minimum section is decreased gradually. Because the corresponding Mach number at the throat decreases, the losses from strong shock are reduced and the efficiency must increase. In this way, without the necessity of attaining higher Mach numbers for starting the diffusor, a higher contraction ratio can be used, and therefore higher efficiency can be expected. An example of a variable-geometry diffusor is shown in Figure 141. The design shows the diffusor in starting position; the section B is

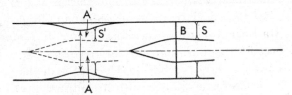

Fig. 141. *Scheme of variable geometry diffusor.*

the minimum section. When the diffusor has started and the strong shock S has passed B, the central body can be moved upstream (dotted position of the figure). The section A' has less area than the section B, and therefore the shock S' occurs for a Mach number which is less than the Mach number corresponding to S, and the losses produced by the shock are lower.

Another system for reducing the limitations of the starting conditions can be obtained in some applications by designing the diffusor with criteria different from the design criteria examined before. In the diffusor examined before, when the compression occurs outside the diffusor, it occurs with a strong shock, because this compression is produced by fixing only the value of the back pressure, and practically no deviation is accepted across the shock (Figure 142a). Because the shock is very nearly a normal shock, the losses

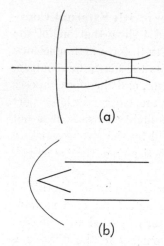

Fig. 142. *Scheme of diffusor that eliminates the formation of the normal shock in front of the diffusor for every stream condition.*

across the shock are very large and are the maximum possible. If formation of a normal shock is avoided, even when the compression is outside as in Figure 142*b*, the losses across the shock are reduced, and therefore the contraction ratio can be larger and the starting limitations reduced (equation 320*a*). A large gain in the pressure recovery can be obtained if the diffusor is so designed as to produce in every condition a part of the compression outside. If a part of the compression is produced gradually outside by deviation of the stream in front of the diffusor, the diffusor is practically equivalent to a diffusor designed for a lower Mach number. Now the diagrams of Figure 137 and Figure 139 show that the starting limitations are very important for high Mach number, but do not reduce sensibly the efficiency for Mach numbers near one; therefore reduction of the Mach number in front of the diffusor permits a notable increase in efficiency.

In Figure 143 a scheme of a diffusor having a part of the compression outside is shown. The Mach number of the undisturbed flow is equal to 2.00, but along the surface *OB* a deviation is produced, and in front of the intake of the diffusor the Mach number is 1.4; therefore the inlet *BCE* must be designed for $M = 1.4$. Because the maximum pressure recovery p_0'/p_0 for a diffusor with a contraction ratio corresponding to $M = 1.4$ is of the order of 99 per cent (Figure 139) while for a diffusor with a contraction ratio corresponding to conditions for $M = 2.0$ is of the order of 83 per cent, the diffusor considered permits a large gain in pressure recovery.

In the diffusor with external compression the contraction ratio can approach practically the theoretical contraction ratio because the external compression can be extended very near the Mach number 1.0 and there no limitations for starting conditions exist. Because the compression occurs in front of the diffusor, also the flow outside the diffusor undergoes a compression that occurs across a shock wave (shock equals *AF* in Figure 143). The shock wave, that is eliminated by expansion waves produced along *CE*, produces a drag (because it produces an increase in entropy), which will increase if the external compression increases. The drag depends on the intensity and extent of the shock wave *AF*. In order to reduce the drag to a minimum for a given value of external compression, and therefore for a given strength of the shock at *A*, it is necessary to reduce to a minimum the extent of the shock *AF*, and to decrease as fast as possible the intensity of the shock AF with a strong expansion along CE. Therefore the distance CC_1 must be the shortest possible. In practical cases a compromise between increase in efficiency and increase in

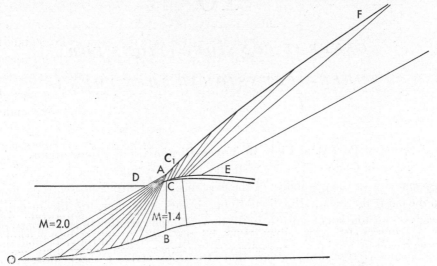

Fig. 143. *Scheme of diffusor having external compression.*

drag must be found. It is interesting to observe that for a given diffusor with external compression the variation of pressure recovery as a function of Mach number is more gradual than for a diffusor with only internal compression. Indeed by increasing the flight Mach number the stream tube that enters the diffusor increases; therefore the contraction ratio of the diffusor increases when the Mach number increases. Figure 144 shows the mechanism of the increase of the mass flow. In the diffusor considered, for simplicity of discussion, the external compression is produced by a finite deviation. If the diffusor is a two-dimensional diffusor, the stream line that passes through B and that defines the stream tube must be parallel to OC. Because when the Mach number increases, the shock in front becomes more inclined and

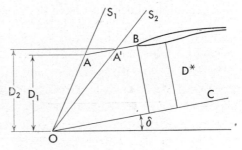

Fig. 144. *Machanism of the variation of the dimensions of stream tube that go inside the diffusor with external compression when the stream Mach numbers changes.*

moves from S_1 to S_2, the height of the stream tube D increases; therefore the corresponding contraction ratio D/D^* increases. For three-dimensional diffusors the phenomena are analogous.

GENERAL CONSIDERATIONS FOR

THREE-DIMENSIONAL PHENOMENA

Existence of Potential Flow in Three-Dimensional Phenomena. As was shown in Chapter 1, the possibility of the existence of potential flow is associated with the possibility of the existence of a continuous isentropic flow in the entire flow field. If a discontinuity occurs in the flow, the discontinuity produces a variation of entropy in the flow, and the variation must be constant in order to obtain again isentropic flow, with different entropy, behind the discontinuity. Because the variation of entropy across a shock for a given Mach number in front of the shock is a function only of the inclination of the shock, the condition of irrotationality for two-dimensional phenomena with shock must correspond to a plane shock. When three-dimensional flow is considered, other forms of shock fronts are compatible with the condition of potential flow behind the shock. Indeed, if the flow in front of a shock is uniform, in order to obtain the same variation of entropy the intersection of the shock front with the planes which contain the vectorial velocity before and behind the shock must have the same inclination with respect to the undis-

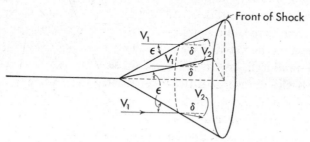

Fig. 145. *Axial symmetrical conical shock.*

turbed velocity at all points on the shock front. This condition is satisfied, for example, if the front of the shock is a cone of revolution (Figure 145), with its axis parallel to the direction of undisturbed velocity, or by many other shock forms as, for example, a shock derived by the combination of a conical shock and a plane shock. Because the shock cannot extend with the same intensity to infinity (this condition corresponds to a body of infinite drag), in all aerodynamic phenomena a zone of rotational flow exists. Sometimes the zone in which the flow is rotational is outside the zone, which must be analyzed in order to obtain the required information, and therefore the potential flow theory must be used. However, it is necessary to remember that the flow analyzed in aerodynamic problems is, generally rotational, and the hypothesis of the existence of potential flow is not exact. This hypothesis can be accepted as a good approximation in many three-dimensional problems, as the variation of entropy across the shock is generally small, because the bodies analyzed usually have small shock drag (equivalent to a small variation of entropy). When the shock has a large change of intensity in the field considered the accuracy of the hypothesis decreases. If that occurs, it becomes necessary to use the analytical expressions for rotational flow. In this case the analytical solution of the problems, which is more complicated, has been found only for a few particular cases.

The Equations of Potential Flow. In three-dimensional flow problems three different types of coordinate systems are usually used: the Cartesian coordinate, the polar coordinate, and the cylindrical coordinate systems. The choice of the coordinate system usually depends on the facility of expressing analytically the boundary conditions. The Cartesian coordinate system is usually used in general three-dimensional phenomena, while the polar coordinate system and the cylindrical coordinate system are particularly useful for conical phenomena or for phenomena with some symmetry, such as for bodies of revolution. The expressions of the potential flow motion are different for the three types of coordinate systems. The differential equation of potential flow in Cartesian coordinates can be obtained in the same way as for two-dimensional flow, from the continuity equation (equation 2), from Euler's equation (equation 1c), and from the hypothesis that the rotation components in the flow (equation 13) are zero. Using the same transformation as in Chapter 2 (equations 53 and 54), the following equation is obtained:

$$\frac{\partial u}{\partial x}\left(1 - \frac{u^2}{a^2}\right) + \frac{\partial v}{\partial y}\left(1 - \frac{v^2}{a^2}\right) + \frac{\partial w}{\partial z}\left(1 - \frac{w^2}{a^2}\right) - 2\,\frac{\partial u}{\partial y}\frac{uv}{a^2}$$
$$- 2\,\frac{\partial u}{\partial z}\frac{uw}{a^2} - 2\,\frac{\partial v}{\partial z}\frac{vw}{a^2} = 0 \qquad (324)$$

or if ϕ is the potential function expressed by

$$u = \frac{\partial \phi}{\partial x}; \ v = \frac{\partial \phi}{\partial y}; \ w = \frac{\partial \phi}{\partial z} \qquad (325)$$

then

$$\frac{\partial^2 \phi}{\partial x^2}\left(1 - \frac{u^2}{a^2}\right) + \frac{\partial^2 \phi}{\partial y^2}\left(1 - \frac{v^2}{a^2}\right) + \frac{\partial^2 \phi}{\partial z^2}\left(1 - \frac{w^2}{a^2}\right) - \frac{2uv}{a^2}\frac{\partial^2 \phi}{\partial x \partial y}$$

$$- \frac{2uw}{a^2}\frac{\partial^2 \phi}{\partial x \partial z} - \frac{2vw}{a^2}\frac{\partial^2 \phi}{\partial y \partial z} = 0 \qquad (326)$$

Cartesian coord.

and

$$\left.\begin{aligned}
du &= \frac{\partial^2 \phi}{\partial x^2}\,dx + \frac{\partial^2 \phi}{\partial y \partial x}\,dy + \frac{\partial^2 \phi}{\partial x \partial z}\,dz \\[4pt]
dv &= \frac{\partial^2 \phi}{\partial x \partial y}\,dx + \frac{\partial^2 \phi}{\partial y^2}\,dy + \frac{\partial^2 \phi}{\partial y \partial z}\,dz \\[4pt]
dw &= \frac{\partial^2 \phi}{\partial x \partial z}\,dx + \frac{\partial^2 \phi}{\partial y \partial z}\,dy + \frac{\partial^2 \phi}{\partial z^2}\,dz.
\end{aligned}\right\} \qquad (327)$$

If the polar coordinate system is used and r, η, and φ are the symbols of the independent variables which define the position of every point P (Figure 146),

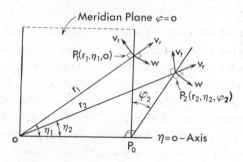

oP_2P_0–Meridian Plane φ_2= Const.

Fig. 146. *Polar coordinates.*

the velocity at the point P can be resolved into a component parallel to r,

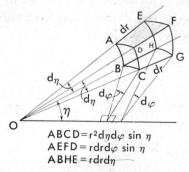

$ABCD = r^2 d\eta d\varphi \sin \eta$
$AEFD = rdrd\varphi \sin \eta$
$ABHE = rdrd\eta$

Fig. 147. *Elementary volume in polar coordinates.*

v_r, a component in the meridian plane $\varphi =$ constant, perpendicular to r, v_t, and a component w perpendicular to the plane $\varphi =$ constant. In this case, if ρ is the density of the flow, the continuity equation in polar coordinates can be obtained by considering that the mass flow in the elementary volume A, B, C, D, E, F, G, H, (Figure 147) must be independent of time. Evaluating the differences of mass flow which overflows from the opposite surfaces of the elementary volume in a unit time, the sum of the differences must be equal to zero, and therefore the continuity equation becomes

$$\frac{\partial}{\partial r}(\rho r^2 \sin \eta v_r) + \frac{\partial}{\partial \varphi}(\rho r w) + \frac{\partial}{\partial \eta}(\rho r \sin \eta v_t) = 0 \qquad (328)$$

or

$$2 \sin \eta v_r + r \sin \eta v_r \frac{1}{\rho}\frac{\partial \rho}{\partial r} + r \sin \eta \frac{\partial v_r}{\partial r} + \frac{\partial w}{\partial \varphi} + w \frac{1}{\rho}\frac{\partial \rho}{\partial \varphi}$$

$$+ v_t \cos \eta + v_t \sin \eta \frac{\partial \rho}{\partial \eta}\frac{1}{\rho} + \sin \eta \frac{\partial v_t}{\partial \eta} = 0. \qquad (329)$$

The conservation of energy equation gives

$$\frac{\gamma}{\gamma - 1}\frac{p}{\rho} + \frac{1}{2}(v_r^2 + v_t^2 + w^2) = \text{constant} \qquad (330)$$

from which, differentiating with respect to φ, η, and r, and substituting a^2 for $dp/d\rho$,

$$\left.\begin{aligned}
\frac{1}{\rho}\frac{\partial \rho}{\partial \varphi} &= -\frac{1}{a^2}\left(v_r \frac{\partial v_r}{\partial \varphi} + v_t \frac{\partial v_t}{\partial \varphi} + w \frac{\partial w}{\partial \varphi}\right) \\[2mm]
\frac{1}{\rho}\frac{\partial \rho}{\partial \eta} &= -\frac{1}{a^2}\left(v_r \frac{\partial v_r}{\partial \eta} + v_t \frac{\partial v_t}{\partial \eta} + w \frac{\partial w}{\partial \eta}\right) \\[2mm]
\frac{1}{\rho}\frac{\partial \rho}{\partial r} &= -\frac{1}{a^2}\left(v_r \frac{\partial v_r}{\partial r} + v_t \frac{\partial v_t}{\partial r} + w \frac{\partial w}{\partial r}\right).
\end{aligned}\right\} \qquad (331)$$

If a velocity potential exists, the components v_r, v_t, and w are defined by

$$\left.\begin{aligned}
v_r &= \frac{\partial \phi}{\partial r}; \quad \frac{\partial v_r}{\partial \varphi} = \frac{\partial^2 \phi}{\partial r \partial \varphi}; \quad \frac{\partial v_r}{\partial \eta} = \frac{\partial^2 \phi}{\partial r \partial \eta} \\[2mm]
v_t &= \frac{\partial \phi}{r \partial \eta}; \quad \frac{\partial v_t}{\partial \varphi} = \frac{\partial^2 \phi}{r \partial \eta \partial \varphi}; \quad \frac{\partial v_t}{\partial r} = \frac{\partial^2 \phi}{r \partial r \partial \eta} - \frac{1}{r^2}\frac{\partial \phi}{\partial \eta} \\[2mm]
w &= \frac{1}{r \sin \eta}\frac{\partial \phi}{\partial \varphi}; \quad \frac{dw}{\partial r} = \frac{1}{r \sin \eta}\frac{\partial^2 \phi}{\partial r \partial \varphi} - \frac{1}{r^2 \sin \eta}\frac{\partial \phi}{\partial \varphi} \\[2mm]
\frac{\partial w}{\partial \eta} &= \frac{1}{r \sin \eta}\frac{\partial^2 \phi}{\partial \eta \partial \varphi} - \frac{\cos \eta}{r \sin^2 \eta}\frac{\partial \phi}{\partial \varphi}.
\end{aligned}\right\} \qquad (332)$$

Substituting equations (331) and (332) in equation (329), the following differential equation is obtained:

$$\left(1 - \frac{w^2}{a^2}\right)\frac{\partial w}{\partial \varphi} + \sin \eta \left(1 - \frac{v_t^2}{a^2}\right)\frac{\partial v_t}{\partial \eta} + r \sin \eta \frac{\partial v_r}{\partial r}\left(1 - \frac{v_r^2}{a^2}\right)$$

$$- \frac{2 v_t w}{a^2}\frac{\partial v_t}{\partial \varphi} - 2r \sin \eta \frac{v_r v_t}{a^2}\frac{\partial v_t}{\partial r} - 2r \sin \eta \frac{v_r w}{a^2}\frac{\partial w}{\partial r}$$

$$+ \sin \eta v_r \left(2 + \frac{v_t^2 + w^2}{a^2}\right) + \cos \eta v_t \left(1 + \frac{w^2}{a^2}\right) = 0 \qquad (333)$$

or

$$\left(1 - \frac{w^2}{a^2}\right)\frac{\partial^2\phi}{\partial\varphi^2} + \sin^2\eta\left(1 - \frac{v_t^2}{a^2}\right)\frac{\partial^2\phi}{\partial^2\eta} + r^2\sin^2\eta\,\frac{\partial^2\phi}{\partial r^2}\left(1 - \frac{v_r^2}{a^2}\right)$$

$$- \frac{2v_t w}{a^2}\sin\eta\,\frac{\partial^2\phi}{\partial\eta\partial\varphi} - 2r\sin^2\eta\,\frac{v_r v_t}{a^2}\frac{\partial^2\phi}{\partial\eta\partial r} - \frac{2v_r w}{a^2}r\sin\eta\,\frac{\partial^2\phi}{\partial r\partial\varphi}$$

$$+ r\sin^2\eta\,\frac{\partial\phi}{\partial r}\left(2 + \frac{v_t^2 + w^2}{a^2}\right) + \cos\eta\sin\eta\,\frac{\partial\phi}{\partial\eta}\left(1 + \frac{w^2}{a^2}\right) = 0. \quad (333a)$$

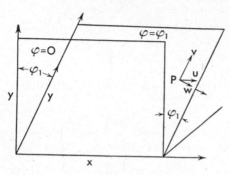

Fig. 148. *Cylindrical coordinates.*

The equation is equivalent to equation (326), but in polar coordinates.

If cylindrical coordinates are assumed, the independent variables are x, y, and φ (Figure 148), and the potential function is

$$\phi = \phi\,(x, y, \varphi).$$

The components of the velocity are u, v, in every meridian plane, and w, in a direction perpendicular to the meridian plane, and are defined by the following expressions:

$$u = \frac{\partial\phi}{\partial x}; \qquad v = \frac{\partial\phi}{\partial y}; \qquad w = \frac{\partial\phi}{y\partial\varphi}. \quad (334)$$

The differential equation of the potential flow can be obtained from equations (1c) and (2) and assumes the following form in cylindrical coordinates:

$$\left(1 - \frac{u^2}{a^2}\right)\frac{\partial^2\phi}{\partial x^2} + \left(1 - \frac{v^2}{a^2}\right)\frac{\partial^2\phi}{\partial y^2} + \left(1 - \frac{w^2}{a^2}\right)\frac{1}{y^2}\frac{\partial^2\phi}{\partial\varphi^2} - \frac{2uv}{a^2}\frac{\partial^2\phi}{\partial x\partial y}$$

$$- \frac{2uw}{a^2}\frac{1}{y}\frac{\partial^2\phi}{\partial\varphi\partial x} - \frac{2uw}{a^2}\frac{1}{y}\frac{\partial^2\phi}{\partial\varphi\partial y} + \frac{v}{y}\left(1 + \frac{w^2}{a^2}\right) = 0. \quad (335)$$

In practical applications it is necessary to find a solution of either equation (326), (333), or (335) which represents a flow that satisfies the boundary conditions. Generally the solution is very difficult to determine; therefore some simplifying hypotheses are usually accepted which permit elimination of some of the terms of equations (326), (333), or (335), thus permitting their solution. The simplifying hypotheses are usually based on the assumption that the variations of some of the components of the velocity due to the flow phenomenon are small in comparison with the speed of sound a. The simplified equation permits simpler determination of an analytical solution of flow problem, thus permitting in many cases, the determination of the flow for boundary conditions interesting to aeronautical problems.

The Equation of Potential Flow in the Approximate Form. In the differential equation of potential flow all coefficients of the second derivative of the potential function are functions of the ratio of the velocity components to the speed of sound. Generally the aerodynamic problem which must be investigated is connected with the flow that wets a body of good aerodynamic shape. Therefore the deviation of the streamline from the direction of the undisturbed flow is small, and the variations of the velocity components with respect to the undisturbed velocity components are small. In order to obtain simpler equations of motion, the variations of the velocity components due to the presence of the body will be considered so small and gradual that the second and higher powers of the disturbance velocity components u_2, v_2, w_2, and their derivatives may be considered negligible (see Chapter 2, last paragraph) compared to the first and zero power terms. In this case equations (326), (333) and (335) can be transformed. To accomplish the transformation it is useful to divide the velocity components into two parts, the components of of the undisturbed stream, u_1 v_1, and w_1 that are known, and the components of the disturbance velocity u_2, v_2, and w_2 which must be determined. If the velocity of the undisturbed stream is in the direction of the x-axis, it is possible to write:

$$u_1 = V_1; \qquad v_1 = 0; \qquad w_1 = 0$$

or

$$\phi_1 = V_1 x.$$

Therefore

$$\left. \begin{array}{l} u = V_1 + u_2 = V_1 + \dfrac{\partial \phi_2}{\partial x} \\[2mm] V = + v_2 = \dfrac{\partial \phi_2}{\partial y}; \qquad w = + w_2 = \dfrac{\partial \phi_2}{\partial z} \end{array} \right\} \tag{336}$$

In the approximation accepted the values of the order of $u_2{}^2/a^2$, $v_2{}^2/a^2$, and $w_2{}^2/a^2$ are neglected, and equation (326) becomes much more simple because many terms disappear. As was shown in Chapter 2, the terms $(u_2 V_1/a^2)$ $(\partial^2\phi/\partial x^2)$ and the like can also be considered of the order of magnitude of $u_2{}^2/a^2$, and therefore equation (326) becomes

$$\left(1 - \frac{V_1{}^2}{a^2}\right) \frac{\partial^2\phi_2}{\partial x^2} + \frac{\partial^2\phi_2}{\partial y^2} + \frac{\partial^2\phi_2}{\partial z^2} = 0. \tag{337}$$

If a is the value of the speed of sound at the point P considered, using the energy equation (equation 5), it is possible to write with the approximation accepted (equation 97):

$$a^2 = a_1{}^2 - (\gamma - 1)(u V_1). \tag{338}$$

Therefore V_1/a becomes in equation (337) equivalent to the Mach number of the undisturbed stream, M_1. The potential flow equation for a phenomenon in which the disturbances can be considered small becomes

$$(1 - M_1{}^2) \frac{\partial^2 \phi}{\partial x^2} + \frac{\partial^2 \phi}{\partial y^2} + \frac{\partial^2 \phi}{\partial z^2} = 0. \tag{339}$$

If ϕ_2 is the potential function that gives the disturbance velocity $\phi = \phi_1 + \phi_2$; therefore

$$(1 - M_1{}^2) \frac{\partial^2 \phi_2}{\partial x^2} + \frac{\partial^2 \phi_2}{\partial y^2} + \frac{\partial^2 \phi_2}{\partial z^2} = 0. \tag{339a}$$

The function ϕ in equation (339) represents a velocity potential. However with the approximation accepted of small disturbances, equation (339) is also valid if ϕ denotes an acceleration potential, one of the velocity components u, v, w, or a property of the state of the fluid, such as pressure or enthalpy. This can be shown if equation (339) is differentiated with respect to time, with respect to the x, y, z coordinates, or by using simple transformations, if the state of the fluids is considered. Equation (339) cannot be used in the range of $M_1 = 1$, because in this range the first term of the equation becomes small and of the same order of magnitude as the terms neglected.

The cylindrical coordinate system is usually used when the body considered has axial symmetry. In this case the x-axis is taken coincident with the axis of the body, and the meridian plane $\varphi = 0$ is assumed coincident with the plane that contains the undisturbed velocity. Therefore

$$\begin{aligned} u &= u_1 + u_2 \\ v &= v_1 + v_2 \\ w &= w_1 + w_2 \end{aligned} \tag{340}$$

where $u_1 = V_1 \cos \alpha$, $v_1 = V_1 \sin \alpha \cos \varphi$, and $w_1 = -V_1 \sin \alpha \sin \varphi$ (α being the inclination between the x-axis and the direction of velocity). In general, the hypothesis of small disturbances can be accepted only when the angle of attack α of the body is small; therefore in this consideration $\sin \alpha$ can be considered as very small and $\cos \alpha$ can be considered as equal to one; therefore v^2 and w^2 can be considered small in comparison to a^2. In this case equation (335) can be simplified and becomes

$$(1 - M_1{}^2) \frac{\partial^2 \phi}{\partial x^2} + \frac{\partial^2 \phi}{\partial y^2} + \frac{1}{y^2} \frac{\partial^2 \phi}{\partial \varphi^2} + \frac{1}{y} \frac{\partial \phi}{\partial y} = 0. \tag{341}$$

Equations (339) and (341), which are all approximate expressions of the flow, are not exactly equivalent, because the values of the terms neglected are not the same, therefore they do not give exactly the same degree of approximation if applied to the same phenomenon.

Preliminary Considerations on the Solution of the Differential Equations of Motion in Approximate Form.   Equations of Sinks, Sources, and Doublets.   In the aerodynamics of incompressible flow in order to represent analytically the flow field around moving bodies, schemes derived from electrodynamics are used.   In this way, by applying the analytical treatment developed for some electric phenomena to the corresponding aerodynamic phenomena, solutions of given aerodynamic problems are found.   Now the same schemes, called in aerodynamics *sources*, *sinks*, and *doublets*, can also be used in compressible flow with some modification of the analytical expressions, when the hypothesis of small disturbances is accepted.   Indeed the flow field produced by sources, sinks, or doublets conforms to the differential equations of the flow in the approximate form (References 33 and 34).   If superimpositions and distributions of sources, sinks and doublets are considered, the flow field produced still corresponds to a solution of the flow motion equations in the approximate form because the coefficients of the differential equation (339) are constant.   Therefore the problem of finding a solution when the hypothesis of small disturbances is accepted corresponds to the problem of finding a distribution of sources, sinks, or doublets which can generate a flow which will satisfy the boundary conditions that define the problem.   The demonstration that the sources, sinks, or doublets conform to the differential equation of motion in the approximate form can be obtained in the following way. Considering equation (339) it is possible to write the equation in this form:

$$(a^2 - V_1^2) \frac{\partial^2 \phi}{\partial x^2} + a^2 \frac{\partial^2 \phi}{\partial y^2} + a^2 \frac{\partial^2 \phi}{\partial z^2} = 0. \tag{342}$$

Considering fixed spatial coordinates in place of coordinates moving with the body, because the phenomenon analyzed is steady,

$$x = x_1 + V_1 t.$$

Therefore

$$\frac{dx}{dt} = V_1$$

and

$$\frac{\partial \phi}{\partial t} = \frac{\partial \phi}{\partial x} V_1$$

and equation (342) becomes

$$\frac{\partial^2 \phi}{\partial t^2} = a^2 \left[\frac{\partial^2 \phi}{\partial x^2} + \frac{\partial^2 \phi}{\partial y^2} + \frac{\partial^2 \phi}{\partial z^2} \right]. \tag{342a}$$

Equation (342) has, among others, solutions of the form

$$\phi = f_1 (x - at) + f_2 (x + at) \tag{343}$$

where f_1 and f_2 are arbitrary functions of the given argument.   Equation (343) represents expanding plane wave fronts which proceed with the velocity of sound (Reference 35).

If the expansion which proceeds with spherical symmetry from a point is considered (source or sink), and

$$r = \sqrt{x^2 + y^2 + z^2}$$

from equation (333a) it is possible to obtain (because $v_r = \partial r/\partial t$ and the derivation with respect to φ and η is zero with existing spherical symmetry)

$$\frac{\partial^2 \phi}{\partial t^2} = a^2 \left[\frac{\partial^2 \phi}{\partial r^2} + \frac{2}{r} \frac{\partial \phi}{\partial r} \right] \tag{344}$$

and therefore

$$\phi = -\frac{1}{r} f(at - r) \tag{345}$$

as can be verified by differentiation. If an expansion from a point which proceeds with circular symmetry in a plane is considered and

$$r = \sqrt{x^2 + y^2}$$

from equation (341), putting $V_1 = dx/dt$

$$\frac{\partial^2 \phi}{\partial t^2} = a^2 \left[\frac{\partial^2 \phi}{\partial x^2} + \frac{\partial^2 \phi}{\partial y^2} + \frac{1}{y} \frac{\partial \phi}{\partial y} \right] \tag{346}$$

and the function ϕ is still given by equation (345), as can be verified by differentiation; therefore equation (346) represents the motion of a two-dimensional circular wave diverging from a point in the axis $y = 0$.

The function f is again an arbitrary function of the argument $\xi = (at - r)$. If $f(\xi)$ is constant, equation (345) gives the usual source potential. If $f(\xi)$ is zero for all negative values of ξ and other than zero for $\xi > 0$, the potential ϕ represents the potential of a disturbance that starts at the time zero at the origin (r equal to zero) and is at

$$r = at$$

at the time t; therefore it represents an expansion which moves with the velocity of sound. The radial velocity changes with r and becomes infinity at the origin.

$$\frac{\partial \phi}{\partial r} = \frac{1}{r^2} f(\xi) + \frac{1}{r} f'(\xi). \tag{347}$$

Because the hypothesis of small variations of velocity is assumed, the solution cannot be used near the origin, but only in those regions in which, for the given intensity of the source, the velocity is small.

For aerodynamic applications it is interesting to study a source system in motion with constant velocity. Consider a row of sources placed on the

x-axis which begin to flow at different times and move at constant speed. The rule will be accepted that, if the position of the sources is x, and the time at which every source begins is t, the relation must exist that

$$-\frac{\partial x}{\partial t} = u_1 = \text{constant.} \tag{348}$$

For this condition, if the first source is at $(x = 0)$ and begins at time $(t = 0)$, a source at the position x_1 begins to flow at the time t_1, given by

$$-\frac{x_1}{u_1} = t_1. \tag{348a}$$

In this case the potential at any point x, y, z, at the time t for all sources at the position x_1 is given by

$$\phi = -\int_{-\infty}^{t} \frac{f\left[a(t - t_1) - r\right] dt_1}{r} \tag{349}$$

where

$$r = \sqrt{(x - x_1)^2 + y^2 + z^2}. \tag{350}$$

Placing

$$\xi = a(t - t_1) - r, \text{ and } x_1 = -u_1 t_1 \tag{351}$$

from equations (350) and (351) an expression in t_1 can be obtained:

$$t_1^2 (a^2 - u_1^2) + 2t_1 \left[a (\xi - at) - u_1 x\right] + (\xi - at)^2$$
$$- (x^2 + y^2 + z^2) = 0 \tag{352}$$

that gives on differentiation

$$dt_1 = \frac{d\xi \left[\xi - a (t - t_1)\right]}{a (\xi - at) - u_1 x + (a^2 - u_1^2) t_1}. \tag{352a}$$

Using in equation (352a) the solution of the quadratic equation (352) that gives the value of t_1 and arranging the terms conveniently, equation (349) becomes

$$\phi = -\int_0^{\xi_1} \frac{f(\xi) \, d\xi}{\sqrt{\left(x + u_1 t - \dfrac{u_1}{a} \xi\right)^2 + \left(1 - \dfrac{u_1^2}{a^2}\right)(y^2 + z^2)}}. \tag{353}$$

If the coordinate system is assumed to be moving with the sources system, the new coordinate x is given by $x + u_1 t$, and if the variable $\xi' = u_1 \xi / a$ is used instead of ξ, the equation (354) becomes

$$\phi = -\int_0^{\xi'_1} \frac{f(\xi') \, d\xi'}{\sqrt{(x_1 - \xi')^2 + \left(1 - \dfrac{u_1^2}{a^2}\right)(y_1^2 + z_1^2)}}. \tag{354}$$

The potential ϕ satisfies the equation of motion. Therefore, in order to determine the solution of a given problem it is necessary to find a source distribution $f(\xi')$ which produces a flow that satisfies the boundary conditions. If the sources placed along the x-axis are two-dimensional sources defined by equation (346), equation (351) has the form

$$\phi = - \int_0^{\xi_1} \frac{f(\xi)\, d\xi}{\sqrt{(x-\xi)^2 + \left(1 - \frac{u_1^2}{a^2}\right) y^2}}. \tag{354a}$$

The value of the integral of equation (354) can be imaginary, because u_1^2/a^2 is larger than one; therefore the rule must be held that it is possible to integrate only over the real values of the integrand, and zero is substituted for the imaginary values. The value of the upper limit ξ_1 of the integral represents the end of the source phenomenon given by the expression $f(\xi)$; but it is necessary to remember that the sources which correspond to values of ξ for which the expression under the root is negative must not be considered. Physically, the exclusion means that the source can influence the flow only in the Mach cone that starts from the source.

The zone of the fore cone must also be excluded from the integration, since no waves of the source system get into it. Therefore it is necessary to consider only values corresponding to positive values of $(x - \xi)$. If a point P (Figure 149) in the Mach cone is considered, it is found that in supersonic flow (differing from subsonic flow) the point P is reached by waves produced from the two sides, A and B; therefore in equation (354) a factor of 2 must be added, that can be considered incorporated in the expression $f(\xi)$.

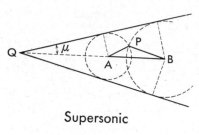

Supersonic

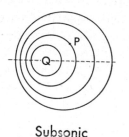

Subsonic

Fig. 149. *Supersonic and subsonic source.*

When lifting surfaces are considered, it is usually necessary to pass from the use of sources to the use of doublets. The doublet is composed of a sink and a source of the same intensity and of opposite sign, placed at a distance h from each other. If the distance h decreases and tends to become zero, and the intensity Q of the source increases in a manner such that the product Qh does not change, the limit of Qh as h becomes zero represents a doublet. The use of doublets permits determination of expressions for lifting surfaces as in the subsonic case. The energy equation with the hypothesis of small disturbances gives

$$\int_p^{p_1} \frac{dp}{\rho} = V_1 u.$$

Performing an integration by parts and introducing equations of the type of equation (331), in the approximation accepted

$$p_1 - p = \rho_1 V_1 u. \qquad (355)$$

If a wing is considered moving in a uniform stream and u_u is the velocity component along a line parallel to the x-axis on the upper part of the wing, and u_l is the corresponding component on the lower part (different from u_u because the surface is a lifting surface), there exists a potential difference behind the wing having the value

$$\Gamma = \int_{x_1}^{x_2} (u_u - u_l) \, dx \qquad (355a)$$

where $x_1 \, x_2$ is the wing chord, because only along the chord can p_u be different from p_l, and therefore u_u is different from u_l. Equation (355a) using equation (355) becomes

$$\rho_1 V_1 \Gamma = \int_{x_1}^{x_2} (p_u - p_l) \, dx. \qquad (356)$$

Equation (356) gives the value of the lift for a unit length in the y direction; therefore integration along the y-axis furnishes the Kutta Joukowsky law, which is also valid for supersonic flow with the approximation accepted. Now it is possible to show that, with the hypothesis of small disturbances, an acceleration potential must exist in the flow, and it is also possible to show that, corresponding to the difference of pressure across the lifting surface there is an equally large difference in the acceleration potential. Now because a doublet distribution represents a difference of potential, it is possible to represent the difference in pressure across the lifting surface with a corresponding doublet distribution.

Consider Euler's equation (1) or (1a). The equation is composed of two equal terms, the first is given by a gradient (grad P); therefore the second term must also be a gradient, so it is possible to write

$$\frac{dV}{dt} = \text{grad } \varphi. \qquad (357)$$

Therefore a potential function φ must exist which represents an acceleration potential. Projecting equation (357) along the x-axis (see equation 1b) gives

$$\frac{\partial \varphi}{\partial x} = -\frac{1}{\rho} \frac{\partial p}{\partial x} = \frac{du}{dt} = \frac{\partial u}{\partial x} (V_1 + u_2) + \frac{\partial u}{\partial y} v_2 + \frac{\partial u}{\partial z} w_2$$

or with the hypothesis of small disturbances

$$\frac{\partial \varphi}{\partial x} = V_1 \frac{\partial u}{\partial x}$$

or

$$\varphi = V_1 u. \tag{358}$$

Therefore, from equation (355)

$$p_l - p_u = (\varphi_u - \varphi_l) \, \rho_1. \tag{359}$$

Now, the difference of the potential φ across the lifting surface can be represented by the potential of a doublet distribution along the surface. Indeed, assume that a source distribution of intensity Q exists in the lower part and a sink distribution of the same intensity (and opposite sign) exists in the upper part of the lifting surface; if the distance between the two distributions h becomes smaller and approaches zero, while Q increases in such a way that Qh remains constant, the difference of potential across the surface is

$$\varphi_u - \varphi_l = Qh. \tag{360}$$

The potential of the doublet distribution can be computed in this way: Consider a lifting surface placed in the plane $z = 0$, having a source distribution in the plane $z = -h/2$ and a sink distribution in the plane $z = +h/2$. The potential resulting from both distributions can be thought of as arising from the removal of a source distribution from $z = h/2$ and placing it at $z = -h/2$. Because h is small,

$$\varphi = h \frac{\partial \phi_Q}{\partial z} \tag{361}$$

where ϕ_Q is the potential of the source distribution. From equation (358) it is found that the velocity potential corresponding to a doublet distribution is given by

$$V_1 \frac{\partial \phi_D}{\partial x} = \varphi_u - \varphi_l = \varphi \tag{361a}$$

or

$$\phi_D = \frac{1}{V_1} \int_{-\infty}^{x_1} \varphi dx = k \int_{-\infty}^{x_1} \frac{\partial \phi_Q}{\partial z} dx. \tag{362}$$

Equation (362) permits determination of the flow field represented by the doublet distribution.

Projecting equation (357) along the y- and z-axis (equations 1 and 1b),

$$\frac{\partial \varphi}{\partial y} = \frac{dv}{dt} = V_1 \frac{\partial v}{\partial x}$$

$$\frac{\partial \varphi}{dz} = \frac{dw}{dt} = V_1 \frac{\partial w}{\partial x}.$$

Since v and w are zero for the undisturbed stream, the components v and w at the point x are

$$v = \frac{1}{V_1} \int_{-\infty}^{x} \frac{\partial \varphi}{\partial y} \, dx$$

$$w = \frac{1}{V_1} \int_{-\infty}^{x} \frac{\partial \varphi}{\partial z} \, dx$$

The velocity components v and w do not disappear at infinity behind the lifting surface. A free vortex system exists behind the lifting surface, the energy of which is related to the induced drag, while the flow field is defined by the potential difference Γ.

CHAPTER

11

AERODYNAMIC PHENOMENA FOR BODY OF REVOLUTION, ANALYZED BY USING THE THEORY OF SMALL DISTURBANCES

The Method of Small Disturbances for a Body of Revolution. To study the problem of aerodynamic phenomena around a body of revolution, the cylindrical coordinate system is considered the most suitable. The x-axis is assumed coincident with the axis of the body, and the y-axis normal to the x-axis in the meridian plane in the direction of the radius of every circular cross section of the body. The meridian plane is defined by the angle φ between the meridian plane which contains the direction of the undisturbed velocity and the meridian plane considered (Figure 150). The angle of attack α of the body is the angle between the direction of the undisturbed velocity and the axis x of the body, in the meridian plane $\varphi = 0$.

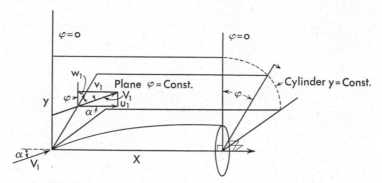

Fig. 150. *Body of revolution referred to cylindrical coordinates.*

At every point the velocity V can be divided into three components: along the x- and y-axis, and normal to the meridian plane. The components can be defined in the following form:

210

$$u = u_1 + u_2 = u_1 + \frac{\partial \phi_2}{\partial x} = V_1 \cos \alpha + \frac{\partial \phi_2}{\partial x}$$

$$v = v_1 + v_2 = v_1 + \frac{\partial \phi_2}{\partial y} = V_1 \sin \alpha \cos \varphi + \frac{\partial \phi_2}{\partial y} \qquad \qquad (363)$$

$$w = w_1 + w_2 = - V_1 \sin \alpha \sin \varphi + \frac{\partial \phi_2}{y \partial \varphi}$$

where u_1, v_1, and w_1 are components of the undisturbed velocity corresponding to the potential ϕ_1 of the undisturbed stream, and ϕ_2 is the potential function which defines the variation of the flow generated by the presence of the body. This potential function always exists, because the hypothesis of small disturbances is accepted. Because with the hypothesis accepted α must be small, the differential equation (341) of the flow motion becomes, using the definitions of equations (363):

$$(1 - M_1^2) \frac{\partial^2 \phi_2}{\partial x^2} + \frac{\partial^2 \phi_2}{\partial y^2} + \frac{1}{y^2} \frac{\partial^2 \phi_2}{\partial \varphi^2} + \frac{1}{y} \frac{\partial \phi_2}{\partial y} = 0 \qquad (364)$$

where, following the considerations of Chapter 10, in equation (341a), the terms v_1 and w_1 are also considered small (of the same order of magnitude of the disturbance velocity components). The solution of equation (364) is of the form (References 36 and 37)

$$\phi_2 = \phi_2' + \phi_2'' \qquad (365)$$

where ϕ_2' is a function only of x and y and is defined by the equation (Reference 33*)

$$(1 - M_1^2) \frac{\partial^2 \phi_2'}{\partial x^2} + \frac{\partial^2 \phi_2'}{\partial y^2} + \frac{1}{y} \frac{\partial \phi_2'}{\partial y} = 0 \qquad (366)$$

which is the equation that defines the flow for the case of the body with axis in the direction of the velocity. In analogy with the phenomena in subsonic flow ϕ_2'' is given by

$$\phi_2'' (x, y, \varphi) = F (xy) \cos \varphi \qquad (367)$$

where

$$F(xy) = \frac{\partial \phi_2'}{\partial y} . \qquad (368)$$

It can be shown that the function ϕ_2'' is a solution of equation (364) in the following way: Substituting the value of ϕ_2'' given by equation (367) in equation (364), equation (364) becomes

$$(1 - M_1^2) \frac{\partial^2 F}{\partial x^2} + \frac{\partial^2 F}{\partial y^2} - \frac{1}{y^2} F + \frac{1}{y} \frac{\partial F}{\partial y} = 0. \qquad (369)$$

* The treatment of bodies of revolution with the small disturbances theory, which was extended in Reference 36 and in Reference 37 to bodies of revolution with angle of attack, was given here for the first time.

Differentiating equation (366) with respect to y,

$$(1 - M_1^2) \frac{\partial^2}{\partial x^2} \left(\frac{\partial \phi_2'}{\partial y} \right) + \frac{\partial^2}{\partial y^2} \left(\frac{\partial \phi_2'}{\partial y} \right) + \frac{1}{y} \frac{\partial}{\partial y} \left(\frac{\partial \phi_2'}{\partial y} \right) - \frac{1}{y^2} \left(\frac{\partial \phi_2'}{\partial y} \right) = 0. \quad (370)$$

Assuming

$$\frac{\partial \phi_2'}{\partial y} = F$$

equation (369) is coincident with equation (370); therefore equation (367) is a solution of equation (364).

The potential function that defines the phenomenon can therefore be expressed in the form

$$\phi = \phi_1 + \phi_2$$

or

$$\phi = \phi_1' + \phi_2' + \phi_1'' + \phi_2''$$
$$= x V_1 \cos \alpha + \phi_2' + y V_1 \sin \alpha \cos \varphi + \frac{\partial \phi_2'}{\partial y} \cos \varphi. \quad (371)$$

The potential function $(\phi_1' + \phi_2')$ defines the phenomenon for the case of axial symmetry or zero angle of attack. To determine the effect of the angle of attack it is necessary to determine only the variation of the phenomenon dependent on the presence of cross flow due to the angle of attack which is represented by the function $(\phi_2' + \phi_1'')$. The part ϕ_1 is assumed independent of the angle of attack, and u_1 is assumed equal to V_1 (because α is small). The determination of the flow around a body of revolution can be considered therefore divided in two parts. The first part consists in determination of the value of the potential function ϕ_2' which, with ϕ_1', represents the phenomenon for the body in axis with the undisturbed flow. The second part consists in determination of ϕ_2'' which, with ϕ_1'', gives the variation of the phenomenon with respect to the preceding case when the body changes angle of attack.

The possibility of superimposing the effect of the axial flow on the effect of the cross flow, which is derived from the hypothesis of small disturbances, notably simplifies the problem and permits rapid determination of the aerodynamic properties of a body at small angles of attack. In equation (364) it is assumed that the angle of attack is very small so that u_1 can be considered equal to V_1 and constant, and v_1 and w_1 very small. Really u_1 changes with the cosine, and v_1 and w_1 with the sine of the angle of attack; therefore the solutions are correct only in a first approximation or for very small angles of attack.

Slender Body with Axial Symmetrical Flow. If the body has its axis parallel to the flow, in order to determine the phenomenon a potential function ϕ_2' which satisfies equation (366) and the boundary condition must be determined. As is shown in Chapter 10, the potential function ϕ_2' can be obtained as the potential given by a source distribution (equation 354a) (References 33 and 38).

Because in equation (366) u_1 is greater than a, equation (366) (identical to equation 346) represents the motion of a circular two-dimensional wave diverging from a center placed in the position $y = 0$. The steady flow around a body of revolution can be interpreted as a two-dimensional circular wave motion with a source at the origin variable with time (equation 354a). In the coordinate system moving with the body this representation corresponds to a variable distribution of sources along the x-axis. The position of the sources and the law of variation of the strength of the sources along the x-axis depend on the shape of the body. The problem is reduced to determination of the source distribution as a function of the shape of the body.

The solution of equation (366) is given by the expression (equation 354a)

$$\phi_2' = \int_0^{\xi_1} \frac{f(\xi) \, d\xi}{\sqrt{(x-\xi)^2 - B^2 y^2}} \qquad (372)$$

where the term B is given by the expression

$$B = \sqrt{M_1^2 - 1} \qquad (373)$$

and the function $f(\xi)$ is an unknown function of the parameter ξ. The integral is taken over the entire interval in which the function in the integral is defined.

For supersonic flow ($M_1 > 1$) the function in the integral becomes imaginary when

$$(x - \xi)^2 - B^2 y^2 < 0, \text{ or when } \xi > x - By.$$

Therefore the limits of the integral are $\xi = 0$ and $\xi = x - By$.

Substituting for the value ξ the expression

$$\xi = x - By \cosh z \qquad (374)$$

equation (372) becomes

$$\phi_2' = \int_{\cosh^{-1} \frac{x}{By}}^{0} f(x - By \cosh z) \, dz \qquad (375)$$

As discussed in Chapter 10, the limit of differentiation has a physical meaning. Indeed, if the body begins at the point $A(x = 0)$ and a point P is considered (Figure 151), the flow at P undergoes variations that are generated only by disturbances produced

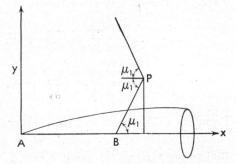

Fig. 151. *Body of revolution in axis with the undisturbed stream.*

in the fore Mach cone which starts at P. These disturbances must be represented by sources placed along the zone AB. In front of A the flow is undisturbed flow, and behind B the sources cannot influence the point P. The sources therefore must be distributed along a segment that goes from ξ equal to zero to ξ equal to AB, where AB is equal to

$$x_B = x_P - y_P \cot \mu_1 \quad \text{where} \quad \cot \mu_1 = \sqrt{M_1^2 - 1} = B.$$

Cone with Axis Parallel to the Undisturbed Velocity (Reference 33). If the function $f(x - By \cosh z)$ of equation (375) is assumed proportional to $x - By \cosh z$, equation (375) becomes

$$\phi_2' = K_1 \int_{\cosh^{-1} \frac{x}{By}}^{0} (x - By \cosh z) \, dz. \tag{376}$$

Equation (376) permits direct integration

$$\phi_2' = K_1 \left[-x \cosh^{-1} \frac{x}{By} + \sqrt{x^2 - B^2 y^2} \right] \tag{377}$$

where K_1 is the constant of integration having the dimensions of a velocity. In this case the disturbance velocity components become

$$\frac{d\phi_2'}{dx} = K_1 \int_{\cosh^{-1} \frac{x}{By}}^{0} dz \tag{377a}$$

and

$$\frac{d\phi_2'}{dy} = K_1 \int_{\cosh^{-1} \frac{x}{By}}^{0} - B \cosh z \, dz. \tag{377b}$$

Therefore the velocity components are

$$u = \frac{\partial \phi}{\partial x} = \frac{\partial \phi_2'}{\partial x} + V_1 = V_1 - K_1 \cosh^{-1} \frac{x}{By} \tag{378}$$

$$v = \frac{\partial \phi}{\partial y} = \frac{\partial \phi_2'}{\partial y} = K_1 B \sqrt{\frac{x^2}{B^2 y^2} - 1}.$$

Equation (378) shows that the components of the velocity are constant for constant value of x/y, and therefore are constant along every straight line that passes through the point $x = 0$, $y = 0$. The potential ϕ_2 given by equation (376) corresponds to a conical phenomenon. Equation (378) can be used to determine the pressure distribution around a circular cone with axis parallel to the flow. If η_0 is the angle at the vertex of the cone (angle between the x-axis and a generatrix) the value of x/y along the cone is given by

$$\frac{y}{x} = \tan \eta_0.$$

But v/u at the cone must be equal to $\tan \eta_0$ or

$$\tan \eta_0 = \frac{K_1 B \sqrt{\dfrac{x^2}{B^2 y^2} - 1}}{V_1 - K_1 \cosh^{-1} \dfrac{x}{By}} \tag{379}$$

and

$$K_1 = \frac{V_1 \tan \eta_0}{\sqrt{\cot^2 \eta_0 - B^2} + \tan \eta_0 \cosh^{-1} \dfrac{\cot \eta_0}{B}}. \tag{380}$$

In order to obtain real values for K_1 in equation (380), the value of $\cot \eta_0$ must be larger than B, or the value of η_0 must be smaller than the Mach angle μ, the cotangent of which is equal to B.

From equations (378) and (380) it is possible to determine the pressure distribution and therefore the drag coefficient for cones at every Mach number.

Indeed, with the approximation accepted (equation 355)

$$\frac{\Delta p}{\frac{1}{2}\rho_1 V_1^2} = -\frac{2u_2}{V_1}. \tag{381}$$

For every value of η_0 and M_1 the value of K/V_1 can be determined (equation 380)

$$\frac{K_1}{V_1} = \frac{\tan \eta_0}{\sqrt{\cot^2 \eta_0 - B^2} + \tan \eta_0 \cosh^{-1} \dfrac{\cot \eta_0}{B}} \tag{382}$$

$$\left(\cosh^{-1} \frac{\cot \eta_0}{B} = \left[\log_e \frac{\cot \eta_0}{B} + \sqrt{\left(\frac{\cot \eta_0}{B} \right)^2 - 1} \right] \right)$$

and u_2/V_1, v_2/V_1, are given by

$$\frac{u_2}{V_1} = -\frac{K_1}{V_1} \cosh^{-1} \frac{\cot \eta_0}{B} = -\frac{1}{2} c_p \tag{383}$$

$$\frac{v_2}{V_1} = \frac{K_1}{V_1} B \sqrt{\frac{\cot^2 \eta_0}{B^2} - 1}. \tag{384}$$

The system gives a good approximation if the angle of the cone is not very large and for Mach numbers not too near one. In Figure 152 some values of the pressure coefficient $(p - p_1)/\tfrac{1}{2}\rho_1 V_1^2$ obtained with this theory are plotted

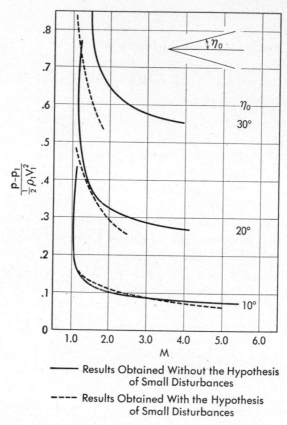

Fig. 152. *Pressure coefficient versus Mach number for cones of different angle.*

as functions of the Mach number. For comparison, the same values obtained theoretically without the hypothesis of small disturbances are also shown.

The Flow around a Slender, Sharp-Nose Body of Revolution with Axis Parallel to the Direction of the Undisturbed Velocity. Consider a slender, sharp-nose body of revolution of given shape (Figure 153). For every point P_n of the body the values of y_n and x_n are known, and therefore the value of ξ_n given by

$$\xi_n = x_n - By_n \tag{385}$$

can be calculated. At the point P_n the additional velocities u_2 and v_2 are produced by the source distribution placed along the segment AB_n corresponding to ξ_n. If $f(\xi)$ is the function that defines the source distribution, it is possible to write, using equations (375) and (374)

$$u_2 = \int_{\cosh^{-1}\frac{x}{By}}^{0} f'\,(x - By \cosh z)\,dz \tag{386}$$

$$v_2 = \int_{\cosh^{-1}\frac{x}{By}}^{0} -f'\,(x - By \cosh z)\,B \cosh z\,dz \tag{387}$$

where $f'(\xi)$ is the function which represents the derivative of $f(\xi)$ with respect to ξ.

If a curve made up of straight segments tangent to the curve is substituted for the curve that represents $f(\xi)$ as a function of ξ, (Figure 153), along every

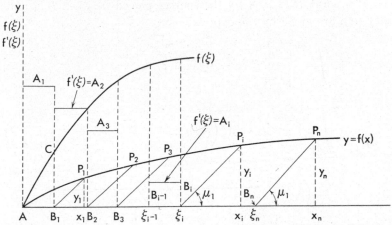

Fig. 153. *The determination of source distribution for a body of revolution.*

segment of the curve $f(\xi)$, the value of $f'(\xi)$ is constant, and the curve which represents the function $f'(\xi)$ as a function of ξ is a step-shaped line as represented in Figure 153. In this case a summation can be substituted for the integrals of equations (386) and (387) and the velocity at the points P_1, P_2, P_u can be determined. If the straight line AC is substituted for the curve of $f(\xi)$ as a function of ξ between A and B_1 (Figure 153), $f'(\xi)$ is constant in this interval; therefore the velocity components at the point P_1 of coordinate x_1 $= \xi_1 + By_1$ are given by (equation 378)

$$u_{2,1} = -A_1\,\cosh^{-1}\frac{x_1}{By_1}$$

$$v_{2,1} = A_1\,B\sqrt{\frac{x_1^2}{B^2y_1^2} - 1}$$

where A_1 is a constant. The hypothesis of $f'(\xi)$ constant corresponds to substitution for the body AP_1 of a cone which passes through P_1. But at P_1 the velocity must be tangent to the body, and, because the cone that passes P_1 is substituted for the body in the approximation accepted, the boundary condition is given by

$$\frac{dy}{dx} = \frac{y_1}{x_1} = \frac{v_2}{V_1 + u_2}.$$

Since v_2 and u_2 are functions only of x_1 and y_1, which are known, the value of A_1 can be determined in the same way as for the cone equation (382).

For a point P_n of coordinates (x_n, y_n) the corresponding values of u_2 and v_2, u_{2n}, and v_{2n} can be obtained in the following way: For every zone of $\xi_i - \xi_{i-1}$ between two points B_{i-1} and B_i (Figure 153), in which the value of $f'(\xi)$ is assumed constant and equal to A_i, the velocity components Δu_{2n} and Δv_{2n}, induced at a point $P_n(x_n, y_n)$ by the sources placed between B_{i-1} and B_i of intensity $f(\xi)$, are given by the expressions

$$\Delta u_{2n} = + \int_{\cosh^{-1}\frac{x_n - \xi_{i-1}}{By_n}}^{\cosh^{-1}\frac{x_n - \xi_i}{By_n}} f'(x - By \cosh z)\, dz$$

$$= A_i \int_{\cosh^{-1}\frac{x_n - \xi_{i-1}}{By_n}}^{\cosh^{-1}\frac{x_n - \xi_i}{By_n}} dz = A_i \left(\cosh^{-1}\frac{x_n - \xi_i}{By_n} - \cosh^{-1}\frac{x_n - \xi_{i-1}}{By_n} \right)$$

and

$$\Delta v_{2n} = - \frac{A_i}{y_n} \left(\sqrt{(x_n - \xi_i)^2 - B^2 y_n^2} - \sqrt{(x_n - \xi_{i-1})^2 - B^2 y_n^2} \right).$$

The total induced velocity components are therefore given by the following summations:

$$\left. \begin{aligned}
u_{2n} &= \sum_{i=1}^{n} A_i \left(\cosh^{-1}\frac{x_n - \xi_i}{By_n} - \cosh^{-1}\frac{x_n - \xi_{i-1}}{By_n} \right) \\
v_{2n} &= - \sum_{i=1}^{n} A_i B \left(\sqrt{\frac{(x_n - \xi_i)^2}{B^2 y_n^2} - 1} - \sqrt{\frac{(x_n - \xi_{i-1})^2}{B^2 y_n^2} - 1} \right)
\end{aligned} \right\} \quad (388)$$

Equations (388) are obtained by considering the effect of every zone in which $f(\xi)$ is constant. Now for the point P_2 at x_2 and y_2 the summation has only two terms, and therefore only two constants must be determined, A_1 and A_2. The constant A_1 is known from the consideration of P_1, and therefore when the boundary condition

$$\frac{v_2}{V_1 + u_2} = \left(\frac{dy}{dx}\right)_{P_2} = \frac{v_2}{V_1} \qquad (389)$$

is imposed at P_2, using equations (388), equation (389) represents an equation in which only the term A_2 is unknown and can be determined. For P_3 three constants are necessary, A_1, A_2, and A_3. The constants A_1 and A_2 are already determined; therefore, from the condition that the velocity must be in the direction P_2P_3 at P_3 (equation 389), the value of A_3 can be determined. Proceeding in a similar way the values of all constants can be determined, and therefore it is possible to determine the value of the velocity along the entire body. From equation (381) the corresponding pressure distribution can be determined. For example, if the body shown in Figure 154 is consid-

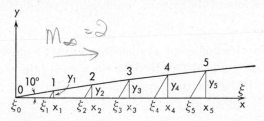

Fig. 154. *Shape of the body analyzed in the numerical example.*

ered, and the flight Mach number is equal to 2, the pressure distribution along the body at zero angle of attack can be performed in the following way. Six points along the body are chosen: the points $0, 1, 2, 3, 4, 5$. For every point the following geometrical quantities are determined: x_n, y_n, $(dy/dx)_n$, and ξ_n, where ξ_n for every point is given by equation (385), and $B = \sqrt{M^2 - 1}$ is equal to $\sqrt{3}$. Because the shape considered for the zone $0-1$ is a cone of $10°$ half angle, the value of the constant A_1/V_1 from equation (382) is equal to

$$\frac{A_1}{V_1} = \frac{\tan 10°}{\sqrt{\cot^2 10° - 3} + \tan 10° \cosh^{-1} \dfrac{\cot 10°}{\sqrt{3}}} = 0.03079$$

and

$$\frac{u_{2,1}}{V_1} = -\frac{A_1}{V_1} \cosh^{-1} \frac{\cot 10°}{\sqrt{3}} = -0.05712.$$

The pressure coefficient between 0 and 1 is equal to $c_p = 0.114$. In order to determine the pressure in the point 2, the value of A_2/V_1 must be calculated, using equation (388). Because $x_2 = 2$, $y_2 = 0.3347$, $\xi_2 = 1.4203$, and $\xi_1 = 0.6946$,

$$-\frac{v_{2,2}}{V_1} = \sqrt{3} \times 0.03079 \left[\sqrt{\left(\frac{2 - 0.6946}{\sqrt{3} \times 0.33471} \right)^2 - 1} - \sqrt{\frac{4}{3 \times 0.33471^2} - 1} \right]$$

$$+ \frac{A_2}{V_1} \sqrt{3} \left\{ \sqrt{\left(\frac{2 - 1.4203}{\sqrt{3} \times 0.33471} \right)^2 - 1} - \sqrt{\left(\frac{2 - 0.6946}{\sqrt{3} \times 0.33471} \right)^2 - 1} \right\}.$$

$$\frac{u_{2,2}}{V_1} = 0.03079 \left(\cosh^{-1} \frac{2 - 0.6946}{\sqrt{3} \times 0.33471} - \cosh^{-1} \frac{2}{\sqrt{3} \times 0.33471} \right)$$
$$+ \frac{A_2}{V_1} \left(\cosh^{-1} \frac{2 - 1.4203}{\sqrt{3}\,(0.33471)} - \cosh^{-1} \frac{2 - 0.6946}{\sqrt{3}\,(0.33471)} \right)$$

In equation (389) $(dy/dx)_2 = v_{2,2}/V_1$ where $(\partial y/\partial x)_2 = 0.158$; therefore the value of A_2/V_1 can be determined; $A_2/V_1 = 0.02354$. In a similar way, the values of A_3/V_1, A_4/V_1, and A_5/V_1 can be determined and the values of 0.01681, 0.01069, and 0.00517 are obtained. From the value of A, the value of u_2/V_1 and therefore of the pressure coefficients can be determined.

$$c_{p_2} = 0.097; \qquad c_{p_3} = 0.080; \qquad c_{p_4} = 0.063; \qquad c_{p_5} = 0.047.$$

For a body of revolution of small diameter a direct expression that gives a first approximation can be determined for the value of the source distribution (Reference 38). Differentiating equation (372) with respect to y, equation (387) is obtained; substituting equation (374) in equation (387) gives

$$\frac{\partial \phi_2'}{\partial y} = \frac{1}{y} \int_0^{x - By} \frac{f'(\xi)(x - \xi)\,d\xi}{\sqrt{(x - \xi)^2 - B^2 y^2}}. \tag{390}$$

Now near the axis of the body (the source distribution is at the axis $y = 0$)

$$\lim_{y \to 0} \frac{\partial \phi_2'}{\partial y} = \frac{1}{y} \int_0^x f'(\xi)\,d\xi = \frac{f(x) - f(0)}{y} \tag{391}$$

The term $f(0)$ is zero if the body has a sharp nose at the point $x = 0$. When the value of the radius y of the body is small it is possible to assume

$$(v_2)_y = (v_2)_{y=0} = \left(\frac{\partial \phi_2'}{\partial y} \right)_{y=0} = \frac{f(x)}{y} \tag{392}$$

but if S is the section of the body, it is possible to write

$$\frac{dS}{dx} = 2\pi y \frac{dy}{dx}. \tag{393}$$

The boundary conditions give

$$\frac{dy}{dx} = \frac{v_2}{V_1 + u_2} = \frac{v_2}{V_1} \tag{394}$$

and therefore with the same order of approximation,

$$\frac{f(x)}{yV_1} = \frac{dy}{dx} \tag{395}$$

or (equation 393)

$$f(x) = \frac{V_1}{2\pi} \frac{dS}{dx}. \tag{396}$$

In the approximation accepted, the source distribution is proportional to the variation of the cross section of the body and therefore can be determined directly from the boundary conditions. The pressure coefficient at every point P can be determined by using equation (381)

$$(c_p)_P = -\frac{2u_2}{V_1} = -\frac{2}{V_1}\int_0^{x_P - By_P} \frac{f'(\xi)\,d\xi}{\sqrt{(x_P - \xi)^2 - B^2 y_P^2}} \tag{397}$$

which becomes

$$(c_p)_P = -\frac{1}{\pi}\int_0^{x_P - By_P} \frac{d^2S}{d\xi^2}\frac{d\xi}{\sqrt{(x_P - \xi)^2 - B^2 y_P^2}}. \tag{398}$$

If the shape of the body is defined by an analytical expression, the derivative $d^2S/d\xi^2$ can be obtained in analytical form as a function of ξ, and therefore the value of the pressure coefficient can be obtained in analytical form evaluating the integral of equation (398).

The Flow around an Open Nose Body of Revolution with Axis Parallel to the Direction of the Undisturbed Flow (Reference 39). The theory

of small disturbances can be applied to a body of revolution with an open nose if the flow that goes into the open nose is supersonic. If S is the section at the nose of the body (Figure 155a), at S the flow can be divided into two parts, the internal flow, or the flow that goes into the nose, and the external flow, which wets the external surface of the body.

If the internal shape of the body or the transformations that the internal flow undergoes are such that there is a supersonic flow at the section S, the internal flow cannot interfere with the external flow, because all variations

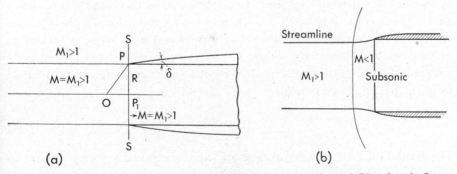

(a)   (b)

Fig. 155. *Open nose body of revolution, with* (a) *supersonic, and* (b) *subsonic flow at the entrance.*

in the flow can begin at the section S when the two masses of flow are separated. If the internal flow is subsonic, an external transformation must occur with a strong shock in front of the body (Figure 155b). The external flow that wets the body then has physical characteristics dependent on the internal flow transformations, and the phenomena cannot be separated.

If the internal flow is supersonic, it can be represented by a cylinder of the same diameter as the nose, and the body can be considered schematically as a cylinder wetted by the undisturbed flow that changes section at S (Figure 155a). To solve the problem it is therefore necessary to determine the potential function of the supplementary flow velocity, produced by the disturbances that are produced at S. Because the variations of velocity begin at the point P, the source distribution must be such that it does not produce any variation in front of P, but must produce a variation at P and behind the point P. The source distribution must therefore begin at the point O determined by the relation (Figure 155),

$$OP_1 = RB$$

where R is the radius of the open nose.

The function $f(\xi)$ must be determined by the condition that $f(\xi)$ is zero in front of the point O, and $f(\xi) \neq O$ after O, where O can be considered as the origin of the coordinates.

For determining the value of $f'(\xi)$ at every point of the axis the same procedure determined for a sharp body can be used, based on the principle of satisfying the boundary conditions. It is evident that at the point P the flow undergoes a finite variation of direction which is much stronger than the variation which occurs at a sharp nose, because at the point P the phenomenon is two-dimensional.

Application of the Equations of Small Disturbances for Flow around a Body of Revolution in Yaw. In paragraph 1 of this chapter it is shown that if the hypothesis of small disturbances is acceptable for the phenomenon considered, the variations of the velocity produced by a body of revolution in yaw can be obtained by adding to the variations produced by the body with axis parallel to the flow some incremental variations that can be obtained from the potential function $(\phi_2 +'' \phi_1'')$ given by

$$\phi_1'' + \phi_2'' = yV_1 \sin \alpha \cos \varphi + \frac{\partial \phi_2'}{\partial y} \cos \varphi \qquad (399)$$

The term $V_1 \sin \alpha$ is the component of the undisturbed velocity normal to the axis of the body, which is assumed coincident with the x-axis, and ϕ_2' is the potential function that gives the variation of the velocity produced by the body when it is on axis with the flow (References 36 and 37).

Using for the function ϕ_2' the expression of equation (375), the potential $(\phi_1'' + \phi_2'')$ becomes

$$\phi_1'' + \phi_2'' = yV_1 \sin \alpha \cos \varphi - \cos \varphi\, B \int_{\cosh^{-1}\frac{x}{By}}^{0} m\,(x - By \cosh z) \cosh z\, dz \quad (400)$$

where $m(x - By \cosh z)$ is a function that must be determined in terms of the boundary condition.

Cone in Yaw. For the cone with axis parallel to the flow the function ϕ_2' is given by equation (376)

$$\phi_2' = K \int_{\cosh^{-1}\frac{x}{By}}^{0} (x - By \cosh z)\, dz \qquad (401)$$

where K is a constant. It is therefore possible to write

$$\phi_2'' = \cos \varphi \frac{\partial \phi_2'}{\partial y} = - K_2\, B \cos \varphi \int_{\cosh^{-1}\frac{x}{By}}^{0} (x - By \cosh z) \cosh z\, dz \quad (402)$$

where the constant K_2 must be determined in such a way as to satisfy the boundary conditions, but

$$\int_{\cosh^{-1}\frac{x}{By}}^{0} (x - By \cosh z) \cosh z\, dz = \frac{1}{2} yB \cosh^{-1} \frac{x}{By} - \frac{x}{2}\sqrt{\frac{x^2}{B^2 y^2} - 1} \quad (402a)$$

and therefore

$$\phi'' = \phi_1'' + \phi_2'' = yV_1 \sin \alpha \cos \varphi - K_2 B \cos \varphi \left[\frac{By}{2} \cosh^{-1} \frac{x}{By} - \frac{x}{2}\sqrt{\frac{x^2}{B^2 y^2} - 1} \right]. \quad (403)$$

The value $\partial \phi_2'' / \partial x$ and $\partial \phi_2'' / \partial y$ can be determined using equation (403)

$$\frac{\partial \phi_2''}{\partial x} = K_2\, B \cos \varphi \sqrt{\frac{x^2}{B^2 y^2} - 1} \qquad (404)$$

and

$$\frac{\partial \phi''}{\partial y} = v_1 - K_2 B \cos \varphi \left[\frac{B}{2} \cosh^{-1} \frac{x}{By} + \frac{x}{2y} \sqrt{\frac{x^2}{B^2 y^2} - 1} \right]. \qquad (405)$$

Considering the total phenomenon the components of the velocity are given by

$$\left. \begin{aligned} u &= \frac{\partial \phi'}{\partial x} + \frac{\partial \phi''}{\partial x} \\[2mm] v &= \frac{\partial \phi'}{\partial y} + \frac{\partial \phi''}{\partial y} \end{aligned} \right\} \qquad (406)$$

and therefore

$$\left.\begin{array}{l} u = u_1 - K_1 \cosh^{-1}\dfrac{x}{By} + K_2\, B\cos\varphi\sqrt{\dfrac{x^2}{B^2y^2}-1} \\[3mm] v = v_1 + K_1\, B\sqrt{\dfrac{x^2}{B^2y^2}-1} - K_2\, B\cos\varphi\left(\dfrac{B}{2}\cosh^{-1}\dfrac{x}{By}\right. \\[5mm] \left.\hspace{3cm} + \dfrac{x}{2y}\sqrt{\dfrac{x^2}{B^2y^2}-1}\right). \end{array}\right\} \quad (407)$$

The values of u and v are constant for constant values of x/y, and therefore are constant along every straight line that passes through the origin of the coordinates; the functions $(\phi_2' + \phi_2'')$ represent a conical field.

If η_0 is the angle of the cone, constant for every value of φ (circular cone), the value of the constants K_1 and K_2 can be determined. The constant K_1 corresponds to the axial-flow phenomenon and is given by equation (380). The constant K_2 must also be determined by imposing the condition that at the surface of the cone the velocity must be tangent to the cone; therefore the velocity must be inclined at η_0, or

$$\frac{v}{u} = \tan\eta_0. \quad (408)$$

Because the term

$$\frac{v'_2}{u_1 + u'_2} = \frac{K_1 B\sqrt{\dfrac{x^2}{B^2y^2}-1}}{u_1 - K_1\cosh^{-1}\dfrac{x}{By}} = \tan\eta_0$$

it is evident from equation (408) that the following relation must be valid:

$$\frac{v_2''}{u_2''} = \frac{v_1 - K_2 B\cos\varphi\left(\dfrac{B}{2}\cosh^{-1}\dfrac{x}{By} + \dfrac{x}{2y}\sqrt{\dfrac{x^2}{B^2y^2}-1}\right)}{K_2 B\cos\varphi\sqrt{\dfrac{x^2}{B^2y^2}-1}} = \tan\eta_0. \quad (408a)$$

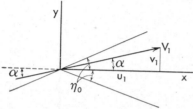

Fig. 156. *Cone with angle of attack.*

From equation (408a) the value of K_2 can be determined as a function of η_0 and of v_1 which is a function of the angle of attack α, $v_1 = V_1 \sin\alpha \cos\varphi$ (Figure 156). K_2 is independent of the value of $\cos\varphi$.

$$K_2 = \frac{V_1 \sin \alpha}{\frac{B^2}{2} \cosh^{-1} \frac{\cot \eta_0}{B} + \frac{B}{2} \cot \eta_0 \sqrt{\frac{\cot^2 \eta_0}{B^2} - 1} + \sqrt{1 - B^2 \tan^2 \eta_0}} \qquad (409)$$

or

$$\frac{K_2}{V_1} = \frac{\sin \alpha}{\frac{B^2}{2} \cosh^{-1} \frac{\cot \eta_0}{B} + \frac{B}{2} \cot \eta_0 \sqrt{\frac{\cot^2 \eta_0}{B^2} - 1} + \sqrt{1 - B^2 \tan \eta_0^2}} .$$

Using the symbol $\zeta = \dfrac{\cot \eta_0}{B}$, the result is

$$\frac{K_2}{V_1} = \frac{\alpha}{\frac{B^2}{2} \left(\cosh^{-1} \zeta + \zeta \sqrt{\zeta^2 - 1} + \frac{2}{\zeta B^2} \sqrt{\zeta^2 - 1} \right)} . \qquad (409a)$$

The lift coefficient of the cone is

$$C_L = \frac{4}{VS} \int_0^\infty y \, dx \int_0^\pi u \cos \varphi \, d\varphi.$$

Therefore

$$C_L = \frac{2 \cot \eta_0}{\pi V_1} \int_0^\pi K_2 B \sqrt{\frac{\cot \eta_0^2}{B^2} - 1} \cos^2 \varphi \, d\varphi$$

or

$$\frac{dC_L}{d\alpha} = \frac{2 \zeta \sqrt{\zeta^2 - 1}}{\cosh^{-1} \zeta + \zeta \sqrt{\zeta^2 - 1} + \frac{2}{\zeta B^2} \sqrt{\zeta^2 - 1}} .$$

Some values of $dc_L/d\alpha$ for different Mach numbers and values of η_0 are shown in Figure 157. For comparison data obtained without the assumption of the small disturbances theory are also shown (see Chapter 12). The results of the two determinations agree fairly well only for low Mach numbers and for very small angles of the cones. The values obtained for $\eta_0 = 0$ coincide with the values given by equation (426).

Lift and Moment for Bodies of Revolution in Yaw (very slender bodies of revolution). As was shown before, the flow around a body of revolution in yaw is given by the potential function

$$\phi' + \phi'' = \phi_1' + \phi_2' + \phi_1'' + \phi_2''$$

where ϕ_2' and ϕ_2'' are defined by equation (371).

In the linearized theory that is used to obtain equation (371) the angle of attack of the body is assumed small, and therefore it is possible to consider the

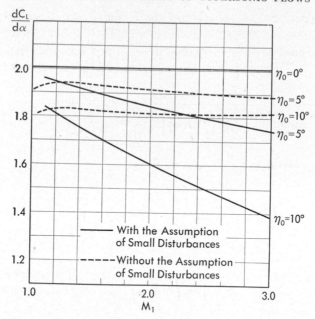

Fig. 157. *Lift coefficient curve slope versus Mach number for cones with different cone angles.*

drag equivalent to the force in the direction of the axis of the body, and the lift equivalent to the normal component. From equation (381), neglecting all terms of higher order, the pressure variation can be expressed in the form

$$\Delta p = - u_2 \rho_1 V_1. \tag{410}$$

Now with this approximation the drag becomes independent of the velocities corresponding to the potential function ϕ'', while the lift is independent of the velocity components corresponding to the potential ϕ'. The drag of the body with small angle of attack then becomes the same as for zero angle of attack, while the lift can be determined as a function only of the potential ϕ''.

Indeed, if the force component in the direction of the x-axis is considered equivalent to the drag, and if for the origin of the cylindrical coordinate φ the meridian plane which contains the undisturbed velocity is considered, it appears from equation (404) that the variation of pressure derived from $\partial\phi''/\partial x$ is equal and of opposite sign along the meridian planes corresponding to ϕ and $(\pi - \phi)$. The resultant of the pressure variations dependent on ϕ'' in the direction of the x-axis is therefore zero.

When the lift is considered, it can be written in the form

$$L = 2 \int_0^\pi d\phi \int_0^\infty -\Delta p y \cos\phi \, dx = 2\rho_1 V_1 \int_0^\pi d\phi \int_0^\infty u_2 y \cos\phi \, dx \tag{411}$$

where u_2 represents the variation of the x component of velocity along the surface of the body. The lift is not influenced by the part of u represented by $\partial \phi_2'/\partial x$, because this part is independent of φ (equation 386), and the integration of $\cos \varphi\, d\varphi$ from 0 to π in the equation (411) gives zero as the resultant value.

The value of the lift can therefore be written in the form

$$L = 2\rho_1 V_1 \int_0^\pi \int_0^\infty \frac{\partial \phi''}{\partial x}\, y \cos \varphi\, d\varphi\, dx \tag{411a}$$

and the moment about the vertex can be calculated from the equation

$$M = 2\rho_1 V_1 \int_0^\pi \int_0^\infty \frac{\partial \phi''}{\partial x}\, xy \cos \varphi\, d\varphi\, dx. \tag{412}$$

To obtain the values of L and M it is necessary to determine a function ϕ_2'' that satisfies the boundary conditions.

A simple general solution of the problem has not yet been found; therefore to obtain numerical results, a step-by-step procedure must be used. Some analytical expressions can be obtained if additional simplifying hypotheses are introduced.

With the approximation accepted before, the flow around a body of revolution in yaw can be represented by four potential functions ϕ_1', ϕ_2', ϕ_1'', and ϕ_2''. Because the potential function $\phi_1' + \phi_2'$ satisfies the boundary conditions and produces a stream that is tangent to the body, the potential function $(\phi_1'' + \phi_2'')$ must also produce a flow that must satisfy the boundary conditions. The boundary conditions would be expressed exactly in the following form:

$$\left(\frac{dy}{dx}\right)_{\varphi,r} = \left[\frac{v_1 + \dfrac{\partial \phi_2''}{\partial y}}{\dfrac{\partial \phi_2''}{\partial x}}\right]_{\varphi,r}. \tag{413}$$

However since the value of $\partial \phi_2''/\partial x$ is very small (small angle of attack), and since the inclination of the body meridian section $(dy/dx)_r$ with respect to the x-axis is also small (hypothesis of small disturbances), the boundary conditions can be expressed in the approximate form

$$\frac{\partial \phi_2''}{\partial y} + \frac{\partial \phi_1''}{\partial y} = v_1 + \frac{\partial \phi_2''}{\partial y} = 0. \tag{413a}$$

From differentiation of equation (400)

$$\frac{\partial \phi''}{\partial y} = \frac{\partial \phi_1''}{\partial y} + \frac{\partial \phi_2''}{\partial y} = v_1 + \cos \varphi\, B^2 \int_{\cosh^{-1}\frac{x}{By}}^0 m'(x - By \cosh z) \cosh^2 z\, dz. \tag{414}$$

Therefore if r is the radius of a section of the body, the boundary conditions are given by

$$V_1 \sin \alpha = - \frac{\partial \phi_2''}{\partial y} \frac{1}{\cos \varphi} = - B^2 \int_{\cosh^{-1} \frac{x}{Br}}^{0} m'(x - Br \cosh z) \cosh^2 z \, dz. \quad (415)$$

As in the preceding analysis, it is convenient to use the function $\xi = x - By \cosh z$ as an independent variable for equation (415). In this case equation (415) becomes

$$V_1 \sin \alpha = \frac{1}{r^2} \int_{0}^{x - Br} \frac{m'(\xi)(x - \xi)^2 \, d\xi}{\sqrt{(x - \xi)^2 - B^2 r^2}} \quad (416)$$

In the first approximation, it is possible to assume r to be small and approaching zero, in which case equation (416) becomes

$$V_1 \sin \alpha = \frac{1}{r^2} \int_{0}^{x - Br} m'(\xi)(x - \xi) d\xi. \quad (417)$$

Equation (417) can be integrated by parts, and it produces

$$V_1 \sin \alpha = \frac{1}{r^2} \left[-x \, m(0) + Br m(x - Br) + \int_{0}^{x - Br} m(\xi) d\xi \right] \quad (418)$$

but $m(0)$ is zero, because the body begins at the point $x = 0$. Therefore for $x = 0$ the flow is still undisturbed flow, and if r is small and Br is negligible, it follows that

$$V_1 \sin \alpha = \frac{1}{r^2} \int_{0}^{x} m(x) \, dx \quad \text{or} \quad m(x) = 2 V_1 r \frac{dr}{dx} \sin \alpha. \quad (419)$$

If S is a section of the body $S = \pi r^2$, it is then possible to write

$$\alpha \frac{V_1}{\pi} \frac{dS}{dx} = m(x) \quad (420)$$

Equation (420) permits determination of the value of $\partial \phi''/\partial x$, which appears in equation (411a). From equation (401),

$$\frac{\partial \phi''}{\partial x} = - B \cos \varphi \int_{\cosh^{-1} \frac{x}{By}}^{0} m'(x - By \cosh z) \cosh z \, dz \quad (421)$$

or substituting the value of ξ for $x - By \cosh z$

$$\frac{\partial \phi''}{\partial x} = B \cos \varphi \int_{0}^{x - By} \frac{m'(\xi)(x - \xi) d\xi}{By \sqrt{(x - \xi)^2 - B^2 y^2}}. \quad (422)$$

With the hypothesis of r approaching zero

$$\left[\frac{\partial \phi''}{\partial x}\right]_r = \frac{\cos \varphi}{r} \int_0^x m'(x)\, dx = \frac{\cos \varphi}{r} m(x) \tag{423}$$

and from equation (420)

$$\left[\frac{\partial \phi''}{\partial x}\right]_r = \frac{V_1 \cos \varphi}{\pi r} \frac{dS}{dx} \alpha. \tag{424}$$

Substituting equation (424) in equations (411) and (411a),

$$L = \rho_1 V_1^2 S_b\, \alpha \tag{425}$$

where S_b is the base section of the body, or

$$C_L = 2\, \alpha \tag{426}$$

where α is the angle of attack of the body.

Using equation (424) in equation (412) the moment becomes

$$M = \rho_1 V_1^2 S_m l\, \alpha \tag{427}$$

where the volume of the body is expressed as $S_m l$ (S_m is the mean section of the body and l the length of the body).

The moment arm from the vertex is

$$d = \frac{M}{L} = \left(\frac{S_m}{S_b}\right) l. \tag{428}$$

Equations (426) and (428) show that a body of revolution inclined at small angles with respect to the direction of flight has, in the first approximation, a lift that is proportional to the angle of attack and has a center of pressure position which is independent of Mach number and of the value of lift. The results are identical to those found in subsonic incompressible flow.

Lift and Moment for Bodies of Revolution in Yaw. In order to determine values of C_L and C_M, equations (426) and (427) can be applied only for very slender bodies of revolution for which dS/dx is a continuous function. For different cases it is possible to determine the phenomenon using the value of $\partial \phi_2''/\partial y$ given by equation (415) if a step-by-step calculation is introduced (Reference 37).

Proceeding in a similar way as for the analysis of the body of revolution on the axis with the undisturbed flow, assume that the distribution of the function $m(\xi)$ along the ξ axis is represented by a given curve as shown in Figure 158. At every point P_1, P_2, and P_n of the body a corresponding value of ξ can be determined. Therefore, the corresponding point A_n in the curve can be determined from the expression $\xi_n = x_n - By_n$. The curve that represents the function m between any two points A_{n-1} and A_n is not a straight line, but if the points A_{n-1} and A_n are very near each other an equivalent straight line can be substituted with good approximation for the curve $m(\xi)$. With this substitution the derivative between the points A_{n-1} and A_n becomes a constant.

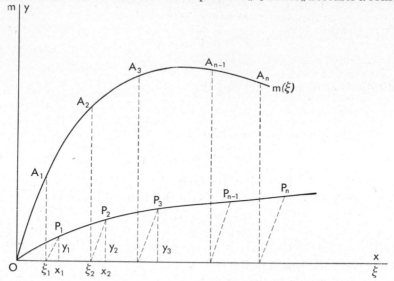

Fig. 158. *Doublet distribution for axial symmetrical body with angle of attack.*

If the substitution is made between all the points A considered, and if in place of the actual curve for the function m, a curve made up of straight segments is used, the calculation of the function $m(\xi)$ can be accomplished with the same system used for the body on the axis with the flow. In the zone between the origin O and the first point $A_{1(x_1 y_1)}$ the curve that gives m as a function of ξ can be expressed in the form

$$m_{A_1} = b_1 \xi$$

where b_1 is a constant. Therefore the integral in equation (415) which imposes the boundary conditions can be solved and from the value of v_1, the value of b_1 can be calculated.

$$V_1 \sin \alpha = -B^2 b_1 \int_{\cosh^{-1} \frac{x_1}{By_1}}^{0} \cosh^2 z\, dz \tag{429}$$

or

$$V_1 \sin \alpha = \frac{B^2 b_1}{2} \left[\cosh^{-1} \frac{x_1}{By_1} + \frac{x_1}{By_1} \sqrt{\frac{x_1^2}{B^2 y_1^2} - 1} \right]. \tag{429a}$$

In equation (429) the incidence of the body α and the coordinates of the point $A_1(x_1, y_1)$ are known; therefore the value of b_1 can be determined. Equation (429a) which gives the constant b_1 for a cone, is different from equation (409) because the boundary conditions are considered in the approximate form of equation (413a).

For the point P_2, an analogous expression can be written if the function m between A_1 and A_2 is expressed in the form

$$m_{A_1 A_2} = b_2\,(\xi_2 - \xi_1).$$

Equation (415) for the point P_2 becomes

$$V_1 \sin \alpha = - B^2 b_1 \int_{\cosh^{-1} \frac{x_2}{B y_2}}^{\cosh^{-1} \frac{x_2 - \xi_1}{B y_2}} \cosh^2 z\,dz$$

$$- B^2 b_2 \int_{\cosh^{-1} \frac{x_2 - \xi_1}{B y_2}}^{0} \cosh^2 z\,dz \qquad (430)$$

Indeed, the first integral must extend from $\xi = 0$ to $\xi_1 = (x_1 - B y_1)$, while the second integral must extend from ξ_1 to ξ_2. Therefore, z must go from

$$x_2 - B y_2 \cosh z = 0$$

to

$$x_2 - B y_2 \cosh z = \xi_1$$

in the first integral, and from

$$x_2 - B y_2 \cosh z = \xi_1$$

to

$$x_2 - B y_2 \cosh z = \xi_2 = x_2 - B y_2$$

in the second.

By performing the integration the following expression can be obtained from equation (430):

$$V_1 \sin \alpha = - \frac{B^2}{2} \left\{ b_1 \left(\cosh^{-1} \frac{x_2 - \xi_1}{B y_2} - \cosh^{-1} \frac{x_2}{B y_2} \right) - b_2 \left(\cosh^{-1} \frac{x_2 - \xi_1}{B y_2} \right) \right.$$

$$+ b_1 \left[\frac{x_2 - \xi_1}{B y_2} \sqrt{\left(\frac{x_2 - \xi_1}{B y_2} \right)^2 - 1} - \frac{x_2}{B y_2} \sqrt{\frac{x_2^2}{B^2 y_2^2} - 1} \right]$$

$$\left. - b_2 \left(\frac{x_2 - \xi_1}{B y_2} \right) \sqrt{\frac{(x_2 - \xi_1)^2}{B^2 y_2^2} - 1} \right\} \qquad (431)$$

where the only unknown value is the value of b_2. The value of the constant b_n for every point P_n can be determined in a similar way. The general equation is

$$V_1 \sin \alpha = \frac{B^2 b_1}{2} \sum_{i=1}^{i=n} \frac{b_i}{b_1} \left\{ \left(\cosh^{-1} \frac{x_n - \xi_{i-1}}{B y_n} - \cosh^{-1} \frac{x_n - \xi_i}{B y_n} \right) \right.$$

$$+ \left[\frac{x_n - \xi_{i-1}}{B y_n} \sqrt{\left(\frac{x_n - \xi_{i-1}}{B y_n} \right)^2 - 1} - \frac{x_n - \xi_i}{B y_n} \sqrt{\left(\frac{x_n - \xi_i}{B y_n} \right)^2 - 1} \right] \right\} \qquad (432)$$

where the values of the constants b_1, b_{n-1}, are determined from the considerations of the preceding points. The values of the constants b_1, b_2, b_n are proportional to the value $V_1 \sin \alpha$, and therefore when the angle of attack α changes, the values of b_1 change with the sine of the angle α (equation 429) while the values of b_i/b_1 do not change. Therefore calculation of the constant b_n/b_1 must be made for every Mach number that appears in B. However the results of the calculation can be used for every angle of attack for which the theory can be applied.

The lift coefficient can be calculated with equation (411a) in which a summation of terms that contain the constants b_1, b_2, and b_n can be substituted for the value of the integral that contains $\partial \phi'' / \partial x$. Indeed, for every point P_n, the value of $\partial \phi_2'' / \partial x$ given by equation (421) can be determined by considering zone by zone every zone in which m' is constant. Therefore the value of $\partial \phi_2'' / \partial x$ is equivalent to a summation of the type

$$\left(\frac{\partial \phi_2''}{\partial x} \right)_{P_n} = + B \cos \varphi \sum_{i=1}^{n} b_i \left[\sqrt{\frac{(x_n - \xi_{i-1})^2}{B^2 y_n^2} - 1} - \sqrt{\frac{(x_n - \xi_i)^2}{B^2 y_n^2} - 1} \right] \quad (433)$$

where x_n and y_n are the coordinates of the point P_n, and b_i and ξ_i are known. The function $\partial \phi_2'' / \partial x$ in equation (433) can be represented as a function of x by a step-by-step diagram, and its value can be considered constant between every two points P_{n-1}, P_n. The value of the function $y = f(x)$ that defines the surface of the body between the two points can be expressed, in the approximation accepted, in the form

$$y = (y_{n-1}) + \frac{y_n - y_{n-1}}{x_n - x_{n-1}} (x - x_{n-1}). \quad (434)$$

The integral that appears in the equation of the lift for the zone of the body between the points P_{n-1} and P_n then becomes

$$\int_{x_{n-1}}^{x_n} \frac{\partial \phi''}{\partial x} y dx = \int_{x_{n-1}}^{x_n} \frac{\partial \phi_2''}{\partial x} y dx = \frac{1}{2} \left(\frac{\partial \phi_2''}{\partial x} \right)_n (y_n + y_{n-1}) (x_n - x_{n-1}) \quad (435)$$

where equation (433) must be substituted for $\partial \phi_2'' / \partial x$ at the point P_n. To obtain higher precision, it is possible to consider, in equation (435) and in the subsequent equations (436) and (437), the value $(\partial \phi_2'' / \partial x)_{[n+(n-1)]/2}$, calculated at a point intermediate between P_n and P_{n-1} in place of the value $(\partial \phi_2'' / \partial x)_n$ at P_n. However, if the steps considered are small, the difference is not important (Reference 39).

Using equations (411a) and (435)

$$L = 2\rho_1 V_1 \int_0^\pi \frac{B\cos^2\phi}{2}\, d\varphi \sum_{n=1}^{n=N} (y_n + y_{n-1})(x_n - x_{n-1}) \sum_{i=1}^{n} b_i$$
$$\left[\sqrt{\frac{(x_n - \xi_{i-1})^2}{B^2 y_n{}^2} - 1} - \sqrt{\frac{(x_n - \xi_i)^2}{B^2 y_n{}^2} - 1} \right] \quad (436)$$

or

$$C_L = \frac{Bb_1}{y_m{}^2 V_1} \sum_{n=1}^{n=N} (y_n + y_{n-1})(x_n - x_{n-1}) \sum_{i=1}^{n} \frac{b_i}{b_1}\left[\sqrt{\frac{(x_n - \xi_{i-1})^2}{B^2 y_n{}^2} - 1} \right.$$
$$\left. - \sqrt{\frac{(x_n - \xi_i)^2}{B^2 y_n{}^2} - 1} \right] \quad (437)$$

where the point P_N is the last point of the body, and y_m is the radius of the surface of reference and usually is the maximum radius of the body. The lift coefficient given from equation (437) contains the constants b_i/b_1 which are obtained from the boundary conditions given by equation (432).

Equation (432) shows that the constants b_i are proportional to $\sin \alpha$. Equation (432) can be transformed by using constants h_i defined by the equation

$$b_i = \frac{2h_i}{B^2} V_1 \sin \alpha = \frac{2h_i v_1 \cdot}{B^2 \cos \varphi}. \quad (438)$$

The constants h_i are independent of the angle of attack of the body, therefore equation (432) that determines the values of the constants becomes

$$1 = \sum_{i=1}^{i=n} h_i \left[\left(\cosh^{-1}\frac{x_n - \xi_{i-1}}{By_n} - \cosh^{-1}\frac{x_n - \xi_i}{By_n} \right) \right.$$
$$\left. + \left(\frac{x_n - \xi_{i-1}}{By_n}\sqrt{\left(\frac{x_n - \xi_{i-1}}{By_n}\right)^2 - 1} - \frac{x_n - \xi_i}{By_n}\sqrt{\left(\frac{x_n - \xi_i}{By_n}\right)^2 - 1} \right) \right] \quad (439)$$

and the lift coefficient becomes

$$C_L = \frac{2\alpha}{By_m{}^2} \sum_{n=1}^{n=N} (y_n + y_{n-1})(x_n - x_{n-1}) \sum_{i=1}^{i=n} h_i \left[\sqrt{\left(\frac{x_n - \xi_{i-1}}{By_n}\right)^2 - 1} \right.$$
$$\left. - \sqrt{\left(\frac{x_n - \xi_i}{By_n}\right)^2 - 1} \right]. \quad (440)$$

The lift coefficient is proportional to the angle of attack and changes when the Mach number changes (because B changes). If the value of $(\partial\phi_2''/\partial x)_{[n+(n-1)]/2}$ is taken for the value of $\partial\phi_2''/\partial x$ in equation (435), equation (440) becomes

$$C_L = \frac{2\alpha}{By_m^2} \sum_{n=1}^{n=N} (y_n + y_{n-1}) \left(\frac{x_n - x_{n-1}}{2}\right) \left\{ \sum_{i=1}^{i=n} h_i \left[\sqrt{\left(\frac{x_n - \xi_{i-1}}{By_n}\right)^2 - 1} - \right. \right.$$

$$\left. \sqrt{\left(\frac{x_n - \xi_i}{By_n}\right)^2 - 1} \right] + \sum_{i=1}^{i=n-1} h_i \left[\sqrt{\left(\frac{x_{n-1} - \xi_{i-1}}{By_{n-1}}\right)^2 - 1} - \sqrt{\left(\frac{x_{n-1} - \xi_i}{By_{n-1}}\right)^2 - 1} \right] \right\}$$

$$(440a)$$

For the determination of the moment given by equation (412) the expression

$$\int_{x_{n-1}}^{x_n} \frac{\partial \phi_2}{\partial x} \, xy \, dx$$

must be calculated. Substituting the value given by equation (434) for y, the expression becomes

$$\int_{x_{n-1}}^{x_n} \left(\frac{\partial \phi_2''}{\partial x}\right)_{n-1} xy \, dx = \left(\frac{\partial \phi_2''}{\partial x}\right)_m \int_{x_{n-1}}^{x_n} xy \, dx$$

$$= \frac{x_n - x_{n-1}}{6} \left[3y_{n-1}(x_n + x_{n-1}) \right.$$

$$\left. + (y_n - y_{n-1})(2x_n + x_{n-1}) \right] \left(\frac{\partial \phi_2''}{\partial x}\right)_n. \qquad (441)$$

Substituting equation (441) in equation (412),

$$C_m = \frac{B}{y_m^2 l} \sum_{n=1}^{n=N} \frac{(x_n - x_{n-1})}{3} \left[3y_{n-1}(x_{n-1} + x_n) \right.$$

$$\left. + (y_n - y_{n-1})(2x_n + x_{n-1}) \right] \sum_{i=1}^{n} \frac{b_i}{V_1}$$

$$\left[\sqrt{\frac{(x_n - \xi_{i-1})^2}{B^2 y_n^2} - 1} - \sqrt{\frac{(x_n - \xi_i)^2}{B^2 y_n^2} - 1} \right] \qquad (442)$$

where l is the length of the reference for the moment coefficient which usually corresponds to the length of the body. Substituting the constants h_i for the constants b_i, (equation 438), the moment coefficient becomes

$$C_m = \frac{2\alpha}{By_m^2 l} \sum_{n=1}^{n=N} \frac{x_n - x_{n-1}}{3} \left[3y_{n-1}(x_n + x_{n-1}) \right.$$

$$\left. + (y_n - y_{n-1})(2x_n + x_{n-1}) \right] \sum_{i=1}^{i=n} h_i \left[\sqrt{\frac{(x_n - \xi_{i-1})^2}{B^2 y_n^2} - 1} \right.$$

$$\left. - \sqrt{\frac{(x_n - \xi_1)^2}{B^2 y_n^2} - 1} \right]. \qquad (443)$$

If, to be more exact, the average value between the point n and the point $n-1$ is assumed for the value of $\partial\phi''/\partial x$ in equation (441), the moment coefficient becomes

$$
C_m = \frac{2\alpha}{By^2{}_m l} \sum_{n=1}^{n=N} \frac{x_n - x_{n-1}}{6}\left[3y_{n-1}\left(x_n + x_{n-1}\right)\right.
$$

$$
\left. + \left(y_n - y_{n-1}\right)\left(2x_n + x_{n-1}\right)\right]\left\{\sum_{i=1}^{i=n} h_i\left[\sqrt{\left(\frac{x_n - \xi_{i-1}}{y_n B}\right)^2 - 1}\right.\right.
$$

$$
\left.- \sqrt{\left(\frac{x_n - \xi_i}{y_n B}\right)^2 - 1}\right] + \sum_{i=1}^{i=n-1} h_i\left[\sqrt{\left(\frac{x_{n-1} - \xi_{i-1}}{By_{n-1}}\right)^2 - 1}\sqrt{\left(\frac{x_{n-1} - \xi_i}{By_{n-1}}\right)^2 - 1}\right]\right\}
$$

$$(443a)$$

If the body is an open nose body of revolution, the calculation of the lift and moment coefficients does not change, because the expressions in the integration in equations (411a) and (412) do not change. Only the limits of integration change and must extend from BR_N to infinity, or if the body is of length l, to the end of the body that has for its abscissa the point $(BR_N + l)$. R_N is the radius of the nose (Reference 39).

Because the moments are taken with respect to the origin of the axis, that is, in front of the body of BR_N, it is necessary to transfer the moment to determine the moment coefficient with respect to any point on the body.

It is apparent that the approximation of the small-disturbance theory to determine lift and moment of bodies of revolution in yaw is smaller than the approximation of the same theory to determine drag for bodies without angle of attack. This is so because, for the same shape of body, the disturbances increase with the angle of attack, and because for practical calculations it is necessary to make some other simplifying hypotheses which reduce the precision of the results. The theory can be applied with good approximation if the angle of attack of the body is small and if the body is a thin body of good aerodynamic shape.

12

PHENOMENA FOR CONICAL BODIES —

HODOGRAPH SYSTEM

The General Equations of Conical Field. In Chapter 11, by assuming the disturbances produced by the bodies to be small, solutions for conical bodies of revolution with and without angle of attack were found. The results are approximate and do not take into account all losses across the shock waves which are generated at the vertex of the cone, and do not give the position of the shock. It is possible, in some cases, to obtain a solution for the supersonic flow around a conical body without a limiting hypothesis for the disturbances by using the general equations of potential flow. As is shown in Chapter 10, the hypothesis of potential flow is exact for a conical body of revolution with axis parallel to the flow.

If the body is an infinite conical body and the flow is a perfect flow, the flow must have the same physical properties along every straight line that passes

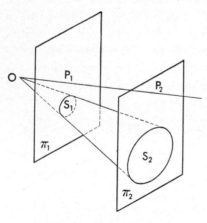

Fig. 159. *Conical flow.*

through the vertex of the cone. Indeed, if two sections of the cone, S_1 and S_2, parallel to each other, are considered (Figure 159), because there is no scale effect in a perfect flow, the flow field must be geometrically similar and kinematically equal in the two corresponding sections; therefore the speed at every two points P_1 and P_2, which are in the same straight line which passes through O and which also are in the two planes π_1 and π_2 which contain S_1 and S_2, must be the same and must have the same direction. The consideration is valid also for a cone of finite length if the flow is all supersonic, because in perfect supersonic flow disturbances produced downstream cannot interfere with the phenomena upstream. When, behind the shock or at the cone, the velocity is subsonic, the consideration can no longer be applied to a finite cone, because every variation introduced in the flow at the end of the cone can propagate upstream; therefore the phenomenon is a function of the position of the section S considered with respect to the end of the conical body. In this case, a conical phenomenon does not correspond to a finite conical body.

If, for the study of the conical field, the polar coordinate system is used, and r is the radius, η the angle between the radius vector and the axis of the cone in the meridian plane, and φ the angular coordinate of the meridian plane with respect to a plane which contains the direction of the velocity and the axis of the cone (Figure 160), the existence of a conical flow corresponds to

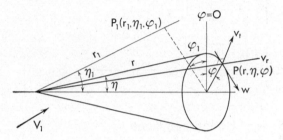

Fig. 160. *Velocity components in conical coordinates.*

the condition that the velocity components are independent of the value of the radius r. If ϕ is the flow potential, the potential function for a conical field must have the form

$$\phi = rF(\eta, \varphi) \tag{444}$$

The components of the velocity along the radius r, (v_r), normal to the radius r in the meridian plane $\varphi = $ constant, (v_t), and normal to the meridian plane (w), (Figure 160) are

$$v_r = \frac{\partial \phi}{\partial r} = F; \quad v_t = \frac{\partial \phi}{r \partial \eta} = \frac{\partial F}{\partial \eta}; \quad w = \frac{\partial \phi}{r \sin \eta \partial \varphi} = \frac{1}{\sin \eta} \frac{\partial F}{\partial \varphi} \tag{445}$$

In the equation of potential flow in polar coordinates (equation 333), because F is not a function of r, the terms

$$\frac{\partial v_r}{\partial r}, \quad \frac{\partial v_t}{\partial r}, \quad \frac{\partial w}{\partial r}$$

are equal to zero; therefore equation (333) becomes

$$\sin^2 \eta \left(1 - \frac{v_t^2}{a^2}\right) \frac{\partial^2 F}{\partial \eta^2} - \frac{2wv_t}{a^2} \sin \eta \frac{\partial^2 F}{\partial \eta \partial \varphi} + \left(1 - \frac{w^2}{a^2}\right) \frac{\partial^2 F}{\partial \varphi^2}$$

$$+ \sin^2 \eta F \left(2 - \frac{w^2 + v_t^2}{a^2}\right) + \frac{1}{2} \sin 2\eta \frac{\partial F}{\partial \eta} \left(1 + \frac{w^2}{a^2}\right) = 0 \tag{446}$$

or

$$\sin \eta \left(1 - \frac{v_t^2}{a^2}\right)\frac{\partial v_t}{\partial \eta} - \frac{2wv_t}{a^2}\frac{\partial v_t}{\partial \varphi} + \left(1 - \frac{w^2}{a^2}\right)\frac{\partial w}{\partial \varphi}$$

$$+ \sin \eta \, v_r \left(2 - \frac{w^2 + v_t^2}{a^2}\right) + \cos \eta \, v_t \left(1 + \frac{w^2}{a^2}\right) = 0. \qquad (446a)$$

Equation (446) shows that the phenomenon is dependent only on two position variables, η and φ, and therefore conical phenomena, from the analytical point of view, are analogous to two-dimensional phenomena. The velocity

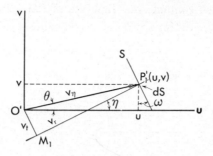

Hodograph Plane

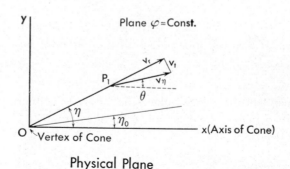

Physical Plane

Fig. 161. *Hodograph diagram for conical flow.*

at a point P can be divided into two components, the velocity v_η in the meridian plane which contains P_1, (plane of the axis of the cone and of the point P_1), and a component w normal to the plane. The component v_η in the meridian plane is the resultant of the components v_r and v_t. For every meridian plane $\varphi =$ constant, along every line $\eta =$ constant, the velocity v_η is constant in intensity and direction, because the phenomenon is conical; therefore for every value of η in the meridian plane there is a corresponding value of v_η, and in the hodograph plane it is possible to design, for every plane $\varphi =$ constant, the diagram which gives the distribution of the velocity v_η as a function of η. The diagram can be obtained in the following manner (Figure 161). If, in a plane, two axes u and v are considered parallel to the x- and y-axes of the physical plane, and a vector equal to v_η is plotted for every value of η in the plane uv (hodograph plane), it is possible to obtain, in the plane uv, a diagram S which is the locus of the points P_1, which defines the velocity v_η in direction and intensity. Therefore for every value of η there is a corresponding point P_1' in the hodograph plane which defines the component v_η in the meridian plane along the radius of coordinate η. Designing, from the point P_1', the line $P_1'M_1$ parallel to the radius OP_1, and from O' the normal to $P_1'M_1$ because $O'P_1'$ corresponds to v_η, $P_1'M_1$ corresponds to the component v_r, and $O'M_1$ to the component $v_{t.}$,

If u and v are the components of v_η along the two coordinate axes,

$$u = v_r \cos \eta - v_t \sin \eta \tag{447}$$

$$v = v_r \sin \eta + v_t \cos \eta \tag{448}$$

but for the condition of a conical field from equation (445),

$$\frac{\partial v_r}{\partial \eta} = \frac{\partial F}{\partial \eta} = v_t. \tag{449}$$

Therefore

$$\left.\begin{aligned}
\frac{du}{d\eta} &= - \left(v_r + \frac{\partial v_t}{\partial \eta} \right) \sin \eta \\
\frac{dv}{d\eta} &= \left(v_r + \frac{\partial v_t}{\partial \eta} \right) \cos \eta
\end{aligned}\right\} \tag{450}$$

If S is the diagram locus of the points P_1' in the hodograph plane, from equation (450) it appears that

$$\left(\frac{dS}{d\eta} \right)^2 = \left(\frac{du}{d\eta} \right)^2 + \left(\frac{dv}{d\eta} \right)^2$$

or

$$\frac{dS}{d\eta} = v_r + \frac{\partial v_t}{\partial \eta}. \tag{451}$$

Equations (450) and (451) show that the element dS is normal to the direction $\eta = $ constant; indeed, if ω is the angle between the normal to the curve S and the u-axis (Figure 161), then

$$du = - dS \sin \omega$$

$$dv = + dS \cos \omega.$$

Therefore from equation (450) and (451) it appears that ω is equal to η, and $P_1'M_1$ inclined at η with the u axis, is normal to dS. This consideration permits, in some conditions, determination of the diagram S in the meridian plane $\varphi = $ constant by a step-by-step construction, and simplifies the problem, which is reduced to determination of the value of the quantity $\partial v_t / \partial \eta$ for every point P. Indeed, from equation (451) is obtained

$$dS = \left(v_r + \frac{\partial v_t}{\partial \eta} \right) d\eta. \tag{452}$$

Therefore the radius of curvature of the diagram S as a function of η is equal to $(v_r + \partial v_t / \partial \eta)$, and because it must be normal to S, the radius must be in the direction of v_r. Now take along the line $P_1 M_1$ that represents v_r, a radius $P_1 A_1$, equal to $(v_r + dv_t / d\eta)$ (Figure 162); if the value of $(v_r + dv_t / d\eta)$ is considered constant for a small variation of η (equal to $\Delta \eta$), from P_1' a point

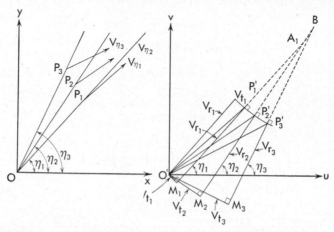

Fig. 162. *Construction of the hodograph diagram for conical flow.*

P_2' can be obtained, which gives the velocity v_η for a value of η corresponding to $(\eta + \Delta \eta)$ (equation (452). Now if the value of the velocity v_η for a given value of η is known, the point P_1' can be designed; and if the value of $\partial v_t / \partial \eta$ is known, the value of $R = P_1' A_1$ can be calculated, and the point P_2' corresponding to a variation of η can be determined graphically. When the point P_2' is known, the values of $v_{r(P_2)}$ ($M_2 P_2'$) and $v_{t(P_2)}$ ($M_2 O'$) are known; therefore if the value $(\partial v_t / \partial \eta)_{P_2}$ can be calculated, the new radius $P_2' B$, inclined at $(\eta + \Delta \eta)$ with respect to the axis, can be determined from equation (452). The new point P_3' along the circle of radius $P_2' B$ at η corresponding to $(\eta + 2\Delta \eta)$ can be determined. The point P_3' defines the velocity v_η along the radius inclined at $(\eta + 2\Delta \eta)$ in the meridian plane $\varphi = $ constant. Thus, proceeding step by step, the entire flow can be determined. Therefore the calculation of the flow field for a conical phenomenon can be reduced to determination of the value of $\partial v_t / \partial \eta$ at every point of the meridian plane.

Now equation (446a) gives the value of $(v_r + \partial v_t / \partial \eta)$ as a function of the other quantities and it is possible to transform equation (446a) into an equation which contains the radius of the hodograph R in place of

$$v_r + \frac{\partial v_t}{\partial \eta}.$$

Equation (446a) after the substitution becomes

$$\left(1 - \frac{v_t^2}{a^2}\right) R = \frac{2}{\sin \eta} \frac{v_t w}{a^2} \frac{\partial v_t}{\partial \varphi} - \cot \eta v_t \left(1 + \frac{w^2}{a^2}\right)$$
$$- \left(1 - \frac{w^2}{a^2}\right)\left(v_r + \frac{1}{\sin \eta} \frac{\partial w}{\partial \varphi}\right) \tag{453}$$

Equation (453) shows that the radius of the hodograph diagram is a function of the velocity components and of the derivatives of the velocity components with respect to the variable φ. Therefore the flow field of every conical phenomenon can be determined, with the approximations of potential flow, with a step-by-step calculation, if the velocity components are known along a closed line around the cross section of the body in the zone of the perturbations produced by the body. If, for example, the cross section of a conical shock wave and the stream Mach number are known, the velocity components behind the shock can be determined from the shape of the shock, because across the shock only the component v_n normal to the front of the shock changes (equation 110), and therefore v_r does not change. From the distribution of the velocity components along the cross section of the shock, the local derivatives $\partial w/\partial \varphi$ and $\partial v_t/\partial \varphi$ can be determined. Using equation (453), the radius of the hodograph diagram in every meridian plane can be evaluated, from which the velocity distribution along another surface near the surface of the shock, but closer to the body, can be obtained. In this way, the entire flow field between the shock and the body can be obtained step by step. In a similar way, if the velocity distribution around the body is known, the flow field around the body can be obtained.

Because the radius R used in the hodograph plane has the dimension of a velocity, as appears from equation (453), the scale of R in the hodograph diagram is determined, and is equal to the scale of u and v or of v_η. The sign of R is determined from equation (450); at the point P_1 the radius R can be plotted along the straight line P_1C_1 in the direction P_1C_1 or in the direction P_1C_2 (Figure 163). Because OP_1 is positive and

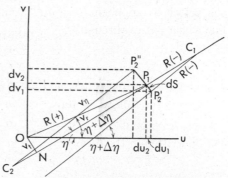

Fig. 163. *The orientation of the radius of curvature in the hodograph diagram.*

v_r, represented by NP_1, is positive in the convention accepted, if R is positive, it must be in the same direction as v_r; therefore the center of the circle must be C_2. If R is negative, it must be in the opposite direction and the center must be C_1. The new point in the first case is P_2'' and in the second case is P_2'. The equations (450) agree with the convention because, if R is positive and $\Delta\eta$ positive, dv must be positive and du negative, as happens for dv_2 and du_2; while if R is negative, du_1 must be positive and dv_1 must be negative, as happens in the case C_1P_2'. A different numerical integration can be substituted for the step-by-step integration considered before, by assuming, for the variation of $\Delta\eta$ considered, the values v_t, $\partial v_t/\partial\eta$, and $\partial w/\partial\eta$ constant; but the hypothesis of $(v_r + \partial v_t/\partial\eta)$ constant, in the step $\Delta\eta$, gives, in general, much greater accuracy than the hypothesis of v_t, $\partial v_t/\partial\eta$ and $\partial w/\partial\eta$ constant, because $(v_r + \partial v_t/\partial\eta)$ is, in general, larger than v_t, and its variation is much smaller.

For some cases of conical flow, use of rectangular coordinates may be more convenient. In this case, the general equation of potential flow in rectangular coordinates given by equation (326) must be substituted for equation (446). The condition of the conical field can be expressed in this form (Figure 164). If the origin of the coordinates is coincident with the vertex of the cone, when the point P considered moves along a straight line which passes through the origin, the variations of the velocity components must be zero. The variations of

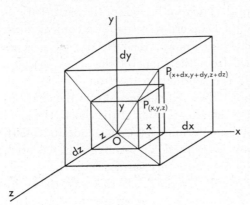

Fig. 164. *Conical flow in Cartesian coordinates.*

the velocity components are du, dv, and dw. If P moves along a straight line which passes through O,

$$\frac{dx}{x} = \frac{dy}{y} = \frac{dz}{z} = \frac{1}{k}.$$

Therefore, the terms du, dv, and dw given by

$$du = \frac{\partial u}{\partial x}\,dx + \frac{\partial u}{\partial y}\,dy + \frac{\partial u}{\partial z}\,dz = \phi_{xx}dx + \phi_{xy}dy + \phi_{xz}dz$$

can be written in the form

$$
\left.
\begin{aligned}
kdu &= \phi_{xx}x + \phi_{xy}y + \phi_{xz}z = 0 \\
kdv &= \phi_{yx}x + \phi_{yy}y + \phi_{yz}z = 0 \\
kdw &= \phi_{zx}x + \phi_{zy}y + \phi_{zz}z = 0
\end{aligned}
\right\}
\qquad (454)
$$

From equations (454) three of the six second derivatives of ϕ can be eliminated, and for the solution of a general conical field problem, only three second derivatives of ϕ must be determined as in equation (446a). Equation (454) can be written in the form

$$\left.\begin{aligned}
\phi_{xz} &= \phi_{zx} = -\phi_{xx}\frac{x}{z} - \phi_{yx}\frac{y}{z}\\[2mm]
\phi_{yz} &= \phi_{zy} = -\phi_{xy}\frac{x}{z} - \phi_{yy}\frac{y}{z}\\[2mm]
\phi_{zz} &= \phi_{xx}\frac{x^2}{z^2} + 2\phi_{xy}\frac{xy}{z^2} + \phi_{yy}\frac{y^2}{z^2}
\end{aligned}\right\} \qquad (454a)$$

Cone of Revolution with Axis Parallel to the Flow. When the phenomenon is conical with axial symmetry, all variations of the physical quantities disappear in the direction normal to every meridian plane; therefore in equations (446) and (453) all derivatives with respect to φ disappear. For axial symmetric phenomenon equation (446) becomes

$$\sin\eta\left(1 - \frac{v_l^2}{a^2}\right)\frac{\partial^2 F}{\partial\eta^2} + F\left(2 - \frac{v_l^2}{a^2}\right) + \cos\eta\,\frac{\partial F}{\partial\theta} = 0 \qquad (455)$$

and equation (453) (Reference 40) becomes

$$R = -\frac{v_t\cot\eta + v_r}{1 - \dfrac{v_t^2}{a^2}}. \qquad (456)$$

Equation (456) can be transformed in terms containing the velocity components relative to the limiting velocity V_l.

$$\frac{R}{V_l} = -\frac{(v_t/V_l)\cot\eta + v_r/V_l}{1 - (v_t^2/V_l^2)(V_l^2/a^2)}$$

but $V^2 = v_r^2 + v_t^2$, and V^2/a^2 is given as a function of V/V_l from equation (85b) in Chapter 2,

$$\frac{V_l^2}{V^2} - 1 = \frac{2}{\gamma - 1}\frac{a^2}{V^2}.$$

Therefore

$$\frac{v_t^2}{a^2} = \frac{v_t^2/V_l^2}{1 - V^2/V_l^2}\frac{2}{\gamma - 1}$$

and

$$\frac{R}{V_l} = -\frac{v_t/V_l\cot\eta + v_r/V_l}{1 - \dfrac{2}{\gamma - 1}\dfrac{v_t^2/V_l^2}{1 - v_t^2/V_l^2 - v_r^2/V_l^2}}. \qquad (457)$$

Equation (457) permits determination of the radius of the hodograph diagram for every value of η as a function of v_r/V_l and v_t/V_l corresponding to the η considered. Because from the value of $R(\eta)$ the values of v_r/V_l and v_t/V_l for a value of $(\eta + \Delta\eta)$ can be determined, equation (457) permits determination of the complete flow field of the conical phenomenon. If, in the hodograph plane, the velocities relative to the limiting velocities are plotted, the radius R must also be plotted in the same scale; therefore equation (457) gives the value which must be used in the construction.

The practical procedure can be as follows: the value of v_r/V_l and v_t/V_l for a given value of η must be fixed with criteria that will be discussed later. From the values of v_r/V_l and v_t/V_l fixed for the value of η considered, a corresponding point P_1' in the hodograph plane can be determined. In Figure 165, O_1N_1', inclined at η with respect to the u-axis, is equal to v_r/V_l; and $N_1'P_1'$, normal to O_1N_1', is equal to v_t/V_l. With equation (457) the value of $(R/V_l)_\eta$ can be determined. Along the line $P_1'N_1$, parallel to O_1N_1' at P_1', a segment equal to $(R/V_l)_\eta$ must be taken, and the point C_1 determined $[P_1'C_1 = (R/V_l)_\eta]$. The direction in which the segment equal to $(R/V_l)_\eta$ must be taken

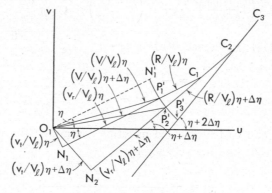

Fig. 165. *Construction of the hodograph diagram for cone of revolution in axis with the free stream.*

is determined by the convention discussed before, and must be as in Figure 165 if R/V_l is negative. From the point C_1 a circle $P_1'P_2'$ can be drawn and a point $P_2'(\eta + \Delta\eta)$ can be obtained along the radius $C_1P_2'N_2$ inclined at $(\eta + \Delta\eta)$ with respect to the u-axis. The segment $O'P_2'$ gives the value of $(V/V_l)_{\eta + \Delta\eta}$, and the segments N_2P_2' and N_2O_1 give the corresponding v_r/V_l and v_t/V_l components. With equation (457) the value of $(R/V_l)_{\eta + \Delta\eta}$ can be determined. Because the radius must be in the direction of $(v_r/V_l)_{\eta + \Delta\eta}$, taken along the line $N_2P_2C_1$, a segment equal to $(R/V_l)_{\eta + \Delta\eta}$, the new center of the curvature of the hodograph diagram at P_2', C_2, can be determined. Drawing a circle $P_2'P_3'$ with center C_2, the point $(P_3')_{\eta + \Delta\eta}$, along the radius C_2P_3'

inclined with respect to the u-axis at $(\eta + 2\Delta\eta)$, can be determined. Proceeding in a similar way, all values of v_r/V_l and v_t/V_l for every value of η, corresponding to the values of v_r/V_l and v_t/V_l for the value of η fixed at the beginning, can be determined. In the practical applications the system of calculation can be either numerical and graphic or only numerical by means of the following equations,

$$(v_t)_{\eta+\Delta\eta} = (v_t)_\eta \cos \Delta\eta + (R - v_r)_\eta \sin \Delta_\eta$$
$$(v_r)_{\eta+\Delta\eta} = (v_t)_\eta \sin \Delta\eta - (R - v_r)_\eta \cos \Delta\eta + (R)_\eta$$

In order to choose the value of η from which to start the construction and to fix the corresponding values of v_r/V_l and v_t/V_l, it is convenient to remember that, at the surface of the cone, the velocity must be in a radial direction and v_t must be zero; therefore if for the initial value of η the angle of the cone η_0 is chosen, in order to know the initial conditions, it is enough to fix the corresponding value of v_r/V_l; then the entire flow field can be determined. To determine the phenomenon it is necessary only to determine the free-stream Mach number corresponding to the value of v_r/V_l fixed at the surface of the cone.

The determination of the free-stream velocity corresponding to the value of v_r/V_l fixed at the surface of the cone can be accomplished, considering the equilibrium across the shock wave which is produced by the cone.

If the phenomenon is conical, the shock wave must start from the vertex of the cone, and the intersection of the front of the shock with the meridian plane must be a straight line. Indeed, if P_1 is a point on the shock wave, along the straight line OP_1 (Figure 166), the velocity must be constant; and because across the shock at P_1 the velocity V_1/V_l becomes V/V_l, for every point of the line OP_1 the velocity V_1/V_l must undergo the same transformation. Along the line OP_1 the equations of shock must be applied. Let η_S be the polar coordinate of the shock and let v_r/V_l and

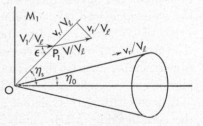

Fig. 166. *Determination of the position of the conical shock for axial symmetrical phenomena.*

v_t/V_l be the corresponding velocity components for $\epsilon = \eta_S$, obtained from the equations of shock (Figure 166). From equations (105) and (110) of Chapter 3

$$\frac{v_r}{V_l} = \frac{V_1}{V_l} \cos \eta_S \tag{458}$$

and from equation (124)

$$\frac{- v_t/V_l}{V_1/V_l \sin \eta_S} = \frac{2}{\gamma + 1} \left(\frac{1}{M_1^2 \sin^2 \eta_S} + \frac{\gamma - 1}{2} \right) \tag{459}$$

because the value of V_l does not change across the shock (equation 151). But M_1 is given in terms of V_1/V_l by equation (85b); therefore it is possible to write

$$-\frac{v_t}{V_l} = \frac{V_1}{V_l} \sin \eta_S \frac{2}{\gamma + 1} \left[\left(\frac{V_l^2}{V_1^2} - 1 \right) \frac{\gamma - 1}{2} \frac{1}{\sin^2 \eta_S} + \frac{\gamma - 1}{2} \right]$$

or because

$$\frac{v_r}{V_l} = \frac{V_1}{V_l} \cos \eta_S$$

$$-\frac{v_t}{V_l} = \frac{\gamma - 1}{\gamma + 1} \frac{v_r}{V_l} \cot \eta_S \left[\left(\frac{V_l}{v_r} \right)^2 - 1 \right]. \tag{460}$$

Equation (460) gives, for every value of η_S, a relation between v_r and v_t, but the construction of the hodograph diagram also gives a relation between v_r and v_t for every value of η; therefore from the two different relations the condition of equilibrium for which shock and conical flow can exist can be determined; from this, the angle of the shock and the free-stream Mach number can be obtained. A practical way of obtaining the value of η_S consists in determination of the value of v_t'/V_l from equation (460) for some values of η, using for v_r/V_l the value v_r/V_l given by the hodograph diagram for the corresponding value of η considered. When the value of v_t'/V_l is equal to the value of v_t/V_l obtained from the hodograph diagram for the corresponding η, shock and conical flow can exist, and the corresponding value of η gives the actual position of the shock; therefore, plotting v_t'/V_l and v_t/V_l as functions of η, the value of η_S can be determined from the intersection of the two curves. From the value of η_S and of the corresponding v_r/V_l from equation (458), the value of V_1/V_l can be determined, and from equation (85b) the free-stream Mach number can be determined. For different treatments of the same phenomenon see references 41 and 42.

Instead of fixing the value of v_r/V_l at the cone and determining from this the corresponding Mach number of the undisturbed stream, it is possible by knowing the Mach number of the undisturbed stream to start the calculation by fixing the value of the angle of shock η_S, and from this to determine the flow field and the angle of the cone that gives, at the Mach number considered, the chosen angle of shock. In order to obtain a physical solution, the angle of the shock must be larger than the Mach angle.

The calculation in this case starts with determination of the value of v_r/V_l and v_t/V_l behind the shock, from the value of M_1 and η_S chosen, with equations (458) and (459). From the values of v_r/V_l and v_t/V_l for the value of η_S chosen, the entire hodograph diagram can be constructed, and the angle of the cone can be found. The value of η_0 of the cone, which corresponds to the value η_S of the front of the shock chosen, for the Mach number considered, is determined from the condition that for η_0 the value of v_t/V_l must be zero; therefore the radius $(R)\eta_0$ must be on the straight line that passes through O_1.

From the value of v_r/V_l at the cone, the pressure can be determined as a function of the pressure of the undisturbed stream. Indeed, from equation (121) the value of the pressure behind the shock can be determined; while with equation (85a) the pressure on the body, as a function of the pressure behind the shock, can be calculated from the value of V/V_l behind the shock and at the body.

Considerations on the Results of the Cone Calculations.

A practical example of calculation of a cone is given in Figure 167. The angle of cone considered is 30°, and the value of v_r/V_l at the cone is fixed equal to 0.42. From the calculations, an angle of shock of 54°12' is found and a corresponding Mach number, $M = 1.708$, is obtained for the free stream. In Figure 167a the shape of the stream lines obtained from the preceding calculations is shown. As it appears from the figure and as it is possible to deduce from equation (457) (R is negative), when the value of η increases, the inclination of the velocity with respect to the axis of the body decreases; therefore the deviation across the shock is less than the angle of the cone, and the stream lines are curved in the zone between the shock and the cone. The velocity moving from the shock decreases and the pressure increases; the velocity at the cone is less than behind the shock, and the pressure is greater. The compression behind the shock is isentropic, and therefore without losses. The shock losses are connected only with the variation of pressure across the shock. Conical compression is therefore in part isentropic, and therefore is more efficient than two-dimensional compression (gives less increase of entropy for the same increase in pressure).

The angle of deviation across the shock is less than the angle of cone; and for a given Mach number, when the deviation across the shock is the maximum possible, the angle of the cone is larger than the angle of the corresponding wedge. Therefore for a given Mach number the maximum angle of cone for which the shock is still attached is larger than the corresponding angle in the two-dimensional case. In Figure 168 the maximum angles for cone and wedge, for which it is still possible to have an attached shock, are plotted as functions of the Mach angle. When the angle of the shock corresponds to the value that gives maximum deviation across the shock for the Mach number considered, the flow behind the shock is all subsonic. For an angle of shock less than the value of maximum deviation, the flow behind the shock can be in part supersonic and in part subsonic. If calculations are made, assuming a value of the angle of shock larger than the value corresponding to maximum deviation, an angle of cone must be found smaller than the value corresponding to maximum deviation; because if the deviation permissible across the shock decreases, the corresponding angle to cone must also decrease. Therefore for

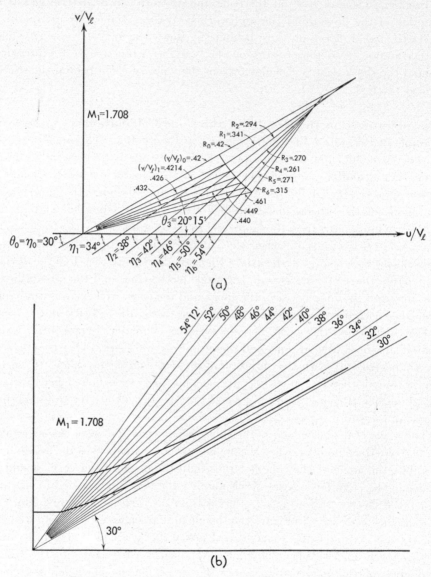

Fig. 167. *Example of graphical calculation of the flow around a cone of 30° angle at stream Mach number 1.708. (a) Construction of the hodograph diagram. (b) Construction of the stream lines.*

every Mach number and for every angle of cone, two possible conditions of equilibrium exist as for the two-dimensional case, one with a weak shock and another with a strong shock. The velocity at the cone is notably different for the two cases.

For the same reasons discussed for the wedge, if the shock is produced only

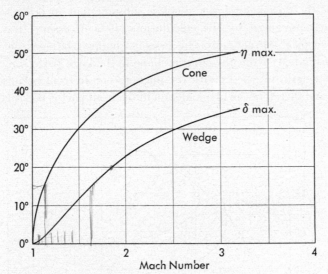

Fig. 168. *Maximum angle of cone and of the wedge that permits an attached shock versus Mach number.*

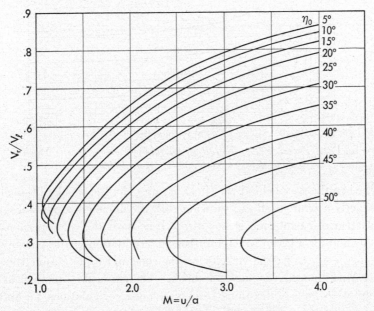

Fig. 169. *Velocity at the surface of the cone versus Mach number for cones of different cone angles. (The velocity is given as ratio to the limiting velocity.)*

by a deviation of the stream produced by a body, the shock that is actually found is weak, and the flow behind the shock is supersonic, but if the shock is generated also by an increase of the back pressure, the shock can be strong. In this case, the flow behind the shock is subsonic, but in order to obtain a phenomenon represented by the calculations, it is necessary that the phenomenon be conical. Practically, this does not happen, because the necessary deviation of the body from the conical shape in the back part (the cone must have a finite length) interferes with the phenomenon in front because the flow is subsonic; and therefore the phenomenon in the front part is no longer conical.

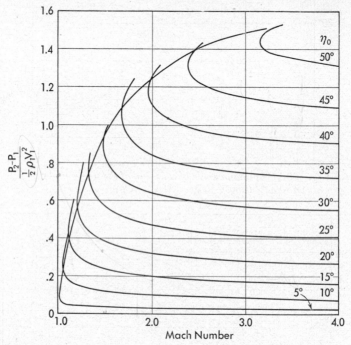

Fig. 170. *Pressure coefficient at the surface of the cone versus Mach number for cones of different cone angles (from Reference 93).*

Usually, when the flow behind the shock is subsonic, the shock obtained is no longer exactly a straight shock, showing that the phenomenon is not conical.

The system of calculation is not direct because it does not permit, for a given cone and for a given Mach number, determination of the phenomenon; but it is necessary to fix the velocity on the cone and to determine the corresponding Mach number or angle of shock. Therefore, for practical use it is very helpful to have indications from systematic calculations for different angles of cone and for different Mach numbers. Some results of cone calculations are shown in Figure 169 and following. In Figure 169 the value of v_r/V_1 at the cone surface, as a function of the Mach number is plotted for constant value of the angle of the cone. In Figure 170, the coefficient of pressure $(p_2 - p_1)/\frac{1}{2}\rho V^2$ at the cone, and in Figure 171 the angles of shock for different angles of cone are plotted as functions of the stream Mach numbers. As it appears from the curves, for every Mach number and for a given cone, two solutions exist. The curves are extended only in a small part of the strong shock zone. In order to obtain data for the entire flow field between the shock and the surface of the cone, a special diagram can be made using the diagram of the shock and the diagram of the velocity in the hodograph plane (Reference 43). For every Mach number of the free stream in the hodograph plane, a

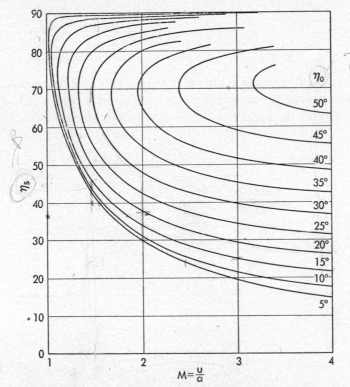

Fig. 171. *Angle of the shock versus Mach number for cones of different cone angles (from Reference 43).*

shock polar curve exists which gives the value of the velocity behind the shock as a function of the deviation across the shock. In the hodograph plane, from the direction and intensity of velocity behind the shock, the value of the angle of the corresponding cone can be obtained with the construction explained before, and the hodograph diagram that gives the velocity as a function of η can be determined. If $O'B$ is the velocity behind the shock for the Mach number considered (Figure 172), and the undisturbed velocity is in the direction of the u-axis (u_1), the angle δ between $O'B$ and u-axis is the deviation across the shock. From the value of $O'B$ and η_S the entire hodograph diagram AB can be determined; and when a line that contains a radius

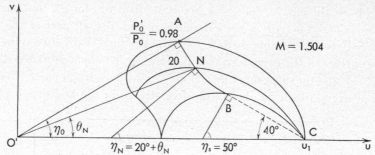

Fig. 172. *Construction and use of the apple curve diagram.*

passing through the point O' is obtained, the value of η_0 is determined. If the point B moves along the shock polar curve, the point A, which gives the value of the velocity at the surface of the cone, describes another curve that, from

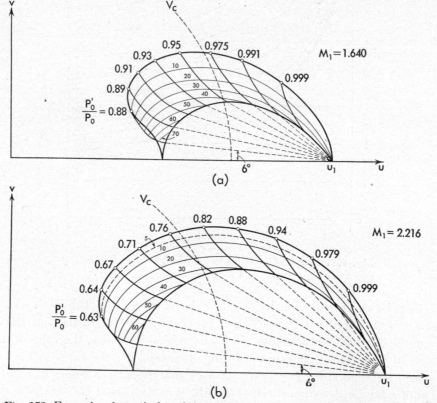

Fig. 173. *Examples of practical apple curve diagrams.* (a) $M_1 = 1.640$, (b) $M_1 = 2.126$.

its form, is called an *apple curve*. The two curves, together with a hodograph diagram and with some values of the losses across the shock, permit determination of the flow field between the cones and shock.

A diagram of this type is shown in Figure 172. The use of the curve is the following: given the angle of the cone η_0, the points A and B are determined. The normal to BC gives the value of η_S. For every point N, between A and B along the hodograph, the segment ON gives the intensity and direction (θ) of the velocity, while the corresponding value of η is determined, remembering that the normal to the diagram AB at the point N must be inclined at η_N with the u-axis. To simplify the determination of the value of η, some envelope curves of points having constant values of $(\eta - \theta)$ are also drawn. The values of losses of total pressure across the shock p_0'/p_0 are also indicated. Figures 173 a, b, c, d, show some of the actual diagrams constructed for different Mach numbers.

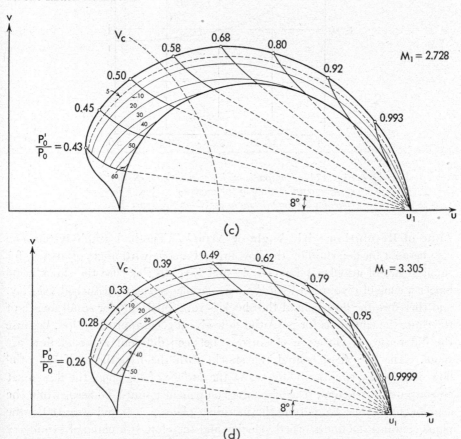

Fig. 173 *(continued). Examples of practical apple curve diagrams.* (c) $M_1 = 2.728$, (d) $M_1 = 3.305$ *(from Reference 43).*

Experimental results obtained from projectile tests or from tunnel tests agree with the theoretical data. Figure 174 shows a comparison between experimental and theoretical values of the angle of shock. The determination was made with firing tests by Taylor and Maccoll (Reference 42). Shadow and schlieren photographs are shown in Figures 175 and 176.

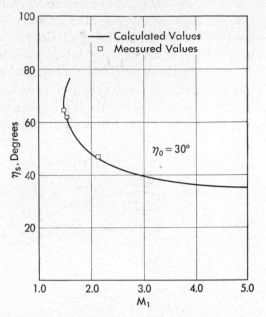

Fig. 174. *Comparison between calculated and experimental values of the angle of the shock for cones with different cone angle (from Reference 41).*

Cone of Revolution with Angle of Attack. The hodograph system can also be used for determining the flow around a cone with angle of attack, for small angles of attack (References 44 and 45). In this case the shock is no longer a cone of revolution with the axis parallel to the undisturbed velocity, and therefore the flow behind the shock is rotational, but for small angles of the cone, the equations for potential flow give a good approximation, because the differences of variation of entropy between different zones of flow are small. The flow field behind the shock, with the hypothesis of potential flow, is given by equation (446a). At the surface of the cone, the flow must be tangent to the cone; therefore the component v_t must be zero, while the component w must be zero at the meridian plane $\varphi = 0$ and $\varphi = 180°$; the plane contains the undisturbed velocity and therefore is a plane of symmetry of the phenomenon. The maximum value of w at the surface of the cone occurs in the zone of $\varphi \sim 90°$ and depends on the angle of attack, but for small

Fig. 175. *Shadow photograph of the flow around a cone of 30° angle at M = 2.13.*

Fig. 176. *Schlieren photograph of the flow around a cone of 20° angle at M ∞ 2.13.*

255

values of the angle of attack its maximum value is also small, and the ratio w^2/a^2 can be considered negligible with respect to one. With this hypothesis, the flow field near the surface of the cone is given by the equation

$$\sin^2 \eta \frac{\partial^2 F}{\partial \eta^2} + \frac{1}{2} \sin 2\eta \frac{\partial F}{\partial \eta} + \frac{\partial^2 F}{\partial^2 \varphi} + 2 \sin^2 \eta F = 0. \tag{461}$$

Equation (461) is a differential equation of the second order of the elliptic type and permits an analytical solution. A solution of the equation is of the type (Reference 46)

$$F = A_0 + A_1 \cos \varphi + B_1 \sin \varphi + \cdots \tag{462}$$

where A_0, A_1, and B_1 are functions of η alone. For $\varphi = 0$, $\partial F/\partial \varphi = 0$, because $w = (1/\sin \eta)(\partial F/\partial \varphi) = 0$; therefore all terms which contain the sines of φ or of $n\varphi$ must be zero, and the equation becomes

$$F = A_0 + A_1 \cos \varphi + \cdots \tag{463}$$

and because along the surface of the cone η is constant, the functions A_0, A_1, and the like have constant values along the cone.

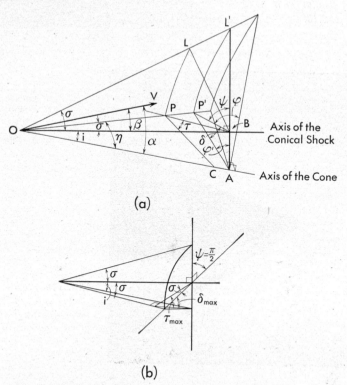

(a)

(b)

Fig. 177. *The equilibrium condition at the shock for a circular cone with angle of attack.*

Equation (463) in order to be a physical solution of the problem must give a flow field in agreement with the flow behind a conical shock; therefore equation (463) must be analyzed in relation to the condition of existence of the shock.

Now consider a circular conical shock of axis OB, and consider a plane normal to the axis OB (Figure 177). If OA is the axis of the cone that produces the shock and OV is the direction of the undisturbed velocity, inclined at α with the axis of the cone, it is possible to demonstrate that such a conical shock, in the approximation accepted, produces behind the shock a flow in agreement with equation (463).

If OP is a generatrix of the conical shock, resolve the velocity vector into components along OP (component v_{r_1}), along PB (component v_{n_1}), and in normal direction to the plane OPB (component w_1); using the symbols of Figure 177, it is found that

$$\left. \begin{aligned}
v_{r_1} &= V_1 \cos \beta \cos \sigma + V_1 \sin \beta \sin \sigma \cos \psi \\
v_{n_1} &= V_1 \cos \beta \sin \sigma - V_1 \sin \beta \cos \sigma \cos \psi \\
w_1 &= - V_1 \sin \beta \sin \psi
\end{aligned} \right\} \quad (464)$$

Across the shock the components v_{r_1} and w_1 do not change, while the component v_{n_1} changes in intensity and becomes v_{n_2}. Transforming the coordinate system and referring the velocity behind the shock to the polar coordinate system in axis with the axis OA of the cone, the result is

$$v_{r_2} = v_{r_1}$$

$$w_2 = w_1 \cos \tau - v_{n_2} \sin \tau = - \sin \beta \, V_1 \sin \psi \cos \tau - v_{n_2} \sin \tau \quad (464a)$$

where τ is the angle between lines CP and BP, in perpendicular direction to OP.

Because the hypothesis is accepted that w_2 is small and that w_2^2/V_1^2 can be neglected, equation (464a) indicates that the angles τ and β must be also considered small and the terms containing τ^2 and β^2 can be neglected.

For $\psi = \pi/2$ the value of w_2 is maximum, and for this condition (Figure 177b)

$$\tan i = \tan \tau \sin \sigma \quad \text{and} \quad \tan \delta = \tan \tau \cos \sigma$$

Therefore, the angles i and δ are small and of the same order as τ. But (see Figure 177)

$$\tan \varphi' = \tan \varphi \cos i; \quad P'A = \frac{\sin \sigma \sin (\varphi' + \delta)}{\sin \varphi'}, \text{ and } \delta = i \cot \sigma \sin \varphi' \quad (464b)$$

Therefore, neglecting terms of the order of τ^2 the result is

$$\sin \eta = \sin \sigma \left(1 + \frac{\delta}{\tan \varphi'} \right) \qquad \cos \eta = \cos \sigma - i \sin \sigma \cos \varphi \quad (464c)$$

Because i is constant, the first of equations (464) becomes

$$v_{r_1} = v_{r_2} = V_1 f_1(\eta) + \alpha f_2(\eta) \cos \varphi.$$

In the approximation accepted, the flow field defined by the first two terms of equation (463) can exist, and the corresponding shock is a circular conical shock out of axis with the conical body and with the undisturbed velocity.

Using equation (463), the flow conditions around the cone can be determined; indeed, the terms w^2/a^2 and $w(\partial w/\partial \eta)$ are zero in the meridian plane $\varphi = 0$, $\varphi = \pi$, and are negligible in every other plane $\varphi = $ constant, therefore equation (446) becomes

$$\sin^2 \eta \left(1 - \frac{v_t^2}{a^2}\right) \frac{\partial^2 F}{\partial \eta^2} + \frac{\partial^2 F}{\partial \varphi^2} + \sin^2 \eta F \left(2 - \frac{v_t^2}{a^2}\right) + \sin \eta \cos \eta \frac{\partial F}{\partial \eta} = 0. \quad (465)$$

If the function F has the form (equation 463)

$$F = F_0 + F_1 \cos \varphi \quad (466)$$

the term $\dfrac{\partial^2 F}{\partial \varphi^2}$ is given by

$$\frac{\partial^2 F}{\partial \varphi^2} = -F_1 \cos \varphi = -F + F_0 \quad (466a)$$

and in the meridian plane $\varphi = 0$ and $\varphi = \pi$

$$F_{\varphi=0} = F_0 + F_1; \quad F_{\varphi=\pi} = F_0 - F_1 \quad (466b)$$

$$\left(\frac{\partial^2 F}{\partial \varphi^2}\right)_{\varphi=0} = -F_1; \quad \left(\frac{\partial^2 F}{\partial \varphi^2}\right)_{\pi} = +F_1 \quad (466c)$$

The first term F_0 of equation (466) can be obtained directly; indeed, if in equation (466), F_1 is zero, equation (465) becomes equal to equation (455); therefore F_0 is the potential function that gives the flow around the cone for zero angle of attack, and can be determined as explained before. When the value of $F_0 = v_{r_0}$ is known as function of η in the meridian plane, from the calculation of the cone without angle of attack, equation (465) can be written in the form

$$\left(1 - \frac{v_t^2}{a^2}\right)\left(\frac{\partial^2 F}{\partial \eta^2} + F\right) = -F + \frac{F - F_0}{\sin^2 \eta} - \frac{\partial F}{\partial \eta} \cot \eta \quad (467)$$

or

$$\left(1 - \frac{v_t^2}{a^2}\right) R = -v_r + \frac{F - F_0}{\sin^2 \eta} - v_t \cot \eta$$

Now suppose that the value of $F_0 = v_{r_0}$ and F_1 are known, for $\eta = \eta_0$, the left side of equation (467) using equation (466a) can be evaluated; therefore, the radius of the hodograph diagram, $\partial^2 F/\partial \eta^2 + F$, in every plane $\varphi = $ constant (for example, $\varphi = 0$) can be obtained. If a, v_t and v_r are values relative to the limiting velocity, a^2 is (equation 85b)

$$a^2 = \frac{\gamma - 1}{2} (1 - v_r{}^2 - v_t{}^2)$$

The values of $\partial F/\partial \eta$ and F for $\eta = \eta_0 + \Delta \eta$ can be obtained as for the case of $\alpha = 0$ with one construction in a plane $\varphi = $ constant. Because $F_{0(\eta + \Delta \eta)}$ and $(\partial F_0/\partial \eta)_{(\eta + \Delta \eta)}$ are known from the calculation of the cone with the axis parallel to the flow, the radius of the hodograph diagrams for $\eta = \eta_0 + \Delta \eta$ can be also determined; and therefore, step-by-step all the values of v_r and v_t as function of η can be evaluated; for example, in the plane $\varphi = 0$ is $F = F_0 + F_1$ and $\partial F/\partial \eta = \partial F_0/\partial \eta + \partial F_1/\partial \eta$, and in the plane $\varphi = \pi$ is $F = F_0 - F_1$ and $\partial F/\partial \eta = \partial F_0/\partial \eta - \partial F_1/\partial \eta$.

Another analytical expression can be preferred for the numerical calculations; equation 467, in the approximation accepted, can be transformed in the form

$$F_1{}''\left(1 - \frac{F_0{}'^2}{a_0{}^2}\right) + F_1{}'\left[\cot \eta + \left(\frac{2F_0{}'}{a_0{}^2} + \frac{\gamma - 1}{a_0{}^4} F_0{}'^3\right)\frac{(F_0 + F_0{}' \cot \eta)}{1 - \dfrac{F_0{}'^2}{a^2}}\right]$$

$$+ F_1\left[2 - \frac{F_0{}'^2}{a_0{}^2} - \frac{1}{\sin^2 \eta} + \frac{\gamma - 1}{a_0{}^4} \frac{F_0 + F_0{}' \cot \eta}{1 - \dfrac{F_0{}'^2}{a^2}} F_0 F_0{}'^2\right] = 0 \qquad (468)$$

where F_0, a_0, and $F_0{}'$ are the quantities obtained at the same η for the cone in axis with the flow, and $F' = (\partial F/\partial \eta)$, $F'' = \partial^2 F/\partial \eta^2$.

To determine the position of the shock and therefore the value of the Mach number of the undisturbed stream and the angle of attack corresponding to the chosen values of F_0 and F_1, it is necessary to consider the equilibrium at the shock in the plane $\varphi = 0$ and $\varphi = \pi$. For every value of η in the meridian plane $\varphi = 0$ and $\varphi = \pi$ corresponding values of v_r and v_t have been found from the hodograph construction. The equilibrium at the shock imposes the condition that along the shock the following relation must exist (equation 460):

$$-v_t = \frac{\gamma - 1}{\gamma + 1} v_r \cot \epsilon \left(\frac{1}{v_r{}^2} - 1\right) \qquad (460a)$$

where ϵ is the angle of the shock with respect to the direction of the undisturbed stream. For every value of η the value of ϵ can be determined with equation (460a), and therefore the value of α given by

$$\alpha = \eta - \epsilon; \qquad\qquad \varphi = 0$$
$$\alpha = \epsilon - \eta; \qquad\qquad \varphi = \pi$$

can be determined. Because

$$\frac{V_1}{V_t} = v_r \cos \epsilon$$

the corresponding value of the stream velocity also can be determined. Therefore, for every value of η in the plane $\varphi = 0$ and $\varphi = \pi$, a value of α and a value of V_1 are obtained.

When V_1/V_l and α calculated at $\varphi = 0$ are equal to V_1/V_l and α calculated at $\varphi = \pi$, the values of V_1/V_l and α corresponding to the values of F_0 and F_1 are determined. The determination can be accomplished by plotting in a diagram the value of α as a function of the corresponding value of V_1/V_l (for the same value of η) for $\varphi = 0°$ and $\varphi = \pi$; two curves are obtained, and the intersection gives the value of α and V_1/V_l corresponding to the constants F_0 and F_1. From the corresponding values of η the angle of the shock in the plane $\varphi = 0°$ and $\varphi = 180°$ can be determined. However, this determination in the practical calculations is not necessary, because the value of F_0 must be equal to the value of v_{r0}/V_l at the cone for zero angle of attack. Now when angle of attack is considered, the value of F_0 must be chosen equal to v_r/V_l for the same cone at zero angle of attack for the M_1 considered, which fixes the value of M_1, while the term F_1 can be considered as the term which fixes the angle of attack. In this case V_1/V_l is known, therefore the value of α can be obtained directly from the analysis of the shock equilibrium only in one of the two planes $\varphi = 0, \varphi = \pi$.

The angle σ of the shock produced by the cone at small angles of attack, in the approximation accepted, is equal to the angle η_s of the shock produced by the same cone at zero angle of attack, for the same stream Mach number. Indeed, from equations (464) and (466), and from Figure 177, at the surface of the shock the result is

$$v_{r_1} = V_1 \cos \sigma + \beta V_1 \sin \sigma \cos \varphi$$
$$= F_0 (\sigma + i \cos \varphi) + F_1 (\sigma + i \cos \varphi) \cos \varphi \qquad (468a)$$

and because i and F_1 are small of the order of w

$$v_{r_1} = F_0 (\sigma) + i F_0' (\sigma) \cos \varphi + F_1 (\sigma) \cos \varphi$$

or

$$F_0 (\sigma) = V_1 \cos \sigma \qquad (468b)$$

and

$$V_1 \beta \sin \sigma = i F_0' (\sigma) + F_1 (\sigma) \qquad (468c)$$

$F_0 (\sigma)$ corresponds to the radial component of the velocity at the coordinate σ for zero angle of attack; therefore from equation (458) it must be

$$\sigma = \eta_s$$

The ratio β/α is given by equation (468c)

$$\frac{\beta}{\alpha} = \frac{F_0' (\sigma) + F_1 (\sigma)/\alpha}{V_1 \sin \sigma + F_0' (\sigma)}$$

But $F_1 (\sigma)/\alpha$ is independent from α (see equation (468)); therefore, in the approximation accepted β/α is constant for a given cone and a given stream Mach number, while F_1/α is a function of the coordinate η and is also constant at the surface of the cone and independent from the angle of attack.

13

CHARACTERISTIC SYSTEM FOR

THREE-DIMENSIONAL PHENOMENA

The Characteristic System for Axial Symmetrical Phenomena (Potential Flow Theory).

The Equations of the Characteristic System. The differential equation of potential flow in cylindrical coordinates has been given in Chapter 10, equation (335). When the phenomenon has axial symmetry (the body considered is a body of revolution with its axis parallel to the undisturbed flow), the phenomenon remains the same in every meridian plane. Therefore it is possible to consider the variation of the flow properties in only one plane, because no variations occur in a direction normal to any meridian plane. If x is the axis of symmetry and y is the axis normal to x in the meridian plane, and u and v are the components of the velocity along x and y, the equation of potential flow is

$$\left(1 - \frac{u^2}{a^2}\right)\frac{\partial^2\phi}{\partial x^2} + \left(1 - \frac{v^2}{a^2}\right)\frac{\partial^2\phi}{\partial y^2} - \frac{2uv}{a^2}\frac{\partial^2\phi}{\partial x\partial y} + \frac{v}{y} = 0. \tag{469}$$

Equation (469) for potential flow of axial symmetrical phenomena is of the same type as equation (58) considered in Chapter 2 for two-dimensional phenomena, and differs only by the last term v/y.

For equation (469) it is possible to repeat all the considerations made for equation (58). Equation (469) can be of hyperbolic, parabolic, or elliptic type. The type is determined by the value of the expression

$$\left(1 - \frac{u^2}{a^2}\right)\left(1 - \frac{v^2}{a^2}\right) - \frac{u^2v^2}{a^4} = 1 - \frac{V^2}{a^2}. \tag{470}$$

If equation (470) is less than zero, equation (469) is of the hyperbolic type, and some characteristic surfaces can be determined in the flow. If the phenomenon has axial symmetry, the surfaces are surfaces of revolution. In every meridian plane two families of characteristic lines can be determined from the intersection of the characteristic surfaces with the plane considered (References 47 and 48).

The characteristic lines can be determined in the same way as for two-dimensional phenomena (Chapter 2, paragraph 3). Using the parameters defined by the following expressions:

$$\left.\begin{array}{c} H = 1 - \dfrac{u^2}{a^2} \\[2mm] L = 1 - \dfrac{v^2}{a^2} \\[2mm] K = - \dfrac{uv}{a^2} \\[2mm] N = \dfrac{v}{y} \end{array}\right\} \quad (471)$$

the inclination of the characteristic lines is given by (equation 69)

$$\left.\begin{array}{c} \lambda_1 = \left(\dfrac{dy}{dx}\right)_{\mathrm{I}} = \dfrac{K}{H} - \dfrac{1}{H}\sqrt{K^2 - HL} \\[4mm] \lambda_2 = \left(\dfrac{dy}{dx}\right)_{\mathrm{II}} = \dfrac{K}{H} + \dfrac{1}{H}\sqrt{K^2 - HL} \end{array}\right\} \quad (472)$$

or if μ is the Mach angle and θ is the inclination of the velocity direction with respect to the axis of symmetry x,

$$\left.\begin{array}{c} \lambda_1 = \left(\dfrac{dy}{dx}\right)_{\mathrm{I}} = \tan(\theta + \mu) \\[4mm] \lambda_2 = \left(\dfrac{dy}{dx}\right)_{\mathrm{II}} = \tan(\theta - \mu) \end{array}\right\} \quad (473)$$

Along every characteristic line a variation of the flow properties occurs which can be determined in a way similar to that in Chapter 2.

The variation of the velocity components along the characteristic line can be written in the form (equation 71)

$$\left.\begin{array}{c} du = \left(\dfrac{\partial u}{\partial x} + \lambda\,\dfrac{\partial u}{\partial y}\right) dx \\[4mm] dv = \left(\dfrac{\partial v}{\partial x} + \lambda\,\dfrac{dv}{dy}\right) dx \end{array}\right\} \quad (474)$$

Remembering that $\partial u/\partial y = \partial v/\partial x$ (potential flow) and transforming equation (474) in a similar way as for equation (74), the following expressions can be obtained:

$$\frac{dy}{dx} = \lambda_1$$

$$du + \lambda_2 dv + \frac{N}{H} dx = 0$$

$\left.\right\}$ first family (475)

$$\frac{dy}{dx} = \lambda_2$$

$$du + \lambda_1 dv + \frac{N}{H} dx = 0$$

$\left.\right\}$ second family (476)

Equations (475) and (476) define the variation of velocity along every characteristic line. While an analytical solution of the two equations is not known, the differential equations (475) and (476) permit the step-by-step calculation of the variation of the flow properties along every characteristic line and therefore permit numerical determination of the flow phenomenon. Equations (475) and (476) can be transformed into equations which permit easier numerical computation. The equations can be written in the following form (Reference 13)

(477)

$$\frac{dy}{dx} = \tan(\mu + \theta)$$

$$\frac{du}{dx} + \tan(\theta - \mu)\frac{dv}{dx} + \frac{v}{Hy} = 0$$

$\left.\right\}$ first family

(477a)

(478)

$$\frac{dy}{dx} = \tan(\theta - \mu)$$

$$\frac{du}{dx} + \tan(\theta + \mu)\frac{dv}{dx} + \frac{v}{Hy} = 0$$

$\left.\right\}$ second family

(478a)

Using equation (76) and remembering that

$$H = 1 - \frac{u^2}{a^2} = 1 - M^2 \cos^2\theta = 1 - \frac{\cos^2\theta}{\sin^2\mu}$$

the following equations can be obtained from (477a) and (478a):

$$\frac{dV}{V} + d\theta \left[\frac{\sin\theta - \tan(\theta \mp \mu)\cos\theta}{\cos\theta + \tan(\theta \mp \mu)\sin\theta}\right]$$
$$+ \frac{dx}{y}\left[\frac{\sin\theta\sin^2\mu}{\sin^2\mu - \cos^2\theta}\right]\left[\frac{1}{\cos\theta + \tan(\theta \mp \mu)\sin\theta}\right] = 0 \quad (479)$$

where the minus sign is for equation (477a) and the plus sign is for equation (478a), but

$$\frac{\sin\theta - \tan(\theta \mp \mu)\cos\theta}{\cos\theta + \tan(\theta \mp \mu)\sin\theta} = \frac{\sin\theta\cos(\theta \mp \mu) - \sin(\theta \mp \mu)\cos\theta}{\cos\theta\cos(\theta \mp \mu) + \sin(\theta \mp \mu)\sin\theta} = \mp\tan\mu$$

while

$$\left[\frac{\sin\theta\sin^2\mu}{\sin^2\mu-\cos^2\theta}\right]\left[\frac{1}{\cos\theta+\tan(\theta\mp\mu)\sin\theta}\right]=\frac{\sin\theta\sin^2\mu\cos(\theta\mp\mu)}{(\sin^2\mu-\cos^2\theta)\cos\mu}$$

$$=-\frac{\sin\mu\tan\mu\sin\theta}{\cos(\theta\pm\mu)}.$$

Therefore, placing

$$l=+\frac{\sin\mu\sin\theta\tan\mu}{\cos(\mu+\theta)} \tag{480}$$

and

$$m=\frac{\sin\mu\sin\theta\tan\mu}{\cos(\theta-\mu)} \tag{481}$$

equations (477) and (478) become

$$\left.\begin{array}{l}\dfrac{dy}{dx}=\tan(\mu+\theta) \qquad\qquad\text{(482)}\\[2ex]\dfrac{dV}{V}-d\theta\tan\mu-l\dfrac{dx}{y}=0 \qquad\text{(482a)}\end{array}\right\}\ \text{first family}$$

$$\left.\begin{array}{l}\dfrac{dy}{dx}=\tan(\theta-\mu) \qquad\qquad\text{(483)}\\[2ex]\dfrac{dV}{V}+d\theta\tan\mu-m\dfrac{dx}{y}=0 \qquad\text{(483a)}\end{array}\right\}\ \text{second family}$$

Equations (482) and (483) are similar to equations (77a) and (77b) because

$$\tan\mu=\frac{\sin^2\mu}{\sqrt{1-\sin^2\mu}}=\frac{1}{\sqrt{M^2-1}}$$

and differ only by the term $l\,dx/y$ or $m\,dx/y$.

Equations (482) and (483) can be used for practical numerical applications by substituting finite differences for the differential terms $d\theta$ and dV. If the flow

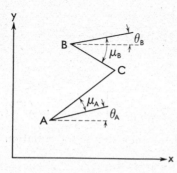

quantities are known in two points A and B (Figure 178), the values of θ and μ are known in points A and B. Therefore the tangent to the characteristic line of the first family at A, inclined at an angle $(\mu_A+\theta_A)$ (equation 482), and the tangent to the characteristic line of the second family at B, inclined at an angle $(\theta_B-\mu_B)$ (equation 483), can be drawn. The two tangents meet at a point C; if the distance between A and B is small, the tangents can be substituted in place of the character-istic lines. If infinitesimal terms of order

Fig. 178.   *Construction of the characteristic rut.*

higher than $d\theta$ and dV are neglected, the quantities μ, θ, l, m, and y in equations (482) and (483) can be considered constant and equal to the values at A and B, respectively. Therefore, applying equations (482a) and (483a), the values of ΔV and $\Delta\theta$ along AC and BC can be determined, and V and θ at C can be obtained. When the values of θ_C, V_C, and μ_C have been determined in the first approximation, a second approximation that considers also second order terms can be obtained by using the average of the values at A and C, or at B and C, for the inclination of the characteristic lines and for all values of the quantities that appear in the coefficients of equations (482) and (483). Equations (482) and (483) can be transformed into expressions which are more practical for numerical applications. For practical use it is better to use a nondimensional coefficient, dividing V by the limiting velocity V_l,

$$W = \frac{V}{V_l}.$$

Equations (482) and (483) can be transformed into equations with only one unknown quantity.

Indeed

$$dV_A = V_C - V_A$$

$$dV_B = V_C - V_B = V_C - V_A + V_A - V_B = +dV_A + V_A - V_B \quad (484)$$

$$d\theta_A = \theta_C - \theta_A$$

$$d\theta_B = \theta_A - \theta_B + d\theta_A.$$

Therefore, combining equations (482a) and (483a), the first approximation is

$$\left(\tan\mu_B + \frac{W_A}{W_B}\tan\mu_A\right)d\theta_A = 1 - \frac{W_A}{W_B} - (\theta_A - \theta_B)\tan\mu_B$$

$$+ (x_C - x_B)\frac{m_B}{y_B} - \frac{l_A}{y_A}(x_C - x_A)\frac{W_A}{W_B} \quad (485)$$

$$\frac{dW_A}{W_A} = \tan\mu_A\, d\theta_A + \frac{l_A}{y_A}(x_C - x_A) \quad (486)$$

$$\theta_C = \theta_A + d\theta_A \text{ (radians)} \quad (487)$$

$$W_C = W_A + dW_A \quad (488)$$

$$\sin^2\mu_C = \frac{\gamma - 1}{2}\left(\frac{1}{W_C^2} - 1\right) \text{ (from equation 85b)} \quad (489)$$

Equations (485) to (489) permit a numerical step-by-step determination of the flow around every body of revolution for supersonic flow. For different systems of numerical applications, see References 49 and 50.

Consider now the case in which a discontinuity of curvature of the profile of the body must be analyzed (Figure 179). Because a variation of direction occurs at A, the velocity along AC must be different than the velocity along AB. The effect of variation of the velocity direction at A is transmitted in a zone of flow which is behind a characteristic line of the first family "a" which starts from A; therefore, the flow in zone I of Figure 179 is not influenced by the variation of direction that occurs in A, the disturbance affects zone II,

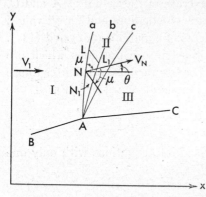

Fig. 179. *The characteristic system for the flow around a corner in a body of revolution.*

and in zone III the disturbance is completely transmitted. The line "a" can be designed in terms of the values V/V_l and θ of zone I. Consider now another characteristic line of the first family "b" near the characteristic "a", and consider from a point N of "a" a characteristic line of the second family; this characteristic line crosses the characteristic line "b" at a point N_1. To determine the variation of velocity along the line NN_1, equation (483a) must be used in which the last term is dx. Consider the variation of abscissas along the characteristic line. Now if N moves along "a" in the direction of the point A, N' moves along "b", and the difference between x_N and x_{N_1} decreases and becomes zero when N is at A; therefore the third term of equation (483a) in dx/y becomes smaller when N moves toward A, and at A disappears. In A in order to pass from the characteristic line "a" to the characteristic line "b" equation (483a) becomes

$$\frac{dV}{V} + d\theta \tan \mu = 0. \tag{490}$$

Equation (490) is equal to equation (77b) for two-dimensional flow; therefore the expansion around the corner at A is regulated by the same law as the two-dimensional case. The same considerations can be applied for deviation with shock. These results permit determination of the flow in zone II in the following way: the variation of direction θ that occurs at A is divided into smaller steps $\Delta\theta$. For every small deviation $\Delta\theta$ considered the velocity V and direction of velocity θ at A are known (equation 80 or equivalent table); therefore the tangent to the characteristic line "b" at A can be drawn. Now from the characteristic line "a" the characteristic line "b" corresponding to the first step $\Delta\theta$ can be calculated because from a point N of "a", and from A a point N_1 along "b" can be obtained. From N_1 and a point L of "a" a point L_1 can be determined, and therefore the entire line "b" can be determined. From line "b" the line "c" corresponding to the next step of expansion $\Delta\theta$ can be determined, and in similar way all other characteristic lines can be computed.

Application of the System of Characteristics to Determination of the Flow Properties along a Pointed Body of Revolution. Bodies of revolution that can be analyzed with the characteristic system can be divided into three groups: sharp nose bodies, bodies that have an open nose, and bodies that represent a supersonic duct, such as nozzles for circular supersonic tunnels.

When a sharp nose body of revolution is analyzed, the calculations can be conducted in the following way (Figure 180). At the nose of the body the phenomenon is conical because the nose in any case can be considered a cone of very small height ON, and therefore the calculation can be started by determining the conical flow field at the nose. From the cone calculations the characteristic line A_0F_0 corresponding to the conical phenomenon can be determined by using equation (482). Indeed, for every value of η (η_{B_0}), the value of μ_{B_0} and θ_{B_0} are known, and therefore the inclination of the characteristic line between two points B_0

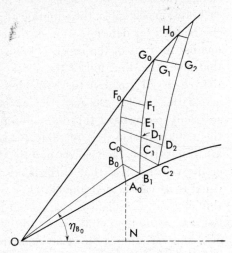

Fig. 180. *Practical method of calculation of the flow around a sharp nose body of revolution.*

and A_0 can be drawn, using the average value of the inclination with respect to the x-axis given by

$$\frac{\theta_{B_0} + \theta_{A_0} + \mu_{B_0} + \mu_{A_0}}{2}.$$

Proceeding in a similar way the line A_0F_0 can be drawn. From the point B_0 the tangent to the characteristic line of the second family can be also drawn (equation 483). The tangent meets the body at B_1. At B_1 the direction of the stream θ_{B_1} is known because it is given by the boundary conditions; therefore, using equation (483a), the velocity W_{B_1} can be determined, using the corresponding values at B_0 for the coefficients of equation (483a). If the variations between B_0 and B_1 are large, a second approximation can be calculated. From B_1 the tangent to the characteristic line of the first family can be drawn, and from a point C_0 on the line A_0F_0 the tangent to the characteristic line of the second family can be drawn. Using equation (485) the point C_1 can be determined. In a similar way, all the points B_1, C_1, D_1, E_1, F_1 can be determined.

For the point G_0 the calculation is slightly different. G_0 is determined from the point F_1. Because G_0 is a point on the shock, the equation of shock must be used, in place of equation (483a). For calculating the shock front from the point F_1 the following considerations must be made: when the expansion lines that are generated from the body meet the shock, the shock decreases in intensity and changes direction. The variation of entropy across the shock changes, and therefore the flow becomes rotational. Assuming the effect of the rotation negligible, the equation of potential flow and the equation of shock can be used for determination of the shape of the shock. Because the Mach number in front of the shock is known, it is possible to construct a diagram that gives the direction of the shock ϵ, the Mach number M_2, and therefore the velocity W (relative to V_L) behind the shock, as functions of the deviation across the shock. Because the deviation across the shock decreases, it is sufficient to construct this diagram for values of δ less than across OF_0. From this determination it is possible to calculate the point G_0. If W_{F_1} and θ_{F_1} are, respectively, the velocity and the direction of the velocity at F_1, the value of the velocity $W_{\theta F}$ that corresponds to a deviation across the shock at G_0 equal to θ_{F_1} can be determined. For the deviation $\delta = \theta_{F_1}$ and for the law of this shock the gradient $dW_{\theta F_1}/d\delta$ can be determined. The value is given by the tangent at the point $\delta = \theta_{F_1}$ to the curve that represents W as a function of δ. If a variation of direction $d\theta$ occurs from F_1 to G_0 along the characteristic line $F_1 G_0$, the direction of the velocity at G_0 must be $\theta_{F_1} + d\theta$; therefore the deviation across the shock at G_0 must be $\delta = \theta_{F_1} + d\theta$, and the corresponding velocity must be

$$W_{G_0} = W_{\theta F_1} + \left(\frac{dW}{d\delta}\right)_{\theta F_1} d\theta.$$

The variation of velocity from F_1 to G_0 becomes

$$dW = W_{G_0} - W_{F_1} = W_{\theta F_1} + \left(\frac{dW}{d\delta}\right)_{\theta F_1} d\theta - W_{F_1}.$$

Therefore, equation (482a) becomes

$$\frac{W_{\theta F_1}}{W_{F_1}} - 1 + \left(\frac{dW}{d\delta}\right)_{\theta F_1} \frac{d\theta}{W_{F_1}} - \tan \mu_{F_1} \, d\theta - \frac{X_{G_0} - X_{F_1}}{y_{F_1}} l_{F_1} = 0. \quad (491)$$

All other terms of equation (491) are known, and therefore the value of $d\theta$ can be determined. If $d\theta$ is determined, the value of δ can be determined from the expression

$$\delta = d\theta + \theta_{F_1} \quad (492)$$

and therefore the value of ϵ corresponding to G_0 can be found, and the line $G_0 H_0$ can be designed.

If C_1 is the first known point of the line $B_1C_1G_0$ the tangent to the characteristic line of the first family can be designed, from C_1. Therefore the point C_2 can be determined on the body. At C_1 the direction of the velocity is known; therefore in equation (483a) the term $d\theta$ is known, and from equation (483a) the value of dW can be determined, and the tangent to the characteristic line C_2D_2 can be designed. The point D_2 is found from the points C_2 and D_1. Proceeding in a similar way, the entire flow around the body can be determined. If the length of some steps becomes too large, intermediate points (G_1) can be considered, assuming linear variation of the flow properties between G_0 and G_2.

In Figure 181 an example of the calculation of the velocity of the flow at a few points around a body of revolution is shown. The calculation has been

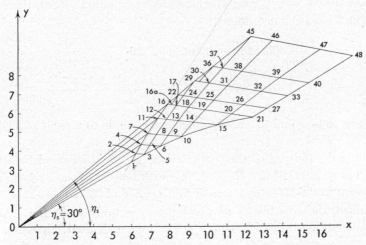

Fig. 181. *A numerical example of calculation of the flow around a sharp nose body of revolution at $M = 3.07$.*

performed for a Mach number equal to 3.07. The first part of the body is a cone of 30°; therefore the calculation starts with determination of the conical flow. From the calculation of the conical flow field the angle of the shock is

$$\eta_s = 39° \ 25'$$

and for the points 1, 2, 4, 7, 11, and 16 the following properties are obtained:

Point	$\eta°$	θ	W	μ	x	y
1	30°	30°	0.6400	32° 28′	6.000	3.462
2	32°	28°	0.6414	32° 20′	6.220	3.880
4	34°	26° 15′	0.6438	32° 6′	6.509	4.380
7	36°	24° 40′	0.6477	31° 44′	6.876	4.982
11	38°	23°	0.6516	31° 22′	7.390	5.753
16	39° 25′	21° 49′	0.6560	30° 58′	7.902	6.473

From the values of θ and μ the first characteristic line inclined at an angle of $(\mu + \theta)$ can be determined, and the positions of points 1, 2, 4, 7, 11, and 16 can be obtained from the position of the point 1, and therefore the values of x and y of the last two columns are obtained. The angle of the conical shock is $39° 25'$; therefore for $M = 3.07$ and for values of inclinations ϵ decreasing from the value of $39° 25'$, the variations across the shock of the flow properties have been determined. For every value of ϵ a value of M_2 and a value of δ are obtained (equations 126 and 125). From M_2, equation (85b), the value of W is computed, and W and ϵ as functions of δ have been plotted, and the value of $\partial W/\partial \delta$ has been determined and plotted as a function of δ. From the point 2 the tangent to the characteristic line of the second family has been drawn inclined at an angle of $-4° 20'$ with respect to the x-axis, and point 3 on the body has been obtained. At 3 the direction θ_3 of the body is $28° 20'$; the position is $x_3 = 6.700$, $y_3 = 3.843$; therefore, using equation (483a), the velocity W at point 3 has been determined:

$$\frac{W_3}{0.6414} = 1 - \frac{\pi}{180} (28° 20' - 28°) \tan 32° 20'$$

$$+ \frac{\sin 28° \sin 32° 20' \tan 32° 20'}{\cos (28° - 32° 20')} \cdot \frac{6.700 - 6.220}{3.880}.$$

W_3 is shown to be equal to 0.6517, which corresponds to a value of μ equal to $31° 21'$.

Designing the tangent to the characteristic line of the second family from 4 inclined at an angle of $(26° 15' - 32° 6')$ with respect to the x-axis and from 3 the tangent to the first characteristic line inclined of $(28° 20' + 31° 21')$, point 5 is obtained, the coordinates of which are $x_5 = 6.979$ and $y_5 = 4.333$. In order to determine W_5 and θ_5, equation (486) must be used; therefore

$$\left(\tan 32° 6' + \frac{0.6517}{0.6438} \tan 31° 21'\right) (\theta_5 - 28° 20')$$

$$= 1 - \frac{0.6517}{0.6438} - (28° 20' - 26° 15') \frac{\pi}{180} \tan 32° 6'$$

$$+ \frac{6.979 - 6.509}{4.380} \times \frac{\sin 26° 15' \sin 32° 6' \tan 32° 6'}{\cos (26° 15' - 32° 6')}$$

$$- \frac{6.979 - 6.700}{3.843} \times \frac{0.6517}{0.6438} \times \frac{\sin 28° 20' \tan 31° 21' \sin 31° 21'}{\cos (31° 21' + 28° 20')}.$$

Therefore θ_5 is obtained.

Using in a similar way equations (486) to (489), μ_5 and W_5 are obtained. If greater accuracy is required, the points 3 and 5 can be recalculated using the average values between 2 and 3 for the coefficients, in order to obtain a second approximation at 3, and the average values of 3 and 5 or of 4 and 5 in order to obtain a second approximation for the point 5.

In a similar way all other points to point 17 have been determined. Between 16 and 17, point 16a has been extrapolated by assuming linear variation along the characteristic line, and point 22 at the shock has been determined. Point 16a has the following properties: $x_{16a} = 8.100$, $y_{16a} = 6.442$, $W_{16a} = 0.6586$, $\theta_{16a} = 21°\ 46'$, $\mu_{16a} = 30°\ 43'$. The position obtained for point 22 on the shock is $x_{22} = 8.500$; $y_{22} = 6.962$. For determination of the flow properties at point 22, equation (491) has been used. From the calculations of the shock law, it is shown that for a deviation across the shock equal to θ_{16a} (21° 46'), the velocity W behind the shock is $W_{\theta_{16a}} = 0.6553$, and $dW/d\delta$ is equal to -0.585 if δ is in radians; therefore the following expression has been written:

$$1 = \frac{0.6553}{0.6586} - \frac{0.585}{0.6586}\ d\theta - \tan 30°\ 43'\ d\theta$$
$$- \frac{\sin 30°\ 43'\ \tan 30°\ 43'\ \sin 21°\ 46'}{\cos\ (30°\ 43' + 21°\ 46')}\ \frac{8.500 - 8.100}{6.442}.$$

θ_{22} is equal to $20°\ 58'$, and $W_{22} = 0.6636$; $\epsilon_{22} = 38°\ 25'$.

In similar way, all the other points have been determined. In order to determine the pressure on the body, the ratio p/p_0' for the value of W at the point considered must be determined; the value of p_{16}/p_0' for the point 16 on the shock can be obtained from the value of W_{16} equation (85b), and the ratio p_{16}/p_1 is given by the law of shock; therefore

$$\frac{p}{p_1} = \frac{p}{p_0'}\ \frac{p_0'}{p_{16}}\ \frac{p_{16}}{p_1}.$$

Application of the Characteristic System to a Slender Open-Nose Body of Revolution or to a Circular Effusor. Determination of the Shape of a Perfect Effusor. The system of characteristics can be applied in a similar way to an open-nose body of revolution (Figure 182). At the point A the flow undergoes a finite variation of direction which is a variation of compression; therefore at A a shock wave is formed. Because at A the phenomenon can be considered as two-dimensional, the flow at A can be determined, and the tangent to the shock front AB can be designed. Assuming that at D the flow has the same properties as at A, with equation (491) the flow properties at B can be determined, and from B the flow at C can be determined with equation (483a), because $d\theta$ from B to C is known. When the

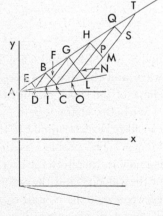

Fig. 182. *System of calculation of the flow around an open nose body of revolution.*

velocity at B is determined a second approximation can be obtained; assuming a continuous variation of the flow properties from A to B, the properties at D can be determined from an intermediate point E between A and B, and from D it is possible to recalculate B. The successive calculations are identical to the calculation for pointed nose of revolution. For accurate calculations some points I, O, etc., must be inserted between the points D, C, and L obtained as intersections of the characteristic lines with the body. In Figures 183 and 184 a practical calculation is shown.

In Figure 183 the characteristic net is shown for $M_1 = 1.525$. At 1 the shock is determined with the two-dimensional law. Point 3 is determined from 2, in which the flow is considered equal to 1. Interpolating a point between 1

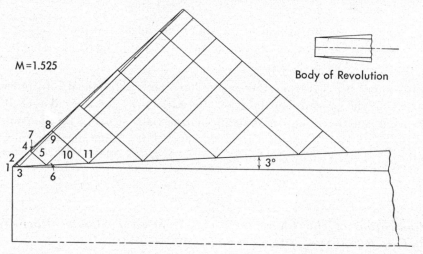

Fig. 183. *Example of the practical characteristic net for an open nose body of revolution at $M = 1.525$ (from Reference 51).*

and 3, points 4, 5 and 6 are determined. In Figure 184 the shape of the shock wave and the shape of the streamlines are shown. For comparison, also the shape of the shock obtained experimentally is shown (Reference 51).

With the characteristic system the flow into a circular supersonic effusor can also be determined if the flow properties at a section of the effusor are known. The problem is the following (Figure 185): The flow in section S_1 is known; therefore for every point P of section S_1 the intensity and direction of the velocity and the velocity of sound are known; the shape of the effusor between sections S_1 and S_2 is fixed, and the flow at S_2 must be determined. The system of calculation is not very different from the system used for a pointed nose of revolution. If the flow is supersonic at section S_1, the characteristic lines can be designed for every point P of section S_1 and the velocity at the points Q, obtained by the intersection of two characteristic lines, can be determined. Because there the direction of the velocity is known, the points

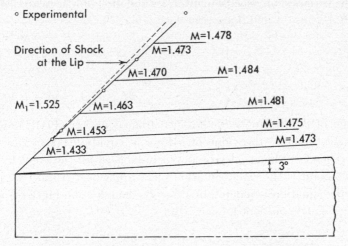

Fig. 184. *Shape of the shock wave and of the streamlines for an open nose body of revolution at M = 1.525. For comparison, the shape of the shock obtained from experiments is shown (from Reference 51).*

at the walls can also be determined. Therefore the system permits determination of the entire flow field. Some complications occur for the points on the axis. In equations (482a) and (483a) the last term ldx/y or mdx/y becomes

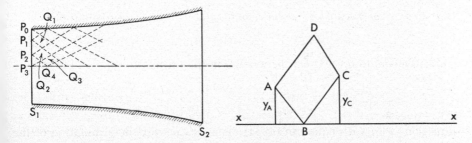

Fig. 185. *System of calculation of the supersonic flow into a circular tube.*

Fig. 186. *The flow conditions at the axis of the channel.*

indeterminate $(0/0)$ at the axis, because y and θ become zero. However, the indetermination in the numerical calculations can be eliminated if some points near the axis are considered. Indeed, if B is a point on the x-axis (Figure 186), the value of W at B must be determined from the value of the flow at A, while point C must be determined from D and B. At A equation (483a) exists:

$$\frac{dW}{W_A} + \tan \mu_A d\theta - \frac{l_A dx}{y_A} = 0 \qquad (483a)$$

and because y_A is other than zero, the equation is determinate. At the axis θ must be zero; therefore along AB the variation of direction must be $\Delta\theta = \theta_A$. If the variation of velocity in intensity and direction are assumed constant along AB, because A and B are near each other,

$$W_B = W_A + \frac{dW}{dx}\Delta x \tag{493}$$

$$\theta_B = \theta_A + \frac{d\theta}{dx}\Delta x = 0 \tag{494}$$

The value of $d\theta/dx$ can be determined from equation (494) because Δx is known, and therefore the value of dW/dx in equation (483a) can be determined. Therefore the usual procedure can be used for the point B.

For the point C the same equation (482) applied at B must be used, but because the equation is indeterminate at B, the equation must be applied at C where θ_C and V_C are not known. But

$$\theta_C = \Delta\theta = \int_{x_B}^{x_C} \frac{d\theta}{dx}\,dx$$

Therefore, assuming $d\theta/dx$ and dV/dx constant along BC, at C equation (482a) becomes

$$\frac{1}{W_B + \Delta W}\frac{dW}{dx} - \tan_{C\mu}\frac{d\theta}{dx} - \frac{\sin\theta_C\tan\mu_C\sin\mu_C}{\cos(\mu_C + \theta_C)}\frac{1}{y_C} = 0. \tag{495}$$

But $\sin\theta_C = \theta_C$ because θ_C is very small, and as a first approximation

$$W_B \cong W_C \quad \text{and} \quad \mu_C \cong \mu_B.$$

Therefore equation (495) can be written in the form

$$\frac{1}{W_B}\Delta W - \tan\mu_B\,\Delta\theta - \frac{\Delta\theta\tan\mu_B\sin\mu_B}{\cos\mu_B}\frac{\Delta x}{y_C} = 0. \tag{496}$$

Equation (496) with equation (483a) along DC permits determination of the values of ΔW and $\Delta\theta$. Knowing the value of ΔW, a second approximation can be obtained using the value of $(W_B + \Delta W)$ and the corresponding $\Delta\theta$ and θ in equation (496). Near the axis the variation of direction for small variation of velocity is large; therefore the calculations require small steps.

The system of characteristics also permits determination of the shape of a perfect effusor or of an effusor that has uniform velocity at section S_2 (Figure 187). If the velocity at S_1 is the velocity of sound, a small expansion $\Delta\theta$ can be considered at P_0, and therefore the characteristics lines at P_0 after the expansion can be designed, because the first characteristic line is straight if the velocity at S_1 is uniform.

At P_0 a finite variation of direction can be introduced (the effusor in this case is the shortest possible) (Figure 187a), or a wall with gradual curvature can be assumed (line P_0P_n of Figure 187b). If a finite variation of direction θ occurs at P_0, the expansion θ must be analyzed considering a finite number of

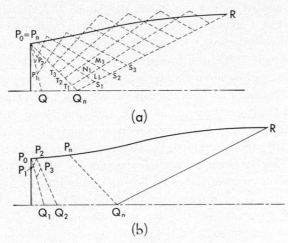

Fig. 187. *System of calculation of the shape of a perfect effusor.*

small increments $\Delta\theta$. At P_0 the expansion occurs with the two-dimensional law; therefore for every increment $\Delta\theta$, the velocity and the Mach angle can be determined at P_0 as in the two-dimensional case (Chapter 2). Therefore the tangent from P_0 to the characteristic line corresponding to each increment $\Delta\theta$ can be drawn. The flow properties at P_1 are known; if uniform flow and $M = 1$ are assumed to exist in the minimum section, the velocity along the characteristic line P_0P_1Q corresponding to an infinitesimal expansion at P_0 of $\Delta\theta$ is determined, because the velocity along P_0P_1Q is constant. From the points P_1 and P_0, the point P_2 can be determined and the properties of flow at P_2 can be calculated. In a similar way all other points of the other characteristic lines can be obtained. Every characteristic line that starts at P_0 crosses the axis at a point Q in which the flow properties can be determined. When a point Q_n is attained at the axis at which the Mach number is equal to the required design Mach number, the expansion from P_0 is stopped. Then from P_0 the wall shape which gives uniform flow at the end of the effusor must be determined.

If the expansion occurs gradually along a given wall P_0P_n (Figure 187b), the calculations can be made in similar manner. From the point P_1 the characteristic of the second family that meets the wall can be drawn, and at the wall the intensity of the velocity can be determined, because the direction is known. When the required design Mach number is attained at the point Q_n on the axis, the wall no longer has an arbitrary shape. From the point P_n on the wall that is on the characteristic line of the first family that passes at Q_n, the correct shape which gives uniform flow must be determined. If R is the end of the curved wall of the effusor, the shape P_nR must be determined in such a way that it gives a velocity at R and along Q_nR equal to the velocity at Q_n and parallel to the axis. If the velocity along RQ_n is uniform, the characteristic line which starts from Q_n must be straight. Therefore from the point Q_n, the line RQ_n can be immediately determined. For every point S of this line the characteristic of the other family can be designed, and therefore from the points T of the characteristic line P_nQ_n and from the points S of the line RQ_n, the flow in the zone P_nRQ_n can be determined. If the flow properties in the zone P_nRQ_n are determined, the stream line that passes through P_n can be designed. This stream line fixes the shape of the effusor. The point R is also determined in terms of the mass flow that goes into the effusor, because the mass flow at S_1 is known, and the density at RQ_n can be determined by using isentropic expansion. Other stream tubes between P_0Q, P_n, and RQ_n can be designed and the ratio of the end sections of the stream tubes can be used in order to have an idea of the precision of the calculations.

The Characteristic System for Axial Symmetrical Phenomena (Rotational Flow Theory). When a curved shock of some intensity exists in the flow, the flow behind the shock must be considered rotational because the variation of entropy is not constant along the shock. In this case, in place of the characteristic system for potential flow, the characteristic system for rotational flow must be considered. While consideration of the presence of rotation in two-dimensional phenomena requires a much longer system of calculations than for potential flow, and therefore the higher precision is expensive, in the three-dimensional case the system of calculation for rotational flow is not much longer than for potential flow because the procedure is a step-by-step procedure for both cases.

The determination of the differential equation for rotational flow can be obtained in a manner similar to that for two-dimensional phenomena. A special stream function ψ can be considered defined by the equation (Reference 16),

$$\left. \begin{array}{l} \psi_y = yu\,(1 - W^2)^{\frac{1}{\gamma-1}} \\[2mm] \psi_x = -\,yv\,(1 - W^2)^{\frac{1}{\gamma-1}} \end{array} \right\} \qquad (497)$$

where u and v are the components along the x and y axis of the velocity W in the meridian plane of the body of revolution, and W is the velocity at the point considered measured with respect to the limiting velocity

$$W = \frac{V}{V_l} \tag{498}$$

The speed of sound is also measured with respect to V_l

$$c = \frac{a}{V_l} \tag{499}$$

Therefore, u, v, W, and c are nondimensional numbers. The use of V_l as a unit of measurement is not necessary but the calculations are notably simplified, because V_l is constant. Proceeding in a manner similar to that for two-dimensional phenomena (Chapter 5), the following expression can be obtained from the continuity equation:

$$\frac{\partial}{\partial x}\left[\frac{u\,(v_x - u_y)}{1 - W^2}\right] + \frac{\partial}{\partial y}\left[\frac{v\,(v_x - u_y)}{1 - W^2}\right] = 0 \tag{500}$$

$$\frac{\partial}{\partial x}\left[yu\,(1 - W^2)^{\frac{1}{\gamma - 1}}\right] + \frac{\partial}{\partial y}\left[yv\,(1 - W^2)^{\frac{1}{\gamma - 1}}\right] = 0. \tag{501}$$

From these two equations the following equation can be obtained

$$u\,\frac{\partial}{\partial x}\left[\frac{v_x - u_y}{y\,(1 - W^2)^{\frac{\gamma}{\gamma - 1}}}\right] + v\,\frac{\partial}{\partial y}\left[\frac{v_x - u_y}{y\,(1 - W^2)^{\frac{\gamma}{\gamma - 1}}}\right] = 0. \tag{502}$$

Equation (500) is automatically satisfied by equation (497) but equations (501) or (502) are satisfied only when

$$\frac{v_x - u_y}{y\,(1 - W^2)^{\frac{\gamma}{\gamma - 1}}} = f\,(\psi). \tag{503}$$

Since $(1 - W^2)^{\frac{\gamma}{\gamma - 1}}$ along the stream lines is proportional to the local pressure, it can be concluded that for three-dimensional symmetrical phenomena the vortex strength, along each stream line and between two discontinuities, is proportional to the pressure moment yp relative to the axis of symmetry.

Equation (503) is a function only of the stream function ψ; therefore, proceeding in a manner similar to that of Chapter 5, the following differential equation can be obtained:

$$\left(1 - \frac{u^2}{c^2}\right)\psi_{xx} - \frac{2uv}{c^2}\,\psi_{xy} + \left(1 - \frac{v^2}{c^2}\right)\psi_{yy} - \frac{\psi_y}{y}$$
$$- y^2\,(1 - W^2)^{\frac{\gamma + 1}{\gamma - 1}}\left(\frac{W^2}{c^2} - 1\right)f\,(\psi) = 0. \tag{504}$$

Equation (504) is similar to equation (469), and calling

$$1 - \frac{u^2}{c^2} = H$$

$$1 - \frac{v^2}{c^2} = L$$

$$-\frac{uv}{c^2} = K$$

$$-\frac{\psi_y}{y} - y^2 (1 - W^2)^{\frac{\gamma+1}{\gamma-1}} \left(\frac{w^2}{c^2} - 1\right) f(\psi) = N$$

$$\left.\right\} \quad (505)$$

the following expression is obtained (Reference 51):

$$H\psi_{xx} + 2K\psi_{xy} + L\psi_{yy} + N = 0 \qquad (506)$$

which is an equation similar to the equation for potential flow and differs only in the term N. Because the inclination of the characteristics lines λ_1 and λ_2 is independent of the term N, the values of λ_1 and λ_2 are identical for potential flow and for rotational flow:

$$\lambda_1 = \left(\frac{dy}{dx}\right)_I = \tan(\theta + \mu); \quad \lambda_2 = \left(\frac{dy}{dx}\right)_{II} = \tan(\theta - \mu) \qquad (507)$$

From equation (506) the following equation can be obtained as for potential flow:

$$\psi_{xx} + \tan(\theta - \mu)\psi_{xy} + \frac{N}{H} = 0$$

$$\psi_{xx} + \tan(\theta + \mu)\psi_{xy} + \frac{N}{H} = 0. \qquad (508)$$

The term N contains the expression $f(\psi)$ defined by equation (503) but

$$\psi_x^2 + \psi_y^2 = \text{grad}^2(\psi) = y^2 W^2 (1 - W^2)^{\frac{2}{\gamma-1}} = \left(\frac{d\psi}{dn}\right)^2. \qquad (509)$$

When n is the normal to the stream lines, and

$$\frac{\text{curl } V \times V}{a^2} = \frac{1}{g\gamma R} \text{grad } S = \frac{1}{g\gamma R} \frac{dS}{dn} \qquad (510)$$

because the entropy is constant along every stream line,

$$f(\psi) = \frac{\gamma - 1}{2g\gamma} \frac{1}{R} \frac{dS}{dn} \frac{1}{yW(1 - W^2)^{\frac{1}{\gamma-1}}}. \qquad (511)$$

Substituting equation (511) in equation (508) and performing the differentiation of equation (497), equation (508) becomes

$$\frac{dW}{W} - \tan \mu \, d\theta - \frac{dx}{y} l + \frac{dx}{dn} \frac{dS}{g\gamma R} \frac{\sin^3 \mu}{\cos(\mu + \theta)} = 0 \quad \text{first family} \quad (512)$$

$$\frac{dW}{W} + \tan \mu \, d\theta - \frac{dx}{y} m - \frac{dx}{dn} \frac{dS}{g\gamma R} \frac{\sin^3 \mu}{\cos(\theta - \mu)} = 0 \quad \text{second family} \quad (513)$$

Equation (512) is similar to equations (482a) and (483a), and differs only in the term which contains the entropy, and can be used in the same manner.

In practical applications, the same numerical system proposed for the potential flow can be used: if the flow is known in two points A and B, near each other (Figure 188), the tangents to the two characteristics at A and B can be designed, and assuming the characteristics coincident with the tangent, the point C can be determined in the first approximation. Along AC equation (512) must be applied and along BC equation (513) must be applied. The terms containing dS/dn in equations (512) and (513) are not known and must be determined for the calculations. If S is known at A and B, assuming a linear variation of entropy between A and B in a normal direction to the stream lines, it is possible to write

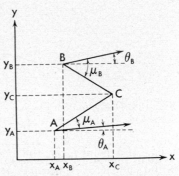

Fig. 188. *Determination of a point of the flow with the characteristic system for rotational flow.*

$$\frac{dS}{dn} = \frac{S_B - S_A}{(x_C - x_A) \dfrac{\sin \mu_A}{\cos(\mu_A + \theta_A)} + (x_C - x_B) \dfrac{\sin \mu_B}{\cos(\theta_B - \mu_B)}} . \quad (514)$$

Equations (512) and (513) can be combined with equation (514) and equations (516) to (519) can be obtained when the following parameters are introduced:

$$\left. \begin{array}{l} f = (x_C - x_B) \sin \mu_B \cos(\mu_A + \theta_A) \\[2mm] e = (x_C - x_A) \sin \mu_A \cos(\theta_B - \mu_B) \end{array} \right\} \quad (515)$$

$$\left(\tan \mu_B + \frac{W_A}{W_B} \tan \mu_A \right) d\theta_A = 1 - \frac{W_A}{W_B} - (\theta_A - \theta_B) \tan \mu_B + (x_C - x_B)\frac{m_B}{y_B}$$

$$- (x_C - x_A)\frac{W_A}{W_B}\frac{l_A}{y_A} + \frac{S_B - S_A}{g\gamma R} \frac{f \sin^2 \mu_B + e \dfrac{W_A}{W_B}\sin^2 \mu_A}{f + e} \quad (516)$$

$$\frac{dW_A}{W_A} = \tan \mu_A \, d\theta_A + \frac{(x_C - x_A)l_A}{y_A} - \frac{S_B - S_A}{\gamma R g}\frac{e \sin^2 \mu_A}{f + e} \quad (517)$$

$$\theta_C = \theta_A + d\theta_A \quad (518)$$

$$W_C = W_A + dW_A \quad (519)$$

$$\sin^2 \mu_C = \frac{\gamma - 1}{2}\left(\frac{1}{W_C^2} - 1 \right) \quad (520)$$

$$S_C = S_A + (S_B - S_A) \frac{e}{f + e} \tag{521}$$

Equations (516) to (521) are similar to equations (486) to (490), and equations (516) and (517) differ from equations (486) and (487) by the last term which contains the entropy.

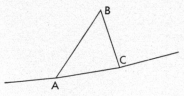

For numerical calculations a system analogous to the system for potential flow can be used, which permits a step-by-step calculation for determining the flow field. For a general point, equations (516) and (517) must be used, while for a point on the body the value of $d\theta$ is known as the direction is known;

Fig. 189. *Determination of a point of the body.*

therefore equations (512) or (513) must be used. If a point C on the body is analyzed (Figure 189), the entropy at C is the same as at A, because AC is a stream line. Therefore the value of dS/dn for equation (512) along BC is given by the equation

$$\frac{dS}{dn} = \frac{(S_B - S_A) \cos (\theta_B - \mu_B)}{(x_C - x_B) \sin \mu_B}.$$

For a point on the shock an equation similar to equation (491) must be used. The expression $d\Delta S/d\delta$ which represents the variation of ΔS across the shock as a function of the variation of the deviation across the shock must be determined. The expression $d\Delta S/d\delta$ can be determined directly, because for a given M for every value of δ the value of variation of pressure and density across the shock, and therefore the variation of entropy ΔS, can be determined. If B is the point that must be calculated and AB is the shock (Figure 190), assuming that the flow at B has the same direction as at C ($\theta_B = \theta_C$), the variation of

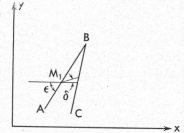

Fig. 190. *Determination of a point of the shock.*

entropy ΔS_{θ_C} and the velocity W_{θ_C} behind the shock corresponding to a deviation across the shock θ_C can be determined. Because the direction at B is different, the value of W at B is different from W_{θ_C} and the variation of entropy is different from ΔS_{θ_C}, but if the slopes of the curves W as functions of δ, and of ΔS as a function of δ are known, it is possible to write

$$\Delta S_B = \Delta S_{\theta_C} + \left(\frac{d\Delta S}{d\delta}\right)_{\theta_C} \Delta \theta$$

$$W_B = W_{\theta_C} + \left(\frac{dw}{d\delta}\right)_{\theta_C} \Delta \theta \tag{522}$$

then the equation of the variation of θ along BC becomes

$$\frac{W_{\theta_C} - W_C}{W_C} + \left(\frac{dW}{d\delta}\right)_{\theta_C} \frac{\Delta\theta}{W_C} - \tan \mu_C \, \Delta\theta - \frac{(x_B - x_C)}{y_C} l_C$$

$$+ \frac{\sin^2 \mu_C}{g\gamma R}\left[\Delta S_{\theta_C} - \Delta S_C + \left(\frac{d\Delta S}{d\delta}\right)_{\theta_C} \Delta\theta\right] = 0. \quad (523)$$

With equation (523) the flow at the point B can be determined, because when $\Delta\theta$ is known, the deviation δ across the shock is determined and W_B is determined.

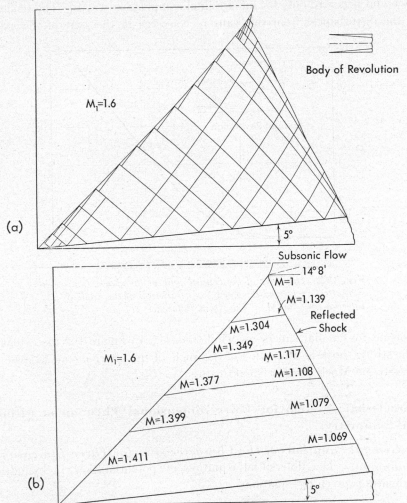

Fig. 191. *Example of* (a) *a practical characteristic net, and* (b) *results of the calculations for the internal flow on a circular conical inlet at M = 1.6 (from Reference 51).*

In Figure 191 a practical determination of the flow along an internal cone is shown (from Reference 51). As is shown in Figure 191, the shock increases in intensity moving towards the axis and becomes a normal shock at the axis. This phenomenon does not depend on the particular boundary conditions chosen, but is general for supersonic flow in circular channels. If a shock is produced at the wall of the channel, the shock increases in intensity moving from the wall toward the axis, becoming a strong shock near the axis (the flow behind the shock is subsonic), and a normal shock at the axis. The zone in which a strong shock exists increases with the increase of the intensity of the shock and it is zero only for infinitesimal compression waves. The tendency for the disturbances from the walls to converge in the zone of the axis is

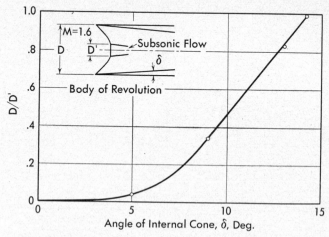

Fig. 192. *Diameter of the central zone of the shock, that gives subsonic flow behind the shock, as a function of the angle of the internal cone for M = 1.6 (from Reference 51).*

important for circular supersonic wind tunnels. In Figure 192 the extension of the strong shock as a function of the angle of the internal cone is given for a free-stream Mach number equal to 1.6.

Characteristic System for Three-Dimensional Phenomena without Axial Symmetry.

The General Equations of the Characteristics for Three-Dimensional Phenomena. The differential equation of potential flow in cylindrical coordinates is given by equation

$$\left(1 - \frac{u^2}{a^2}\right)\frac{\partial^2 \phi}{\partial x^2} + \left(1 - \frac{v^2}{a^2}\right)\frac{\partial^2 \phi}{\partial y^2} + \left(1 - \frac{w^2}{a^2}\right)\frac{1}{y^2}\frac{\partial^2 \phi}{\partial \phi^2} - \frac{2uv}{a^2}\frac{\partial^2 \phi}{\partial x \partial y}$$
$$- \frac{2uw}{a^2}\frac{1}{y}\frac{\partial^2 \phi}{\partial \phi \partial x} - \frac{2vw}{a^2}\frac{1}{y}\frac{\partial^2 \phi}{\partial \phi \partial y} + \frac{v}{y}\left(1 + \frac{w^2}{a^2}\right) = 0 \quad (524)$$

where u, v, and w are the respective velocity components along the x-axis (coincident with the axis of the body), along the y-axis (normal to x in the meridian plane) and in a direction normal to the meridian plane, respectively, and φ is the angular coordinate of the meridian plane. Equation (524) is an equation with second order partial derivatives of the hyperbolic type because V is larger than a. Therefore characteristic surfaces exist which are the singular surfaces of the Cauchy theorem. (See Chapter 2, Reference 3.)

If the equation of the singular surfaces is

$$y = f(x, \varphi) \tag{525}$$

equation (525) must be satisfied by the relation

$$a_{11}f_x'^2 - a_{12}f_x' + a_{22} + a_{13}f_x'f_\varphi' - a_{23}f_\varphi' + a_{33}f_\varphi'^2 = 0 \tag{526}$$

where

$$a_{11} = 1 - \frac{u^2}{a^2}; \qquad a_{22} = 1 - \frac{v^2}{a^2}; \qquad a_{44} = 1 + \frac{w^2}{a^2};$$

$$a_{12} = \frac{-2uv}{a^2}; \qquad a_{23} = \frac{-2vw}{a^2}\frac{1}{y};$$

$$a_{13} = \frac{-2uw}{a^2}\frac{1}{y}; \qquad a_{33} = \left(1 - \frac{w^2}{a^2}\right)\frac{1}{y^2} \tag{527}$$

or

$$f_x'^2 + 1 + \frac{f_\varphi'^2}{y^2} - \frac{u^2}{a^2}f_x'^2 + \frac{2uv}{a^2}f_x' - \frac{v^2}{a^2} - \frac{2uw}{a^2}\frac{f_\varphi'}{y^2}f_x'$$
$$+ \frac{2uw}{a^2}\frac{f_\varphi'}{y} - \frac{w^2}{a^2}\frac{f_\varphi'^2}{y^2} = 0 \tag{528}$$

but

$$\frac{f_x'}{\sqrt{1 + f_x'^2 + \frac{f_\phi'^2}{y^2}}}; \quad \frac{-1}{\sqrt{1 + f_x'^2 + \frac{f_\varphi'^2}{y^2}}}; \text{ and } \frac{f_\varphi'}{y\sqrt{1 + f_x'^2 + \frac{f_\varphi'^2}{y^2}}} \tag{529}$$

are the direction cosines of the normal n to the surface (equation 525) at a generical point, while u/V, v/V, and w/V are the direction cosines of the velocity; therefore dividing equation (528) by the factor

$$1 + f_x'^2 + \frac{f_\varphi'^2}{y^2}$$

and multiplying by the factor $\dfrac{a^2}{V^2}$ produces

$$\cos^2(V, n) = \frac{a^2}{V^2}$$

or

$$\cos(V, n) = \frac{a}{V}\cdot \tag{530}$$

Therefore it can be concluded that the characteristic surfaces defined by equation (525) are the envelope surfaces of the Mach cones, with vertices at the points from which the disturbance in the flow begins to propagate. The surfaces divide the region of undisturbed flow from the region of flow in which the disturbance is propagated. For every line contained in a plane normal to the x-axis, two families of characteristics surfaces pass, the normals of which are symmetrically inclined with respect to the direction of the velocity.

For numerical application of the characteristic system in three-dimensional flow, the intersections of the characteristic surfaces with the meridian planes and with the parallel planes can be considered, and then the variation of the velocity properties along the intersection lines can be determined (Reference 44). With the equations of the intersection lines, it is possible to proceed with a step-by-step process and to determine the flow properties in the entire field if the initial conditions are known. The initial conditions can be determined, for example, if the front part of the body considered is a pointed body of revolution or an open-nose body not necessarily of revolution. For this case, the shock at the lip follows the two-dimensional law, and therefore the system used for a body of revolution with axis parallel to the flow can be applied. When the initial conditions at a characteristic surface are known, in order to determine the flow field, the law of variation of the flow properties along the intersection of the characteristics surfaces with parallel and meridian plane must be determined.

If σ_1 is the intersection of a characteristic surface of a given family with a meridian plane, the variations du, dv, and $d(yw)$ along the line σ_1 will be considered. If $d\sigma_1$ is an element of the curve which has the components dx and dy along the x-axis and the y-axis, respectively,

$$\left.\begin{aligned} du &= (p_{11} + p_{12}f_x') \, dx \\ dv &= (p_{12} + p_{22}f_x') \, dx \\ d(yw) &= (p_{13} + p_{23}f_x') \, dx \end{aligned}\right\} \tag{531}$$

where

$$p_{ik} = \frac{\partial^2 \phi}{\partial x_i \, \partial x_k} \quad \text{and} \quad f_x' = \frac{dy}{dx} \tag{532}$$

and x_i or x_k is one of the three independent variables x (subscript 1), y (subscript 2), and z (subscript 3). For analogy with the characteristic system for a body of revolution with axis parallel to the flow, call the expression f_x'

$$f_x' = \lambda_1 = \left(\frac{dy}{dx}\right)_{\varphi = \text{const.}}$$

and

$$f_\varphi' = k = \left(\frac{dy}{d\varphi}\right)_{x = \text{const.}}$$

Then

$$p_{12} = \frac{dv}{dx} - p_{22}\lambda_1; \qquad p_{13} = \frac{d\,(yw)}{dx} - \lambda_1 p_{23};$$

$$p_{11} = \frac{du}{dx} - \lambda_1 \frac{dv}{dx} + \lambda_1^2 p_{22}. \qquad\qquad (533)$$

Substituting equations (533) in equation (524), the equation becomes

$$a_{11}\left(\frac{du}{dx} - \lambda_1 \frac{dv}{dx} + \lambda_1^2 p_{22}\right) + a_{12}\left(\frac{dv}{dx} - \lambda_1 p_{22}\right) + a_{22}p_{22}$$

$$+ a_{13}\left[\frac{d\,(yw)}{dx} - \lambda_1 p_{23}\right] + a_{23}p_{23} + \frac{v}{y}a_{44} + a_{33}p_{33} = 0. \qquad (534)$$

Adding and subtracting equal terms to equation (526), the equation becomes

$$p_{22}\,(a_{11}\lambda_1^2 - a_{12}\lambda_1 + a_{22}) - a_{13}p_{23}\lambda_1 + a_{23}p_{23} + a_{33}p_{33} =$$
$$- \lambda_1 a_{13}\,(kp_{22} + p_{23}) + a_{23}\,(p_{22}k + p_{23}) + a_{33}\,(p_{33} - k^2 p_{22}). \qquad (535)$$

Now consider a parallel plane, $x = $ constant, and call τ_1 the intersection of the same characteristic surface with a parallel plane $x = $ constant.

Then

$$(d\tau_1)^2 = (dy)^2 + (yd\varphi)^2; \qquad \frac{dv}{d\tau_1} = \frac{dv}{d\varphi}\,d\varphi/d\tau_1 + \frac{dv}{dy}\frac{dy}{d\tau}.$$

Therefore

$$bp_{22} + p_{23} = y\sqrt{1 + \frac{k^2}{y^2}\frac{dv}{d\tau_1}}$$

$$p_{33} - k^2 p_{22} = y\sqrt{1 + \frac{k^2}{y^2}}\left[\frac{d\,(yw)}{d\tau_1} - k\frac{dv}{d\tau_1}\right]. \qquad (536)$$

Placing

$$A = \frac{v}{y}a_{44} \qquad\qquad (537)$$

and

$$B_1 = y\sqrt{1 + \frac{k^2}{y^2}}\left[\frac{dv}{d\tau_1}\,(a_{23} - \lambda_1 a_{13} - ka_{33}) + a_{33}\frac{d(yw)}{d\tau_1}\right] \qquad (538)$$

and substituting equation (535) in equation (534), the following expression is obtained:

$$a_{11}\frac{du}{dx} + (a_{12} - a_{11}\lambda_1)\frac{dv}{dx} + a_{13}\frac{d\,(yw)}{dx} + A + B_1 = 0. \qquad (539)$$

Equation (528) with the new symbols becomes

$$a_{11}\lambda^2 - a_{12}\lambda + a_{22} + a_{13}\lambda k - a_{23}k + a_{33}k^2 = 0 \qquad (540)$$

and is an equation of the second order in λ or k. Equation (540) has two solutions, λ_1 and λ_2, which are the inclinations of the intersections with a meridian plane of the two characteristic surfaces of different families that pass through every point. For every point the following conditions exist:

$$\left(\frac{dy}{dx}\right)_{\varphi \,=\, \text{const.}} = \lambda_1, \qquad \left(\frac{dy}{d\varphi}\right)_{x \,=\, \text{const.}} = k \tag{541}$$

first family

$$a_{11}\frac{du}{dx} + (ka_{13} + \lambda_2 a_{11})\frac{dv}{dx} + a_{13}\frac{d\,(yw)}{dx} + A + B_1 = 0 \tag{542}$$

$$\left(\frac{dy}{dx}\right)_{\varphi \,=\, \text{const.}} = \lambda_2, \qquad \left(\frac{dy}{d\varphi}\right)_{x \,=\, \text{const.}} = k \tag{543}$$

second family

$$a_{11}\frac{du}{dx} + (ka_{13} + \lambda_1 a_{11})\frac{dv}{dx} + a_{13}\frac{d\,(yw)}{dx} + A + B_2 = 0 \tag{544}$$

where B_2 corresponds to B_1 for σ_2 (λ_2 must be substituted in place of λ_1 in equation 538).

Using the condition of irrotationality or proceeding in a similar way as in the preceding consideration, an expression can be obtained for the variation of the velocity along the intersection of the characteristic surface with the parallel plane $x = $ constant. The expression is

$$a_{13}\frac{du}{d\varphi} + (a_{23} - ka_{33})\frac{dv}{d\varphi} + a_{33}\frac{d\,(yw)}{d\varphi} + A + C_1 = 0. \tag{545}$$

$$C_1 = \sqrt{1 + \lambda_1^2}\left[\frac{dv}{d\sigma_1}(-ka_{13} + a_{12} - \lambda_1 a_{11}) + a_{11}\frac{du}{d\sigma_1}\right]. \tag{546}$$

For the surface τ_2, the term C_1 changes in a manner analogous to the term B_1

Equations (541) to (546) are general for three-dimensional problems and can be used whenever the initial conditions of the flow along a characteristic surface are known. To explain the practical system for using equations (541) to (546), the following application is considered.

Application of the Characteristic System for Three-Dimensional Phenomena.

A body of revolution in yaw with a pointed nose is considered, and a shape made up of truncated cones is substituted for the shape of the body. In order to determine the flow around such a body, the expansions around the corner made by the truncated cones, and the flow along the truncated cones must be determined. It is assumed that the flow around the first part of the body, that in the example considered, is a cone of revolution in yaw, is known. If OA is the first part of the body (Figure 193) and a variation of direction occurs at A, the deviation produces a disturbance in the flow which is transmitted in a zone of flow behind a characteristic surface which

starts from the circle AA' of the body. The propagation occurs with a series
of Mach cones having vertices along the circle AA', and, when the entire dis-

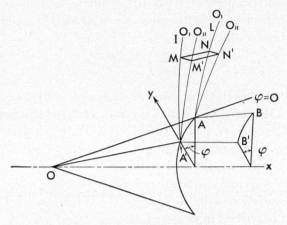

Fig. 193. *Characteristic system for body of revolution
with angle of attack, expansion around the corner.*

turbance is propagated, the velocity at AA' has a new direction tangent to the
body $ABA'B'$. The characteristic surface behind which the disturbance is
transmitted can be determined. Every meridian plane $\varphi = $ constant intersects the characteristic surface along a characteristic line that passes through
the point A (Figure 193) of the body and is defined by the equation

$$y = y_A + \lambda_1 (x - x_A). \tag{547}$$

The slope of the curve that corresponds to the coefficient λ_1 can be determined
from equation (540). Because the body considered is a body of revolution,
at the section AA', $f'(\varphi) = 0$ (the characteristic surface for $x = x_A$ passes
through AA' for which $y = $ constant). Therefore equation (540) becomes

$$a_{11}\lambda^2 - a_{12}\lambda + a_{22} = 0. \tag{548}$$

Therefore λ_1 at AA' is known in every meridian plane.

If the body is not one of revolution, the line AA' is a known intersection of
the characteristic surface, and therefore the value of k can be calculated and
the value of λ_1 can be obtained from equation (540). When part of the line
AA' is not in the same plane $x = $ constant, the intersection of characteristic
surface and the body can still be determined because the characteristic surface is made up of Mach cones. Their intersections with the body give
a line that permits determination of the value of k.

Assuming $x - x_A = x_1 - x_A$ small, in equation (547) λ_1 can be considered
constant in every meridian plane between x_1 and x_A, and therefore the value of

y for every value of φ for the plane $x = x_1$ can be calculated with equation (547), and the intersection of the characteristic surface with the parallel plane $x = x_1$ can be determined. If NM is the intersection of the characteristic surface with the plane $x = x_1$, the value of y at M and N is known from equation (547). Therefore the value

$$\left(\frac{dy}{d\varphi}\right)_{x_1} = k \tag{549}$$

can be calculated, and the new value of $\lambda_1(\varphi)$ along NM can be determined with equation (540) because the flow in front of the characteristic surface is known. The tangents NL and MI to the characteristic surface at N and M can be designed. So, proceeding step by step, the complete characteristic surface of the first family can be determined.

Consider now a second characteristic surface O_{II} along which a disturbance produced by a variation of direction $\Delta\theta$ at A is transmitted. The equation of O_{II} near A can be written in the form

$$y = y_A + \lambda_{II}(x - x_A).$$

But at A

$$k_A = (f_\varphi')_A = 0$$

because the characteristic surfaces O_{II} and O_I meet along AA'. In the meridian plane $\varphi = 0$, which is the plane of symmetry for the flow phenomenon (the plane that contains the undisturbed velocity)

$$w = 0$$

therefore, λ is known in terms of the components u and v (equation 540), and

$$\left.\begin{aligned} \lambda_{1,2} &= \frac{uv}{u^2 - a^2} \pm \frac{a\sqrt{v^2 - a^2}}{u^2 - a^2} = \tan(\theta \pm \mu) \\[2ex] \tan\theta &= \frac{v}{u} \\[2ex] \sin\mu &= \frac{a}{V} \end{aligned}\right\} \tag{550}$$

If du and dv are the increments in the plane $\varphi = 0$, du and dv at A are also known, because the value of θ at A along O_{II} is given, and du and dv are given by the two-dimensional law, from considerations similar to those given in page 266 equation (490). Consider now a point N along the characteristic surface O_I in the plane $\varphi = 0$. At N the values of λ_1 and λ_2 are known; therefore in the plane $\varphi = 0$, the tangent to the second characteristic surface corresponding to λ_2 can be drawn. Because the tangent to the surface O_{II} at A in the plane $\varphi = 0$ is known, the point N', which is the intersection of the two tangents, can be determined. At N' the component w is also zero and using the symbols

$$\Delta u = u_{N' \longrightarrow A} - u_N$$
$$\Delta v = v_{N' \longrightarrow A} - v_N$$
$$du = - u_{N' \longrightarrow A} + u_{N'}$$
$$dv = - v_{N' \longrightarrow A} + v_{N'}$$

(551)

from equation (542) is obtained

$$du + \lambda_2 dv + \frac{A + B_2}{a_{11}} (x_{N'} - x_N) + \Delta u + \lambda_2 \Delta v = 0 \qquad (552)$$

$$du + \lambda_1 dv + \frac{A + B_1}{a_{11}} (x_{N'} - x_A) = 0 \qquad (553)$$

where du and dv are the variations of velocity along the line AN'. The terms λ_2, A, B_2, and a_{11} in equation (552) are the values at the point N, while the terms λ_1, A, B_1, the a_{11} in equation (553) are the values at the point A on O_{II}. The values of the coefficients A and B_1 at the point A of O_{II} are the same as at the point A of O_I because $dw/d\varphi$ does not change from O_I to O_{II}. Therefore the term $d(yw)/d\tau$ does not change. In this way it is possible with equations (552) and (553) to determine the flow at the point N' in the meridian plane $\varphi = 0$.

It is necessary now to determine the flow properties in the other meridian planes along the characteristic surface O_{II}. The characteristic surface O_{II} corresponds to a small deviation of the stream along AA' which is constant in all the meridian planes. Therefore the value of dv/du at A' is known and is equal to the value at A. At A', k is known (for a body of revolution k is zero) and w has the same value if A' is considered on the surface O_I or on the surface O_{II}, because w is tangent to the characteristic surfaces. Thus passing from O_I to O_{II} the component w cannot undergo any discontinuous variation. Therefore, the quantities $\partial(wy)/\partial\varphi$, $\partial(yw)/\partial\tau$ along AA' have the same known value in all the characteristic surfaces O_I, O_{II}, O_n, that exists at O_I. Using equation (545), in which k is known (in this case is equal to zero), the value of dv and du at A' can be determined, because dv/du is known and all the coefficients that appear in equation (542) are known and correspond to the flow properties at A' in O_I in the meridian plane considered.

If the flow at the point A' of the surface O_{II} is determined, the value of the tangent to the intersection of O_{II} with the meridian plane can be determined, using equation (548), or in the general case, using equation (540) and a point M' in the plane, $x = x_{N'} = $ constant can be determined. The point M can be found on O_I and along the characteristic line of the other family from M' in the meridian plane, and by determining the variation of the flow along A', M', MM', and $N'M'$, the flow in M' can be calculated.

$$y_{M'} = y_{A'} + \lambda (\varphi) (x_{N'} - x_{A'}) \tag{554}$$

where, in this case

$$a_{11} \lambda^2 (\varphi) - a_{12} \lambda (\varphi) + a_{22} = 0$$

and a_{11}, a_{12}, and a_{22} are the coefficients corresponding to the point A' of O_{II}. Along $A'M'$ equation (542) must be applied where $dx = x_{M'} - x_{A'}$, $du = u_{M'} - u_{A'}$, $dv = v_{M'} - v_{A'}$, $d(wy) = (wy)_{M'} - (wy)_{A'}$, and the coefficients of the expression are calculated at the point A'.

Along MM' equation (544) must be used where du, dv, $d(yw)$, and dx are the differences between corresponding values in M' and M, while k is given by the equation

$$k (\varphi) = \frac{\lambda (\varphi) - \lambda (\varphi = 0)}{\Delta \varphi} dx \tag{555}$$

Along $M'N'$ equation (545) must be used in a similar manner. From the three equations, the values of $u_{M'}$, $v_{M'}$, and $w_{M'}$ can be determined and another point L' along $A'N'$ can be determined, as the value of $dv/d\tau$, and $d(yw)/d\tau$ between M_1 and N_1 are now known. Proceeding in a similar way, the entire expansion around the corner AA' can be determined.

In order to determine the flow properties along the straight part of the body AB, the following considerations can be made (Figure 194). If, from a point N of the last characteristic line that starts from A, the characteristic line of

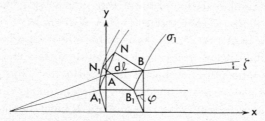

Fig. 194. *The determination of the flow along the cone of the body with constant inclination.*

the opposite family NB is designed in the meridian plane, a point B is determined on the body for which the following relations can be written: If dl is the distance along the body between A and B and ζ is the inclination of the body on the axis, then from the definition of w, v, and u

$$d (yw)_{\varphi = \text{const}} = \frac{\partial (yw)}{\partial x} dx + \frac{d (yw)}{dy} dy.$$

Therefore

$$y_B w_B = y_A w_A + d\,(yw)$$

$$d\,(yw) = \left(\frac{\partial u}{\partial \varphi} \cos \zeta + \frac{dv}{\partial \varphi} \sin \zeta\right) dl. \tag{556}$$

The quantities $\partial u / \partial \varphi$ and $\partial v / \partial \varphi$ must be calculated at the point A of the same meridian plane as B and therefore are known from the preceding calculations. Thus, the value $y_B w_B$ can be determined.

In the meridian plane $\varphi = 0$, w is zero; the boundary conditions give the relation

$$\frac{dv_B}{du_B} = \tan \zeta \tag{557}$$

and from equation (544)

$$du_B + \lambda_1 dv_B + \frac{A + B_2}{a_{11}}\,(x_B - x_N) = 0. \tag{558}$$

Therefore u_B and v_B can be determined, and the tangent at B to the characteristic line σ_1 can be designed.

From B the flow at a point B' in the meridian plane φ can be determined for the same distance dl, because two equations can be written that give the variation of velocity components along BB_1 (equation 557) and along $N_1 B_1$ (equation 544), which with equation (556) permits the determination of the flow at B_1. Proceeding in the same way, the entire flow around the body of revolution can be determined.

CHAPTER

14

PRESSURE DRAG OF SUPERSONIC WINGS

Introductory Considerations. In Chapter 7 the aerodynamic characteristics of supersonic profiles as functions of their geometry were considered; therefore the aerodynamic characteristics of the rectangular wing of infinite span have been determined. In general, for wings of finite span and of various plan form, the aerodynamic phenomena are different and more complicated than those of the two-dimensional profiles, and it is not possible, at present, to make a theoretical analysis with the same approximation obtained for two-dimensional profiles. When wings of finite span are considered, the hypothesis that the theory of small disturbances can be applied is usually accepted, and it is also assumed that the wing is very thin. With these two hypotheses the drag at the zero-lift condition, and the lift-curve slope of wings for different plan forms have been determined. In the following paragraphs, some considerations on the relation between the plan form of the wings and their aerodynamic characteristics will be developed, and the pressure drag for wings of different shape will be determined.

Wing Plan Form Which Eliminates Tip Effect. In the aerodynamics of subsonic flow, it is shown that when a wing of infinite span is considered, and the flow is assumed perfect, the drag obtained is zero; however, for a wing of finite span in a perfect flow a drag exists. This drag, which is called *induced drag*, is a consequence of the lift of the wing, and depends on the aspect ratio and plan form of the wing. The induced drag is the only drag that can be found in a perfect flow. In aerodynamics of supersonic flow, a drag is found even if perfect flow and wings of infinite aspect ratio are considered. This drag is dependent on the shape of the profile and on the lift (equation 266). When a wing of finite span is considered, a different value of the drag is generally found; however, with special configuration of the wing tips, it is possible to obtain a wing of finite span with the same drag characteristics as the infinite-span wing (Reference 25).

Consider, for example, a flat plate of infinite length (Figure 195), and on the wing two points, A and B, along the leading edge. If the flow on every

292

point of the span is supersonic and some small transformations are produced
along the leading edge in the zones CA and BD, those disturbances are trans-

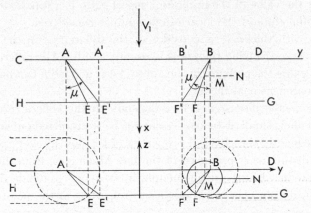

Fig. 195. *Flat plate of finite aspect ratio without tip effect.*

mitted in the flow in a zone defined by the envelope of Mach cones, with vertex
along CA and BD at the points at which the disturbances are produced. The
zones of the wing influenced by the disturbances are the zones $CAEH$ and
$DBFG$, where the lines AE and BF are the intersections of the Mach cones
from A and B with the wing. Consequently in the zone $AEFB$ no variation of
flow characteristics occurs for the disturbances produced along BD and CA.
If the disturbances are produced at points of the wing in the zones $BFDG$ and
$CAHE$, for example along MN, the disturbances are still inside the zone
defined by the envelope of Mach cones with vertices along CA or BD (Figure
195), and cannot affect the flow in the zone $AEBF$. Therefore if the part of
the wing outside the zone $AEBF$ is eliminated and the wing $AEBF$ is considered, that wing must have the same flow characteristics as the wing of infinite
span, and consequently the same pressure distribution. The lines AE and BF
change with angle of attack of the flat plate but are all outside a line AE' or
BF' inclined at the Mach angle with respect to the chord; therefore on the
flat plate $AE'BF'$ the pressure distribution found in Chapter 7 (page 118 or 131)
exists.

The pressure for the trapezoidal flat plate is constant on the entire upper
surface and on the entire lower surface; therefore the focus of the profile for
the trapezoidal wing moves from the 50 per cent station of the chord in the
direction of the leading edge, because the center of pressure of the triangular
zones $AA'E'$ and $BB'F$ is at $\frac{1}{3}$ of the chord from the leading edge. Its position
can be easily determined as a function of the angle of the line AE'.

The possibility of cutting the plate along the lines AE' and BF' is dependent
on the aspect ratio considered. When the aspect ratio decreases, the distance

$E'F'$ decreases and becomes zero for a given value of the aspect ratio. This value is the minimum for which the criterion considered can be applied. It is evident that the value of the minimum aspect ratio is a function of the angle $AE'A'$, and therefore of the local Mach number considered.

If a wing with thickness is considered, the differences in the phenomena are small because the wing thickness is usually small. The differences can be evaluated because the pressure in the zones $AA'E$ and $BB'F$ can be determined with the two-dimensional theory.

The phenomenon discussed before depends on the general property that, in supersonic flow, small disturbances cannot be transmitted outside the Mach cone. Consequently the physical properties of the flow at every point depend only on the disturbances produced in the fore Mach cone from the point, and alterations produced in the phenomenon, in every zone outside the fore cone from a point, do not change the physical properties in the point considered.

Infinite Sweptback Wings. In all the preceding analysis, the wing of infinite span and the wing with trapezoidal plan form considered have the leading edge and the trailing edge perpendicular to the direction of the stream; therefore in the zone of the wing, the stream lines are plane and are contained in the plane perpendicular to the leading edge. Now the two-dimensional theory can be applied also to the flow around an infinite wing with constant cross section, when the leading edge is inclined with respect to the direction perpendicular to the undisturbed velocity. In this case, the streamlines are no longer plane, but the phenomenon must be the same in every plane perpendicular to the leading edge; therefore the component of the velocity in the direction of the leading edge w must be constant in the entire flow and independent of the shape of the wing. If X is the angle of sweepback (Figure 196), the component w is given by

$$w = V_1 \sin \text{X}. \qquad (559)$$

The phenomena for the sweptback wing of infinite span in a perfect flow can be assumed to be obtained by moving the wing in the direction of the leading edge with the velocity w, in a flow moving in a direction perpendicular to the leading edge with a velocity $V_1 \cos \text{X}$. Because the component w does not produce any variation of pressure, the phenomena must correspond to those for a straight wing at a velocity $V_1 \cos$ X. However, the component w must be considered when viscous forces are analyzed in the boundary layer.

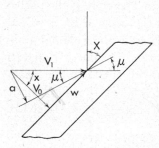

Fig. 196. *Infinite sweptback wing less inclined than the Mach wave.*

The possibility of resolving the undisturbed velocity into two components, normal and parallel, respectively, to the leading edge, shows that the angle of sweepback of an infinite wing is equivalent to reduction of the value of the undisturbed velocity from the aerodynamic point of view, and, since the temperature of the flow is not affected by such resolution, the effective Mach number that must be considered is reduced by adoption of an angle of sweepback. The resolution of the velocity into two components permits determination of the pressure forces for the infinite sweptback wing, from the lift and drag coefficients corresponding to the section of the wing in the plane perpendicular to the leading edge. The Mach number that must be considered in the determination of the coefficients of the forces is $(M_0 = M_1 \cos X)$, where M_1 is the Mach number of the undisturbed flow. The angle of attack of the wing must also be measured in the plane perpendicular to the leading edge. The pressure drag determined in this way has the direction of $V_1 \cos X$; therefore to obtain the component of the force in the direction V_1 which gives the pressure drag for the wing, the drag determined before must be reduced in proportion to the cosine of the angle of sweepback.

If C_{L_0} and C_{D_0} are, respectively, the lift and drag coefficients corresponding to the angle of attack of the wing measured in the plane perpendicular to the leading edge for the Mach number $(M_0 = M_1 \cos X)$, the lift is given by

$$L = \frac{1}{2} C_{L_0} \rho s \, V_1^2 \cos^2 X. \qquad \longleftarrow \text{———} \qquad (560)$$

The profile drag in the V_1 direction is given by

$$D_p = \frac{1}{2} C_{D_0} \rho s \, V_1^2 \cos^3 X. \qquad \longleftarrow \text{———} \qquad (561)$$

If C_L and C_D are the coefficients of the sweptback wing determined in the usual way, and C_f is the corresponding friction drag coefficient,

$$C_{L_0} \cos^2 X = C_L$$

and

$$C_{D_0} \cos^3 X + C_f = C_D. \qquad (562)$$

The phenomena for sweptback wings can be divided into two groups: the phenomena for wings with low angle of sweepback, for which $(M_0 = M_1 \cos X)$ Supersonic is larger than one, and the phenomena for wings with large angle of sweepback, for which $(M_0 = M_1 \cos X)$ is less than one. Subsonic

For the first group of wings, the coefficients C_{L_0} and C_{D_0} must be determined in terms of supersonic aerodynamic theory, while for the second group the normal component is subsonic, and therefore the flow phenomena must be considered, using subsonic theory.

For the first group, applying the small-disturbances theory (the variation of pressure is proportional to the deviation, and the term that contains η^2

is not considered), it is possible to obtain (by equation 243), the following (Reference 25):

$$C_{D0} = \frac{4}{\sqrt{M_1^2 \cos^2 X - 1}} \left[\alpha^2 + \frac{1}{2} (F_2 + D_2) \right] \tag{563}$$

$$C_{L0} = \frac{4}{\sqrt{M_1^2 \cos^2 X - 1}} \alpha. \tag{564}$$

From equations (564) and (562) the fineness ratio of the wing can be determined:

$$\frac{D}{L} = \frac{C_{D0} \cos^3 X + C_f}{C_{L0} \cos^2 X} = \frac{C_{D0} \cos X}{C_{L0}} + \frac{C_f}{C_{L0} \cos^2 X}$$

or using expressions (563) and (564)

$$\frac{D}{L} = \frac{1}{\alpha} \left[\frac{\sqrt{M_1^2 \cos^2 X - 1}}{4 \cos^2 X} C_f + \frac{1}{2} (F_2 + D_2) \cos X \right] + \alpha \cos X. \tag{565}$$

Assuming C_f constant, the angle of attack α that gives the minimum value of D/L of equation (7) is given by

$$\alpha_{\text{opt}} = \sqrt{\frac{C_f}{4} \frac{\sqrt{M_1^2 \cos^2 X - 1}}{\cos^3 X} + \frac{1}{2} (F_2 + D_2)} \tag{566}$$

and the corresponding minimum value of D/L is

$$\left(\frac{D}{L} \right)_{\text{min}} = \sqrt{2C_f \frac{M_1}{M_0} \sqrt{M_0^2 - 1} + 2 \frac{M_0^2}{M_1^2} (F_2 + D_2)}. \tag{567}$$

For the infinite straight wing with the same approximation, the value of $(D/L)_{\text{min}}$ is given by

$$\left(\frac{D}{L} \right)_{\text{min}} = \sqrt{2C_f \sqrt{M_1^2 - 1} + 2 (F_2 + D_2)}. \tag{568}$$

For average values of friction drag coefficient, a small diminution of $(D/L)_{\text{min}}$ is obtained by using a wing with an angle of sweepback. When the Mach number is very high, in which case the importance of the terms dependent on the form of the profile decreases, the value of $(D/L)_{\text{min}}$ is no longer decreased by the angle of sweepback.

The second group of wings corresponds to an angle of sweepback for which $(M_0 = M_1 \cos X)$ is less than one (Reference 52). Since

$$\frac{V_1}{V_0} = \cos X; \qquad \frac{V_1}{a} = \sin \mu; \qquad \frac{V_0}{a} < 1$$

the second group corresponds to the condition

$$\cos X > \sin \mu. \tag{569}$$

For this condition the leading edge of the wing is inclined with respect to the direction of the velocity more than the Mach wave (Figure 197). In this case, the flow phenomena on the wing are of the subsonic type and must be considered with subsonic or transonic theory. The drag of the wing is given by

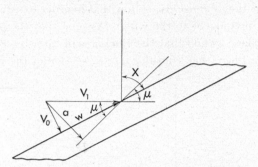

Fig. 197. *Infinite sweptback wing more inclined than the Mach wave.*

subsonic law, and shock losses can occur only if M_0 is very near to one. If M_0 is near one, the shock does not occur near the leading edge but along the profile, as happens for profiles in the supersonic zone of the transonic region. If M_0 is small, no shock losses can be verified, although V_1 is supersonic.

It is natural that the absence of shocks is derived from the hypothesis of infinite wings, because when a wing of finite span is considered, the shock losses appear immediately in every case. Indeed, at the tips of the wing, the component $V_1 \sin X$ takes part in the aerodynamic phenomena, and the pressure distribution at the tips depends on both the two components; then the supersonic quality of the flow appears again, and, three-dimensional phenomena must be considered.

Determination of the Source Distribution for Symmetrical Wings of Finite Aspect Ratio at Zero Angle of Incidence. The determination of the pressure distribution and of the pressure drag for three-dimensional thin symmetrical wings can be obtained by using the theory of small disturbances. Consider a stream with supersonic speed V_1 and a wing of symmetrical cross section placed in the stream at zero angle of attack. The presence of the wing produces a variation of the stream velocity; therefore in the zone of the wing three components, u_2, v_2, and w_2, of the variation of the velocity with respect to the undisturbed velocity, can be considered.

Let ϕ_2 be the potential function of the additive flow that has the velocity components u_2, v_2, and w_2 along the x-, y-, and z-axes; and assume that the undisturbed flow is in the x direction. The accepted approximation of the small-disturbances theory defines the potential function ϕ_2 by the following equation (equation 339):

$$(1 - M_1{}^2) \frac{\partial^2 \phi_2}{\partial x^2} + \frac{\partial^2 \phi_2}{\partial y^2} + \frac{\partial^2 \phi_2}{\partial z^2} = 0. \tag{570}$$

The potential function ϕ_2 must give a flow that in order to satisfy the boundary conditions, must be tangent to the wing. Assume that the plane of the wing is placed on the plane xy and that the thickness of the wing is measured along the z-axis (Figure 198); then consider a cross section of the wing in the plane

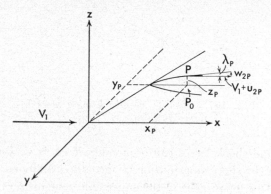

Fig. 198. *The boundary conditions for a three-dimensional wing.*

xz and a general point P of the contour of the wing in this cross section. The stream must be tangent to the wing at P; therefore the components of the speed in the xz plane must give a resultant tangent to the cross section at P. Using the subscript P to indicate that the quantity is considered at the point P, the boundary condition can be expressed in the form

$$\frac{w_{2P}}{V_1 + u_{2P}} = \left(\frac{dz}{dx}\right)_P = \lambda_P \qquad \mathcal{B.C.} \tag{571}$$

where λ_P is the slope of the cross section at P. With the approximation accepted, the term u_{2P} can be neglected; therefore (Figure 198)

$$\frac{w_{2P}}{V_1} = \left(\frac{dz}{dx}\right)_P = \lambda_P. \tag{571a}$$

Since the thickness of the wing is small, (the small-disturbance theory is accepted in the analysis) the value of the velocity w_{2P} at P can be assumed, with good approximation, practically equal to the value w_{2P_0} of the velocity calculated at the point P_0 of the same coordinates x and y but in the plane $z = 0$ (the approximation can be accepted because z_P is small); therefore in equation (571) the value of w_{2P_0} calculated for the coordinates x_P, y_P and 0, which can be determined more easily than the value of w_{2P} at $P(x_P y_P z_P)$, will be used. In order to determine the potential function ϕ_2 that satisfies the given boundary conditions, a source distribution in the plane $z = 0$ will be considered for the upper surface and another of opposite sign for the lower surface (References 53 and 54).

If ξ and η are the coordinates of a source of intensity C in the plane $z = 0$, the potential of the source is given by equation (354):

$$\phi_2 = \frac{-C}{\sqrt{(x - \xi)^2 - B^2 \left[(y - \eta)^2 + z^2\right]}} \tag{572}$$

where

$$B = \sqrt{M_1^2 - 1}.$$

Therefore the potential of a source distribution of area $d\xi d\eta$ and coordinates ξ and η, in the plane $(z = 0)$, is given by

$$d\phi_2 = \frac{-C\, d\xi d\eta}{\sqrt{(x - \xi)^2 - B^2 \left[(y - \eta)^2 + z^2\right]}}. \tag{573}$$

The source distribution of intensity $+C$ and area $d\eta d\xi$, that exists at the position ξ, η of the plane $z = 0$, induces at a point P of coordinates x, y, and z, a velocity, the component of which along the z-axis is given by

$$w_P = \frac{\partial}{\partial z}\left[d\phi_2\right] = -\frac{CB^2\, z d\xi d\eta}{\left\{(x - \xi)^2 - B^2 \left[(y - \eta)^2 + z^2\right]\right\}^{3/2}}. \tag{574}$$

If the point P is outside the area in which the source distribution is placed, when z is equal to zero w_P is equal to zero; therefore the source distribution $C\, d\xi d\eta$ at $(\xi, \eta, 0)$ does not induce any vertical component of the velocity at every point P of the plane $z = 0$ outside of the area $d\xi d\eta$.

If the point P is in the zone of the plane in which the source distribution $C\, d\xi d\eta$ is placed, when z goes to zero, the denominator of equation (574) tends to approach zero, because $(x - \xi)$ and $(y - \eta)$ have infinitesimal values; therefore the limit of equation (574) for z approaching zero can no longer be evaluated directly from equation (574). In this case, the value can be determined in the following way: consider a point P, slightly above the plane $z = 0$, in the zone of the source distribution [Figure 199]. The zone of the source distribution, that can induce a velocity at a point P of coordinates (x, y, z) in supersonic flow, is the zone contained in the fore cone that has its vertex at P, its axis parallel to the velocity, and its semiangle equal to μ. If the point P has the projection P_0 in the plane $(z = 0)$ (P_0 is inside the element $d\xi d\eta$ considered), the part of the element $d\xi d\eta$ that can influence P is the part contained in $B_1 A_0 B_0 A_1$, where $B_1 A_0 B_0 A_1$ is the intersection of the plane $(z = 0)$ with the fore cone from P. Because the cone is a circular cone with its axis parallel to V_1, the intersection is a ~~parabola~~ HYPERBOLA the coordinates η', ξ' of which are defined by equation (575):

$$B^2\left[(y - \eta')^2 + z^2\right] = (x - \xi')^2. \tag{575}$$

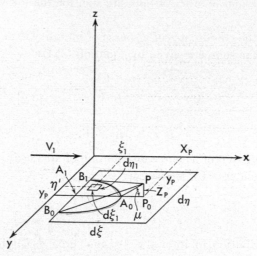

Fig. 199.   *The induction due to sources placed in the fore cone from the point considered.*

The potential at P of the source distribution contained in $B_1A_0B_0A_1$ is given by

$$\phi = -C \int_{x_{A_1}}^{x_{A_0}} d\xi' \int_{y_{B_1A_0}}^{y_{B_0A_0}} \frac{d\eta'}{\sqrt{(x - \xi')^2 - B^2\left[(y - \eta')^2 + z^2\right]}} \tag{576}$$

where the limits of integration of the double integral of equation (576) are given by the values ξ' and η' defined by equation (575). However

$$\int \frac{d\eta'}{\sqrt{(x - \xi')^2 - B^2\left[(x - \eta')^2 + z^2\right]}} = \frac{1}{B}\sin^{-1}\frac{B(y - \eta')}{\sqrt{(x - \xi')^2 - B^2z^2}}.$$

Since $(y - \eta')$ is negative along B_0A_0 and positive along B_1A_0, using the limits of integration defined by equation (575), π is found to be the value of the first definite integral of equation (576). Since

$$x_{A_0} = x_P - Bz_P$$

then

$$\phi_2 = -\frac{C}{B}\int_{x_{A_1}}^{x_P - Bz_P} \pi d\xi' = -\frac{\pi C}{B}\left[x_P - Bz - x_{A1}\right]$$

or

$$\frac{\partial \phi_2}{\partial z} = w_2 = \pi C. \tag{577}$$

If the value of z approaches zero, the value of w does not change; therefore the induced velocity at P_0 is equal to

$$w_{2P_0} = \pi C. \tag{578}$$

The value given by equation (578) is the total vertical velocity. Indeed as has been shown before, the source distribution on zones far from P does not produce induced velocity w at the point P_0.

Since the value of w_P is fixed by the boundary conditions (equation 571a), equation (578) gives the value of the intensity of the source distribution which satisfies the boundary conditions.

The pressure distribution on the wing is given by equation (355), which can be written (not considering the terms of higher order) as

$$C_P = \frac{P - P_1}{\dfrac{1}{2}\rho_1 V_1{}^2} = -\frac{2u_2}{V_1} = -\frac{2\phi_{2x}}{V_1} \tag{579}$$

where the potential function is given by equation (573) and the value of the constant C is given by the boundary conditions (equations 578 and 571a). The horizontal component of the perturbation ϕ_{2x} at any point is affected by all source elements in the field and therefore must be determined by integration over the entire fore cone from that point.

Determination of the Components along the x-Axis of the Distur-bance Velocity Induced by Source Distributions of Constant Intensity and Different Plan Form. In the preceding paragraph, it was shown that the intensity of the source distribution that produces a flow which satisfies given boundary conditions is proportional at every point to the slope of the cross section in the plane ($y = $ constant). From the source distribution, the x component of the velocity must be determined in order to determine the pressure distribution (equation 579). The x component of the induced velocity at a point can be determined as the sum of all velocities induced by all source distributions that exist in the flow. Indeed with the approximation of the small-disturbances theory, the coefficients of equation (570) are constant; therefore superimposition of different potential distributions is possible. Consequently determination of the pressure distribution for a given wing can be made in the following way: Every wing can be assumed to be constituted by an envelope of a finite or infinite number of planes tangent to the wing. For every flat surface of the wing the value of dz/dx is constant; therefore the corresponding intensities of the sources are constant and known. For every plane surface of every plan form the corresponding induced velocity in the direction of the x-axis can be determined in the entire flow; therefore from the sum of all velocity induced from all source distributions at a given point, the pressure at the point can be determined (equation 579) (Reference 53).

If the profile of the wing in the plane (y = constant) is obtained with straight lines, as are the diamond-shaped profile and the trapezoidal profile, the number of planes that constitute the envelope of the wing is finite. Then the value of ϕ_{2x} is given by the summation of a finite and small number of terms, and it is possible to obtain an analytical expression for the pressure distribution and for the total drag of the wing. If the profile has a continuous curvature, the value of ϕ_{2x} is given by an integral, that in some cases can be evaluated directly, or can generally be evaluated by substituting for the continuous line of the profile a polygon with a finite number of straight segments.

Determination of the pressure distribution on a wing is therefore reduced to the problem of determining the x component of the velocity, ϕ_{2x}, for a given plan form of a source distribution of constant intensity. In this paragraph indications for determining this component ϕ_{2x} will be given.

The induced velocity ϕ_{2x} produced by a given plan form of source distribution, in general, can be determined with superimposition of source distributions of simple form of a given intensity, as will be shown later; therefore these simple forms will be considered first.

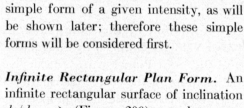

Fig. 200. *Source distribution for infinite two-dimensional flat plate.*

Infinite Rectangular Plan Form. An infinite rectangular surface of inclination $dz/dx = \lambda$ (Figure 200) can be represented by a rectangular source distribution of the intensity (equation 578)

$$\pi C = w_2 = \lambda V_1$$

The component of the velocity along the x-axis can be determined by the two-dimensional theory and is given by equation (101) (see page 42).

$$u^* = \frac{u_2}{\cos X} = -V_1 \cos X \frac{\lambda}{\cos X} \tan \mu^*.$$

Therefore

$$\phi_{2x} = u_2 = -\lambda V_1 \tan \mu^* \cos X$$

where μ^* is the Mach angle corresponding to the velocity component normal to the leading edge of the wing, and

$$\tan \mu^* = \frac{1}{\sqrt{M^{*2} - 1}}.$$

If

$$\sqrt{M^2 - 1} = B; \qquad \tan X = k; \qquad n = \frac{k}{B} \tag{580}$$

$\tan \mu^*$ becomes

$$\tan \mu^* = \frac{\sqrt{1 + k^2}}{\sqrt{B^2 - k^2}}$$

and

$$\cos X = \frac{1}{\sqrt{1 + k^2}}.$$

Therefore the value of ϕ_{2x} can be written in the form

$$\phi_{2x} = \frac{-\lambda V_1}{\sqrt{B^2 - k^2}} = \frac{-w}{B\sqrt{1 - n^2}}. \tag{581}$$

The pressure coefficient C_P becomes

$$C_P = \frac{P - P_1}{\frac{1}{2}\rho V^2} = \frac{2\lambda}{B\sqrt{1 - n^2}} \tag{582}$$

where λ is the slope in the plane ($y = $ constant), and not the slope of the profile in the plane perpendicular to the leading edge.

Infinite Triangular Plan Form. $k_1 > B.$ Any triangular surface can be obtained from the sum or differences of triangular surfaces having a side of

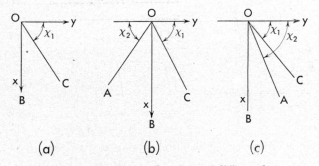

(a)   (b)   (c)

Fig. 201. *Triangular flat plates of different form.*

the triangle in the direction of the x-axis (Figure 201a). If the inclinations of the two sides of the triangle OA and OC are of opposite sign (Figure 201b), the source distribution can be considered as the sum of two source distributions of the type considered before (Figure 201a) of the same intensity, and, in general, with different values of the angle X. If the inclination of the two sides is of the same sign (Figure 201c), the source distribution can be considered as corresponding to the difference of two source distributions COB and AOB, of the same intensity and sign. Therefore from the analysis of a source distribution of the type of Figure 201a, the value of ϕ_{2x} for the source distribution as in Figure 201b and 201c can be determined. For the analysis of the plan form as in Figure 201a, two cases must be considered: the case in which the angle X_1 is larger than $(\pi/2 - \mu_1)$ (Figure 202), or using the definitions of equation (580) in which

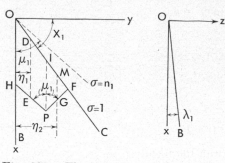

Fig. 202. *The induction in a point of the flat plate due to a triangular source distribution* $(n_1 > 1)$.

$$k_1 > B; \qquad n > 1$$

(where $k_1 = \tan X, B = \cot \mu_1$ and $n = k_1/B$), and the case in which X_1 is less than $(\pi/2 - \mu_1)$, or $k_1 < B$.

Assume at first $k_1 > B$; the plane OBC can be represented as a source distribution in the plane $z = 0$ extended in the zone OCB and of intensity

$$\pi C = w = \lambda_1 V_1. \tag{583}$$

Consider a point P on the zone OCB (Figure 202). If PH and PF are the Mach lines that pass through P, the only part of the source distribution that can induce a velocity at the point P is that in the zone $OHPF$. Therefore the potential function ϕ_2 at P can be written in the form (equation 576)

$$\phi_2 = -\frac{w}{\pi} \left[\int_0^{y_P} d\eta \int_{k_1\eta}^{x_P - B(y_P - \eta)} f(\xi, \eta)d\xi \right.$$

$$\left. + \int_{y_P}^{y_F} d\eta \int_{k_1\eta}^{x_P + B(y_P - \eta)} f(\xi, \eta)d\xi \right] \tag{584}$$

where

$$f(\xi, \eta) = \frac{1}{\sqrt{(x_P - \xi)^2 - B^2 (y_P - \eta)^2 - B^2 z_P^2}}$$

and z_P in the approximation accepted is assumed equal to zero. Indeed, in the zone $HPIO$ for every value of $\eta = \eta_1$ the integral with respect to ξ must be extended from D to E where

$$\xi_D = k_1\eta$$

and

$$\xi_E = x_P - B(y_P - \eta)$$

($B = \cot \mu_1$ and HP is inclined at μ_1 with the x-axis), while in the zone IPF for every ($\eta = \eta_2$) the integral with respect to ξ must be extended from M to G, where

$$\xi_M = k_1\eta$$

and

$$\xi_G = x_P - B(\eta - y_P), \text{ or } \xi_G = x_P + B(y_P - \eta).$$

The integrals with respect to η must be extended from $\eta = 0$ to $\eta = y_P$ for the first part, and from $\eta = y_P$ to $\eta = y_F$ for the second part. Since F is on the line defined by

$$x = k_1 y$$

and on the line PF defined by $(\xi - x_P) = B(y_P - \eta)$,

$$y_F = \frac{x_P + By_P}{k_1 + B}. \tag{585}$$

The expression in the integral (equation 584) becomes infinite for $\xi = x_P - B(y_P - \eta)$ and $z_P = 0$. By performing the integration and determining the principal values, the following expression can be obtained:

$$\phi_2 = -\frac{w}{\pi} \int_0^{y_F} \cosh^{-1} \frac{x_P - k_1\eta}{B \mid y_P - \eta \mid} \, d\eta \tag{586}$$

where $|y_P - \eta|$ indicates the absolute value of $(y_P - \eta)$. The x component of the additive velocity at P becomes

$$\phi_{2x} = \frac{\partial\phi_2}{\partial x} = -\frac{w}{\pi} \int_0^{y_F} \frac{d\eta}{\sqrt{(x_P - k_1\eta)^2 - B^2(y_P - \eta)^2}} \tag{587}$$

and performing the integration, since in the case considered, $k_1 > B$,

$$\phi_{2x} = -\frac{w}{\pi} \frac{1}{\sqrt{k_1^2 - B^2}} \cosh^{-1} \frac{k_1 x_P - B^2 y_P}{B(x_P - k_1 y_P)}. \tag{588}$$

If the symbols $n_1 = k_1/B$ and

$$\sigma = \frac{k_1 y_P}{x_P} \tag{589}$$

are introduced

$$\phi_{2x} = -\frac{w}{\pi B \sqrt{n_1^2 - 1}} \cosh^{-1} \frac{n_1^2 - \sigma}{n_1(1 - \sigma)} \tag{590}$$

where

$$n_1 > 1 > \sigma$$

$$[\cosh^{-1} a = \log_e (a + \sqrt{a^2 - 1})].$$

Equation (590) shows that ϕ_{2x} is a function only of the ratio of the coordinates of the point P_1 considered, and not of the absolute value of the coordinates.

ϕ_{2x} is constant if the value y/x or the value of σ remains constant, thus it is constant along every straight line that starts from O. The phenomenon considered is conical.

The source distribution considered before produces also an induced velocity outside the surface, that can be determined (Figure 203). If the point P

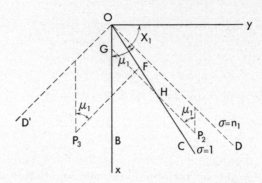

Fig. 203. *The induction in points outside of the flat plate due to a triangular source distribution $(n_1 > 1)$.*

considered is placed between the Mach wave $(\sigma = n_1)$ from O and the inclined side of the triangle in the plane $z = 0$, $(\sigma = 1)$, $P = P_2 \, (x_P, y_P)$, the potential function for P_2 is given by (see equation 584)

$$\phi_2 = -\frac{w}{\pi} \int_0^{y_H} d\eta \int_{k_1\eta}^{x_P - B(y_P - \eta)} f\,(\xi, \eta)\,d\xi \tag{591}$$

where

$$y_H = \frac{x_P - By_P}{k_1 - B}.$$

Therefore

$$\phi_{2x} = -\frac{w}{\pi} \int_0^{y_H} d\eta \, \frac{1}{\sqrt{(x_P - k_1\eta)^2 - B^2\,(y_P - \eta)^2}} \tag{592}$$

or

$$\phi_{2x} = -\frac{w}{\pi} \frac{1}{\sqrt{k_1^2 - B^2}} \cosh^{-1} \frac{k_1 x_P - B^2 y_P}{B\,(k_1 y_P - x_P)} \tag{592a}$$

or

$$\phi_{2x} = -\frac{w}{\pi B} \frac{1}{\sqrt{n_1^2 - 1}} \cosh^{-1} \frac{n_1^2 - \sigma}{n_1\,(\sigma - 1)} \tag{592b}$$

where

$$n_1 > \sigma > 1.$$

If the point considered is between the Mach wave from O, OD', and the side of the triangle parallel to the x-axis ($P = P_3$), the upper limit in the integral in equation (591) is $[x_P + B(y_P - \eta)]$, but the induced velocity ϕ_{2x} is still given by equation (592), and the value of y_F is:

$$y_F = \frac{x_P + By_P}{k_1 + B}.$$

Therefore

$$\phi_{2x} = -\frac{w}{\pi B}\frac{1}{\sqrt{n_1^2 - 1}}\cosh^{-1}\frac{n_1^2 - \sigma}{n_1(-\sigma + 1)} \qquad (593)$$

where

$$n_1 > 1; \qquad \sigma < 0 < n_1.$$

Assuming σ positive and assuming for k_1 the absolute value, equation (593) becomes

$$\phi_{2x} = -\frac{w}{\pi B}\frac{1}{\sqrt{n_1^2 - 1}}\cosh^{-1}\frac{n_1^2 + \sigma}{n_1(\sigma + 1)}. \qquad (593a)$$

Outside the Mach waves $D'O$ or DO no influence can exist in the flow from the source distribution BOC; therefore ϕ_{2x} is equal to zero. Equations (590), (592b), and (593) give the value of ϕ_{2x} in the plane $z = 0$, but will be used also for determining the pressure at points $P(z \neq 0)$ of the profile because in the hypothesis of small disturbances the hypothesis of thin wings is included; and the same approximation accepted for the z component of the induced velocity is accepted for the x component. From equations (579), (590), (592b), and (593a) the pressure distribution can be determined.

Infinite Triangular Plan Form. $k_1 < B$. If the angle X_1 is less than $(\pi/2 - \mu)$, or if k_1 is less than B (Figure 204), three possible positions for the points P can be considered. If the point P is in front of the Mach wave OD, that starts from O (P equal to P_1), the effect at P_1 of the limitation of the surface OBC along the line OB is zero because the fore cone from P_1 does not intersect the line OB. The flow can be considered as two-dimensional, and ϕ_{2x} is given by equation (581)

$$\phi_{2x} = -\frac{w}{B\sqrt{1 - n_1^2}}; \qquad n_1 = \frac{k_1}{B}; \qquad n_1 < \sigma < 1. \qquad (594)$$

If the point P considered is between the Mach wave OD ($\sigma = n_1$) and the side OB of the triangle OBC ($\sigma = 0$) ($P = P_2$), then the induced velocity at the point P, can be considered as produced by two source distributions: the source distribution $P_2 HOL$ that produces a velocity distribution at P_2 given by equation (594), and the source distribution HOI of the same intensity and of opposite sign as the source distribution considered before. The source distribution HOI produces an induced velocity at P_2 given by

$$\phi_{2x}' = - \frac{(-w)}{\pi} \int_{y_H}^{0} \frac{d\eta}{\sqrt{(x_P - k_1\eta)^2 - B^2 (\eta - y_P)^2}} \tag{595}$$

where

$$y_H = \frac{x_P - By_P}{k_1 - B} \quad \text{and} \quad k_1 < B.$$

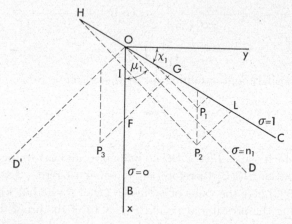

Fig. 204. *The induction due to a triangular source distribution* $(n_1 < 1)$.

Performing the integration in equation (595), because $k_1 < B$, ϕ_{2x} becomes

$$\phi_{2x}' = \frac{w}{\pi B \sqrt{1 - n_1^2}} \cos^{-1} \frac{\sigma - n_1^2}{n_1 (1 - \sigma)} . \tag{596}$$

Therefore the induced velocity at P_2 is given by

$$\phi_{2x} = - \frac{w}{B \sqrt{1 - n_1^2}} \left[1 - \frac{1}{\pi} \cos^{-1} \frac{\sigma - n_1^2}{n_1 (1 - \sigma)} \right] \tag{597}$$

where

$$0 < \sigma < n_1 < 1$$

If the point P considered is between the Mach wave OD' and the side OB (Figure 204), $(P = P_3)$, the induction at P_3, is given by the source distribution OFG, and the x component of the induced velocity is given by:

$$\phi_{2x} = - \frac{w}{\pi} \int_{y_H}^{0} \frac{d\eta}{\sqrt{(x_P - k_1\eta)^2 - B^2 (y_P - \eta)^2}}$$

$$= - \frac{w}{\pi B \sqrt{1 - n_1^2}} \cos^{-1} \frac{n_1^2 - \sigma}{n_1 (1 - \sigma)} \tag{598}$$

If y_{P3} is assumed positive and $(\sigma > 0)$, and for k_1 the absolute value is considered,

$$\phi_{2x} = -\frac{w}{\pi B \sqrt{1 - n_1^2}} \cos^{-1} \frac{\sigma + n_1^2}{n_1(1 + \sigma)} \qquad (598a)$$

where $|n_1| < 1$, $|n_1| > \sigma > 0$.

Superimposition of Triangular Source Distributions. Triangular Surface Symmetrical with Respect to the x-Axis.

From the determination of ϕ_{2x} for a triangular source distribution with one edge in the direction of the undisturbed stream, the value of ϕ_{2x} for any kind of triangular source distribution can be determined. If the triangular distribution is symmetrical with respect to the x-axis and $k_1 > B$ (Figure 205) the induced velocity at a point P_1 inside the surfaces is given by

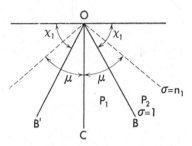

Fig. 205. *Superimposition of two triangular source distributions, $n_1 > 1$ and $n_1 = n_2$.*

$$\phi_{2x} = -\frac{w_1}{\pi B \sqrt{n_1^2 - 1}} \left[\cosh^{-1} \frac{n_1^2 - \sigma}{n_1(1 - \sigma)} + \cosh^{-1} \frac{n_1^2 + \sigma}{n_1(1 + \sigma)} \right]. \qquad (599)$$

Indeed, for the source distributions BCO and $B'CO$ equations (590) and (593a), respectively, must be used. Transforming $\cosh^{-1} a$ into $\log(a + \sqrt{a^2 - 1})$ and performing the operation in parenthesis, equation (599) becomes

$$\phi_{2x} = -\frac{2w}{\pi B \sqrt{n_1^2 - 1}} \cosh^{-1} \sqrt{\frac{n_1^2 - \sigma^2}{1 - \sigma^2}} \qquad (599a)$$

where $n_1 > 1 > \sigma$, and $k_1 > B$.

If the point P_2 is outside the source distribution BOB' but inside the Mach waves starting from O, equations (592b) and (593a) must be used for determining the induced velocity.

$$\phi_{2x} = -\frac{w}{\pi B \sqrt{n_1^2 - 1}} \left[\cosh^{-1} \frac{n_1^2 + \sigma}{n_1(\sigma + 1)} + \cosh^{-1} \frac{n_1^2 - \sigma}{n_1(\sigma - 1)} \right] \qquad (600)$$

and performing the operation in parentheses

$$\phi_{2x} = \frac{2w}{\pi B \sqrt{n_1^2 - 1}} \cosh^{-1} \sqrt{\frac{n_1^2 - 1}{\sigma^2 - 1}} \qquad (600a)$$

where $1 < \sigma < n_1$.

If the distribution is symmetrical, $X_1 = X_2$, and k_1 is less than B (Figure 206),

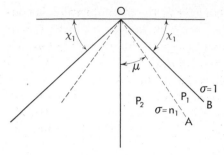

Fig. 206. *Superimposition of two triangular source distributions, $n_1 < 1$ and $n_1 = n_2$.*

and the ϕ_{2x} for a point P_1 for which σ is less than one but greater than n_1 (point P_1 placed between the edge of the wing OB and the Mach wave OA from O) is still given by equation (594), because the other side of the wing does not interfere with the flow outside the Mach wave from O. If σ is less than n_1 (point P_2 inside the Mach wave OA), ϕ_{2x} is given by equations (597) and (598a)

$$\phi_{2x} = -\frac{w}{\pi B\sqrt{1 - n_1^2}}\left[\pi - \cos^{-1}\frac{\sigma - n_1^2}{n_1(1 - \sigma)} + \cos^{-1}\frac{\sigma + n_1^2}{n_1(1 + \sigma)}\right]$$

or using the transformations

$$\cos^{-1}\alpha \pm \cos^{-1}\beta = \cos^{-1}\left[\alpha\beta \mp \sqrt{(1 - a^2)(1 - \beta^2)}\right]$$

and $\sin^{-1}\alpha = \frac{1}{2}\cos^{-1}(1 - 2\alpha^2)$

$$\phi_{2x} = -\frac{w}{\pi B\sqrt{1 - n_1^2}}$$
$$\left[\pi - 2\sin^{-1}\sqrt{\frac{n_1^2 - \sigma^2}{1 - \sigma^2}}\right] \quad (601)$$

where $0 < \sigma < n_1 < 1$.

Using equations (599) and (601), the x component of the induced velocity for a triangular symmetrical surface can be determined; therefore with equations (571a) and (579) the value of the expression $C_P B/\lambda$ can be determined as a function of σ and n_1. In Figure 207 the value of $C_P B/\lambda$ as a function of σ for different values of n_1 is given. For n_1 less than one, the part of the wing between ($\sigma = 1$) and ($\sigma = n_1$) has a constant pressure coefficient (the phenomenon is two-dimensional). For ($n_1 = 1$) and ($X = \pi/2 - \mu$) the pressure coefficient becomes infinite at ($\sigma = 1$) (leading edge of the wing). It is

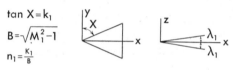

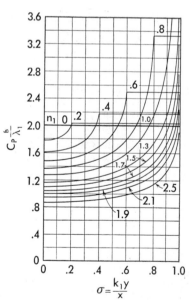

Fig. 207. *Pressure distribution in an isosceles triangular flat plate for different values of n_1 (from Reference 53).*

evident that in this field the small-disturbances theory can no longer be applied. For n_1 less than one, the diagram of C_P as a function of σ presents a slope discontinuity for ($\sigma = n_1$). The discontinuity depends on the assumption that μ is constant in the entire flow, and therefore that the expansion does not occur gradually across infinitesimal conical waves, but across only one wave with discontinuity, and there is no physical counterpart. If the integration of the pressure is made over the surface between ($\sigma = 0$) and ($\sigma = 1$), the value of the integral is constant and independent of n_1, when n_1 is less than one. Therefore the drag in this field is independent of the value of the angle X of the surface.

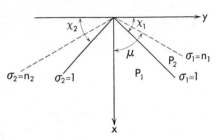

Fig. 208. *Superimposition of two triangular source distributions, $n_1 > 1$, $n_2 > 1$, and $n_1 \neq n_2$.*

Unsymmetrical Triangular Surface. If the triangular surface considered is unsymmetrical, and X_1 and X_2 are of opposite sign (Figure 208), ϕ_{2x} in the entire flow can be obtained in a similar way as for the symmetrical wing. If X_1 and X_2 are greater than $(\pi/2 - \mu)$ and the point P is inside the surface ($\sigma < 1$), ϕ_{2x} can be determined from equations (590) and (593).

$$\phi_{2x} = -\frac{w}{\pi B}\left[\frac{1}{\sqrt{n_1^2 - 1}} \cosh^{-1}\frac{n_1^2 - \sigma_1}{n_1(1 - \sigma_1)}\right.$$
$$\left. + \frac{1}{\sqrt{n_2^2 - 1}} \cosh^{-1}\frac{\sigma_2 + n_2^2}{n_2(\sigma_2 + 1)}\right] \quad (602)$$

where
$$n_1 = \frac{k_1}{B}; \quad n_2 = \frac{k_2}{B}; \quad k_1 = \tan X_1; \quad k_2 = \tan X_2 > 0;$$

$$\sigma_1 = \frac{k_1 y}{x}; \quad \sigma_2 = \frac{k_2 y}{x}; \quad n_1 > 1; \quad n_2 > 1; \quad 0 < \sigma_1 < 1.$$

If σ_2 is expressed as a function of σ_1,

$$\sigma_2 = \frac{k_2}{k_1}\sigma_1 = \frac{n_2}{n_1}\sigma_1$$

ϕ_{2x} becomes

$$\phi_{2x} = -\frac{w}{\pi B}\left[\frac{1}{\sqrt{n_1^2 - 1}} \cosh^{-1}\frac{n_1^2 - \sigma_1}{n_1(1 - \sigma_1)}\right.$$
$$\left. + \frac{1}{\sqrt{n_2^2 - 1}} \cosh^{-1}\frac{\sigma_1 + n_2 n_1}{n_2 \sigma_1 + n_1}\right]. \quad (603)$$

When $1 < \sigma_1 < n_1$, the value of ϕ_{2x} is given by

$$\phi_{2x} = - \frac{w}{\pi B}\left[\frac{1}{\sqrt{n_1{}^2 - 1}} \cosh^{-1} \frac{n_1{}^2 - \sigma_1}{n_1 (\sigma_1 - 1)} \right.$$

$$\left. + \frac{1}{\sqrt{n_2{}^2 - 1}} \cosh^{-1} \frac{n_1 n_2 + \sigma_1}{n_1 + n_2 \sigma_1} \right]. \qquad (604)$$

When $n_1 < 1$, $n_2 < 1$ if $P = P_1$, or (Figure 209) $1 > \sigma_1 > n_1$

$$\phi_{2x} = - \frac{w}{B\sqrt{1 - n_1{}^2}}. \qquad (605)$$

If $1 > \sigma_2 > n_2$ and $P = P_2$

$$\phi_{2x} = - \frac{w}{B\sqrt{1 - n_2{}^2}}. \qquad (605a)$$

If $0 < \sigma_1 < n_1$, and $P = P_3$

$$\phi_{2x} = - \frac{w}{\pi B}\left[\frac{\pi}{\sqrt{1 - n_1{}^2}} - \frac{1}{\sqrt{1 - n_1{}^2}} \cos^{-1} \frac{\sigma_1 - n_1{}^2}{n_1 (1 - \sigma_1)} \right.$$

$$\left. + \frac{1}{\sqrt{1 - n_2{}^2}} \cos^{-1} \frac{\sigma_1 + n_2 n_1}{n_2 \sigma_1 + n_1} \right]. \qquad (606)$$

When $n_1 > 1$ and $n_2 < 1$ (Figure 210) four different zones must be considered for the point P.

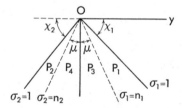

Fig. 209. *Superimposition of two triangular source distributions, $n_1 < 1$, $n_2 < 1$, and $n_1 \neq n_2$.*

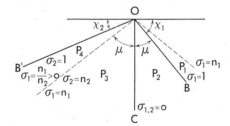

Fig. 210. *Superimposition of two triangular source distributions, $n_1 > 1$ and $n_2 < 1$.*

If $1 < \sigma_1 < n_1$ and $P = P_1$, ϕ_{2x} is given by the equation

$$\phi_{2x} = - \frac{w}{\pi B}\left[\frac{1}{\sqrt{n_1{}^2 - 1}} \cosh^{-1} \frac{n_1{}^2 - \sigma_1}{n_1 (\sigma_1 - 1)} \right.$$

$$\left. + \frac{1}{\sqrt{1 - n_2{}^2}} \cos^{-1} \frac{\sigma_1 + n_2 n_1}{n_2 \sigma_1 + n_1} \right]. \qquad (607)$$

If $0 < \sigma_1 < 1 < n_1$ and $P = P_2$, ϕ_{2x} is given by the expression

$$\phi_{2x} = -\frac{w}{\pi B}\left[\frac{1}{\sqrt{n_1^2 - 1}}\cosh^{-1}\frac{n_1^2 - \sigma_1}{n_1(1 - \sigma_1)}\right.$$

$$\left. + \frac{1}{\sqrt{1 - n_2^2}}\cos^{-1}\frac{\sigma_1 + n_2 n_1}{n_2 \sigma_1 + n_1}\right]. \qquad (608)$$

If the other side of the wing is considered $OB'C$, and for the point P a positive value of σ is considered, where $P = P_3$ and $n_2 > \sigma_2 > 0$,

$$\phi_{2x} = -\frac{w}{\pi B}\left[\frac{\pi}{\sqrt{1 - n_2^2}} - \frac{1}{\sqrt{1 - n_2^2}}\cos^{-1}\frac{\sigma_1 - n_1 n_2}{n_1 - n_2 \sigma_1}\right.$$

$$\left. + \frac{1}{\sqrt{n_1^2 - 1}}\cosh^{-1}\frac{n_1 + \sigma_1}{n_1(\sigma_1 + 1)}\right]. \qquad (609)$$

While if $1 > \sigma_2 > n_2$ or $P = P_4$,

$$\phi_{2x} = -\frac{w}{\pi B}\frac{1}{\sqrt{1 - n_2^2}}. \qquad (610)$$

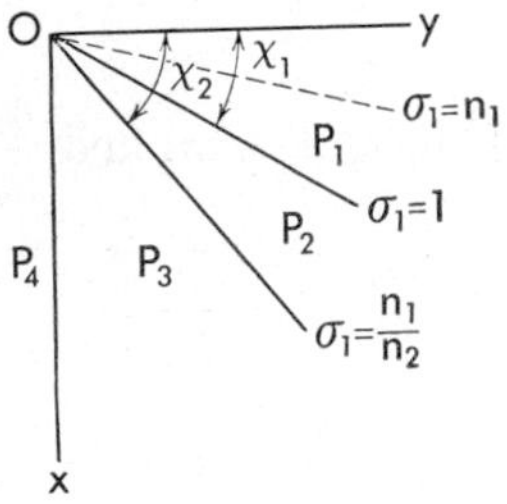

Fig. 211. *Superimposition of two triangular source distributions of opposite sign.*

When the inclinations of the two edges of the triangular surface are of the same sign, the source distribution can be considered as a difference of two source distributions similar to the distribution considered in the second and third paragraphs; therefore the following expression for ϕ_{2x} can be obtained (Figure 211). If

$$n_2 > n_1 > 1, \qquad \sigma_1 = \frac{k_1 y}{x}$$

and

$$n_1 > \sigma_1 > 1 \qquad \text{or} \qquad P = P_1,$$

$$\phi_{2x} = -\frac{w}{\pi}\left[\frac{1}{\sqrt{n_1^2 - 1}}\cosh^{-1}\frac{n_1^2 - \sigma_1}{n_1(\sigma_1 - 1)}\right.$$

$$\left. - \frac{1}{\sqrt{n_2^2 - 1}}\cosh^{-1}\frac{n_1 n_2 - \sigma_1}{n_2 \sigma_1 - n_1}\right]. \qquad (611)$$

If $n_1 > 1 > \sigma > \dfrac{n_1}{n_2}$ or $P = P_2$,

$$\sigma_1 = \frac{y k_1}{x}$$

and

$$\phi_{2x} = -\frac{w}{\pi}\left[\frac{1}{\sqrt{n_1^2 - 1}}\cosh^{-1}\frac{n_1^2 - \sigma_1}{n_1(1 - \sigma_1)}\right.$$

$$\left. - \frac{1}{\sqrt{n_2^2 - 1}}\cosh^{-1}\frac{n_1 n_2 - \sigma_1}{n_2 \sigma_1 - n_1}\right]. \qquad (612)$$

When the points P_3 and P_4 are considered, (P_4 has $\sigma < 0$; therefore the absolute value of σ is considered for the point P_4) ϕ_{2x} at P_3 and P_4 becomes

$$\phi_{2x_{P_3}} = -\frac{w}{\pi}\left[\frac{1}{\sqrt{n_1^2 - 1}}\cosh^{-1}\frac{n_1^2 - \sigma_1}{n_1(1 - \sigma_1)}\right.$$
$$\left. - \frac{1}{\sqrt{n_2^2 - 1}}\cosh^{-1}\frac{n_1 n_2 - \sigma_1}{n_1 - n_2\sigma_1}\right]. \qquad (613)$$

$$(\phi_{2x})_{P_4} = -\frac{w}{\pi}\left[\frac{1}{\sqrt{n_1^2 - 1}}\cosh^{-1}\frac{n_1^2 + \sigma_1}{n_1(\sigma_1 + 1)}\right.$$
$$\left. - \frac{1}{\sqrt{n_2^2 - 1}}\cosh^{-1}\frac{n_1^2 + \sigma_1}{n_2\sigma_1 + n_1}\right]. \qquad (613a)$$

If $n_1 < 1 < n_2$ and $n_1 < \sigma_1 < 1$,

$$\phi_{2x} = -\frac{w}{B\sqrt{1 - n_1^2}}. \qquad (614)$$

If $n_1 < 1 < n_2$ and $\dfrac{n_1}{n_2} < \sigma_1 < n_1$,

$$\phi_{2x} = -\frac{w}{B\pi}\left[\frac{\pi}{\sqrt{1 - n_1^2}} - \frac{1}{\sqrt{1 - n_1^2}}\cos^{-1}\frac{\sigma_1 - n_1^2}{n_1(1 - \sigma_1)}\right.$$
$$\left. - \frac{1}{\sqrt{n_2^2 - 1}}\cosh^{-1}\frac{n_2 n_1 - \sigma_1}{n_2\sigma_1 - n_1}\right]. \qquad (615)$$

If $n_1 < 1 < n_2$ and $\dfrac{n_1}{n_2} > \sigma_1 > 0$,

$$\phi_{2x} = -\frac{w}{B\pi}\left[\frac{\pi}{\sqrt{1 - n_1^2}} - \frac{1}{\sqrt{1 - n_1^2}}\cos^{-1}\frac{\sigma_1 - n_1^2}{n_1(1 - \sigma_1)}\right.$$
$$\left. - \frac{1}{\sqrt{n_2^2 - 1}}\cosh^{-1}\frac{n_2 n_1 - \sigma_1}{n_1 - n_2\sigma_1}\right]. \qquad (615a)$$

If the point is on the negative side of the y-axis where $P = P_4$, assuming σ_1 positive, ϕ_{2x} becomes

$$\phi_{2x} = -\frac{w}{B\pi}\left(\cos^{-1}\frac{\sigma_1 + n_1^2}{n_1(1 + \sigma_1)} - \cosh^{-1}\frac{n_1 n_2 + \sigma_1}{n_1 + n_2\sigma_1}\right). \qquad (615b)$$

It is interesting to observe that the value of ϕ_{2x} in this approximation is a function only of the slope of the surface in the plane ($y = $ constant), and is independent of the slope of the surface in the plane ($x = $ constant); therefore the same induced velocity and the same pressure distribution are obtained if, for example, a flat surface OAB and a double wedge $OA'CB'$ with the same plan form and cross section slope ($dz/dx = \lambda$) are considered (Figure 212).

Plan Form of Any Shape. With proper composition of triangular and two-dimensional flat surfaces, every plan form can be considered. For example, if a surface *ABC* is analyzed (Figure 213*a*), the surface can be represented with two source distributions: the triangular source distribution *CDB* of in-

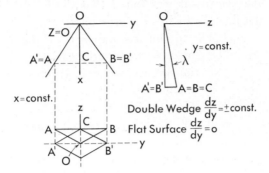

Fig. 212. *The equivalence between triangular flat plate and double wedge surface.*

tensity corresponding to the slope of the surface *ABC*, and a source distribution *BAD* of same intensity and opposite sign.

If the surface *ABCDE* is considered (Figure 213*b*), it can be represented by the composition of a source distribution *AFE* and by source distributions of opposite sign *BFG*, *CGH*, *DHE*. In the zone *ABI*, if *BI* is a Mach wave from *B*, no induction produced by the source distributions of negative sign exists. In the zone *BICL*, the distribution *BFG* of opposite sign than the distribution *AEF* must also be considered. In the zone *LCDM* the distribution *AFE* and the distributions *BFG* and *CGH* must be considered, while for points in the zone *DME* the distribution *DEH* must also be considered. Every other plan form can be considered in a similar manner.

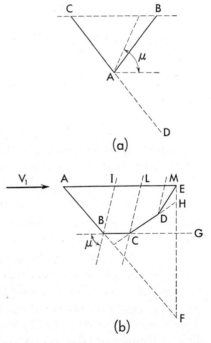

(a)

(b)

Fig. 213. *Superimposition of several source distributions of simple shape.*

Discussion of the Necessity for Analysis of the Hypothesis of Zero Lift.
On page 297 the hypothesis was accepted that the wings considered must have a symmetrical profile and zero angle of attack. The results of the preceding paragraph permit discussion of the necessity for that hypothesis, and analysis

of the possibility of applying the preceding system of calculations to some cases of wings with lift.

In the preceding analysis it was found that the flow field around a wing corresponds to the flow given by a source distribution of intensity proportional to the w component of the induced velocity in the plane $z = 0$. In order to determine the pressure distribution on the wing, it is important to know the w component and therefore the source distribution contained in the plane $z = 0$ and in the fore cone of every point of the wing. It is not important to know the distribution of the w component behind the wing because a source distribution in this zone cannot induce any velocity in the wing. Now if the wing has such a plan form that it can produce a variation of flow velocity in some zones outside the wing, contained in the fore Mach cone from any point of the wing, it is necessary to impose the hypothesis that the wing is symmetrical and has zero angle of attack. ~ Indeed in this case, only for this condition, the w component in the plane $(z = 0)$ is zero outside the wing. The hypothesis is no longer necessary if the wing does not induce any velocity in the flow contained in the fore Mach cone from every point of the wing, and outside the zone of the wing. If that happens, lifting surfaces can also be considered with this system. In order to clarify this concept, consider a triangular wing (Figure 214). If the wing has a value of X larger than $(\pi/2 - \mu)$, an induced velocity exists in the zone ACE. If the wing has a symmetrical profile and zero angle of attack, the value of λ is equal for the upper and lower surfaces; therefore the source distributions on the wing for the upper and lower surfaces have the same intensity. The value of ϕ_{2x} and the corresponding value of the pressure induced by the distributions that represent the upper and lower surfaces are equal at AEC, and no discontinuity occurs across the plane $(z = 0)$; therefore no vertical component exists in this zone. If the wing is not symmetrical or has an angle of attack, the values of λ of the upper and lower surfaces are no longer equal; therefore the corresponding source distributions that represent the wing are different. In the zone ACE different values of ϕ_{2x}, and consequently different values of the corresponding pressures are found when the upper side or lower sides of the plane $z = 0$ are considered. Across the plane $z = 0$, a discontinuity of pressure is found at ACE. This discontinuity of pressure can exist if a solid plate exists at ACE, but cannot exist if there is no plate at ACE, in which case a w component must exist in this zone. This w component corresponds to a source distribution in the zone ACE, which cannot be determined directly from the shape of the body, and therefore

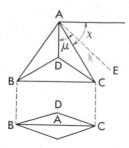

Fig. 214. *Triangular diamond-shaped profile wing.*

in this case the system cannot be used. If the flow in front of the wing is not influenced by the wing, the discontinuity of pressure no longer exists, and the system can also be used for phenomena which are not symmetrical with respect to the plane ($z = 0$).

If, for example, a triangular wing as in Figure 214 is considered, but $X < \pi/2 - \mu$, variations in the flow begin along the edges of the wings AB and AC, and therefore the upper part of the phenomenon cannot interfere with the lower part of the phenomenon in the zone of the wing. At the trailing edge of the wing, BC, a discontinuity of pressure can be found if the phenomenon is not symmetrical, and therefore a w component will exist in the actual phenomenon. However the corresponding source distribution cannot change the flow condition on the wing, because any source can change the flow only in the Mach cone with its apex in the source. The system of using source distributions on the wing gives the actual pressure distribution with the same order of accuracy as the simplifying hypothesis accepted.

The possibility of analysis of nonsymmetrical phenomena with the system of sources and sinks distribution discussed before can be easily defined if the concepts of supersonic leading edge and supersonic trailing edge are used (Reference 54).

A wing has a leading edge that can be called *supersonic* if the tangent to every point of the leading edge in the plane of the wing is in front of the Mach wave ($k_1 < B$), because in this case the component normal to the leading edge is supersonic. A leading edge can be called *subsonic* when the tangent to every point of the leading edge is behind the Mach wave ($k_1 > B$).

In the same way, a trailing edge can be defined as supersonic when the tangent to the trailing edge is in front of the Mach wave. For example, for the wing shown in Figure 215, the part of the leading edge AB is supersonic, while the part BC is subsonic. The part of the trailing edge DC is subsonic, while the part DE is supersonic.

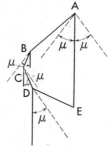

Using the preceding definitions, it is possible to conclude that nonsymmetrical phenomena can be analyzed with the method of sources and sink distributions only if the leading edge and trailing edge of the wings are all supersonic, whereas if the leading edge or the trailing edge are in part or completely subsonic, only symmetrical phenomena can be analyzed.

Fig. 215. *Supersonic and subsonic leading and trailing edges.*

Superimposition of Source Distributions of Different Type and Its Application to Practical Problems. The pressure distribution on wings of different shape can be determined with the superimposition of the source distributions considered in the preceding paragraph. Some examples of the practical use of the method will be given in this paragraph to explain the use and to demonstrate some interesting aspects of the phenomena for three-dimensional wings.

Profile Drag Distribution along a Chord of a Symmetrical Sweptback Wing. In the first paragraph of this chapter the infinite sweptback wing was considered, and it was shown that if the angle of sweepback is larger than $(\pi/2 - \mu)$, where μ is the Mach angle of the undisturbed stream, no pressure drag can be found for the wing, with the hypothesis of perfect flow. In practical cases a pressure drag will exist at the tips of the wing; therefore if a sweptback wing symmetrical with respect to the planes $(z = 0)$ and $(y = 0)$ is considered, a drag for the different profiles of the wing will be obtained. In this application the wing will be considered as two half wings, equal and symmetrical with respect to the plane $(y = 0)$. The profile of the wing will be considered as the section of the wing with the plane $(y = $ constant), and will be assumed to be of a constant shape, either a diamond-shaped profile as in the first part of the paragraph, or a circular-arc profile, as in the second part of the paragraph. To simplify the problem, the leading and the trailing

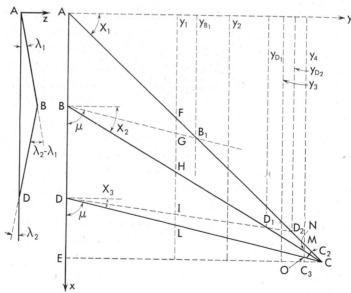

Fig. 216. *Diamond-shaped sweptback wing.*

edges will be considered straight lines. The wing will be considered extended to the point C of Figure 216 (C is at infinity if the chord of the wing is constant); if the wing has a tip, for example along the line C_2C_3, the effect of the tip can be considered independently.

If the wing has a diamond-shaped profile (Figure 216), the wing $ABDC$ can be represented as three source distributions of constant intensity and triangular plan form. The first source distribution has the plan form AEC and intensity

$$\pi c_1 = w_1 = \lambda_1 V_1 \tag{616}$$

where λ_1 is the slope of the segment AB. The second source distribution has the plan form BCE and intensity

$$\pi c_2 = w_2 = (\lambda_2 - \lambda_1) V_1 \tag{616a}$$

where λ_2 is the slope of the segment BD. The third source distribution has the plan form DEC and intensity of source

$$\pi c_3 = w_3 = -\lambda_2 V_1 \tag{616b}$$

The induced velocity ϕ_{2x} at every point of the plane $z = 0$ is given by equations (599), (600), or (601) as a function of the position, or of the value of the angle of sweepback of the triangular source distribution. The pressure at every point can be immediately calculated with equation (579), in which the ϕ_{2x} is the sum of the three induced velocities produced by the three source distributions considered.

For example, if the inclinations X_1 of the leading edge AC, X_2 of the line of the maximum thickness BC, and X_3 of the trailing edge DC, are larger than $(\pi/2 - \mu)$, four different possible positions y_1, y_2, y_3, and y_4 must be considered for the profile. If $y = y_1$, four different zones must be considered along the profile. In the zone FG the inclination is λ_1, and the induction is produced only by the source distribution AEC, since the zone is in front of the Mach line BB_1 from B. The induction in this zone can be determined with equation (599a) in which w_1 is given by equation (616). In the zone GH, the inclination still is λ_1 but the induced velocity ϕ_{2x} is produced by the source distribution AEC, (ϕ_{2x}'), and by the source distribution BEC of intensity c_2 (equation 616a) (ϕ_{2x}''). ϕ_{2x}' is calculated with equation (599a), and ϕ_{2x}'' is calculated with equation (600a), where a new value of σ must be determined by assuming the point B for the origin of coordinates. In the zone HI the induced velocity is still produced by the source distributions ACE and BEC, but the inclination of the surface is λ_2, and the induction produced by BCE must be calculated with equation (599a). In the zone IL the induction is also produced by the source distribution DCE of intensity c_3 (equation 616b), that can be calculated with equation (600a) (the value of σ in this case must be evaluated from the point D), and must be added to the induction determined as in HI. If the profile MNO is considered ($y = y_4$), because the profile is behind the line DD_2, at every point of the profile the induction produced by all three of the source distributions exists, and therefore $\phi_{2x} = \phi_{2x}' + \phi_{2x}'' + \phi_{2x}'''$. For intermediate positions y_2 and y_3, the induction is given in some parts by the sum of two inductions $\phi_{2x}' + \phi_{2x}''$, and in some parts by the sum of three.

If X_1, X_2, or X_3 are less than $(\pi/2 - \mu)$, in place of equation (599a), equation (601) must be used in the analysis. When the pressure coefficient is determined in every point of the profile, the drag coefficient of the profile and the profile drag distribution as functions of y can be obtained.

For the case considered the drag coefficient can be obtained analytically, while for other cases it can be obtained either analytically or graphically (Reference 55).

If the front part of the chord of the profile corresponding to ABC is assumed equal to $(1 - r)c$, and the part corresponding to BDC is equal to rc, where c is the chord of the profile, the force corresponding to the zone FH of the profile at $(y = y_1)$ can be expressed in the following way:

$$C_{D1} = 2 \int_F^H \frac{\Delta p_1 \lambda_1}{\frac{1}{2}\rho_1 V_1^2 c} \, dx + 2 \int_G^H \frac{\Delta p_2 \lambda_1}{\frac{1}{2}\rho_1 V_1^2 c} \, dx \tag{617}$$

where

$$\frac{\Delta p_1}{\frac{1}{2}\rho_1 V_1^2} = -\frac{2\phi_{2x}'}{V_1}; \qquad \frac{\Delta p_2}{\frac{1}{2}\rho_1 V_1^2} = -\frac{2\phi_{2x}''}{V_1}.$$

The coefficient 2 in equation (617) depends on the fact that the upper and lower surfaces are considered at the same time. But ϕ_{2x}' is given by equation (599a)

$$\phi_{2x}' = -\frac{2w_1}{\pi B} \frac{1}{\sqrt{n_1^2 - 1}} \cosh^{-1} \sqrt{\frac{n_1^2 - \sigma^2}{1 - \sigma_1^2}} \tag{618}$$

where

$$n_1 = \frac{k_1}{B}; \qquad k_1 = \tan X_1; \qquad \sigma_1 = \frac{k_1 y_1}{X_1}$$

or if ξ is the coordinate of the profile with respect to the leading edge F,

$$\sigma_1 = \frac{k_1 y_1}{k_1 y_1 + \xi}$$

$$w_1 = -\lambda_1 V_1$$

and

$$\lambda_1 = \frac{\tau}{2(1 - r)}$$

where τ is the percentage thickness of the profile. ϕ_{2x}'' is given by equation (600a)

$$\phi_{2x}'' = -\frac{2w_2}{\pi B} \frac{1}{\sqrt{n_2^2 - 1}} \cosh^{-1} \sqrt{\frac{n_2^2 - 1}{\sigma_2^2 - 1}} \tag{618a}$$

where

$$\sigma_2 = \frac{k_2 y_1}{k_1 y_1 + \xi - (1 - r)c_0}$$

and c_0 is the root chord of the wing. (σ must be calculated with respect to the point B.)

$$n_2 = \frac{k_2}{B}; \quad k_2 = \tan X_2; \quad w_2 = (\lambda_2 - \lambda_1)V_1$$

and

$$\lambda_2 - \lambda_1 = -\frac{\tau}{2r(1-r)}$$

but

$$dx = \frac{-k_1 y_1}{\sigma_1^2} d\sigma_1; \quad dx = \frac{-k_2 y_1}{\sigma_2^2} d\sigma_2 \qquad (619)$$

and in the first integral of equation (617) for X_F

$$\sigma_1 = 1.$$

For X_H,

$$\sigma_H = \frac{k_1 y}{(1-r)c_0 + k_2 y}.$$

In the second integral of equation (617) corresponding to X_H, $\sigma_2 = 1$, and for X_G, $\sigma_2 = n_2$; therefore equation (617) becomes

$$C_{D1} = \frac{2\tau^2 k_1 y_1}{(1-r)^2 \pi Bc \sqrt{n_1^2 - 1}} \int_{\sigma_1 = 1}^{\sigma_1 = \frac{k_1 y_1}{(1-r)c_0 + k_2 y_1}} \cosh^{-1} \sqrt{\frac{n_1^2 - \sigma_1^2}{1 - \sigma_1^2}} \frac{d\sigma_1}{\sigma_1^2}$$
$$- \frac{2\tau^2 k_2 y_1}{r(1-r)^2 \pi Bc \sqrt{n_2^2 - 1}} \int_{\sigma_2 = 1}^{\sigma_2 = n_2} \cosh^{-1} \sqrt{\frac{n_2^2 - 1}{\sigma_2^2 - 1}} \frac{d\sigma_2}{\sigma_2^2}. \qquad (620)$$

In a similar way the drag C_{D2} in the part HI and in the part IL, given by the three source distributions, can be evaluated, because HL is inclined at λ_2, and $\lambda_2 = -\frac{\tau}{2r}$. Therefore

$$C_{D2} = -\frac{2\tau^2 k_1 y_1}{(1-r)r \pi Bc \sqrt{n_1^2 - 1}} \int_{\sigma = \frac{k_1 y_1}{(1-r)c_0 + k_2 y_1}}^{\sigma = \frac{k_1 y_1}{c_0 + k_3 y_1}} \cosh^{-1} \sqrt{\frac{n_1^2 - \sigma_1^2}{1 - \sigma_1^2}} \frac{d\sigma_1}{\sigma_1^2}$$

$$+ \frac{2\tau^2 k_2 y_1}{(1-r)r^2 \pi Bc_0 \sqrt{n_2^2 - 1}} \int_{\sigma_2 = 1}^{\sigma_2 = \frac{k_2 y_1}{k_3 y_1 + rc_0}} \cosh^{-1} \sqrt{\frac{n_2^2 - \sigma_2^2}{1 - \sigma_2^2}} \frac{d\sigma_2}{\sigma_2^2} - \frac{2\tau^2 k_3 y_1}{r^2 \pi Bc_0 \sqrt{n_3^2 - 1}}$$

$$\times \int_{\sigma = 1}^{\sigma = n_3} \cosh^{-1} \sqrt{\frac{n_3^2 - 1}{\sigma_3^2 - 1}} \frac{d\sigma_3}{\sigma_3^2} \qquad (620a)$$

but

$$\int \cosh^{-1} \sqrt{\frac{n_1^2 - \sigma_1^2}{1 - \sigma_1^2}} \frac{d\sigma_1}{\sigma_1^2} = - \frac{1 + \sigma_1}{\sigma_1} \log_e \frac{\sqrt{n_1^2 - 1} + \sqrt{n_1^2 - \sigma_1^2}}{\sqrt{\sigma_1 + 1}}$$

$$+ \frac{1 - \sigma_1}{2\sigma_1} \log_e (1 - \sigma_1) + \log_e 2[n_1^2 - \sigma_1 + \sqrt{(n_1^2 - \sigma_1^2)(n_1^2 - 1)}]$$

$$= N\sigma_1 \qquad (620b)$$

while

$$\int \cosh^{-1} \sqrt{\frac{n_2^2 - 1}{\sigma_2^2 - 1}} \frac{d\sigma_2}{\sigma_2^2} = - \frac{\sigma_2 + 1}{\sigma_2} \log \frac{\sqrt{n_2^2 - 1} + \sqrt{n_2^2 - \sigma_2^2}}{\sqrt{\sigma_2 + 1}}$$

$$+ \frac{1 - \sigma_2}{2\sigma_2} \log (\sigma_2 - 1) + \log 2 [n_2^2 - \sigma_2 + \sqrt{(n_2^2 - \sigma_2^2)(n_2^2 - 1)}]$$

$$= Q\sigma_2 \qquad (620c)$$

and

$N\sigma_1$ for $(\sigma_1 = 1)$ is $(N\sigma_1 = \log_e 2)$, while $Q\sigma_2$ for $(\sigma_2 = n_2)$ is $(Q_{n2} = \log_e 2n_2)$.
Therefore for a profile between $(y = 0)$ and $(y = y_{B1})$ the total drag coefficient of the profile referred to the chord c_0 is given by

$$C_D = - \frac{2y\tau^2}{\pi c_0 r^2 (1 - r)^2} \left\{ \frac{n_1}{\sqrt{n_1^2 - 1}} \left(N_1 r - r (1 - r) N_2 - r^2 \log 2 \right) \right.$$

$$+ \frac{n_2}{\sqrt{n_2^2 - 1}} \left[(1 - r)N_3 + r \log 2n_2 - \log 2 \right]$$

$$\left. + \frac{n_3}{\sqrt{n_3^2 - 1}} (1 - r)^2 \log n_3 \right\} \qquad (621)$$

where N_1 is given by equation $(620b)$ for

$$\sigma_{H1} = \frac{k_1}{k_2 + (1 - r)\dfrac{c_0}{y}} \qquad (622)$$

N_2 is given by equation $(620b)$ for

$$\sigma_{L1} = \frac{k_1}{k_3 + \dfrac{c_0}{y}} \qquad (623)$$

N_3 is given by equation $(620b)$ for

$$\sigma_{L2} = \frac{k_2}{k_3 + \dfrac{rc_0}{y}} \cdot \qquad (624)$$

Equation (621) can be applied for

$$0 < y < \frac{(1 - r)c_0}{k_1 - B}, \quad \left[y_{B1} = \frac{(1 - r)c_0}{k_1 - B} \right] \qquad (625)$$

or if

$$\frac{rc_0}{k_2 - B} < \frac{(1 - r)c_0}{k_1 - B}$$

for

$$0 < y < \frac{rc_0}{k_2 - B} , \quad \left[y_{D_1} = \frac{rc_0}{k_2 - B} \right]. \tag{626a}$$

For $y = 0$

$$C_D = \frac{2\tau^2}{\pi B (1 - r)r} \frac{1}{\sqrt{n_2^2 - 1}} \log \left(n_2 + \sqrt{n_2^2 - 1} \right). \tag{627}$$

For

$$\frac{(1 - r)c_0}{k_1 - B} < y < \frac{rc_0}{k_2 - B} \tag{628}$$

$$C_D = \frac{2y\tau^2}{\pi c_0 r^2 (1 - r)^2} \left\{ \left[N_1 r - N_2 r (1 - r) - r^2 \log 2 \right] \frac{n_1}{\sqrt{n_1^2 - 1}} \right.$$

$$+ \frac{n_2}{\sqrt{n_2^2 - 1}} \left[(1 - r) N_3 + rQ_1 - \log 2 \right] + \frac{n_3}{\sqrt{n_3^2 - 1}} (1 - r)^2 \log n_3 \right\} \tag{629}$$

where Q_1 is given by equation (620c) for

$$\sigma_{F_2} = \frac{k_2}{k_1 - (1 - r)\dfrac{c_0}{y}}.$$

If

$$\frac{rc_0}{k_2 - B} < y < \frac{(1 - r)c_0}{k_1 - B} \tag{630}$$

the drag coefficient is given by

$$C_D = \frac{2\tau^2 y}{\pi c_0 r^2 (1 - r)^2} \left\{ \left[N_1 r - r (1 - r) N_2 - r^2 \log 2 \right] \frac{n_1}{\sqrt{n_1^2 - 1}} \right.$$

$$+ \frac{n_2}{\sqrt{n_2^2 - 1}} \left[N_3 (1 - r) - \log 2 + r \log 2n_2 \right]$$

$$+ \frac{n_3}{\sqrt{n_3^2 - 1}} \left[(1 - r)Q_2 - r (1 - r) \log 2n_3 - (1 - r)^2 \log 2 \right] \right\} \tag{631}$$

where Q_2 is given by equation (620c) for

$$\sigma_{H_3} = \frac{k_3}{k_2 - r\dfrac{c_0}{y}}.$$

For the condition $\dfrac{(1 - r)c_0}{k_1 - B} < y < \dfrac{c_0}{k_1 - B}$

or
$$\frac{rc_0}{k_2 - B} < y < \frac{c_0}{k_1 - B}, \quad \left(y_{D_2} = \frac{c_0}{k_1 - B}\right) \tag{632}$$

$$C_D = \frac{2\tau^2 y}{\pi c_0 r^2 (1 - r)^2} \left\{ \left[N_1 r - r(1 - r) N_2 - r^2 \log 2 \right] \frac{n_1}{\sqrt{n_1^2 - 1}} \right.$$

$$+ \frac{n_2}{\sqrt{n_2^2 - 1}} \left[N_3 (1 - r) + rQ_1 - \log 2 \right]$$

$$\left. + \frac{n_3}{\sqrt{n_3^2 - 1}} \left[(1 - r)Q_2 - r(1 - r) \log 2n_3 - (1 - r)^2 \log 2 \right] \right\}. \tag{633}$$

If $y > \dfrac{c_0}{k_1 - B}$ \hfill (634)

$$C_D = \frac{2\tau^2 y}{\pi c_0 r^2 (1 - r)^2} \left\{ \left[N_1 r - r(1 - r) N_2 - r^2 \log 2 \right] \frac{n_1}{\sqrt{n_1^2 - 1}} \right.$$

$$+ \frac{n_2}{\sqrt{n_2^2 - 1}} \left[(1 - r) N_3 + Q_1 r - \log 2 \right]$$

$$\left. + \frac{n_3}{\sqrt{n_3^2 - 1}} \left[(1 - r)Q_2 - r(1 - r)Q_3 - (1 - r)^2 \log 2 \right] \right\} \tag{635}$$

where Q_3 is given by equation (620c) for

$$\sigma_{F_3} = \frac{k_3}{k_1 - \dfrac{c_0}{y}}.$$

In a similar way, analogous expressions can be obtained for $(k_3 < B)$ or $(k_2 < B)$ or $(k_1, k_2, k_3 < B)$.

In Figure 217 the drag-coefficient distribution along the span for a swept-back wing of constant chord is shown. The profile is a symmetrical profile with $(1 - r) = r$ and the angle of sweepback is $60°$. The calculations have been made for $M = 1.40$, $M = 1.80$, and for $M = 1.90$. For all three Mach numbers $k_1 = k_2 = k_3 > B$. The values of C_D/τ^2, where τ is the percentage thickness, are plotted as ordinates, and the values of y/c are plotted as abscissas in the diagram. As shown in the diagram, the drag decreases noticeably and tends to approach zero for large values of y/c. The variation of the drag coefficient along the span becomes lower if the value of B becomes larger, and the Mach wave from the vertex approaches the leading edge of the wing. For comparison, the values of C_D/τ^2 for a two-dimensional wing of the same cross section are also shown.

In a similar way, analogous calculations for different types of profiles can be developed. In order to give an example of the system of calculation for wings with profiles of gradual curvature, the following simple case will also be examined. A sweptback wing symmetrical with respect to the plane

$(y = 0)$, with constant chord and symmetrical circular-arc profile is considered, and the variation of the profile pressure drag distribution along the span is determined. The wing considered (Figure 218) has the leading edge behind the Mach cone from the vertex. The flow around the wing considered can be

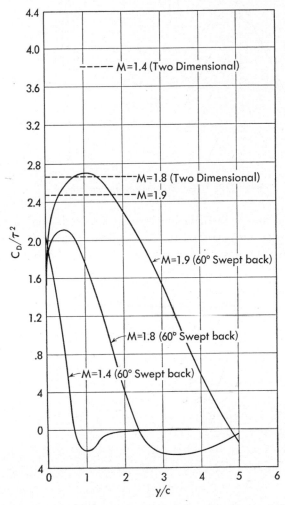

Fig. 217. *Profile drag along the span of a diamond-shaped sweptback wing of constant chord for different Mach numbers.*

represented by a potential function given by superimposition of different source distributions. Initially a source distribution is considered, having triangular plan form, constant and finite intensity C, proportional to the inclination λ_1 of the profile at the leading edge. Then an infinite series of source distributions is superimposed, having the same plan form and intensity

$-(d\lambda/dx)\,dx$, in which $d\lambda/dx$ is the variation of the direction of the tangent to the profile at any point C of abscissa x, along the profile. Every distribution of the series has the vertex along the chord AB at the corresponding point C.

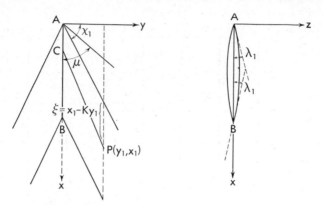

Fig. 218. *Circular-arc profile sweptback wing.*

Finally another source distribution is superimposed, having triangular plan form and intensity proportional to $-\lambda_1$, and starting at B. The distribution turns the flow in the direction of the plane $(z = 0)$ behind the wing. If the

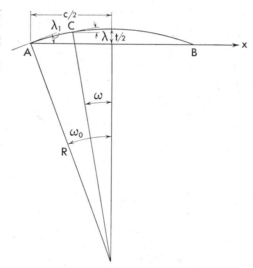

Fig. 219. *Geometrical parameters of a circular-arc profile.*

profile AB is thin, the intensity of the triangular source distribution that starts at every point of A can be determined in the following way. If R is the radius of the circular-arc profile (Figure 219) and $2\omega_0$ is the angle at the center corresponding to the profile,

$$\frac{c}{2} = R \sin \omega_0; \quad \frac{t}{2} = R - R \cos \omega_0$$

or because ω_0 is small (thin profile)

$$\frac{c}{2} = R\omega_0; \quad \frac{t}{2} = R \frac{\omega_0^2}{2}; \quad x = R(\omega_0 - \omega); \quad \lambda_1 = \omega_0$$

$$\lambda = \omega = \omega_0 - \frac{x}{R}; \quad \lambda = \frac{4t}{c}\left(\frac{1}{2} - \frac{x}{c}\right);$$

$$\frac{d\lambda}{dx} = -\frac{4t}{c^2} = -\frac{2\lambda_1}{c}; \quad \lambda_1 = \frac{2t}{c} = 2\tau.$$

For every point P along a profile at a distance y_1 from the center, at a position ξ along the chord, the coordinates are (Figure 218)

$$x_1 = \xi + k_1 y_1$$

$$y = y_1.$$

Therefore the induction at P given by the source distribution of constant intensity proportional to λ_1 is given by (equation 599a)

$$\phi_{2x}' = \frac{2\lambda_1 V_1}{\pi B \sqrt{n_1^2 - 1}} \cosh^{-1} \sqrt{\frac{n_1^2 - \sigma_1^2}{1 - \sigma_1^2}} \tag{636}$$

where

$$\sigma_1 = \frac{k_1 y_1}{\xi + k_1 y_1}; \quad n_1 = \frac{k_1}{B}$$

The induction at P given by the source distribution of constant intensity proportional to $d\lambda/dx$ starting at a point C, of coordinates $(x_c, 0)$, is given by

$$\frac{d\phi_{2x}''}{dx} = \frac{-4\lambda_1 V_1}{c_0 \pi B \sqrt{n_1^2 - 1}} \cosh^{-1} \sqrt{\frac{n_1^2 - \sigma_2^2}{1 - \sigma_2^2}}$$

when

$$\sigma_2 = \frac{k_1 y_1}{\xi + k_1 y_1 - x_c} < 1$$

or by

$$\frac{d\phi_{2x}''}{dx} = \frac{-4\lambda_1 V_1}{c_0 \pi B \sqrt{n_1^2 - 1}} \cosh^{-1} \sqrt{\frac{n_1^2 - 1}{\sigma_2^2 - 1}}$$

when

$$\sigma_2 = \frac{k_1 y_1}{\xi + k_1 y_1 - x_c} > 1.$$

But

$$dx_c = \frac{k_1 y_1}{\sigma_2^2} d\sigma.$$

Therefore

$$\phi_{2x}'' = \frac{-4\lambda_1 k_1 y_1 V_1}{c_0 \pi B \sqrt{n_1{}^2 - 1}} \left[\int_{\sigma=\sigma_1}^{\sigma_2=1} \cosh^{-1} \sqrt{\frac{n_1 - \sigma_2{}^2}{1 - \sigma_2{}^2}} \frac{d\sigma_2}{\sigma_2{}^2} \right.$$
$$\left. + \int_{\sigma=1}^{\sigma_2=n_1} \cosh^{-1} \sqrt{\frac{n_1{}^2 - 1}{\sigma_2{}^2 - 1}} \frac{d\sigma_2}{\sigma_2{}^2} \right]. \quad (636a)$$

The limit of integration $\sigma_2 = n_1$ depends on the fact that the source distribution at C cannot interfere with the flow at the point P if σ_2 is larger than n_1 where $(\sigma_2 = n_1)$ corresponds to the condition that CP coincides with the Mach wave from C. If the point P is in such a position that the source distribution proportional to $-\lambda_1$ existing at B can interfere with P, or if

$$\sigma_B = \frac{k_1 y_1}{\xi + k_1 y_1 - c_0} < n_1$$

the value of ϕ_{2x}'' becomes

$$\phi_{2x}'' = -\frac{4\lambda_1 k_1 y_1 V_1}{c_0 \pi B \sqrt{n_1{}^2 - 1}} \left[\int_{\sigma_2=\sigma_1}^{\sigma_2=1} \cosh^{-1} \sqrt{\frac{n_1{}^2 - \sigma_2{}^2}{1 - \sigma_2{}^2}} \frac{d\sigma_2}{\sigma_2{}^2} \right.$$
$$\left. + \int_{\sigma_2=1}^{\sigma_2=\sigma_B} \cosh^{-1} \sqrt{\frac{n_1{}^2 - 1}{\sigma_2{}^2 - 1}} \frac{d\sigma_2}{\sigma_2{}^2} \right] \quad (637)$$

and the induction ϕ_{2x}''' must also be considered:

$$\phi_{2x}''' = -\frac{2\lambda_1}{\pi B \sqrt{n_1{}^2 - 1}} \cosh^{-1} \sqrt{\frac{n_1{}^2 - 1}{\sigma_B{}^2 - 1}}. \quad (638)$$

The integral that appears in equation (636a) can be evaluated, and the following expression can be obtained for the pressure coefficient at a point P of the profile:

$$C_P = \frac{8\tau}{\pi B \sqrt{n_1{}^2 - 1}} \left[\cosh^{-1} \sqrt{\frac{n_1{}^2 - \sigma_1{}^2}{1 - \sigma_1{}^2}} - \frac{2y_1 k_1}{c_0} (N_2 - N_1) + A \right] \quad (639)$$

where

$$\sigma_B = \frac{k_1 y_1}{\xi + k_1 y_1 - c_0}; \quad \sigma_1 = \frac{k_1 y_1}{\xi + k_1 y_1}$$

and if $\sigma_B > n_1$,

$$N_2 = \log 2n_1; \quad A = 0. \quad (640)$$

If $\sigma_B < n_1$,

$$N_2 = -\frac{\sigma_B + 1}{\sigma_B} \log_e \frac{\sqrt{n_1{}^2 - \sigma_B{}^2} + \sqrt{n_1{}^2 - 1}}{\sqrt{\sigma_B + 1}} - \frac{\sigma_B - 1}{2\sigma_B} \log_e (\sigma_B - 1)$$
$$+ \log_e 2 \left[n_1{}^2 - \sigma_B + \sqrt{(n_1{}^2 - 1)(n_1{}^2 - \sigma_B{}^2)} \right]. \quad (641)$$

$$A = \cosh^{-1} \sqrt{\frac{n_1^2 - 1}{\sigma_B^2 - 1}} \tag{642}$$

while

$$N_1 = -\frac{1 + \sigma_1}{\sigma_1} \log_e \frac{\sqrt{n_1^2 - 1} + \sqrt{n_1^2 - \sigma_1^2}}{\sqrt{\sigma_1 + 1}} + \frac{1 - \sigma_1}{2\sigma_1} \log_e (1 - \sigma_1)$$
$$+ \log 2 \left[n_1^2 - \sigma_1 + \sqrt{(n_1^2 - 1)(n_1^2 - \sigma_1^2)} \right] \tag{643}$$

for every condition.

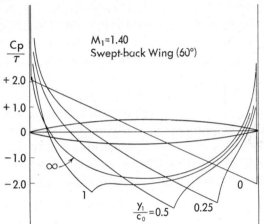

Fig. 220. *Pressure distribution along the chord of a 60° sweptback wing at M = 1.60 for different span stations (from Reference 55).*

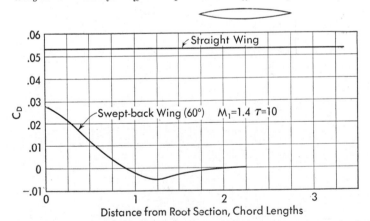

Fig. 221. *Profile drag distribution along the span of a 60° sweptback wing with a symmetrical circular arc profile 10 per cent thick (from Reference 55).*

Some values of C_P/τ have been calculated for $(M = 1.4)$ for a wing with 60° sweepback, and the results are shown in Figure 220; while Figure 221 shows the profile drag distribution along the span for the wing considered.

If the wing has a tip of different form as, for example, in Figure 222, the calculations can be developed in two steps. In the first step the induction on *ABDE* is determined by assuming the existence of a source distribution corresponding to the wing *ACB*. In the second step the effect of a source distribution of opposite sign than the source representing the wing in the area *DEC* is evaluated. The source *DEC* can change the phenomenon only in the zone *DE'E*. (*DE'* is a Mach wave from *D*.)

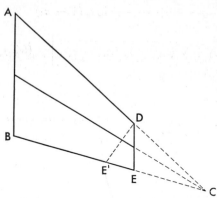

Fig. 222.   *Analysis of the tip effect.*

Drag of a Diamond-Shaped Profile Triangular Wing with Zero Lift. Equations (599a), (600a) and (601) will be used in this paragraph for determination of the profile drag for a triangular plan form wing. To simplify the problem the profile of the wing will be assumed diamond-shaped and symmetrical with respect to the chord. The wing that will be analyzed is shown

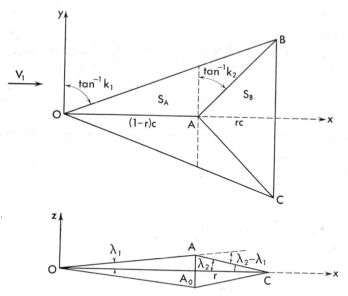

Fig. 223.   *Geometrical parameters of a diamond-shaped profile triangular wing.*

in Figure 223, and in the first part of these considerations the drag for the wing moving with the sides *OB* and *OC* as leading edges will be considered, and later the drag for the wing moving with the side BC as leading edge will be calculated (Reference 53).

For the determination of the potential function that satisfies the boundary conditions, it is convenient to consider two source distributions of constant strength. In the zone $OBAC$ the strength of the source distribution is

$$\pi w_1 = \pi \lambda_1 V_1$$

where λ_1 is the slope of the profile in the parts OAB and OAC, and in the zone ABC, the strength of the source distribution must be

$$\pi w_2' = \pi \lambda_2 V_1.$$

However, for simplicity of calculation it is convenient to consider the source distribution w_1 extended to the entire zone OBC, and therefore to consider in the zone ABC the source distribution

$$\pi w_2 = \pi (\lambda_2 - \lambda_1) V_1.$$

In the analysis the following geometrical parameters will be used (Figure 223):

k_1, tangent of the angle between the y-axis and the leading edge

k_2, tangent of the angle between the y-axis and the line AB of the maximum thickness of the profiles

$1 - r$, position of the maximum thickness along the chord in percentage of the chord

For the wing three possibilities must be considered:

1. The Mach wave from O is less inclined with respect to the x-axis than the lines OB and AB
2. The Mach wave from O is more inclined with respect to the x-axis than the leading edge OB but less than the line BC
3. The Mach wave from O is more inclined than either of the lines OB and AB.

Because the tangent of the angle between the Mach wave and the y-axis is given by

$$B = \sqrt{M^2 - 1}$$

the three conditions correspond to

$$1. \quad B > k_1 > k_2$$
$$2. \quad k_1 > B > k_2$$
$$3. \quad k_1 > k_2 > B$$

or, using the parameters n_1 and n_2 defined by

$$n_1 = \frac{k_1}{B} \quad \text{and} \quad n_2 = \frac{k_2}{B}, \tag{644}$$

$$
\left.
\begin{array}{ll}
1. & 1 > n_1 > n_2 \\
2. & n_1 > 1 > n_2 \\
3. & n_1 > n_2 > 1
\end{array}
\right\} \qquad (645)
$$

If $1 > n_1 > n_2$, the wing drag can be calculated by determining three different contributions to the value of the induced velocity ϕ_{2x}: the drag dependent on the induction produced by the source distribution proportional to w_1 over s_A (area of the zone OAB), the induction produced by the source distribution proportional to w_1 over s_B (area of zone ABC), and the induction produced by the source distribution proportional to w_2 over s_B. The source distribution proportional to w_2 does not induce velocity in the zone OAB

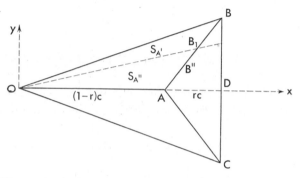

Fig. 224. *Triangular wing with supersonic leading edge.*

because AB is more inclined than the Mach wave from A, $1 > n_2$. For $1 > n_1 > n_2$ the drag of the zone of the wing OAB (Figure 224) can be determined with equation (601); therefore the first part of the drag coefficient is given by

$$
\frac{D_{11}}{\frac{1}{2}\rho_1 V_1^2} = \frac{4\lambda_1^2}{B\sqrt{1 - n_1^2}} \left\{ \int_{s_{A'}} ds + \int_{s_{A''}} \left[1 - \frac{2}{\pi} \sin^{-1} \sqrt{\frac{n_1^2 - \sigma_1^2}{1 - \sigma_1^2}} \right] ds \right\} \qquad (646)
$$

where $s_{A'}$ is the area OBB_1, and $s_{A''}$ is the area OAB_1. If a point B'' along AB is considered, the area of the zone OAB'' is given by

$$
s_{OAB''} = \frac{(1 - r)c}{2} \, y_{B''} = s_T (1 - r)^2 \frac{\sigma}{1 - r\sigma}
$$

where s_T is the total area of the wing; therefore

$$
ds = s_T (1 - r)^2 \frac{d\sigma}{(1 - r\sigma)^2}. \qquad (647)
$$

Using equation (647), equation (646) can be written in the form

$$\frac{D_{11}}{\frac{1}{2}\rho_1 V_1^2 s_T} = \frac{8\lambda_1^2}{B\pi} G_1(n, r) \tag{648}$$

where

$$G_1(n, r) = \frac{(1-r)^2}{\sqrt{1-n^2}} \int_0^1 \left[\frac{\pi}{2} - \sin^{-1}\sqrt{\frac{n^2 - \sigma^2}{1 - \sigma^2}}\right] \frac{d\sigma}{(1 - \sigma r)^2} \tag{649}$$

The second part of the drag, depending on the induction of the source distribution, proportional to w_1 over the area s_B in which the slope is λ_2, is given by

$$\frac{D_{21}}{\frac{1}{2}\rho_1 V_1^2 s_T} = \frac{8\lambda_1\lambda_2}{B\pi}\left[G(n_1, 0) - G(n_1, r)\right] \tag{650}$$

where the expression $G(n_1, 0)$ represents the value of the integral (649) extended to the total area s_T that corresponds in equation (649) to the condition $r = 0$.

The third part of the drag can be obtained in a similar way, and since the intensity of the source is proportional to $(\lambda_2 - \lambda_1)$ and acts over the zone of the profile inclined at λ_2, it is given by

$$\frac{D_{22}}{\frac{1}{2}\rho_1 V_1^2 s_T} = \frac{8\lambda_2(\lambda_2 - \lambda_1)}{B\pi}\frac{s_B}{s_T} G_1(n_2, 0). \tag{651}$$

The value of $G_1(n, r)$ can be obtained by determining the real part of the integral (649) with an integration by parts, and is

$$G_1(n, r) = \frac{1-r}{1+r}\left\{\frac{r}{1-n^2}\cos^{-1}n + \frac{1}{\sqrt{1 - r^2 n^2}}\left[\frac{\pi}{2} + \sin^{-1}(rn)\right]\right\} \tag{652}$$

and $G_1(n, 0)$ is given by

$$G_1(n, 0) = \frac{\pi}{2}.$$

Substituting the thickness of the profile for the slopes λ_1 and λ_2 of the profile, and using the following relations

$$\lambda_1 = \frac{t}{2c}\frac{1}{1-r}$$

$$\lambda_2 = -\frac{t}{2c}\frac{1}{r}$$

$$\lambda_2 - \lambda_1 = -\frac{t}{2c}\frac{1}{r(1-r)}$$

$$\left.\begin{array}{c} \\ \\ \\ \end{array}\right\} \tag{653}$$

or using the percentage thickness τ

$$\lambda_1 = \frac{\tau}{2(1-r)}$$

$$\lambda_2 - \lambda_1 = -\frac{\tau}{2r(1-r)}$$

the drag coefficient for the case considered becomes

$$C_D = \frac{2\tau^2}{\pi B (1-r)^2} \left\{ \frac{1}{\sqrt{1-n_1^2}} \cos^{-1} n + \frac{1}{r\sqrt{1-r^2 n_1^2}} \left[\frac{\pi}{2} + \sin^{-1}(rn_1) \right] \right\} \quad (654)$$

where

$$n_1 < 1 \quad \text{and} \quad 0 < r < 1.$$

The value of C_D for the value of n equal to zero, becomes

$$C_D = \frac{\tau^2}{B(1-r)r} \quad (655)$$

which corresponds to the drag coefficient for a straight wing in the approximation accepted.

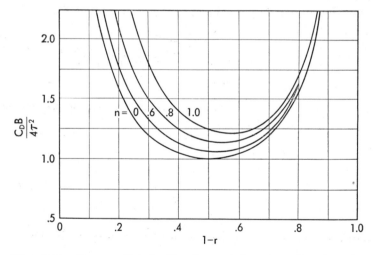

Fig. 225. *Drag coefficient of a diamond-shaped profile triangular wing with supersonic leading edges, as function of the maximum thickness position, for different values of sweepback (from Reference 53).*

In Figure 225 the values of $C_D B/4\tau^2$ as functions of $(1-r)$ for different values of n are shown. The minimum drag coefficient is obtained for a straight wing ($n = 0$) and the maximum thickness at 50 per cent of the chord. The last result is dependent on the assumption of the small-disturbances theory, and as shown in Chapter 7, is no longer exact if a more accurate analysis is made.

If $n_1 > 1 > n_2$ (Figure 226) the drag can be determined in the same way using for the front part equation (599a).

$$\frac{D_{11}}{\frac{1}{2}\rho_1 V_1^2 s_T} = \frac{8\lambda_1^2}{B\pi} G_2(n_1, r) \tag{656}$$

where

$$G_2(n_1, r) = \frac{(1 - r)^2}{\sqrt{n_1^2 - 1}} \int_0^1 \frac{1}{(1 - \sigma r)^2} \cosh^{-1}\sqrt{\frac{n_1^2 - \sigma^2}{1 - \sigma^2}}\, d\sigma. \tag{657}$$

The second part of the drag dependent on the source distribution w_1/π in the zone ABD, is given by

$$\frac{D_{21}}{\frac{1}{2}\rho_1 V_1^2 s_T} = \frac{8\lambda_2\lambda_1}{B\pi} [G_2(n_1, 0) - G_2(n_1, r)]. \tag{658}$$

The third part of the drag dependent on the source distribution in the zone ABD is equal to the value calculated for the first case given by equation (651)

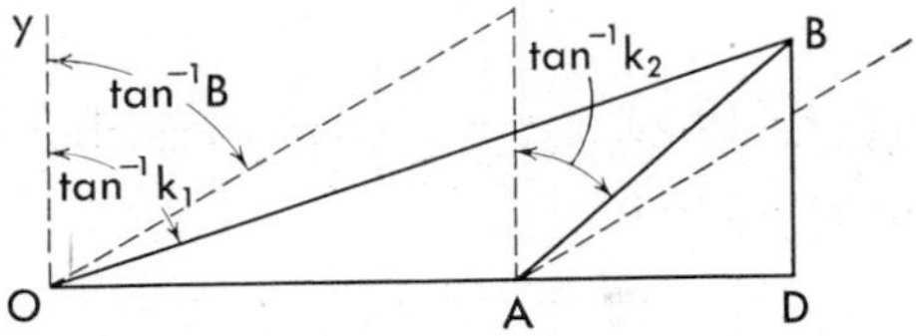

$$\frac{D_{22}}{\frac{1}{2}\rho_1 V_1^2 s_T} = \frac{8\lambda_2(\lambda_2 - \lambda_1)}{B\pi} \frac{s_B}{s_T} G_1(n_2, 0). \tag{659}$$

Fig. 226. *Triangular wing with subsonic leading edge and supersonic line of maximum thickness.*

The integral of equation (657) can be evaluated by using integration by parts, and for $rn_1 < 1$ the real value is

$$G_2(n, r) = \frac{1 - r}{1 + r}\left[\frac{\log_e n}{\sqrt{n^2 - 1}} + \frac{r \cosh^{-1} n}{\sqrt{n^2 - 1}} \right.$$
$$\left. + \frac{2}{\sqrt{1 - r^2 n^2}} \tan^{-1}\left(\frac{\sqrt{1 - r^2 n^2}}{n + \sqrt{n^2 - 1} - rn}\right)\right]. \tag{660}$$

The condition $rn_1 < 1$ is equivalent to the condition $rk_1 < B$, but

$$r = \frac{k_2}{k_1}.$$

Therefore $rn_1 < 1$ corresponds to $k_2 < B$, which is true for the case considered.

For $r = 0$, equation (660) becomes

$$G_2(n, 0) = \frac{\log_e n}{\sqrt{n^2 - 1}} + \sin^{-1}\frac{1}{n}. \tag{661}$$

The total drag coefficient can be obtained from equations (656), (658), and (659) for $(n_1 > 1)$ and $(n_1 r < 1)$ is

$$C_D = \frac{2\tau^2}{\pi B}\left[\frac{G_2\,(n_1, r)}{r(1-r)^2} + \frac{1}{r\,(1-r)}\left(\frac{\pi}{2} - \frac{\log_e n_1}{\sqrt{n_1^2 - 1}} - \sin^{-1}\frac{1}{n_1}\right)\right]. \quad (662)$$

In the third case where $n_1 > n_2 > 1$ (Figure 227), to the three parts consid-

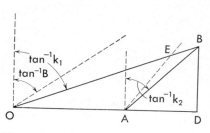

ered before in the determination of the drag, there must be added a fourth part, which is the drag dependent on the component ϕ_{2x} induced in the zone AEB by the source distribution $(w_2 - w_1)/\pi$ of the zone ADB. The first three parts are similar to those considered for the case where $n_1 > 1 > n_2$, but the value of the integral (657) is different because $k_2 > B$, and therefore $rn_1 > 1$. The integral (657) for $(rn_1 > 1)$ has the value

Fig. 227. *Triangular wing with subsonic leading edge and subsonic line of maximum thickness.*

$$G_2'\,(n, r) = \frac{1-r}{1+r}\left\{\frac{\log_e n}{\sqrt{n^2 - 1}} + \frac{r\cosh^{-1} n}{\sqrt{n^2 - 1}}\right.$$

$$\left. + \frac{1}{r^2n^2 - 1}\log_e\left[1 + \frac{2\sqrt{r^2n^2 - 1}}{n\,(1 - r) + \sqrt{n^2 - 1} - \sqrt{r^2n^2 - 1}}\right]\right\}. \quad (663)$$

The three parts of the drag become

$$\frac{D_{11}}{\frac{1}{2}\rho_1 V_1^2 s_T} = \frac{8\lambda_1^2}{\pi B}\,G_2'\,(n_1, r) \quad (664)$$

$$\frac{D_{21}}{\frac{1}{2}\rho_1 V_1^2 s_T} = \frac{8\lambda_1\lambda_2}{\pi B}\,[G_2\,(n_1, 0) - G_2'\,(n_1, r)] \quad (665)$$

$$\frac{D_{22}}{\frac{1}{2}\rho_1 V_1^2 s_T} = \frac{8\lambda_2\,(\lambda_2 - \lambda_1)}{\pi B}\,\frac{s_B}{s_T}\,G_2\,(n_2, 0) \quad (666)$$

The drag contribution due to the induction of the source distribution $(w_2 - w_1)/\pi$ in the zone AEB can be written

$$\frac{D_{12}}{\frac{1}{2}\rho_1 V_1^2 s_T} = \frac{8\lambda_1\,(\lambda_2 - \lambda_1)}{\pi B}\,\frac{s_B}{s_T}\,F\,(n_2, r) \quad (667)$$

where, using equation (600a), $F(n_2, r)$ is

$$F(n_2, r) = \frac{(1 - r)^2}{\sqrt{n_2^2 - 1}}\int_1^{n_2} \frac{1}{(\sigma - r)^2}\cosh^{-1}\sqrt{\frac{n_2^2 - 1}{\sigma^2 - 1}}\,d\sigma. \quad (668)$$

Evaluating the integral of equation (668) gives

$$F(n_2, r) = \frac{1-r}{1+r} \left\{ \frac{\log_e n_2}{\sqrt{n_2^2 - 1}} \right.$$

$$\left. + \frac{r}{\sqrt{n_2^2 - r^2}} \log_e \left[\frac{n_2^2 - r + \sqrt{(n_2^2 - r^2)(n_2^2 - 1)}}{n_2(1-r)} \right] \right\} \quad (669)$$

or remembering that $n_2 = rn_1$,

$$F(n_2, r) = \frac{1-r}{1+r} \left\{ \frac{\log n_1 r}{\sqrt{n_1^2 r^2 - 1}} \right.$$

$$\left. + \frac{1}{\sqrt{n_1^2 - 1}} \log_e \left[\frac{rn_1^2 - 1 + \sqrt{(r^2 n_1^2 - 1)(n_1^2 - 1)}}{n_1(1-r)} \right] \right\} . \quad (670)$$

From equations (664), (665), (666), (667), and (670) the drag coefficient for $(n_1 > 1)$, $(n_1 r > 1)$ can be evaluated and is given by

$$C_D = \frac{2\tau^2}{\pi B} \left\{ \frac{G_2'(n_1, r)}{r(1-r)^2} - \frac{F(n_2, r)}{(1-r)^2} \right.$$

$$\left. + \frac{1}{r(1-r)} \left[\frac{\log_e n_1 r}{\sqrt{n_1^2 r^2 - 1}} - \frac{\log_e n_1}{\sqrt{n_1^2 - 1}} + \sin^{-1} \frac{1}{rn_1} - \sin^{-1} \frac{1}{n_1} \right] \right\} . \quad (671)$$

Equations (662) and (671) give the values of the drag coefficients for the case of $(n_1 > 1)$ (leading edge more inclined than the Mach wave) for different positions of the maximum thickness. In Figure 228 some values of $C_D B/4\tau^2$ are shown as a function of the percentage position of the maximum thickness along the chord $(1 - r)$ for different values of n_1. As it is shown in the figure, the drag coefficient is higher than for a two-dimensional wing $(n = 0)$, when the maximum thickness is in the back part of the wing where $(1 - r)$ is large, and decreases notably only if the maximum thickness of the profile is very near the leading edge where $(1 - r)$ is small.

It is necessary to remember that the only drag considered in this discussion is the pressure drag, while the drag due to the viscosity, that is a large part of the total drag, is not considered. The drag due to the viscosity depends also upon the position of the maximum thickness, because it depends upon the pressure distribution along the wing; therefore the optimum position of the maximum thickness can be obtained only if both components of the drag are considered. On the other hand, the value found for the position of the thickness corresponding to minimum pressure drag is dependent on the simplifications accepted, and therefore somewhat different conclusions would be obtained if a more accurate theory were used.

If the direction of movement of the wing is reversed, the drag coefficient can still be evaluated by using a superimposition of source distributions (Figure 229). If the inclination of AD is X_1, and that of AB is X_2, by using the same definition used before, the coefficients k_1 and k_2 can be determined and the coefficients n_1 and n_2 can be obtained.

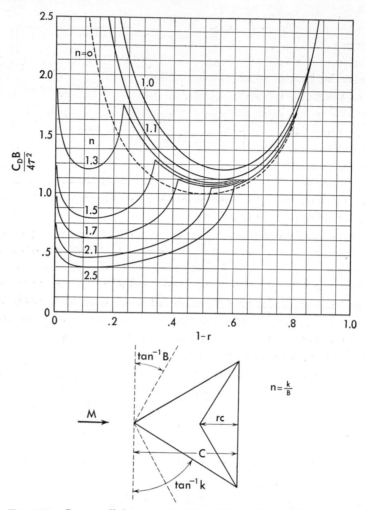

Fig. 228. *Drag coefficient as a function of the position of the maximum thickness for a diamond-shaped profile triangular wing with subsonic leading edge (from Reference 53).*

If $n_1 > 1$ and $n_2 > 1$, the drag coefficient of the wing can be represented by two source distributions: a source distribution of plan form ABC and intensity w_1/π where

$$w_1 = \lambda_1 V_1 \tag{672}$$

and a source distribution $ABCD$ of intensity w_2/π where

$$w_2 = (\lambda_2 - \lambda_1) V_1. \tag{672a}$$

The effect of the first source distribution w_1/π can be evaluated by considering the two zones of the wing of different inclination, the zone ADC and the zone $ADCB$. In ADC the source distribution w_1/π induces a velocity component ϕ_{2x}, that in the zone ALC can be obtained from two-dimensional considerations. In the zone $AF'L$, the velocity component ϕ_{2x} is the sum of the two-dimensional value, as in ALI, and of the value $\phi_{2x}{}'$ dependent on the tip effect at A, which can be determined as produced by a source distribution $-w_1/\pi$ in the zone $A'AB$. The velocity component ϕ_{2x} in $F'LFD$ can be obtained as

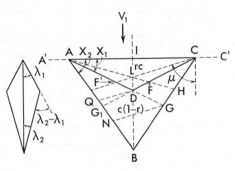

Fig. 229. *Diamond-shaped profile triangular wing with inverted direction of motion.*

the sum of the two-dimensional value and of the values $\phi_{2x}{}'$ and $\phi_{2x}{}''$ produced by the tip effect at A and C, which can be determined by assuming a source distribution at $A'AB$ and BCC' of intensity $-w_1/\pi$. Because the induction of the source BCC' at DLF' is equal to the induction of the source $A'AB$ at LDF, the drag corresponding to the pressure on ADC will be determined by evaluating the drag D_{11}, corresponding to the ϕ_{2x} over ADC computed with the two-dimensional theory, and the drag D_{13} corresponding to $\phi_{2x}{}'$ over ADF and $F'DC$ (which are identical).

If $ID = rc$ and $BD = (1 - r)c$

$$\frac{D_{11}}{\frac{1}{2}\rho_1 V_1^2 s_T} = \frac{\tau^2}{rB} \tag{673}$$

and if

$$\sigma_2 = \frac{k_2 y}{x} \quad \text{and} \quad \sigma_1 = \frac{k_1 y}{x}$$

because the area ADF can be expressed in the form

$$ds = \frac{2 s_T n_1}{n_2} \frac{d\sigma_1}{(1 + \sigma_1)^2} \tag{674}$$

and the expression of $\phi_{2x}{}'$ is given by equation (607) D_{13} is given by

$$\frac{D_{13}}{\frac{1}{2}\rho_1 V_1^2 s_T} = -\frac{4 n_1^2}{n_2^2} \frac{\tau^2}{B \pi r^2} \int_{n_2/n_1}^{n_2} \left[\frac{1}{\sqrt{n_2^2 - 1}} \cosh^{-1} \frac{n_2^2 - \sigma_2}{(\sigma_2 - 1)n_2} \right.$$
$$\left. + \cos^{-1} \frac{\sigma_2}{n_2} \right] \frac{d\sigma_2}{\left(1 + \dfrac{n_1}{n_2}\sigma_2\right)^2} \tag{675}$$

or, integrating,

$$\frac{D_{13}}{\frac{1}{2}\rho_1 V_1{}^2 s_T} =$$

$$-\frac{4n_1}{n_2}\frac{\tau^2}{B\pi r^2}\left[-\frac{n_2 - n_1}{2(n_1 + n_2)}\frac{1}{\sqrt{n_2{}^2 - 1}}\log_e \frac{n_1 n_2 - 1 + \sqrt{n_1{}^2 - 1)(n_2{}^2 - 1)}}{n_2 - n_1}\right.$$

$$\left. + \frac{1}{2}\cos^{-1}\frac{1}{n_1} - \frac{n_2}{n_1 + n_2}\frac{1}{\sqrt{n_1{}^2 - 1}}\log_e n_1\right]. \quad (675a)$$

The drag D_{12} due to induction of the source distribution ABC of intensity w_1/π over $ADBC$ can be determined by computing the drag due to the induction over a surface ABC of inclination λ_2, and subtracting the value of the drag due to the induction over a surface ADC of inclination λ_2 that can be obtained directly from equations (673) and (675a). The drag due to the induction over ABC can be obtained by using the criteria developed on page 315, in order to evaluate the tip effect. Proceeding in a similar way as for equation (675), the following expression is obtained:

$$\frac{D_{12}}{\frac{1}{2}\rho_1 V_1{}^2 s_T} = -\frac{\tau^2}{rB} + \frac{D_{13}}{\frac{1}{2}\rho_1 V_1{}^2 s_T}\frac{r}{1 - r}$$

$$+ \frac{2\tau^2}{\pi B r (1 - r)}\left[\cos^{-1}\frac{1}{n_2} - \frac{1}{\sqrt{n_2{}^2 - 1}}\log_e n_2\right]. \quad (676)$$

The source distribution $ADCB$ of intensity w_2/π can be analyzed as being composed of two source distributions AGB and CG_1B, identical and symmetrical, of intensity w_2/π and of a source distribution DG_1GB of intensity $-w_2/\pi$. Then the drag due to the induction of a source distribution $ADCB$ can be evaluated by calculating the drag D_{21} due to the induction of a source distribution AGB of intensity w_2/π, over the surface ADF of inclination λ_1, the drag D_{23} over the surface $DFGH$ of inclination λ_2 and the drag D_{22} over the surface AGB of inclination λ_2. The drags D_{33} and D_{34} due to the induction of the source distribution $BGDG_1$ of intensity $-w_2/\pi$ over the surface G_1DGB of inclination λ_2, and over the surface G_1DQ of inclination λ_2 respectively (where AH and DQ are Mach waves) must also be determined. The effect of the source distribution AGB in NGB, due to the tip GB, is equal to and of opposite sign from the similar effect due to the source distribution DG_1GB on the same surface, and therefore its evaluation is not necessary.

Using for ϕ_{2x} the expression of equations (599) to (615), the values of the drag coefficients can be evaluated. The value of D_{21} can be found by using for ϕ_{2x} the expression given by equation (611) and for the elemental area the expression

$$ds = 2\,\frac{n_1}{n_2}\,s_T\,\frac{d\sigma_1}{(1+\sigma_1)^2}\,.$$

Therefore the following expression can be obtained for D_{21}

$$\frac{D_{21}}{\frac{1}{2}\rho_1 V_1^2 s_T} = -\frac{2\tau^2}{r^2\,(1-r)\pi B}\frac{n_1}{n_2}\frac{n_2-n_1}{n_2+n_1}\left[\frac{1}{\sqrt{n_1^2-1}}\log_e n_1\right.$$

$$\left.+\frac{1}{\sqrt{n_2^2-1}}\log_e\frac{n_1 n_2 - 1 + \sqrt{(n_1^2-1)(n_2^2-1)}}{n_2-n_1}\right].\qquad(677)$$

The value of D_{23} can be found as the difference of the drag due to the induction over the surface AGH of inclination λ_2, and the drag due to the induction over the surface ADF of inclination λ_2 that is proportional to the value obtained in equation (677). For the induction over AGH equation (611) must be used, while the elemental surface is given by the expression

$$ds = 2n_2 n_1 s_T\,\frac{d\sigma_1}{(n_1+n_2\sigma_1)^2}\,.\qquad(678)$$

For the drag D_{23} the following expression can be obtained:

$$\frac{D_{23}}{\frac{1}{2}\rho_1 V_1^2 s_T} = \frac{4\tau^2}{r\,(1-r)^2\pi B}\frac{n_2-n_1}{n_1+n_2}\frac{1}{\sqrt{n_2^2-1}}\log_e\frac{+n_2\sqrt{n_1^2-1}+n_1\sqrt{n_2^2-1}}{\sqrt{n_2^2-n_1^2}}$$

$$+\frac{r}{1-r}\frac{D_{21}}{\frac{1}{2}\rho_1 V_1^2 s_T}\qquad(679)$$

The value of the drag D_{22} can be evaluated by using equation (612) for ϕ_{2x}, and using for the elemental surface the expression given in equation (678). Thus the following expression is obtained:

$$\frac{D_{22}}{\frac{1}{2}\rho_1 V_1^2 s_T} =$$

$$\frac{2\tau^2}{\pi Br\,(1-r)^2}\frac{n_2-n_1}{n_1+n_2}\left[\frac{1}{\sqrt{n_2^2-1}}\log_e\left(n_2\frac{n_1 n_2 + 1 - \sqrt{(n_1^2-1)(n_2^2-1)}}{n_2+n_1}\right)\right.$$

$$\left.+\left(\frac{1}{\sqrt{n_1^2-1}}-\frac{1}{\sqrt{n_2^2-1}}\right)\log_e\frac{n_1 n_2 - 1 + \sqrt{(n_1^2-1)(n_2^2-1)}}{n_2-n_1}\right].\qquad(680)$$

The value of D_{33} can be calculated by using for ϕ_{2x} the value given by equation (609), while the elemental area is given by the expression

$$ds = s_R\,\frac{n_1+n_2}{n_1}\,\frac{d\sigma_1}{\left(1+\sigma_1\dfrac{n_2}{n_1}\right)^2}$$

where s_R is the area of the surface G_1DGB; therefore

$$ds = x s_T \; \frac{(n_2 - n_1)^2 n_1}{n_2 \,(n_1 + \sigma_1 n_2)^2} \; d\sigma_1 \tag{681}$$

D_{33} becomes

$$\frac{D_{33}}{\frac{1}{2}\rho_1 V_1{}^2 s_T} = - \frac{2\tau^2}{(1 - r)^2 r \pi B} \frac{(n_1 - n_2) n_1}{(n_1 + n_2) n_2}\left[\frac{1}{\sqrt{n_2{}^2 - 1}} \; \log_e \left(1\right.\right.$$

$$+ \frac{2\sqrt{n_2{}^2 - 1}}{n_2 + n_1 + \sqrt{n_1{}^2 - 1} - \sqrt{n_2{}^2 - 1}}\right) + \frac{\log_e n_1}{\sqrt{n_1{}^2 - 1}} - \frac{n_2 \log_e (n_1 + \sqrt{n_1{}^2 - 1})}{n_1 \sqrt{n^2 - 1}}\bigg]. \tag{682}$$

The value of D_{34} can be calculated in a similar way. The elemental surface can be expressed in the form

$$ds = \frac{1}{2}\frac{n_1}{n_2} \, s_T \, \frac{d\sigma_1}{(n_1 + n_2 \sigma_1)^2} \, (n_2 - n_1)^2$$

and the value of D_{34} is given by the expression

$$\frac{D_{34}}{\frac{1}{2}\rho_1 V_1{}^2 s_T} = - \frac{2\tau^2}{(1 - r) r^2 \pi B} \frac{(n_2 - n_1) n_1}{(n_2 + n_1) n_2}\left[\frac{\log_e n_1}{\sqrt{n_1{}^2 - 1}}\right.$$

$$+ \frac{1}{\sqrt{n_2{}^2 - 1}} \; \log_e \left(\frac{n_2 n_1 + 1 - \sqrt{n_1{}^2 - 1}\sqrt{n_2{}^2 - 1}}{n_1 + n_2}\right)\bigg]. \tag{683}$$

The total drag D is given by

$$D = D_{11} + D_{12} + D_{13} + D_{21} + D_{22} + D_{23} + D_{33} + D_{34}. \tag{684}$$

In a similar way, if $n_1 < 1$ and $n_2 > 1$ the drag is given by a summation of different terms

$$D = D_{11} + D_{12} + D_{23} + D_{22} + D_{33} \tag{684a}$$

where

$$\frac{D_{11}}{\frac{1}{2}\rho_1 V_1{}^2 s_T} = \frac{- D_{12}}{\frac{1}{2}\rho_1 V_1{}^2 s_T} = \frac{\tau^2}{Br}$$

$$D_{23} = \frac{\tau^2}{Br(1 - r)} \frac{2}{\pi}\left[\cos^{-1}\frac{1}{n_2} - \frac{1}{\sqrt{n_2{}^2 - 1}} \log_e n_2\right]$$

$$\frac{D_{22}}{\frac{1}{2}\rho_1 V_1{}^2 s_T} = \frac{2\tau^2}{r(1 - r)^2}\frac{n_2 - n_1}{n_1 + n_2}\frac{1}{B\pi}\left[\frac{1}{\sqrt{1 - n_1{}^2}}\cos^{-1}\frac{1 - n_1 n_2}{n_1 - n_2} + \frac{\log_e n_2}{\sqrt{n_2{}^2 - 1}}\right]$$

$$\frac{D_{33}}{\frac{1}{2}\rho_1 V_1{}^2 s_T} = \frac{(n_2 - n_1)^2}{(n_2 + n_1) n_2}\frac{2\tau^2}{\pi Br(1 - r)^2}\left[\frac{+ r}{1 - r}\frac{1}{\sqrt{n_2{}^2 - 1}}\log_e(n_2 - \sqrt{n_2{}^2 - 1})\right.$$

$$\left. - \frac{1}{1 - r}\frac{\cos^{-1} n_1}{\sqrt{1 - n_1{}^2}}\right]. \tag{685}$$

If $n_1 < n_2 < 1$

$$D = D_{22} + D_{33} \tag{686}$$

where

$$\frac{D_{22}}{\frac{1}{2}\rho_1 V_1^2 s_T} = 2\frac{n_2 - n_1}{n_2 + n_1}\frac{\tau^2}{Br\,(1-r)^2\sqrt{1-n_1^2}}$$

$$\frac{D_{33}}{\frac{1}{2}\rho_1 V_1^2 s_T} =$$

$$\frac{(n_2 - n_1)^2}{(n_1 + n_2)n_2}\frac{2\tau^2}{r\,(1-r)^2\pi B}\left[\frac{r}{1-r}\frac{\cos^{-1} n_2}{\sqrt{1-n_2^2}} - \frac{1}{1-r}\frac{\cos^{-1} n_1}{\sqrt{1-n_1^2}}\right]. \tag{687}$$

When the calculations are performed for different values of $r/(1-r)$ and of the parameters n_1 and n_2, an interesting result obtained is that the drag coefficient for this type of wing is coincident, in the approximation accepted, with the drag coefficient of the same wing but moving in the opposite direction, as is considered in the first part of the paragraph, if the Mach number and the geometrical parameters are the same, $(1-r)/r$ constant and $(n_1 = n_2')$, $(n_2 = n_1')$ where the index refers to the wing moving in the opposite direction. The coincidence of the drag coefficient for zero lift when the direction of the movement is reversed is not peculiar to the type of wing considered, but occurs generally for all types of wing if the phenomenon is analyzed by assuming that all the approximations accepted are correct. The drag distribution and pressure distribution on the wings are different when the direction of the movement is reversed (Reference 54).

Drag of Wing Having Diamond-shaped Plan Form and Diamond-shaped Profile for Zero Lift. The wing considered in this paragraph will be a diamond plan form wing with symmetrical diamond-shaped profile. The position of the maximum thickness for every section in the plane ($y = $ constant) will be assumed to be placed along a straight line BB' perpendicular to the chord of the profile (Figure 230). No difficulties will be found if the wing in Figure 230a is examined, but the equations are slightly more involved. The wing considered can be defined geometrically by the root section the geometric parameters of which are the percentage thickness

$$\frac{t}{c} = \tau$$

and the inclinations of the sides of the diamond-shaped profile λ_1, and λ_2, which are defined by the parameters $(1-r)$ and r (the ratio $r/(1-r) = A$ will also be considered as a parameter in the analysis).

$$\lambda_1 = \frac{\tau}{2(1-r)}; \qquad \lambda_2 = -\frac{\tau}{2r}. \tag{688}$$

To define the plan form, the two angles X_1 and X_2 must be fixed. The Mach

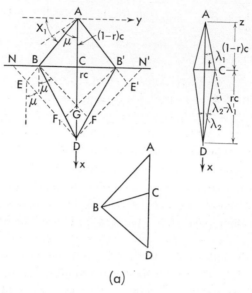

(a)

Fig. 230.   *Wing having diamond-shaped plan form and diamond-shaped profile.*

angle μ gives the value of the speed.   Using the tangents of the angles X_1 and X_2, the following parameters will be used:

$$k_1 = \tan X_1; \qquad\qquad k_2 = \tan X_2; \qquad\qquad B = \sqrt{M_1^2 - 1};$$

$$n_1 = \frac{k_1}{B}; \qquad\qquad n_2 = \frac{k_2}{B};$$

$$n_2 = n_1 \frac{r}{1-r} = n_1 A. \tag{689}$$

The flow around the wing can be represented by the potential due to two different source distributions: a source distribution of intensity

$$C_1 = \frac{w_1}{\pi} = \frac{\lambda_1 V_1}{\pi} \tag{690}$$

and plan form $ABDB_1$, and a source distribution of intensity

$$C_2 = \frac{w_2}{\pi} = \frac{(\lambda_2 - \lambda_1) V_1}{\pi} \tag{690a}$$

and plan form BB_1D.

In order to determine the pressure on the wing and from that the drag coefficient, the x component of the induced velocity produced by the source distribution must be found. The first source distribution can be analyzed by considering two source distributions, the source of intensity w_1/c extended at the surface $AEDE'$, where ED and $E'D$ are inclined at μ with respect to the x-axis, and the source distribution BED or $B'E'D'$ of intensity $-w_1/c$. The first source distribution produces an induced velocity ϕ_{2x}' that can be determined with equations (599a) or (601). The second source distribution BED produces an induced velocity ϕ_{2x}'' in the zone BDF, that exists only if $n_2 > 1$, and can be determined by using the considerations stated on page 311. The second source distribution $BB'D$ can also be considered as the resultant of two source distributions. The source NDN' of intensity $(\lambda_2 - \lambda_1)V_1/\pi$, produces in $BB'D$ an induced velocity component ϕ_{2x}' that can be calculated as for two-dimensional phenomena. The source distributions NBD and $N'B'D$ (ND and $N'D$ inclined at μ with respect to x) of intensity $-(\lambda_2 - \lambda_1)V_1/\pi$ produce over BFD and $B'F'D$ an induced velocity ϕ_{2x}'', that can be determined by using the considerations stated on page 311.

For determination of drag, different cases must be considered for the values of n_1 and n_2. If $n_1 > 1$ and $n_2 > 1$ the drag can be considered composed of five terms. The first term depends on the induction of the source distribution $AEDE'$ over the surface BAB' of the inclination λ_1. This term, D_{11}, is identical to a corresponding term calculated for the triangular wing; using equation (656) and (661),

$$\frac{D_{11}}{\frac{1}{2}\rho_1 V_1^2 s_T} = \frac{2\tau^2}{B\pi\,(1-r)}\left[\frac{\log_e n_1}{\sqrt{n_1^2-1}} + \sin^{-1}\frac{1}{n_1}\right]. \qquad (691)$$

The part of the drag, D_{12}, dependent on the induction of the source distribution $AEDE'$ over BB_1D inclined at λ_2 can be determined as the difference of the drag over $ABB'D$ and the drag over $BB'A$, and can be expressed in the form

$$\frac{D_{12}}{\frac{1}{2}\rho_1 V_1^2} = \frac{8\lambda_2\lambda_1}{B\pi\sqrt{n_1^2-1}}\int_{s_T}\cosh^{-1}\sqrt{\frac{n_1^2-\sigma^2}{1-\sigma^2}}\,ds$$

$$+ \frac{2s_T\tau^2}{B\pi r}\left[\frac{\log_e n_1}{\sqrt{n_1^2-1}} + \sin^{-1}\frac{1}{n_1}\right].$$

The elemental area for the zone $ABDB$ is given by

$$ds = \frac{s_T}{1-r}\frac{d\sigma}{(1+A\sigma)^2}.$$

Therefore, performing the integration, the following expression is obtained for D_{12}:

$$\frac{D_{12}}{\frac{1}{2}\rho_1 V_1{}^2 s_T} = \frac{2\tau^2}{B\pi}\frac{(1+A)^2}{A}\left\{\frac{1}{1+A}\sin^{-1}\frac{1}{n_1} - \frac{2A}{1-A^2}\frac{\log_e n_1}{\sqrt{n_1{}^2-1}}\right.$$

$$+\frac{A}{1-A}\frac{\cosh^{-1}n_1}{\sqrt{n_1{}^2-1}} - \frac{1}{(1-A)\sqrt{n_2{}^2-1}}\log_e\left[1\right.$$

$$\left.\left.+\frac{2\sqrt{n_2{}^2-1}}{(A+1)n_1+\sqrt{n_1{}^2-1}-\sqrt{n_2{}^2-1}}\right]\right\}. \qquad (692)$$

The source BED of intensity $-w_1/\pi$ induces a velocity component ϕ_{2x}' in the zone BDF given by equation (604); therefore the corresponding drag D_{13} is given by

$$\frac{D_{13}}{\frac{1}{2}\rho_1 V_1{}^2} = \frac{-4\lambda_1\lambda_2}{B\pi}4rs_T\int_1^{n_2}\left[\frac{1}{\sqrt{n_2{}^2-1}}\cosh^{-1}\frac{n_2{}^2-\sigma_2}{n_2(1-\sigma_2)}\right.$$

$$\left.+\frac{1}{\sqrt{n_1{}^2-1}}\cosh^{-1}\frac{n_2 n_1+\sigma_2}{n_1\sigma_2+n_2}\right]\frac{d\sigma_2}{(1+\sigma_2)^2}$$

where $\sigma_2 = \dfrac{k_2 y}{x}$.

Performing the integration, the following expression is obtained:

$$\frac{D_{13}}{\frac{1}{2}\rho_1 V_1{}^2 s_T} = \frac{2\tau^2}{B\pi(1-r)}\frac{n_1+n_2}{n_1-n_2}\left\{\frac{\log n_2}{\sqrt{n_2{}^2-1}} - \frac{1}{\sqrt{n_1{}^2-1}}\log_e\left[\frac{n_1 n_2+1}{n_1+n_2}\right.\right.$$

$$\left.\left.+\sqrt{\left(\frac{(n_1 n_2+1)}{n_1+n_2}\right)^2-1}\right]\right\}. \qquad (693)$$

The source distribution $NN'D$ of intensity w_2/π induces a velocity component ϕ_{2x} in the zone BB_1D that can be calculated with the two-dimensional theory; therefore the corresponding drag D_{22} can easily be evaluated.

$$\frac{D_{22}}{\frac{1}{2}\rho_1 V_1{}^2 s_T} = \frac{\tau^2}{(1-r)rB}. \qquad (694)$$

The source distribution NBD of intensity $-w_2/\pi$, induces a velocity component ϕ_{2x}' in the zone BDF given by equation (607) (in which n_2 is zero), and therefore the corresponding drag D_{23} can be evaluated in the following way:

$$\frac{D_{23}}{\frac{1}{2}\rho_1 V_1{}^2} = \frac{16rs_T(\lambda_1-\lambda_2)\lambda_2}{B\pi}\int_1^{n_2}\left(\frac{1}{\sqrt{n_2{}^2-1}}\cosh^{-1}\frac{n_2-\sigma_2}{(1-\sigma_2)n_2}\right.$$

$$\left.+\cos^{-1}\frac{\sigma_2}{n_2}\right)\frac{d\sigma_2}{(1+\sigma_2)^2}$$

and performing the integration, the following expression is obtained:

$$\frac{D_{23}}{\frac{1}{2}\rho_1 V_1{}^2 s_T} = - -\frac{2\tau^2}{r(1-r)B\pi}\left[\cos^{-1}\frac{1}{n_2} - \frac{1}{\sqrt{n_2{}^2-1}}\log_e n_2\right]. \quad (695)$$

In a similar way the following expressions can be obtained for the different possible combinations of the values of n_1 and n_2. If $n_1 > 1$ and $n_2 = 1$, D_{11} and D_{22} are given by equations (691) and (694); D_{13} and D_{23} are zero; and D_{12} is given by

$$\frac{D_{12}}{\frac{1}{2}\rho_1 V_1{}^2 s_T} = \frac{2\tau^2}{B\pi}\frac{(1+A)^2}{A}\left[\frac{1}{1+A}\sin^{-1}\frac{1}{n_1} - \frac{2A}{1-A^2}\frac{\log_e n_1}{\sqrt{n_1{}^2-1}}\right.$$

$$\left. + \frac{A}{1-A}\frac{\cosh^{-1}n_1}{\sqrt{n_1{}^2-1}} - \frac{1}{1-A}\left(1-\frac{\sqrt{n_1{}^2-1}}{1+n_1}\right)\right]. \quad (696)$$

If $n_1 > 1$ and $n_2 < 1$, D_{11} and D_{22} do not change; D_{13} and D_{23} are zero; and D_{12} is given by

$$\frac{D_{12}}{\frac{1}{2}\rho_1 V_1{}^2 s_T} = \frac{2\tau^2}{B\pi}\frac{(1+A)^2}{A}\left\{\frac{1}{1+A}\sin^{-1}\frac{1}{n_1} - -\frac{2A}{1-A^2}\frac{\log_e n_1}{\sqrt{n_1{}^2-1}}\right.$$

$$+ \frac{A}{1-A}\frac{\cosh^{-1}n_1}{\sqrt{n_1{}^2--1}} - - \frac{1}{1-A}\frac{1}{\sqrt{1-n_2{}^2}}\left[\sin^{-1}\frac{n_2 n_1+1}{n_2+n_1} - \sin^{-1}n_2\right]\right\}. \quad (697)$$

If $n_1 = 1$ and $n_2 > 1$

$$\frac{D_{11}}{\frac{1}{2}\rho_1 V_1{}^2 s_T} = \frac{\tau^2}{(1-r)B}; \qquad \frac{D_{22}}{\frac{1}{2}\rho_1 V_1{}^2 s_T} = \frac{\tau^2}{B}\frac{1}{r(1-r)} \quad (698)$$

$$\frac{D_{12}}{\frac{1}{2}\rho_1 V_1{}^2 s_T} = \frac{2\tau^2}{r(1-r)\pi B}\left[\frac{1-r}{2}\pi - \frac{r}{2r-1}\right.$$

$$\left. + \frac{(r-1)^2}{(2r-1)\sqrt{2r-1}}\cosh^{-1}A\right]. \quad (699)$$

D_{23} is given by equation (695), and D_{13} is obtained from

$$\frac{D_{13}}{\frac{1}{2}\rho_1 V_1{}^2 s_T} = \frac{2\tau^2}{B\pi\sqrt{n_2{}^2-1}}\frac{1}{1-r}(1+n_2)\left[1-\frac{\log_e n_2}{n_2-1}\right]. \quad (700)$$

If $n_1 = 1$ and $n_2 < 1$, D_{23} and D_{13} are zero; and D_{22} and D_{11} are given by equation (698). D_{12} is obtained from

$$\frac{D_{12}}{\frac{1}{2}\rho_1 V_1{}^2 s_T} = \frac{2\tau^2}{B\pi r (1 - r)}\left[\pi \frac{1 - r}{2} - \frac{r}{2r - 1} - \frac{1 - r}{1 - 2r}\frac{\cos^{-1} n_2}{\sqrt{1 - n_2{}^2}}\right]. \quad (701)$$

If $n_1 < 1$ and $n_2 < 1$, the total drag D can de evaluated because D_{13} and D_{23} are zero; therefore

$$\frac{D}{\frac{1}{2}\rho_1 V_1{}^2 s_T} = \frac{2\tau^2}{Br (1 - r)}\left[1 - \frac{r}{2r - 1}\frac{\cos^{-1} n_1}{\pi \sqrt{1 - n_1{}^2}} - \frac{1}{\pi}\frac{r - 1}{2r - 1}\frac{\cos^{-1} n_2}{\sqrt{1 - n_2{}^2}}\right]. \quad (702)$$

If $n_1 < 1$ and $n_2 > 1$, D_{11} and D_{22} are given by equation (698); D_{23} is given by equation (695). D_{12} and D_{13} are obtained from

$$\frac{D_{12}}{\frac{1}{2}\rho_1 V_1{}^2 s_T} = \frac{\tau^2}{Br (1 - r)}\left[1 - r - \frac{r}{2r - 1}\frac{2}{\pi}\frac{\cos^{-1} n_1}{\sqrt{1 - n_1{}^2}}\right.$$
$$\left. + \frac{2}{\pi}\frac{r - 1}{2r - 1}\frac{1}{\sqrt{n_2{}^2 - 1}}\log_e (n_2 - \sqrt{n_2{}^2 - 1})\right]. \quad (703)$$

$$\frac{D_{13}}{\frac{1}{2}\rho_1 V_1{}^2 s_T} = \frac{2\tau^2}{B\pi \sqrt{n_2{}^2 - 1}}\frac{1}{1 - r}\frac{n_1 + n_2}{n_1 - n_2}\left(\log_e n_2\right.$$
$$\left. - \frac{\sqrt{n_2{}^2 - 1}}{\sqrt{1 - n_1{}^2}}\cos^{-1}\frac{n_1 n_2 + 1}{n_1 + n_2}\right). \quad (704)$$

When $n_1 < 1$ and $n_2 = 1$, D_{11} and D_{22} are given by equation (698); D_{13} and D_{23} are zero; and D_{12} is given by

$$\frac{D_{12}}{\frac{1}{2}\rho_1 V_1{}^2 s_T} = \frac{2\tau^2}{B (1 - r)r}\left[\frac{1 - r}{2} - \frac{r}{2r - 1}\frac{\cos^{-1} n_1}{\pi \sqrt{1 - n_1{}^2}} - \frac{1}{\pi}\frac{r - 1}{2r - 1}\right]. \quad (705)$$

If $n_1 = 1$ and $n_2 = 1$, the total drag becomes

$$\frac{D}{\frac{1}{2}\rho_1 V_1{}^2 s_T} = \frac{4\tau^2}{B}\left(2 - \frac{8}{3\pi}\right). \quad (706)$$

In Figure 231 some results obtained from this analysis for different values of n_1 and $(1 - r)$ are shown. In the diagram the value of $C_D B / 4\tau^2$ is plotted as a function of the parameter $(1 - r)$ that gives the position of the maximum thickness for different values of n_1. With the approximation of this theory, the minimum drag for a two-dimensional wing occurs when $r = (1 - r)$ and is $C_{D_0} = 4\tau^2/B$. For the conditions for which $C_D B/4\tau^2$ is less than one, the drag of the wing is less than the minimum drag of a two-dimensional wing, of same thickness. The results also show that if the direction of motion of the wing is reversed, the drag coefficient does not change for the same Mach number.

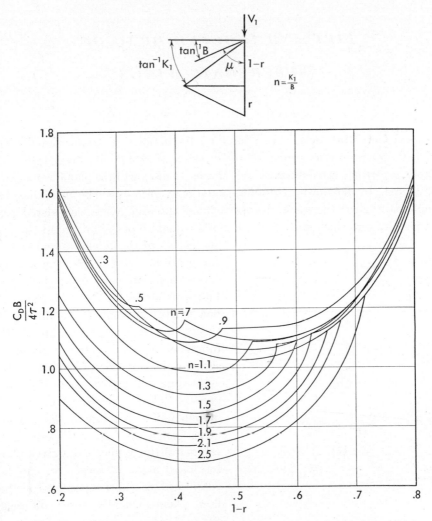

Fig. 231. *Drag coefficient as a function of the position of the maximum thickness for a diamond plan form wing, having a diamond-shaped profile.*

Indeed, reversing n_2, n_1, $(1 - r)$, and r, the same $C_D B/4\tau^2$ is obtained. It can be shown that the wave drag is dependent, in the approximation accepted, only on the source distribution representing the flow. The source distribution is inverted, but not changed, when the flow direction is inverted.

15

LIFT AND INDUCED DRAG OF

SUPERSONIC WINGS

General Considerations. In Chapter 7 the lift of a two-dimensional wing has been determined as a function of the shape of profile; in this chapter the lift of a supersonic three-dimensional wing as a function of the plan form will be considered. In all following considerations the hypothesis will be made that the small-disturbances theory can be applied, and the wing will be considered as a flat plate of zero thickness. With the approximation of the linearized theory, the effects of the thickness and of the camber of the wing profiles can be considered separately, by using the possibility of superimposition of different flow fields. Indeed, in the linearized theory each linear combination of the functions ϕ_1, ϕ_2 ... that separately satisfies the equation of motion in the approximate form (equation 339) also gives a solution of the equation of motion (339). Therefore the flow phenomena for a wing of given thickness and camber of the profile, and a given plan form and angle of incidence, can be considered as superimposition of the flow phenomena for three different wings having the same plan form but different shapes. For example, the wing a of Figure 232, at the angle of incidence α, can be considered as the combination of three wings of the same plan form: the wing b, having zero angle of attack and a symmetrical profile, but having the same thickness distribution along the chord and

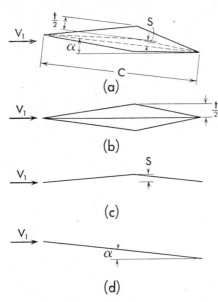

Fig. 232. *Effect of the thickness and of the camber in the lift of a supersonic wing.*

350

the span; the wing c, of zero thickness and zero angle of attack, but having the same camber distribution; and the wing d, of zero thickness and zero camber, having the same angle of attack. Superimposition of the flow fields of the wings b, c, and d, gives the flow field for the wing a. Since the wing b has zero lift, the effect of the thickness of the wing on the lift is zero by the approximation of the linearized theory. The wing c gives a lift that is constant, because if the angle of incidence of the wing a changes, the lift of the wing c does not change; therefore the wing c, or the camber, affects only the angle of zero lift, without changing the lift curve slope. The lift curve slope depends only on the wing d, and therefore on the plan form of the wing.

The mechanism of lift for supersonic wings changes when the component of the undisturbed velocity normal to the leading or trailing edge passes from supersonic to subsonic values; therefore a preliminary general discussion of the physics of the phenomena will be useful (Reference 54).

Consider a two-dimensional flat plate moving in a perfect flow with subsonic velocity: the equation of motion admits a solution that gives a flow without circulation and therefore without lift. When the pressure and velocity distribution along the profile corresponding to this flow field are determined, an infinite velocity is found along leading edge and trailing edge of the profile. The presence of viscosity in the actual phenomenon produces a separation of the flow at the trailing edge, with consequent formation of a vortex, the starting vortex, that produces a circulation around the wing. The intensity of the circulation around the wing is stated by the Kutta-Joukowski theorem, which imposes the condition that the flow must be smooth at the trailing edge. Therefore for subsonic speed the physical solution of the equation of the flow motion is the solution with smooth flow at the trailing edge, and therefore the solution that satisfies the Kutta-Joukowski condition.

When the circulation around the flat plate is considered, it is found that the

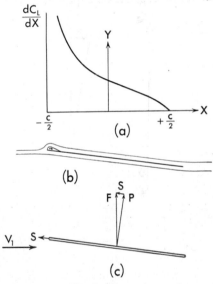

Fig. 233. *The leading edge vortex and the suction force in a flat plate in subsonic flow.*

flow around the leading edge still has infinite velocity (Figure 233a); therefore separation of the flow must be expected also at the leading edge. The separation that depends on the zero radius of the leading edge produces a vortex region that, for conditions below stalling, is restricted only to the zone of the leading edge (Figure 233b). If the thickness of the flat plate near the leading edge is increased, and a nose with a small but finite radius of curvature is considered, the infinite velocity at the leading edge decreases to a large but finite value, and the separation region disappears. Because of the large velocity, the pressure at the leading edge is very low, and therefore a suction force (S) exists at the leading edge (Figure 233c). The suction force eliminates the drag of the wing because it changes the direction of the resulting force from the direction normal to the chord of the wing, as must be the case if only the force P, given by the pressure normal to the plate, is considered, to the direction normal to the undisturbed stream (F).

Therefore in subsonic flow, a round leading edge must be used in order to avoid the vortex dissipation. In this case, a suction force exists and the drag due to lift becomes zero as is expected as a consequence of the hypothesis of potential flow.

When the two-dimensional flat plate is considered moving in a perfect flow, but with supersonic velocity, a finite difference of pressure is found between upper and lower surfaces (Chapter 7, page 118), and therefore no suction force can be expected at the leading edge. In this case the resultant of the pressures is perpendicular to the chord of the plate, and has a component in the direction of movement that constitutes a drag (Figure 234). The existence of the drag component agrees with the existence of an increase in entropy across the shock waves produced by the flat plate.

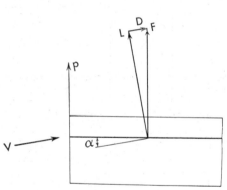

Fig. 234. *The pressure distribution in a flat plate in supersonic flow.*

Similar considerations can be made if three-dimensional lifting surfaces are considered: if the component of the undisturbed velocity normal to the leading edge is greater than the speed of sound (if the leading edge is *super-sonic*), the phenomena at the leading edge are locally equivalent to those for a two-dimensional flat plate at the Mach number corresponding to the normal component of the velocity. Therefore no suction forces must be expected, because a finite density of lift is found at the leading edge. In the actual wing a sharp leading edge must be used in order to reduce the shock losses. (Similar considerations can be made as in Chapter 7, page 117.)

If the component of the velocity normal to the leading edge is subsonic (the leading edge is *subsonic*), the phenomena locally are analogous to the phenomena corresponding to a subsonic flat plate. Therefore if the leading edge has an appropriate radius in order to avoid local separation, a suction force is developed, that decreases the drag due to lift. In this case less induced drag must be expected.

In the category of subsonic leading edges there can also be considered the case in which the normal component of the undisturbed velocity is slightly higher than the speed of sound; because in this case, if the wing has some thickness or an angle of attack, a detached shock must be expected on the basis of two-dimensional considerations. In the approximation of small disturbances this leading edge is considered as a supersonic leading edge, but in the actual phenomena, because of the presence of thickness, the normal flow component at the leading edge is subsonic.

In the analysis of the flow phenomena at the trailing edge, an analogous distinction must be considered: if the trailing edge is supersonic (the component of the velocity normal to the trailing edge is greater than the speed of sound), a finite density of lift will be found at the trailing edge, and therefore a possible physical flow condition will always be found. If the trailing edge is subsonic (the normal component of the velocity is less than the speed of sound), a solution with infinite density of lift at the trailing edge can be found. This solution is not physical. In order to obtain a physical solution of the problem, the Kutta-Joukowski condition must be satified. This can be obtained by imposing the condition that the lift density be zero along the trailing edge, and therefore a different solution must be found.

In Chapter 10, page 207, it was shown that, when the small-disturbances theory approximation is accepted, a lifting surface can be considered equivalent to an acceleration potential distribution, which can be represented by a doublet distribution. From the consideration of the potential of the doublet distribution it is found that an induced velocity exists at infinity. Thus an induced drag must exist, which is connected with the doublet distribution. This drag, produced by the vortex sheet that follows the doublet distribution, can be called *induced vortex drag* and must be added to the wave drag. Therefore the drag due to lift can be divided into induced vortex drag and induced wave drag.

When the leading edge and the trailing edge are all supersonic, the flow of the upper surface cannot interfere with the flow of the lower surface in the zone in front of the wing or in the zone of the wing. Therefore, the lift of the wing can be calculated by using, in place of a doublet distribution, a source and sink distribution as in the drag determination (Chapter 14). If interference exists between the upper flow and the lower flow in the zone of the wing, the equilibrium at the subsonic leading edge or trailing edge must be considered and doublet distributions must be used.

Supersonic Lifting Line and Elementary Lifting Surface. Consider a source distribution of constant intensity C along the y axis from $y = -\infty$ to $y = \infty$. The corresponding potential can be obtained from equation 354 and is

$$\phi_Q = -C \int \frac{d\eta}{\sqrt{(x - \xi)^2 - B^2 \left[(y - \eta)^2 + z^2\right]}} \tag{707}$$

When $B = \sqrt{M^2 - 1}$, ξ and η are the source coordinates and ξ in this case is zero. The expression 707 is to be integrated between limits when the expression under the root becomes zero.

Substituting for brevity reasons

$$\frac{x^2}{B^2} - z^2 = m^2 > 1, \qquad y - \eta = n \tag{708}$$

equation (707) becomes

$$\phi_Q = -\frac{C}{B} \int_{n_1}^{n_2} \frac{dn}{\sqrt{m^2 - n^2}} = -\frac{C}{B} \left[\sin^{-1} \frac{n}{m} \right]_{n_1}^{n_2} \tag{709}$$

where in this case $n_1 = -m$ and $n_2 = +m$. Therefore, $\phi = -\pi C/B$. Thus the potential jumps from zero to the value $-\pi C/B$ on the surface of the wedge defined by $z = \pm x/B$. Consider now a source distribution of constant density C/C_0 extended from $x = 0$ to $x = C_0$ and from $y = -\infty$ to $y = +\infty$ (two-dimensional flat plate). The corresponding potential is given by

$$\phi_Q = -\frac{C}{C_0} \int d\xi \int \frac{d\eta}{\sqrt{(x - \xi)^2 - B^2 \left[(y - \eta)^2 + z^2\right]}}$$

The expression is to be integrated between limits where the expression under the root becomes zero; therefore

$$\phi_Q = -\frac{\pi C}{B}$$

for points whose fore Mach wedge contains the entire source distribution from $x = 0$ to $x = c_0$, while the potential is

$$\phi_Q = -\frac{\pi C}{C_0 B}(x \mp Bz)$$

for points whose fore Mach cone contains only a part of the source distribution (m must be larger than one). From the potential of the source distribution an acceleration potential ϕ can be derived by means of equation 361 which represents a two-dimensional lifting surface.

$$\varphi = h \frac{\partial \Phi_Q}{\partial z} = \pm \frac{\pi C}{C_0} h$$

for points contained between the two wedges,

$$x = Bz \quad \text{and} \quad x - C_0 = Bz,$$

while it is zero for points outside of this zone.

From equation (358) it results that:

$$u_2 = \pm \frac{\pi C}{C_0} \frac{h}{V_1}, \quad C_P = \mp \frac{2\pi C}{C_0} \frac{h}{V_1^2}$$

and

$$C_L = \frac{4\pi C}{C_0} \frac{h}{V_1^2}$$

Therefore

$$\Gamma = \frac{2\pi Ch}{V_1}$$

and from equation (362)

$$\phi_D = \frac{\Gamma}{2\pi C} \int_0^{x_1} \frac{\partial \phi_Q}{\partial z} \, dx \tag{710}$$

The vertical component of the disturbance velocity w_2 can be obtained from the consideration that because the pressure variation occurs in normal direction to the Mach wedges from the leading and trailing edges of the surface, the variation of velocity must occur in the same direction; therefore, the following relation must exist between the two components of the disturbance velocity u_2 and w_2.

$$w_2 = - u_2 \cot \mu = \mp \frac{\pi C}{C_0} \frac{hB}{V_1}$$

This equation is equivalent to equation 578 where h is assumed equal to V_1/B. The angle of attack of the surface is represented by

$$\alpha = \frac{w_2}{V_1} = \frac{\pi C}{C_0} \frac{hB}{V_1^2}.$$

Therefore,

$$C_L = \frac{4\alpha}{B} = 4\alpha \tan \mu$$

and

$$C_D = 4\alpha^2 \tan \mu$$

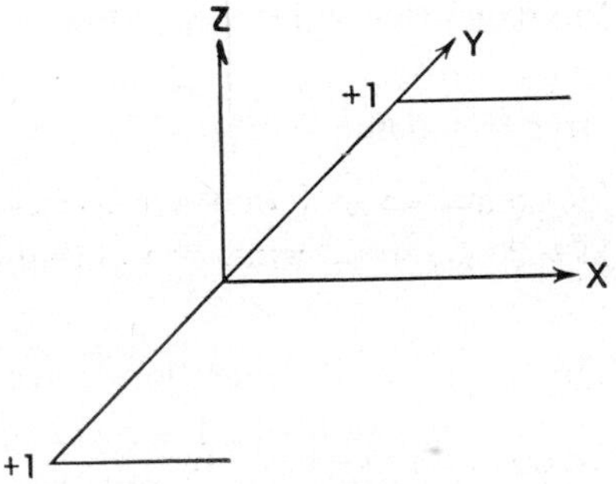

These values of C_L and C_D correspond to the values that can be obtained with the same approximation from equation 103, or 268.

Fig. 235.   *The horseshoe vortex in supersonic flow.*

Consider now a lifting line of length equal to 2, placed along the y-axis in the $z = 0$ plane, from $y = -1$ to $y = 1$ (Figure 235); and suppose that the intensity of the line is constant. If Γ_0 is the circulation of the line (constant) the potential function of the lifting line can be obtained from equation (710) (see Reference 56).

$$\phi_D = \frac{\Gamma_0}{2\pi} \int_{-\infty}^{x_1} \frac{\partial \phi_Q}{\partial z} \, dx \qquad (710a)$$

where ϕ_Q is the potential of a line source corresponding in position to the lifting line of unitary strength. ϕ_Q is given by equation (354) which in this case has the form of equation (707) or (709), where $n_2 = y - 1$ and $n_1 = y + 1$. From equation (709) is obtained

$$- B \frac{d\phi_Q}{dz} = \frac{zn_2}{m^2 \sqrt{m^2 - n_2^2}} - \frac{zn_1}{m^2 \sqrt{m^2 - n_1^2}} \qquad (711)$$

But

$$\int \frac{zn_2 dx}{m^2 \sqrt{m^2 - n_2^2}} = - \frac{B^3}{2} \int \frac{n_2 z d\zeta}{\zeta \sqrt{\zeta^2 + B^2\zeta (z^2 - n_2^2) - B^4\zeta^2 n_2^2}}$$

$$= \frac{B}{2} \tan^{-1} \frac{z^2\Omega - x^2 (y - 1)^2}{2x (y - 1)z \sqrt{\Omega}} \qquad (712)$$

where $\zeta = x^2 - B^2z^2 = B^2m^2$ $\Omega = x^2 - B^2 [(y - 1)^2 + z^2]$

The value $\Omega = 0$ defines the surface of the Mach cone that starts from the ends of the lifting line ($y = \pm 1$, $x = 0$, $z = 0$). Outside this Mach cone the value of the expression given by the integral of equation (712) is imaginary; therefore outside the Mach cone from the ends of the lifting line, the value of the integral must be considered equal to zero. In this case in equation (707) integration must be extended from 0 to x because the zone between $-\infty$ and 0 is outside the Mach cone. For $x = 0$ the integral is equal to $\pi/2$. In the velocity considerations $\pi/2$ can be neglected and the potential of the lifting line, after trigonometric transformations, can be expressed in the form

$$\phi_D = \frac{\Gamma_0}{2\pi} \tan^{-1} \frac{x (y - 1)}{z\sqrt{\Omega}} + \text{similar term for the cone at } (y = -1) \qquad (713)$$

This potential is other than zero only within the two Mach cones arising at the ends of the lifting line, while it is zero in the other remaining space.

For a complete circuit about each of the cone axes ($y = \pm 1$) and ($z = 0$) the arc tangent increases to 2π; therefore at the axis of the cone a vortex of circulation Γ_0 exists. The circulation Γ_0 extended between -1 and $+1$ in the direction of the y-axis, continues in the direction of the x-axis producing two free vortices, and together they produce a *horseshoe vortex* similar to the subsonic vortex.

The velocity components corresponding to the potential are given by

$$u = \frac{\partial \phi_D}{\partial x} = B \frac{\Gamma_0}{2\pi} \frac{(y-1)z}{(x^2 - Bz^2)\sqrt{\Omega}} \tag{714}$$

$$v = \frac{\partial \phi_D}{\partial y} = -\frac{\Gamma_0}{2\pi} \frac{xz}{[z^2 + (y-1)^2]\sqrt{\Omega}} \tag{714a}$$

$$w = \frac{\partial \phi_D}{\partial z} = \frac{\Gamma_0}{\pi} \frac{x(y-1)(\Omega - B^2 z^2)}{[z^2\Omega + (y-1)^2 x^2]\sqrt{\Omega}}. \tag{714b}$$

All three velocity components become infinite at the surface of the cone. On the cone axis, u is equal to zero; v and w become infinite as r becomes zero (r radius from the axis).

In addition to the two Mach cones that arise from the ends, the lifting line generates two plane waves, which enclose a wedge space, and produce the induced wave drag.

In supersonic flow, analysis of the flow phenomena for a finite wing cannot be made by substituting for the wing a lifting line of variable circulation along the span, as has been done in the subsonic case, because singularities at the lifting line position exist which notably complicate the problem of determining the drag depending on the vortex sheet. The difficulty depends on the fact that the lifting line is the locus of the vertices of all the Mach cones that are extended downstream and therefore must be a line with singularities.

In order to overcome the difficulty it is necessary to pass from the concept of a lifting line to the concept of a lifting surface, which requires a more complicated analysis. A lifting surface can be obtained from a doublet surface distribution, the potential of which can be derived from the potential of a source surface distribution.

If, in the plane of the wing ($z = 0$), a source distribution $D(\xi, \eta)$ is considered, the corresponding potential is given by (equation 351)

$$\phi_Q = \iint \frac{D(\xi, \eta)\,d\xi d\eta}{\sqrt{(x-\xi)^2 - B^2(y-\eta)^2 - B^2 z^2}} \tag{715}$$

and a corresponding doublet potential is given by

$$\phi_D = k \frac{\partial}{\partial z} \iint \frac{D(\xi, \eta)d\xi d\eta}{\sqrt{(x-\xi)^2 - B^2(y-\eta)^2 - B^2 z^2}}. \tag{716}$$

But the z component of the velocity corresponding to the source potential of equation (707) is

$$w = \frac{\partial \phi_Q}{\partial z} \tag{717}$$

and (as shown in Chapter 14, equation 577), in the plane $z = 0$, it is proportional to the intensity of the local source distribution, or

$$w_{z=0} (x, y) = \pi D (\xi, \eta). \tag{718}$$

Therefore for $\xi = x$ and $\eta = y$

$$\phi_{D_{z=0}} (x, y) = k\pi D.$$

Then in the plane of the wing ($z = 0$) the velocity component u is given by

$$u_{z=0} = \left(\frac{\partial \phi_D}{\partial x}\right)_{z=0} = k\pi \frac{\partial D (x, y)}{\partial x} = k\pi \frac{\partial D (\xi, \eta)}{\partial \xi} \tag{719}$$

and the pressure is given by

$$\frac{\Delta p}{\frac{1}{2}\rho V^2} = - \frac{4\pi}{V} k \frac{\partial D}{\partial x}. \tag{720}$$

Behind a lifting surface of finite span an induced velocity exists, which can be determined with equations similar to equations (714, 714a, and 714b). Indeed, consider a lifting surface of chord $d\xi$ and span equal to 2, and of constant intensity of circulation γ, placed as the lifting line of Figure 235. The lifting surface is equivalent to an infinite number of infinitesimal lifting lines of circulation γ span equal to 2, placed along the chord $d\xi$. Along the axis of the Mach cone with the apex at the ends of every lifting line a free vortex exists of intensity γ. Because the axes of all Mach cones from the tips of the lifting lines are coincident, along these axes (parallel to the x-axis at $y = \pm 1$) a vortex of circulation $\gamma d\xi$ exists. The two vortices produce an induced velocity behind the lifting surface in the zone inside the Mach cones from the tips, that can be determined with equations (714).

Any lifting surface with variable lift distribution along the span and the chord of the wing can be considered as a superimposition of several elementary lifting surfaces. Every lifting surface has constant intensity of circulation, but the value of the intensity of circulation, the span of the surface, and the position along the chord change from one to another. In this case the free vortices can be determined directly from the lift distribution and, from the distribution of the vortices, the velocity induced at any point behind the wing can be determined with equations (714), (714a), and (714b).

The circulation and the starting point of the free vortices produced by the lifting surface can be directly determined from the pressure distribution. Indeed, the circulation of the free vortex, starting from any point of the wing, is given by the variation of circulation along the span, and can be determined with equation 356, and is

$$\rho_1 V_1 \gamma_{(x,y)} = (\partial P / \partial y)_{(x,y)}.$$

In the zone near the axis of the free vortex the velocity components given by equation (714) behave exactly as in the zone near a vortex filament in incompressible flow; therefore the induced velocity in zones far behind the wing (exactly at $x = \infty$) can be determined with the equation of Biot-Savart for incompressible vortex.

Triangular Wing.

First Approximation for a Very Slender Wing. With the hypothesis of perfect flow, the flow motion around a flat plate of triangular plan form must be of conical type, and therefore the potential function ϕ that defines the flow can be expressed in the form (Chapter 12, page 237)

$$\phi\,(\,x,\,y,\,z) \;=\; xF\left(\frac{y}{x}\,,\,\frac{z}{x}\right). \tag{721}$$

Indeed the velocity components obtained from the potential function must be functions only of the ratio of two spatial coordinates. The velocity components in this case are

$$
\left.
\begin{aligned}
\frac{\partial \phi}{\partial x} &= F - \frac{y}{x}\,\frac{\partial F}{\partial \left(\frac{y}{x}\right)} - \frac{z}{x}\,\frac{\partial F}{\partial \left(\frac{z}{x}\right)}\\[2ex]
\frac{\partial \phi}{\partial y} &= \frac{\partial F}{\partial \left(\frac{y}{x}\right)}\\[2ex]
\frac{\partial \phi}{\partial z} &= \frac{\partial F}{\partial \left(\frac{z}{x}\right)}\,.
\end{aligned}
\right\} \tag{722}
$$

If the auxiliary coordinates

$$\eta = \frac{y}{x} \qquad \text{and} \qquad \xi = \frac{z}{x}$$

are introduced, from equation (722) are obtained

$$
\left.
\begin{aligned}
\frac{\partial^2 \phi}{\partial x^2} &= \frac{1}{x}\left(\eta^2\,\frac{\partial^2 F}{\partial \eta^2} + 2\xi\eta\,\frac{\partial^2 F}{\partial \xi \partial \eta} + \xi^2\,\frac{\partial^2 F}{\partial \xi^2}\right)\\[2ex]
\frac{\partial^2 \phi}{\partial y^2} &= \frac{1}{x}\,\frac{\partial^2 F}{\partial \eta^2}\\[2ex]
\frac{\partial^2 \phi}{\partial z^2} &= \frac{1}{k}\,\frac{\partial^2 F}{\partial \xi^2}
\end{aligned}
\right\} \tag{723}
$$

Using equations (723) the equation of motion in the approximate form (equation 339) becomes (Reference 57)

$$\frac{\partial^2 F}{\partial \eta^2}\left[1 - B^2\eta^2\right] + \frac{\partial^2 F}{\partial \xi^2}\left[1 - B^2\xi^2\right] - 2\xi\eta B^2\,\frac{\partial F}{\partial \eta \partial \xi} = 0 \tag{724}$$

where

$$B = \sqrt{M_1^2 - 1}.$$

If the body is very slender the terms η and ξ at the surface of the wing are very small and for small Mach numbers the square terms $B^2\eta^2$ and $B^2\xi^2$ can be neglected; therefore equation (724) becomes

$$\frac{\partial^2 F}{\partial \eta^2} + \frac{\partial^2 F}{\partial \xi^2} = 0 \qquad (725)$$

which is the Laplace equation for two-dimensional incompressible flow.

Consider now a lifting triangular surface in the plane ($z = 0$) and at an angle of attack α, with plan form symmetrical with respect to the plane zx (Figure 236a). Equation (725) suggests that the expression for the potential function that defines the flow around such a wing must be similar to the expression

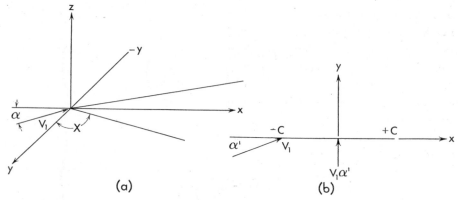

Fig. 236. *The lift in a very slender triangular wing and its similarity to a flat plate in subsonic flow.*

that gives the potential function for a flat plate in incompressible flow. For the flat plate considered (Figure 236b), a symmetrical solution must be obtained; therefore if the vertical velocity component is $V\alpha'$, the potential function has the form (Reference 58)

$$\phi = \pm \ V\alpha' \ \sqrt{c^2 - x^2}.$$

If for the triangular flat plate the vertical component is $V_1\alpha$ the function F can be expressed in the form

$$F = \pm \ V_1\alpha\sqrt{c^2 - \eta^2} \qquad (726)$$

where $\pm c$ is the value of η at the plate edges.

From equations (726) and (722) is obtained

$$u = F - \eta \ \frac{\partial F}{\partial \eta} = V_1\alpha \left(\frac{c^2}{\sqrt{c^2 - \eta^2}} \right). \qquad (727)$$

The difference in pressure between upper and lower surfaces is (equation 381)

$$\frac{\Delta p}{\frac{1}{2}\rho V_1{}^2} = \frac{4u}{V_1} = 4\alpha \, \frac{c^2}{\sqrt{c^2 - \eta^2}} \cdot \tag{728}$$

Because the elemental area of the wing is $ds = x^2 d\eta/2$, and the total area $x^2 c$, the lift coefficient of the wing is (Reference 59)

$$C_L = 2\pi c\alpha. \tag{729}$$

Or, introducing the aspect ratio A of the wing $\left(A = \dfrac{4c^2 x^2}{cx^2} \right)$

$$C_L = \frac{\pi A \alpha}{2} \cdot \tag{729a}$$

Equation (729a) is valid only for wings of very small aspect ratio.

Triangular Wing with Supersonic Leading Edge. In order to determine the lift of a triangular flat plate when the leading edge is outside the Mach cone, the system of source and sink distribution developed in Chapter 14 can be used (the trailing edge is also supersonic).

The pressure distribution on the wing is given by the expression

$$C_p = -\frac{2\phi_{2x}}{V_1} \tag{730}$$

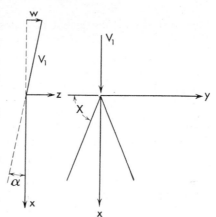

Fig. 237. *The lift of a triangular flat plate with supersonic leading edge.*

where ϕ_{2x} is given by equation (601), Chapter 14, and is

$$\phi_{2x} = -\frac{w}{B\sqrt{1 - n^2}} \tag{731}$$

outside the Mach cone, and

$$\phi_{2x} = -\frac{w}{B\sqrt{1 - n^2}} \left(1 - \frac{2}{\pi} \sin^{-1} \sqrt{\frac{n^2 - \sigma^2}{1 - \sigma^2}} \right) \tag{731a}$$

inside the Mach cone, where (Figure 237)

$$w = V_1\alpha; \quad n = \frac{k}{B}; \quad k = \tan \mathrm{X}; \quad \sigma = \frac{ky}{x}; \quad B = \sqrt{M_1{}^2 - 1}.$$

Therefore the pressure difference between two corresponding points on the upper and lower surface is

$$\Delta C_p = \frac{4\alpha}{B\sqrt{1 - n^2}} \tag{732}$$

outside the Mach cone, and

$$\Delta C_p = \frac{4\alpha}{B\sqrt{1 - n^2}}\left(1 - \frac{2}{\pi}\sin^{-1}\sqrt{\frac{n^2 - \sigma^2}{1 - \sigma^2}}\right) \tag{732a}$$

inside the Mach cone.

(Figure 207 of Chapter 14 shows the pressure distribution along the wing for different values of n; λ in this case is equal to $\pm\alpha$.)

The lift coefficient of the wing can be obtained by performing the following integration:

$$C_L = \frac{4\alpha}{B\sqrt{1 - n^2}}\left(1 - \frac{2}{\pi}\int_0^{+n}\sin^{-1}\sqrt{\frac{n^2 - \sigma^2}{1 - \sigma^2}}\,d\sigma\right). \tag{733}$$

Integrating by parts results in

$$\int_0^{+n}\sin^{-1}\sqrt{\frac{n^2 - \sigma^2}{1 - \sigma^2}}\,d\sigma = \frac{\pi}{2}\left(1 - \sqrt{1 - n^2}\right). \tag{734}$$

Therefore the lift coefficient becomes (Reference 53)

$$C_L = \frac{4\alpha}{\sqrt{M_1^2 - 1}}. \tag{735}$$

The value of C_L given by equation (735) is identical to the value obtained for a two-dimensional wing with no sweepback, when the same approximation is considered, and is independent of the value of the angle of sweepback.

The total induced drag is proportional to the angle of attack because no suction forces exist, and therefore has the form

$$C_{Di} = C_L\alpha = \frac{\sqrt{M_1^2 - 1}}{4}\,C_L^2. \tag{735a}$$

Because the phenomenon is conical and therefore the pressure is constant for σ = constant, the center of pressure is at the 2/3 of the root chord from the apex.

An analogous system can be used for every wing with supersonic trailing edges and leading edges.

Triangular Wing with Subsonic Leading Edges. Determination of the Lift. The lift of a triangular flat plate with the leading edge inside the Mach cone has been determined by using the theory of small disturbances, with several different mathematical treatments (References 57, 60, and 61). A treatment that uses methods familar to aerodynamic theory is that which determines the lift of the wing by using a doublet distribution (Reference 61).

If a source distribution is considered in the plane $z = 0$, the potential function of the source distribution is (equation 573, Chapter 14)

$$\phi_Q = \iint \frac{D\,(\xi,\,\eta)d\xi d\eta}{\sqrt{(x-\xi)^2 - B^2\,(y-\eta)^2 - B^2 z^2}}. \qquad (736)$$

By differentiation of equation (736) a doublet distribution can be obtained. The flow that satisfies the boundary conditions around a triangular wing must be a conical flow; therefore in expression (736) the variable h defined by

$$h = \frac{\eta}{\xi} \qquad (737)$$

can be used in place of the independent variable η. The source distribution $D(\xi,\,\eta)$ considered will have the form

$$D\,(\xi,\,\eta) = \xi f\,(h). \qquad (737a)$$

Therefore equation (736) becomes

$$\phi_Q = \int_{-c}^{+c} f\,(h)dh \int_{0}^{\xi_1} \frac{\xi^2 d\xi}{\sqrt{(x-\xi)^2 - B^2\,(y-h\xi)^2 - B^2 z^2}}. \qquad (738)$$

The limits of the first integral of equation (738) are the origin of the coordinates, which coincides with the vertex of the wing, and the value ξ_1 of ξ, of the last source that can affect the flow at the point $P(x,\,y,\,z)$. The value of ξ_1 is given by the value of ξ that makes the radical of the integrand zero. The limits $-c$ and $+c$ of the second integral are the values of h corresponding to the leading edges of the wing. The wing is in the plane $(z = 0)$, and the plane $(y = 0)$ is a plane of symmetry.

The potential of the doublet is given by

$$\phi_D = \int_{-c}^{+c} f\,(h)dh\,\frac{\partial}{\partial z} \int_{0}^{\xi_1} \frac{\xi^2 d\xi}{\sqrt{(x-\xi)^2 - B^2\,(y-h\xi)^2 - B^2 z^2}}. \qquad (739)$$

The first integral of equation (739) can be evaluated and the derivation can be performed.

For reasons of brevity, assume

$$l = x^2 - B^2\,(y^2 + z^2) = x^2\left[1 - B^2\left(\frac{y^2}{x^2} + \frac{z^2}{x^2}\right)\right]$$

$$m = 2\left(B^2 yh - x\right) = 2x\left(B^2\,\frac{y}{x}\,h - 1\right)$$

$$n = 1 - B^2 h^2 \qquad\qquad\qquad (740)$$

$$\zeta = \frac{-m}{2\sqrt{ln}} = -\frac{\left(B^2\,\dfrac{y}{x}\,h - 1\right)}{\sqrt{\left(1 - B^2 h^2\right)\left[1 - B^2\left(\dfrac{y^2}{x^2} + \dfrac{z^2}{x^2}\right)\right]}}.$$

Then

$$\int_0^{\xi_1} \frac{\xi^2 d\xi}{\sqrt{n\xi^2 + m\xi + l}} = \frac{3m\sqrt{l}}{4n^2} - \frac{3m^2 - 4ln}{8n^2\sqrt{n}} \, \text{ctnh}^{-1} \frac{m}{2\sqrt{ln}}$$

because

$$\sqrt{n\xi_1^2 + m\xi_1 + l} = 0.$$

Therefore

$$\frac{\partial}{\partial z} \int_0^{\xi_1} \frac{\xi^2 d\xi}{\sqrt{n\xi^2 + m\xi + l}} = F = \frac{+zB^2}{n^{3/2}}\left[\frac{\zeta}{1 - \zeta^2} + \text{ctnh}^{-1}\zeta\right] \quad (741)$$

or

$$\phi_D = \int_{-c}^{+c} Ff(h)dh. \quad (742)$$

Because ϕ_D given by equation (742) can be expressed in the form (equations 740 and 741)

$$\phi_D = x \int_{-c}^{+c} F\left(\frac{z}{x}, \frac{y}{x}, \frac{\xi}{\eta}\right) f\left(\frac{\xi}{\eta}\right) d\left(\frac{\xi}{\eta}\right) \quad (743)$$

it represents a conical phenomenon. In order to obtain for every conical boundary condition the corresponding intensity of the source distribution, the function $f(h)$ must be determined.

At the surface of the wing, for y/x between $-c$ and $+c$ the velocity component in the z direction, w, must be

$$w_{z=0} = V_1\alpha = \left(\frac{\partial\phi_D}{\partial z}\right)_{z=0} \quad (744)$$

where α is the angle of attack and V_1 is the undisturbed velocity. From equation (742) is obtained

$$w_{z=0} = \int_{-c}^{+c} \left(\frac{\partial F}{\partial z}\right)_{z=0} f(h)dh$$

or using equations (741) and (740),

$$w_{z=0} = \frac{B^2}{(1 - B^2h^2)^{3/2}} \int_{-c}^{+c} \left(\frac{\zeta}{1 - \zeta^2} + \text{ctnh}^{-1}\zeta\right)_{z=0} f(h)dh. \quad (745)$$

Because the phenomenon is conical

$$\frac{\partial w}{\partial \left(\frac{y}{x}\right)} = 0. \quad (746)$$

Using equations (745) and (740) is obtained

$$-\frac{1}{2}\frac{\partial w}{\partial\left(\dfrac{y}{x}\right)} = \int_{-c}^{+c}\frac{f(h)\sqrt{1 - B^2\left(\dfrac{y}{x}\right)^2}}{\left(h - \dfrac{y}{x}\right)^3}\,dh$$

$$= \sqrt{1 - B^2\left(\frac{y}{x}\right)^2}\int_{-c}^{+c}\frac{f(h)\,dh}{\left(h - \dfrac{y}{x}\right)^3} = 0. \qquad (747)$$

Equation (747) is of the same form as the integral equation obtained when the incompressible flow normal to a two-dimensional flat plate is constructed by use of a doublet distribution. The solution obtained in the incompressible flow case can therefore suggest an expression for the function $f(h)$, that will satisfy the boundary conditions (Reference 58).

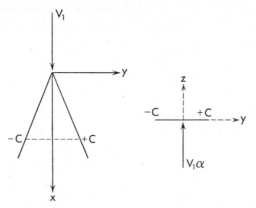

Fig. 238. *The lift of a triangular flat plate with subsonic leading edge.*

In subsonic two-dimensional incompressible flow, the potential of a doublet placed in the plane ($z = 0$) along the y-axis is given by (Figure 238)

$$\phi_D = \frac{z}{(y - \eta)^2 + z^2}. \qquad (748)$$

The corresponding induced velocity in the z direction, w, in the plane ($z = 0$) is given by

$$w_{(z = 0)} = \frac{1}{(y - \eta)^2}. \qquad (749)$$

If $g(\eta)$ is the doublet distribution along the y-axis from $-c$ to $+c$ that satisfies the boundary condition, it follows that

$$w_{z=0} = \int_{-c}^{+c} \frac{g(\eta)d\eta}{(y - \eta)^2} . \tag{750}$$

Along the surface of the plate the vertical velocity component must be constant; therefore

$$-\frac{1}{2}\frac{\partial w}{\partial y} = 0 = \int_{-c}^{+c} \frac{g(\eta)d\eta}{(y - \eta)^3} . \tag{751}$$

Equation (751) is of the same type as equation (747); therefore it suggests for the doublet distribution $f(h)$ an expression of the same type as the doublet distribution $g(\eta)$. The distribution $g(\eta)$ must give a symmetrical solution with respect to the z-axis because a symmetrical solution must be expected for the triangular wing, and therefore is the symmetrical distribution without circulation that must be considered.

Now the doublet distribution for the flat plate is equivalent to the difference of potential between the upper and lower surfaces of the flat plate which, for incompressible flow without circulation, is given by the following expression:

$$\Delta\phi = 2V_1\alpha\sqrt{c^2 - y^2}. \tag{752}$$

Therefore for the function $f(h)$ an expression of the form

$$f(h) = I\sqrt{c^2 - h^2} \tag{753}$$

must be considered.

Equation (753) is a physical solution of the problem, as can be verified by substituting equation (753) in equation (745).

The value of the constant I must be obtained from equation (745). The integration of equation (745) is involved, but can be accomplished by using integrations by parts.

In order to obtain the value of the intensity I the value of w from equation (745) must be calculated. The calculation can be made for the lines $(z = 0)$ and $(y = 0)$.

Performing the integration gives

$$w = \pi I E \left(\sqrt{1 - B^2c^2} \right) = V_1\alpha \tag{754}$$

where $E \sqrt{1 - B^2c^2}$ is the complete elliptic integral of the second kind, with the parameter

$$k = \sin\alpha = \sqrt{1 - B^2c^2}. \tag{755}$$

The value of the elliptic integral is available in tables as a function of the parameter k (see Reference 62).

Equation (754) permits determination of the intensity of the doublet distribution as a function of the angle of incidence of the wing.

In order to determine the lift of the wing, the velocity component u must be determined; indeed

$$\frac{2\Delta p}{\frac{1}{2}\rho_1 V_1^2} = + \frac{4u}{V_1}. \tag{756}$$

The u component of the induced velocity can be determined by using equation (719). The source distribution is given by equation (737a)

$$D = \xi f(h) = \xi I \sqrt{c^2 - h^2} = \frac{\xi V_1 \alpha \sqrt{c^2 - h^2}}{\pi E \left(\sqrt{1 - B^2 c^2}\right)}. \tag{757}$$

Therefore

$$\frac{2\Delta p}{\frac{1}{2}\rho V^2} = \frac{4\alpha c^2}{\sqrt{c^2 - h^2}\, E\left(\sqrt{1 - c^2 B^2}\right)}. \tag{758}$$

By integration of $(2\Delta p\, dh)/\frac{1}{2}\rho V^2$ from $-c$ to $+c$ the value of the lift coefficient is obtained as

$$C_L = \frac{1}{2c} \int_{-c}^{+c} \frac{2\Delta p}{\frac{1}{2}\rho V^2}\, dh = \frac{2\pi c\alpha}{E\sqrt{(1 - B^2 c^2)}}. \tag{759}$$

Equation (759) shows that the lift curve slope is a function only of the parameters B and c.

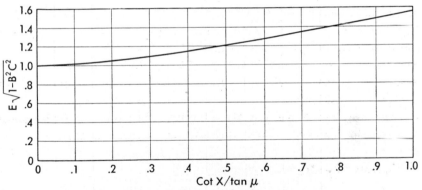

Fig. 239. *The value of the function E versus* cot $X/\tan \mu$.

The value of the elliptical integral E is shown in Figure 239 as a function of the value Bc. The value Bc corresponds to (cot $X/\tan \mu$) where $(\pi/2 - X)$ is the semi-angle at the apex of the triangular wing, and μ is the Mach angle.

In equation (759) if Bc approaches zero, $E(\sqrt{1 - B^2 c^2})$ approaches unity, and the lift curve slope becomes

$$\frac{dC_L}{d\alpha} = 2\pi c$$

which corresponds to the value of equation (729). If Bc is equal to one $(X = \pi/2 - \mu)$, E is equal to $\pi/2$, c is equal to $1/(\sqrt{M_1^2 - 1})$, and C_L becomes

$$C_L = \frac{4\alpha}{\sqrt{M_1^2 - 1}} \qquad (760)$$

which is the value for the two-dimensional case or for supersonic leading edge as was shown on page 362.

The ratio of the lift of the triangular wing C_{L_A} to the lift of the two-dimensional wing C_{L_∞} (equation 760) is

$$\frac{C_{L_A}}{C_{L_\infty}} = \frac{\pi Bc}{2E\sqrt{1 - B^2 c^2}} \cdot \qquad (761)$$

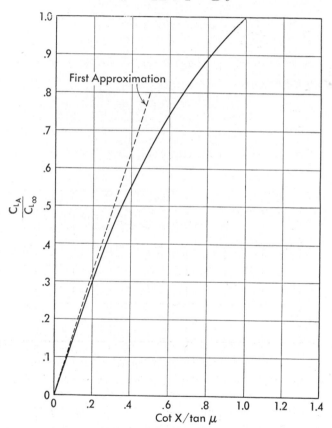

Fig. 240. *The ratio of the lift coefficient of the triangular wing to the lift coefficient of the two-dimensional wing as a function of* cot $X/\tan \mu$ (*from Reference 61*).

The ratio is a function only of $Bc = (\cot X/\tan \mu)$. The value of C_{L_A}/C_{L_∞} as a function of $(\cot X/\tan \mu)$ is shown in Figure 240.

In Figure 241 the lift curve slope for two wings as a function of the stream Mach number is shown. When Bc is equal to one, the lift curve slope is equal to the two-dimensional value.

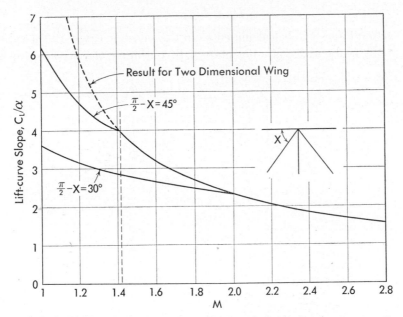

Fig. 241. *Lift-curve slope as a function of Mach number for two swept-back wings* $X = 60°$ *and* $X = 45°$ *(from Reference 61).*

From the pressure distribution obtained for the triangular wing the lift for every type of wing with supersonic trailing edge, derived from the triangular wing with subsonic or supersonic leading edges, can be obtained. For example, lift or wings such as those shown in Figure 242 can be determined.

Triangular Wing with Subsonic Leading Edge. Determination of the Induced Drag. As was discussed on page 351, when the leading edge of the wing is subsonic, and is sharp, a vortex separation occurs in the zone of the leading edge. The separation can be eliminated by using a round leading edge. In this way a suction force exists at the leading edge that deviates the resultant of the pressure from the direction normal to the chord, and reduces the drag due to lift. The existence of suction forces in the triangular wing with subsonic leading edge increases somewhat the value of the optimum L/D of the wing. The maximum value of the suction force that can be expected is obtained when the suction force is extended to the entire leading edge. The value of this maximum can be calculated.

Without suction force

$$D_i = L\alpha \tag{762}$$

while if F is the suction force at the leading edge,

$$D_i = L\alpha - F. \tag{763}$$

The suction forces can be calculated as in the subsonic case. In the subsonic case at the leading edge of a flat plate a discontinuity of velocity component

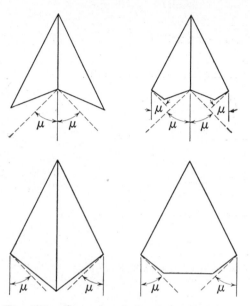

Fig. 242. *Examples of plan forms that can be analyzed by the theory of triangular wing.*

in the direction of the chord of the plate occurs. The discontinuity produces a vortex. If the circulation of the vortex at the leading edge is called Γ and the flow is compressible flow, the value of Γ can be expressed in the form (Reference 58)

$$\Gamma_{d\to 0} = \frac{2G}{\sqrt{1 - M_1^2}\sqrt{d}} \tag{764}$$

when d is the distance in the direction normal to the leading edge, G is a constant, and $\sqrt{1 - M_1^2}$ is the compressibility factor (M_1 is the Mach number corresponding to the component of the velocity normal to the leading edge.)

The suction force produced by the vortex Γ, is given by

$$F_n = \frac{\rho\pi G^2}{\sqrt{1 - M_1^2}}. \tag{765}$$

The velocity at the leading edge of the plate is given by

$$u_{d \to 0} = \frac{G}{\sqrt{1 - M_1{}^2}\sqrt{d}} \cdot \qquad (766)$$

For the triangular wing the equation of the flat plate can be used, because locally the phenomenon is the same as two-dimensional. The component of the velocity along the wing in the direction normal to the leading edge is (Figure 243)

$$U = u \cos X - v \sin X = \frac{uc - v}{\sqrt{1 + c^2}} \qquad (767)$$

because $c = \cot X$, but from equation (757),

$$u = \pi \frac{\partial D}{\partial x} = \pm \frac{Ic^2\pi}{\sqrt{c^2 - \left(\dfrac{y}{x}\right)^2}} \qquad (768)$$

$$v = \pi \frac{\partial D}{\partial y} = \mp \frac{I\pi\dfrac{y}{x}}{\sqrt{c^2 - \left(\dfrac{y}{x}\right)^2}} \cdot \qquad (768a)$$

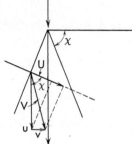

Fig. 243. *Determination of the suction force.*

Therefore

$$U = \pm \frac{cI\pi\sqrt{1 + c^2}}{\sqrt{c^2 - \left(\dfrac{y}{x}\right)^2}} = \pm \frac{I\pi\sqrt{\dfrac{cr}{2}}}{\sqrt{d}} \qquad (768b)$$

where $r = x\sqrt{1 + c^2}$ is the distance of a point on the leading edge from the apex.

The suction force for an element dr of the leading edge in the direction normal to the leading edge from equations (765) and (766) is

$$\frac{dF_n}{dr} = \frac{\rho\pi cr I^2\pi^2\sqrt{1 - M_n{}^2}}{2} \cdot \qquad (769)$$

If the root chord of the wing is indicated by C_0, the value of F_n can be obtained by integrating equation (769) from r equal to zero to r equal to $C_0\sqrt{1 + c^2}$; therefore

$$F_n = \frac{\rho\pi^3 I^2 C_0{}^2 c\,(1 + c^2)\sqrt{1 - M_n{}^2}}{4} \cdot \qquad (770)$$

The component F in the flight direction is given by

$$F = 2F_n \cos X = \frac{\rho\pi^3 c^2\sqrt{1 + c^2}\,C_0{}^2 I^2\sqrt{1 - M_n{}^2}}{2} \cdot \qquad (771)$$

Substituting in equation (771) the value of I given by equation (754), and for $\sqrt{1 - M_n^2}$ the corresponding expression

$$\sqrt{1 - M_n^2} = \frac{\sqrt{1 - B^2 c^2}}{\sqrt{1 + c^2}} \cdot \tag{772}$$

The induced coefficient becomes

$$C_D = \frac{L\alpha - F}{\frac{1}{2} \rho_1 V_1^2 S} = \frac{C_L^2}{\pi A}\left[2E\left(\sqrt{1 - B^2 c^2}\right) - \sqrt{1 - B^2 c^2} \right] \tag{773}$$

where A is the aspect ratio of the wing and the term $C_L^2/\pi A \sqrt{1 - B^2 c^2}$ represents the suction forces. When $Bc = 1$ or when the leading edge becomes sonic, the suction forces disappear and the induced drag becomes $[E(0) = \pi/2]$

$$C_{D_i} = \frac{C_L^2}{A} \tag{774}$$

but $A = 4 \cot X = 4 \tan \mu = \dfrac{4}{\sqrt{M_1^2 - 1}} \cdot$

Therefore equation (774) is equivalent to equation (735a).

If Bc approaches zero, because $E(1)$ is equal to one, the induced drag becomes

$$C_{D_{i Bc \to 0}} = \frac{C_L^2}{\pi A} \tag{775}$$

which is the value found for very slender wings and is the value obtained for incompressible flow.

Rectangular Wing. The aerodynamic phenomena for a wing with rectangular plan form are different from the phenomena for a two-dimensional wing only in the zone of the tips contained within the Mach cones, having their apexes at the ends of the leading edge (see Chapter 14, page 293). In this zone the effect of the tips changes the flow from two-dimensional, and the variation is such that, at the tips, conical flow exists. (Indeed, for the tips of a rectangular wing the same considerations made in Chapter 12, page 236, can be applied.)

Determination of the flow field at the tips of the wing is possible with the approximation of the small-disturbances theory, and various different mathematical treatments have been developed (References 56 and 57). Here the treatment that uses the scheme of doublet distribution will be given (Reference 56).

In the second paragraph of this chapter it was shown that in supersonic flow, doublet distributions can be substituted for lifting surfaces. In a rectangular wing (Figure 244) the lift must go to zero at the tip of the wing (lines AB and A_1B_1), while it must have a constant value in the zone between the two end Mach cones (zone ACC_1A_1). In the zones ABC and $A_1B_1C_1$, the phenomenon must be conical; therefore the lift distribution can be considered as obtained by superimposition of an infinite number of constant and infinitesimal lift distributions of trapezoidal plan form (ADA_1D_1) with different values of the angle X. The angle X that defines the plan form of the trapezoidal infinitesimal wing must have values between $\pi/2$ and $(\pi/2 - \mu)$, where μ is the Mach angle. In this way, in the zone between the two Mach cones (zone ACC_1A_1), a constant lift distribution is obtained, while within the Mach cones the lift remains constant along every straight line from the apexes A and A_1 of the cones, and therefore the phenomenon is conical.

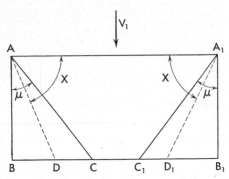

Fig. 244. *The rectangular flat plate.*

The problem of determining the lift distribution of the rectangular wing is transformed into the problem of determining the intensity of the lift distribution of the trapezoidal wings as a function of the angle X, in order to satisfy the boundary conditions. The boundary conditions are satisfied if the resultant of the induced velocities produced by the infinitesimal lift distribution is such that the flow is tangent to the wing.

Now the induced velocity produced by a trapezoidal wing with constant lift distribution can be determined.

Trapezoidal Lift Distribution of Constant Intensity. If a trapezoidal wing, of angle X and lift intensity γ_0 constant on the entire surface is analyzed (Figure 245), the velocity induced by every strip, $d\xi$, of the surface can be calculated by using equation (714b). If the strip considered is placed along the axis ($\xi = 0$) from -1 to $+1$, the vertical component of the induced velocity (downwash) produced by the lifting element $\gamma_0 \, d\xi$ in the plane ($z = 0$), is given by

$$dw = -\frac{\gamma_0}{2\pi} d\xi \frac{\sqrt{x^2 - B^2(y-1)^2}}{x(1-y)} \tag{776}$$

while for an element of surface extended from $-\eta$ to $+\eta$ at the distance ξ from the leading edge, the downwash is given by

$$dw = -\frac{\gamma_0}{2\pi} d\xi \frac{\sqrt{(x-\xi)^2 - B^2(y-\eta)^2}}{(x-\xi)(\eta-y)}. \tag{777}$$

The downwash is zero outside of the Mach cone with apex at the ends of the element.

The velocity induced by the entire distribution at a point $P(x, y, 0)$ is

$$w = -\frac{\gamma_0}{2\pi} \int_{\xi=0}^{\xi=\xi^*} \frac{\sqrt{(x-\xi)^2 - B^2 (y-\eta)^2}}{(x-\xi)(\eta-y)} \, d\xi. \tag{778}$$

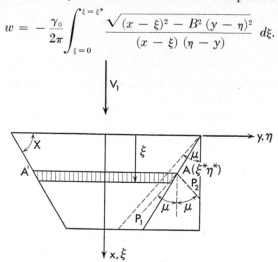

Fig. 245. *The induction due to a trapezoidal circulation distribution of constant intensity.*

The upper limit ξ^* corresponds to the value of ξ of the last strip AA', of surface that can affect the point $P(x, y, 0)$ (Figure 245). Now the coordinates ξ^*, η^*, of the point A are given by the following expression:

$$\frac{\eta^* - y}{x - \xi^*} = \tan \mu = \pm \frac{1}{B} \tag{779}$$

or

$$\frac{\eta^* - y}{x - \xi^*} B = \pm 1 \tag{779a}$$

and

$$\frac{1 - \eta^*}{\xi^*} = \cot X. \tag{780}$$

The plus-or-minus sign in equation (779) corresponds to the two possible positions of the point P with respect to the point A, the position P_1, and the position P_2.

Equation (778) can be transformed by introducing the following parameters:

$$\tau = B \frac{\eta - y}{x - \xi} \tag{781}$$

$$h = B \frac{1 - y}{x} \tag{781a}$$

$$\Theta = \frac{1}{n} = B \cot X = B \frac{1 - \eta}{\xi} \tag{781b}$$

because η is the ordinate of the end points of the lifting elements. In this case the lower limit of the integral, $\xi = 0$, corresponds to $\eta = 1$, and

$$\tau_1 = B \frac{1 - y}{x} = h$$

while the upper limit, $\xi = \xi^*$, corresponds to $\tau = \pm 1$ (equation 779). But

$$d\tau = + B \frac{d\eta}{x - \xi} + B \frac{\eta - y}{(x - \xi)^2} d\xi$$

or because

$$B \left(\frac{1 - \eta}{\xi} \right) = \Theta = B \cot X = \text{constant}$$

$$d\tau = + \frac{d\xi}{x - \xi} (\tau - \Theta).$$

Therefore equation (778) becomes

$$w = - \frac{\gamma_0}{2\pi} B \int_{\tau = h}^{\tau = \pm 1} \frac{\sqrt{1 - \tau^2}}{\tau} \frac{d\tau}{\tau - \Theta}. \tag{782}$$

For equation (782) three cases must be considered (Figure 246). The first case is when the point P is on the lifting surface ($P = P_1$),

$$h > \Theta$$

and in the upper limit the plus sign must be considered.

The second case is when $P = P_2$,

$$0 < h < \Theta$$

or

$$0 < \frac{1 - y}{x} < \frac{1 - \eta}{\xi}.$$

The point P is outside the lifting surface but

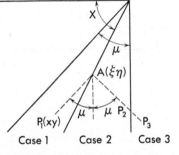

Fig. 246. *The three possible positions of the point P in which the induction must be determined.*

is in the rectangular wing. In this case the integration in equation (782) must be extended from $\tau = h$ to $\tau = -1$ or from

$$B \frac{\eta - y}{x - \xi} = B \frac{1 - y}{x} > 0$$

to

$$B \left(\frac{\eta - y}{x - \xi} \right) = - 1.$$

In this case a position must be considered in which $\tau = 0$. For $\tau = 0$ the integral of equation (782) has a singularity and the value of w must be determined by using the expression

$$w = -\frac{\gamma_0}{2\pi} B \lim_{e \to 0} \left[\int_{\tau=h}^{\tau=e} \frac{\sqrt{1-\tau^2}}{\tau} \frac{d\tau}{\tau-\theta} + \int_{\tau=-e}^{\tau=-1} \frac{\sqrt{1-\tau^2}}{\tau} \frac{d\tau}{\tau-\theta} \right]. \quad (782a)$$

The third case is when the point is outside the rectangular wing, $h < 0$ ($P = P_3$). The upper limit in this case is minus, and τ is always negative.

The integral

$$\int_h^{\pm 1} \frac{\sqrt{1-\tau^2}}{\tau} \frac{d\tau}{\tau-\theta} = F(h, \theta) \quad (783)$$

can be calculated by elementary methods.

If it is assumed that

$$\sqrt{1-\tau^2} = r\tau - 1 \quad (784)$$

and

$$\psi = \frac{1+\sqrt{1-h^2}}{h} \quad (784a)$$

$F(h, \theta)$ becomes

$$F(h, \theta) = \int_{r=1}^{r=\psi} \frac{(1-r^2)^2 dr}{r(1+r^2)[2r-\theta(1+r^2)]} \quad (785)$$

but

$$\frac{(1-r^2)^2}{r(1+r^2)[2r-\theta(1+r^2)]} = -\frac{2}{1+r^2} - \frac{1}{\theta r}$$
$$+ \frac{\sqrt{1-\theta^2}}{\theta} \left(\frac{1}{r-r_2} - \frac{1}{r-r_1} \right) \quad (786)$$

where

$$r_{1,2} = \frac{1 \pm \sqrt{1-\theta^2}}{\theta}. \quad (787)$$

Therefore when $h > \theta$ for the function $F(h, \theta)$, the following expression is obtained:

$$F(h,\theta) = \frac{\pi}{2} - 2\tan^{-1}\psi - \frac{\log\psi}{\theta}$$
$$+ \frac{\sqrt{1-\theta^2}}{\theta} \log\left[\frac{1+\sqrt{1-\theta^2}}{\theta} \frac{\psi\theta-1+\sqrt{1-\theta^2}}{1-\psi\theta+\sqrt{1-\theta^2}} \right] \quad (788)$$

When the point P considered is outside the trapezoidal lifting surface, but in the rectangular wing, if the expression

$$m = \frac{1+\sqrt{1-e^2}}{e}$$

is introduced, the first integral of equation (782a) becomes

$$\int_{+h}^{+e} \frac{\sqrt{1-\tau^2}}{\tau} \frac{d\tau}{\tau - \Theta} = + 2 \tan^{-1} m - 2 \tan^{-1} \psi + \frac{\log m}{\Theta} - \frac{\log \psi}{\Theta}$$

$$+ \frac{\sqrt{1-\Theta^2}}{\Theta} \log \frac{m\Theta - 1 - \sqrt{1-\Theta^2}}{m\Theta - 1 + \sqrt{1-\Theta^2}} \frac{\Theta\psi - 1 + \sqrt{1-\Theta^2}}{\Theta\psi - 1 - \sqrt{1-\Theta^2}}$$

and the second integral becomes

$$\int_{-e}^{-1} \frac{\sqrt{1-\tau^2}}{\tau} \frac{d\tau}{\tau - \Theta} = - \frac{\pi}{2} + 2 \tan^{-1} m - \frac{\log m}{\Theta}$$

$$+ \frac{\sqrt{1-\Theta^2}}{\Theta} \log \frac{m\Theta + 1 - \sqrt{1-\Theta^2}}{m\Theta + 1 + \sqrt{1-\Theta^2}} .$$

When $e \to 0$, $m \to \infty$; therefore the function $F(h, \Theta)$ has the form

$$F(h, \Theta) = \frac{3}{2} \pi - 2 \tan^{-1} \psi - \frac{\log \psi}{\Theta}$$

$$+ \frac{\sqrt{1-\Theta^2}}{\Theta} \log \frac{1 + \sqrt{1-\Theta^2}}{\Theta} \frac{\Theta\psi - 1 + \sqrt{1-\Theta^2}}{\Theta\psi - 1 - \sqrt{1-\Theta^2}} . \quad (788a)$$

Lift Distribution for a Rectangular Wing. For a rectangular wing, in the central zone contained between the two Mach the cones with their apex at the ends of the leading edge, a constant induced velocity exists, due to the plane waves at the leading edge.

With the approximation of the small-disturbances theory, the value of the vertical component of the induced velocity is given by

$$w_{\text{waves}} = - \alpha_0 V_1 = - \frac{1}{2} \frac{\Gamma_0}{\tan \mu} . \quad (789)$$

Indeed, the difference in pressure between upper and lower surfaces is given by (equation 355)

$$p_u - p_l = \Delta p = \rho_1 V_1 \Gamma_0 \quad (790)$$

and from equation (103) is obtained

$$p_u - p_l = 2\rho_1 V_1^2 \alpha_0 \tan \mu. \quad (790a)$$

Equation (789) gives the value of the intensity of circulation (constant) that exists in the central part of the wing.

At the ends of the wing the circulation must be zero, and in the zone of Mach cones at the tips the intensity of circulation can be expressed in the form

$$\Gamma(h) = \Gamma_0 f(h) \quad (791)$$

because the phenomenon is conical.

In the zone of the tips a vortex distribution in the direction of the x-axis exists which produces an induced vertical velocity w_n; therefore the boundary conditions at the tips can be written in the form

$$\alpha_0 = \alpha\,(h) - \frac{w_n}{V_1} \tag{792}$$

where

$$\alpha\,(h) = \frac{1}{2}\,\frac{\Gamma(h)}{V_1 \tan \mu}. \tag{793}$$

The variation of circulation intensity from the zone h to the zone $(h + dh)$ is given by

$$d\Gamma(h) = \Gamma_0 f'(h)dh. \tag{794}$$

Therefore it is possible to assume that the circulation distribution of the wing is obtained by superimposition of an infinite number of trapezoidal circulation distributions. The intensity of the distribution is such that, for a value of Θ equal to the h considered in (794), it must be

$$\Gamma\,(\Theta) = \Gamma_0 f'\,(h) = \Gamma_0 f'\,(\Theta) \tag{795}$$

The velocity induced at every point $P(x, y, 0)$ inside the Mach cone by the circulation distribution of intensity as in equation (795) is given by (equations 782 and 783)

$$dw\,(h) = BF\,(h, \Theta)\,\frac{\Gamma_0 f'\,(\Theta)d\Theta}{2\pi}. \tag{796}$$

Therefore the induced velocity along every line ($h = $ constant) is given by

$$w\,(h) = -\,\frac{\Gamma_0}{2\pi \tan \mu} \int_{\Theta=0}^{\Theta=1} F\,(h\Theta) f'(\Theta)d\Theta. \tag{797}$$

Substituting in equation (792) equations (789), (791), and (797), the boundary conditions can be expressed in the form

$$f\,(h) + \frac{1}{\pi} \int_{\Theta=0}^{\Theta=1} f'\,(\Theta)F(\Theta, h)d\Theta = 1. \tag{798}$$

The function $F(h, \Theta)$ is given by equation (782) and presents a singularity for $h = \Theta$ (an infinity occurs in the value within integral for the condition $h = \Theta$). Therefore equation (798) must be determined by using the expression

$$f\,(h) + \frac{1}{\pi} \lim_{\epsilon \to 0} \left[\int_{\Theta=0}^{\Theta=h-\epsilon} f'\,(\Theta)F(h, \Theta)d\Theta \right.$$

$$\left. + \int_{\Theta=h+\epsilon}^{\Theta=1} f'\,(\Theta)f(h, \Theta)d\Theta \right] = 1. \tag{799}$$

Differentiation with respect to h gives

$$f'(h) + \frac{1}{\pi}\left[f'(h)F_1(h, h) + \int_{\Theta=0}^{\Theta=h} f'\Theta\, \frac{\partial F(h, \Theta)}{\partial h}\, d\Theta - f'(h)F_2(h, h) \right.$$

$$\left. + \int_{\Theta=h}^{\Theta=1} f'\Theta\, \frac{\partial F(h\,\Theta)}{\partial h}\, d\Theta \right] = 0. \qquad (800)$$

In equation (800) the term $F_1(h, h)$ is the principal value of equation (788) for Θ equal to h, and the term $F_2(h, h)$ is the principal value of expression (788a) for Θ equal to h; therefore the expression

$$\frac{1}{\pi} f'(h) \left[F_1(h, h) - F_2(h, h) \right]$$

can be obtained from the value of the limit of the difference of expressions (788) and (788a) for $\Theta \to h$. The limit gives for the expression the value of $-\pi$; therefore equation (800) becomes

$$\int_{\Theta=0}^{\Theta=1} f'(\Theta)\, \frac{\partial F(\Theta, h)}{\partial h}\, d\Theta = 0. \qquad (801)$$

After differentiation within the integral, equation (801) becomes

$$\frac{\sqrt{1 - h^2}}{h} \int_{\Theta=0}^{\Theta=1} \frac{f'(\Theta)}{h - \Theta}\, d\Theta = 0 \qquad (802)$$

or

$$\int_{\Theta=0}^{\Theta=1} \frac{f'(\Theta)}{h - \Theta}\, d\Theta = 0. \qquad (803)$$

For equation (803) the following solution can be found:

$$f(\Theta) = \frac{1}{\pi} \cos^{-1}(1 - 2\Theta). \qquad (804)$$

Lift, Drag, and Moment of the Rectangular Wing. The lift of the rectangular wing can be considered as composed of the lift of the central zone, between the two end Mach cones, and of the lift of the surface contained inside the Mach cones. If A is the aspect ratio, and S the surface of the wing, the first part of the lift is given by

$$L_1 = \rho_1 V_1 \Gamma_0 S \left(1 - \frac{\tan \mu}{A} \right). \qquad (805)$$

The lift of the second part is given by

$$L_2 = \rho_1 V_1 \frac{S}{A} \tan \mu \int_{\Theta=0}^{\Theta=1} \Gamma(\Theta) \, d\Theta = \tan \mu \, \rho_1 V_1 \frac{S}{A} \Gamma_0 \int_{\Theta=0}^{\Theta=1} f(\Theta) \, d\Theta.$$

Because

$$\int_0^1 f(\Theta) \, d\Theta = \frac{1}{2}$$

the total lift is

$$L = \rho_1 V_1 \Gamma_0 S \left(1 - \frac{1}{2} \frac{\tan \mu}{A} \right) \tag{806}$$

and

$$C_L = 4\alpha_0 \tan \mu \left(1 - \frac{1}{2} \frac{\tan \mu}{A} \right). \tag{807}$$

Because the lift coefficient of the infinite wing $C_{L\infty}$ is, with the approximation accepted,

$$C_{L\infty} = 4\alpha_0 \tan \mu$$

the lift coefficient of the rectangular wing can be expressed in the form

$$C_L = C_{L\infty} \left[1 - \frac{1}{2} \frac{\tan \mu}{A} \right]. \tag{808}$$

The drag of the wing also can be divided in two parts: the drag of the central zone of the wing and the drag of the tips.

The drag of the central zone can be determined with the two-dimensional theory and is

$$D_1 = \alpha_0 L = \frac{\rho_1}{2} \Gamma_0^2 \frac{S}{\tan \mu} \left(1 - \frac{\tan \mu}{A} \right). \tag{809}$$

The wave drag of the tips is given by (equation 793)

$$D_2 = 2\rho_1 \int_0^1 \Gamma \frac{\Gamma}{2 \tan \mu} \, dS \tag{810}$$

because $\Gamma/(2 \tan \mu)$ is the induced downwash velocity. The elemental triangular surface can be expressed in the form

$$dS = \tan \mu \frac{S}{2A} \, d\Theta \tag{811}$$

and

$$\Gamma = \Gamma_0 f(\Theta) \tag{812}$$

Therefore the wave drag of the tips is

$$D_2 = \frac{S}{A} \frac{\rho_1}{2} \Gamma_0^2 \int_0^1 \left[f(\Theta) \right]^2 d\Theta \qquad (813)$$

At the tips of the wing a free vortex distribution exists that also produces an induced drag, D_3. This part of the drag can be expressed in the form

$$D_3 = 2\rho \int_0^1 \Gamma w_n dS. \qquad (814)$$

But

$$w_n = \frac{1}{2} \frac{\Gamma_0}{\tan \mu} \left[1 - f(\Theta) \right]. \qquad (815)$$

Therefore the total drag is given by

$$D = D_1 + D_2 + D_3 = \frac{\rho}{2} \Gamma_0^2 \frac{S}{\tan \mu} \left[1 - \frac{1}{2} \frac{\tan \mu}{A} \right] \qquad (816)$$

and

$$C_D = 4\alpha_0^2 \tan \mu \left[1 - \frac{1}{2} \frac{\tan \mu}{A} \right] = \frac{C_L^2}{4 \tan \mu \left(1 - \frac{1}{2} \frac{\tan \mu}{A} \right)} \qquad (817)$$

If the lift coefficient is constant, the drag increases when the aspect ratio of the wing decreases.

Using the value of the drag, C_{D_∞}, of an infinite wing for the same lift coefficient, equation (817) can be written in the form

$$C_D = C_{D_\infty} \frac{1}{1 - \frac{1}{2} \frac{\tan \mu}{A}}. \qquad (818)$$

If the axis of reference is at the leading edge, the moment of the wing is

$$m = 2\rho V_1^2 \alpha_0 Sc \left[\frac{1}{2} - \frac{1}{3} \frac{\tan \mu}{A} \right] \tan \mu \qquad (819)$$

where c is the chord of the wing; therefore

$$C_m = - 4\alpha_0 \tan \mu \left[\frac{1}{2} - \frac{1}{3} \frac{\tan \mu}{A} \right] = C_L \frac{A - 2/3 \tan \mu}{2A - \tan \mu}. \qquad (820)$$

Equations (808), (817), and (820) are valid until the aspect ratio of the wing becomes so small that the Mach cones at the tips overlap on the surface of the wing.

When a zone of the wing exists that is inside both Mach cones from the ends of the leading edge, equations (808), (817), and (820) are no longer valid, but the flow field and the pressure distribution can still be determined with the same system. Indeed, past the tip of the wing a flow field has been found that satisfies the boundary conditions, and the boundary conditions and law of motion are still satisfied if the two flow fields of the tips are superimposed, because the approximate form of the motion is used.

The pressure coefficient in the zone in which the two Mach cones overlap is given by

$$C_p = \frac{2\Gamma(h)}{V_1} \qquad (821)$$

but from equations (792) and (793)

$$\frac{1}{2}\frac{\Gamma(h)}{V_1 \tan \mu} = \alpha(h) = \alpha_0 - \frac{w_{h_1}}{V_1} - \frac{w_{h_2}}{V_1} \qquad (822)$$

where w_{h_1} is the vertical velocity component induced by one of the tips and w_{h_2} is the vertical velocity component induced by the other tip. (The values of h_1 and h_2 are the values of h for the point examined, considered respectively in each of the two ends of the wings.) The value of w_h is given by equation (815)

$$w_h = \frac{1}{2}\frac{\Gamma_0}{\tan \mu}\left[1 - \frac{1}{\pi}\cos^{-1}(1 - 2\Theta)\right]. \qquad (823)$$

Therefore

$$C_p = 4\alpha_0 \frac{\tan \mu}{\pi}\left[\cos^{-1}(1 - 2\Theta_1) + \cos^{-1}(1 - 2\Theta_2) - \pi\right]. \qquad (824)$$

Again Θ_1 and Θ_2 are the values of Θ for a given point of the wing when the two opposite ends of the wings are considered.

When the aspect ratio of the wing has such a value that the Mach cones reach the ends of the trailing edge ($A = \tan \mu$) (Figure 247), for every point P of the trailing edge (line DE) the following relation exists between Θ_1 and Θ_2:

$$\Theta_1 + \Theta_2 = \frac{1 - \eta_1}{\xi \tan \mu} + \frac{1 - \eta_2}{\xi \tan \mu} = 1.$$

Therefore

$$\cos^{-1}(1 - 2\Theta_1) = \pi - \cos^{-1}(1 - 2\Theta_2) \qquad (825)$$

and (Reference 57)

$$C_p = 0. \qquad (826)$$

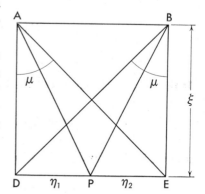

Fig. 247. *The wing plan form that has zero pressure difference at the trailing edge.*

Figure 248 shows the lift distribution on the surface of the wing for $A = \tan \mu$. If the aspect ratio of the wing is less than $\tan \mu$, the zone of the wing behind the

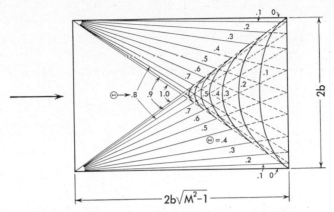

Fig. 248. *The lines of constant pressure in a rectangular wing with zero pressure difference at the trailing edge.*

line *DE*, placed at a distance from the leading edge of $\tan \mu$ times the span of the wing, has negative lift.

APPENDIX

(1) BIBLIOGRAPHY

Works of General Character

ACKERET, J., "Gasdynamik," *Handbuch der Physik*, Berlin, Springer, 1927, Band 7, Chapter 5.

BUSEMANN, A., "Gasdynamik," *Handbuch der Experimental Physik*, Leipzig, Akademi-cher Verlage, 1931, Vol. 4, Part 1.

TAYLOR, G. I. and MACCOLL, J. W., The Mechanics of Compressible Fluids, *Aerodynamic Theory*, Editor Durand, W. F., Berlin, Springer, 1935, Vol. III, Div. H.

TAYLOR, G. I. and MACCOLL, J. W., *Atti del V Convegno Volta* della R. Accademia d'Italia. *Convegno di Scienze Fisiche Matematiche e Naturali:* Roma 1935.

FERRARI, C., *Aerodinamica*, Turin, Arti Grafiche Viretto, 1939, Parte III, Dinamica dei Fluidi Compressibili.

SAUER, R., *Theoretische Einführung in die Gasdynamik*, Berlin, Springer, 1943.

LIEPMANN, H. W. and PUCKETT, A. E., *Introduction to the Aerodynamics of Compressible Fluids*, New York, John Wiley and Sons, 1947.

VON KÁRMÁN, TH., "Supersonic Aerodynamics — Principles and Applications — Tenth Wright Brothers Lecture," *Journal of the Aeronautical Sciences* 14, No. 7 (1947).

See also:

LAMB, H., *On Wave Propagation in Two Dimensions — Hydrodynamics*, Cambridge Dover Publication, 1932.

RAYLEIGH, T. W. S., *The Theory of Sound*. Reprinted Dover Publications, New York, 1945.

Specific References

1. DE SANT, VENANT B. and WANTZEL, L., *Journal de l'Ecole Polytecnique*, 27, 85 (1839).
2. HUGONIOT, H., *Comptes Rendus de L'Academie des Sciences*, 103, 1178 (1880).
3. WEBSTER, C. A., *Partial Differential Equations of Mathematical Physics*, New York, G. E. Stechert Co., 1933, Chapter VI.
4. PRANDTL, L. and BUSEMANN, A., *Stodola Festschrift*, Orell Füssli Verlag, Zurich, 429 (1929).
5. FERRARI, C., *Aerodinamica*, Turin, Arti Grafiche Viretto, 1939, Vol. 3, 43.
6. PRANDTL, L., *Physicalische Zeitschrift*, 8, 23 (1907).
7. BUSEMANN, A., *Handbuch der Experimental Physic*, Leipzig Akademische Verlagsgesell-schaft, 1931, Tell I, Gasdynamik.
8. ACKERET, J., *Zeitschrift für Flugtechnik und Motorluftschiffahrt*, 16 (1925).
9. HUGONIOT, H., *Journal de l'Ecole Polytecnique*, 57, 58 (1889).
10. MEYER, TH., *Mitteilungen über Forschungsarbeiten*, 62, (1908).
11. CROCCO, L., *L'Aerotecnica*, 17, (1937).
12. BUSEMANN, A., *Vorträge aus dem Gebiete der Aerodynamik (Aachen, 1929)*, Berlin, Von Gilles, Hopf and von Karman, 162 (1930).
13. FERRARI, C., *Atti della Reale Accademia delle Scienze di Torino*, 75 (1939).
14. BECKER, R., *Zeitschrifts für Physik*, 8, 321 (1922).
15. THOMAS, L. H., *Journal of Chemical Physics*, 12, 11 (1944).
16. CROCCO, L., *Atti della Reale Accademia dei Lincei*, 23-6 (1936).
17. FERRI, A., *National Advisory Committee for Aeronautics*, Technical Note No. 1135 (1946).

18. von Karman, Th. and Tsien, H. S., *Journal of Aeronautical Sciences*, 5, 4, (1938).

19. Crocco, L., *Monografie Scientifiche di Aeronautica*, Rome (1946).

20. Mach, E. and L., *Sitzungsberichte der Wiener Akademie*, 1035 (1893).

21. Cranz, L., *Lehrbuch der Ballistik*, Berlin, Springer, 1927, Vol. 3.

22. Tremblot, R., *Publications du Ministere de l'Air*, No. 10 (1932).

23. Panetti, M., *Atti del V Convegno "Volta,"* Rome, Reale Accademia d'Italia, 1935.

24. Schardin, H., *Forschung auf dem Gebiete des Ingenieurwesens*, 5 Forschungsheft 367 B, (1934).

25. Busemann, A., *Atti del V Convegno "Volta,"* Rome, Reale Accademia d'Italia, 1935.

26. Ferrari, C., *Aerodinamica*, Turin, Arti Grafiche Viretto, 1939, Vol. 3, 173.

27. Busemann, A. and Walchner, O., *Forschung auf dem Gebiete des Ingenieurswesens*, 4 (1933).

28. Ferri, A., *Atti di Guidonia*, No. 17 (1939).

29. Walchner, O., *Luftfahrtforschung*, 14, No. 2 (1937).

30. Ferri, A., *Atti di Guidonia*, No. 37–38 (1940).

31. Eggink, G., *Deutsche Luftfahrtforschung*, Forschungsbericht No. 1756 (1943).

32. Kantrowitz, A. and Donaldson, C. DuP., *National Advisory Committee for Aeronautics*, Wartime Report No. L-713 (1945).

33. von Karman, Th. and Moore, N. B., *Transactions of the American Society of Mechanical Engineers*, 54 (1932).

34. Prandtl, L., *Luftfahrtforschung*, 13, No. 10 (1936).

35. Lamb, H., *Hydrodynamics*, New York, Dover Publications, 1945, Chap. 8; 278.

36. Ferrari, C., *L'Aerotecnica*, 17, No. 6 (1937).

37. Tsien, H. S., *Journal of the Aeronautical Sciences*, 5, No. 12, 1938.

38. von Karman, Th., *Atti del V Convegno "Volta,"* Rome, Reale Accademia d'Italia (1935).

39. Brown, C. E. and Parker, H. M., *National Advisory Committee for Aeronautics*, Wartime Report L-720 (1946).

40. Busemann, A., *Zeitschrift für angewandte Mathematik und Mechanik*, 9, Heft. 6 (1929).

41. Taylor, G. I. and Maccoll, T. W., *Proceedings of the Royal Society*, Series A, 139. No. 838 (1933).

42. Bourguard, F., *Comptes Rendus*, No. 194 (1932).

43. Hantsche, W. and Wendt, H., *Jahrbuch 1942 der Deutschen Luftfahrtforschung*, Heft. 7 (1942).

44. Ferrari, C., *Atti della Reale Accademia delle Scienze di Torino*, 72 (1936).

45. Sauer, R., *Luftfahrtforschung*, 19 (1942).

46. Byerly, W. E., *Fourier's Series and Spherical Harmonics*, Boston, Ginn and Company, 1893, Chapter 6.

47. Ferrari, C., *Atti del V Convegno Volta*, Rome, Reale Accademia d'Italia, 1935, or *l'Aerotecnica*, 16, No. 2 (1936).

48. Frankl, F. J., *Izvetia Akademii*, RKKA 1 (1934).

49. Guderley, A., *Jahrbuch 1940 der Deutschen Luftfahrtforschung*, Heft. 1 (1940).

50. Sauer, R., *Deutsche Luftfahrtforschung*, Forschungsbericht No. 1269 (1940).

51. Ferri, A., *National Advisory Committee for Aeronautics*, Technical Note No. 1135 (1946).

52. Jones, R. T., *National Advisory Committee for Aeronautics*, Technical Note No. 1032 and 1033 (1946).

53. Puckett, A. E., *Journal of the Aeronautical Sciences*, 13, No. 9 (1946).

54. von Karman, Th., *Journal of the Aeronautical Sciences*, 14, No. 7 (1947).

55. Jones, R. T., *National Advisory Committee for Aeronautics*, Technical Note No. 1107 (1946).

56. SCHLICHTING, H., *Deutsche Luftfahrtforschung, Jahrbuch 1937*.

57. BUSEMANN, A., *Deutsche Akademie für Luftfahrtforschung, Jahrbuch 1942-1943*, **7B**, No. 3 (1943).

58. VON KARMAN, TH. and BURGERS, J. M., *Aerodynamic Theory*, Vol. II, Div. E, Chapter 1, Editor Durand, W. F., Berlin, Springer, 1935.

59. JONES, R. T., *National Advisory Committee for Aeronautics*, Technical Notes No. 1032–1033 (1946).

60. STEWART, H. J., *Quarterly of Applied Mathematics*, IV, No. 3, (1946).

61. BROWN, C. E., *National Advisory Committee for Aeronautics*, Technical Note No. 1183 (1946).

62. JANKE and ENDE, *Tables of Functions*, New York, G. E. Stechert & Co. (1938).

63. BURCHER, M. A., *National Advisory Committee for Aeronautics*, Report Memorandum No. L7K26 (1947).

64. NIECE, M. J., *National Advisory Committee for Aeronautics*, Technical Note No. 1673 (1948).

(2) SYMBOLS OFTEN USED

Latin symbols

A aspect ratio of the wing

a speed of sound

B $\sqrt{M_1^2 - 1}$ or cot μ

c chord of a profile

C_D drag coefficient

C_L lift coefficient

c_m pitching-moment coefficient

c_p pressure coefficient

c_p specific heat at constant pressure (energy per degree for unit weight in mechanical units)

c_v specific heat at constant volume (energy per degree for unit weight in mechanical units)

D drag

g acceleration of gravity

I total heat (mechanical units, energy per unit mass)

L lift

M Mach number

m viscosity coefficient or mass flow

N characteristic number corresponding to $\dfrac{C_1 + C_2}{2}$ equation (94)

p pressure

Q heat (energy per unit mass, mechanical units)

R gas constant (length per degree)

r radius in polar or spherical coordinates

S entropy (energy per degree per unit mass, mechanical units)

T absolute temperature

t time (Chapter 1) or thickness of the profile

u velocity component in the x direction

v velocity component in the y direction

V_c critical stream velocity (velocity of sound at $M = 1$, equation 83)

V_l limiting velocity (maximum possible velocity, equation 85)

W $\dfrac{V}{V_l}$ ratio of the local velocity to the limiting velocity

w velocity component in the z-axis direction

xyz Cartesian coordinates

Greek symbols

α angle of attack

β angle between the shock and the velocity behind the shock

γ $\dfrac{C_p}{C_v} = 1.40$ in the numerical applications

δ $= (\epsilon - \beta)$, deviation of the velocity direction across the shock

ϵ angle between the front of the shock and the velocity in front of the shock

ζ Cartesian coordinates $(\xi \eta \zeta)$

η polar or spherical coordinate $(r\eta\varphi)$ or Cartesian coordinate $(\zeta\eta\xi)$

θ inclination of the vector velocity with the x-axis in the xy-plane

λ inclination of the characteristic lines, or tangent to the wing profile

μ Mach angle

ν angle of expansion from $(M = 1)$ to the stream Mach number

ξ Cartesian coordinate $(\xi\eta\zeta)$

ρ density

ϕ potential function

φ polar $(r\eta\varphi)$ or cylindrical coordinate $(xy\varphi)$

X   angle of sweepback (measured between the edge of the wing and the normal to the direction of the velocity)

Subscripts

0   tank conditions for undisturbed stream $(V = 0)$

1   conditions of the undisturbed stream

n normal component

t tangent component

T total

(3) TABLES USEFUL IN THE ANALYSIS OF
SUPERSONIC FLOW

All the tables are determined assuming $\gamma = 1.40$.

TABLE I: Isentropic transformations.

The table gives as a function of the Mach number M (column 1) the following quantities (part of the numerical values are taken from reference 63):

Column 2   The ratio of the stream static pressure p to the stagnation pressure p_0 — the ratio is determined using equation (41).

Column 3   The ratio of the stream temperature T to the stagnation temperature T_0 — the ratio is determined using equation (349).

Column 4   The ratio of the stream density ρ to the stagnation density ρ_0 — the ratio is determined with equation 6.

Column 5   The ratio of the cross section of the stream tube when the Mach number is equal to one (A_{cr}) to the cross section of the same stream tube when the Mach number has the value given by column 1 — the ratio is determined with equation (51a).

Column 6   The ratio of the local velocity to the limiting velocity (maximum possible velocity obtained expanding the air to zero pressure) — the ratio is determined with equation (85b).

Column 7   The value of the Mach angle μ (determined with equation 52).

Column 8   The value of the deviation of expansion ν necessary to obtain the given stream Mach number from $M = 1$. The value is determined with equation (81).

TABLE 1

M	$\dfrac{p}{p_0}$	$\dfrac{T}{T_0}$	$\dfrac{\rho}{\rho_0}$	$\dfrac{A_{cr}}{A}$	$\dfrac{V}{V_l}$
.00	1.0000	1.0000	1.0000	.00000	.00000
.01	.9999	1.0000	1.0000	.01728	.00447
.02	.9997	.9999	.9998	.03455	.00894
.03	.9994	.9998	.9996	.05180	.01342
.04	.9989	.9997	.9992	.06905	.01789
.05	.9983	.9995	.9988	.08625	.02236
.06	.9975	.9993	.9982	.1035	.02683
.07	.9966	.9990	.9976	.1206	.03130
.08	.9955	.9987	.9968	.1377	.03577
.09	.9944	.9984	.9960	.1548	.04024
.10	.9930	.9980	.9950	.1718	.04471
.11	.9916	.9976	.9940	.1887	.04916
.12	.9900	.9971	.9928	.2056	.05361
.13	.9883	.9966	.9916	.2224	.05805
.14	.9864	.9961	.9903	.2391	.06249
.15	.9844	.9955	.9888	.2557	.06693
.16	.9823	.9949	.9873	.2723	.07137
.17	.9800	.9943	.9857	.2887	.07581
.18	.9777	.9936	.9840	.3051	.08024
.19	.9751	.9928	.9822	.3213	.08466
.20	.9725	.9921	.9803	.3374	.08908
.21	.9697	.9913	.9783	.3534	.09349
.22	.9669	.9904	.9762	.3693	.09790
.23	.9638	.9895	.9740	.3851	.1023
.24	.9607	.9886	.9718	.4007	.1067
.25	.9575	.9877	.9694	.4162	.1111
.26	.9541	.9867	.9670	.4315	.1155
.27	.9506	.9856	.9645	.4468	.1199
.28	.9470	.9846	.9619	.4618	.1242
.29	.9433	.9835	.9592	.4767	.1286
.30	.9395	.9823	.9564	.4914	.1330
.31	.9355	.9811	.9535	.5059	.1373
.32	.9315	.9799	.9506	.5203	.1417
.33	.9274	.9787	.9476	.5345	.1460
.34	.9231	.9774	.9445	.5486	.1503
.35	.9188	.9761	.9413	.5624	.1546
.36	.9143	.9747	.9380	.5761	.1590
.37	.9098	.9733	.9347	.5896	.1632
.38	.9052	.9719	.9313	.6029	.1675
.39	.9004	.9705	.9278	.6159	.1718
.40	.8956	.9690	.9243	.6288	.1761
.41	.8907	.9675	.9207	.6415	.1804
.42	.8857	.9659	.9170	.6541	.1846
.43	.8807	.9643	.9132	.6664	.1888
.44	.8755	.9627	.9094	.6784	.1931
.45	.8703	.9611	.9055	.6903	.1973
.46	.8650	.9594	.9016	.7019	.2015
.47	.8596	.9577	.8976	.7134	.2057
.48	.8541	.9560	.8935	.7246	.2099
.49	.8486	.9542	.8894	.7356	.2141
.50	.8430	.9524	.8852	.7464	.2182

TABLE 1 (Continued)

M	$\dfrac{p}{p_0}$	$\dfrac{T}{T_0}$	$\dfrac{\rho}{\rho_0}$	$\dfrac{A_{cr}}{A}$	$\dfrac{V}{V_l}$
.50	.8430	.9524	.8852	.7464	.2182
.51	.8374	.9506	.8809	.7569	.2224
.52	.8317	.9487	.8766	.7672	.2265
.53	.8259	.9468	.8723	.7773	.2306
.54	.8201	.9449	.8679	.7872	.2348
.55	.8142	.9430	.8634	.7969	.2389
.56	.8082	.9410	.8589	.8063	.2429
.57	.8022	.9390	.8544	.8155	.2470
.58	.7962	.9370	.8498	.8244	.2511
.59	.7901	.9349	.8451	.8331	.2551
.60	.7840	.9328	.8405	.8416	.2592
.61	.7778	.9307	.8357	.8499	.2632
.62	.7716	.9286	.8310	.8579	.2672
.63	.7654	.9265	.8262	.8657	.2712
.64	.7591	.9243	.8213	.8733	.2752
.65	.7528	.9221	.8164	.8806	.2791
.66	.7465	.9199	.8115	.8877	.2831
.67	.7401	.9176	.8066	.8945	.2870
.68	.7338	.9153	.8016	.9011	.2910
.69	.7274	.9130	.7966	.9076	.2949
.70	.7209	.9107	.7916	.9138	.2988
.71	.7145	.9084	.7865	.9197	.3026
.72	.7080	.9061	.7814	.9255	.3065
.73	.7016	.9037	.7763	.9309	.3103
.74	.6951	.9013	.7712	.9362	.3142
.75	.6886	.8989	.7660	.9413	.3180
.76	.6821	.8964	.7609	.9461	.3218
.77	.6756	.8940	.7557	.9507	.3256
.78	.6691	.8915	.7505	.9551	.3294
.79	.6625	.8890	.7452	.9592	.3331
.80	.6560	.8865	.7400	.9632	.3369
.81	.6495	.8840	.7347	.9669	.3406
.82	.6430	.8815	.7295	.9704	.3443
.83	.6365	.8789	.7242	.9737	.3480
.84	.6300	.8763	.7189	.9769	.3517
.85	.6235	.8737	.7136	.9797	.3553
.86	.6170	.8711	.7083	.9824	.3590
.87	.6106	.8685	.7030	.9849	.3626
.88	.6041	.8659	.6977	.9872	.3662
.89	.5977	.8632	.6924	.9893	.3698
.90	.5913	.8606	.6870	.9912	.3734
.91	.5849	.8579	.6817	.9929	.3769
.92	.5785	.8552	.6764	.9944	.3805
.93	.5721	.8525	.6711	.9958	.3840
.94	.5658	.8498	.6658	.9969	.3875
.95	.5595	.8471	.6604	.9979	.3910
.96	.5532	.8444	.6551	.9987	.3945
.97	.5469	.8416	.6498	.9992	.3980
.98	.5407	.8389	.6445	.9997	.4014
.99	.5345	.8361	.6392	.9999	.4048
1.00	.5283	.8333	.6339	1.0000	.4083

TABLE 1 (Continued)

M	$\dfrac{p}{p_0}$	$\dfrac{T}{T_0}$	$\dfrac{\rho}{\rho_0}$	$\dfrac{A_{cr}}{A}$	$\dfrac{V}{V_l}$	μ	ν
1.00	.5283	.8333	.6339	1.0000	.4083	90.00	0
1.01	.5221	.8306	.6287	.9999	.4116	81.93	.045
1.02	.5160	.8278	.6234	.9997	.4150	78.64	.126
1.03	.5099	.8250	.6181	.9993	.4184	76.14	.230
1.04	.5039	.8222	.6129	.9987	.4217	74.06	.351
1.05	.4979	.8193	.6077	.9980	.4250	72.25	.488
1.06	.4919	.8165	.6024	.9971	.4284	70.63	.637
1.07	.4860	.8137	.5972	.9961	.4317	69.16	.797
1.08	.4801	.8108	.5920	.9949	.4349	67.81	.968
1.09	.4742	.8080	.5869	.9936	.4382	66.55	1.15
1.10	.4684	.8052	.5817	.9921	.4414	65.38	1.34
1.11	.4626	.8023	.5766	.9906	.4446	64.28	1.53
1.12	.4568	.7994	.5714	.9888	.4478	63.23	1.74
1.13	.4511	.7966	.5663	.9870	.4510	62.25	1.95
1.14	.4455	.7937	.5612	.9850	.4542	61.31	2.16
1.15	.4399	.7908	.5562	.9829	.4574	60.41	2.38
1.16	.4343	.7879	.5511	.9806	.4605	59.55	2.61
1.17	.4287	.7851	.5461	.9783	.4636	58.73	2.84
1.18	.4232	.7822	.5411	.9758	.4667	57.93	3.07
1.19	.4178	.7793	.5361	.9732	.4698	57.18	3.32
1.20	.4124	.7764	.5311	.9705	.4729	56.44	3.56
1.21	.4070	.7735	.5262	.9676	.4759	55.74	3.81
1.22	.4017	.7706	.5213	.9647	.4790	55.05	4.07
1.23	.3965	.7677	.5164	.9617	.4820	54.39	4.32
1.24	.3912	.7648	.5115	.9586	.4850	53.75	4.57
1.25	.3861	.7619	.5067	.9553	.4880	53.13	4.83
1.26	.3809	.7590	.5019	.9520	.4910	52.53	5.09
1.27	.3759	.7561	.4971	.9486	.4939	51.94	5.36
1.28	.3708	.7532	.4923	.9451	.4968	51.36	5.63
1.29	.3659	.7503	.4876	.9415	.4997	50.82	5.90
1.30	.3609	.7474	.4829	.9378	.5026	50.28	6.16
1.31	.3560	.7445	.4782	.9342	.5055	49.76	6.44
1.32	.3512	.7416	.4736	.9302	.5084	49.25	6.72
1.33	.3464	.7387	.4690	.9263	.5112	48.75	7.00
1.34	.3417	.7358	.4644	.9223	.5140	48.27	7.28
1.35	.3369	.7329	.4598	.9183	.5168	47.79	7.56
1.36	.3323	.7300	.4553	.9141	.5196	47.33	7.84
1.37	.3277	.7271	.4508	.9099	.5224	46.88	8.13
1.38	.3232	.7242	.4463	.9057	.5252	46.44	8.41
1.39	.3187	.7213	.4418	.9013	.5279	46.01	8.70
1.40	.3142	.7184	.4374	.8969	.5307	45.58	8.99
1.41	.3098	.7155	.4330	.8926	.5334	45.17	9.28
1.42	.3055	.7126	.4287	.8880	.5361	44.77	9.57
1.43	.3012	.7097	.4244	.8834	.5388	44.37	9.86
1.44	.2969	.7069	.4201	.8788	.5414	43.98	10.15
1.45	.2927	.7040	.4158	.8742	.5441	43.60	10.44
1.46	.2886	.7011	.4116	.8695	.5467	43.23	10.73
1.47	.2845	.6982	.4074	.8647	.5493	42.86	11.03
1.48	.2804	.6954	.4032	.8599	.5519	42.51	11.32
1.49	.2764	.6925	.3991	.8551	.5545	42.16	11.61
1.50	.2724	.6897	.3950	.8502	.5571	41.81	11.91

TABLE 1 (Continued)

M	$\dfrac{p}{p_0}$	$\dfrac{T}{T_0}$	$\dfrac{\rho}{\rho_0}$	$\dfrac{A_{cr}}{A}$	$\dfrac{V}{V_l}$	μ	ν
1.50	.2724	.6897	.3950	.8502	.5571	41.81	11.91
1.51	.2685	.6868	.3909	.8453	.5596	41.47	12.20
1.52	.2646	.6840	.3869	.8404	.5622	41.14	12.51
1.53	.2608	.6811	.3829	.8354	.5647	40.81	12.80
1.54	.2570	.6783	.3789	.8304	.5672	40.49	13.09
1.55	.2533	.6754	.3750	.8254	.5697	40.18	13.39
1.56	.2496	.6726	.3711	.8203	.5722	39.87	13.68
1.57	.2459	.6698	.3672	.8152	.5746	39.56	13.97
1.58	.2423	.6670	.3633	.8102	.5771	39.27	14.27
1.59	.2388	.6642	.3595	.8050	.5795	38.97	14.57
1.60	.2353	.6614	.3557	.7999	.5819	38.68	14.86
1.61	.2318	.6586	.3520	.7947	.5843	38.40	15.16
1.62	.2284	.6558	.3483	.7895	.5867	38.12	15.46
1.63	.2250	.6530	.3446	.7843	.5891	37.84	15.75
1.64	.2217	.6502	.3409	.7791	.5914	37.57	16.04
1.65	.2184	.6475	.3373	.7739	.5938	37.31	16.33
1.66	.2152	.6447	.3337	.7686	.5961	37.04	16.63
1.67	.2120	.6419	.3302	.7633	.5984	36.78	16.93
1.68	.2088	.6392	.3267	.7581	.6007	36.53	17.23
1.69	.2057	.6364	.3232	.7529	.6030	36.28	17.52
1.70	.2026	.6337	.3197	.7476	.6052	36.03	17.81
1.71	.1996	.6310	.3163	.7423	.6075	35.79	18.10
1.72	.1966	.6283	.3129	.7371	.6097	35.55	18.40
1.73	.1936	.6256	.3095	.7318	.6119	35.31	18.69
1.74	.1907	.6229	.3062	.7265	.6141	35.08	18.98
1.75	.1878	.6202	.3029	.7212	.6163	34.85	19.27
1.76	.1850	.6175	.2996	.7160	.6185	34.62	19.56
1.77	.1822	.6148	.2964	.7107	.6207	34.40	19.85
1.78	.1794	.6121	.2932	.7055	.6228	34.18	20.14
1.79	.1767	.6095	.2900	.7002	.6249	33.96	20.43
1.80	.1740	.6068	.2868	.6949	.6271	33.75	20.72
1.81	.1714	.6041	.2837	.6897	.6292	33.54	21.01
1.82	.1688	.6015	.2806	.6845	.6313	33.33	21.30
1.83	.1662	.5989	.2776	.6792	.6333	33.12	21.59
1.84	.1637	.5963	.2745	.6741	.6354	32.92	21.88
1.85	.1612	.5936	.2715	.6689	.6375	32.72	22.16
1.86	.1587	.5910	.2686	.6636	.6395	32.52	22.45
1.87	.1563	.5884	.2656	.6583	.6415	32.33	22.74
1.88	.1539	.5859	.2627	.6533	.6435	32.13	23.02
1.89	.1516	.5833	.2598	.6482	.6455	31.94	23.31
1.90	.1492	.5807	.2570	.6430	.6475	31.76	23.59
1.91	.1470	.5782	.2542	.6379	.6495	31.57	23.87
1.92	.1447	.5756	.2514	.6328	.6515	31.39	24.15
1.93	.1425	.5731	.2486	.6277	.6534	31.21	24.43
1.94	.1403	.5705	.2459	.6226	.6553	31.03	24.71
1.95	.1381	.5680	.2432	.6176	.6572	30.85	24.99
1.96	.1360	.5655	.2405	.6125	.6592	30.68	25.27
1.97	.1339	.5630	.2378	.6075	.6611	30.50	25.55
1.98	.1318	.5605	.2352	.6025	.6629	30.33	25.83
1.99	.1298	.5580	.2326	.5975	.6648	30.17	26.11
2.00	.1278	.5556	.2301	.5926	.6667	30.00	26.38

TABLE 1 (Continued)

M	$\dfrac{p}{p_0}$	$\dfrac{T}{T_0}$	$\dfrac{\rho}{\rho_0}$	$\dfrac{A_{cr}}{A}$	$\dfrac{V}{V_l}$	μ	ν
2.00	.1278	.5556	.2301	.5926	.6667	30.00	26.38
2.01	.1258	.5531	.2275	.5877	.6685	29.84	26.66
2.02	.1239	.5506	.2250	.5828	.6703	29.67	26.93
2.03	.1220	.5482	.2225	.5779	.6722	29.51	27.20
2.04	.1201	.5458	.2200	.5730	.6740	29.35	27.48
2.05	.1182	.5433	.2176	.5682	.6758	29.20	27.75
2.06	.1164	.5409	.2153	.5634	.6776	29.04	28.02
2.07	.1146	.5385	.2128	.5586	.6793	28.89	28.29
2.08	.1128	.5361	.2105	.5538	.6811	28.74	28.56
2.09	.1111	.5337	.2081	.5491	.6828	28.59	28.83
2.10	.1094	.5313	.2058	.5444	.6846	28.44	29.10
2.11	.1077	.5290	.2035	.5397	.6863	28.29	29.36
2.12	.1060	.5266	.2013	.5350	.6880	28.14	29.63
2.13	.1043	.5243	.1990	.5304	.6897	28.00	29.90
2.14	.1027	.5219	.1968	.5258	.6914	27.86	30.17
2.15	.1011	.5196	.1946	.5212	.6931	27.72	30.43
2.16	.0996	.5173	.1925	.5167	.6948	27.58	30.69
2.17	.0980	.5150	.1903	.5122	.6964	27.44	30.95
2.18	.0965	.5127	.1882	.5077	.6981	27.30	31.21
2.19	.0950	.5104	.1861	.5032	.6997	27.17	31.47
2.20	.0935	.5081	.1841	.4988	.7013	27.04	31.73
2.21	.0921	.5059	.1820	.4944	.7030	26.90	31.99
2.22	.0906	.5036	.1800	.4900	.7046	26.77	32.25
2.23	.0892	.5014	.1780	.4856	.7061	26.64	32.51
2.24	.0878	.4991	.1760	.4813	.7077	26.52	32.77
2.25	.0865	.4969	.1740	.4770	.7093	26.39	33.02
2.26	.0851	.4947	.1721	.4727	.7109	26.26	33.27
2.27	.0838	.4925	.1702	.4685	.7124	26.14	33.52
2.28	.0825	.4903	.1683	.4643	.7140	26.01	33.78
2.29	.0812	.4881	.1664	.4601	.7155	25.89	34.03
2.30	.0800	.4859	.1646	.4560	.7170	25.77	34.28
2.31	.0787	.4837	.1628	.4519	.7185	25.65	34.53
2.32	.0775	.4816	.1610	.4478	.7200	25.53	34.78
2.33	.0763	.4794	.1592	.4437	.7215	25.42	35.03
2.34	.0751	.4773	.1574	.4397	.7230	25.30	35.28
2.35	.0740	.4752	.1556	.4357	.7245	25.18	35.53
2.36	.0728	.4731	.1539	.4317	.7259	25.07	35.77
2.37	.0717	.4709	.1522	.4278	.7274	24.96	36.02
2.38	.0706	.4688	.1505	.4239	.7288	24.85	36.26
2.39	.0695	.4668	.1489	.4200	.7302	24.73	36.51
2.40	.0684	.4647	.1472	.4161	.7317	24.62	36.75
2.41	.0673	.4626	.1456	.4123	.7331	24.52	36.99
2.42	.0663	.4606	.1440	.4085	.7345	24.41	37.23
2.43	.0653	.4585	.1424	.4048	.7359	24.30	37.47
2.44	.0643	.4565	.1408	.4010	.7372	24.20	37.71
2.45	.0633	.4544	.1392	.3973	.7386	24.09	37.95
2.46	.0623	.4524	.1377	.3937	.7400	23.99	38.18
2.47	.0613	.4504	.1362	.3900	.7413	23.88	38.42
2.48	.0604	.4484	.1347	.3864	.7427	23.78	38.66
2.49	.0595	.4464	.1332	.3828	.7440	23.68	38.89
2.50	.0585	.4444	.1317	.3793	.7454	23.58	39.12

TABLE 1   (Continued)

M	$\dfrac{p}{p_0}$	$\dfrac{T}{T_0}$	$\dfrac{\rho}{\rho_0}$	$\dfrac{A_{cr}}{A}$	$\dfrac{V}{V_l}$	μ	ν
2.50	.0585	.4444	.1317	.3793	.7454	23.58	39.12
2.51	.0576	.4425	.1303	.3757	.7467	23.48	39.35
2.52	.0567	.4405	.1288	.3722	.7480	23.38	39.58
2.53	.0559	.4386	.1274	.3688	.7493	23.28	39.81
2.54	.0550	.4366	.1260	.3653	.7506	23.19	40.05
2.55	.0542	.4347	.1246	.3619	.7519	23.09	40.28
2.56	.0533	.4328	.1232	.3585	.7532	22.99	40.51
2.57	.0525	.4309	.1219	.3552	.7544	22.90	40.74
2.58	.0517	.4289	.1205	.3519	.7557	22.81	40.97
2.59	.0509	.4271	.1192	.3486	.7569	22.71	41.19
2.60	.0501	.4252	.1179	.3453	.7582	22.62	41.41
2.61	.0493	.4233	.1166	.3421	.7594	22.53	41.63
2.62	.0486	.4214	.1153	.3389	.7606	22.44	41.86
2.63	.0478	.4196	.1140	.3357	.7619	22.35	42.08
2.64	.0471	.4177	.1128	.3325	.7631	22.26	42.30
2.65	.0464	.4159	.1115	.3294	.7643	22.17	42.52
2.66	.0457	.4141	.1103	.3263	.7655	22.08	42.74
2.67	.0450	.4122	.1091	.3232	.7667	22.00	42.96
2.68	.0443	.4104	.1079	.3202	.7678	21.91	43.18
2.69	.0436	.4086	.1067	.3172	.7690	21.82	43.40
2.70	.0430	.4068	.1056	.3142	.7702	21.74	43.62
2.71	.0423	.4051	.1044	.3112	.7713	21.65	43.84
2.72	.0417	.4033	.1033	.3083	.7725	21.57	44.06
2.73	.0410	.4015	.1022	.3054	.7736	21.49	44.27
2.74	.0404	.3998	.1010	.3025	.7748	21.41	44.48
2.75	.0398	.3980	.0999	.2996	.7759	21.32	44.69
2.76	.0392	.3963	.0989	.2968	.7770	21.24	44.90
2.77	.0386	.3945	.0978	.2940	.7781	21.16	45.11
2.78	.0380	.3928	.0967	.2912	.7792	21.08	45.32
2.79	.0374	.3911	.0957	.2884	.7803	21.00	45.53
2.80	.0368	.3894	.0946	.2857	.7814	20.92	45.74
2.81	.0363	.3877	.0936	.2830	.7825	20.85	45.95
2.82	.0357	.3860	.0926	.2803	.7836	20.77	46.16
2.83	.0352	.3844	.0916	.2777	.7846	20.69	46.37
2.84	.0347	.3827	.0906	.2750	.7857	20.62	46.58
2.85	.0341	.3810	.0896	.2724	.7868	20.54	46.79
2.86	.0336	.3794	.0886	.2698	.7878	20.47	46.99
2.87	.0331	.3777	.0877	.2673	.7888	20.39	47.19
2.88	.0326	.3761	.0867	.2648	.7899	20.32	47.39
2.89	.0321	.3745	.0858	.2622	.7909	20.24	47.59
2.90	.0317	.3729	.0849	.2598	.7919	20.17	47.79
2.91	.0312	.3712	.0840	.2573	.7929	20.10	47.99
2.92	.0307	.3696	.0831	.2549	.7940	20.03	48.19
2.93	.0302	.3681	.0822	.2524	.7950	19.96	48.38
2.94	.0298	.3665	.0813	.2500	.7959	19.89	48.58
2.95	.0293	.3649	.0804	.2477	.7969	19.82	48.78
2.96	.0289	.3633	.0796	.2453	.7979	19.75	48.98
2.97	.0285	.3618	.0787	.2430	.7989	19.68	49.18
2.98	.0281	.3602	.0779	.2407	.7999	19.61	49.37
2.99	.0276	.3587	.0770	.2384	.8008	19.54	49.56
3.00	.0272	.3571	.0762	.2362	.8018	19.47	49.75

TABLE 1 (Continued)

M	$\dfrac{p}{p_0}$	$\dfrac{T}{T_0}$	$\dfrac{\rho}{\rho_0}$	$\dfrac{A_{cr}}{A}$	$\dfrac{V}{V_l}$	μ	ν
3.00	$.2722\text{x}10^{-1}$	.3571	$.7623\text{x}10^{-1}$	.2362	.8018	19.47	49.76
3.01	.2682	.3556	.7541	.2339	.8027	19.40	49.95
3.02	.2642	.3541	.7461	.2317	.8037	19.34	50.14
3.03	.2603	.3526	.7382	.2295	.8046	19.27	50.33
3.04	.2564	.3511	.7303	.2273	.0056	19.20	50.52
3.05	.2526	.3496	.7226	.2252	.8066	19.14	50.71
3.06	.2489	.3481	.7149	.2230	.8075	19.07	50.90
3.07	.2452	.3466	.7074	.2209	.8084	19.01	51.09
3.08	.2416	.3452	.6999	.2188	.8093	18.95	51.28
3.09	.2380	.3437	.6925	.2168	.8102	18.88	51.46
3.10	.2345	.3422	.6852	.2147	.8111	18.82	51.65
3.11	.2310	.3408	.6779	.2127	.8119	18.76	51.84
3.12	.2276	.3393	.6708	.2107	.8128	18.69	52.02
3.13	.2243	.3379	.6637	.2087	.8137	18.63	52.20
3.14	.2210	.3365	.6568	.2067	.8146	18.57	52.39
3.15	.2177	.3351	.6499	.2048	.8153	18.51	52.57
3.16	.2146	.3337	.6430	.2028	.8162	18.45	52.75
3.17	.2114	.3323	.6363	.2009	.8170	18.39	52.93
3.18	.2083	.3309	.6296	.1990	.8179	18.33	53.11
3.19	.2053	.3295	.6231	.1971	.8187	18.27	53.29
3.20	.2023	.3281	.6165	.1953	.8196	18.21	53.47
3.21	.1993	.3267	.6101	.1934	.8204	18.15	53.65
3.22	.1964	.3253	.6037	.1916	.8213	18.09	53.83
3.23	.1936	.3240	.5975	.1898	.8222	18.04	54.00
3.24	.1908	.3226	.5912	.1880	.8230	17.98	54.18
3.25	$.1880\text{x}10^{-1}$	.3213	$.5851\text{x}10^{-1}$	.1863	.8239	17.92	54.35
3.26	.1853	.3199	.5790	.1845	.8247	17.86	54.53
3.37	.1826	.3186	.5730	.1828	.8255	17.81	54.70
3.28	.1799	.3173	.5671	.1810	.8263	17.75	54.88
3.29	.1773	.3160	.5612	.1794	.8271	17.70	55.05
3.30	.1748	.3147	.5554	.1777	.8279	17.64	55.22
3.31	.1722	.3134	.5497	.1760	.8287	17.58	55.39
3.32	.1698	.3121	.5440	.1743	.8295	17.53	55.56
3.33	.1673	.3108	.5384	.1727	.8303	17.48	55.73
3.34	.1649	.3095	.5329	.1711	.8311	17.42	55.90
3.35	.1625	.3082	.5274	.1695	.8318	17.37	56.07
3.36	.1602	.3069	.5220	.1679	.8326	17.31	56.24
3.37	.1579	.3057	.5166	.1663	.8333	17.26	56.41
3.38	.1557	.3044	.5113	.1648	.8340	17.21	56.58
3.39	.1534	.3032	.5061	.1632	.8348	17.16	56.74
3.40	.1512	.3019	.5009	.1617	.8355	17.10	56.91
3.41	.1491	.3007	.4958	.1602	.8362	17.05	57.07
3.42	.1470	.2995	.4908	.1587	.8370	17.00	57.24
3.43	.1449	.2982	.4858	.1572	.8377	16.95	57.40
3.44	.1428	.2970	.4808	.1558	.8384	16.90	57.56
3.45	.1408	.2958	.4759	.1543	.8392	16.85	57.73
3.46	.1388	.2946	.4711	.1529	.8399	16.80	57.89
3.47	.1368	.2934	.4663	.1515	.8407	16.75	58.05
3.48	.1349	.2922	.4616	.1501	.8414	16.70	58.21
3.49	.1330	.2910	.4569	.1487	.8421	16.65	58.37
3.50	.1311	.2899	.4523	.1473	.8427	16.60	58.53

TABLE 1 (Continued)

M	$\dfrac{p}{p_0}$	$\dfrac{T}{T_0}$	$\dfrac{\rho}{\rho_0}$	$\dfrac{A_{cr}}{A}$	$\dfrac{V}{V_l}$	μ	ν
3.50	$.1311\mathrm{x}10^{-1}$	.2899	$.4523\mathrm{x}10^{-1}$	.1473	.8427	16.60	58.53
3.51	.1293	.2887	.4478	.1459	.8434	16.55	58.69
3.52	.1274	.2875	.4433	.1446	.8441	16.50	58.85
3.53	.1256	.2864	.4388	.1432	.8447	16.46	59.00
3.54	.1239	.2852	.4344	.1419	.8454	16.41	59.16
3.55	.1221	.2841	.4300	.1406	.8460	16.36	59.32
3.56	.1204	.2829	.4257	.1393	.8467	16.31	59.47
3.57	.1188	.2818	.4214	.1380	.8474	16.27	59.63
3.58	.1171	.2806	.4172	.1367	.8481	16.22	59.78
3.59	.1155	.2795	.4131	.1355	.8488	16.17	59.94
3.60	.1138	.2784	.4089	.1342	.8494	16.13	60.09
3.61	.1123	.2773	.4049	.1330	.8501	16.08	60.24
3.62	.1107	.2762	.4008	.1318	.8508	16.04	60.40
3.63	.1092	.2751	.3968	.1306	.8514	15.99	60.55
3.64	.1076	.2740	.3929	.1294	.8521	15.95	60.70
3.65	.1062	.2729	.3890	.1282	.8527	15.90	60.85
3.66	.1047	.2718	.3852	.1270	.8533	15.86	61.00
3.67	.1032	.2707	.3813	.1258	.8539	15.81	61.15
3.68	.1018	.2697	.3776	.1247	.8546	15.77	61.30
3.69	.1004	.2686	.3739	.1235	.8552	15.72	61.45
3.70	$.9903\mathrm{x}10^{-2}$	.2675	.3702	.1225	.8558	15.68	61.60
3.71	.9767	.2665	.3665	.1213	.8564	15.64	61.74
3.72	.9633	.2654	.3629	.1202	.8570	15.59	61.89
3.73	.9500	.2644	.3594	.1191	.8577	15.55	62.04
3.74	.9370	.2633	.3558	.1180	.8583	15.51	62.18
3.75	$.9242\mathrm{x}10^{-2}$	.2623	$.3524\mathrm{x}10^{-1}$	.1169	.8589	15.47	62.33
3.76	.9116	.2613	.3489	.1159	.8596	15.42	62.47
3.77	.8991	.2602	.3455	.1148	.8602	15.38	62.61
3.78	.8869	.2592	.3421	.1138	.8608	15.34	62.76
3.79	.8748	.2582	.3388	.1127	.8614	15.30	62.90
3.80	.8629	.2572	.3355	.1117	.8620	15.26	63.04
3.81	.8512	.2562	.3322	.1107	.8626	15.22	63.19
3.82	.8396	.2552	.3290	.1097	.8632	15.18	63.33
3.83	.8283	.2542	.3258	.1087	.8637	15.14	63.47
3.84	.8171	.2532	.3227	.1077	.8643	15.09	63.61
3.85	.8060	.2522	.3195	.1068	.8648	15.05	63.75
3.86	.7951	.2513	.3165	.1058	.8654	15.01	63.89
3.87	.7844	.2503	.3134	.1049	.8660	14.98	64.03
3.88	.7739	.2493	.3104	.1039	.8665	14.94	64.16
3.89	.7635	.2484	.3074	.1030	.8671	14.90	64.30
3.90	.7532	.2474	.3044	.1021	.8676	14.86	64.44
3.91	.7431	.2464	.3015	.1011	.8682	14.82	64.58
3.92	.7332	.2455	.2986	.1002	.8687	14.78	64.71
3.93	.7233	.2446	.2958	.09933	.8692	14.74	64.85
3.94	.7137	.2436	.2929	.09844	.8697	14.70	64.98
3.95	.7042	.2427	.2902	.09756	.8702	14.66	65.12
3.96	.6948	.2418	.2874	.09669	.8707	14.63	65.25
3.97	.6855	.2408	.2846	.09583	.8713	14.59	65.39
3.98	.6764	.2399	.2819	.09498	.8718	14.55	65.52
3.99	.6675	.2390	.2793	.09413	.8723	14.51	65.65
4.00	.6586	.2381	.2766	.09329	.8728	14.48	65.78

TABLE 2: Numerical relations for the two-dimensional characteristics system. The table gives as a function of the characteristic number N (column 1) the following quantities:

Column 2 The value of ν, deviation of expansion from Mach number 1.

Column 3 The value of the stream Mach number (determined from column 2 with equation (81)).

Column 4 The ratio of the local static pressure p to the critical static pressure p^* corresponding to the pressure for ($M = 1$).

Column 5 The Mach angle μ determined with equation (52) from column 3.

TABLE 2

N	ν	M	$\dfrac{p}{p^*}$	μ	N	ν	M	$\dfrac{p}{p^*}$	μ
1000	0°	1.0000	1.00000	90°	963	37°	2.4107	.12735	24°30'
999	1°	1.0813	.90724	67°37'	962	38°	2.4525	.11970	24° 4'
998	2°	1.1327	.85100	61°59'	961	39°	2.4946	.11177	23°37'
997	3°	1.1764	.80486	58°13'	960	40°	2.5373	.10454	23°12'
996	4°	1.2185	.76192	55° 9'	959	41°	2.5812	.09770	22°48'
995	5°	1.2577	.72329	52°39'	958	42°	2.6256	.09117	22°23'
994	6°	1.2938	.68896	50°37'	957	43°	2.6712	.08500	21°59'
993	7°	1.3298	.65588	48°45'	956	44°	2.7175	.07917	21°36'
992	8°	1.3648	.62488	47° 6'	955	45°	2.7650	.07359	21°13'
991	9°	1.4000	.59484	45°35'	954	46°	2.8118	.06848	20°50'
990	10°	1.4350	.56608	44°10'	953	47°	2.8601	.06363	20°28'
989	11°	1.4690	.53921	42°54'	952	48°	2.9112	.05895	20° 5'
988	12°	1.5032	.51325	41°42'	951	49°	2.9613	.05466	19°44'
987	13°	1.5368	.48875	40°36'	950	50°	3.0122	.05065	19°23'
986	14°	1.5706	.46512	39°33'	949	51°	3.0650	.04660	19° 2'
985	15°	1.6046	.44233	38°33'	948	52°	3.1188	.04310	18°42'
984	16°	1.6382	.42075	37°37'	947	53°	3.1735	.03985	18°22'
983	17°	1.6721	.39995	36°44'	946	54°	3.2263	.03669	18° 3'
982	18°	1.7064	.37981	35°53'	945	55°	3.2866	.03375	17°43'
981	19°	1.7408	.36053	35° 4'	944	56°	3.3455	.03103	17°24'
980	20°	1.7753	.34210	34°16'	943	57°	3.4065	.02843	17' 4'
979	21°	1.8098	.32454	33°32'	942	58°	3.4682	.02605	16°45'
978	22°	1.8446	.30768	32°49'	941	59°	3.5300	.02382	16°27'
977	23°	1.8796	.29152	32° 8'	940	60°	3.5945	.02175	16° 9'
976	24°	1.9148	.27610	31°29'	939	61°	3.6605	.01984	15°51'
975	25°	1.9503	.26136	30°50'	938	62°	3.7283	.01838	15°33'
974	26°	1.9860	.24727	30°14'	937	63°	3.7975	.01643	15°16'
973	27°	2.0235	.23324	29°37'	936	64°	3.8699	.01489	14°58'
972	28°	2.0600	.22034	29° 2'	935	65°	3.9425	.01350	14°42'
971	29°	2.0968	.20805	28°29'	934	66°	4.0175	.01223	14°25'
970	30°	2.1320	.19690	27°58'	933	67°	4.0950	.01103	14° 8'
969	31°	2.1726	.18483	27°24'	932	68°	4.175	.00990	13°56'
968	32°	2.2105	.17430	26°54'	931	69°	4.256	.00889	13°35'
967	33°	2.2485	.16400	26°24'	930	70°	4.340	.00800	13°19'
966	34°	2.2879	.15406	25°55'	929	71°	4.427	.00720	13° 3'
965	35°	2.3290	.14480	25°25'	928	72°	4.517	.00646	12°47'
964	36°	2.3693	.13582	24°58'	927	73°	4.610	.00577	12°32'

* See chart 1 of the appendix.

TABLE 2 (Continued)

N	ν	M	$\frac{p}{p^*}$	μ	N	ν	M	$\frac{p}{p^*}$	μ
926	74°	4.704	.00510	12°16′	909	91°	7.008	.000455	8° 7′
925	75°	4.802	.00450	12° 1′	908	92°	7.202	.000381	7°54′
924	76°	4.905	.00400	11°46′	907	93°	7.407	.000318	7°41′
923	77°	5.010	.00354	11°31′	906	94°	7.622	.000265	7°28′
922	78°	5.119	.00313	11°16′	905	95°	7.853	.000220	7°15′
921	79°	5.231	.00277	11° 1′	904	96°	8.092	.000182	7° 3′
920	80°	5.348	.002413	10°47′	903	97°	8.343	.000149	6°50′
919	81°	5.472	.002105	10°32′	902	98°	8.616	.0001194	6°37′
918	82°	5.599	.001835	10°17′	901	99°	8.902	.0000965	6°25′
917	83°	5.730	.001598	10° 3′	900	100°	9.210	.0000770	6°12′
916	84°	5.865	.001383	9°41′	899	101°	9.535	.0000614	5°59′
915	85°	6.007	.001193	9°27′	898	102°	9.881	.0000481	5°47′
914	86°	6.152	.001023	9°14′	897	103°	10.260	.0000377	5°34′
913	87°	6.307	.000879	9° 1′	896	104°	10.665	.0000294	5°21′
912	88°	6.472	.000751	8°47′	895	105°	11.088	.0000224	5° 9′
911	89°	6.642	.000638	8°34′	894	106°	11.552	.0000168	4°57′
910	90°	6.821	.000540	8°20′					

TABLE 3: Numerical relations between flow quantities in front and behind normal shock waves. The table gives as a function of the Mach number in front of the shock M_1 of column 1, the following quantities:

Column 2   The Mach number behind a normal shock M_{2n}, calculated with equation (129).

Column 3   The ratio of the static pressure behind the normal shock P_{2n} to the pressure P_1 in front of the normal shock. The ratio is calculated using equation (127).

Column 4   The ratio between stagnation pressure behind a normal shock P_{0n} and the stagnation pressure P_0 in front of a normal shock. The ratio is determined with equation (216).

TABLE 3

M_1	M_{2n}	$\dfrac{P_{2n}}{P_1}$	$\dfrac{P_{0n}}{P_0}$	M_1	M_{2n}	$\dfrac{P_{2n}}{P_1}$	$\dfrac{P_{0n}}{P_0}$
1.00	1.0000	1.000	1.0000	1.30	.7860	1.805	.9794
1.01	.9901	1.024	1.0000	1.31	.7809	1.836	.9776
1.02	.9805	1.047	1.0000	1.32	.7760	1.866	.9758
1.03	.9712	1.071	1.0000	1.33	.7712	1.897	.9738
1.04	.9620	1.095	.9999	1.34	.7664	1.928	.9718
1.05	.9531	1.120	.9998	1.35	.7618	1.960	.9697
1.06	.9444	1.144	.9998	1.36	.7572	1.991	.9676
1.07	.9360	1.169	.9996	1.37	.7527	2.023	.9653
1.08	.9277	1.194	.9994	1.38	.7483	2.055	.9630
1.09	.9196	1.220	.9992	1.39	.7440	2.088	.9607
1.10	.9118	1.245	.9989	1.40	.7397	2.120	.9582
1.11	.9041	1.271	.9986	1.41	.7355	2.153	.9557
1.12	.8966	1.297	.9982	1.42	.7314	2.186	.9531
1.13	.8892	1.323	.9978	1.43	.7274	2.219	.9504
1.14	.8820	1.350	.9973	1.44	.7235	2.253	.9476
1.15	.8750	1.376	.9967	1.45	.7196	2.286	.9448
1.16	.8682	1.403	.9961	1.46	.7157	2.320	.9420
1.17	.8615	1.430	.9953	1.47	.7120	2.354	.9390
1.18	.8549	1.458	.9946	1.48	.7083	2.389	.9360
1.19	.8485	1.486	.9937	1.49	.7047	2.424	.9330
1.20	.8422	1.514	.9928	1.50	.7011	2.458	.9298
1.21	.8360	1.542	.9918	1.51	.6976	2.494	.9266
1.22	.8300	1.570	.9907	1.52	.6941	2.529	.9233
1.23	.8241	1.598	.9896	1.53	.6907	2.564	.9200
1.24	.8183	1.627	.9883	1.54	.6874	2.600	.9166
1.25	.8126	1.656	.9871	1.55	.6841	2.636	.9132
1.26	.8071	1.686	.9857	1.56	.6809	2.673	.9098
1.27	.8016	1.715	.9842	1.57	.6777	2.709	.9062
1.28	.7963	1.745	.9827	1.58	.6746	2.746	.9025
1.29	.7911	1.775	.9811	1.59	.6715	2.783	.8989

TABLE 3 (Continued)

M_1	M_{2n}	$\dfrac{P_{2n}}{P_1}$	$\dfrac{P_{0n}}{P_0}$	M_1	M_{2n}	$\dfrac{P_{2n}}{P_1}$	$\dfrac{P_{0n}}{P_0}$
1.60	.6684	2.820	.8952	2.10	.5613	4.978	.6742
1.61	.6655	2.858	.8914	2.11	.5598	5.028	.6696
1.62	.6625	2.895	.8877	2.12	.5583	5.077	.6649
1.63	.6596	2.933	.8838	2.13	.5568	5.126	.6603
1.64	.6568	2.971	.8799	2.14	.5554	5.176	.6557
1.65	.6540	3.010	.8760	2.15	.5540	5.226	.6511
1.66	.6512	3.048	.8720	2.16	.5525	5.277	.6465
1.67	.6485	3.087	.8680	2.17	.5511	5.327	.6419
1.68	.6458	3.126	.8640	2.18	.5498	5.378	.6373
1.69	.6431	3.166	.8598	2.19	.5484	5.429	.6327
1.70	.6405	3.205	.8557	2.20	.5471	5.480	.6281
1.71	.6380	3.245	.8516	2.21	.5457	5.532	.6236
1.72	.6355	3.285	.8473	2.22	.5444	5.583	.6191
1.73	.6330	3.325	.8431	2.23	.5431	5.635	.6145
1.74	.6305	3.366	.8389	2.24	.5418	5.687	.6100
1.75	.6281	3.406	.8346	2.25	.5406	5.740	.6055
1.76	.6257	3.447	.8302	2.26	.5393	5.792	.6011
1.77	.6234	3.488	.8259	2.27	.5381	5.845	.5966
1.78	.6210	3.530	.8215	2.28	.5368	5.898	.5921
1.79	.6188	3.572	.8171	2.29	.5356	5.952	.5877
1.80	.6165	3.613	.8127	2.30	.5344	6.005	.5833
1.81	.6143	.3656	.8082	2.31	.5332	6.059	.5789
1.82	.6121	3.698	.8038	2.32	.5321	6.113	.5745
1.83	.6099	3.710	.7993	2.33	.5309	6.167	.5702
1.84	.6078	3.783	.7948	2.34	.5297	6.222	.5658
1.85	.6057	3.826	.7902	2.35	.5286	6.276	.5615
1.86	.6036	3.870	.7857	2.36	.5275	6.331	.5572
1.87	.6016	3.913	.7811	2.37	.5264	6.386	.5529
1.88	.5996	3.957	.7765	2.38	.5253	6.442	.5486
1.89	.5976	4.001	.7720	2.39	.5242	6.498	.5444
1.90	.5956	4.045	.7674	2.40	.5231	6.554	.5401
1.91	.5937	4.090	.7627	2.41	.5221	6.610	.5359
1.92	.5918	4.134	.7581	2.42	.5210	6.666	.5317
1.93	.5899	4.179	.7535	2.43	.5200	6.722	.5276
1.94	.5880	4.224	.7488	2.44	.5189	6.779	.5234
1.95	.5862	4.270	.7442	2.45	.5179	6.836	.5193
1.96	.5844	4.315	.7395	2.46	.5169	6.894	.5152
1.97	.5826	4.361	.7349	2.47	.5159	6.951	.5111
1.98	.5808	4.407	.7302	2.48	.5149	7.009	.5071
1.99	.5790	4.454	.7255	2.49	.5140	7.067	.5030
2.00	.5773	4.500	.7209	2.50	.5130	7.125	.4990
2.01	.5757	4.547	.7162	2.51	.5120	7.184	.4950
2.02	.5740	4.594	.7115	2.52	.5111	7.242	.4911
2.03	.5723	4.641	.7069	2.53	.5102	7.301	.4871
2.04	.5707	4.689	.7022	2.54	.5092	7.360	.4832
2.05	.5691	4.736	.6975	2.55	.5083	7.420	.4793
2.06	.5675	4.784	.6928	2.56	.5074	7.479	.4754
2.07	.5659	4.832	.6882	2.57	.5065	7.539	.4715
2.08	.5643	4.881	.6835	2.58	.5056	7.599	.4677
2.09	.5628	4.929	.6789	2.59	.5047	7.660	.4639

TABLE 3 (Continued)

M_1	M_{2n}	$\dfrac{P_{2n}}{P_1}$	$\dfrac{P_{0n}}{P_0}$	M_1	M_{2n}	$\dfrac{P_{2n}}{P_1}$	$\dfrac{P_{0n}}{P_0}$
2.60	.5039	7.720	.4601	3.10	.4695	11.05	.3012
2.61	.5030	7.781	.4564	3.11	.4690	11.12	.2986
2.62	.5022	7.842	.4526	3.12	.4685	11.19	.2960
2.63	.5013	7.903	.4489	3.13	.4679	11.26	.2935
2.64	.5005	7.965	.4452	3.14	.4674	11.34	.2910
2.65	.4996	8.026	.4416	3.15	.4669	11.41	.2885
2.66	.4988	8.088	.4379	3.16	.4664	11.48	.2860
2.67	.4980	8.150	.4343	3.17	.4659	11.56	.2835
2.68	.4972	8.213	.4307	3.18	.4654	11.63	.2811
2.69	.4964	8.276	.4271	3.19	.4618	11.71	.2786
2.70	.4956	8.338	.4236	3.20	.4643	11.78	.2762
2.71	.4949	8.402	.4201	3.21	.4639	11.85	.2738
2.72	.4941	8.465	.4166	3.22	.4634	11.93	.2715
2.73	.4933	8.528	.4131	3.23	.4629	12.01	.2691
2.74	.4926	8.592	.4096	3.24	.4624	12.08	.2668
2.75	.4918	8.656	.4062	3.25	.4619	12.16	.2645
2.76	.4911	8.721	.4028	3.26	.4614	12.23	.2622
2.77	.4903	8.785	.3994	3.27	.4610	12.31	.2600
2.78	.4896	8.850	.3961	3.28	.4605	12.38	.2577
2.79	.4889	8.915	.3928	3.29	.4600	12.46	.2555
2.80	.4882	8.980	.3895	3.30	.4596	12.54	.2533
2.81	.4875	9.046	.3862	3.31	.4591	12.62	.2511
2.82	.4868	9.111	.3829	3.32	.4587	12.69	.2489
2.83	.4861	9.177	.3797	3.33	.4582	12.77	.2468
2.84	.4854	9.243	.3765	3.34	.4578	12.85	.2446
2.85	.4847	9.310	.3733	3.35	.4573	12.93	.2425
2.86	.4840	9.376	.3701	3.36	.4569	13.00	.2404
2.87	.4833	9.443	.3670	3.37	.4565	13.08	.2383
2.88	.4827	9.510	.3639	3.38	.4560	13.16	.2363
2.89	.4820	9.578	.3608	3.39	.4556	13.24	.2342
2.90	.4814	9.645	.3577	3.40	.4552	13.32	.2322
2.91	.4807	9.713	.3547	3.41	.4548	13.40	.2302
2.92	.4801	9.781	.3517	3.42	.4544	13.48	.2282
2.93	.4795	9.849	.3487	3.43	.4540	13.56	.2263
2.94	.4788	9.918	.3457	3.44	.4535	13.64	.2243
2.95	.4782	9.986	.3428	3.45	.4531	13.72	.2224
2.96	.4776	10.06	.3398	3.46	.4527	13.80	.2205
2.97	.4770	10.12	.3369	3.47	.4523	13.88	.2186
2.98	.4764	10.19	.3340	3.48	.4519	13.96	.2167
2.99	.4758	10.26	.3312	3.49	.4515	14.04	.2148
3.00	.4752	10.33	.3283	3.50	.4512	14.13	.2129
3.01	.4746	10.40	.3255	3.51	.4508	14.21	.2111
3.02	.4740	10.47	.3227	3.52	.4504	14.29	.2093
3.03	.4734	10.54	.3200	3.53	.4500	14.37	.2075
3.04	.4729	10.62	.3172	3.54	.4496	14.45	.2057
3.05	.4723	10.69	.3145	3.55	.4492	14.54	.2039
3.06	.4717	10.76	.3118	3.56	.4489	14.62	.2022
3.07	.4712	10.83	.3091	3.57	.4485	14.70	.2004
3.08	.4706	10.90	.3065	3.58	.4481	14.79	.1987
3.09	.4701	10.97	.3038	3.59	.4478	14.87	.1970

TABLE 3 (Continued)

M_1	M_{2n}	$\dfrac{P_{2n}}{P_1}$	$\dfrac{P_{0n}}{P_0}$	M_1	M_{2n}	$\dfrac{P_{2n}}{P_1}$	$\dfrac{P_{0n}}{P_0}$
3.60	.4474	14.95	.1953	3.80	.4407	16.68	.1645
3.61	.4471	15.04	.1936	3.81	.4404	16.77	.1631
3.62	.4467	15.12	.1920	3.82	.4401	16.86	.1617
3.63	.4463	15.21	.1903	3.83	.4398	16.95	.1603
3.64	.4460	15.29	.1887	3.84	.4395	17.04	.1589
3.65	.4456	15.38	.1871	3.85	.4392	17.13	.1576
3.66	.4453	15.46	.1855	3.86	.4389	17.22	.1563
3.67	.4450	15.55	.1839	3.87	.4386	17.31	.1549
3.68	.4446	15.63	.1823	3.88	.4383	17.40	.1536
3.69	.4443	15.72	.1807	3.89	.4380	17.49	.1523
3.70	.4439	15.81	.1792	3.90	.4377	17.58	.1510
3.71	.4436	15.89	.1777	3.91	.4375	17.67	.1497
3.72	.4433	15.98	.1761	3.92	.4372	17.76	.1485
3.73	.4430	16.07	.1746	3.93	.4369	17.85	.1472
3.74	.4426	16.15	.1731	3.94	.4366	17.94	.1460
3.75	.4423	16.24	.1717	3.95	.4363	18.04	.1448
3.76	.4420	16.33	.1702	3.96	.4360	18.13	.1435
3.77	.4417	16.42	.1687	3.97	.4358	18.22	.1423
3.78	.4414	16.50	.1673	3.98	.4355	18.31	.1411
3.79	.4410	16.59	.1659	3.99	.4352	18.41	.1399
				4.00	.4350	18.50	.1388

TABLE 4: Numerical relations between flow quantities in front and behind shock waves. The table gives as a function of the Mach number in front of the shock of column 1 the following quantities (from reference 64).*

Column 2 The inclination of the shock ϵ_m that gives the maximum deviation. The value has been calculated with equation (134).

Column 3 The inclination of the shock ϵ_s that gives sonic velocity ($M = 1$) behind the shock. The value has been calculated with equation (131).

Column 4 The maximum deviation possible across the shock δ_m corresponding to the value ϵ_m.

Column 5 The deviation δ_s corresponding to sonic velocity behind the shock and to the value ϵ_s.

Column 6 The deviation ν that gives sonic velocity when the transformation is isentropic (from table 1).

Column 7 The Mach number M_{2m} behind the shock corresponding to the maximum deviation.

TABLE 4

M_1	m		s		δ_m		δ_s		ν		M_{2m}
	deg	min	deg	min	deg	min	deg	min	deg	min	
1.0	90		90		0		0		0		1.000
1.1	76	18	73	14	1	31	1	24	1	20	.9710
1.2	71	59	68	5	3	57	3	42	3	34	.9500
1.3	69	24	65	7	6	40	6	19	6	10	.9357
1.4	67	42	63	20	9	26	9	1	8	59	.9268
1.5	66	36	62	15	12	6	11	41	11	55	.9212
1.6	65	50	61	39	14	39	14	15	14	52	.9187
1.7	65	19	61	22	17	0	16	38	17	49	.9185
1.8	64	59	61	17	19	11	18	50	20	43	.9196
1.9	64	47	61	21	21	10	20	52	23	35	.9216
2.0	64	40	61	29	22	59	22	43	26	23	.9243
2.1	64	37	61	41	24	37	24	23	29	6	.9274
2.2	64	37	61	54	26	6	25	54	31	44	.9306
2.3	64	41	62	9	27	28	27	17	34	17	.9331
2.4	64	42	62	24	28	42	28	32	36	45	.9374
2.5	64	48	62	39	29	48	29	40	39	7	.9397
2.6	64	52	62	53	30	49	30	42	41	25	.9426
2.7	64	57	63	7	31	45	31	39	43	37	.9464
2.8	65	3	63	21	32	35	32	30	45	44	.9489
2.9	65	9	63	33	33	21	33	17	47	47	.9514
3.0	65	15	63	46	34	4	34	1	49	46	.9537
3.1	65	20	63	58	34	44	34	40	51	39	.9565
3.2	65	25	64	8	35	20	35	17	53	28	.9589
3.3	65	31	64	18	35	53	35	51	55	13	.9606
3.4	65	36	64	28	36	24	36	22	56	55	.9627
3.5	65	41	64	37	36	52	36	50	58	32	.9645
3.6	65	46	64	45	37	18	37	17	60	5	.9660
3.7	65	51	64	54	37	43	37	41	61	36	.9674
3.8	65	56	65	2	38	5	38	4	63	2	.9685
3.9	65	59	65	9	38	27	38	25	64	26	.9708
4.0	66	3	65	15	38	47	38	45	65	47	.9721

* See chart 2 of appendix.

TABLE 5: Numerical relations between flow quantities in front and behind inclined shock waves (from reference 64).

The table gives for different Mach numbers (column 1) (varying from 1 to 4 with steps of 0, 05), as function of the inclination of the shock (given in column 2), the following quantities:

Column 3 The deviation across the shock, calculated with equation 126.

Column 4 The Mach number behind the shock, calculated with equation 125.

Column 5 The ratio of the pressures behind p_2 and in front p_1 of the shock, calculated with equation 121.

Column 6 The ratio of the densities before p_1 and behind the shock, calculated with equation 122.

Column 7 The variation of entropy across the shock (in mechanical units (ft^2 sec^2 per degree Fahrenheit), determined with equation 150.

Chart 2 of the appendix gives the shock polar diagram from which the same relations can be obtained.

TABLE 5

M_1	ϵ (deg.)	ϵ (min.)	δ (deg.)	δ (min.)	M_2	$\dfrac{p_2}{p_1}$	$\dfrac{\rho_1}{\rho_2}$	ΔS
1.05	72	15	0	0	1.050	1.000	1.000	0
	73		0	16	1.037	1.010	.9932	. . . .
	76		0	25	1.014	1.044	.9695	.0010
	79		0	33	.991	1.073	.9511	.0454
	82		0	32	.973	1.095	.9375	.1284
	85		0	23	.961	1.110	.9283	.1739
	88		0	10	.954	1.118	.9234	.2035
	90		0		.953	1.120	.9225	.2865
1.10	65	23	0	0	1.100	1.100	1.000	0
	68		0	40	1.063	1.047	.9678	.0494
	71		1	11	1.025	1.095	.9370	.2095
	74		1	27	.993	1.138	.9120	.3359
	77		1	31	.965	1.174	.8921	.8437
	80		1	22	.940	1.202	.8768	.9465
	83		1	4	.928	1.224	.8658	1.293
	86		0	39	.918	1.238	.8587	1.601
	90		0		.912	1.245	.8554	1.828
1.15	60	24	0	0	1.150	1.000	1.000	0
	63		0	57	1.105	1.058	.9604	.0188
	66		1	47	1.058	1.121	.9217	.2421
	69		2	20	1.016	1.178	.8896	.8121
	72		2	37	.980	1.229	.8633	1.412
	75		2	39	.948	1.273	.8420	2.427
	78		2	27	.922	1.310	.8253	3.541
	81		2	2	.902	1.339	.8126	4.332
	84		1	27	.887	1.359	.8038	5.105
	87		0	45	.879	1.372	.7985	5.475
	90		0	0	.875	1.376	.7968	5.487

TABLE 5　(Continued)

M_1	ϵ		δ		M_2	$\dfrac{p_2}{p_1}$	$\dfrac{\rho_1}{\rho_2}$	ΔS
	(deg.)	(min.)	(deg.)	(min.)				
1.20	56	26	0	0	1.200	1.000	1.000	0
	59		1	12	1.149	1.068	.9543	.0178
	62		2	20	1.095	1.143	.9090	.5286
	65		3	9	1.045	1.213	.8712	1.317
	68		3	41	1.001	1.278	.8398	1.952
	71		3	56	.962	1.335	.8140	4.327
	74		3	53	.928	1.386	.7930	6.135
	77		3	34	.899	1.428	.7762	7.808
	80		3	0	.877	1.463	.7634	9.647
	83		2	15	.859	1.488	.7541	11.114
	86		1	20	.848	1.505	.7482	12.043
	90		0	0	.842	1.514	.7454	12.307
1.25	53	8	0	0	1.250	1.000	1.000	0
	54		0	31	1.230	1.026	.9815	....
	57		2	4	1.166	1.116	.9249	.1531
	60		3	20	1.108	1.201	.8778	.9405
	63		4	17	1.055	1.281	.8385	2.517
	66		4	55	1.006	1.355	.8057	4.948
	69		5	15	.963	1.422	.7786	7.532
	72		5	15	.924	1.482	.7563	10.655
	75		4	57	.891	1.534	.7383	13.550
	78		4	22	.863	1.578	.7241	16.587
	81		3	31	.841	1.612	.7134	18.752
	84		2	28	.826	1.636	.7059	20.695
	87		1	16	.817	1.651	.7015	22.118
	90		0	0	.813	1.656	.7000	22.229
1.30	50	17	0	0	1.300	1.000	1.000	0
	53		1	43	1.235	1.091	.9398	.0207
	56		3	20	1.169	1.189	.8841	.9998
	59		4	39	1.109	1.282	.8378	2.668
	62		5	38	1.053	1.370	.7992	5.357
	65		6	18	1.002	1.453	.7670	9.144
	68		6	38	.956	1.528	.7403	13.304
	71		6	37	.914	1.596	.7182	17.718
	74		6	16	.878	1.655	.7003	22.297
	77		5	36	.848	1.705	.6860	26.324
	80		4	28	.828	1.726	.6803	28.213
	83		3	26	.804	1.776	.6672	32.790
	86		2	2	.792	1.795	.6622	34.762
	90		0	0	.786	1.805	.6598	35.832
1.35	47	47	0	0	1.350	1.000	1.000	0
	50		1	35	1.293	1.081	.9459	.2332
	53		3	28	1.221	1.190	.8835	.8012
	56		5	2	1.155	1.295	.8319	2.943
	59		6	17	1.094	1.396	.7890	6.531
	62		7	13	1.037	1.491	.7532	11.222
	65		7	49	.985	1.580	.7233	16.531
	68		8	3	.938	1.661	.6986	22.793
	71		7	55	.895	1.734	.6781	28.932
	74		7	26	.858	1.798	.6615	34.981
	77		6	36	.826	1.852	.6483	40.592
	80		5	15	.806	1.875	.6430	43.000

TABLE 5 (Continued)

M_1	ϵ (deg.)	ϵ (min.)	δ (deg.)	δ (min.)	M_2	$\dfrac{p_2}{p_1}$	$\dfrac{\rho_1}{\rho_2}$	ΔS
1.35	83		4	1	0.781	1.928	0.6308	48.958
	86		2	22	.768	1.949	.6262	51.435
	90		0	0	.762	1.960	.6239	52.835
1.40	45	35	0	0	1.400	1.000	1.000	0
	47		1	7	1.361	1.056	.9616	.0168
	50		3	17	1.279	1.175	.8912	.7618
	53		5	8	1.211	1.292	.8333	2.773
	56		6	40	1.144	1.405	.7853	6.944
	59		7	52	1.082	1.513	.7453	12.268
	62		8	45	1.024	1.616	.7120	19.157
	65		9	16	.971	1.712	.6843	26.968
	68		9	25	.922	1.799	.6613	35.244
	71		9	12	.878	1.878	.6422	43.735
	74		8	35	.840	1.946	.6268	51.279
	77		7	35	.807	2.004	.6145	58.225
	80		6	2	.785	2.029	.6096	61.135
	83		4	36	.760	2.086	.5982	68.769
	86		2	43	.746	2.109	.5939	71.876
	90		0	0	.740	2.120	.5918	73.225
1.45	43	36	0	0	1.450	1.000	1.000	0
	44		0	21	1.438	1.017	.9880	.0524
	47		2	46	1.354	1.145	.9077	.3804
	50		4	54	1.275	1.273	.8421	2.590
	53		6	43	1.204	1.398	.7881	6.588
	56		8	13	1.135	1.519	.7433	12.621
	59		9	24	1.072	1.636	.7061	20.816
	62		10	13	1.021	1.746	.6751	29.965
	65		10	41	.959	1.848	.6492	40.298
	68		10	46	.909	1.942	.6277	50.600
	71		10	27	.864	2.026	.6100	61.012
	74		9	42	.826	2.100	.5956	70.544
	77		8	34	.790	2.162	.5841	79.032
	80		6	48	.767	2.188	.5795	82.727
	83		5	11	.740	2.250	.5690	91.785
	86		3	3	.727	2.274	.5650	95.562
	90		0	0	.720	2.286	.5630	97.685
1.50	41	49	0	0	1.500	1.000	1.000	0
	45		2	47	1.405	1.146	.9074	.3339
	48		5	5	1.322	1.283	.8373	2.643
	51		7	5	1.246	1.419	0.7799	7.361
	54		8	46	1.174	1.551	.7325	14.752
	57		10	8	1.107	1.680	.6932	24.227
	60		11	9	1.045	1.802	.6605	35.484
	63		11	49	.986	1.917	.6332	47.745
	66		12	6	.932	2.024	.6105	60.597
	69		11	59	.882	2.121	.5916	73.519
	72		11	25	.837	2.208	.5761	85.625
	75		10	26	.797	2.282	.5636	96.758
	78		9	0	.764	2.345	.5538	106.52
	81		7	10	.737	2.394	.5463	114.27
	84		5	0	.717	2.430	.5411	120.18
	87		2	34	.705	2.451	.5381	123.69
	90		0	0	.701	2.458	.5370	124.97

TABLE 5 (Continued)

M_1	ϵ		δ		M_2	$\dfrac{p_2}{p_1}$	$\dfrac{\rho_1}{\rho_2}$	ΔS
	(deg.)	(min.)	(deg.)	(min.)				
1.55	40	11	0	0	1.550	1.000	1.000	0
	43		2	36	1.461	1.137	.9124	.2618
	46		5	5	1.375	1.284	.8370	2.758
	49		7	15	1.294	1.430	.7756	7.822
	52		9	8	1.219	1.574	.7253	16.209
	55		10	42	1.148	1.714	.6836	27.196
	58		11	55	1.081	1.849	.6490	40.282
	61		12	47	1.018	1.977	.6201	53.883
	64		13	18	.960	2.098	.5960	70.187
	67		13	23	.905	2.208	.5760	86.652
	70		13	3	.855	2.308	.5595	100.703
	73		12	15	.811	2.397	.5460	114.735
	76		10	59	.772	2.472	.5351	127.18
	79		9	16	.739	2.534	.5266	137.84
	82		7	7	.714	2.582	.5204	146.19
	85		4	37	.696	2.615	.5162	151.95
	88		1	53	.686	2.633	.5140	155.23
	90		0	0	.684	2.636	.5135	155.77
1.60	38	41	0	0	1.600	1.000	1.000	0
	41		2	16	1.524	1.119	.9230	.1492
	44		4	55	1.433	1.275	.8413	2.321
	47		7	16	1.347	1.431	.7753	8.033
	50		9	19	1.268	1.586	.7214	17.068
	53		11	4	1.193	1.738	.6770	29.336
	56		12	29	1.123	1.886	.6403	44.264
	59		13	35	1.056	2.027	0.6097	51.249
	62		14	18	.993	2.162	.5842	79.141
	65		14	38	.934	2.287	.5630	97.414
	68		14	32	.880	2.401	.5453	115.37
	71		13	58	.830	2.503	.5308	132.45
	74		12	55	.786	2.593	.5190	148.21
	77		11	22	.748	2.669	.5095	162.13
	80		9	21	.722	2.701	.5058	173.06
	83		6	52	.692	2.776	.4971	181.56
	86		4	4	.676	2.805	.4938	187.21
	90		0	0	.668	2.820	.4922	190.04
1.65	37	18	0	0	1.650	1.000	1.000	0
	38		0	44	1.626	1.037	.9742	.0741
	41		3	40	1.526	1.200	.8778	1.074
	45		7	5	1.406	1.422	.7789	7.728
	48		9	19	1.322	1.587	.7208	16.545
	51		11	15	1.243	1.752	.6735	30.582
	54		12	53	1.169	1.912	.6343	47.195
	57		14	11	1.098	2.067	.6019	66.274
	60		15	8	1.032	2.216	.5748	86.781
	63		15	42	.969	2.355	.5522	108.07
	66		15	51	.910	2.484	.5334	129.27
	69		15	33	.856	2.602	.5179	149.64
	72		14	45	.806	2.706	.5051	168.66
	75		13	27	.762	2.797	.4947	185.57
	78		11	36	.725	2.872	.4866	200.02
	81		9	15	.695	2.932	.4804	211.67
	84		6	27	.672	2.975	.4761	220.27
	87		3	19	.659	3.001	.4736	225.50
	90		0	0	.654	3.010	.4728	227.26

TABLE 5 (Continued)

M_1	ϵ		δ		M_2	$\dfrac{p_2}{p_1}$	$\dfrac{\rho_1}{\rho_2}$	ΔS
	(deg.)	(min.)	(deg.)	(min.)				
1.70	36	2	0	0	1.700	1.000	1.000	0
	37		1	2	1.665	1.055	.9628	.1818
	40		4	3	1.562	1.226	.8646	1.610
	44		7	34	1.439	1.460	.7642	9.630
	47		9	53	1.350	1.637	.7058	20.803
	50		11	54	1.272	1.812	.6580	36.407
	53		13	37	1.195	1.984	.6188	55.689
	56		15	0	1.122	2.151	.5862	77.555
	59		16	4	1.052	2.311	.5591	101.14
	62		16	44	0.987	2.462	0.5365	125.46
	65		17	1	.925	2.602	.5177	149.93
	68		16	49	.867	2.732	.5021	173.35
	71		16	8	.815	2.848	.4892	195.27
	74		14	55	.768	2.949	.4787	215.00
	77		13	9	.726	3.034	.4704	232.17
	80		10	49	.698	3.070	.4670	239.48
	83		7	58	.666	3.155	.4594	256.95
	86		4	43	.649	3.189	.4564	263.86
	90		0	0	.641	3.205	.4550	267.45
1.75	34	51	0	0	1.750	1.000	1.000	0
	36		1	16	1.707	1.068	.9543	.1680
	39		4	21	1.602	1.248	.8537	2.002
	42		7	7	1.505	1.433	.7744	5.679
	45		9	35	1.414	1.620	.7109	19.498
	48		11	47	1.330	1.807	.6594	35.868
	51		13	41	1.249	1.991	.6172	56.587
	54		15	17	1.172	2.172	.5824	80.500
	57		16	33	1.099	2.346	.5535	106.72
	60		17	29	1.029	2.513	.5295	134.17
	63		18	0	.963	2.670	.5094	161.99
	66		18	6	.901	2.815	.4927	189.16
	69		17	43	.844	2.947	.4789	214.78
	72		16	48	.792	3.065	.4675	238.48
	75		15	19	.745	3.167	.4583	259.45
	78		13	14	.705	3.252	.4511	277.31
	81		10	34	.672	3.318	.4566	291.52
	84		7	23	.648	3.367	.4418	301.90
	87		3	48	.633	3.396	.4395	308.21
	90		0	0	.628	3.406	.4388	310.30
1.80	33	45	0	0	1.800	1.000	1.000	0
	35		1	25	1.751	1.077	.9485	.1551
	38		4	33	1.643	1.266	.8452	2.365
	41		7	24	1.544	1.460	.7642	9.580
	44		9	58	1.451	1.657	.6997	22.427
	47		12	13	1.364	1.855	.6475	40.908
	50		14	13	1.280	2.052	.6050	54.347
	53		15	54	1.201	2.244	.5699	91.046
	56		17	16	1.125	2.431	.5409	120.44
	59		18	18	1.053	2.611	.5167	151.22
	62		18	57	.984	2.780	.4966	182.40
	65		19	11	.919	2.938	.4798	212.98
	68		18	56	.859	3.083	.4659	242.15
	71		18	9	.803	3.213	.4544	269.00
	74		16	48	.753	3.326	.4450	293.12

TABLE 5 (Continued)

M_1	ϵ		δ		M_2	$\dfrac{p_2}{p_1}$	$\dfrac{\rho_1}{\rho_2}$	ΔS
	(deg.)	(min.)	(deg.)	(min.)				
1.80	77		14	49	.709	3.422	.4376	313.73
	80		12	12	.678	3.499	.4319	330.80
	83		9	1	.645	3.557	.4277	343.47
	86		5	21	.625	3.595	.4251	351.77
	90		0	0	.617	3.613	.4239	356.00
1.85	32	43	0	0	1.850	1.000	1.000	0
	34		1	29	1.799	1.082	.9454	.0761
	37		4	42	1.687	1.280	.8389	3.029
	40		7	37	1.585	1.483	.7560	10.761
	43		10	14	1.490	1.691	.6902	25.168
	46		12	35	1.400	1.899	.6372	45.795
	49		14	39	1.314	2.108	.5941	71.556
	52		16	26	1.232	2.313	.5588	101.48
	55		17	54	1.153	2.513	.5295	134.09
	58		19	3	1.078	2.705	.5052	171.91
	61		19	49	1.007	2.888	.4850	203.15
	64		20	11	.939	3.059	.4681	237.22
	67		20	4	.876	3.217	.4540	269.74
	70		19	27	.817	3.359	.4424	300.20
	73		18	14	.763	3.485	.4329	327.61
	76		16	23	.716	3.593	.4253	351.39
	79		13	52	.676	3.681	.4193	371.09
	82		10	43	.643	3.749	.4150	386.58
	85		7	0	.620	3.796	.4120	397.11
	88		2	52	.608	3.821	.4105	402.93
	90		0	0	.606	3.826	.4102	405.62
1.90	31	45	0	0	1.900	1.000	1.000	0
	33		1	28	1.848	1.083	.9449	.1927
	36		4	46	1.734	1.289	.8348	2.962
	39		7	45	1.628	1.501	.7495	11.832
	42		10	26	1.530	1.719	.6822	27.594
	45		12	51	1.437	1.939	.6284	50.345
	48		15	0	1.349	2.159	.5846	78.759
	51		16	52	1.265	2.377	.5489	111.52
	54		18	27	1.184	2.590	.5194	147.61
	57		19	41	1.106	2.796	.4949	185.39
	60		20	35	1.032	2.992	.4745	223.46
	63		21	5	.962	3.177	.4574	261.49
	66		21	8	.895	3.348	.4433	297.92
	69		20	39	.833	3.504	.4315	331.73
	72		19	36	.776	3.643	.4219	362.52
	75		17	55	.725	3.763	.4141	389.54
	78		15	31	.681	3.863	.4079	412.39
	81		12	26	.645	3.942	.4033	430.64
	84		8	43	.618	3.999	.4001	443.81
	87		4	30	.601	4.033	.3981	452.76
	90		0	0	.596	4.045	.3975	454.52
1.95	30	51	0	0	1.950	1.000	1.000	0
	32		1	23	1.901	1.079	.9471	.1650
	35		4	45	1.782	1.293	.8328	3.053
	38		7	48	1.674	1.515	.7449	12.620
	41		10	34	1.573	1.743	.6758	29.754
	44		13	3	1.478	1.974	.6208	54.438

TABLE 5 (Continued)

M_1	ϵ (deg.)	ϵ (min.)	δ (deg.)	δ (min.)	M_2	$\dfrac{p_2}{p_1}$	$\dfrac{\rho_1}{\rho_2}$	ΔS
1.95	47		15	17	1.386	2.206	.5764	85.426
	50		17	14	1.299	2.437	.5401	121.25
	53		18	54	1.216	2.663	.5103	160.67
	56		20	15	1.136	2.882	.4855	200.76
	59		21	16	1.059	3.098	.4649	251.41
	62		21	54	.986	3.292	.4478	285.66
	65		22	6	.917	3.477	.4335	325.83
	68		21	47	.851	3.647	.4216	363.54
	71		20	54	.791	3.799	.4118	397.89
	74		19	23	.737	3.935	.4038	430.70
	77		17	9	.689	4.045	.3975	454.48
	80		14	11	.649	4.136	.3926	475.59
	83		10	31	.617	4.204	.3891	491.55
	86		6	15	.596	4.248	.3869	501.92
	90		0	0	.586	4.270	.3858	507.06
2.00	30	0	0	0	2.000	1.000	1.000	0
	31		1	15	1.956	1.072	.9515	.0751
	34		4	40	1.833	1.293	.8329	2.885
	37		7	48	1.721	1.524	.7419	12.999
	40		10	36	1.617	1.762	.6709	31.470
	43		13	11	1.519	2.004	.6146	58.128
	46		15	29	1.426	2.248	.5693	91.374
	49		17	31	1.336	2.491	.5324	130.44
	52		19	16	1.250	2.731	.5022	173.24
	55		20	44	1.167	2.965	.4771	218.21
	58		21	52	1.088	3.190	.4563	264.12
	61		22	37	1.012	3.403	.4390	309.67
	64		22	58	.940	3.603	.4246	353.67
	67		22	49	.872	3.787	.4125	395.23
	70		22	7	.773	3.954	.4026	433.42
	73		20	47	.751	4.101	.3945	467.44
	76		18	44	.709	4.227	.3880	497.03
	79		15	55	.655	4.330	.3829	521.38
	82		12	21	.619	4.410	.3791	540.28
	85		8	5	.594	4.464	.3766	553.29
	88		3	19	.580	4.494	.3753	560.45
	90		0	0	.577	4.500	.3750	561.72
2.05	29	12	0	0	2.050	1.000	1.000	0
	30		1	0	2.013	1.059	.9598	.0336
	33		4	32	1.886	1.288	.8351	2.667
	36		7	43	1.771	1.527	.7406	13.094
	39		10	37	1.664	1.775	.6673	32.672
	42		13	14	1.563	2.029	.6095	61.108
	45		15	37	1.467	2.284	.5632	97.103
	48		17	43	1.374	2.541	.5257	138.82
	51		19	34	1.286	2.795	.4950	185.00
	54		21	7	1.200	3.042	.4696	233.68
	57		22	22	1.118	3.282	.4486	283.54
	60		23	15	1.040	3.511	.4310	333.09
	63		23	44	.965	3.726	.4164	381.21
	66		23	46	.894	3.925	.4043	426.60
	69		23	14	.828	4.107	.3942	468.77
	72		22	6	.766	4.268	.3859	506.65
	75		20	15	.711	4.408	.3792	539.66

TABLE 5 (Continued)

M_1	ϵ (deg.)	(min.)	δ (deg.)	(min.)	M_2	$\dfrac{p_2}{p_1}$	$\dfrac{\rho_1}{\rho_2}$	ΔS
2.05	78		17	37	.663	4.524	.3739	567.34
	81		14	11	.623	4.616	.3699	589.36
	84		9	58	.594	4.683	.3671	605.33
	87		5	10	.575	4.723	.3655	614.90
	90		0	0	.569	4.736	.3650	618.04
2.10	28	26	0	0	2.100	1.000	1.000	0
	29		0	43	2.073	1.043	.9706	.0119
	32		4	19	1.941	1.278	.8395	2.431
	35		7	35	1.823	1.526	.7410	13.010
	38		10	32	1.712	1.784	.6652	33.503
	41		13	14	1.608	2.048	.6057	63.611
	44		15	40	1.509	2.316	.5582	101.86
	47		17	51	1.414	2.585	.5199	146.68
	50		19	47	1.323	2.852	.4887	196.12
	53		21	26	1.235	3.115	.4629	248.57
	56		22	47	1.151	3.369	.4416	302.28
	59		23	48	1.070	3.614	.4238	355.83
	62		24	26	.992	3.844	.4090	407.99
	65		24	37	.918	4.060	.3967	457.66
	68		24	16	.849	4.256	.3865	503.91
	71		23	20	.784	4.433	.3780	545.66
	74		21	41	.726	4.588	.3712	582.41
	77		19	16	.674	4.718	.3657	613.80
	80		16	0	.630	4.823	.3615	639.05
	83		11	54	.596	4.902	.3585	657.99
	86		7	6	.573	4.953	.3565	670.39
	90		0	0	.561	4.978	.3556	676.56
2.15	27	43	0	0	2.150	1.000	1.000	0
	28		0	22	2.139	1.022	.9846	.0020
	31		4	4	1.999	1.265	.8458	2.102
	34		7	23	1.876	1.520	.7432	12.711
	37		10	25	1.763	1.787	.6644	33.790
	40		13	10	1.656	2.062	.6030	65.350
	43		15	40	1.554	2.342	.5542	105.89
	46		17	56	1.456	2.624	.5151	153.61
	49		19	56	1.362	2.905	.4832	206.46
	52		21	41	1.272	3.182	.4570	262.52
	55		23	8	1.185	3.452	.4353	320.29
	58		24	16	1.101	3.712	.4173	378.01
	61		25	2	1.028	3.959	.4023	434.36
	64		25	22	.944	4.190	.3898	488.25
	67		25	12	.872	4.402	.3794	538.44
	70		24	28	.804	4.596	.3708	584.34
	73		23	3	.742	4.765	.3638	625.23
	76		20	51	.686	4.911	.3581	660.21
	79		17	47	.639	5.030	.3537	688.94
	82		13	51	.600	5.122	.3505	711.13
	85		9	6	.572	5.185	.3483	726.45
	88		3	45	.557	5.220	.3472	734.85
	90		0	0	.554	5.226	.3469	736.44
2.20	27	2	0	0	2.200	1.000	1.000	0
	30		3	43	2.059	1.245	.8553	1.720
	33		7	7	1.932	1.508	.7471	11.985
	36		10	13	1.815	1.784	.6650	33.590

TABLE 5 (Continued)

M_1	ϵ (deg.)	ϵ (min.)	δ (deg.)	δ (min.)	M_2	$\dfrac{p_2}{p_1}$	$\dfrac{\rho_1}{\rho_2}$	ΔS
2.20	39		13	2	1.705	2.070	.6014	66.331
	42		15	36	1.600	2.362	.5512	109.03
	45		17	56	1.499	2.657	.5110	159.44
	48		20	0	1.403	2.952	.4784	215.51
	51		21	51	1.310	3.244	.4517	275.34
	54		23	24	1.220	3.529	.4297	337.15
	57		24	39	1.134	3.805	.4114	399.12
	60		25	32	1.051	4.069	.3962	459.85
	63		26	2	.972	4.316	.3835	518.05
	66		26	3	.896	4.546	.3730	572.59
	69		25	30	.826	4.755	.3642	622.62
	72		24	18	.761	4.941	.3570	667.37
	75		22	20	.701	5.122	.3512	706.33
	78		19	31	.650	5.234	.3466	738.68
	81		15	47	.607	5.342	.3431	764.31
	84		11	9	.574	5.418	.3407	782.94
	87		5	47	.554	5.465	.3393	794.15
	90		0	0	.547	5.480	.3388	798.01
2.25	26	23	0	0	2.250	1.000	1.000	0
	29		3	20	2.122	1.222	.8670	1.226
	32		6	48	1.990	1.492	.7528	11.034
	35		9	58	1.869	1.776	.6670	32.878
	38		12	51	1.755	2.072	.6009	66.707
	41		15	29	1.648	2.376	.5491	111.22
	44		17	53	1.544	2.683	.5078	164.30
	47		20	2	1.445	2.992	.4744	223.75
	50		21	57	1.349	3.301	.4472	289.97
	53		23	36	1.257	3.601	.4247	352.90
	56		24	57	1.168	3.893	.4062	419.20
	59		25	58	1.083	4.173	.3907	484.09
	62		26	36	1.001	4.438	.3778	546.70
	65		26	47	.923	4.685	.3671	605.74
	68		26	27	.849	4.911	.3581	660.25
	71		25	28	.781	5.114	.3508	709.13
	74		23	45	.718	5.291	.3448	751.96
	77		21	10	.663	5.441	.3400	788.50
	80		17	40	.615	5.562	.3364	817.71
	83		13	12	.578	5.652	.3337	839.54
	86		7	54	.553	5.711	.3321	853.92
	90		0	0	.541	5.740	.3313	860.86
2.30	25	46	0	0	2.300	1.000	1.000	0
	28		2	53	2.186	1.194	.8814	.7943
	31		6	27	2.050	1.472	.7601	9.925
	34		9	40	1.925	1.763	.6704	31.579
	37		12	37	1.808	2.069	.6016	66.296
	40		15	18	1.697	2.383	.5479	112.53
	43		17	46	1.591	2.704	.5053	168.02
	46		20	0	1.489	3.027	.4711	229.53
	49		21	59	1.390	3.349	.4432	294.87
	52		23	43	1.295	3.666	.4203	367.61
	55		25	10	1.212	3.975	.4014	438.08
	58		26	19	1.116	4.272	.3857	507.53
	61		27	6	1.032	4.555	.3726	574.68
	64		27	26	.951	4.819	.3617	638.07

TABLE 5 (Continued)

M_1	ϵ		δ		M_2	$\dfrac{p_2}{p_1}$	$\dfrac{\rho_1}{\rho_2}$	ΔS
	(deg.)	(min.)	(deg.)	(min.)				
2.30	67		27	17	.874	5.063	.3526	696.90
	70		26	32	.803	5.283	.3451	750.17
	73		25	3	.737	5.478	.3389	797.33
	76		22	45	.678	5.644	.3340	837.74
	79		19	29	.626	5.781	.3301	870.83
	82		15	14	.585	5.886	.3273	896.25
	85		10	3	.555	5.958	.3254	913.86
	88		4	9	.537	5.998	.3244	923.31
	90		0	0	.534	6.005	.3242	925.18
2.35	25	11	0	0	2.350	1.000	1.000	0
	27		2	24	2.254	1.161	.8988	.4871
	30		6	1	2.112	1.444	.7702	8.584
	33		9	19	1.983	1.745	.6754	29.851
	36		12	20	1.862	2.059	.6034	65.009
	39		15	5	1.748	2.385	.5477	112.76
	42		17	36	1.639	2.718	.5037	170.62
	45		19	54	1.534	3.055	.4684	236.22
	48		21	58	1.433	3.392	.4399	306.99
	51		23	47	1.335	3.725	.4165	380.88
	54		25	20	1.241	4.050	.3972	455.56
	57		26	35	1.151	4.365	.3812	529.42
	60		27	30	1.064	4.666	.3678	601.08
	63		28		.980	4.949	.3567	669.34
	66		28	2	.901	5.211	.3475	732.57
	69		27	29	.827	5.449	.3398	790.44
	72		26	15	.757	5.661	.3335	841.84
	75		24	13	.694	5.845	.3284	886.40
	78		21	14	.639	5.998	.3244	923.36
	81		17	14	.593	6.119	.3213	952.54
	84		12	13	.558	6.206	.3192	973.52
	87		6	22	.536	6.259	.3180	986.09
	90		0	0	.529	6.276	.3176	990.43
2.40	24	37	0	0	2.400	1.000	1.000	0
	26		1	51	2.325	1.125	.9195	.1502
	29		5	34	2.176	1.413	.7822	7.137
	32		8	55	2.042	1.720	.6818	27.650
	35		12	0	1.919	2.044	.6064	63.094
	38		14	49	1.801	2.381	.5483	112.11
	41		17	23	1.688	2.726	.5028	172.07
	44		19	45	1.581	3.076	.4665	240.56
	47		21	53	1.492	3.428	.4322	329.56
	50		23	47	1.376	3.777	.4132	392.62
	53		25	26	1.280	4.120	.3935	471.78
	56		26	47	1.187	4.452	.3771	550.07
	59		27	49	1.097	4.771	.3636	626.45
	62		28	29	1.011	5.072	.3522	699.18
	65		28	41	.929	5.353	.3428	767.25
	68		28	20	.852	5.610	.3349	829.37
	71		27	21	.780	5.841	.3285	885.40
	74		25	35	.713	6.043	.3232	934.25
	77		22	53	.654	6.213	.3190	975.29
	80		19	10	.604	6.350	.3158	1008.42
	83		14	23	.564	6.454	.3135	1033.08
	86		8	38	.537	6.521	.3120	1049.17
	90		0	0	.523	6.554	.3113	1057.03

TABLE 5 (Continued)

M_1	ϵ		δ		M_2	$\dfrac{p_2}{p_1}$	$\dfrac{\rho_1}{\rho_2}$	ΔS
	(deg.)	(min.)	(deg.)	(min.)				
2.45	24	5	0	0	2.450	1.000	1.000	0
	25		1	15	2.398	1.084	.9439	.0919
	28		5	3	2.243	1.377	.7965	5.580
	31		8	30	2.105	1.692	.6896	25.181
	34		11	37	1.976	2.023	.6106	60.395
	37		14	29	1.855	2.370	.5500	110.28
	40		17	8	1.740	2.727	.5027	172.27
	43		19	33	1.629	3.091	.4651	243.52
	46		21	45	1.522	3.457	.4350	321.33
	49		23	44	1.419	3.822	.4104	403.01
	52		25	28	1.320	4.182	.3902	486.38
	55		26	55	1.224	4.532	.3736	569.31
	58		28	4	1.132	4.870	.3597	650.28
	61		28	52	1.043	5.190	.3481	727.72
	64		29	14	.959	5.491	.3385	800.43
	67		29	6	.879	5.767	.3305	867.49
	70		28	20	.804	6.017	.3239	928.03
	73		26	50	.734	6.238	.3185	981.10
	76		24	26	.671	6.427	.3141	1026.47
	79		21	2	.616	6.582	.3107	1063.68
	82		16	31	.572	6.701	.3082	1092.28
	85		10	56	.540	6.783	.3066	1111.86
	88		4	31	.521	6.828	.3057	1122.61
	90		0	0	.518	6.836	.3055	1124.64
2.50	23	35	0	0	2.500	1.000	1.000	0
	24		0	39	2.477	1.040	.9726	.0099
	27		4	29	2.318	1.336	.8136	4.218
	30		8	0	2.169	1.656	.7000	22.359
	33		11	11	2.036	1.996	.6162	57.183
	36		14	7	1.911	2.353	.5526	107.72
	39		16	49	1.793	2.721	.5033	171.33
	42		19	18	1.679	3.098	.4645	245.26
	45		21	34	1.569	3.479	.4333	326.23
	48		23	37	1.463	3.860	.4081	411.85
	51		25	26	1.361	4.237	.3874	499.41
	54		26	59	1.263	4.606	.3704	586.97
	57		28	15	1.168	4.962	.3562	672.66
	60		29	11	1.077	5.302	.3444	754.91
	63		29	42	.990	5.622	.3346	832.63
	66		29	45	.907	5.919	.3264	904.33
	69		29	13	.829	6.189	.3197	969.50
	72		27	58	.756	6.429	.3141	1027.15
	75		25	53	.690	6.637	.3096	1076.97
	78		22	47	.621	6.810	.3060	1118.26
	81		18	34	.582	6.947	.3033	1150.70
	84		13	13	.545	7.045	.3015	1174.11
	87		6	58	.519	7.105	.3004	1188.32
	90		0	0	.513	7.125	.3000	1193.01
2.55	23	5	0	0	2.550	1.000	1.000	0
	26		3	53	2.385	1.291	.8336	2.876
	29		7	28	2.235	1.616	.7119	19.290
	32		10	44	2.098	1.964	.6230	53.132
	35		13	43	1.969	2.329	.5562	104.01
	38		16	29	1.847	2.709	.5048	169.05

TABLE 5 (Continued)

M_1	ϵ		δ		M_2	$\dfrac{p_2}{p_1}$	$\dfrac{\rho_1}{\rho_2}$	$-\Delta S$
	(deg.)	(min.)	(deg.)	(min.)				
2.55	41		19	1	1.730	3.097	.4644	243.87
	44		21	21	1.618	3.494	.4323	329.59
	47		23	27	1.509	3.891	.4063	418.89
	50		25	21	1.404	4.285	.3850	510.47
	53		27	0	1.306	4.672	.3676	602.80
	56		28	22	1.206	5.048	.3531	693.13
	59		29	25	1.112	5.407	.3411	780.37
	62		30	6	1.022	5.748	.3310	862.79
	65		30	19	.937	6.065	.3227	939.56
	68		29	59	.856	6.354	.3158	1009.10
	71		29	0	.780	6.616	.3100	1071.77
	74		27	12	.710	6.843	.3054	1126.14
	77		24	26	.648	7.036	.3016	1171.71
	80		20	33	.594	7.191	.2988	1208.54
	83		15	29	.552	7.307	.2967	1235.73
	86		9	19	.523	7.383	.2954	1253.54
	90		0	0	.508	7.420	.2948	1262.20
2.60	22	37	0	0	2.600	1.000	1.000	0
	25		3	13	2.460	1.242	.8568	1.650
	28		6	53	2.303	1.572	.7260	15.975
	31		10	14	2.164	1.927	.6310	48.795
	34		13	17	2.029	2.299	.5609	99.355
	37		16	5	1.903	2.690	.5070	165.41
	40		18	41	1.783	3.092	.4650	243.95
	43		21	4	1.667	3.502	.4317	331.00
	46		23	15	1.556	3.914	.4049	424.05
	49		25	13	1.448	4.326	.3831	520.20
	52		26	57	1.344	4.731	.3652	616.90
	55		28	25	1.244	5.126	.3504	712.07
	58		29	35	1.148	5.505	.3381	804.08
	61		30	24	1.056	5.866	.3278	891.44
	64		30	47	.968	6.205	.3193	1000.97
	67		30	40	.891	6.516	.3121	1047.96
	70		29	55	.803	6.798	.3063	1117.32
	73		28	24	.733	7.046	.3015	1174.12
	76		25	57	.666	7.259	.2976	1224.31
	79		22	25	.609	7.433	.2946	1265.36
	82		17	40	.562	7.567	.2924	1296.76
	85		11	44	.527	7.660	.2909	1318.12
	88		4	52	.508	7.711	.2901	1329.92
	90		0	0	.504	7.720	.2899	1332.26
2.65	22	10	0	0	2.650	1.000	1.000	0
	24		2	31	2.538	1.189	.8839	. . . .
	27		6	17	2.375	1.522	.7424	12.917
	30		9	41	2.228	1.882	.6413	43.790
	33		12	48	2.091	2.264	.5667	93.992
	36		15	40	1.961	2.664	.5101	160.88
	39		18	19	1.838	3.078	.4663	241.13
	42		20	45	1.718	3.502	.4317	331.24
	45		23	0	1.604	3.930	.4040	427.82
	48		25	2	1.493	4.358	.3815	527.95
	51		26	51	1.387	4.782	.3632	629.24
	54		28	24	1.284	5.196	.3480	729.13
	57		29	41	1.186	5.596	.3354	826.05

TABLE 5   (Continued)

M_1	ϵ		δ		M_2	$\dfrac{p_2}{p_1}$	$\dfrac{\rho_1}{\rho_2}$	ΔS
	(deg.)	(min.)	(deg.)	(min.)				
2.65	60		30	38	1.091	5.978	.3249	918.56
	63		31	11	1.000	6.338	.3161	1005.37
	66		31	15	.914	6.671	.3089	1085.28
	69		30	44	.832	6.974	.3028	1157.32
	72		29	29	.756	7.244	.2979	1221.07
	75		27	22	.687	7.477	.2939	1275.77
	78		24	11	.625	7.672	.2907	1321.10
	81		19	47	.573	7.826	.2883	1356.78
	84		14	8	.534	7.937	.2866	1382.27
	87		7	24	.508	8.004	.2857	1397.83
	90		0	0	.500	8.026	.2853	1402.90
2.70	21	44	0	0	2.700	1.000	1.000	0
	23		1	46	2.620	1.132	.9154	0.0037
	26		5	37	2.448	1.468	.7615	9.908
	29		9	6	2.296	1.832	.6530	38.562
	32		12	17	2.155	2.222	.5737	87.712
	35		15	12	2.021	2.631	.5141	154.99
	38		17	54	1.893	3.057	.4683	236.84
	41		20	24	1.771	3.494	.4323	329.61
	44		22	42	1.653	3.937	.4036	429.60
	47		24	48	1.540	4.382	.3804	533.67
	50		26	42	1.431	4.824	.3615	639.51
	53		28	21	1.326	5.258	.3459	744.16
	56		29	44	1.225	5.679	.3330	846.19
	59		30	47	1.127	6.082	.3223	943.73
	62		31	30	1.034	6.464	.3133	1035.46
	65		31	45	.945	6.820	.3058	1120.43
	68		31	26	.861	7.145	.2996	1197.59
	71		30	28	.782	7.437	.2945	1266.21
	74		28	38	.709	7.692	.2904	1325.55
	77		25	48	.647	7.908	.2871	1375.64
	80		21	47	.587	8.082	.2845	1415.60
	83		16	29	.542	8.212	.2827	1445.41
	86		9	57	.511	8.297	.2815	1464.79
	90		0	0	.496	8.338	.2810	1474.07
2.75	21	19	0	0	2.750	1.000	1.000	0
	22		0	58	2.705	1.071	.9519	.0583
	25		4	56	2.526	1.409	.7836	6.901
	28		8	29	2.366	1.778	.6666	33.023
	31		11	39	2.217	2.175	.5818	80.901
	34		14	42	2.082	2.592	.5191	147.88
	37		17	28	1.951	3.029	.4709	231.04
	40		20	1	1.826	3.479	.4333	326.03
	43		22	23	1.705	3.937	.4036	429.46
	46		24	32	1.588	4.399	.3796	537.44
	49		26	30	1.477	4.859	.3601	647.59
	52		28	14	1.368	5.312	.3441	757.25
	55		29	42	1.264	5.754	.3309	864.19
	58		30	54	1.165	6.179	.3199	966.93
	61		31	44	1.069	6.583	.3107	1063.86
	64		32	9	.977	6.961	.3031	1152.98
	67		32	3	.890	7.309	.2967	1236.19
	70		31	19	.808	7.624	.2914	1309.77
	73		29	47	.732	7.902	.2872	1374.26

TABLE 5 (Continued)

M_1	ϵ		δ		M_2	$\dfrac{p_2}{p_1}$	$\dfrac{\rho_1}{\rho_2}$	ΔS
	(deg.)	(min.)	(deg.)	(min.)				
2.75	76		27	19	.663	8.140	.2837	1428.95
	79		23	40	.603	8.335	.2810	1473.39
	82		18	44	.553	8.486	.2790	1507.35
	85		12	29	.517	8.589	.2777	1531.02
	88		5	11	.496	9.646	.2770	1543.49
	90		0	0	.492	8.656	.2769	1546.11
2.80	20	56	0	0	2.800	1.000	1.000	0
	21		0	7	2.795	1.008	.9943	....
	24		4	11	2.604	1.347	.8091	4.353
	27		7	50	2.439	1.719	.6824	27.389
	30		11	8	2.288	2.120	.5918	73.021
	33		14	10	2.145	2.547	.5250	139.75
	36		16	59	2.011	2.994	.4743	223.81
	39		19	36	1.882	3.456	.4350	320.95
	42		22	0	1.757	3.929	.4041	427.22
	45		24	14	1.638	4.407	.3792	539.17
	48		26	15	1.523	4.884	.3591	653.23
	51		28	4	1.412	5.358	.3426	768.04
	54		29	38	1.305	5.820	.3291	880.12
	57		30	55	1.203	6.267	.3178	988.02
	60		31	54	1.105	6.693	.3084	1090.41
	63		32	28	1.011	7.095	.3005	1185.63
	66		32	34	.921	7.467	.2940	1272.94
	69		32	4	.836	7.805	.2886	1351.78
	72		30	50	.757	8.107	.2842	1421.21
	75		28	41	.685	8.367	.2806	1480.64
	78		25	26	.620	8.585	.2778	1529.76
	81		20	53	.566	8.756	.2756	1568.17
	84		14	59	.524	8.880	.2741	1595.87
	87		7	51	.498	8.955	.2732	1612.60
	90		0	0	.488	8.980	.2730	1618.43
2.85	20	32	0	0	2.850	1.000	1.000	0
	23		3	24	2.687	1.280	.8386	2.366
	26		7	8	2.514	1.654	.7005	21.972
	29		10	31	2.358	2.061	.6031	65.049
	32		13	37	2.211	2.494	.5320	130.80
	35		16	28	2.072	2.951	.4785	215.30
	38		19	8	1.939	3.425	.4373	314.22
	41		21	36	1.811	3.912	.4050	423.51
	44		23	53	1.689	4.406	.3793	539.08
	47		25	58	1.570	4.902	0.3585	657.96
	50		27	51	1.457	5.394	.3415	777.09
	53		29	31	1.348	5.878	.3275	894.04
	56		30	54	1.243	6.346	.3159	1007.37
	59		31	59	1.142	6.796	.3063	1059.43
	62		32	43	1.045	7.221	.2983	1215.30
	65		32	59	.953	7.617	.2916	1308.29
	68		32	42	.866	7.980	.2860	1392.15
	71		31	44	.784	8.305	.2814	1466.51
	74		29	55	.708	8.590	.2777	1531.03
	77		27	2	.640	8.830	.2747	1584.93
	80		22	55	.581	9.024	.2724	1628.01
	83		17	24	.534	9.169	.2708	1660.18
	86		10	32	.501	9.264	.2698	1681.05
	90		0	0	.485	9.310	.2693	1691.11

TABLE 5 (Continued)

M_1	ϵ		δ		M_2	$\dfrac{p_2}{p_1}$	$\dfrac{\rho_1}{\rho_2}$	ΔS
	(deg.)	(min.)	(deg.)	(min.)				
2.90	20	10	0	0	2.900	1.000	1.000	0
	21		1	12	2.842	1.093	.9382	.1255
	24		5	11	2.651	1.457	.7656	9.189
	27		8	45	2.483	1.856	.6474	40.835
	30		12	0	2.328	2.286	.5630	97.177
	33		14	59	2.182	2.744	.5007	175.55
	36		17	46	2.043	3.223	.4535	271.20
	39		20	21	1.910	3.719	.4169	379.65
	42		22	45	1.783	4.226	.3880	496.86
	45		24	57	1.660	4.739	.3648	618.87
	48		26	58	1.542	5.252	.3461	742.74
	51		28	47	1.428	5.759	.3307	865.63
	54		30	21	1.319	6.255	.3181	985.44
	57		31	39	1.214	6.735	.3075	1100.24
	60		32	38	1.114	7.192	.2988	1208.72
	63		33	14	1.018	7.623	.2915	1309.43
	66		33	20	.926	8.022	.2854	1401.94
	69		32	52	.839	8.385	.2804	1484.81
	72		31	38	.758	8.708	.2762	1557.77
	75		29	29	.684	8.988	.2729	1620.09
	78		26	11	.618	9.221	.2702	1671.56
	81		21	34	0.562	9.405	0.2682	1711.92
	84		15	30	.519	9.538	.2668	1740.89
	87		8	9	.491	9.618	.2660	1758.18
	90		0	0	.481	9.645	.2658	1764.28
2.95	19	49	0	0	2.95	1.000	1.000	0
	20		0	16	2.936	1.021	.9853	.000
	23		4	23	2.735	1.383	.7939	5.986
	26		8	2	2.559	1.784	.6650	33.698
	29		11	21	2.399	2.220	.5741	87.349
	32		14	24	2.248	2.684	.5077	164.62
	35		16	53	2.090	3.174	.4577	260.81
	38		19	52	1.969	3.682	.4193	371.32
	41		22	19	1.838	4.203	.3892	491.51
	44		24	35	1.712	4.732	.3651	617.38
	47		26	39	1.590	5.264	.3457	745.74
	50		28	32	1.474	5.791	.3299	873.54
	53		30	12	1.360	6.309	.3168	998.57
	56		31	36	1.255	6.812	.3060	1118.74
	59		32	42	1.152	7.293	.2970	1232.49
	62		33	26	1.053	7.749	.2895	1338.98
	65		33	44	.959	8.173	.2832	1436.41
	68		33	28	.870	8.561	.2781	1524.82
	71		32	31	.786	8.910	.2738	1602.73
	74		30	41	.708	9.215	.2703	1670.38
	77		27	48	.638	9.473	.2675	1726.62
	80		25	54	.568	9.680	.2654	1771.85
	83		17	57	.529	9.836	.2639	1805.48
	86		10	54	.495	9.937	.2629	1827.06
	90		0	0	.478	9.986	.2624	1837.61
3.00	19	28	0	0	3.000	1.000	1.000	0
	20		0	46	2.960	1.062	.9582	.0375
	23		4	50	2.758	1.436	.7731	8.219

TABLE 5 (Continued)

M_1	ϵ (deg.)	(min.)	δ (deg.)	(min.)	M_2	$\dfrac{p_2}{p_1}$	$\dfrac{\rho_1}{\rho_2}$	ΔS
3.00	26		8	27	2.581	1.851	.6485	40.430
	29		11	44	2.419	2.301	.5606	99.591
	32		14	46	2.267	2.782	.4964	182.65
	35		17	35	2.122	3.287	.4481	284.73
	38		20	12	1.983	3.813	.4109	400.94
	41		22	38	1.850	4.352	.3818	526.62
	44		24	54	1.723	4.900	.3585	657.70
	47		26	59	1.600	5.450	.3398	790.44
	50		28	52	1.483	5.995	.3244	922.61
	53		30	31	1.369	6.531	.3118	1051.46
	56		31	55	1.261	7.050	.3014	1175.15
	59		33	2	1.156	7.548	.2927	1292.26
	62		33	46	1.057	8.019	.2854	1401.11
	65		34	4	.961	8.458	.2794	1501.26
	68		33	49	.871	8.860	.2744	1591.45
	71		32	52	.787	9.221	.2702	1671.32
	74		31	3	.708	9.536	.2669	1740.34
	77		28	9	.637	9.802	.2642	1797.98
	80		23	56	.576	10.017	.2621	1844.15
	83		18	14	.527	10.178	.2606	1878.23
	86		11	4	.493	10.283	.2597	1900.44
	90		0	0	.475	10.333	.2593	1911.41
3.05	19	8	0	0	3.050	1.000	1.0000	0
	20		1	15	2.984	1.103	.9324	.0553
	23		5	16	2.782	1.490	.7534	11.010
	26		8	51	2.603	1.919	.6328	47.836
	29		12	7	2.440	2.384	.5478	112.68
	32		15	7	2.285	2.881	.4856	201.70
	35		17	55	2.139	3.404	.4389	309.65
	38		20	31	1.998	3.947	.4030	431.82
	41		22	57	1.863	4.505	.3748	562.70
	44		25	13	1.734	5.071	.3523	698.86
	47		27	17	1.610	5.639	.3341	836.42
	50		29	10	1.491	6.203	.3193	972.67
	53		30	50	1.376	6.756	.3071	1105.48
	56		32	14	1.266	7.293	.2970	1232.61
	59		33	21	1.161	7.808	.2886	1352.50
	62		34	6	1.060	8.295	.2816	1464.32
	65		34	24	.964	8.749	.2757	1566.64
	68		34	10	.873	9.164	.2709	1659.02
	71		33	13	.788	9.537	.2669	1740.75
	74		31	24	.708	9.863	.2636	1811.04
	77		28	29	.637	10.138	.2610	1869.52
	80		24	14	.575	10.360	.2590	1916.64
	83		18	29	.525	10.526	.2576	1951.67
	86		11	14	.490	10.634	.2567	1974.29
	89		2	54	.473	10.684	.2563	1984.65
	90		0	0	.472	10.686	.2562	1985.15
3.10	18	49	0	0	3.100	1.000	1.0000	0
	20		1	43	3.010	1.145	.9079	.2717
	23		5	41	2.806	1.545	.7346	14.353
	26		9	14	2.621	1.988	.6179	55.921
	29		12	28	2.460	2.469	.5356	126.62
	32		15	27	2.303	2.982	.4754	221.57

TABLE 5 (Continued)

M_1	ϵ (deg.)	(min.)	δ (deg.)	(min.)	M_2	$\dfrac{p_2}{p_1}$	$\dfrac{\rho_1}{\rho_2}$	ΔS
3.10	35		18	14	2.155	3.522	.4302	335.62
	38		20	50	2.012	4.083	.3954	463.34
	41		23	15	1.876	4.659	.3681	599.73
	44		25	30	1.745	5.244	.3464	740.57
	47		27	35	1.619	5.830	.3288	882.83
	50		29	27	1.498	6.413	.3144	1023.28
	53		31	7	1.383	6.985	.3026	1159.52
	56		32	32	1.272	7.539	.2928	1290.06
	59		33	39	1.166	8.071	.2847	1413.16
	62		34	24	1.064	8.574	.2779	1527.55
	65		34	44	.967	9.043	.2722	1632.03
	68		34	29	.875	9.472	.2675	1726.51
	71		33	33	.789	9.857	.2637	1809.79
	74		31	45	.708	10.193	.2605	1881.58
	77		28	50	.636	10.478	.2580	1941.57
	80		24	33	.573	10.703	.2561	1989.35
	83		18	44	.523	10.879	.2547	2025.11
	86		11	24	.488	10.991	.2538	2048.19
	89		2	56	.471	11.042	.2534	2058.69
	90		0	0	.470	11.045	.2534	2059.38
3.15	18	31	0	0	3.150	1.000	1.0000	0
	20		2	9	3.034	1.188	.8845	.6698
	23		6	5	2.830	1.601	.7167	17.961
	26		9	36	2.648	2.058	.6037	64.868
	29		12	48	2.479	2.554	.5240	141.23
	32		15	46	2.321	3.084	.4657	242.24
	35		18	32	2.170	3.642	.4219	362.33
	38		21	8	2.026	4.222	.3882	495.57
	41		23	32	1.888	4.816	.3618	637.43
	44		25	47	1.755	5.420	.3407	783.40
	47		27	51	1.628	6.026	.3237	929.92
	50		29	44	1.506	6.627	.3098	1074.44
	53		31	24	1.390	7.218	.2983	1214.69
	56		32	49	1.277	7.790	.2888	1348.37
	59		33	56	1.170	8.340	.2810	1474.46
	62		34	42	1.067	8.859	.2744	1591.35
	65		35	2	.970	9.343	.2689	1698.35
	68		34	48	.877	9.786	.2644	1794.61
	71		33	53	.790	10.183	.2606	1879.44
	74		32	4	.709	10.531	.2575	1952.69
	77		29	8	.636	10.825	.2551	2013.81
	80		24	51	.572	11.061	.2533	2062.67
	83		18	59	.521	11.239	.2519	2098.79
	86		11	34	.485	11.354	.2511	2122.32
	89		2	59	.468	11.407	.2507	2132.92
	90		0	0	.467	11.410	.2506	2133.42
3.20	18	13	0	0	3.200	1.000	1.0000	0
	20		2	34	3.059	1.055	.8623	1.359
	23		6	27	2.843	1.657	.6997	22.418
	26		9	57	2.670	2.129	.5901	74.520
	29		13	8	2.500	2.641	.5129	156.77
	32		16	5	2.339	3.188	.4564	263.75
	35		18	50	2.187	3.764	.4140	389.52
	38		21	24	2.040	4.362	.3814	528.97

TABLE 5 (Continued)

M_1	ϵ (deg.)	ϵ (min.)	δ (deg.)	δ (min.)	M_2	$\dfrac{p_2}{p_1}$	$\dfrac{\rho_1}{\rho_2}$	ΔS
3.20	41		23	47	1.900	4.975	.3557	675.74
	44		26	4	1.766	5.598	.3353	826.64
	47		28	7	1.637	6.223	.3188	977.62
	50		30	0	1.514	6.844	.3053	1126.41
	53		31	40	1.396	7.453	.2943	1270.16
	56		33	5	1.283	8.045	.2851	1407.01
	59		34	13	1.174	8.611	.2774	1535.69
	62		34	59	1.071	9.147	.2710	1655.19
	65		35	19	.972	9.647	.2657	1764.42
	68		35	6	.879	10.104	.2613	1862.53
	71		34	11	.791	10.514	.2577	1949.11
	74		32	23	.709	10.873	.2547	2023.80
	77		29	27	.635	11.176	.2524	2085.90
	80		25	8	.571	11.420	.2506	2135.45
	83		19	13	.519	11.603	.2493	2172.62
	86		11	43	.483	11.722	.2484	2205.80
	89		3	27	.465	11.777	.2481	2207.39
	90		0	0	.464	11.780	.2480	2207.86
3.25	17	55	0	0	3.250	1.000	1.0000	0
	20		2	59	3.086	1.275	.8411	2.381
	23		6	49	2.809	1.715	.6834	27.089
	26		10	17	2.692	2.201	.5772	84.619
	29		13	26	2.519	2.730	.5023	172.81
	32		16	22	2.357	3.294	.4476	286.08
	35		19	7	2.202	3.888	.4065	404.14
	38		21	41	2.054	4.504	.3748	562.45
	41		24	5	1.912	5.137	.3500	714.81
	44		26	19	1.776	5.780	.3302	870.56
	47		28	23	1.646	6.425	.3142	1025.95
	50		30	15	1.521	7.065	.3011	1178.65
	53		31	56	1.429	7.693	.2904	1325.99
	56		33	21	1.288	8.303	.2815	1466.21
	59		34	29	1.179	8.888	.2740	1597.61
	62		35	16	1.074	9.441	.2679	1719.76
	65		35	36	.975	9.956	.2627	1831.08
	68		35	23	.880	10.427	.2585	1931.61
	71		34	29	.792	10.851	.2549	2019.32
	74		32	41	.709	11.220	.2520	2095.10
	77		29	45	.635	11.533	.2498	2158.45
	80		25	25	.570	11.785	.2480	2208.96
	83		19	27	.517	11.974	.2467	2246.27
	86		11	52	.481	12.097	.2459	2270.58
	89		3	4	.463	12.153	.2456	2281.43
	90		0	0	.462	12.156	.2456	2282.42
3.30	17	35	0	0	3.300	1.000	1.0000	0
	18		0	32	3.268	1.047	.9680	.....
	20		3	22	3.110	1.320	.8208	3.555
	23		7	10	2.901	1.773	.6679	32.532
	26		10	36	2.716	2.275	.5648	95.417
	29		13	44	2.539	2.820	.4922	189.79
	32		16	39	2.374	3.401	.4392	309.14
	35		19	23	2.218	4.013	.3992	447.00
	38		21	56	2.067	4.649	.3685	607.17
	41		24	20	1.924	5.302	.3444	754.63

TABLE 5 (Continued)

M_1	ϵ		δ		M_2	$\dfrac{p_2}{p_1}$	$\dfrac{\rho_1}{\rho_2}$	ΔS
	(deg.)	(min.)	(deg.)	(min.)				
3.30	44		26	34	1.787	5.964	.3252	915.30
	47		28	38	1.654	6.629	.3097	1074.96
	50		30	30	1.529	7.289	.2971	1231.29
	53		32	11	1.409	7.937	.2866	1382.34
	56		33	36	1.293	8.566	.2780	1525.56
	59		34	44	1.183	9.169	.2708	1660.07
	62		35	31	1.078	9.738	.2648	1784.22
	65		35	52	.977	10.270	.2598	1897.56
	68		35	40	.882	10.756	.2557	1999.51
	71		34	46	.793	11.192	.2523	2089.26
	74		32	58	.710	11.573	.2495	2166.48
	77		30	2	.634	11.896	.2473	2230.92
	80		25	41	.569	12.156	.2456	2282.41
	83		19	41	.516	12.350	.2443	2320.12
	86		12	1	.479	12.477	.2436	2344.95
	89		3	6	.461	12.535	.2432	2356.21
	90		0	0	.460	12.538	.2432	2356.67
3.35	17	22	0	0	3.350	1.000	1.0000	0
	20		3	44	3.135	1.365	.8014	5.064
	23		7	10	2.825	1.832	.6531	38.510
	26		10	54	2.735	2.349	.5531	107.19
	29		14	1	2.559	2.911	.4826	207.54
	32		16	55	2.381	3.510	.4311	333.09
	35		19	38	2.210	4.141	.3924	476.78
	38		22	11	2.081	4.796	.3626	632.66
	41		24	34	1.935	5.469	.3392	795.35
	44		26	48	1.796	6.151	.3206	960.51
	47		28	52	1.664	6.836	.3055	1124.67
	50		30	44	1.536	7.517	.2932	1285.01
	53		32	25	1.415	8.184	.2831	1439.07
	56		33	50	1.298	8.832	.2747	1585.62
	59		34	59	1.187	9.453	.2677	1722.56
	62		35	47	1.081	10.041	.2619	1849.43
	65		36	8	.980	10.588	.2571	1964.84
	68		35	56	.884	11.089	.2530	2068.30
	71		35	3	.794	11.539	.2497	2159.53
	74		33	15	.710	11.931	.2470	2237.90
	77		30	19	.634	12.264	.2449	2303.50
	80		25	56	.568	12.531	.2432	2355.54
	83		19	54	.514	12.732	.2420	2394.22
	86		12	10	.491	12.862	.2413	2419.05
	89		3	9	.458	12.922	.2409	2430.52
	90		0	0	.457	12.926	.2409	2431.31
3.40	17	6	0	0	3.400	1.000	1.0000	0
	18		1	20	3.361	1.121	.9216	.3557
	21		5	23	3.042	1.565	.7280	15.651
	24		8	59	2.881	2.065	.6024	65.946
	27		12	15	2.696	2.613	.5164	151.75
	30		15	17	2.521	3.205	.4550	267.45
	33		18	6	2.354	3.834	.4097	405.84
	36		20	45	2.196	4.493	.3753	560.16
	39		23	14	2.044	5.175	.3487	724.10
	42		25	34	1.899	5.872	.3277	892.88
	45		27	44	1.761	6.577	.3108	1062.65

TABLE 5 (Continued)

M_1	ϵ		δ		M_2	$\dfrac{p_2}{p_1}$	$\dfrac{\rho_1}{\rho_2}$	ΔS
	(deg.)	(min.)	(deg.)	(min.)				
3.40	48	29	44		1.628	7.282	.2972	1229.91
	51		31	33	1.502	7.979	.2860	1391.92
	54		33	9	1.381	8.661	.2768	1547.13
	57		34	29	1.262	9.320	.2692	1694.75
	60		35	32	1.155	9.949	.2628	1829.58
	63		36	12	1.050	10.540	.2575	1954.93
	66		36	23	.950	11.089	.2530	2068.30
	69		35	59	.855	11.588	.2494	2169.44
	72		34	50	.766	12.032	.2464	2258.45
	75		32	4	.684	12.417	.2439	2333.35
	78		29	18	.610	12.731	.2420	2395.19
	81		24	22	.547	12.990	.2406	2443.70
	84·		17	41	.498	13.173	.2396	2478.08
	87		9	22	.466	13.283	.2390	2498.82
	90		0	0	.455	13.320	.2388	2505.96
3.45	16	51	0	0	3.450	1.000	1.0000	0
	18		1	42	3.346	1.159	.8999	.4693
	21		5	43	3.113	1.617	.7118	19.243
	24		9	17	2.907	2.131	.5899	74.797
	27		12	32	2.717	2.695	.5064	166.63
	30		15	32	2.539	3.305	.4467	288.56
	33		18	21	2.371	3.952	.4027	432.93
	36		20	59	2.210	4.631	.3693	593.00
	39		23	27	2.056	5.333	.3435	762.36
	42		25	47	1.910	6.051	.3230	936.17
	45		27	57	1.770	6.777	.3067	1111.59
	48		29	57	1.636	7.502	.2934	1281.49
	51		31	46	1.504	8.220	.2826	1447.34
	54		33	22	1.387	8.922	.2736	1605.36
	57		34	43	1.270	9.601	.2662	1754.71
	60		35	45	1.159	10.248	.2600	1893.51
	63		36	26	1.053	10.858	.2549	2020.94
	66		36	38	.952	11.422	.2506	2136.31
	69		36	14	.856	11.936	.2470	2239.14
	72		35	5	.767	12.394	.2441	2328.84
	75		32	57	.684	12.790	.2417	2405.02
	78		29	33	.610	13.119	.2398	2467.98
	81		24	36	.546	13.380	.2384	2497.27
	84		17	53	.496	13.568	.2375	2542.10
	87		9	29	.464	13.619	.2369	2573.13
	90		0	0	.453	13.720	.2367	2580.25
3.50	16	36	0	0	3.500	1.000	.0000	0
	17		0	36	3.462	1.055	.9625	....
	20		4	46	3.209	1.505	.7482	11.778
	23		8	26	2.997	2.015	.6122	59.476
	26		11	45	2.800	2.580	.5206	145.61
	29		14	49	2.617	3.193	.4561	264.53
	32		17	40	2.443	3.847	.4089	418.39
	35		20	21	2.277	4.535	.3734	570.04
	38		22	52	2.131	5.251	.3461	742.39
	41		25	14	1.970	5.985	.3247	920.04
	44		27	27	1.819	6.730	.3076	1099.16
	47		29	30	1.688	7.478	.2938	1275.69
	50		31	23	1.557	8.220	.2826	1447.18

TABLE 5   (Continued)

M_1	ϵ (deg.)	ϵ (min.)	δ (deg.)	δ (min.)	M_2	$\dfrac{p_2}{p_1}$	$\dfrac{\rho_1}{\rho_2}$	ΔS
3.50	53		33	7	1.433	8.949	.2733	1611.78
	56		34	30	1.313	9.656	.2656	1766.51
	59		35	40	1.200	10.334	.2592	1911.35
	62		36	28	1.091	10.975	.2539	2042.66
	65		36	51	.987	11.573	.2495	2152.46
	68		36	41	.889	12.120	.2458	2275.07
	71		35	49	.797	12.610	.2428	2370.67
	74		34	2	.711	13.039	.2403	2452.74
	77		31	5	.633	13.402	.2383	2521.04
	80		26	40	.565	13.695	.2368	2575.43
	83		20	31	.510	13.913	.2357	2615.70
	86		12	31	.472	14.056	.2350	2641.81
	89		3	15	.453	14.121	.2347	2653.77
	90		0	0	.451	14.125	.2347	2654.47
3.55	16	22	0	0	3.550	1.000	1.0000	0
	17		0	58	3.489	1.090	.9402	.1433
	20		5	5	3.238	1.553	.7319	14.698
	23		8	43	3.021	2.078	.5998	67.626
	26		12	1	2.822	2.659	.5107	159.87
	29		15	3	2.635	3.289	.4480	285.05
	32		17	54	2.460	3.962	.4021	435.15
	35		20	34	2.292	4.671	.3676	602.31
	38		23	5	2.132	5.407	.3411	780.18
	41		25	26	1.979	6.162	.3203	962.95
	44		27	39	1.834	6.928	.3037	1146.00
	47		29	42	1.696	7.698	.2903	1326.89
	50		31	35	1.564	8.462	.2793	1502.04
	53		33	16	1.439	9.212	.2703	1669.53
	56		34	42	1.318	9.939	.2629	1827.35
	59		35	52	1.203	10.637	.2567	1974.95
	62		36	41	1.094	11.296	.2515	2110.35
	65		37	5	.990	11.911	.2472	2233.82
	68		36	55	.891	12.473	.2436	2343.96
	71		36	3	.798	12.978	.2406	2441.09
	74		34	17	.712	13.420	.2382	2524.31
	77		31	20	.633	13.793	.2363	2588.67
	80		26	54	.564	14.093	.2348	2638.79
	83		20	42	.509	14.318	.2338	2689.23
	86		12	42	.469	14.465	.2331	2715.95
	89		3	18	.450	14.532	.2328	2727.85
	90		0	0	.449	14.536	.2328	2728.51
3.60	16	8	0	0	3.600	1.000	1.0000	0
	17		1	19	3.465	1.126	.9189	.0356
	20		5	23	3.263	1.602	.7163	18.007
	23		8	59	3.044	2.142	.5878	76.282
	26		12	16	2.843	2.739	.5013	174.56
	29		15	17	2.654	3.387	.4402	306.06
	32		18	7	2.476	4.079	.3956	462.38
	35		20	46	2.305	4.808	.3621	635.32
	38		23	17	2.144	5.565	.3363	818.37
	41		25	38	1.990	6.341	.3161	1006.11
	44		27	51	1.844	7.130	.2999	1193.84
	47		29	54	1.704	7.921	.2869	1378.49

TABLE 5 (Continued)

M_1	ϵ		δ		M_2	$\dfrac{p_2}{p_1}$	$\dfrac{\rho_1}{\rho_2}$	ΔS
	(deg.)	(min.)	(deg.)	(min.)				
3.60	50		31	47	1.571	8.706	.2762	1557.16
	53		33	28	1.444	9.478	.2674	1727.56
	56		34	54	1.323	10.226	.2602	1888.50
	59		36	4	1.207	10.943	.2542	2038.24
	62		36	54	1.097	11.621	.2489	2169.45
	65		37	17	.992	12.253	.2449	2301.30
	68		37	8	.893	12.832	.2415	2413.29
	71		36	17	.799	13.351	.2386	2511.45
	74		34	31	.712	13.805	.2363	2595.91
	77		31	34	.633	14.189	.2344	2665.81
	80		27	7	.564	14.498	.2330	2721.83
	83		20	54	.507	14.729	.2319	2762.93
	86		12	49	.468	14.880	.2313	2789.74
	89		3	19	.449	14.949	.2310	2801.83
	90		0	0	.447	14.953	.2310	2802.74
3.65	15	54	0	0	3.650	1.000	.10000	0
	18		3	3	3.453	1.318	.8217	3.597
	21		6	55	3.213	1.830	.6537	38.249
	24		10	22	2.998	2.405	.5448	116.07
	27		13	32	2.799	3.037	.4702	232.78
	30		16	28	2.611	3.719	.4169	379.76
	33		19	14	2.434	4.444	.3775	548.35
	36		21	49	2.264	5.203	.3477	731.01
	39		24	16	2.103	5.989	.3246	921.31
	42		26	35	1.951	6.792	.3064	1114.11
	45		28	44	1.805	7.605	.2918	1305.54
	48		30	44	1.666	8.417	.2799	1492.14
	51		32	33	1.534	9.221	.2702	1671.50
	54		34	9	1.408	10.006	.2622	1841.85
	57		35	31	1.288	10.766	.2556	2001.93
	60		36	35	1.173	11.491	.2501	2150.14
	63		37	17	1.064	12.173	.2455	2285.79
	66		37	31	.960	12.805	.2416	2408.32
	69		37	9	.862	13.380	.2384	2516.99
	72		36	2	.770	13.892	.2358	2612.02
	75		33	54	.685	14.335	.2337	2692.72
	78		30	30	.608	14.705	.2320	2758.78
	81		25	28	.542	14.996	.2308	2810.27
	84		18	34	.491	15.206	.2299	2847.39
	87		9	52	.457	15.334	.2294	2869.56
	90		0	0	.446	15.376	.2292	2876.98
3.70	15	41	0	0	3.700	1.000	1.0000	0
	18		3	21	3.479	1.359	.8041	5.102
	21		7	11	3.237	1.885	.6406	44.156
	24		10	37	3.021	2.476	.5346	127.94
	27		13	45	2.818	3.125	.4620	250.85
	30		16	41	2.629	3.826	.4102	404.07
	33		19	25	2.448	4.571	.3719	578.54
	36		22	1	2.278	5.352	.3429	766.95
	39		24	27	2.114	6.159	.3204	962.36
	42		26	45	1.960	6.984	.3026	1159.67
	45		28	55	1.813	7.819	.2884	1355.26
	48		30	54	1.673	8.654	.2769	1545.54

TABLE 5 (Continued)

M_1	ϵ (deg.)	(min.)	δ (deg.)	(min.)	M_2	$\dfrac{p_2}{p_1}$	$\dfrac{\rho_1}{\rho_2}$	ΔS
3.70	51		32	43	1.540	9.480	.2675	1728.47
	54		34	20	1.413	10.287	.2597	1901.59
	57		35	42	1.292	11.067	.2532	2064.01
	60		36	46	1.177	11.812	.2478	2214.25
	63		37	28	1.067	12.513	.2433	2352.02
	66		37	43	.962	13.163	.2396	2476.39
	69		37	22	.863	13.754	.2365	2586.61
	72		36	15	.771	14.280	.2340	2682.84
	75		34	7	.685	14.735	.2319	2764.36
	78		30	43	.608	15.115	.2303	2831.36
	81		25	40	.542	15.414	.2291	2883.64
	84		18	44	.490	15.630	.2282	2920.32
	87		9	58	.456	15.761	.2277	2943.39
	90		0	0	.444	15.805	.2275	2950.81
3.75	15	28	0	0	3.750	1.000	1.0000	0
	18		3	39	3.506	1.400	.7873	6.776
	21		7	27	3.263	1.940	.6281	50.411
	24		10	51	3.043	2.548	.5249	140.21
	27		13	58	2.838	3.215	.4542	269.45
	30		16	53	2.646	3.935	.4037	428.93
	33		19	37	2.464	4.700	.3664	609.50
	36		22	12	2.291	5.502	.3382	803.26
	39		24	38	2.126	6.331	.3163	1003.82
	42		26	56	1.970	7.179	.2990	1205.69
	45		29	5	1.821	8.037	.2852	1391.39
	48		31	5	1.680	8.894	.2740	1599.23
	51		32	54	1.546	9.742	.2648	1785.17
	54		34	30	1.418	10.571	.2572	1961.46
	57		35	52	1.296	11.373	.2509	2126.34
	60		37	6	1.186	12.138	.2457	2278.71
	63		37	40	1.070	12.858	.2413	2418.46
	66		37	54	.964	13.526	.2377	2544.18
	69		37	34	.865	14.133	.2347	2656.08
	72		36	27	.772	14.673	.2322	2753.23
	75		34	20	.685	15.141	.2302	2835.86
	78		30	55	.608	15.531	.2286	2903.55
	81		25	51	.541	15.838	.2274	2956.35
	84		18	53	.488	16.060	.2266	2994.16
	87		10	3	.455	16.195	.2261	3016.89
	90		0	0	.442	16.240	.2259	3024.28
3.80	15	15	0	0	3.800	1.000	1.0000	0
	17		2	34	3.624	1.273	.8418	2.328
	20		6	30	3.368	1.804	.6600	35.512
	23		9	59	3.137	2.405	.5447	116.10
	26		13	10	2.925	3.071	.4670	239.51
	29		16	8	2.727	3.793	.4122	396.33
	32		18	54	2.538	4.564	.3722	576.93
	35		21	32	2.361	5.376	.3421	772.71
	38		24	1	2.192	6.219	.3189	976.54
	41		26	21	2.031	7.085	.3007	1183.35
	44		28	33	1.879	7.963	.2863	1384.22
	47		30	36	1.734	8.844	.2746	1588.04
	50		32	28	1.596	9.720	.2650	1780.24

TABLE 5 (Continued)

M_1	ϵ (deg.)	(min.)	δ (deg.)	(min.)	M_2	$\dfrac{p_2}{p_1}$	$\dfrac{\rho_1}{\rho_2}$	ΔS
3.80	53		34	10	1.465	10.579	.2571	1962.64
	56		35	37	1.340	11.401	.2506	2129.67
	59		36	48	1.222	12.212	.2452	2292.69
	62		37	39	1.136	12.967	.2407	2438.95
	65		38	4	1.001	13.672	.2369	2571.26
	68		37	57	.899	14.316	.2338	2689.05
	71		37	7	.803	14.895	.2312	2792.42
	74		35	22	.714	15.400	.2291	2880.82
	77		32	26	.632	15.828	.2274	2954.38
	80		27	56	.561	16.172	.2262	3013.13
	83		21	36	.503	16.430	.2252	3056.29
	86		13	17	.462	16.598	.2247	3084.18
	89		3	27	.442	16.675	.2244	3096.82
	90		0	0	.441	16.680	.2244	3097.73
3.85	15	3	0	0	3.850	1.000	1.0000	0
	17		2	51	3.655	1.312	.8243	3.462
	20		6	45	3.392	1.856	.6472	40.898
	23		10	12	3.159	2.474	.5349	127.38
	26		13	23	2.946	3.157	.4592	243.39
	29		16	19	2.734	3.898	.4059	420.41
	32		19	5	2.553	4.690	.3669	606.90
	35		21	42	2.373	5.523	.3375	808.22
	38		24	11	2.203	6.388	.3150	1017.35
	41		26	31	2.041	7.277	.2973	1228.64
	44		28	42	1.886	8.178	.2832	1423.73
	47		30	45	1.741	9.083	.2718	1640.95
	50		32	38	1.602	9.981	.2625	1836.43
	53		34	19	1.470	10.864	.2548	2021.90
	56		35	47	1.345	11.719	.2485	2195.86
	59		36	58	1.225	12.758	.2432	2431.05
	62		37	49	1.112	13.315	.2388	2504.68
	65		38	15	1.003	14.038	.2351	2638.48
	68		38	8	.901	14.700	.2321	2757.79
	71		37	19	.804	15.294	.2295	2862.02
	74		35	34	.714	15.813	.2275	2942.33
	77		32	38	.632	16.252	.2259	3025.35
	80		28	8	.561	16.605	.2246	3085.16
	83		21	46	.501	16.870	.2237	3128.90
	86		13	24	.461	17.043	.2232	3157.50
	89		3	29	.440	17.122	.2229	3170.36
	90		0	0	.439	17.126	.2229	3171.00
3.90	14	51	0	0	3.900	1.000	1.0000	0
	17		3	8	3.679	1.350	.8076	4.524
	20		6	59	3.418	1.907	.6350	40.704
	23		10	25	3.181	2.542	.5255	139.05
	26		13	34	2.964	3.244	.4518	275.36
	29		16	30	2.761	4.004	.3998	444.78
	32		19	16	2.570	4.817	.3618	637.36
	35		21	52	2.386	5.671	.3332	844.31
	38		24	20	2.214	6.560	.3112	1058.43
	41		26	40	2.050	7.471	.2940	1274.21
	44		28	52	1.895	8.396	.2802	1487.37
	47		30	54	1.747	9.325	.2691	1694.37

TABLE 5 (Continued)

M_1	ϵ (deg.)	(min.)	δ (deg.)	(min.)	M_2	$\dfrac{p_2}{p_1}$	$\dfrac{\rho_1}{\rho_2}$	ΔS
3.90	50		32	47	1.608	10.247	.2600	1892.88
	53		34	28	1.475	11.152	.2526	2081.24
	56		35	56	1.348	12.030	.2464	2257.39
	59		37	8	1.228	12.872	.2412	2420.62
	62		37	59	1.114	13.668	.2369	2570.33
	65		38	25	1.005	14.409	.2334	2705.87
	68		38	18	.902	15.088	.2304	2826.46
	71		37	30	.805	15.698	.2279	2932.18
	74		35	45	.715	16.230	.2260	3008.81
	77		32	49	.632	16.681	.2244	3097.97
	80		28	19	.560	17.044	.2232	3157.53
	83		21	55	.501	17.316	.2223	3201.68
	86		13	30	.459	17.492	.2217	3230.39
	89		3	30	.439	17.573	.2215	3243.46
	90		0	0	.438	17.578	.2215	3244.11
3.95	14	40	0	0	3.950	1.000	1.0000	0
	17		3	24	3.707	1.389	.7914	5.742
	20		7	13	3.441	1.963	.6232	52.900
	23		10	38	3.205	2.613	.5165	151.47
	26		13	46	2.985	3.332	.4446	294.11
	29		16	41	2.778	4.112	.3939	469.90
	32		19	26	2.584	4.945	.3568	668.50
	35		22	2	2.399	5.822	.3290	880.96
	38		24	29	2.224	6.733	.3076	1099.96
	41		26	49	2.059	7.669	.2908	1320.30
	44		29	0	1.902	8.618	.2773	1537.36
	47		31	3	1.754	9.570	.2665	1747.86
	50		32	56	1.614	10.516	.2577	1949.57
	53		34	37	1.480	11.444	.2504	2140.49
	56		36	5	1.353	12.345	.2444	2319.36
	59		37	17	1.187	13.208	.2394	2484.70
	62		38	8	1.116	14.025	.2352	2636.29
	65		38	35	1.007	14.786	.2317	2773.19
	68		38	28	.903	15.483	.2288	2895.03
	71		37	40	.806	16.108	.2264	2992.18
	74		35	57	.715	16.654	.2245	3093.50
	77		33	0	.632	17.116	.2229	3169.55
	80		28	29	.560	17.489	.2217	3229.18
	83		22	4	.500	17.767	.2209	3274.19
	86		13	36	.458	17.949	.2203	3302.83
	89		3	32	.438	18.032	.2201	3316.12
	90		0	0	.436	18.036	.2201	3316.92
4.00	14	29	0	0	4.000	1.000	1.0000	0
	17		3	39	3.733	1.429	.7759	7.820
	20		7	27	3.467	2.017	.6119	59.660
	23		10	50	3.226	2.683	.5078	164.23
	26		13	57	3.004	3.421	.4377	313.26
	29		16	51	2.795	4.221	.3882	495.42
	32		19	35	2.598	5.075 ——	.3521	699.85
	35		22	11	2.412	5.975 ——	.3250	917.71
	38		24	38	2.235	6.909	.3041	1141.61
	41		26	58	2.069	7.868	.2877	1366.26
	44		29	9	1.911	8.841	.2746	1587.26

TABLE 5 (Continued)

M_1	ϵ		δ		M_2	$\dfrac{p_2}{p_1}$	$\dfrac{\rho_1}{\rho_2}$	ΔS
	(deg.)	(min.)	(deg.)	(min.)				
4.00	47		31	14	1.768	9.818	.2640	1801.39
	50		33	4	1.619	10.788	.2554	2006.14
	53		34	46	1.485	11.740	.2479	2190.53
	56		36	14	1.357	12.664	.2424	2380.55
	59		37	26	1.235	13.549	.2375	2548.28
	62		38	18	1.119	14.386	.2335	2701.78
	65		38	44	1.009	15.167	.2301	2840.29
	68		38	39	.905	15.881	.2272	2963.41
	71		37	51	.807	16.522	.2249	3071.60
	74		36	7	.716	17.082	.2230	3163.69
	77		33	21	.632	17.556	.2215	3240.53
	80		28	40	.559	17.938	.2204	3301.04
	83		22	13	.499	18.224	.2195	3346.19
	86		13	42	.457	18.410	.2190	3365.66
	89		3	34	.436	18.495	.2188	3378.91
	90		0	0	.435	18.500	.2187	3289.42

INDEX

profiles of minimum drag, 133, 137

rectangular wing, 371
reflection of expansion or shock waves, 75, 79
rotational flow, 4
  characteristics system, 82, 276

schlieren apparatus, 114
shadow apparatus, 113
shock drag, 58
shock polar curve, 50
shock wave equations, 45, 46
shock waves, formation of, 16
shock wave theory, 43
sink and source distribution, 205, 213, 299
slender body of revolution, 210
small disturbances theory, 40, 201, 210, 292, 350
  bodies of revolution, 210
  two-dimensional, 40
source distribution, 205, 213, 299
source line, 354
speed of sound, 9
spherical coordinates, 198
starting conditions, 181
starting Mach number, 186
static pressure, measurements, 94
stream function for rotational flow, 84, 276
strong shock, 49
strophoid, 51
subsonic leading edge, 317, 352
subsonic trailing edge, 317, 352
suction forces, 351, 370
supersonic biplane, 154

supersonic diffusors, 179
  efficiency, 191
  variable geometry, 193
  with external compression, 194
supersonic leading edge, 317, 352
supersonic trailing edge, 317, 352
sweep-back wing, 294, 318

temperature measurements, 99
thickness, effect on the drag, 138, 338, 349
  effect on the lift, 350
total head pressure, 95
total head tube, 95
trailing edge, subsonic or supersonic, 317, 352
trapezoidal lift distribution, 373
trapezoidal wing, 292
triangular wing, drag, 330
  lift, 359
  slender wing, 359
  supersonic leading edge, 332, 361
  subsonic leading edge, 336, 362
two-dimensional diffusors, 179
  flow, 19
two-dimensional effusors, 161

velocity direction, measurements, 95

wings, diamond plan form, 343
  drag, 126, 292
  lift, 123, 350
  rectangular, 379
  sweep back, 294, 318
  trapezoidal, 292
  triangular, 330, 359
  two-dimensional, 117

aero Engr